THE GLOBAL EXPERIENCE

Readings in World History to 1500

Volume I

THIRD EDITION

THE GLOBAL EXPERIENCE
Readings in World History to 1500
Volume I

Philip F. Riley
Frank A. Gerome
Robert L. Lembright
Henry A. Myers
Chong-Kun Yoon
James Madison University

Prentice Hall, Upper Saddle River, New Jersey 07458

Library of Congress Cataloging-in-Publication Data

The Global experience / [edited by] Philip F. Riley . . . [et al.].— 3rd ed.
   p. cm.
   Contents: v. 1. Readings in world history to 1500.
   ISBN 0-13-310798-1 (v. 1)
   1. World history. I. Riley, Philip F.
   D20.G56   1998
   909—dc21   97-2038
                                  CIP

Editorial Director: Charlyce Jones Owen
Editorial Assistant: Holly Brown
Production Liaison: Fran Russello
Project Manager: Linda B. Pawelchak
Manufacturing Manager: Nick Sklitsis
Prepress and Manufacturing Buyer: Lynn Pearlman
Cover Director: Jayne Conte
Marketing Manager: Sheryl Adams

This book was set in 10/11 Times Roman
by The Composing Room of Michigan, Inc.,
and was printed and bound by RR Donnelley & Sons
Company. The cover was printed by Phoenix Color Corp.

Reprinted with corrections June, 1999

Printed in the United States of America
10 9 8 7 6 5 4 3

ISBN 0-13-310798-1

Prentice-Hall International (UK) Limited, *London*
Prentice-Hall of Australia Pty. Limited, *Sydney*
Prentice-Hall Canada Inc., *Toronto*
Prentice-Hall Hispanoamericana, S.A., *Mexico*
Prentice-Hall of India Private Limited, *New Delhi*
Prentice-Hall of Japan, Inc., *Tokyo*
Prentice-Hall Asia Pte. Ltd., *Singapore*
Editora Prentice-Hall do Brasil, Ltda., *Rio de Janeiro*

For
Raymond C. Dingledine Jr.
1919–1990
Teacher, Scholar, Friend

CONTENTS

A WORLD IN CHANGE

PREFACE

This anthology is a brief, balanced collection of primary materials organized chronologically and focused on global themes.

In preparing this collection, we had three concerns in mind. First, any informed understanding of the world at the end of the twentieth century must begin with history. We believe the most useful mode of historical study—particularly for college students—is world history. Because men and women make history, the documents we have chosen depict the variety of their experiences over time on a global scale. To help students study and appreciate these experiences, we have included excerpts both from classic texts and from less familiar but equally illustrative material. The resulting selection of readings illustrates patterns of global change and exchange, as well as the distinct achievements of the major civilizations.

Second, to encourage the comparative study of world history and to reinforce the underlying links between civilizations, we have organized the readings into chronological sections. By doing so, we hope to underscore global patterns of development and, at the same time, give our readers access to documents of special interest.

Third, to help with the understanding and retention of our reading selections, particularly those likely to be unfamiliar to students, we have included introductory comments as well as questions to consider. We hope this material will help students gain a better understanding of the text and connect their historical study to contemporary problems and issues.

Our students, particularly in their questions and criticisms, have shaped our work from the outset more than they know. Many of our colleagues at James Madison University have also helped immeasurably. Michael J. Galgano, Head, Department of History, has assisted us at every turn: He enthusiastically found for us the means and time to complete this project. Martha B. Caldwell, William H. Ingham, Caroline Marshall, Daniel McFarland, and Jacqueline Walker provided insights and suggestions to make this a better book. Mary Louise Loe not only contributed the sections on Russian and Soviet history but helped us throughout our work. Nicholas Miller of Boise State University and John A. Murphy of University College, Cork, Republic of Ireland, and John O. Hunwick of Northwestern University kindly advised us on Serbian, Irish, and African selections.

The third edition of *The Global Experience: Readings in World History* contains new sections, new selections, and new translations, as well as some changes in the selections published in our second edition. Among the new selections in Volume I are: A Greek Creation Story: Hesiod's *Theogony;* A Hindu Creation Story: *Rig Veda;* Hittite Laws; Hatshepsut: Successful Female Pharaoh; Sun Tzu, *The Art of War;* Sappho, *Lyric Songs;* The *Kama Sutra;* Hsuan-tsang, The Land and People of India; Aristotle, *Politics;* Polybius, Why Romans and Not Greeks Govern the World; Cicero, *The Laws;* Hippocrates, *On the Sacred Disease;* Pliny the Elder, *The Nature Story;* The Yellow Emperor, Nei-ching (Canon of Medicine); Paulus Orosius, *History Against the Pagans; The Institutes of Justinian;* Sayings (*Hadith*) Ascribed to the Prophet; Kai Kaus, "Scientific Physiognomy and the Purchase of Slaves"; Gregory of Tours, *History of the Franks;* Law Code of the Visigoths; Sir John Mandeville, "The Land of Prester John"; Martín Fernández de Figueroa, Confronting the Moors in Somalia; Anna Comnena, *The Alexiad;* Peter Abelard, *The Story of My Misfortunes;* St. Hildegard of Bingen, *Know the Ways;* Julian(a) of Norwich, *Showings;* The Good Man of Paris; The *Domestroi, Rules for Russian Households in the Time of Ivan the Terrible;* Ibn Al-Wadī, *An Essay on the Report of the Pestilence;* Vlad Tsepes, "The Impaler": The Real Dracula or How the Enemy of the Ottomans Became a Legend; Heinrich von Staden, *The Land and Government of Muscovy;* St. Francis Xavier on the Japanese: "The Best People Who Have Yet Been Discovered"; *The Travels of Mendes Pinto;* Antonio de Montesinos, Sermon to Colonists, 1511; and Bartolomé de Las Casas, *Destruction of the Indies* and The Only Method of Converting the Indians. In this volume we have included new sections on science in the ancient world and on spirituality and mysticism. We have also expanded our comparative selections on laws and increased our selections by women.

Among the new additions to Volume II are Vasco da Gama, *Journey to India;* an anonymous first-hand account, *Commerce, Slavery, and Religion in North Africa;* Thomas Nelson, *Slavery and the Slave Trade with Brazil;* Sophia, *Woman Not Inferior to Man;* Jean-Jacques Rousseau, *Sophie or The Woman;* Friedrich List, *National System of Political Economy;* Catherine II (the Great) of Russia, *The Instruction to the Commissioners for Composing a New Code of Laws,* and Lieutenant General Iakobii, "Secret Instructions to Agents of the Russian Empire in Alaska"; Taisuke Mitamuri, The Palace Eunuchs of Imperial China; Thomas Jefferson, The Declaration of Independence; Program of the Serb Society of National Defense; Irish National Identity and Destiny: Three Views; Fustel de Coulanges, "What Is a Nation?"; Heinrich von Treitschke, *A Word About the Jews Among Us;* President Millard Fillmore, "Letter to the Emperor of Japan"; President Theodore Roosevelt, The Roosevelt Corollary; Francisco García Calderón, "The North American Peril"; V.I. Lenin, "Tasks of the Youth League: Bourgeois and Communist Morality"; Nadezhda K. Krupskaya, "What a Communist Ought to Be Like"; Ethnic Cleansing in Northwestern Bosnia: Three Witnesses; Alain Destexhe, *Rwanda and Genocide in the Twentieth Century;* Adolf Hitler, The Obersalzberg Speech; William Faulkner, *Acceptance Speech: 1949 Nobel Prize for Literature;* Palestinian Declaration of Independence; Robert Bartley, "The Case for Optimism"; The United Nations Declaration on Human Rights; Carolyn Forché, "The Colonel"; Theresa Andrews, *Letters from a 1990s Bush Doctor;* Richard Preston, "Back in the Hot Zone"; Deng Xiaoping, A Market Economy for Socialist Goals; John Paul II, *Cen-*

tesimus Annus. In this volume we have added three sections dealing with problems and challenges of the turn of this century; we have increased the number of articles by women; and we have substantially expanded our coverage of Africa, nationalism, and ethnic struggles.

In making these revisions, we were guided by the advice and criticism of our colleagues, J. Chris Arndt, Ann Crabb, Steven W. Guerrier, Raymond M. Hyser, William McBride, David Owusa-Ansah, Harry Stansbury, and, in his role as teacher of world civilization, Michael J. Galgano. Sheila Riley helped with the final editing of all three editions; Marcella Smith worked on the third. Gordon Miller, reference librarian, and JMU's Interlibrary Loan staff headed by Darlene Newman and Debra Ryman tirelessly and skillfully assisted us in obtaining materials. Sarah C. ("Kate") Raikes discharged the ongoing and occasionally stressful duties involved with computer work and correspondence in support of the project for the two-and-a-half years the third edition was in progress.

We continue to welcome comments and criticism, which we appreciate in connection with our ongoing project of updating and improving this work. Please send your comments and suggestions to Philip F. Riley or Henry A. Myers, Department of History, James Madison University, Harrisonburg, VA 22807.

Philip F. Riley
Henry A. Myers

THE GLOBAL EXPERIENCE

Readings in World History to 1500

Volume I

EARLY CIVILIZATIONS

Global Conceptions of the Cosmos and Creation

With the dawn of civilization, people sought understanding of the universe and the conditions of their own existence as they described the will or clash of wills that made things the way they were. The resulting creation stories parallel the human experience of birth, with a god or gods arising out of chaos, a primordial ocean, or void to create the universe. Humanity could be formed from tears, blood, or the earth itself with duties of worship and obedience to the will of the god or gods. Once these myths and the postcreation stories that followed them with a certain logic had been established, they were celebrated at festivals or in rites, often by religious leaders or monarchs whose right to govern was substantiated by these myths.

The best-known creation story of the Hebrews, Genesis, developed between 1000 and 400 B.C. from oral and written traditions. Although the Hebrews were influenced by previous accounts of creation, they contributed the idea that there was only one creator god, who stood outside time and space, from whose thought or Word the universe began. In the Hebrew account, God made a conscious decision to create human beings, who were placed in the Garden of Eden. Evil came to this idyllic paradise when a snake persuaded Adam and Eve to disobey God's law and eat out of the Tree of Knowledge. For their original sin, or willful disobedience, humans were forever driven from Paradise.

Like most other ancient peoples, the Greeks perceived forces of nature as gods. They had no holy scriptures setting forth their deities, but they treated the stories of their earliest known poets generally as authoritative when they told of gods and goddesses, as Homer did around 800 B.C. Some fifty years later, Hesiod, who lived in rural Boeotia on the central-eastern Greek mainland, attempted to bring together stories of deities in his *Theogony (Origins of the Gods)*. In his creation story, the "older gods" came into being as the raw forces of nature. Later, Zeus, son of Cronos, and the other "younger gods," who were more humanlike in motives and activities, would take control of the universe from those senior deities. In contrast with many other creation accounts, the Greek stories of divine origins do not lend themselves to enhancing the power of priests or rulers.

In the East, the Japanese creation story *Nihongi* (A.D. 712) contains similar elements to those of the Mediterranean world. Before the separation of earth and heaven, there was a chaotic egglike mass until the divine couple Izanagi and Izanami, male and female, created the islands of Japan. Once this had been accomplished, the divine pair made their beautiful daughter, the Sun-Goddess,

1

ruler of Heaven. Her authority was soon challenged by her wicked and rude brother, Mikoto, whose actions so disturbed the Sun-Goddess that she retired into a cave, turning day into night until she was tricked into returning. Eventually, the Sun-Goddess's descendants ruled the earth as emperors of Japan.

In India, creation accounts evolved for many centuries before stabilizing in a combination of elements acceptable to most Hindus. These include portrayals of a single, original deity with unlimited creative power ("the One"), similar to the world soul in several other religions and some philosophies, such as Greco-Roman Stoicism, and the story of a cosmic sacrifice establishing a hierarchy of being from the parts of the huge but vulnerable deity, Purusa or Purusha.

1

The Hebrew Creation Story: *Genesis*

In the Hebrew creation story, God creates the world in six days. He gives Adam and Eve the Garden of Eden as their home until they commit the "Original Sin."

QUESTIONS TO CONSIDER

1. Discuss the differences or similarities of Genesis to the other creation stories.
2. Might one say that the Hebrew account is more sophisticated or refined than the others? If so, why? If not, why not?
3. How does the role of human beings in Genesis compare with that found among the Greeks (see Reading 2) or the Japanese (see Reading 3)?
4. There are two creation accounts of men and women in Genesis. What are the political and social implications of these differing accounts?

Chapter 1

In the beginning God created the heaven and the earth.

And the earth was without form, and void; and darkness was upon the face of the deep. And the Spirit of God moved upon the face of the waters.

And God said, Let there be light: and there was light.

And God saw the light, that it was good: and God divided the light from the darkness.

And God called the light Day, and the darkness he called Night. And the evening and the morning were the first day.

And God said, Let there be a firmament in the midst of the waters, and let it divide the waters from the waters.

From Genesis: 1–3 (King James Version); slightly modernized.

And God made the firmament, and divided the waters which were under the firmament from the waters which were above the firmament: and it was so.

And God called the firmament Heaven. And the evening and the morning were the second day.

And God said, Let the waters under the heaven be gathered together unto one place, and let the dry land appear: and it was so.

And God called the dry land Earth; and the gathering together of the waters called he Seas: and God saw that it was good.

And God said, Let the earth bring forth grass, the herb yielding seed, and the fruit tree yielding fruit after his kind, whose seed is in itself, upon the earth: and it was so.

And the earth brought forth grass, and herb yielding seed after his kind, and the tree yielding fruit, whose seed was in itself, after his kind: and God saw that it was good.

And the evening and the morning were the third day.

And God said, Let there be lights in the firmament of the heaven to divide the day from the night; and let them be for signs, and for seasons, and for days, and years:

And let them be for lights in the firmament of the heaven to give light upon the earth: and it was so.

And God made two great lights; the greater light to rule the day, and the lesser light to rule the night: he made the stars also.

And God set them in the firmament of the heaven to give light upon the earth,

And to rule over the day and over the night, and to divide the light from the darkness: and God saw that it was good.

And the evening and the morning were the fourth day.

And God said, Let the waters bring forth abundantly the moving creature that hath life, and fowl that may fly above the earth in the open firmament of heaven.

And God created great whales, and every living creature that moveth, which the waters brought forth abundantly, after their kind, and every winged fowl after his kind: and God saw that it was good.

And God blessed them, saying, Be fruitful, and multiply, and fill the waters in the seas, and let fowl multiply in the earth.

And the evening and the morning were the fifth day.

And God said, Let the earth bring forth the living creature after his kind, cattle, and creeping thing, and beast of the earth after his kind: and it was so.

And God made the beast of the earth after his kind, and cattle after their kind, and every thing that creepeth upon the earth after his kind: and God saw that it was good.

And God said, Let us make man in our image, after our likeness: and let them have dominion over the fish of the sea, and over the fowl of the air, and over the cattle, and over all the earth, and over every creeping thing that creepeth upon the earth.

So God created man in his own image, in the image of God created he him; male and female created he them.

And God blessed them, and God said unto them, Be fruitful, and multiply, and replenish the earth, and subdue it: and have dominion over the fish of the sea, and over the fowl of the air, and over every living thing that moveth upon the earth.

And God said, Behold, I have given you every herb bearing seed, which is upon the face of all the earth, and every tree in which is the fruit of a tree yielding seed; to you it shall be for meat.

And to every beast of the earth, and to every fowl of the air, and to every thing that creepeth upon the earth, wherein there is life, I have given every green herb for meat: and it was so.

And God saw everything that he had made, and, behold, it was very good. And the evening and the morning were the sixth day.

Chapter 2

Thus the heavens and the earth were finished, and all the host of them.

And on the seventh day God ended his work which he had made; and he rested on the seventh day from all his work which he had made.

And God blessed the seventh day and sanctified it: because in it he had rested from all his work which God created and made.

These are the generations of the heavens and of the earth when they were created, in the day that the Lord God made the earth and the heavens,

And every plant of the field before it was in the earth, and every herb of the field before it grew: for the Lord God had not caused it to rain upon the earth, and there was not a man to till the ground.

But there went up a mist from the earth, and watered the whole face of the ground.

And the Lord God formed man of the dust of the ground, and breathed into his nostrils the breath of life; and man became a living soul.

And the Lord God planted a garden eastward in Eden; and there he put the man whom he had formed.

And out of the ground made the Lord God to grow every tree that is pleasant to the sight, and good for food; the tree of life also in the midst of the garden, and the tree of knowledge of good and evil.

And a river went out of Eden to water the garden; and from thence it was parted and became into four heads.

The name of the first is Pishon: that is it which compasseth the whole land of Havilah, where there is gold;

And the gold of that land is good: there is bdellium and the onyx stone.

And the name of the second river is Gihon: the same is it that compasseth the whole land of Ethiopia.

And the name of the third river is Haddekel: that is it which goeth toward the east of Assyria. And the fourth river is Euphrates.

And the Lord God took the man, and put him into the garden of Eden to dress it and to keep it.

And the Lord God commanded the man, saying, Of every tree of the garden thou mayest freely eat:

But of the tree of knowledge of good and evil, thou shall not eat of it: for in the day that thou eatest thereof thou shalt surely die.

And the Lord God said, It is not good that the man should be alone; I will make him an help mate for him.

And out of the ground the Lord God formed every beast of the field, and every fowl of the air; and brought them unto Adam to see what he would call them: and whatsoever Adam called every living creature, that was the name thereof.

And Adam gave names to all cattle, and to the fowl of the air, and to every beast of the field; but for Adam there was not found an help mate for him.

And the Lord God caused a deep sleep to fall upon Adam, and he slept: and he took one of his ribs, and closed up the flesh instead thereof;

And the rib, which the Lord God had taken from man, made he a woman, and brought her unto the man.

And Adam said, This is now bone of my bones, and flesh of my flesh: she shall be called Woman, because she was taken out of Man.

Therefore shall a man leave his father and his mother, and shall cleave unto his wife: and they shall be one flesh.

And they were both naked, the man and his wife, and were not ashamed.

Chapter 3

Now the serpent was more subtil than any beast of the field which the Lord God had made. And he said unto the woman, Yea, hath God said, Ye shall not eat of every tree of the garden?

And the woman said unto the serpent, We may eat of the fruit of the trees of the garden:

But of the fruit of the tree which is in the midst of the garden, God hath said, Ye shall not eat of it, neither shall ye touch it, lest ye die.

And the serpent said unto the woman, ye shall not surely die:

For God doth know that in the day ye eat thereof, then your eyes shall be opened, and ye shall be as gods, knowing good and evil.

And when the woman saw that the tree was good for food, and that it was pleasant to the eyes, and a tree to be desired to make one wise, she took of the fruit thereof, and did eat, and gave also unto her husband with her; and he did eat.

And the eyes of them both were opened, and they knew that they were naked; and they sewed fig leaves together, and made themselves aprons.

And they heard the voice of the Lord God walking in the garden in the cool of the day: and Adam and his wife hid themselves from the presence of the Lord God amongst the trees of the garden.

And the Lord God called unto Adam, and said unto him, Where art thou?

And he said, I heard thy voice in the garden, and I was afraid, because I was naked; and I hid myself.

And he said, Who told thee that thou wast naked? Hast thou eaten of the tree, whereof I commanded thee that thou shouldest not eat?

And the man said, The woman whom thou gavest to be with me, she gave me of the tree, and I did eat.

And the Lord God said unto the woman, What is this that thou hast done? And the woman said, The serpent beguiled me, and I did eat.

And the Lord God said unto the serpent, Because thou hast done this, thou art cursed above all cattle, and above every beast of the field; upon thy belly shalt thou go, and dust shalt thou eat all the days of thy life:

And I will put enmity between thee and the woman, and between thy seed and her seed; it shall bruise thy head, and thou shalt bruise his heel.

Unto the woman he said, I will greatly multiply thy sorrow and thy conception; in sorrow thou shalt bring forth children; and thy desire shall be to thy husband, and he shall rule over thee.

And unto Adam he said, Because thou has hearkened unto the voice of thy wife, and hast eaten of the tree, of which I commanded thee, saying, Thou shalt not eat of it: cursed is the ground for thy sake; in sorrow shalt thou eat of it all the days of thy life;

Thorns also and thistles shall it bring forth to thee; and thou shalt eat the herb of the field:

In the sweat of thy face shalt thou eat bread, till thou return unto the ground; for out of it wast thou taken: for dust thou art, and unto dust shalt thou return.

And Adam called his wife's name Eve; because she was the mother of all living.

Unto Adam also and to his wife did the Lord God make coats of skins, and clothed them.

And the Lord God said, Behold, the man is become as one of us, to know good and evil: and now, lest he put forth his hand, and take also of the tree of life, and eat, and live for ever:

Therefore the Lord God sent him forth from the garden of Eden, to till the ground from whence he was taken.

So he drove out the man; and he placed at the east of the garden of Eden Cherubims, and a flaming sword which turned every way, to keep the way of the tree of life.

2

A Greek Creation Story: Hesiod's *Theogony*

This account begins creation with the Greek "old gods." Although they were to be superseded in considerable part by the more anthropomorphic "new gods," none of them were totally erased from the Greek religious system. Tartarus, for example, yielded most of the underworld to Hades (Pluto) but became a place-name for its bottom pit (from whence "the Tartars"; see Reading 78), and Erebos became the semi-darkness on the way to the underworld. Aphrodite (Venus), whose domain was heterosexual love, can be seen either as the first of the new gods to take over the functions of an older one (Eros) or as one of the older deities herself and one of the few to arrive in the classical world with her powers unchallenged. Eros shrank into the cute, winged, cherubic figure we recognize on stereotypical valentines, more familiar by his Roman name, "Cupid." The Furies, whose domain was blood vengeance—a frequent and dreaded threat in early societies—later took on a law-enforcement role as Aeschylus portrayed them in his classic play *Eumenides (The Right-Thinking Ones)*. In Greek cosmology, aether was the totally pure airspace reserved for gods above the atmosphere that mortals breathed. "Adamant" was the (mythical) hardest of all metals and stones, available only to gods; later it evolved into one of the names for "diamonds."

QUESTIONS TO CONSIDER

1. Where might Hesiod's sources have gotten the idea of Heaven and Earth conceiving offspring in a union?
2. What aspects of Hesiod's creation story do you suppose later Greeks who thought of themselves as eminently civilized wanted to suppress or amend?

3. Do you think that perhaps the idea of the Oedipus or Edipus complex goes all the way back to Greek ideas of the creation?
4. Are there any similarities between the Greek and Japanese creation stories (see Reading 3)?

Chaos was at the beginning, but broad-bosomed Gaia [Earth] soon followed as solid footing for all the immortals who live on the snowy peak of Olympus. Gloomy Tartarus established himself in a deep hole within a broad-pathed Earth. Eros, most handsome of the immortals, also came to be the god who makes other gods and men stumble with their limbs and minds alike.

Black Night and Erebus emerged from Chaos. Then Night bore Aether and Day, whom she had conceived in love with Erebus. Gaia's own first-born was starry Ouranos [Heaven], her own equal, to cover her all around and to provide a secure abode for all the blessed gods forever. Then she brought forth long Hills, the beautiful homes of Nymphs, goddesses who live in their clefts. She also bore—without love—Pontus, the barren sea depths and the raging billows. She then lay with Heaven and bore deep-swirling Oceanos. Later she bore cunning, scheming Kronos, who hated his brutal, self-indulgent father.

She went on to bear the arrogant, offensive Cyclopes: Brontes, Stereopes, and spirited Arges; they were to make and give Zeus thunder and the lightning bolt. They resembled other gods except for having only one eye: their name [Cyclopes = the round-eyed] comes from the one round eye set in the middle of the forehead of each one. Their work displayed great strength and craftsmanship. Finally, Heaven and Earth bore three sons, Kottos, Gyes and Briareos, all unspeakably violent, strong and insolent children. From the shoulders of each stretched a hundred arms, flailing about, making it impossible for anyone to come close. Each had fifty heads on his shoulders over all those arms: nothing could withstand the overwhelming strength of these monstrous creatures. They were the most terrible of the children of Gaia, and their own father hated them from the first. As soon as each was born, Heaven would stuff him away in a secret place far down in Earth and would not let him come up to see the light.

Ouranos gloated over this wickedness of his. Vast Gaia, however, groaned from having her insides strained and stretched, devised a crafty, evil plan. First she created adamant and from it a huge sickle. Then she called on her beloved sons, urging them to join her in vengeance, for her heart was heavy with grief and anger.

"My children, your father is evil and reckless. Do as I say, and we shall avenge his wicked crime against us. He was the first to begin shameful acts."

Those were her words, but fear froze all her sons, and none said a word until finally great but crooked Kronos took heart and answered his dear mother: "I volunteer for this deed, Mother, for I do not love my evil father; he *was* the first to think up shameful acts."

This is what he said, and vast Gaia was greatly pleased. She hid him in a place of ambush, gave him the serated sickle and revealed the whole plot to him. After a while Ouranos came, bringing Night with him: he spread himself fully over Gaia as he lay with her. From his hiding place, Heaven's son stretched his left hand forward and, with the jagged teeth of the heavy, long sickle in his right hand, quickly severed his father's genitals and threw them

From Hesiod, "Theogonia," in *Die Hesiodische Theogonie,* ed. F.G. Welcher (Elberfeld: R.L. Friderich, 1865), pp. 30–33; translated by Henry A. Myers.

behind him. They fell with marvelous results: From all the bloody drops that spurted out and fell Gaia conceived the mighty Furies, also the huge giants in gleaming armor who hold long spears, and those Nymphs everywhere called "Meliae" [Ash-tree Nymphs].

Kronos threw the sickle-severed genitals from land into the stormy sea, where the waves swept them away for a long time. White foam attached itself to the immortal flesh and, in it a girl developed. At first she approached holy Cythera, but afterwards she came to the island of Cyprus. There she came up on land, a beautiful and awesome goddess, and grass grew up around her from under her shapely feet. Gods and men call her "Aphrodite," since she developed in the foam (aphros), also "Cythera" since she first arrived at Cythera, "Cyprogenes," since she first emerged on stormy Cyprus, or "Philommedes" [members-living] because of the genitalia from which she developed. Eros went along with her, and pretty Desire followed her when she first came on land and when she went to join the assemblage of gods. Among gods and men she has been honored from the first; the fond whisperings of girls pay tribute to her. Her power is in smiles and tricks, sweet delights of love and charm.

But great Ouranos condemned his own sons, calling them "Titans" [those who strain], for he said that they had strained insolently and done a terrible deed which would later be avenged.

And Night bore fearsome Doom and black Fate, as well as Death, Sleep and the whole tribe of Dreams. . . .

3

A Japanese Creation Story: *Nihongi*

The two oldest sources on Japanese mythology and history, *Kojiki (Record of Ancient Matters)* and *Nihongi (Chronicle of Japan),* completed in A.D. 712 and A.D. 720 respectively, tell about the creation of heaven and earth and the divine origins of the land of Japan and its reigning family. According to the *Nihongi,* Amaterasu-o-Mikami, the Sun-Goddess and progenitrix of the Japanese imperial line, was chosen by her divine parents, Izanagi-no-Mikoto and Izanami-no-Mikoto, to rule the plain of High Heaven (Takama-no-hara). The grandson of the Sun-Goddess, Ninigi-no-Mikoto, descended on Taka-chiho-no-mine, a sacred mountain top in modern Kyushu, and his grandson, Jimmu, finally established his rule as the first emperor of Japan in 660 B.C. Akihito (r. 1989–   ), the reigning monarch of Japan today, is regarded as the 125th direct descendant of Emperor Jimmu. The following selection is an excerpt from *Nihongi.*

QUESTIONS TO CONSIDER

1. Compare and contrast the creation epic of Japan with Genesis (see Reading 1).
2. How do you compare Amaterasu-o-Mikami, the Sun-Goddess of Japan, with Gaia in the Greek creation story (see Reading 2)?

Of old, Heaven and Earth were not yet separated, and the In and Yo[1] not yet divided. They formed a chaotic mass like an egg which was of obscurely defined limits and contained germs.

The purer and clearer part was thinly drawn out, and formed Heaven, while the heavier and grosser element settled down and became Earth. . . .

Thereafter Divine Beings were produced between them.

Hence, it is said that when the world began to be created, the soil of which lands were composed floated about in a manner which might be compared to the floating of a fish sporting on the surface of the water.

At this time a certain thing was produced between Heaven and Earth. It was in form like a reed-shoot. Now this became transformed into a God, and was called Kuni-no-toko-tachi-no-Mikoto. . . . [and seven other deities including Izanagi-no-Mikoto and Izanami-no-Mikoto]. . . .

Being formed by the mutual action of Heavenly and Earthly principles, they were made male and female. From Kuni-no-toko-tachi-no-Mikoto to Izanagi-no-Mikoto and Izanami-no-Mikoto are called the seven generations of the age of the Gods.

Izanagi-no-Mikoto and Izanami-no-Mikoto stood on the floating bridge of Heaven, and held counsel together, saying: "Is there not a country beneath?" Thereupon they thrust down the jewel-spear of Heaven and groping about therewith found the Ocean. The brine which dripped from the point of the spear coagulated and became an island which received the name of Ono-goro-jima.[2]

The two Deities thereupon descended and dwelt in this island. Accordingly they wished to become husband and wife together, and to produce countries.

So they made Ono-goro-jima the pillar of the center of the land.

Now the male deity turning by the left, and the female deity by the right, they went around the pillar of the land separately. When they met together on one side, the female deity spoke first and said: "How delightful! I have met with a lovely youth." The male deity was displeased, and said: "I am a man, and by right should have spoken first. How is it that on the contrary thou, a woman, shouldst have been the first to speak? This was unlucky. Let us go round again." Upon this the two deities went back, and having met anew, this time the male deity spoke first, and said: "How delightful! I have met a lovely maiden."

Then he inquired of the female deity, saying: "In thy body, is there aught formed?" She answered, and said: "In my body there is a place which is the source of femininity." The male deity said: "In my body again there is a place which is the source of masculinity. I wish to unite this source-place of my body to the source-place of thy body." Hereupon the male and female first became united as husband and wife.

Now when the time of birth arrived [they gave birth to one island after another, in all eight islands which were known as Oho-ya-shima country][3] . . .

They next produced the sea, then the rivers, and then the mountains. Then they produced Ku-ku-no-chi, the ancestor of the trees, and next the ancestor of herbs, Kaya-no-hime.

After this Izanagi-no-Mikoto and Izanami-no-Mikoto consulted together, saying: "We have now produced the Great-eight-island country, with the mountains, rivers, herbs,

[1]The basic dualism of nature in Chinese philosophy. Yo or Yang in Chinese represents male: light, hot, and positive; and In or Yin in Chinese is female: dark, cold, and negative.
[2]The islets off the coast of the larger island of Ahaji in western Japan.
[3]Land-of-the-Eight-Great-Islands, old name for Japan.

From W.G. Aston, trans., *Nihongi, Chronicles of Japan from the Earliest Times to* A.D. *607*, Transactions and Proceedings of The Japan Society, Supplement I (London: Kegan, Paul, Trench, Trubner & Co., 1896), pp. 1–45.

and trees. Why should we not produce someone who shall be lord of the universe? They then together produced the Sun-Goddess, who was called [Amaterasu-o-Mikami].

The resplendent luster of this child shone throughout all the six quarters. Therefore the two Deities rejoiced, saying: "We have had many children, but none of them have been equal to this wondrous infant. She ought not to be kept long in this land, but we ought of our own accord to send her at once to Heaven, and entrust to her the affairs of Heaven."

At this time Heaven and Earth were still not far separated, and therefore they sent her up to Heaven by the ladder of Heaven.

They next produced the Moon God.

His radiance was next to that of the Sun in splendor. This God was to be the consort of the Sun-Goddess, and to share in her government. They therefore sent him also to Heaven. . . .

Their next child was Sosa-no-wo-no-Mikoto.

This God had a fierce temper and was given to cruel acts. Moreover he made a practice of continually weeping and wailing. So he brought many of the people of the land to an untimely end. Again he caused green mountains to become withered. Therefore the two Gods, his parents, addressed Sosa-no-wo-no-Mikoto, saying: "Thou art exceedingly wicked, and it is not meet that thou shouldst reign over the world. Certainly thou must depart far away to the Nether-Land." So they at length expelled him. . . .

Upon this Sosa-no-wo-no-Mikoto made petition, saying: "I will now obey thy instructions and proceed to the Nether-Land. Therefore I wish for a short time to go to the Plain of High Heaven and meet with my elder sister, after which I will go away for ever." Permission was granted him, and he therefore ascended to Heaven. . . .

Now at first when Sosa-no-wo-no-Mikoto went up to Heaven, by reason of the fierceness of his divine nature there was a commotion in the sea and the hills and mountains groaned aloud. [The Sun Goddess], knowing the violence and wickedness of this Deity, was startled and changed countenance, when she heard the manner of his coming. She said [to herself]: "Is my younger brother coming with good intentions? I think it might be his purpose to rob me of my kingdom." . . .

After this Sosa-no-wo-no-Mikoto's behavior was exceedingly rude. . . . Indignant at this, she straightway entered the Rock-cave of Heaven, and having fastened the Rock-door, dwelt there in seclusion. Therefore, constant darkness prevailed on all sides, and the alternation of night and day was unknown.

Then the eighty myriads of Gods met on the bank of the Tranquil River of Heaven, and considered in what manner they should supplicate her. Accordingly, [a deity][4] with profound device and far-reaching thought, at length gathered long-singing birds of Eternal Land and made them utter their prolonged cry to one another. Moreover, he made [a powerful deity][5] to stand beside the Rock-door. Then [two other deities] dug up a five hundred branched True Sakaki tree[6] of the Heavenly Mt. Kagu.[7] On its upper branches they hung an august five-hundred string of Yasaka jewels.[8] On the middle branches they hung an eight-hand mirror.[9] . . .

Then they recited their liturgy together.

[4]A god named Omoho-kane-no-Kami.

[5]A god named Ta-jikara-wo-no-Kami.

[6]The Sakaki, or cleyera Japonica, is the sacred tree of the Shinto religion of Japan. It is used in Shinto religious ceremonies.

[7]A mountain in Yamato. Heaven is supposed to have a counterpart.

[8]An eight-feet-long sacred curved jewel, which is one of the three Imperial Regalia.

[9]A large size mirror.

Moreover, [another deity][10] took in her hand a spear with Eulalia grass,[11] and standing before the door of the Rock-cave of Heaven, skillfully performed a mimic dance. She took moreover, the true Sakaki tree of the Heavenly Mount Kagu, and made of it a head-dress, she took club moss and made of it braces, she kindled fires, she placed a tub bottom upwards, and gave forth a divinely-inspired utterance.

Now the [Sun-Goddess] heard this, and said: "Since I have shut myself up in the Rock-cave, there ought surely to be continual night in the Central Land of fertile reed plains. How then can [this deity] be so jolly?" So with her august hand, she opened for a narrow space the Rock-door and peeped out. Then the [awaiting powerful deity] forthwith took the [Sun-Goddess] by the hand, and led her out [. . . and the radiance of the Sun-Goddess filled the universe].

4

A Hindu Creation Story: *Rig Veda*

When the Aryans invaded India, they brought with them the diverse pantheon characteristic of the Indo-European peoples, some of them identifiable with prototypes of Greek and Roman deities. The *Rig Veda,* which reflects oral tradition written roughly between 1500 and 700 B.C., is the major source-book of early Hindu religion, containing descriptions and stories of the early universe and its gods, along with much genealogy and rules for sacrifices. A distinctly Hindu deity, however, was Purusa (Purusha), sacrificed by the other gods to fill creation with worthwhile items ranging from the sacred verses of the *Rig Veda* itself to horses and humankind.

QUESTIONS TO CONSIDER

1. How does the depiction of the universe before human existence compare with the early parts of the previous creation stories?
2. How can the sacrifice of Purusha be seen as justification for the social divisions that developed into the Hindu caste system?

Creation Hymn

Then even nothingness was not, nor existence. There was no air then, nor the heavens beyond it. What covered it? Where was it? In whose keeping? Was there then cosmic water, in depths unfathomed?

[10]A terrible female of Heaven named Ama-no-uzume-no Mikoto.
[11]Eulalia japonica, a kind of grass.

From the *Rig Veda,* Book X, 129, translated by A.L. Basham, *The Wonder That Was India* (New York: Grove Press, 1977), pp. 247–48. Reprinted by permission. "To the Purusha" from the *Rig Veda,* Book X, 90, in Edward J. Thomas, *Wisdom of the East: Vedic Hymns* (London: John Murray, 1923), pp. 120–22. Reprinted by permission.

Then there were neither death nor immortality, nor was there then the torch of night and day. The One breathed windlessly and self-sustaining. There was that One then, and there was no other.

At first there was only darkness wrapped in darkness. All this was only unilluminated water. That One which came to be, enclosed in nothing, arose at last, born of the power of heat.

In the beginning desire descended on it—that was the primal seed, born of the mind. The sages who have searched their hearts with wisdom know that which is kin to that which is not.

And they have stretched their cord across the void, and know what was above, and what below. Seminal powers made fertile mighty forces. Below was strength, and over it was impulse.

The Cosmic Sacrifice

Thousand headed was the Purusa, thousand-eyed, thousand-footed. He embraced the earth on all sides, and stood beyond the breadth of ten fingers.

The Purusa is this all, that which was and which shall be. He is Lord of immortality, which he grows beyond through [sacrificial] food.

Such is his greatness, and still greater than that is the Purusa. One fourth of him is all beings. The three fourths of him is the immortal in Heaven.

Three fourths on high rose the Purusa. One fourth of him arose again here [on the earth]. Thence in all directions he spread abroad, as that which eats and that which eats not. . . .

When the Gods spread out the sacrifice with the Purusa as oblation [offering], spring was its ghee [butter offering], summer the fuel, autumn the oblation.

As the sacrifice on the strewn grass they besprinkled the Purusa, born in the beginning. With him the Gods sacrificed, the Sadhyas [demi-gods], and the sages.

From that sacrifice completely offered were born the Verses [*Rig Veda*] and the Saman-melodies [*Sama Veda*]. The metres were born from it. From it was born the Sacrificial formula [*Yajur Veda*].

From it were born horses, and they have two rows of teeth. Cattle were born from it. From it were born goats and sheep.

When they divided the Purusa, into how many parts did they arrange him? What was his mouth? What his two arms? What are his thighs and feet called?

The *brâhman* was his mouth, his two arms were made the *rajanya* [or *kshatriya* = warrior], his two thighs the *vaisya* [trader and agriculturist], from his feet the *sûdra* [servile class] was born.

The moon was born from his spirit, from his eye was born the sun, from his mouth Indra and Agni,[1] from his breath Vayu [wind] was born.

From his navel arose the middle sky, from his head the heaven originated, from his feet the earth, the quarters from his ear. Thus did they fashion the worlds.

Seven were his sticks that enclose the fire, thrice seven were made the faggots. When the Gods spread out the sacrifice, they bound the Purusa as a victim.

---

[1]Indra was the storm and war god, Agni the god of fire.

With the sacrifice the Gods sacrificed the sacrifice. These were the first ordinances. These great powers reached to the firmament, where are the ancient Sadhyas, the Gods.

A Sumerian Heroic Legend

5

The Epic of Gilgamesh

Gilgamesh, the semi-legendary Sumerian king who ruled the city of Uruk around 2700 B.C., is the subject of the world's first great epic poem. Gilgamesh was a roguish king whose lusty appetites were resented by his subjects, who prayed for a deliverer. To punish Gilgamesh for his sins, the gods created the uncivilized Enkidu and sent him to chastise Gilgamesh and spare Uruk further harm. But instead of becoming mortal enemies, Gilgamesh and Enkidu became fast friends and set off together on a series of adventures, detailed in the first half of this epic.

Their first adventure is to secure timber from the distant Cedar Forest, which is guarded by the ogre Humbaba, whom they must kill. Upon their return to Uruk, the fierce Ishtar, goddess of love, tries to entice Gilgamesh into marriage; however, because Gilgamesh and Enkidu spurn Ishtar, she sends down the Bull of Heaven to punish them. Gilgamesh and Enkidu kill this creature, thereby angering the powerful Enlil, king of the gods, who takes his revenge by killing Enkidu. King Gilgamesh is devastated by his friend's death and laments humanity's fate.

The second half of the epic is devoted to Gilgamesh's quest for the secret of life. He descends into the Netherworld in search of Utnapishtim, to whom the gods had granted immortality and from whom he hopes to learn the key to life. When the two meet, Utnapishtim introduces Gilgamesh to the story of the Great Flood, which had killed all life save for Utnapishtim, his family, and the animals he had placed in his great ship. At the end of the Flood tale, Utnapishtim tells Gilgamesh of a certain Plant of Life that can give immortality. Gilgamesh is able to retrieve this plant and bring it back to the living; yet his hopes are dashed when it is eaten by a snake. At the end of the poem, Gilgamesh can only lament the human fate, old age and death.

QUESTIONS TO CONSIDER

1. What elements of this epic do you also find in Homer's *Odyssey* (see Reading 14)?
2. Why was Enkidu created and how was he changed?

3. In the second half of the epic, what is Gilgamesh seeking? Does he succeed in this quest?
4. What part of the epic is the most familiar to you?

I will proclaim to the world the deeds of Gilgamesh. This was the man to whom all things were known; this was the king who knew the countries of the world. He was wise, he saw mysteries and knew secret things, he brought us a tale of the days before the flood. He went on a long journey, was weary, wornout with labour, returning he rested, he engraved on a stone the whole story.

When the gods created Gilgamesh they gave him a perfect body. Shamash the glorious sun endowed him with beauty. Adad the god of the storm endowed him with courage, the great gods made his beauty perfect, surpassing all others, terrifying like a great wild bull. Two thirds they made him god and one third man.

In Uruk he built walls, a great rampart, and the temple of blessed Eanna for the god of the firmament Anu, and for Ishtar the goddess of love. . . .

The Coming of Enkidu

Gilgamesh went abroad in the world, but he met with none who could withstand his arms till he came to Uruk. But the men of Uruk muttered in their houses, "Gilgamesh sounds the tocsin for his amusement, his arrogance has no bounds by day or night. No son is left with his father, for Gilgamesh takes them all, even the children; yet the king should be a shepherd to his people. His lust leaves no virgin to her lover, neither the warrior's daughter nor the wife of the noble; yet this is the shepherd of the city, wise, comely, and resolute."

The gods heard their lament, the gods of heaven cried to the Lord of Uruk, to Anu the god of Uruk. . . . When Anu had heard their lamentation the gods cried to Aruru, the goddess of creation, "You made him, O Aruru, now create his equal; let it be as like him as his own reflection, his second self, stormy heart for stormy heart. Let them contend together and leave Uruk in quiet."

So the goddess conceived an image in her mind, and it was of the stuff of Anu of the firmament. She dipped her hands in water and pinched off clay, she let it fall in the wilderness, and noble Enkidu was created. There was virtue in him of the god of war, of Ninurta himself. His body was rough, he had long hair like a woman's; it waved like the hair of Nisaba, the goddess of corn. His body was covered with matted hair like Samuqan's, the god of cattle. He was innocent of mankind; he knew nothing of the cultivated land.

Enkidu ate grass in the hills with the gazelle and lurked with wild beasts at the water-holes; he had joy of the water with the herds of wild game. But there was a trapper who met him one day face to face at the drinking-hole, for the wild game had entered his territory. On three days he met him face to face, and the trapper was frozen with fear. He went back to his house with the game that he had caught, and he was dumb, benumbed with terror. His face was altered like that of one who has made a long journey. . . .

So the trapper set out on his journey to Uruk and addressed himself to Gilgamesh saying, "A man unlike any other is roaming now in the pastures; he is as strong as a star from

From *The Epic of Gilgamesh,* introduction and translation by N.K. Sandars (New York: Penguin Books, 1972), pp. 61–65, 67–69, 85–86, 89, 108–111, 116–17. Copyright © N.K. Sandars, 1960, 1964, 1970. Reproduced by permission of Penguin Books Ltd.

heaven and I am afraid to approach him. He helps the wild game to escape; he fills in my pits and pulls up my traps." Gilgamesh said, "Trapper, go back, take with you a harlot, a child of pleasure. At the drinking-hole she will strip, and when he sees her beckoning he will embrace her and the game of the wilderness will surely reject him."

Now the trapper returned, taking the harlot with him. After a three days' journey they came to the drinking-hole, and there they sat down; the harlot and the trapper sat facing one another and waited for the game to come. For the first day and for the second day the two sat waiting, but on the third day the herds came; they came down to drink and Enkidu was with them. The small wild creatures of the plains were glad of the water, and Enkidu with them, who ate grass with the gazelle and was born in the hills; and she saw him, the savage man, come from far-off in the hills. The trapper spoke to her: "There he is. Now, woman, make your breasts bare, have no shame, do not delay but welcome his love. Let him see you naked, let him possess your body. When he comes near uncover yourself and lie with him; teach him, the savage man, your woman's art, for when he murmurs love to you the wild beasts that shared his life in the hills will reject him."

She was not ashamed to take him, she made herself naked and welcomed his eagerness; as he lay on her murmuring love she taught him the woman's art. For six days and seven nights they lay together, for Enkidu had forgotten his home in the hills; but when he was satisfied he went back to the wild beasts. Then, when the gazelle saw him, they bolted away; when the wild creatures saw him they fled. Enkidu would have followed, but his body was bound as though with a cord, his knees gave way when he started to run, his swiftness was gone. And now the wild creatures had all fled away; Enkidu was grown weak, for wisdom was in him, and the thoughts of a man were in his heart. So he returned and sat down at the woman's feet, and listened intently to what she said, "You are wise, Enkidu, and now you have become like a god. Why do you want to run wild with the beasts in the hills? Come with me. I will take you to strong-walled Uruk, to the blessed temple of Ishtar and of Anu, of love and heaven; there Gilgamesh lives, who is very strong, and like a wild bull he lords it over men." . . .

And now she said to Enkidu, "When I look at you you have become like a god. Why do you yearn to run wild again with the beasts in the hills? Get up from the ground, the bed of a shepherd." He listened to her words with care. It was good advice that she gave. She divided her clothing in two and with the one half she clothed him and with the other herself; and holding his hand she led him like a child to the sheepfolds, into the shepherds' tents. There all the shepherds crowded round to see him, they put down bread in front of him, but Enkidu could only suck the milk of wild animals. He fumbled and gaped, at a loss what to do or how he should eat the bread and drink the strong wine. Then the woman said, "Enkidu, eat bread, it is the staff of life; drink the wine, it is the custom of the land." So he ate till he was full and drank strong wine, seven goblets. He became merry, his heart exulted and his face shone. He rubbed down the matted hair of his body and anointed himself with oil. Enkidu had become a man; but when he had put on man's clothing he appeared like a bridegroom.

Now Enkidu strode in front and the woman followed behind. He entered Uruk, that great market, and all the folk thronged round him where he stood in the street in strong-walled Uruk. The people jostled; speaking of him they said, "He is the spit of Gilgamesh." "He is shorter." "He is bigger of bone." "This is the one who was reared on the milk of wild beasts. His is the greatest strength." The men rejoiced: "Now Gilgamesh has met his match. This great one, this hero whose beauty is like a god, he is a match even for Gilgamesh."

In Uruk the bridal bed was made, fit for the goddess of love. The bride waited for the bridegroom, but in the night Gilgamesh got up and came to the house. Then Enkidu stepped out, he stood in the street and blocked the way. Mighty Gilgamesh came on and Enkidu met him at the gate. He put out his foot and prevented Gilgamesh from entering the house, so they grappled, holding each other like bulls. They broke the doorposts and the walls shook. Gilgamesh bent his knee with his foot planted on the ground and with a turn Enkidu was thrown. Then immediately his fury died. When Enkidu was thrown he said to Gilgamesh, "There is not another like you in the world. Ninsun, who is as strong as a wild ox in the byre, she was the mother who bore you, and now you are raised above all men, and Enlil has given you the kingship, for your strength surpasses the strength of men." So Enkidu and Gilgamesh embraced and their friendship was sealed. . . .

[After they had become good friends, Gilgamesh and Enkidu set out for the Cedar Forest (possibly southern Turkey or Phoenicia) in order to secure wood for the city. Before they got to the wood, however, they had to kill a fire-breathing ogre called Humbaba. Succeeding in this mission, they returned to Uruk, where Gilgamesh was offered marriage by the goddess of love, Ishtar (or Inanna).]

Gilgamesh opened his mouth and answered glorious Ishtar, "If I take you in marriage, what gifts can I give in return? What ointments and clothing for your body? I would gladly give you bread and all sorts of food fit for a god. I would give you wine to drink fit for a queen. I would pour out barley to stuff your granary; but as for making you my wife—that I will not. How would it go with me? Your lovers have found you like a brazier which smoulders in the cold, a backdoor which keeps out neither squall of wind nor storm, a castle which crushes the garrison, pitch that blackens the bearer, a water-skin that chafes the carrier, a stone which falls from the parapet, a battering-ram turned back from the enemy, a sandal that trips the wearer. Which of your lovers did you ever love for ever? What shepherd of yours has pleased you for all time?" . . .

[Gravely insulted by the king's words, Ishtar asked her father, Anu, to punish Gilgamesh by sending the Bull of Heaven to ravage the land. Gilgamesh and Enkidu managed to kill the bull, whose hind leg Enkidu tore off and flung at the goddess. Such a serious offense against the gods demanded immediate punishment; thus did Enkidu fall ill and die.]

So Enkidu lay stretched out before Gilgamesh; his tears ran down in streams and he said to Gilgamesh, "O my brother, so dear as you are to me, brother, yet they will take me from you." Again he said, "I must sit down on the threshold of the dead and never again will I see my dear brother with my eyes." . . .

[Gilgamesh was unreconciled to the death of his beloved friend Enkidu. He decided to make a long and difficult journey to the Netherworld in order to search for the secret of immortality. There he encountered the Sumerian Akkadian Noah called Utnapishtim (or Ziusudra). Utnapishtim tells Gilgamesh of a Flood that had been sent by the gods to destroy all life except for Utnapishtim and his family.]

"In those days the world teemed, the people multiplied, the world bellowed like a wild bull, and the great god was aroused by the clamour. Enlil heard the clamour and he said to the gods in council, 'The uproar of mankind is intolerable and sleep is no longer possible by reason of the babel.' So the gods agreed to exterminate mankind. Enlil did this, but Ea because of his oath warned me in a dream. He whispered their words to my house of reeds,

'Reed-house, reed-house! Wall, O wall, hearken reed-house, wall reflect; O man of Shur-rupak, son of Ubara-Tutu; tear down your house and build a boat, abandon possessions and look for life, despise worldly goods and save your soul alive. Tear down your house, I say, and build a boat. These are the measurements of the barque as you shall build her: let her beam equal her length, let her deck be roofed like the vault that covers the abyss; then take up into the boat the seed of all living creatures.'

"In the first light of dawn all my household gathered round me, the children brought pitch and the men whatever was necessary. On the fifth day I laid the keel and the ribs, then I made fast the planking. The ground-space was one acre, each side of the deck measured one hundred and twenty cubits, making a square. I built six decks below, seven in all. I divided them into nine sections with bulkheads between. I drove in wedges where needed, I saw to the punt-poles, and laid in supplies. The carriers brought oil in baskets, I poured pitch into the furnace and asphalt and oil; more oil was consumed in caulking, and more again the master of the boat took into his stores. I slaughtered bullocks for the people and every day I killed sheep. I gave the shipwrights wine to drink as though it were river water, raw wine and red wine and oil and white wine. There was feasting then as there is at the time of the New Year's festival; I myself anointed my head. On the seventh day the boat was complete.

"Then was the launching full of difficulty; there was shifting of ballast above and below till two thirds was submerged. I loaded into her all that I had of gold and of living things, my family, my kin, the beast of the field both wild and tame, and all the craftsmen. I sent them on board, for the time that Shamash had ordained was already fulfilled when he said, 'In the evening, when the rider of the storm sends down the destroying rain, enter the boat and batten her down.' The time was fulfilled, the evening came, the rider of the storm sent down the rain. I looked out at the weather and it was terrible, so I too boarded the boat and battened her down. All was now complete, the battening and the caulking; so I handed the tiller to Puzur-Amurri the steersman, with the navigation and the care of the whole boat. . . .

"For six days and six nights the winds blew, torrent and tempest and flood over-whelmed the world, tempest and flood raged together like warring hosts. When the seventh day dawned the storm from the south subsided, the sea grew calm, the flood was stilled; I looked at the face of the world and there was silence, all mankind was turned to clay. The surface of the sea stretched as flat as a roof-top; I opened a hatch and the light fell on my face. Then I bowed low, I sat down and I wept, the tears streamed down my face, for on every side was the waste of water. I looked for land in vain, but fourteen leagues distant there appeared a mountain, and there the boat grounded; on the mountain of Nisir the boat held fast, she held fast and did not budge. One day she held, and a second day on the mountain of Nisir she held fast and did not budge. A third day, and a fourth day she held fast on the mountain and did not budge; a fifth day and a sixth day she held fast on the mountain. When the seventh day dawned I loosed a dove and let her go. She flew away, but finding no resting-place she returned. Then I loosed a swallow, and she flew away but finding no resting-place she returned. I loosed a raven, she saw that the waters had retreated, she ate, she flew around, she cawed, and she did not come back. Then I threw everything open to the four winds, I made a sacrifice and poured out a libation on the mountain top. Seven and again seven cauldrons I set up on their stands, I heaped up wood and cane and cedar and myrtle. When the gods smelled the sweet savour, they gathered like flies over the sacrifice."

[Utnapishtim then revealed to Gilgamesh the secret of immortality. With the aid of his ferryman, Urshanabi, King Gilgamesh secured this mysterious prickly plant, but his hopes for future rejuvenation were not to be.]

"Gilgamesh, I shall reveal a secret thing, it is a mystery of the gods that I am telling you. There is a plant that grows under the water, it has a prickle like a thorn, like a rose; it will wound your hands, but if you succeed in taking it, then your hands will hold that which restores his lost youth to a man."

When Gilgamesh heard this he opened the sluices so that a sweet-water current might carry him out to the deepest channel; he tied heavy stones to his feet and they dragged him down to the water-bed. There he saw the plant growing; although it pricked him he took it in his hands; then he cut the heavy stones from his feet, and the sea carried him and threw him on to the shore. Gilgamesh said to Urshanabi the ferryman, "Come here, and see this marvellous plant. By its virtue a man may win back all his former strength. I will take it to Uruk of the strong walls; there I will give it to the old men to eat. Its name shall be 'The Old Men Are Young Again'; and at last I shall eat it myself and have back all my lost youth." So Gilgamesh returned by the gate through which he had come, Gilgamesh and Urshanabi went together. They travelled their twenty leagues and then they broke their fast; after thirty leagues they stopped for the night.

Gilgamesh saw a well of cool water and he went down and bathed; but deep in the pool there was lying a serpent, and the serpent sensed the sweetness of the flower. It rose out of the water and snatched it away, and immediately it sloughed its skin and returned to the well. Then Gilgamesh sat down and wept, the tears ran down his face, and he took the hand of Urshanabi: "O Urshanabi, was it for this that I toiled with my hands, is it for this I have wrung out my heart's blood? For myself I have gained nothing; not I, but the beast of the earth has joy of it now. Already the stream has carried it twenty leagues back to the channels where I found it. I found a sign and now I have lost it. Let us leave the boat on the bank and go."

After twenty leagues they broke their fast, after thirty leagues they stopped for the night; in three days they had walked as much as a journey of a month and fifteen days. When the journey was accomplished they arrived at Uruk, the strong-walled city. Gilgamesh spoke to him, to Urshanabi the ferryman, "Urshanabi, climb up on to the wall of Uruk, inspect its foundation terrace, and examine well the brickwork; see if it is not of burnt bricks; and did not the seven wise men lay these foundations? One third of the whole is city, one third is garden, and one third is field, with the precinct of the goddess Ishtar. These parts and the precinct are all Uruk."

This too was the work of Gilgamesh, the king, who knew the countries of the world. He was wise, he saw mysteries and knew secret things, he brought us a tale of the days before the flood. He went on a long journey, was weary, worn out with labour, and returning engraved on a stone the whole story.

Law in the Ancient Near East:
Hittites and Hebrews

Law is a basic requirement for security in any civilization. Unless imposed on them by foreign conquerors, legal systems reflect the values of the people who create them. Consequently, it is no surprise to find a commercial people punishing commercial fraud much more severely than an agricultural people or feudal lords giving themselves special privileges at the expense of merchants in societies they control.

Throughout the history of civilization, two themes stand out in the construction of law codes: peace and justice. As we will see in the case of the relatively primitive Germanic tribes at the onset of the Western Middle Ages (see Reading 54), *peace* is the essence of law in this sense: When someone offends another with violence or fraud, a nomadic people who think of themselves as having a valuable population of limited numbers will aim to settle the conflict by letting the guilty party pay his victim or the victim's family enough to settle the matter without a blood feud among families—a dreaded evil for them. On the other hand, people in a settled environment, particularly in an urban one, see justice as the essence of law: this seems to mean punishing the offender severely enough that people believe he has suffered as much or a little more than his victim and enough to deter others in advance from attempting the same act. In sophisticated, urban societies, people who commit acts of violence and fraud are *criminals* who deserve something drastic to happen to them as punishment. No one worries about losing them or hopelessly alienating them: The danger of blood feuds is a minor one in most urban environments.

One thing we do *not* find is early historical confirmation of our experience that laws tend to become more humane, assumedly as people become more civilized. In Europe, we will see the use of capital punishment go from being rare to common between the sixth and seventeenth centuries A.D. In the ancient Near East, the constant coming and going of civilizations, the sudden appearance of nomadic conquerors, and the relegation of some advanced people to the status of being subjects of a new empire make it difficult to ascertain trends in law before Roman times. Often, laws relating to religious offenses are of different degrees of severity from those instituted to combat secular fraud and violence. The same is true of sex offenses, many of which were seen as violations of religious taboos. Here, primitive peoples were apt to think that the danger of angering a god was a worse threat even than a blood feud, whereas urban peoples were sometimes less worried about divine actions and reactions. The whole question of what sort of religion the people had is another important variable. With the Hebrews in the ancient Near East, for example, religion played a much more important part in their law codes than it did for their neighbors.

6

Hittite Laws

While the Amorites were creating their Babylonian Empire, a new language group of peoples called the Indo-European began to invade the ancient world from India to western Europe after 2000 B.C. They were a nomadic people known for their breeding of horses and their development of the war chariot. In religion, the Indo-Europeans at first worshipped chiefly storm and thunder gods, but as they became settled their civilizations generated families of (often competing, occasionally feuding) deities for each aspect of human existence.

Sometime after 2000 B.C., a branch of the Indo-European peoples, the Hittites, invaded and settled in the center of Anatolia (Western Turkey). From their well-fortified capital city of Hattusas (modern Boghazkoy), great warrior kings expanded their realm (in the fourteenth century) to include most of Anatolia, northern Mesopotamia, and a large part of northern Syria. Yet, by 1200 B.C., the Hittite Empire was destroyed either by native Anatolian peoples or by the notorious "Sea Peoples," who were attacking Egypt at the time.

The Hittite laws in the following selection come from several collections of cuneiform tablets that were found in the archives at Hattusas.

QUESTIONS TO CONSIDER

1. Was there legal equality among the Hittites?
2. Why would we say that the Hittite code closely approximates that of the Visigoths (see Reading 54)?

1. If anyone kills a man or a woman in a quarrel, he shall be declared liable for him/her. He shall give four persons, man or woman, and pledge his estate as security.
2. If anyone kills a male or female slave in a quarrel, he shall be declared liable for him/her. He shall give two persons, man or woman, and pledge his estate as security.
3. If anyone strikes a free man or woman and he/she dies, (only) his hand doing wrong, he shall be declared liable for him/her. He shall give two persons and pledge his estate as security.
4. If anyone strikes a male or a female slave and he/she dies, (only) his hand doing wrong, he shall be liable for him/her. He shall give one person and pledge his estate as security.
7. If anyone blinds a free man or knocks out his teeth, they would formerly give one mina of silver; now he shall give twenty shekels of silver and pledge his estate as security.
8. If anyone blinds a male or female slave or knocks out his/her teeth, he shall give ten shekels of silver and pledge his estate as security.
9. If anyone batters a man's head, they would formerly give six shekels of silver; he who was battered would receive three shekels of silver, and they would receive three shekels of silver for the palace. Now the king has abolished the (share) of the palace and only he who was battered receives three shekels of silver.
10. If anyone batters a man so that he falls ill, he shall take care of him. He shall give a man in his stead who can look after his house until he recovers. When he recovers, he shall give him six shekels of silver, and he shall also pay the physician's fee.
Later version of 10: If anyone injures a free man's head, he shall take care of him. He shall give a man in his stead who can look after his house until he recovers. When he recovers, he shall give him ten shekels of silver, and he shall also pay the physician's fee. If it is a slave, he shall pay two shekels of silver.
11. If anyone breaks a free man's hand or foot, he shall give him twenty shekels of silver and pledge his estate as security.
12. If anyone breaks the hand or foot of a male or a female slave, he shall give ten shekels of silver and pledge his estate as security.

From "The Hittite Laws," trans. Albrecht Goetze, in *Ancient Near Eastern Texts Relating to the Old Testament*, 3rd ed. with supplement, ed. James B. Pritchard. Copyright © renewed 1969 by Princeton University Press. Reprinted with permission of Princeton University Press.

Later version of 11 and 12: If anyone breaks a free man's hand or foot, in case he is permanently crippled, he shall give him twenty shekels of silver. But in case he is not permanently crippled, he shall give him ten shekels of silver. If anyone breaks a slave's hand or foot, in case he is permanently crippled, he shall give him ten shekels of silver. But in case he is not permanently crippled, he shall give him five shekels of silver.

13. If anyone bites off a free man's nose, he shall give thirty shekels of silver and pledge his estate as security.
14. If anyone bites off the nose of a male or female slave, he shall give thirty shekels of silver and pledge his estate as security.
17. If anyone causes a free woman to miscarry—if (it is the ninth or) the tenth month, he shall give ten shekels of silver, if (it is) the fifth month, he shall give five shekels of silver and pledge his estate as security.
Later version of 17: If anyone causes a free woman to miscarry, he shall give twenty shekels of silver.
18. If anyone causes a slave-woman to miscarry, if (it is) the tenth month, he shall give five shekels of silver.
22. If a slave runs away and anyone brings him back—if he seizes him in the vicinity, he shall give him shoes; if on this side of the river, he shall give him two shekels of silver; if on the other side of the river, he shall give him three shekels of silver.
23. If a slave runs away and goes to the country of Luwiya, he shall give to him who brings him back six shekels of silver. If a slave runs away and goes to an enemy country, whoever brings him nevertheless back, shall receive him (the slave) himself.
24. If a male or female slave runs away, the man at whose hearth his master finds him/her, shall give a man's wages for one year, (namely) x shekels of silver, or a woman's wages for one year, namely x shekels of silver.
27. If a man takes a wife and carries her to his house, he takes her dowry with her. If the woman dies, they turn her property into (property) of the man, and the man also receives her dowry. But if she dies in the house of her father, and there are children, the man will not receive her dowry.
29. If a girl is betrothed to a man and he has given the bride-price for her, but the parents subsequently abrogate the contract and withhold her from the man, they shall make double compensation.
32. If a slave takes a free woman, the provision of the law is the same for them.
33. If a slave takes a slave-girl, the provision of the law is the same for them.
57. If anyone steals a bull—if it is a weanling, it is not a bull; if it is a yearling, it is not a bull; if it is a two-year-old, that is a bull—they would formerly give thirty (head of) cattle. Now he shall give fifteen (head of) cattle, (specifically) five two-year-olds, five yearlings (and) five weanlings and he shall pledge his estate as security.
60. If anyone finds a bull and removes the brand, (if) its owner traces it out, he shall give seven (head of) cattle; he shall give (specifically) two two-year-olds, three yearlings, and two weanlings and he shall pledge his estate as security.
61. If anyone finds a stallion and removes the brand, (if) its owner traces it out, he shall give seven horses; he shall give (specifically) two two-year-olds, three yearlings, and two weanlings and he shall pledge his estate as security.
94. If a free man steals a house, he shall give (back) the respective goods; they would formerly give for the theft one mina of silver, but now he shall give twelve shekels of silver. If he has stolen much, they shall impose a heavy fine upon him; if he has stolen little, they shall impose a small fine upon him and pledge his estate as security.

98. If a free man sets a house on fire, he shall rebuild the house. Whatever was lost in the house, whether it is man, cattle or sheep, he shall replace as a matter of course.

99. If a slave sets a house on fire, his master shall make compensation in his stead. They shall cut off the slave's nose (and) ears and shall give him back to his master. But if he does not make compensation, he will lose that (slave).

172. If a man saves a free man's life in a year of famine, he shall give (a person) like himself. If he is a slave, he shall give ten shekels of silver.

173. If anyone rejects the judgment of the king, his house shall be made a shambles. If anyone rejects the judgment of a dignitary, they shall cut off his head. If a slave rises against his master, he shall go into the pit.

188. If a man does evil with a sheep, it is a capital crime and he shall be killed. They bring him to the king's court. Whether the king orders him killed or whether the king spares his life, he must not appeal to the king.

189. If a man violates his own mother, it is a capital crime. If a man violates his daughter, it is a capital crime. If a man violates his son, it is a capital crime.

192. If a man's wife dies (and) he marries his wife's sister, there shall be no punishment.

193. If a man has a wife and then the man dies, his brother shall take his wife, then his father shall take her. If in turn also his father dies, one of the brother's sons shall take the wife whom he had. There shall be no punishment.

197. If a man seizes a woman in the mountains, it is the man's crime and he will be killed. But if he seizes her in (her) house, it is the woman's crime and the woman shall be killed. If the husband finds them, he may kill them: there shall be no punishment for him.

198. If he brings them to the gate of the palace and declares: "My wife shall not be killed" and thereby spares his wife's life, he shall also spare the life of the adulterer and shall mark his head. If he says, "Let them die, both of them!" . . . the king may order them killed, the king may spare their lives.

199. If anyone does evil with a pig, (or) a dog, he shall die. They will bring him to the gate of the palace and the king may order them killed, the king may spare their lives; but he must not appeal to the king. If an ox leaps at a man, the ox shall die, but the man shall not die. A sheep may be proffered in the man's stead and they shall kill that. If a pig leaps at a man, there shall be no punishment.

7

Hebrew Laws and Their Covenant

The Hebrew laws composing the third group come from the period of Moses (after 1300 B.C.) and the exodus of the Hebrews from Egypt. Although tradition ascribes the writing of the first five books of the Bible (the Torah or Pentateuch) to Moses, biblical scholars have shown that, in truth, parts of the Torah must have been created over many centuries. Some sections of the Torah reveal a wandering, pastoral people, whereas others describe a settled, highly organized society that borrowed from the Babylonian code to suit its own circumstances.

QUESTIONS TO CONSIDER

1. What elements of the Ten Commandments show a refined moral concern?
2. How were the Hebrews influenced by other law codes?
3. Why do you suppose that sexual perversion was harshly punished in these codes?
4. Do you find legal equality among the Hebrews? Why do you suppose their attitude on equality differs from that of the Hittites?
5. What sin did the Hebrews commit that angered their God?
6. Why might other religions have accepted the Hebrews' act of worship that angered their God?

And God spoke all these words, saying,

I am the Lord thy God, which have brought thee out of the land of Egypt, out of the house of bondage.

Thou shalt have no other gods before me.

Thou shalt not make unto thee any graven image, or any likeness of any thing that is in heaven above, or that is in the earth beneath, or that is in the water under the earth:

Thou shalt not bow down thyself to them, nor serve them: for I the Lord thy God am a jealous God, visiting the iniquity of the fathers upon the children unto the third and fourth generation of them that hate me;

And showing mercy unto thousands of them that love me, and keep my commandments.

Thou shalt not take the name of the Lord thy God in vain; for the Lord will not hold him guiltless that taketh his name in vain.

Remember the sabbath day, to keep it holy.

Six days shalt thou labour, and do all thy work:

But the seventh day is the sabbath of the Lord thy God: in it thou shalt not do any work, thou, nor thy son, nor thy daughter, thy manservant, nor thy maidservant, nor thy cattle, nor thy stranger that is within thy gates:

For in six days the Lord made heaven and earth, the sea and all that in them is, and rested the seventh day: wherefore the Lord blessed the sabbath day, and hallowed it.

Honour thy father and thy mother: that thy days may be long upon the land which the Lord thy God giveth thee.

Thou shalt not kill.

Thou shalt not commit adultery.

Thou shalt not steal.

Thou shalt not bear false witness against thy neighbour.

Thou shalt not covet thy neighbour's house, thou shalt not covet thy neighbour's wife, nor his manservant, nor his maidservant, nor his ox, nor his ass, nor any thing that is thy neighbour's.

And all the people saw the thunderings, and the lightnings, and the noise of the trumpet, and the mountain smoking: and when the people saw it, they removed, and stood afar off.

And they said unto Moses, Speak thou with us, and we will hear: but let not God speak with us, lest we die.

And Moses said unto the people, Fear not: for God is come to prove you, and that his fear may be before your faces, that ye sin not.

Now these are the judgments which thou shalt set before them.

From Exodus, 20:1–26 and 21:1–36 (King James Version); slightly modernized.

If thou buy an Hebrew servant, six years he shall serve: and in the seventh he shall go out free for nothing.

If he came in by himself, he shall go out by himself: if he were married, then his wife shall go out with him.

If his master have given him a wife, and she have born him sons or daughters; the wife and her children shall be her master's, and he shall go out by himself.

And if the servant shall plainly say, I love my master, my wife, and my children, I will not go out free:

Then his master shall bring him unto the judges; he shall also bring him to the door, or unto the door post; and his master shall bore his ear through with an aul; and he shall serve him for ever.

And if a man sell his daughter to be a maidservant, she shall not go out as the menservants do.

If she please not her master, who hath betrothed her to himself, then shall he let her be redeemed: to sell her unto a strange nation he shall have no power, seeing he hath dealt deceitfully with her.

And if he have betrothed her unto his son, he shall deal with her after the manner of daughters.

If he take him another wife; her food, her raiment, her duty of marriage, shall he not diminish.

And if he do not these three unto her, then shall she go out free without money.

He that smiteth a man, so that he die, shall be surely put to death.

And if a man lie not in wait, but God deliver him into his hand; then I will appoint thee a place whither he shall flee.

But if a man come presumptuously upon his neighbour, to slay him with guile; thou shalt take him from mine altar, that he may die.

And he that smiteth his father, or his mother, shall be surely put to death.

And he that stealeth a man, and selleth him, or if he be found in his hand, he shall surely be put to death.

And he that curseth his father, or his mother, shall surely be put to death.

And if men strive together, and one smite another with a stone, or with his fist, and he die not, but keepeth his bed:

If he rise again, and walk abroad upon his staff, then shall he that smote him be quit: only he shall pay for the loss of his time, and shall cause him to be thoroughly healed.

And if a man smite his servant, or his maid, with a rod, and he die under his hand; he shall be surely punished.

Notwithstanding, if he continue a day or two, he shall not be punished: for he is his money.

If men strive, and hurt a woman with child, so that her fruit depart from her, and yet no mischief follow: he shall be surely punished, according as the woman's husband will lay upon him; and he shall pay as the judges determine.

And if any mischief follow, then thou shalt give life for life,

Eye for eye, tooth for tooth, hand for hand, foot for foot,

Burning for burning, wound for wound, stripe for stripe.

And if a man smite the eye of his servant, or the eye of his maid, that it perish; he shall let him go free for his eye's sake.

And if he smite out his manservant's tooth, or his maidservant's tooth; he shall let him go free for his tooth's sake.

If an ox gore a man or a woman that they die: then the ox shall be surely stoned, and his flesh shall not be eaten; but the owner of the ox shall be quit.

But if the ox were wont to push with horn in time past, and it hath been testified to his owner, and he hath not kept him in, but that he hath killed a man or a woman; the ox shall be stoned, and his owner shall also be put to death.

If there be laid on him a sum of money, then he shall give for the ransom of his life whatsoever is laid upon him.

Whether he have gored a son, or have gored a daughter, according to this judgment shall it be done unto him.

If the ox shall push a manservant or a maidservant; he shall give unto their master thirty shekels of silver, and the ox shall be stoned.

And if a man shall open a pit, or if a man shall dig a pit, and not cover it, and an ox or an ass fall therein;

The owner of the pit shall make it good, and give money unto the owner of them; and the dead beast shall be his.

And if one man's ox hurt another's, that he die; then they shall sell the live ox, and divide the money of it; and the dead ox also they shall divide.

Or if it be known that the ox hath used to push in time past, and his owner hath not kept him in; he shall surely pay ox for ox; and the dead shall be his own.
And six years thou shalt sow thy land, and shalt gather in the fruits thereof:

But the seventh year thou shalt let it rest and lie still; that the poor of thy people may eat: and what they leave the beasts of the field shall eat. In like manner thou shalt deal with thy vineyard, and with thy oliveyard.

Six days thou shalt do thy work, and on the seventh day thou shalt rest: that thine ox and thine ass may rest, and the son of thy handmaid, and the stranger, may be refreshed.

And in all things that I have said unto you be circumspect: and make no mention of the name of other gods, neither let it be heard out of thy mouth.

Three times thou shalt keep a feast unto me in the year.

Thou shalt keep the feast of unleavened bread: (thou shalt eat unleavened seven days, as I commanded thee in the time appointed of the month Abib; for in it thou camest out from Egypt: and none shall appear before me empty:)

And the feast of harvest, the firstfruits of thy labours, which thou hast sown in the field: and the feast of in-gathering, which is in the end of the year, when thou hast gathered in thy labours out of the field.

Three times in the year all thy males shall appear before the Lord God.

Thou shalt not offer the blood of my sacrifice with leavened bread; neither shall the fat of my sacrifice remain until the morning.

The first of the firstfruits of thy land thou shalt bring into the house of the Lord thy God. Thou shalt not boil a kid in his mother's milk.

Behold, I send an Angel before thee, to keep thee in the way, and to bring thee into the place which I have prepared.

Beware of him, and obey his voice, provoke him not; for he will not pardon your transgressions: for my name is in him.

But if thou shalt indeed obey his voice, and do all that I speak; then I will be an enemy unto thine enemies, and an adversary unto thine adversaries.

For mine Angel shall go before thee, and bring thee in unto the Amorites, and the Hittites, and the Perizzites, and the Canaanites, and the Hivites and the Jebusites; and I will cut them off.

Thou shalt not bow down to their gods, nor serve them, nor do after their works: but thou shalt utterly overthrow them, and quite breakdown their images.

And ye shall serve the Lord your God, and he shall bless thy bread, and thy water; and I will take sickness away from the midst of thee.

There shall nothing cast their young, nor be barren, in thy land: the number of thy days I will fulfill.

I will send my fear before thee, and will destroy all the people to whom thou shalt come, and I will make all thine enemies turn their backs unto thee.

And I will send hornets before thee, which shall drive out the Hivite, the Canaanite, and the Hittite, from before thee.

I will not drive them out from before thee in one year; lest the land become desolate, and the beast of the field multiply against thee.

By little and little I will drive them out from before thee, until thou be increased, and inherit the land.

And I will set thy bounds from the Red sea even unto the sea of the Philistines, and from the desert unto the river: for I will deliver the inhabitants of the land into your hand; and thou shalt drive them out before thee.

Thou shalt make no covenant with them, nor with their gods.

They shall not dwell in thy land, lest they make thee sin against me: for if thou serve their gods, it will surely be a snare unto thee.

[While Moses was receiving the Ten Commandments, the Hebrews broke God's commandments.]

And when the people saw that Moses delayed to come down out of the mount, the people gathered themselves together unto Aaron, and said unto him, Up, make us gods, which shall go before us; for as for this Moses, the man that brought us up out of the land of Egypt, we know not what is become of him.

And Aaron said unto them, Break off the golden earrings, which are in the ears of your wives, of your sons, and of your daughters, and bring them to me.

And all the people broke off the golden earrings which were in their ears, and brought them unto Aaron.

And he received them at their hand, and fashioned it with a graving tool, after he made it a molten calf: and they said, These be thy gods, O Israel, which brought thee up out of the land of Egypt.

And when Aaron saw it, he built an altar before it; and Aaron made proclamation, and said, Tomorrow is a feast to the Lord.

And they rose up early on the morrow, and offered burnt offerings, and brought peace offerings; and the people sat down to eat and to drink, and rose up to play.

And the Lord said unto Moses, Go, get thee down; for thy people, which thou broughtest out of the land of Egypt, have corrupted themselves:

They turned aside quickly out of the way which I commanded them: they have made them a molten calf, and have worshipped it, and have sacrificed thereunto, and said, These be thy gods, O Israel, which have brought thee up out of the land of Egypt.

And the Lord said unto Moses, I have seen this people, and, behold, it is a stiffnecked people:

Now therefore let me alone, that my wrath may wax hot against them, and that I may consume them: and I will make of thee a great nation.

And Moses besought the Lord his God, and said, Lord, why doth thy wrath wax hot against thy people, which thou hast brought forth out of the land of Egypt with great power, and with a mighty hand?

Wherefore should the Egyptians speak, and say, For mischief did he bring them out, to slay them in the mountains, and to consume them from the face of the earth? Turn from thy fierce wrath, and repent of this evil against thy people.

Remember Abraham, Isaac, and Israel, thy servants, to whom thou swarest by thine own self, and saidst unto them, I will multiply your seed as the stars of heaven, and all this land that I have spoken of will I give unto your seed, and they shall inherit it for ever.

And the Lord repented of the evil which he thought to do unto his people.

And Moses turned, and went down from the mount, and the two tables of the testimony were in his hand: the tables were written on both their sides; on the one side and on the other were they written.

And the tables were the work of God, and the writing was the writing of God, graven upon the tables.

The Origins of Writing in Egypt and China: Wisdom Literature and Oracles

Both the ancient Egyptians and Chinese devised pictorial writing systems. The art work of the New Stone Age had often featured stick figures drawn with less realism than were animals in Old Stone Age cave drawings. People who drew these stick figures could well have sacrificed naturalistic detail, we may suppose, in designing them for communication in the way that simple figures on our own signs for "Reserved for Handicapped" or "Deer Crossing" convey a message.

In Egypt, such pictographs evolved into hieroglyphics, which satisfied the Egyptians well enough as a means for recording their language that they were slow to change them. In China, the earliest pictographs developed into ideographs conveying more abstract concepts. By the time that oracle shells showing the earliest surviving Chinese writing were inscribed, the figures or "characters" had moved far away from being easily deciphered stick figures.

8

Papyrus Lansing: A Schoolbook

The ancient Egyptians had a high regard for education, which meant learning the complicated hieroglyphic writing. Thousands of papyri, writing tablets, and shards of pottery have been preserved. These were covered with exercises that young boys had to reproduce in order to learn the scribal art.

Writing was taught in the "House of Life" by having the students copy ancient texts such as *Instructions,* maxims, prayers, business letters, legal documents, hymns and religious texts, while their teachers made corrections. As the students copied down these texts, they learned spelling, grammar, and the practical and moral ideas contained within them.

It is thought that the scribal profession was open to any male in Egypt. Once a boy had learned how to read and write, he could enter the House of Life as a teacher. If a student really applied himself, other positions in the civil service, even that of governor or vizir or service in the temples might provide employment opportunities. Some of the letters suggest that senior officials wrote instructive letters or literature in order to help a young man advance his career.

The following selection is from a book called the *Papyrus Lansing* and is dated to the late New Kingdom period (after 1200 B.C.). A royal scribe urges his apprentice to work hard as the scribal profession is the best when compared to any other. His apprentice responds with appreciation for his mentor's advice.

QUESTIONS TO CONSIDER

1. Why was the scribe unhappy with his apprentice?
2. Why is the scribal profession the best of all?
3. How does the apprentice show his appreciation for his teacher?

Title

[Beginning of the instruction in letter-writing made by the royal scribe and chief overseer of the cattle of Amen-Re, King of Gods, Nebmare-nakht] for his apprentice, the scribe Wenemdiamun.

Praise of the Scribe's Profession

[The royal scribe] and chief overseer of the cattle of Amen-[Re, King of Gods, Nebmare-nakht speaks to the scribe Wenemdiamun]. [Apply yourself to this] noble profession. . . . You will find it useful. . . . You will be advanced by your superiors. You will be sent on a mission. . . . Love writing, shun dancing; then you become a worthy official. Do not long for the marsh thicket. Turn your back on throw stick and chase. By day write with your fingers; recite by night. Befriend the scroll, the palette. It pleases more than wine. Writing for him who knows it is better than all other professions. It pleases more than bread and beer, more than clothing and ointment. It is worth more than an inheritance in Egypt, than a tomb in the west.

Advice to the Unwilling Pupil

Young fellow, how conceited you are! You do not listen when I speak. Your heart is denser than a great obelisk, a hundred cubits high, ten cubits thick. When it is finished and ready for loading, many work gangs draw it. It hears the words of men; it is loaded on a barge. Departing from Yebu it is conveyed, until it comes to rest on its place in Thebes.

So also a cow is bought this year, and it plows the following year. It learns to listen to the herdsman; it only lacks words. Horses brought from the field, they forget their mothers. Yoked they go up and down on all his majesty's errands. They become like those that bore them, that stand in the stable. They do their utmost for fear of a beating.

But though I beat you with every kind of stick, you do not listen. If I knew another way of doing it, I would do it for you, that you might listen. You are a person fit for writing, though you have not yet known a woman. Your heart discerns, your fingers are skilled, your mouth is apt for reciting.

Writing is more enjoyable than enjoying a basket of . . . and beans; more enjoyable than a mother's giving birth, when her heart knows no distaste. She is constant in nursing her son; her breast is in his mouth every day. Happy is the heart <of>[1] him who writes; he is young each day.

The Idle Scribe Is Worthless

The royal scribe and chief overseer of the cattle of Amen-Re, King of Gods, Nebmare-nakht, speaks to the scribe Wenemdiamun, as follows. You are busy coming and going, and don't think of writing. You resist listening to me; you neglect my teachings.

You are worse than the goose of the shore, that is busy with mischief. It spends the summer destroying the dates, the winter destroying the seed-grain. It spends the balance of the year in pursuit of the cultivators. It does not let seed be cast to the ground without snatching it ? in its fall. ? One cannot catch it by snaring. One does not offer it in the temple. The evil, sharpeyed bird that does no work!

You are worse than the desert antelope that lives by running. It spends no day in plowing. Never at all does it tread on the threshing-floor. It lives on the oxen's labor, without entering among them. But though I spend the day telling you "Write," it seems like a plague to you. Writing is very pleasant! . . .

All Occupations Are Bad Except That of the Scribe

See for yourself with your own eye. The occupations lie before you.

The washerman's day is going up, going down. All his limbs are weak, <from> whitening his neighbors' clothes every day, from washing their linen.

The maker of pots is smeared with soil, like one whose relations have died. His hands, his feet are full of clay; he is like one who lives in the bog.

The cobbler mingles with vats. His odor is penetrating. His hands are red with madder, like one who is smeared with blood. He looks behind him for the kite, like one whose flesh is exposed.

The watchman prepares garlands and polishes vase-stands. He spends a night of toil just as one on whom the sun shines.

The merchants travel downstream and upstream. They are as busy as can be, carrying goods from one town to another. They supply him who has wants. But the tax collectors carry off the gold, that most precious of metals.

---

[1]Words omitted by scribes are represented by the symbols < / >.

The ships' crews from every house (of commerce), they receive their loads. They depart from Egypt for Syria, and each man's god is with him. (But) not one of them says: "We shall see Egypt again!"

The carpenter who is in the shipyard carries the timber and stacks it. If he gives today the output of yesterday, woe to his limbs! The shipwright stands behind him to tell him evil things.

His outworker who is in the fields, his is the toughest of all the jobs. He spends the day loaded with his tools, tied to his tool-box. When he returns home at night, he is loaded with the tool-box and the timbers, his drinking mug, and his whetstones.

The scribe, he alone, records the output of all of them. Take note of it!

The Misfortunes of the Peasant

Let me also expound to you the situation of the peasant, that other tough occupation. [Comes] the inundation and soaks him . . . , he attends to his equipment. By day he cuts his farming tools; by night he twists rope. Even his midday hour he spends on farm labor. He equips himself to go to the field as if he were a warrior. The dried field lies before him; he goes out to get his team. When he has been after the herdsman for many days, he gets his team and comes back with it. He makes for it a place in the field. Comes dawn, he goes to make a start and does not find it in its place. He spends three days searching for it; he finds it in the bog. He finds no hides on them; the jackals have chewed them. He comes out, his garment in his hand, to beg for himself a team.

When he reaches his field he finds <it> ? broken up ? . He spends time cultivating, and the snake is after him. It finishes off the seed as it is cast to the ground. He does not see a green blade. He does three plowings with borrowed grain. His wife has gone down to the merchants and found nothing for ? barter. ? Now the scribe lands on the shore. He surveys the harvest. Attendants are behind him with staffs. Nubians[2] with clubs. One says (to him): "Give grain." "There is none." He is beaten savagely. He is bound, thrown in the well, submerged head down. His wife is bound in his presence. His children are in fetters. His neighbors abandon them and flee. When it's over, there's no grain.

If you have any sense, be a scribe. If you have learned about the peasant, you will not be able to be one. Take note of it! . . .

The Scribe Does Not Suffer Like the Soldier

Furthermore. Look, I instruct you to make you sound; to make you hold the palette freely. To make you become one whom the king trusts; to make you gain entrance to treasury and granary. To make you receive the ship-load at the gate of the granary. To make you issue the offerings on feast days. You are dressed in fine clothes; you own horses. Your boat is on the river; you are supplied with attendants. You stride about inspecting. A mansion is built in your town. You have a powerful office, given you by the king. Male and female slaves are about you. Those who are in the fields grasp your hand, on plots that you have made.

[2]The southern border of ancient Egypt stopped at the First Cataract, near present-day Aswan. This area was known as Nubia, to which the Egyptians traveled for trade in oils, spices, and gold during the Old Kingdom. Later, during the Middle and New Kingdom, the Egyptians ruled Nubia as a province.

Look, I make you into a staff of life! Put the writings in your heart, and you will be protected from all kinds of toil. You will become a worthy official.

Do you not recall the (fate of) the unskilled man? His name is not known. He is ever burdened <like an ass carrying> in front of the scribe who knows what he is about.

Come, <let me tell> you the woes of the soldier, and how many are his superiors: the general, the troop-commander, the officer who leads, the standard-bearer, the lieutenant, the scribe, the commander of fifty, and the garrison-captain. They go in and out in the halls of the palace, saying: "Get laborers!" He is awakened at any hour. One is after him as (after) a donkey. He toils until the Aten (sun) sets in his darkness of night. He is hungry, his belly hurts; he is dead while yet alive. When he receives the grain-ration, having been released from duty, it is not good for grinding.

He is called up for Syria. He may not rest. There are no clothes, no sandals. The weapons of war are assembled at the fortress of Sile. His march is uphill through mountains. He drinks water every third day; it is smelly and tastes of salt. His body is ravaged by illness. The enemy comes, surrounds him with missiles, and life recedes from him. He is told: "Quick, forward, valiant soldier! Win for yourself a good name!" He does not know what he is about. His body is weak, his legs fail him. When victory is won, the captives are handed over to his majesty, to be taken to Egypt. The foreign woman faints on the march; she hangs herself <on> the soldier's neck. His knapsack drops, another grabs it while he is burdened with the woman. His wife and children are in their village; he dies and does not reach it. If he comes out alive, he is worn out from marching. Be he at large, be he detained, the soldier suffers. If he leaps and joins the deserters, all his people are imprisoned. He dies on the edge of the desert, and there is none to perpetuate his name. He suffers in death as in life. A big sack is brought for him; he does not know his resting place.

Be a scribe, and be spared from soldiering! You call and one says: "Here I am." You are safe from torments. Every man seeks to raise himself up. Take note of it!

The Pupil Wishes to Build a Mansion for His Teacher

Furthermore. (To) the royal scribe and chief overseer of the cattle of Amen-Re, King of Gods, Nebmare-nakht. The scribe Wenemdiamun greets his lord: In life, prosperity, and health! This letter is to inform my lord. Another message to my lord. I grew into a youth at your side. You beat my back; your teaching entered my ear. I am like a pawing horse. Sleep does not enter my heart by day; nor is it upon me at night. (For I say): I will serve my lord just as a slave serves his master.

I shall build a new mansion for you <on> the ground of your town, with trees (planted) on all its sides. There are stables within it. Its barns are full of barley and emmer, wheat, ? cumin, ? dates, . . . beans, lentils, coriander, peas, seed-grain, . . . flax, herbs, reeds, rushes, . . . dung for the winter, alfa grass, reeds, . . . grass, produced by the basketful. Your herds abound in draft animals, your cows are pregnant. I will make for you five aruras of cucumber beds to the south.

9

The Oracle Bones of Shang

In the late nineteenth century, Chinese farmers near Anyang, an ancient capital of the Shang dynasty (ca. 1766–1027 B.C. or 1523–1122 B.C.), discovered curious pieces of bone in their fields. Since then, some one hundred thousand pieces of such bone have been dug up at that site. These so-called "dragon bones," often sold as medicine, were actually the undershells of tortoises, the shoulder blades of cattle, and other flat bones. In 1899, Chinese scholars in Peking noticed inscriptions on the dragon bones. This occurrence led to two important historic discoveries: the discovery of the archaelogical sites in Anyang, where excavations began in 1928; and the discovery that the inscriptions were a very ancient form of Chinese writing. The bones were dated from the middle of the second millennium B.C.

These inscriptions, however, are not the only evidence of the development of early Chinese writing. Neolithic potsherds (fragments of broken earthen pots) dating back from the fifth millennium B.C. also have inscriptions, although these await further study. Certainly the inscribed bones and shells provide a link between the archaic signs and present-day Chinese characters. About five thousand signs scratched on the bones and shells have been recognized. These inscriptions have shed light on the life, thought, religion, and government of Shang China. Because these bones and shells were used in a method of divination, they are now called "oracle bones."

In Shang China, the oracle bones were the most important means of communication between humans and the gods. Shang rulers, as well as the people, never made any important decisions without first consulting the Supreme God. Shang diviners inscribed questions on the bones and then heated them with a red-hot bronze rod or live coal. The questions asked included such subjects as the efficacy of sacrifices; the best times for planting, hunting, fishing, and war; the weather; illness; and travel directions and timing. The reply of the Supreme God to these questions was revealed through the shape or direction of the cracks resulting from the heat. Diviners interpreted the meanings of the cracks, and generally replies were either "yes," "no," "lucky," or "unlucky." The answers were inscribed in the bone or shell for a permanent record. Each inscription generally consisted of approximately twelve characters, although some have had as many as sixty characters.

The characters that were used on the oracle bones were basically pictographs, which represented animals, plants, the sun, the moon, water, fire, houses, spears, and human beings. A circle with a dot in the center represented the sun. A crescent represented the moon. Three peaks represented a mountain. A vertical line with two spreading strokes at the bottom and two others at the top stood for a tree.

Because abstract ideas could not be pictured, ideographs were created. For example, one, two, and three were represented by one, two, and three horizontal strokes, respectively. Two trees standing side by side represented a forest. A woman holding a child meant "good." Two women suggested "quarrel."

Table 1 *A Comparison of Sumerian Words with Chinese Oracle-Bone Characters*

	Sumerian	Shang oracle inscription	Modern Chinese
1. *a.* heaven	an	t'ien	天
b. god	dingir	ti	帝
2. earth	ki	t'u	土
3. man	lu	jen	人
4. woman	munus	nü	女
5. mountain	kur	shan	山
6. slave-girl	geme	pei	婢
7. head	sag	shou	首
8. *a.* mouth	ka	k'ou	口
b. speak	dug	yüeh	曰
9. food	ninda	shih	食
	ssu		飤
10. eat	ku	shih (same as in no. 9)	食
		hsiang	饗
11. water	a	shui	水
12. drink	nag	yin	飲
13. *a.* to go	du	chih	之
		wang	往
b. to stand	gub	li	立
14. bird	mushen	chui	佳
		niao	鳥
15. fish	ha	yü	魚
16. ox	gud	mou	牡
17. cow	ab	p'in	牝
18. barley	she	mou	牟、麰
wheat		lai	來
		mai	麥

Source: Ping-ti Ho, *The Cradle of the East* (Hong Kong: The Chinese University of Hong Kong; Chicago: The University of Chicago Press, 1975), pp. 247–48. Copyright © 1975 by The Chinese University of Hong Kong. Reprinted with permission of The University of Chicago Press.

Table 2   *The Development of Chinese Script*

PICTOGRAPHS					
Archaic script	Small seal	Modern script	Forms in writing	Meaning	Rad. no.
		人 儿虎 羊象 馬魚壹車 月 山		*jên,* man	9
				hu, tiger	141
				yang, sheep	123
				hsiang, elephant	—
				niao, bird	196
				yü, fish	195
				hu, wine-vessel	—
				chhê, chariot, car	159
				yüeh, moon	74
				shan, mountain	46

INDIRECT SYMBOLS

射 *shê,* to shoot with a bow; 伐 *fa,* to attack (man being decapitated); 為 *wei,* lead, manage, do (hand leading an elephant by the trunk); 立 *li,* to stand (a man standing); 降 *chiang,* descend (hill and two footprints pointing downwards); 陟 *chih,* to mount (footprints upwards); 至 *chih,* arrive at (arrow hitting target); 回 *hui,* revolve (meander); 曰 *yüeh,* speak (mouth and breath); 甘 *kan,* sweet (mouth and something in it); 高 *kao,* high (picture of a high building); 長 *chang,* senior, grown up, *chhang,* extended (long-haired man walking on stick); 力 *li,* strength (ard or plough); 富 *fu,* blest (picture of a jar); 酉 *yu,* wine-must (jar and liquid inside).

ASSOCIATIVE COMPOUNDS

父 *fu,* father (hand and stick); 婦 *fu,* wife (女 woman and 帚 broom); 好 *hao,* to love, *hao,* good (woman and 子 child); 姦 *wan,* to quarrel (two women); 林 *lin,* forest (two 木 trees); 森 *sên,* umbrageous (three trees); 析 *hsi,* split (tree and 斤 axe); 牧 *mu,* tend cattle (ox and hand wielding whip); 鳴 *ming,* sing (鳥 bird and 口 mouth); 男 *nan,* male, man (employ 力 strength in the 田 fields).

DETERMINATIVE-PHONETIC CHARACTERS

耳 *êrh,* ear, is PHONETIC in: 珥 *êrh,* ear-pendant (determinative 玉 jade, precious stone; word cognate to 耳); 餌 *êrh,* cake (det. 食 food or 鬲 cauldron); 珥 *êrh,* plume (det. 毛 hair); 佴 *êrh,* assistant (det. 亻 人 man); 蛦 *êrh,* bait (det. 虫 worm); 衈 *êrh,* a sacrifice (det. 血 blood; 恥 *chhih,* shame (det. 心 heart); 弭 *mi,* repress, ends of a bow (det. 弓 bow); DETERMINATIVE in: 聞 *wên,* to hear (phonetic 門 *mên*); 聆 *ling,* listen to, apprehend (phon. 令 *ling*); 聾 *lung,* deaf (phon. 龍 *lung*); 聰 *tshung,* acute of hearing, clever (phon. 恩 *tshung*); 聳 *sung,* alarm, excite (phon. 從 *tshung*).

立 **li,** to stand, is PHONETIC in: 笠 *li,* conical hat (det. 竹 bamboo); 粒 *li,* grain of rice (det. 米 rice or 食 food); 苙 *li,* pen for animals, *chi,* hyacinth (det. 艸 herb, plant); 泣 *chhi,* to weep (det. 氵 水 water); 拉 *la,* to pull, break (det. 扌 手 hand); 翋 *la,* to fly (det. 羽 wings); 雴 *li, chhih,* heavy rain (det. 雨 rain); 颯 颭 *sa,* storm (det. 風 wind); DETERMINATIVE in: 站 *chan,* to stop (phon. 占 *chan*); 竚 *chu,* to wait for (phon. 宁 *chu*); 竣 *chün, tsun,* stop work (phon. 夋 *chün*); 靖 *ching,* quiet (phon. 青 *chhing*); 端 *tuan,* extremity, origin, end, principle (phon. 耑 *chuan*); 竭 *chieh,* exhausted (phon. 曷 *ho*).

Source: Joseph Needham, *Science and Civilisation in China,* vol. 1 (New York: Cambridge University Press, 1954), p. 29. Reprinted with permission.

Figure 1   *Oracle shell from the Shang dynasty. The inscribed characters indicate questions being posed to the Supreme God; the heat-induced cracks were interpreted as answers. (Photograph by Wan-go Weng/Collection Academia Sinica, Taipei.)*

A woman with a broom meant "wife." An ear between the two panels of a door meant to "hear."

The preceding material illustrates the development of Chinese writing. Table 1 compares Sumerian words with Chinese oracle characters, and Table 2 displays the evolution of Chinese script. Figure 1 is a photograph of a Shang oracle shell.

QUESTIONS TO CONSIDER

1. How do the oracle bones as writing media compare with those used by the ancient Sumerians and the Egyptians?
2. What principles contributed to the original construction of Chinese characters?

Challenges to Egyptian Tradition

Ancient Egyptians prided themselves on having a state and society that was not only ancient but totally unchanging. Skeptical as the Greeks often were, Egyptians had them convinced by classical Greek times that Egyptian civilization had flourished as it was for ten thousand years. It can be argued, however, that this image of serene continuity represented more of an ideal than reality: certainly Egyptian dynasties came and went much more frequently in most centuries than did those of China. Particularly in the New Kingdom, Egyptian traditions were challenged, even two of the most established ones: male rulership and polytheism.

10

Hatshepsut: Successful Female Pharaoh

From the earliest organization of the Egyptian state, the kings or pharaohs were considered to be divine and thought of as living images of the god Horus, son of the god Osiris and his sister-wife, Isis. This was true until a woman dared to make herself king, in reality as well as in art.

Hatshepsut (ca. 1504–1482 B.C.) was a daughter of Pharaoh Thutmose I and chief queen to Pharaoh Thutmose II, by whom she had a daughter, Nefrure. When her husband died unexpectedly in 1504 B.C., the next pharaoh was a six-year-old boy, Thutmose III, borne by one of his father's minor wives. For a year, Hatshepsut was content to act as regent, but then her ambition was so great that she overthrew her nephew and had herself declared pharaoh in her own right.

For twenty-two years Pharaoh Hatshepsut reigned alone. She was depicted in art as a male, with men's clothing, and wearing the beard of Osiris. Her

Figure 2　*Statue of Hatshepsut.*

main support came from a man named Senmut or Senenmut, who held many titles such as tutor to Hatshepsut's daughter, leader of very famous trade expeditions to the fabled land of Punt, and chief architect of Hatshepsut's tomb at Deir el-Bahri.

Whether Hatshepsut and Senmut died naturally in 1482 B.C. or were violently overthrown is not known. Thutmose III suddenly reappeared and began to erase his aunt's memory through the destruction or obliteration of her inscriptions, statues, and obelisks. She was not counted as one of the true pharaohs in royal annals.

The following selection comes from Hatshepsut's tomb at Deir el-Bahri, where her birth was recorded. In these depictions, Hatshepsut's mother, Queen Aahames, receives and embraces an unexpected divine lover, the creator god Amen, who tells her that she will have a daughter who would rule as pharaoh.

Figure 3 *Hatshepsut kneeling and offering jars of wine.*

QUESTIONS TO CONSIDER

1. What are some of the artistic attributes of a pharaoh?
2. Why was it necessary for Hatshepsut to create this fiction of her birth?
3. Why was her reign such a break with Egyptian tradition?
4. Over the centuries, we frequently find that people in civilizations in which women have *not* been allowed to have lesser political roles as council members or administrators have accepted women as *rulers* (queens and empresses). How would you explain this? Why do you suppose Hatshepsut here and Cleopatra later could rule Egypt successfully, although neither could have served as the governor of an Egyptian province?

The Divine Conception of Queen Hatshepsut

Amen declares the following to these gods [the Great Ennead][1] concerning the heir of the Lord of the Two Lands:

Lo, I have loved the mate whom he [Thothmes] has loved, the Mother of King Ka-Maat-Ra [Hatshepsut], endued with life, the Queen Aahmes. I was the protector of her body when she was exalted. I have endowed her with all lands and foreign countries, that she may lead all the living.

I have joined the Two Lands unto her in contentment. She builds your temples and makes them holy; she keeps fresh your sacrifices and offering tables. Cause the dew in the heavens to come down for her at its proper time, and make a Great Nile[2] for her at its proper time. Extend about her your protection of life and good fortune!

He who shall praise her shall live, but he who shall speak evil of the name of Her Majesty, to him will I give the gift of death forthwith!

The Great Ennead answers:

We have come to extend our protection of life and good fortune about her. She shall build her beautiful monuments in these Two Lands.

[Amen announces his intention to Thoth,[3] who will escort him into the presence of Queen Aahmes. Thoth replies:]

This princess of whom you have spoken, Queen Aahmes is her name. She is more beautiful than all the women in this entire land. She is the wife of the Sovereign, King Aa-Kheper-Ka-Ra ["great is the becoming of the ka of Ra," that is, Thothmes I], given eternal life. His Majesty is a child of royalty, and thou mayest then go!"

And then he came, this august god Amen, Lord of the Two Lands, and he assumed the form of the Majesty of her husband, King Thothmes. They [the god and the form of the king] found her as she was reclining in the beauty of her palace.

She awakened at the fragrant odor of the god, and laughed in joy before His Majesty. And then he came to her straightway. He was passionate for her. He gave his heart unto her. He let her see him in his divine form after he came to her. She rejoiced when she beheld his beauty; his love went through her limbs. The Palace was flooded with the divine fragrance, and all his odors were those of Punt. The dearest and loveliest one—the Majesty of this god did everything that he desired with her. She let him rejoice over her. She kissed him.

Then spoke the Wife and Mother of the God, Queen Aahmes, to the Majesty of this god, Amen, Lord of the Thrones of the Two Lands:

My Lord, how great is thy splendor! Magnificent it is to see thy presence. Thou hast filled my Majesty with thy glory! Thy sweet savor pervades all my members!

Thus she spoke after the Majesty of this god did everything that he desired with her.

Then spoke Amen, Lord of the Thrones of the Two Lands, unto her:

Hat-Shepsut ["foremost in nobility"] shall be the name of this daughter whom I have implanted in thy body. She shall exercise beneficent kingship in this entire land. My spirit

[1]The Great Ennead is a group of nine gods and goddesses, consisting of Ra-Atum, She, Tefnut, Geb, Nut, Osiris, Isis, Set, and Nephthys.

[2]A good inundation.

[3]The god Thoth was the god of wisdom and learning who functioned as the scribe and keeper of the sacred archives.

From Joseph Kaster, trans. and ed., "The Divine Conception of Queen Hatshepsut," in *Wings of the Falcon: Life and Thought of Ancient Egypt* (New York: Holt, Rinehart and Winston, 1968), pp. 119–21. Copyright 1968 by Joseph Kaster.

shall be hers. My power shall be hers. My exaltation shall be hers. My crown shall be hers. She shall rule the Two Lands in kingship, and shall lead all the living over all that the heavens embrace and over all which I shine. I have joined unto her the Two Lands in all her names, and upon the throne of Horus of the Living. She shall be under my divine protection every day, together with the god thereof. She is my beloved daughter, out of my own seed.

11

The Hymn to Aton and Psalm 104

The Egyptian pharaoh Amenhotep IV (ca. 1367 B.C.) and his wife Nefertiti attempted to break completely with traditional Egyptian religion. They substituted the worship of the sun disk, Aton, in place of the hundreds of older gods. This radical change caused a revolution in both literary and artistic styles; intimate family scenes now portrayed the pharaoh as a loving father and husband, and hymns and funeral inscriptions prayed to and through him to reach the new cosmic god.

Evidently, priests opposed the pharaoh's new ideas. In his fifth regnal year, Amenhotep and his family left the capital of Thebes for a new city, which the pharaoh called Akhetaton (meaning the gleaming horizon of Aton). Not content with just changing his residence, the pharaoh also changed his name to Akhenaton (meaning one who is serviceable to Aton) as well as all the names and titles of his family. Orders were given to destroy the old gods' names on the temples and tombs, including those of his father, Amenhotep III.

Once the political and religious changes occurred, knowledge about the royal family—especially Nefertiti—became clouded. The queen disappeared from public view and was, perhaps, replaced in the affections of the pharaoh by a man called Smenkhkare, who may have been Akhenaton's son. Although the pharaoh continued his religious reform unabated, the Egyptian Empire began to disintegrate because of attacks from the Hittite Empire or its client states.

The following Hymn to Aton reflects Akhenaton's belief in the universality and, at the same time, the uniqueness of Aton. It often has been compared with Psalm 104. This selection juxtaposes corresponding passages of the Hymn to Aton (*left column*) and Psalm 104 of the Old Testament (*right column*).

QUESTIONS TO CONSIDER

1. Why was the Aton worship such a dramatic change in Egyptian history?
2. What was the relationship and role of the pharaoh to Aton?
3. Compare the ethical principles of the Hebrews (see Reading 7) and this hymn. What is missing from the *Hymn to Aton?*

Praise of Re Har-akhti, Rejoicing on the Horizon, in his name as Shu Who Is in the Aton-disc,[1] living forever and ever; the living great Aton who is in jubilee, lord of all that the Aton encircles, lord of heaven, lord of earth, lord of the House of Aton in Akhet-Aton,[2] [and praise of] the King of Upper and Lower Egypt, who lives on truth, the Lord of the Two Lands: Nefer-kheperu-Re Wa-en-Re; the Son of Re, who lives on truth, the Lord of Diadems: Akh-en-Aton, long in his lifetime; [and praise of] the Chief Wife of the King, his beloved, the Lady of the Two Lands: Nefer-neferu-Aton Nefert-iti, living, healthy, and youthful forever and ever; (by) the Fan-bearer on the Right Hand of the King . . . Eye. He says:

Thou appearest beautifully on the horizon
     of heaven,
Thou living Aton, the beginning of life!
When thou art risen on the eastern horizon,
Thou hast filled every land with thy
     beauty.
Thou art gracious, great, glistening, and
     high over every land;
Thy rays encompass the lands to the limit
     of all that thou hast made:
As thou art Re, thou reaches to the end of
     them;[3]
(Thou) subduest them (for) thy beloved
     son.[4]
Though thou art far away, thy rays are on
     earth;
Though thou art in *their* faces, *no one
     knows thy* going.

---

[1]The Aton had a dogmatic name written within a royal cartouche and including the three old solar deities, Re, Har-of-the-Horizon, and Shu.

[2]Akhet-Aton was the name of the capital at Tell el-Amarna.

[3]Pun: *Ra* "Re," and *er-ra* "to the end."

[4]Akh-en-Aton.

When thou settest in the western horizon,
The land is in darkness, in the manner of
  death.
They sleep in a room, with heads wrapped
  up,
Nor sees one eye the other.
All their goods which are under their heads
  might be stolen,
(But) they would not perceive (it).
Every lion is come forth from his den;
All creeping things, they sting.
Darkness *is a shroud,* and the earth is in
  stillness,
For he who made them rests in his horizon.

At daybreak, when thou arisest on the
  horizon,
When thou shinest as the Aton by day,
Thou drivest away the darkness and givest
  thy rays.
The Two Lands are in festivity *every day,*
Awake and standing upon (their) feet,
For thou hast raised them up.
Washing their bodies, taking (their)
  clothing,
Their arms are (raised) in praise at thy
  appearance.
All the world, they do their work.
All beasts are content with their pasturage;
Trees and plants are flourishing.
The birds which fly from their nests,
Their wings are (stretched out) in praise to
  thy *Ra.*
All beasts spring upon (their) feet.
Whatever flies and alights,
They live when thou hast risen (for) them.
The ships are sailing north and south as
  well,
For every way is open at thy appearance.
The fish in the river dart before thy face;
Thy rays are in the midst of the great green
  sea.

Creator of seed in women,
Thou who makest fluid into man,
Who maintainest the son in the womb of
  his mother,
Who soothest him with that which stills his
  weeping,

Thou makest darkness, and it is night:
wherein all the beasts of the forest do creep
forth.

The young lions roar after their prey,
and seek their meat from God.

The sun ariseth, they gather themselves together, and lay them down in their
dens.

Man goeth forth unto his work and to
his labour until the evening.

They give drink to every beast of the
field: the wild asses quench their thirst.

By them shall the fowls of the heaven
have their habitation, *which* sing among the
branches.

He watereth the hills from his chambers: the earth is satisfied with the fruit of
thy works.

He causeth the grass to grow for the
cattle, and herb for the service of man: that
he may bring forth food out of the earth;

So is this great and wide sea, wherein
are things creeping innumerable, both small
and great beasts.

There go the ships: *there* is that
leviathan, *whom* thou hast made to play
therein.

Thou nurse (even) in the womb,
Who givest breath to sustain all that he has
    made!
When he descends from the womb to
    breathe
On the day when he is born,
Thou openest his mouth completely,
Thou suppliest his necessities.
When the chick in the egg speaks within
    the shell,
Thou givest him breath within it to
    maintain him.
When thou hast made him his fulfillment
    within the egg, to break it,
He comes forth from the egg to speak at
    his completed (time);
He walks upon his legs when he comes
    forth from it.

How manifold it is, what thou hast made!
They are hidden from the face (of man).
O sole god, like whom there is no other!
Thou didst create the world according to
    thy desire,
Whilst thou wert alone: All men, cattle,
    and wild beasts,

O Lord, how manifold are thy works!
in wisdom hast thou made them all: the earth
is full of thy riches.

Whatever is on earth, going upon (its) feet,
And what is on high, flying with its wings.
The countries of Syria and Nubia, the *land*
    of Egypt,
Thou settest every man in his place,
Thou suppliest their necessities:
Everyone has his food, and his time of life
    is reckoned.

These wait all upon thee; that thou
mayest give *them* their meat in due season.

Their tongues are separate in speech,
And their natures as well;
Their skins are distinguished,
As thou distinguishest the foreign peoples.
Thou makest a Nile in the underworld,
Thou bringest it forth as thou desirest
To maintain the people (of Egypt)[5]
According as thou madest them for thyself,
The lord of all of them, wearying (himself)
    with them,
The lord of every land, rising for them,
The Aton of the day, great of majesty.

[5]The Egyptian believed that their Nile came from the waters under the earth, called by them Nun.

All distant foreign countries, thou makest
   their life (also),
For thou hast set a Nile in heaven,
That it may descend for them and make
   waves upon the mountains,
Like the great green sea,
To water their fields in their towns.[6]
How effective they are, thy plans, O lord
   of eternity!
The Nile in heaven, it is for the foreign
   peoples
And for the beasts of every desert that go
   upon (their) feet;
(While the true) Nile comes from the
   underworld for Egypt.

He sendeth the springs into the valleys, *which* run among the hills.

Thy rays suckle every meadow.
When thou risest, they live, they grow for
   thee.
Thou makest the seasons in order to rear
   all that thou hast made,
The winter to cool them,
And the heat that *they* may taste thee.
Thou hast made the distant sky in order to
   rise therein,
In order to see all that thou dost make.
Whilst thou wert alone,
Rising in thy form as the living Aton,
Appearing, shining, *withdrawing or
   approaching,*
Thou madest millions of forms of thyself
   alone.
Cities, towns, fields, road, and river—
Every eye beholds thee over against them,
For thou art the Aton of the day over *the
   earth*. . . .

Thou art in my heart,
And there is no other that knows thee
Save thy son Nefer-kheperu-Re Wa-en-
   Re,[7]
For thou hast made him well-versed in thy
   plans and in thy strength.[8]

[6]The rain of foreign countries is like the Nile of rainless Egypt.
[7]Even though the hymn was recited by the official Eye, he states that Akh-en-Aton alone knows the Aton.
[8]Pharaoh was the official intermediary between the Egyptians and their gods. The Amarna religion did not change this dogma.

The world came into being by thy hand,
According as thou hast made them.
When thou hast risen they live,
When thou settest they die.
Thou art lifetime thy own self,
For one lives (only) through thee.
Eyes are (fixed) on beauty until thou
    settest.
All work is laid aside when thou settest in
    the west.
(But) when (thou) risest (again),
[*Everything is*] made to flourish for the
    king, . . .
Since thou didst found the earth
And raise them up for thy son,
Who came forth from thy body: the king of
    Upper and Lower Egypt, . . . Akh-en-
    Aton, . . . and the Chief Wife of the King
    . . . Nefert-iti, living and youthful
    forever and ever.

Military Strategy and Tactics: Assyria and China

Situated in the rolling hills north of Babylonia, Assyria was never a major empire until the late tenth century B.C. The land had been invaded time and again by the Akkadians, Babylonians, Kassites, and, finally, the Arameans. In 911 B.C., the Assyrian kings finally confronted the threat posed by the Arameans and expelled them. Thereafter, year by year, the kings went to war and conquered most of the ancient Near East.

The success achieved by Assyria resulted from studying war techniques as a science. The army was divided into light and heavy infantry as well as chariotry, which was supplemented by rolling siege engines. Special schools were set up to teach the techniques of sapping and mining city walls. Conquered areas were welded together through a great system of roads and were controlled by royal governors, supported by garrisons of soldiers. These newly conquered areas saw their populations dispersed or transported throughout Assyria. Booty and tribute kept Assyria constantly expanding. If any city tried to revolt, it could expect swift and severe punishment. The Assyrians were making maximum use of psychological warfare, particularly terror, to encourage quick surrenders of populations marked for annexation and passive acceptance of Assyrian rule once it was in place.

The Chinese took a different approach to warfare. The overall image they projected was one of calm, confident superiority. Their rulers assumed that their own subjects and conquered peoples of any intelligence would recognize the benefits gained from their ties to a wise, paternalistic kingdom. Consequently, terror of the Assyrian type had no place in their scheme of things. Nonetheless, since war was a large part of the real world, Chinese military leaders strove for an understanding of what worked in waging it: speed, restraint, and deception, with actions based on military intelligence in all its forms.

12

Assyrian War Tactics

A typical example of an Assyrian king is Ashurnasirpal (844–859 B.C.). He was at war for most of his reign, attacking northwestern Mesopotamia, Anatolia, Syria, and Phoenicia both for booty and for enlargement of his empire. Nonetheless, he found time to construct a new, six-acre palace at Calah (modern Nimrud) on the Upper Zab, west of the Tigris River—a palace that was well built and beautifully decorated.

The following selection comes from the Assyrian royal archives and describes King Ashurnasirpal's ferocious treatment of rebels.

QUESTIONS TO CONSIDER

1. Why do you suppose that the Assyrian king resorted to such harshness in dealing with rebels?
2. Why would the subjects of Assyria rebel even though they were aware of the consequences?
3. Do you know of a kingdom and peoples who disappeared from history due to Assyrian destruction?

While I was staying in the land of Kutmuhi, they brought me the word: "The city of Sûru of Bît-Halupê has revolted, they have slain Hamatai, their governor, and Ahiababa, the son of a nobody, whom they brought from Bît-Adini, they have set up as king over them." With the help of Adad and the great gods who have made great my kingdom, I mobilized (my) chariots and armies and marched along the bank of the Habur. During my advance I received much tribute from Shulmanu-haman-ilâni of the city of Gardiganni, from Ilu-Adad of the city of Katna,—silver, gold, lead, vessels of copper, and garments of brightly colored wool, and garments of linen. To the city of Sûru of Bît-Halupê I drew near, and the terror of the splendor of Assur, my lord, overwhelmed them. The chief men and the elders of the city, to save their lives, came forth into my presence and embraced my feet, saying: "If it is thy pleasure, slay! If it is thy pleasure, let live! That which thy heart desireth, do!" Ahiababa, the son of nobody, whom they had brought from Bît-Adini, I took captive. In the valor of my heart and with the fury of my weapons I stormed the city. All the rebels they seized and delivered them up. My officers I caused to enter into his palace and his temples.

From Daniel David Luckenbill, ed., *Ancient Records of Assyria and Babylonia,* vol. 1 (New York: Greenwood Press, 1968), pp. 144–45.

His silver, his gold, his goods and his possessions, copper, iron, lead, vessels of copper, cups of copper, dishes of copper, a great hoard of copper, alabaster, tables with inlay, the women of his palaces, his daughters, the captive rebels together with their possessions, the gods together with their possessions, precious stone from the mountains, his chariot with equipment, his horses, broken to the yoke, trappings of men and trappings of horses, garments of brightly colored wool and garments of linen, goodly oil, cedar, and fine sweet-scented herbs, panels(?) of cedar, purple and crimson wool, his wagons, his cattle, his sheep, his heavy spoil, which like the stars of heaven could not be counted, I carried off. Azi-ilu I set over them as my own governor. I built a pillar over against his city gate, and I flayed all the chief men who had revolted, and I covered the pillar with their skins; some I walled up within the pillar, some I impaled upon the pillar on stakes, and others I bound to stakes round about the pillar; many within the border of my own land I flayed, and I spread their skins upon the walls; and I cut off the limbs of the officers, of the royal officers who had rebelled. Ahiababa I took to Nineveh, I flayed him, I spread his skin upon the wall of Nineveh. My power and might I established over the land of Lakê. While I was staying in the city of Sûru, (I received) tribute from all the kings of the land of Lakê,—silver, gold, lead, copper, vessels of copper, cattle, sheep, garments of brightly colored wool, and garments of linen, and I increased the tribute and taxes and imposed them upon them. At that time, the tribute of Haiâni of the city of Hindani,—silver, gold, lead, copper, *umu*-stone, alabaster, purple wool, and (Bactrian) camels I received from him as tribute. At that time I fashioned a heroic image of my royal self, my power and my glory I inscribed thereon, in the midst of his palace I set it up. I fashioned memorial steles and inscribed thereon my glory and my prowess, and I set them up by his city gate.

13

Sun Tzu [Sunzi],[1] *The Art of War*

This is perhaps the world's oldest known treatise on war and strategy. Although the precise date of composition of this martial classic is not known, most Chinese historians and literary critics place it sometime in the early part of the fourth century B.C. Sunzi served as strategist and general under the king of the state of Wu, one of the warring states during the chaotic late Chou [Zhou] period (ca. 1050–256 B.C.).

For well over two millennia, in both war and peace, *The Art of War* has been an important source of wisdom for kings, emperors, feudal lords, generals, and strategists in China, Korea, and Japan. The military thought of Mao Tse-tung [Mao Zedong] was profoundly influenced by Sunzi's work, as evi-

[1]There are at least two ways to transcribe Chinese in the English-speaking world: the Wade-Giles system and the Pinyin system. The Wade-Giles system was first developed by an English Sinologist, Thomas F. Wade, in 1867, and was later modified by Herbert Giles in 1912. It became the standard way of transcribing Chinese. This system is being replaced by the somewhat simpler Pinyin system, the official one of the People's Republic of China, although Wade-Giles continues to be used on Taiwan, where many English-language books are printed. Except where the term is the same in both systems, we will give Pinyin transcriptions in brackets after the Chinese terms when they first occur in the readings.

denced in Mao's writings, such as "On Guerrilla Warfare" and "On Protracted Warfare." *The Art of War* has also received much attention in the West. Since it was first translated into French by a Jesuit named Amiot in 1782, the book has been translated into all major Western languages. Napoleon was supposed to have been an avid reader of it.

QUESTIONS TO CONSIDER

1. How timeless are Sunzi's military strategy and tactics? Discuss.
2. What did Sunzi mean by "All warfare is based on deception"? Explain.

Estimates

War is a matter of vital importance to the State; the province of life or death; the road to survival or ruin. It is mandatory that it be thoroughly studied. Therefore, appraise it in terms of the five fundamental factors and make comparisons of the seven elements later named. So you may assess its essentials.

The first of these factors is moral influence; the second, weather; the third, terrain; the fourth, command; and the fifth, doctrine. By moral influence I mean that which causes the people to be in harmony with their leaders, so that they will accompany them in life and unto death without fear of mortal peril. By weather I mean the interaction of natural forces; the effects of winter's cold and summer's heat and the conduct of military operations in accordance with the seasons. By terrain I mean distances, whether the ground is traversed with ease or difficulty, whether it is open or constricted, and the chances of life or death. By command I mean the general's qualities of wisdom, sincerity, humanity, courage, and strictness. By doctrine I mean organization, control, assignment of appropriate ranks to officers, regulation of supply routes, and the provision of principal items used by the army.

There is no general who has not heard of these five matters. Those who master them win; those who do not are defeated.

Therefore in laying plans compare the following elements, appraising them with the utmost care. If you say which ruler possesses moral influence, which commander is the more able, which army obtains the advantages of nature and the terrain, in which regulations and instructions are better carried out, which troops are the stronger; which has the better trained officers and men; and which administers rewards and punishments in a more enlightened manner; I will be able to forecast which side will be victorious and which defeated. If a general who heeds my strategy is employed he is certain to win. Retain him! When one who refuses to listen to my strategy is employed, he is certain to be defeated. Dismiss him.

Having paid heed to the advantages of my plans, the general must create situations which will contribute to their accomplishment. By "situations" I mean that he should act expediently in accordance with what is advantageous and so control the balance. All warfare is based on deception. Therefore, when capable, feign incapacity; when active, inactivity. When near, make it appear that you are far away; when far away, that you are near.

From Sunzi, trans. Samuel Griffith, *The Art of War* (New York: Oxford University Press, 1963), pp. 63–67, 71, 77–81, 96–101, 144–49. Reprinted by permission of Oxford University Press.

Offer the enemy a bait to lure him; feign disorder and strike him. When he concentrates, prepare against him; where he is strong, avoid him. Anger his general and confuse him. Pretend inferiority and encourage his arrogance. Keep him under a strain and wear him down. When he is united, divide him. Attack where he is unprepared; sally out when he does not expect you. These are the strategist's keys to victory.

Now if the estimates made in the temple before hostilities indicate victory it is because calculations show one's strength to be superior to that of his enemy; if they indicate defeat, it is because calculations show that one is inferior. With many calculations, one can win; with few one cannot. How much less chance of victory has one who makes none at all! By this means I examine the situation and the outcome will be clearly apparent.

Offensive Strategy

Generally in war the best policy is to take a state intact; to ruin it is inferior to this. To capture the enemy's army is better than to destroy it; to take intact a battalion, a company or a five-man squad is better than to destroy them. For to win one hundred victories in one hundred battles is not the acme of skill. To subdue the enemy without fighting is the acme of skill. Thus, what is of supreme importance in war is to attack the enemy's strategy; the next best is to disrupt his alliances; the next best is to attack his army.

The worst policy is to attack cities. Attack cities only when there is no alternative. To prepare the shielded wagons and make ready the necessary arms and equipment requires at least three months; to pile up the earthen ramps against the walls an additional three months will be needed. If the general is unable to control his impatience and orders his troops to swarm up the wall like ants, one-third of them will be killed without taking the city. Such is the calamity of these attacks. Thus, those skilled in war subdue the enemy's army without battle. They capture his cities without assaulting them and overthrow his state without protracted operations.

Your aim must be to take All-under-Heaven intact. Thus your troops are not worn out and your gains will be complete. This is the art of offensive strategy. Consequently, the art of using troops is this: When ten to the enemy's one, surround him, when five times his strength, attack him; if double his strength, divide him. If equally matched you may engage him. If weaker numerically, be capable of withdrawing; and if in all respects unequal, be capable of eluding him, for a small force is but booty for one more powerful.

Now the general is the protector of the state. If this protection is all-embracing, the state will surely be strong; if defective, the state will certainly be weak. Now there are three ways in which a ruler can bring misfortune upon his army: (1) when ignorant that the army should not advance, to order an advance or ignorant that it should not retire, to order a retirement. This is described as "hobbling the army"; (2) when ignorant of military affairs, to participate in their administration. This causes the officers to be perplexed; (3) when ignorant of command problems to share in the exercise of responsibilities. This engenders doubts in the minds of the officers.

Weaknesses and Strengths

Generally, he who occupies the field of battle first and awaits his enemy is at ease; he who comes later to the scene and rushes into the fight is weary. Therefore those skilled in war bring the enemy to the field of battle and are not brought there by him.

One able to make the enemy come of his own accord does so by offering him some advantage. And one able to prevent him from coming does so by hurting him. When the enemy is at ease, be able to weary him; when well fed, to starve him; when at rest, to make him move. Appear at places to which he must hasten; move swiftly where he does not expect you. That you may march a thousand li[2] without wearying yourself is because you travel where there is no enemy. To be certain to take what you attack is to attack a place the enemy does not protect. To be certain to hold what you defend is to defend a place the enemy does not attack. Therefore, against those skilled in attack, an enemy does not know where to defend; against the experts in defense, the enemy does not know where to attack.

He whose advance is irresistible plunges into his enemy's weak positions; he who in withdrawal cannot be pursued moves so swiftly that he cannot be overtaken. When I wish to avoid battle I may defend myself simply by drawing a line on the ground; the enemy will be unable to attack me because I divert him from going where he wishes. If I am able to determine the enemy's dispositions while at the same time I conceal my own then I can concentrate and he must divide. And if I concentrate while he divides, I can use my entire strength to attack a fraction of his. There, I will be numerically superior. Then, if I am able to use many to strike few at the selected point, those I deal with will be in dire straits. The enemy must not know where I intend to give battle. For if he does not know where I intend to give battle he must prepare in a great many places. When he prepares in a great many places, those I have to fight in any one place will be few. One who has few must prepare against the enemy; one who has many makes the enemy prepare against him. If one knows where and when a battle will be fought his troops can march a thousand li and meet on the field. But if one knows neither the battleground nor the day of battle, the left will be unable to aid the right, or the right, the left; the van to support the rear, or the rear, the van. How much more is this so when separated by several tens of li, or, indeed, by even a few!

Therefore, determine the enemy's plans and you will know which strategy will be successful and which will not. Agitate him and ascertain the pattern of his movement. Determine his dispositions and so ascertain the field of battle. Probe him and learn where his strength is abundant and where deficient. The ultimate in disposing one's troops is to be without ascertainable shape. Then the most penetrating spies cannot pry in nor can the wise lay plans against you. Therefore, when I have won a victory I do not repeat my tactics but respond to circumstances in an infinite variety of ways.

Now an army may be likened to water, for just as flowing water avoids the heights and hastens to the lowlands, so an army avoids strength and strikes weakness. And as water shapes its flow in accordance with the ground, so an army manages its victory in accordance with the situation of the enemy. And as water has no constant form, there are in war no constant conditions.

Employment of Secret Agents

Now when an army of one hundred thousand is raised and dispatched on a distant campaign the expenses borne by the people together with the disbursements of the treasury will amount to a thousand pieces of gold daily. There will be continuous commotion both at home and abroad, people will be exhausted by the requirements of transport, and the affairs of seven hundred thousand households will be disrupted. One who confronts his enemy for many years in order to struggle for victory in a decisive battle yet who, because he be-

---

[2]One li is a third of a mile.

grudges rank, honors, and a few hundred pieces of gold, remains ignorant of his enemy's situation, is completely devoid of humanity. Such a man is no general; no support to his sovereign, no master of victory.

Now the reason the enlightened prince and the wise general conquer the enemy whenever they move and their achievements surpass those of ordinary men is foreknowledge. What is called "foreknowledge" cannot be elicited from spirits, nor from gods, nor by analogy with past events, nor from calculations. It must be obtained from men who know the enemy situation. Now there are five sorts of secret agents to be employed. These are native, inside, doubled, expendable, and living. When these five types of agents are all working simultaneously and none knows their method of operation, they are called "The Divine Skein" and are the treasure of a sovereign.

Native agents are those of the enemy's country people whom we employ. Doubled agents are enemy spies whom we employ. Expendable agents are those of our own spies who are deliberately given fabricated information. Living agents are those who return with information. Of all those in the army close to the commander none is more intimate than the secret agent; of all rewards none more liberal than those given to secret agents; of all matters none is more confidential than those relating to secret operations. He who is sage and wise, humane and just, cannot use secret agents. And he who is not delicate and subtle cannot get the truth out of them.

Delicate indeed! Truly delicate! There is no place where espionage is not used.

If plans relating to secret operations are prematurely divulged the agent and all those to whom he spoke of them shall be put to death. Generally in the case of armies you wish to strike, cities which you wish to attack, and people you wish to assassinate, you must know the names of the garrison commander, the staff officers, the ushers, gate keepers, and the bodyguards. You must instruct your agents to inquire into these matters in minute detail. It is essential to seek out enemy agents who have come to conduct espionage against you and to bribe them to serve you. Give them instructions and care for them. Thus doubled agents are recruited and used. It is by means of the doubled agent that native and inside agents can be recruited and employed, and it is by this means that the expendable agent, armed with false information, can be sent to convey it to the enemy. It is by this means also that living agents can be used at appropriate times.

The sovereign must have full knowledge of the activities of the five sorts of agents. This knowledge must come from the doubled agents, and therefore it is mandatory that they be treated with the utmost liberality. And therefore only the enlightened sovereign and the worthy general who are able to use the most intelligent people as agents are certain to achieve great things. Secret operations are essential in war; upon them the army relies to make its every move.

CLASSICAL CIVILIZATIONS

The Early Greeks: Their Gods, Heroes, and Poetry

Greeks differed from other peoples of the ancient Near East in many ways. One difference involved their reducing the conceptual distance between gods and people. Greek gods had human failings on a larger-than-life scale as well as superhuman powers. In the earliest surviving Greek literary works of any importance, we find the poet Homer narrating exciting adventures in which the gods side with humans or against them, but mortal beings are always the focal point. Homer's gods are intent on avenging offenses or insults to themselves, their priests, any semi-divine offspring, and their "special interests." For example, Artemis, goddess of the chase, avenges wanton destruction of wild animals, and Hera, goddess of marriage, gets even with home-wreckers. Somewhat less frequently, Homer's gods reward those who serve them well.

As their civilization developed, the Greeks recognized three types of poetry: (1) the epic, exemplified by Homer, (2) lyric poetry, and (3) the poetry of drama, exemplified by Sophocles (see Reading 28) and other playwrights of the Classical Age. Lyric poetry antedated the Classical Age: It was originally composed as words to be sung to the accompaniment of a lyre. (Lyres are rare among us now, but notice how we still refer to the "lyrics" of a song.) Lyric poetry focused on what the poet believed as an individual, reflecting personal experiences and desires, whereas the epic poets focused much more on descriptions and narratives of their heroes and events than on their own beliefs about them.

14

Homer, *The Odyssey*

Homer is considered the author of two epics, composed about 800 B.C. *The Iliad* describes the Greek siege of Troy. *The Odyssey* presents the return home from Troy of the wily Odysseus. In this selection, Odysseus meets Polyphemus, a savage one-eyed giant. Polyphemus's curse is carried out by his father Poseidon, leading to mounting catastrophes for Odysseus and his men. All ends well, however, when Odysseus returns home safely and kills all the suitors who have been pursuing his faithful wife. This final glorious battle takes place in the halls of his home.

QUESTIONS TO CONSIDER

1. What does Odysseus find striking about the land of the Cyclopes?
2. How do Odysseus and his men become captives in the cave of Polyphemus?
3. When Polyphemus is injured, why do the other Cyclopes show indifference to his fate?

We came to the land of the Cyclopes, a fierce, uncivilized people who never lift a hand to plant or plough but put their trust in Providence. All the crops they require spring up unsown and untilled, wheat and barley and the vines whose generous clusters give them wine when ripened for them by the timely rains. The Cyclopes have no assemblies for the making of laws, nor any settled customs, but live in hollow caverns in the mountain heights, where each man is lawgiver to his children and his wives, and nobody cares a jot for his neighbors.

Not very far from the harbour on their coast, there lies a luxuriant island. This is where we came to land. Some god must have guided us through the murky night, for the ships were in a thick fog, and it was impossible to see ahead. Not a man among us caught sight of the island before our good ships ran aground. We then jumped out on the shore, fell asleep where we were and so waited for the blessed light of day.

When the fresh Dawn came we were delighted with what we saw of the island and set out to explore it. Presently, in order that my company might have something to eat, the Nymphs, those Children of Zeus, set some mountain goats on the move. We let fly at the game; and in a short time Providence had sent us a satisfactory bag. So the whole day long till the sun set we sat and enjoyed this rich supply of meat, and as we looked across at the neighbouring land of the Cyclopes, we could not only see the smoke from their fires but hear the voices and the bleating of their sheep and goats. The sun went down, night fell, and we slept on the sea-shore.

With the first rosy light of Dawn, I assembled my company. "My good friends," I said, "for the time being I want you to stay here, while I go in my own ship with my own crew to find out what kind of men are over there, and whether they are brutal and lawless savages or hospitable and god-fearing people."

Then I climbed into my ship with my men. It was no great distance to the mainland coast. As we approached its nearest point, we made out a cave there, close to the sea. Here large flocks of sheep and goats were penned at night. It was the den of a giant, the lonely shepherd of sequestered flocks, who had no truck with others of his kind but lived aloof in his own lawless way. And what a formidable monster he was! No one would have taken him for a man who ate bread like ourselves; he reminded one rather of some wooded peak in the high hills, lifting itself in solitary state.

I picked out the twelve best men in the company and advanced, leaving the rest of my men on guard. I took with me in a goatskin some dark and mellow wine which had been given to me by Maron son of Euanthes, the priest of Apollo. And a wonderful drink it was. It had been kept secret from everyone in the house but himself, his good wife, and a single stewardess. When they drank this red and honeyed vintage, he used to pour one cupful of wine into twenty of water, and the sweet fumes that came up from the bowl were irresistible.

Well, I filled a big bottle with this wine and took some food in a wallet along with me also; for I had an instant foreboding, though I am no coward, that we were going to find ourselves face to face with some being of colossal strength and ferocity, to whom the law of man and god meant nothing. It took us very little time to reach the cave, but we did not find its owner at home: he was tending his fat sheep in the pastures. So we went inside and had a good look round. There were baskets laden with cheeses, and the folds were thronged with lambs and kids.

Now my men's idea was to make off with some of the cheeses, drive the kids and lambs quickly out of the pens down to the good ship, and so set sail across the salt water. They pleaded with me; but though it would have been far better so, I was not to be persuaded. I wished to see the owner of the cave and had hopes of some friendly gifts from my host. As things fell out, my company were to have an unpleasant surprise when he did put in an appearance.

We lit a fire, killed a beast and made offerings, took some cheeses just for ourselves, and when we had eaten, sat down in the cave to await his arrival. At last he came up, shepherding his flocks and carrying a huge bundle of dry wood to burn at supper-time. With a great din he cast this down inside the cavern, giving us such a fright that we hastily retreated to an inner recess. Meanwhile he drove his fat sheep into the wider part of the cave. He then picked up a huge stone, with which he closed the entrance. It was a mighty slab, such as you couldn't have budged from the ground, not with a score of heavy four-wheeled wagons to help you. Next he sat down to milk his ewes and bleating goats. When he had finished all his jobs, he spied us and began asking questions.

"Strangers!" he said. "And who may you be? Where do you hail from over the highways of the sea? Is yours a trading venture; or are you cruising the main on chance, like roving pirates, who risk their lives to ruin other people?"

Our hearts sank within us. The booming voice and the very sight of the monster filled us with panic. Still, I managed to find words to answer him.

"We are Achaeans," I said, "on our way back from Troy. We meant to sail straight home; but we lost our bearings, as Zeus, I suppose, intended that we should. We are proud to belong to the forces of Agamemnon, who by sacking the great city of Ilium and destroying all its armies, has made himself the most famous man in the world today. We, less fortunate, are visiting you here as suppliants, in the hope that you might give us friendly entertainment or even go further in your generosity. You know the laws of hospitality: I beseech you, good sir, to remember your duty to the gods. For we throw ourselves on your mercy; and Zeus is there to avenge the suppliant and the guest. He is the travellers' god: he guards their steps and he invests them with their rights."

So said I, and promptly he answered me out of his pitiless heart: "Stranger, you must be a fool, or must have come from very far afield, to preach to me of fear or reverence for the gods. We Cyclopes care not a jot for Zeus, nor for the rest of the blessed gods, since we are much stronger than they. It would never occur to me to spare you or your men against my will for fear of trouble from Zeus. But tell me where you moored your good ship. I should like to see her."

He was trying to get the better of me, but I knew enough of the world to see through him and I met him with deceit.

"As for my ship," I answered, "it was wrecked by the Earthshaker Poseidon on the confines of your land. I and my friends here managed to escape with our lives."

To this the cruel brute made no reply. Instead, he jumped up, and reaching out towards my men, seized a couple and dashed their heads against the floor as though they had been puppies. Their brains ran out on the ground and soaked the earth. Limb by limb he tore them to pieces to make his meal, which he devoured like a mountain lion, never pausing till all entrails and flesh, marrow and bones, were all consumed, while we could do nothing but weep and lift our hands to Zeus in horror at the ghastly sight, paralysed by our sense of utter helplessness. When the Cyclops had filled his great belly with this meal of human flesh, he stretched himself out for sleep. And now my manhood prompted me to action: I thought I would draw my sharp sword from the scabbard at my side, creep up to him, and stab him in the breast. But on second thoughts I refrained, realizing that we should have perished there as surely as the Cyclops, for we should have found it impossible to push aside the huge rock with which he had closed the great mouth of the cave. So for the time being we just sat groaning there and waited for the blessed light of day.

No sooner had the tender Dawn shown her roses in the East, than the Cyclops lit up the fire and milked his splendid ewes. This business over and his morning labours done, he once more snatched up a couple of my men and prepared his meal. When he had eaten, he turned his fatted sheep out of the cave, removing the great doorstone without an effort. But he replaced it immediately. Then, he drove his rich flocks off towards the high pasture, while I was left, with murder in my heart, beating about for some scheme by which I might pay him back. The best plan I could think of was this. Lying by the pen, the Cyclops had a huge staff of green olive-wood, which he had cut to carry in his hand when it was seasoned. To us it looked more like the mast of some black ship of twenty oars. That was the impression which its length and thickness made on us. On this piece of timber I set to work. I cut off a length and sharpened it to a point. Then I poked it into the blazing fire to make it hard, and finally I hid it carefully. I then told my company to casts lots among themselves for the dangerous task of helping me to lift the pole and twist it in the Cyclops' eye when he was sound asleep.

Evening came, and with it the Cyclops, shepherding his woolly sheep, which he herded into the broad part of the cave. He raised the great doorstone, set it in its place, and then sat down to milk his ewes and bleating goats. When this business was over and his work finished, he once more seized upon two of us and prepared his supper. Then came my chance. With an ivy-wood bowl of my dark wine in my hands, I went up to him and said: "Here, Cyclops, have some wine to wash down that meal of human flesh, and find out for yourself what kind of vintage was stored away in our ship's hold. I brought it for you by way of offering in the hope that you would be charitable and help me on my homeward way. But your savagery is more than we can bear. Cruel monster, how can you expect to ever have a visitor again from the world of men, after such deeds as you have done?"

The Cyclops took the wine and drank it up. And the delicious draught gave him such exquisite pleasure that he asked me for another bowlful.

"Be good enough," he said, "to let me have some more; and tell me your name, so that I may make you a gift that you will value. We Cyclopes have wine of our own. But this vintage of yours is nectar and ambrosia distilled."

So said the Cyclops, and I handed him another bowlful of the ruddy wine. Three times I filled up for him; and three times the fool drained the bowl to the dregs. At last, when the wine had fuddled his wits, I addressed him with disarming suavity.

"Cyclops," I said, "you wish to know the name I bear. I'll tell it to you; and in return I should like to have the gift you promised me. My name is Nobody. That is what I am called by my mother and father and by all my friends."

The Cyclops answered me with a cruel jest. "Of all his company I will eat Nobody last, and the rest before him. That shall be your gift."

He had hardly spoken before he toppled over and fell face upwards on the floor, where he lay with his great neck twisted to one side, conquered by sleep. His drunkenness made him vomit, and a stream of wine mixed with morsels of men's flesh poured from his throat. I went at once and thrust our pole deep under the ashes of the fire to make it hot, and meanwhile gave a word of encouragement to all my men, to make sure that no one should play the coward and leave me in the lurch. I withdrew the pole from the fire and brought it over to the spot where my men were standing ready. Heaven now inspired them with a reckless courage. Seizing the olive pole, they drove its sharpened end into the Cyclops' eye, while I used my weight from above to twist it home. The fiery smoke from the Cyclops' blazing eyeball singed his lids and brow all round, and the very roots of his eye crackled in the heat. He gave a dreadful shriek, which echoed round the rocky walls, and we backed away from him in terror, while he pulled the stake from his eye, streaming with blood. Then he hurled it away from him with frenzied hands and raised a great shout for the other Cyclopes who lived in neighboring caves. These, hearing his screams, came up from every quarter and gathering outside the cave asked him what ailed him:

"What on earth is wrong with you, Polyphemus? Why must you disturb the peaceful night and spoil our sleep with all this shouting? Is a robber driving off your sheep, or is somebody trying by treachery or violence to kill you?"

Out of the cave came Polyphemus' great voice in reply: "O my friends, it's Nobody's treachery that is doing me to death."

"Well then," they answered, in a way that settled the matter, "if nobody is assaulting you in your solitude, you must be sick. Sickness comes from the almighty Zeus and cannot be helped. All you can do is pray to your father, the Lord Poseidon."

And off they went, while I chuckled to myself at the way in which my happy notion of a false name had taken them in. The Cyclops, still moaning in agonies of pain, groped about with his hands and pushed the rock away from the mouth of the cave. But then he sat himself down in the doorway and stretched out both arms in the hope of catching us in the act of slipping out among the sheep. What a fool he must have thought me! Meanwhile I was cudgelling my brains for the best possible course, trying to hit on some way of saving my friends as well as my own skin. Plan after plan, dodge after dodge, passed through my mind. It was a matter of life or death: we were in mortal peril. And this was the scheme I eventually chose. There were in the flock some well bred, thick-fleeced rams. Those I quietly lashed together in threes. The middle one in each case was to carry one of my followers, while its fellows went on either side to protect him. For myself I chose a full-grown ram who was the pick of the whole flock. Seizing him by the back, I curled myself up under his shaggy belly and lay there upside down, with a firm grip on his wonderful fleece and with patience in my heart. Thus in fear and trembling we waited for the blessed Dawn.

As soon as she arrived, the flock began to scramble out and make for the pastures. Their master, though he was worn out by the agonies he had gone through, passed his hand along the backs of all the animals as they left; but the idiot never noticed that my men were tied up under the breasts of his own woolly sheep. The last of the flock to come up to the doorway was the big ram, burdened by his own fleece and by me with my teeming brain. As he felt him with his big hands the great Polyphemus broke into speech:

"Sweet ram," he said, "what does this mean? Why are you the last of the flock to pass out of the cave, you who have never lagged behind the sheep, you who always steps so proudly out and are the first of them to crop the lush shoots of the grass? Are you grieved for your master's eye, blinded by a wicked man and his accursed friends, when he had robbed me of my wits with wine? Nobody was his name; and I swear that he has not yet saved his skin! Ah, if only you could find a voice to tell me where he's hiding from my fury! Wouldn't I hammer him and splash his brains all over the floor of the cave, till that miserable Nobody had eased my heart of the suffering I owe to him!"

So he passed the ram out; and when we had put a little distance between ourselves and the cave, I freed myself from under my ram and next untied my men from theirs. Then, quickly, though with many a backward look, we drove our long-legged sheep right down to the ship—and a rich, fat flock they made. My dear companions were overjoyed when they caught sight of us survivors, though their relief soon changed to lamentation for their slaughtered friends. I would have none of this weeping, however, bidding them to make haste instead to tumble all the fleecy sheep on board and put to sea.

But before we were out of earshot, I let Polyphemus have a piece of my mind. "Cyclops!" I called. "So he was not such a weakling after all, the man whose friends you meant to overpower and eat in that snug cave of yours! And your crimes came home to roost, you brute, who have not even the decency to refrain from devouring your own guests. Now Zeus and all his fellow-gods have paid you out."

My taunts so exasperated the angry Cyclops that he tore the top off a great pinnacle of rock and hurled it at us. The rock fell just ahead of our blue-painted bows. As it plunged in, the water rose and the backwash, like a swell from the open sea, swept us landward and nearly drove us on the beach. My crew rowed with a will; but when they had brought us across the water to twice our previous distance I was for giving the Cyclops some more of my talk.

"Cyclops, if anyone ever asks you how you came by your unsightful blindness, tell him your eye was put out by Odysseus, Sacker of Cities, the son of Laertes, who lives in Ithaca."

The Cyclops gave a groan. "Alas!" he cried. "So the old prophecy has come home to me with a vengeance! We had a prophet with us once, who was an excellent seer and grew old among us in the practice of his art. He warned me that a man named Odysseus would rob me of my sight. But I always expected some big and handsome fellow of tremendous strength to come along. And now, a puny, good for nothing, little runt fuddles me with wine and then puts out my eye! But come here, Odysseus, so that I may make you some friendly gifts and prevail on the great Earthshaker to see you safely home. For I am his son, and he is the one who will heal me if he's willing—a thing no other blessed god nor any man on earth could do."

To which I shouted in reply: "I only wish I could make as sure of robbing you of life and breath and sending you to Hell, as I am certain that not even the Earthshaker will ever heal your eye."

At this the Cyclops lifted up his hands and prayed to the Lord Poseidon: "Hear me, Poseidon, Girdler of Earth, grant that Odysseus may never reach his home in Ithaca. But if he is destined to reach his native land, let him come late, in evil plight, with all his comrades dead, and when he is landed, by a foreign ship, let him find trouble in his home."

So Polyphemus prayed; and the god of the sable locks heard his prayer. Then once again the Cyclops picked a boulder up—bigger by far, this time—and hurled it with a swing, putting such boundless force into his throw that the rock missed our blue-painted ship by only inches. The water heaved up as it ploughed by into the sea; but the wave that it raised carried us on toward the further shore. And so we reached our island, where the rest of our good ships were awaiting us. Once there, we unloaded the Cyclops' sheep and divided our spoil. My comrades-in-arms did me the special honor, when the sheep were distributed, of presenting me with the big ram. Him I sacrificed on the beach, burning slices from his thighs as an offering to Zeus, who is lord of us all. But Zeus took no notice of my sacrifice; his mind must already have been full of plans for the destruction of all my gallant ships and my trusty band.

15

Sappho, *Lyric Songs*

One of the earliest and greatest writers of Greek lyric poetry was Sappho of the Island of Lesbos, who had a remarkable gift for conveying a wealth of universal emotions in a few lines. Only a small fraction of her work survives, and most of it is in "fragments" copied by later Greek writers. Although these surviving fragments cover a broad spectrum of topics, the recurring theme in them is love for both women and men. Sappho's poetry made its contribution to the modern meaning of "lesbian," but she appears unaware of anything unusual in her sexual orientation. When she refers to "Lesbian bards" as far excelling those from other parts of Greece, she is including her contemporary male poets on Lesbos. Ancient Greeks of both sexes were expected to be heterosexual enough to have conventional families; beyond that the only frequent caution raised was for moderation, in sex as in all things.

QUESTIONS TO CONSIDER

1. Why does Aphrodite figure so prominently in Sappho's poetry? Elsewhere in Greek poems, Aphrodite is described as "faithless" or "merciless." What characteristics does she have for Sappho?
2. Poems 1 and 3 are given in both prose and verse translations. Which do you prefer? Why? Would your reasons apply to Homer's epics as well? Are there grounds for the modern custom of keeping lyric poetry in verse translation while giving the epics in prose?

1a. Immortal Aphrodite

Immortal Aphrodite of the broidered throne, daughter of Zeus, weaver of wiles, I pray thee break not my spirit with anguish and distress, O Queen. But come hither, if ever before thou didst hear my voice afar, and listen, and leaving thy father's golden house camest with chariot yoked, and fair fleet sparrows drew thee, flapping fast their wings around the dark earth, from heaven through mid sky. Quickly arrived they; and thou, blessed one, smiling with immortal countenance, didst ask, what now is befallen me, and why now I call, and what I in my mad heart most desire to see. "What Beauty now wouldst thou draw to love thee? Who wrongs thee, Sappho? For even if she flies she shall soon follow, and if she rejects gifts shall yet give, and if she loves not shall soon love, however loth." Come, I pray thee, now too, and release me from cruel cares, and all that my heart desires to accomplish, accomplish thou, and by thyself my ally.

From *The Songs of Sappho in English Translation by Many Poets* (Mt. Vernon, NY: Peter Pauper Press, 1942): 1a. trans. Henry T. Wharton (1898) p. 9; 3a. trans. Edwin D. Cox (1913) pp. 18–19; 3b. trans. J.M. Edmonds, pp. 20–21; 5. trans. C.M. Bowra, pp. 36–37. Walter Peterson, ed. and trans., *The Lyric Songs of the Greeks* (Boston: The Gorham Press, 1918): 1b. pp. 17–19; 2. pp. 18–19; 4. p. 22; 6–7. pp. 28–29. Percy Osborne, ed. and trans., *The Poems of Sappho* (London: Elkin Matthews, 1909): 8. p. 44. Lord Rennell of Rodd and Edward Arnold, *Love, Worship and Death: Some Renderings from the Greek Anthology:* trans. Rodd (1908), p. 5. C.M. Bowra translation by permission of Oxford University Press.

1b.

Ah! gold-enthroned immortal Aphrodite,
Daughter of Zeus, through wily cunning mighty,
    Goddess revered, to thee I pray:
    My soul-subduing griefs allay.

And hither come thou, if before this ever
Thou didst my distant voice to hear endeavor,
    Leaving thy father's house of gold,
    If e'er thou camest to me of old.

Upon thy radiant chariot thee ascending
Thy beauteous sparrows, across the earth contending,
    Carried thee down from heaven on high,
    And busily their wings did ply.

Scarce had they passed, O goddess, earth's wide portal,
When thou, with smiling countenance immortal,
    Didst ask concerning my distress,
    What misfortune did me oppress:

"Why call'st thou me, what all-consuming passion
Devoureth thee? The Goddess of Persuasion
    Shall whom constrain to do thy will?
    Who, Sappho, dares to do thee ill?

"Though now she spurns thee, soon she'll friendship proffer;
Gifts which she now refuses soon she'll offer;
    Though now thy love she from her fling,
    Soon 'gainst thy will her love she'll bring."

And now again come to me, cares dispelling,
My soul's tempestuous fiery passion quelling.
    My heart's desire for me fulfill,
    And be my friend and ally still.

2. To a Beloved Maiden

That man who sits before thy face,
    Godlike he seems to me.
He hears thy words' sweet charming grace,
    Conversing joyously.

Thou laugh'st a laugh of pure delight;
    But in my breast my heart
Violently flutters at thy sight:
    No sound from me will start.

My tongue is lamed, a fiery glow
    My limbs completely sears;
My eyes see nothing, rumblings low
    Play havoc in my ears.

Hot perspiration downward drops,
    And trembling seizes me.
I am ghastly pale, my life-blood stops,
    Near death I seem to be.

3a. To Anactoria in Lydia

Some say that the fairest thing upon the dark earth is a host of horsemen, and some say a host of foot soldiers, and others again a fleet of ships, but for me it is my beloved. And it is easy to make anyone understand this. When Helen saw the most beautiful of mortals, she chose for best that one, the destroyer of all the honor of Troy, and thought not much of child or dear parent, but was led astray by Love, to bestow her heart far off, for woman is ever easy to lead astray when she thinks of no account what is near and dear. Even so, Anactoria, you do not remember, it seems, when she is with you, one the gentle sound of whose footfall I would rather hear and the brightness of whose shining face I would rather see than all the chariots and mail-clad footmen of Lydia. I know that in this world man cannot have the best; yet to pray for a part of what was once shared is better than to forget it. . . .

3b.

A host of horse or foot may be
To some the fairest sight to see,
To some a fleet of ships; to me
    The loved one passes all.
And easy 'tis to prove my case;
She that had the fairest face
Man ever looked on, set her joy
Upon the ravisher of Troy,
    And heedless of the call
Of parent dear or sweetest child,
Left her home, by Love beguiled
    To give her heart afar.
For ever easy to mislead
Is woman, when she pays no heed
To what is near to her and dear.
Anactory, though far thou'rt gone,
Let us remembered by one
Whose sweet footfall I'd rather hear,
Whose beaming smile I'd rather see,
Than all the Lydian chariotry
    And mighty men of war.
Well wot I no mortal wight

May have the best for his delight;
Yet a one-time happy lot
Is better longed-for than forgot.

4. My Daughter, Cleis

For me a pretty child I claim,
    With form like flowers of gold.
Beloved Cleis is her name,
    Admired by young and old.
Were lovely Lydia all my own,
It could not for her loss atone.

5. To My Brother, Charaxus

Aye, seek the false and shun the true,
And bid your friends go hang for you,
And grieve me in your pride, and say
I bring you shame. Go, have your way,
And flout me till you've had your fill;
I have no fears, and never will,
    For the anger of a child.

Do as you choose; but have a care;
Old birds know how to shun the snare;
The measure of my foe is ta'en;
What once he's done he'll do again;
    I shall not be beguiled.

Be wise in time then, change your heart;
I know the gods will take my part
    Because my spirit's mild.

6. Truly I Want to Die

Truly I want to die,
Such was her weeping when she said good-bye.
    These words she said to me:
    "What sad calamity!
Sappho, I leave you most unwillingly."
    To her I made reply:
    "Go with good heart, but try
Not to forget our love in days gone by.
    Else let me call to mind,
    If your heart proves unkind,

The soft delightful ways you leave behind.
    Many a coronet
    Of rose and violet,
Crocus and dill upon your brow you set:
    Many a necklace too
    Round your soft throat you threw,
Woven with me from buds of ravishing hue,
    And often balm you spread
    Of myrrh upon my head,
And royal ointment on my hair you shed."

7. The Bridegroom

Lift high the roof to give him room—
Ye workmen, lift again—
Like mighty Ares now doth come
The bridegroom taller than tall men.

His rivals he outstrips with ease,
Like Lesbian bards those of all Greece.

8. A Certain Kind of Woman

Like the sweet apple which reddens, far up on the
    high tree-top growing,
Up on the loftiest branch, scarce itself to the gatherers
    showing—
They rathermore could not reach it; although
    of it easily knowing.

9. Death

Death is an evil; for the gods chose breath;
Had Death been good the gods had chosen
    Death.

10. To the Goddess of Evening

Thou, Hesper, bringest homeward all
    That radiant dawn sped far and wide:
The sheep to fold, the goat to stall,
    The children to their mother's side.

The Hindu Tradition

"Hinduism" is the term Westerners have used for the religion of most people living on the Indian subcontinent. Many other religions have originated and flourished in India, however, including Buddhism, Jainism, and Sikhism. Islam has also played a large role in Indian life since around A.D. 1000. Hinduism itself encompasses more than a religion; it includes an entire way of life.

When the Aryan invaders conquered and settled among the native Dravidians in India, the fusion of cultures developed into early Hinduism between approximately 700 B.C. and A.D. 400. In spite of portraying individual divinities in versions much at a variance with one another, Hinduism promoted a comprehensive view of life. It focused on four legitimate goals for which all men and women should strive.

The first and most basic goal was pleasure *(kama).* Wealthy people and the less affluent alike could derive pleasure from elaborate craft traditions in art, music, drama, and story-telling in all forms. Hindus developed the joys of food and, with even more emphasis, sex into highly sophisticated forms, and treatises such as the *Kama Sutra* served to cultivate refinement in enjoying them.

The second goal was the acquisition of wealth *(artha),* illustrated in the following section on Hindu ideas of the proper use of ruling power. The third goal was abiding by law or duty *(dharma).* Hindu law was believed to be eternal and unchanging, revealed to human seers or prophets at the beginning of time (for example, Manu was the recipient of the *Laws of Manu).* The essential structure of the law was the fourfold division of social classes—from priests and warriors at the top to the commoners and servile class (the conquered, darker-skinned people) at the bottom. This structure was the basis of the "caste system," whereby one's occupation and social status were completely determined at birth. Hindu law also postulated that after death each person would enter a new life form based on the good or evil done in the previous life. This process is called transmigration or reincarnation *(samsara).*

A final goal of the Hindus was the quest for liberation *(moksha)* from the process of transmigration. This goal involved a quest for transcending the normal human condition of trying to do good and avoid evil, only to be reborn in another life where the struggle would continue indefinitely. Some Hindus sought, and believed that they could attain, a condition of godlike perfection that would be an end to such a cycle.

The Hindu tradition described three valid paths to end transmigration. The first was the path of action *(karma),* which meant properly performing religious rituals as well as doing one's prescribed duty. Most Hindu thinkers, however, believed that following such a path could only partially lead a person to the ultimate goal. Therefore a second, and more favored, path was that of knowledge *(jhana),* first described in the *Upanishads,* beginning around 700 B.C. This path involved calm contemplation of the universe and the self until one realized that God was present everywhere—including *within* the self. Only a small percentage of all Hindus would ever reach, or even attempt to reach, this mystical experience of oneness with God and the universe. The journey was a long and difficult one that required sacrificing all usual ways of living and thinking for long hours of private meditation.

The final path to liberation involved devotion *(bhakti)* to God. After the time of the *Rig Veda,*[1] the Hindus gradually developed the concept that only one God existed. But Hindus did not all agree on the identity of this God; some believed Vishnu was supreme (as did the writer of the *Bhagavad Gita*), while others favored Shiva. They did agree, however, that a person totally devoted to God, in thinking and love, would be saved by God and granted liberation from transmigration. The worship of the supreme deity, the outpouring of love toward God, and the prayerful hope for divine compassion became the major driving forces of Hinduism. The following text selections can give only a small sample of the great variety of writing produced by Hindu India.

16

The Essence of the Universe

This selection, from one of the earliest *Upanishads* (the *Chandogya Upanishad*), takes the form of a dialogue between a teacher and pupil. It presents the view that the *Brahman*—the Self of the universe, the abstract, divine power that is present everywhere—is the same as the soul or self *(atman)* dwelling within each individual.

QUESTIONS TO CONSIDER

1. How does the dialogue explain the essential reality underlying the world?
2. How essential is this dialogue in the understanding of Hinduism? Why?

"In the beginning, my dear, this world was just being *(sat),* one only, without a second. Some people, no doubt, say: 'In the beginning, verily, this world was just nonbeing *(asat),* one only, without a second; from that nonbeing, being was produced.' But how, indeed, my dear, could it be so?" said he. "How could being be produced from nonbeing? On the contrary, my dear, in the beginning this world was being alone, one only, without a second. Being thought to itself: 'May I be many; may I procreate.' It produced fire. That fire thought to itself: 'May I be many, may I procreate.' It produced water. Therefore, whenever a person grieves or perspires, then it is from fire [heat] alone that water is produced. That water thought to itself: 'May I be many; may I procreate.' It produced food. Therefore, whenever

---

[1]The *Rig Veda* is an anthology of over a thousand hymns of praise arranged in ten books. The hymns are chanted by Brahmans to the various Aryan gods of nature. The *Rig Veda* is the oldest of the four earliest Indian literary works known as *Vedas (Knowledge)*. Vedic India covers the period from about 1500 to 1000 B.C.

it rains, then there is abundant food; it is from water alone that food for eating is produced. . . .

"Bring hither a fig from there." "Here it is, sir." "Break it." "It is broken, sir." "What do you see there?" "These extremely fine seeds, sir." "Of these, please break one." "It is broken, sir." "What do you see there?" "Nothing at all, sir." Then he said to Shvetaketu: "Verily, my dear, that subtle essence which you do not perceive—from that very essence, indeed, my dear, does this great fig tree thus arise. Believe me, my dear, that which is the subtle essence—this whole world has that essence for its Self; that is the Real [*satya*, truth]; that is the Self; that [subtle essence] art thou, Shvetaketu." "Still further may the venerable sir instruct me." "So be it, my dear," said he.

"Having put this salt in the water, come to me in the morning." He did so. Then the father said to him: "That salt which you put in the water last evening—please bring it hither." Even having looked for it, he did not find it, for it was completely dissolved. "Please take a sip of water from this end," said the father. "How is it?" "Salt." "Take a sip from the middle," said he. "How is it?" "Salt." "Take a sip from that end," said he. "How is it?" "Salt." "Throw it away and come to me." Shvetaketu did so thinking to himself: "That salt, though unperceived, still persists in the water." Then Aruni said to him: "Verily, my dear, you do not perceive Being in this world; but it is, indeed, here only: That which is the subtle essence—this whole world has that essence for its Self. That is the Real. That is the Self. That art thou, Shvetaketu."

17

The *Kama Sutra*

The *Kama Sutra* is one of the world's oldest treatises on the art of love, compiled sometime in the fourth century A.D. by a Brahman named Vatsyayana from texts dating back to the fourth century B.C.[1] The word *kama* means desires and pleasures with a strong connotation of sexual love, and *sutra* stands for a scriptural narrative or a collection of precepts and maxims. The *Kama Sutra* is not a pornographic work. The Hindu cultural tradition takes physical love seriously and honestly and views sexual pleasures as the best of all legitimate pleasures. The *Kama Sutra* deals with all aspects of eroticism including detailed instructions on erotic techniques, from stimulation of amorous desires, the art of scratching, and forms of coition to aphrodisiac recipes, marriage, adultery, prostitution, male and female homosexuality, sadomasochism, group sex, and transvestism. The following excerpts are from the chapters on "The Three Aims of Life,"[2] and "Preludes and Conclusions to the Games of Love."

---

[1]In the text, Vatsyayana speaks of himself in the third person, that is, "Vatsyayana's opinion is that . . ." In the text that follows, Vatsyayana's words are in the bold-type sections; these are supplemented by commentaries by Yashodhara, given in italics, and by modern Hindu commentaries in regular Roman type.

[2]In some Hindu treatises, such as this one, the goals of *dharma* (following the moral law) and *moksha* (liberation from reincarnation) are combined.

QUESTIONS TO CONSIDER

1. Compare the place of eroticism in the Western cultural tradition with that of Hindu India.
2. In the *Kama Sutra,* what is the basic standard for distinguishing good from bad love?
3. Does the *Kama Sutra* approach to sex support female equality? Why or why not?

The Three Aims of Life

11   Kama signifies the mental inclination toward the pleasures of touch, sight, taste and smell, to the extent that the practitioner derives satisfaction from it.
Kama is the perception of the power of illusion materialized in an object, since from perception is born desire, attraction and ardor. The tendency to possess oneself of these objects of the senses is eroticism. Eroticism is of two kinds, general or specific.

Particularly concerned with touch, closely connected to selfish pleasure, eroticism is an experience that finds its finality in itself. This is the most general aspect of Eros.
The organs of action are the tongue, the hand, the foot, the anus, and the sexual organ. Of these, leaving aside the pleasures deriving from speech, the highest pleasure is the reciprocal discovery by man and woman of the natural differences of the lower part of their bodies, which are the vulva and the penis. This pleasure is connected with the sense of touch, seated particularly in the organ known as upastha (the sexual organ), which, in the act of procreation, causes wonderful bliss.

This experience is essentially connected with the sense of touch.

A whirl of pleasurable sensations is connected with the perception of the organ of touch. The desire for such experience is the cause of the state of erotic excitement in both man and woman. In the woman, it manifests itself as a diffuse desire for contact with the man, while for the latter, it is desire of the pleasure of touching, especially the thighs and center of the body.

A specific desire is the urge to achieve a result. Seeking for sexual relations has its aim in the pleasure experienced at the moment sperm is emitted. This enjoyment is called the result. From the point of view of touch, this moment is a special experience, because the previous pleasurable sensations did not bear fruit.

Since this experience is oriented toward a goal, the sensation of touch is not its essence. The achievement of a goal is therefore distinct from eroticism.

Kissing, biting, and scratching with the nails, which serve to augment the erotic charge of both men and women, belong to a general eroticism. They are not considered forms of possession.

The fact that the sexual act has a goal poses a difficult problem. Yashodhara considers as a whole the continuity of pleasure, starting from kisses and caresses up to the emission of sperm. Vatsyayana, however, differs from Yashodhara since he considers procreation as the real goal. According to the Arharva Veda, *"Wife! Stretch yourself with pleasure on this bed and procreate sons for your husband. You will be blessed like the Queen of Heaven. You shall awake at dawn, before the rising of the sun."*

From *The Complete Kama Sutra,* translated by Alain Danielou, published by Park Street Press, an imprint of Inner Traditions International, Rochester, VT 05767. Copyright © 1994.

"Prudent men take a wife early, intermingling their bodies as they must. O thou astonishing creature, able to procreate children, unite with your husband!"

"O Supreme God that protectest this woman in whom I have today planted my seed, inspire her so that she realizes my wish, full of desire as I am, and that, opening her thighs, she allows my penis to assail her vagina." "Wife! I made my penis slide effortlessly along the path of your vagina, between your thighs. I marked with red this sublime union connected with the sun."

"Man! With your hand, stroke the vaginal thighs of your wife and joyfully both beget a son so that the sun god will prolong your life."

"Let us throw into the fire, together with the blanket, the defilements we have left in the marriage act."

The meaning of these Vedic texts suggests that:

Love must be made at night so as to avoid fear, doubt, or inconvenience. Before copulating, embraces and caresses must be exchanged so that man and woman experience feelings of pleasure. Once the light is extinguished, caresses are not only made without shyness, but the pleasure is greater. Man and woman must take pleasure in the act with satisfaction and they must both take care not to injure the fetus. At the entry to the vagina, there is a delicate membrane that breaks at the first union. This is why the man must take care not to hurt the girl.

The act must be performed in the normal position, since children begotten in an abnormal posture are deformed. For reasons of hygiene and cleanliness, a bath must be taken after making love.

Sexual behavior is to be learned with the aid of the *Kama Sutra* and the counsel of worthy men, experts in the arts of pleasure.

Through the *Kama Sutra*, Vatsyayana defines the approaches to erotic practice.

Among the means taught by the Kama Sutra, *Vatsyayana suggests an exchange of letters, if the girl is of the same caste and well educated.*

The *Kama Sutra* defines moral and social rules for the couple. If the couple's conduct is in accordance with the teachings of the *Kama Sutra,* their life will be a success from an erotic point of view. The partners will always be satisfied with each other and their spirit will not be touched by any desire to be unfaithful.

The *Kama Sutra* teaches that sighs, flirtation, and foreplay are three most important elements in amorous relations. There are: three kinds of boy; three classes of girl; three sorts of equal copulation; six sorts of unequal copulation; three modes of copulation; nine ways of copulating according to the different modes; nine sorts of copulation according to different moments; making a total of twenty-seven modes of copulation.

During copulation, at what moment and in what way do the man and the woman reach enjoyment?

What problems are faced in the first sexual relation?

What effect does ejaculation have on the woman?

What use are the various positions at the moment of union?

What illness can beset a woman after copulating with an inexpert man?

The *Kama Sutra* gives the answer to all questions that may arise when man and woman unite like milk and water.

This is why the Master explains that an erotic treatise is as important as a treatise on morals or politics.

Preludes and Conclusions to the Game of Love

The preludes and conclusions form part of the act of love. Once stimulated, desire leads to various kinds of amorous relations. The various kinds of amorous relations are as follows:

Ragavat, passionate love, born of physical attraction;

Aharyaraga, love born from habit, the result of affection produced by long co-habitation;

Kritrimaraga, feigned love, without true feeling;

Vyavahitaraga, substitute love, through an interposed party. The man sleeps with his wife, while thinking of another woman;

Potarata, neutral sex, without feeling, practiced with servant-women or female porters;

Khalarata, degrading love, to satiate one's basest instincts, practiced with a corrupt woman or some gross individual.

Such are the various kinds of erotic attraction, whether good or bad.

Ragavat, passionate love born of physical attraction: born in both parties at first sight, this attraction grows with the efforts made to realize it. This kind of attraction is also found on returning from a journey, or on meeting again after a quarrel.

Desire born from a first glimpse of someone's pleasant appearance, which develops with information brought through a messenger and other efforts to manage to unite, is called ragavat, passionate love. It is the same desire felt on returning from a journey, stimulated by absence, or else when, after a quarrel, peace is made and one makes love joyously and with pleasure. This is what is known as passionate love.

This attachment increases until its goal has been attained.
Passionate desire fires itself and lasts until it is fulfilled.

Abaryaraga, affection born of habit: only an ordinary attraction exists to begin with, but little by little, it grows. This is desire born of force of habit.

To begin with only an extraordinary attraction existed, a feeling of congeniality, born of a physical appearance that caused a simple desire, not the union of two hearts. Sexual attraction is consequently relative. At the outset, during their first experiences, they nevertheless feel a certain satisfaction. Later on, sexual attraction is established by routine copulation. They attain true erotic satisfaction. Love born of consummation also leads to true affection.
Ordinary attraction means that the lover or his mistress have a simple desire for each other, but not true erotic attraction. However, a mutual desire develops from such an ordinary attraction by practice, and creates true affection. This is what is termed love born of consummation.

Becoming gradually more excited by practicing the sixty-four positions, with common accord, a true passion grows up.
The woman is aroused by the mere desire for erotic exercises.

Kritrimaraga, feigned love: here, it is a matter of an occasional relation, while true love is for someone else. This is false desire.

Whether for good or bad reasons, it is not a case of true attraction, because the feelings of both one and the other are elsewhere. The woman is tied to another man, and the man to another woman. The enjoyment they experience in making love together is a false passion [kritrimaraga].

In such forms of intercourse, it is better to consult the texts.

In these two kinds of union, unlike the others, there is no spontaneous attraction. At the moment of intercourse, therefore, it is useful to consult about the methods of practicing the various forms of embrace, etc. This is why the texts are useful for information on local customs, conventions, states of mind, etc.

Vyavahitaraga, substitute love: the man whose heart is tied to another makes love with his wife while thinking of the other woman. All the marks of affection and erotic acts take place by the interposition of another party. This is substitute love.

The state of a man who, even without other ties, or without being stimulated by another attachment, makes love without feeling is called false desire. Unless he does it in the hope of begetting a child, he finds no satisfaction due to lack of passion. On the other hand, if he performs with the thought of one he loves in mind, he finds an ardor and excitation in the sexual act, which is expressed in his erotic performance. Since his performance is directed at the one he loves, it is love by substitution of the party. In reality, he is uniting with the girl of his heart.

After which, occasional sexual relations are contemplated.

The first three kinds of spontaneous, habitual, or occasional sexual relations are morally acceptable and are considered pure. The following kinds, on the other hand, are not acceptable, since they should not be practiced by men and women of different social class. Their advantages and inconveniences are described by way of example.

Potarata, neutral sex: this refers to occasional sexual relations, due to the need for sexual satisfaction, with persons of no account, water-bearers, servant-women, inverts, etc.

This concerns water-bearers, or servants of a very lowly condition, but also wandering monks and bisexual scribes. This is neutral sex.

This kind of behavior is not recommended.

This kind of embrace is not respectable, or gracious. It only supplies a semblance of sexual satisfaction. In such cases, there is no need to embrace or kiss, since they are merely a convenience.

Khalarata, degrading sex: this is the case when a prostitute gives her body to a gross peasant to satisfy her perverse taste for adventure with people unlike an agreeable lover. It is the case of the prostitutes, and courtesans who live on their charms, who, not being able to obtain what they desire, make use of gross individuals such as, for example, cowherds. This is degrading sexuality.

It is the same for a gentleman who sleeps with village girls, shepherd girls, cow-girls, etc.

For a gentleman, relations with peasants are degrading; they are merely substitutes for love. Such forms of sexual release, like neutral sex, are only possible if one disguises oneself. Of village girls, the only attractive ones are the cowgirls of the Vraja country; all the others are savages.

For a person who is skilled in the art of love, relations with cowgirls, buffalo keepers, etc., are degrading.

Only when mutual confidence is established, with its moments of passion, quarrels, and so on, can one practice sex without barriers.

18

The Laws of Manu

In the Hindu tradition, Manu was the grandson of the Supreme Being, who set down laws for all to follow. The most influential parts of this sacred law book over the ages have been the assignment of duties to the castes, an explanation of cause and effect in the transmigration process, and rules to follow for achieving liberation from reincarnation.

QUESTIONS TO CONSIDER

1. How does the rigidity of castes follow logically from the Cosmic Sacrifice in the Hindu creation story (see Reading 16)?
2. What reasons does Manu give all castes for abiding by his law and doing their prescribed duties?
3. How does the Hindu concept of transmigration compare with the Christian concepts of resurrection, rewards, and punishments?
4. What is final liberation in Hindu-Buddhist thought? Can one achieve this liberation simply by ending one's life in this world?
5. Compare the Hindu goal of liberation with the Judaic, Christian, and Islamic ideas of salvation.

Duties of the Social Classes

31. For the sake of the prosperity of the worlds, Purusha caused the Brâhmana, the Kshatriya, the Vaisya, and the Sûdra to proceed from his mouth, his arms, his thighs, and his feet.

88. To Brâhmanas he assigned teaching and studying (the Veda), sacrificing for their own benefit and for others, giving and accepting (of alms).

89. The Kshatriya he commanded to protect the people, to bestow gifts, to offer sacrifices, to study the Veda, and to abstain from attaching himself to sensual pleasures.

90. The Vaisya to tend cattle, to bestow gifts, to offer sacrifices, to study the Veda, to trade, to lend money, and to cultivate land.

From G. Buhler, trans., *The Laws of Manu* (Oxford: The Clarendon Press, 1886), pp. 13–14, 24–27, 183–85, 196–97, 198–99, 203–6, 214–15, 483–85, 496–97, *passim.*

91. One occupation only the lord prescribed to the Sûdra, to serve meekly even these other three castes.

92. Man is stated to be purer above the navel than below: hence the self-existent has declared the purest part of him to be his mouth.

93. As the Brâhmana sprang from mouth, as he was the first-born, and as he possesses the Veda, he is by right the lord of this creation.

94. For the Self-existent one, having performed austerities, produced him first from his own mouth, in order that the offerings might be conveyed to the gods and manes[1] and that this universe might be preserved.

95. What created being can surpass him, through whose mouth the gods continually consume the sacrificial meats and the manes the offerings to the dead?

96. Of created beings the most excellent are said to be those which are animated; of the animated, those which subsist by intelligence; of the intelligent, mankind; and of men, Brâhmanas;

97. Of Brâhmanas, those learned in the Veda; of the learned, those who recognize the necessity and the manner of performing those prescribed duties; of those who possess this knowledge, those who perform them; of the performers, those who know the Brahman.

98. The very birth of a Brâhmana is an eternal incarnation of the sacred law; for he is born to fulfill the sacred law, and becomes one with Brahman.

102. In order to clearly settle his duties and those of the other castes according to their order, wise Manu, sprung from the Self-existent, composed these Institutes of the sacred law.

Transmigration

3. Action [karma], which springs from the mind, from speech, and from the body, produces either good or evil results; by action are caused the various conditions of men, the highest, the middling, and the lowest.

4. Know that the mind is the instigator here below, even to that action which is connected with the body, and which is of three kinds, has three locations, and falls under ten heads.

5. Coveting the property of others, thinking in one's heart of what is undesirable, and adherence to false doctrines, are the three kinds of sinful mental action.

6. Abusing others, speaking untruth, detracting from the merits of all men, and talking idly, shall be the four kinds of evil verbal action.

7. Taking what has not been given, injuring creatures without the sanction of the law, and holding criminal intercourse with another man's wife, are declared to be the three kinds of wicked bodily action.

8. A man obtains the result of a good or evil mental act in his mind, that of a verbal act in his speech, that of a bodily act in his body.

9. In consequence of many sinful acts committed with his body, a man becomes in the next birth something inanimate, in consequence of sins committed by speech, a bird or a beast, and in consequence of mental sins he is re-born in a low caste.

10. That man is called a true tridandin in whose mind these three, the control over his speech . . . , the control over his thoughts . . . , and the control over his body . . . , are firmly fixed.

11. That man who keeps this threefold control over himself with respect to all created beings and wholly subdues desire and wrath, thereby assuredly gains complete success. . . .

[1]Venerated spirits of the dead.

52. In consequence of attachment to the objects of the senses, and in consequence of the nonperformance of their duties, fools, the lowest of men, reach the vilest births.

53. What wombs this individual soul enters in this world and in consequence of what actions, learn the particulars of that at large and in due order.

54. Those who committed mortal sins . . . , having passed during large numbers of years through dreadful hells, obtain, after the expiration of that term of punishment, the following births:

55. The slayer of a Brâman enters the womb of a dog, a pig, an ass, a camel, a cow, a goat, a sheep, a deer, a bird, a Candala, and a Pukkasa [two low-caste groups].

56. A Brâman who drinks the spirituous liquor called Sura shall enter the bodies of small and large insects, of moths, or birds, feeding on ordure, and of destructive beasts.

57. A Brâman who steals the gold of a Brâhman shall pass a thousand times through the bodies of spiders, snakes and lizards, of aquatic animals and of destructive Pishacas [ghosts].

58. The violater of a Guru's bed enters a hundred times the forms of grasses, shrubs and creepers, likewise of carnivorous animals and of beasts with fangs and of those doing cruel deeds.

59. Men who delight in doing hurt become carnivorous animals; those who eat forbidden food, worms, thieves, creatures consuming their own kind; those who have intercourse with women of the lower castes, Pretas [another kind of ghost].

The Path to Liberation

1. A twice-born householder, who has thus lived according to the law in the order of householders, may, taking a firm resolution and keeping his organs of sense in subjection, dwell in the forest, duly observing the rules given below.

2. When a householder sees his skin wrinkled, and his hair white, and the sons of his sons, then he may resort to the forest.

3. Abandoning all food raised by cultivation, and all his belongings, he may depart into the forest, either committing his wife to his sons, or accompanied by her.

8. Let him be always industrious in privately reciting the Veda; let him be patient of hardships, friendly towards all of collected mind, always liberal. . . .

25. Having reposited the three sacred fires in himself, according to prescribed rule, let him live without a fire, without a house, wholly silent, subsisting on roots and fruit,

33. But having thus passed the third part of a man's natural term of life in the forest, he may live as an ascetic during the fourth part of his existence, after abandoning all attachment to worldly objects.

42. Let him always wander alone, without any companion, in order to attain final liberation, fully understanding that the solitary man, who neither forsakes nor is forsaken, gains his end.

87. The student, the householder, the hermit, and the ascetic, these constitute four separate orders, which all spring from the order of householders.

88. But all or even any of these orders, assumed successively in accordance with the Institutes of the sacred law, lead the Brâman who acts by the preceding rules to the highest state.

89. And in accordance with the precepts of the Veda . . . the householder is declared to be superior to all of them; for he supports the other three.

19

Bhagavad-Gita

The *Bhagavad-Gita*, "The Song of God," is one of the most popular and revered books in Hindu religious literature. For more than two millennia, it has been the principal source of religious inspiration for many millions of South Asian people. It consists of more than seven hundred line verses in the form of a long philosophical dialogue primarily between Krishna, a manifestation of the Supreme Deity in human form, and Arjuna, a warrior-prince, dealing with questions regarding the relationship between man's real self or soul and the body and life and destiny as a whole. In the first of the following two excerpts from the *Bhagavad-Gita*, Krishna explains the deathless life and the indestructibility of the soul and the importance of caste duties, concepts so central to Hindu religious belief, to Arjuna, who is torn by the feelings of worldly and spiritual obligations. In the second excerpt, the importance of devotion to God in achieving salvation in Hindu religion is described.

QUESTIONS TO CONSIDER

1. Explain what Arjuna's worldly and spiritual obligations are and the reason for his dilemma.
2. What spiritual justifications does Krishna offer to Arjuna for killing the enemy in the battlefield?

Deathless Life and Caste Obligation

How can I use my arrows in battle against Bhīshma, my grandsire, and Droṇa, my venerable teacher, who are worthy rather to be worshipped, O Destroyer of all opponents?

Surely would it be better to eat the bread of beggary in this life than to slay these great-souled masters!

If I kill them, all enjoyment of wealth, all gratified desire, is stained by their blood!

Indeed, scarcely can I tell which would be better, that they or we should conquer, for to destroy those sons of Dhritarāshṭra who oppose us, would be to extinguish forever the savor of life.

Overpowered by my helplessness, and with a mind in confusion, I supplicate Thee! Make clear to me that which is my good; I am Thy disciple. Instruct me, who have sought my refuge in Thee!

There is naught to dispel this sorrow which overpowereth my senses. Were I to obtain undisputed and powerful dominion over all the earth, and mastery over the gods, what then would that avail me?

Arjuna, having thus spoken to Kṛishṇa, Lord of the Senses, made end, saying:
'I shall not fight!' and with these words fell silent.

From *The Song of God*, trans. Dhan Gopal Mukerji. Copyright 1931 by Dhan Gopal Mukerji. Reprinted by permission of Dutton Signet, a division of Penguin Books USA Inc.

But as he remained sorrowing thus in the midst of the two armies, Krishṇa, smiling a little, spoke to him as follows:

Thou hast grieved for those undeserving of grief, Arjuna! Although thou speakest wisely, those who are still wiser mourn neither for the living nor for the dead.

For never hath it been that I was not, nor thou, nor these Kings; nor shall we cease to be, ever.

The self is not interrupted while childhood, youth and old age pass through the flesh; likewise in death the self dieth not, but is released to assume another shape. By this the calm soul is not deluded.

The impressions of the senses, quickened to heat and cold, pain and pleasure, are transitory. Forever on the ebb and flow, they are by their very nature impermanent. Bear them then patiently, O Descendant of Kings!

For the wise man who is serene in pain and pleasure, whom these disturb not, he alone is able to attain Immortality, O Great amongst men!

The unreal can never be; the real can never cease to be. Those who know the truth know that this is so.

The Unnamable Principle which pervadeth all things, none hath power to destroy: know thou certainly that It is indestructible.

By *That,* immortal, inexhaustible, illimitable, Indweller, is the mortality of this flesh possessed. Fight therefore O Descendant of brave Kings!

He who conceiveth this Indweller, this Self, as slayer, or who conceiveth It as slain, is without knowledge. The Self neither slayeth nor is It slain.

It is never born, nor doth It die, nor having once existed, doth It ever cease to be. Ancient, eternal, changeless, ever Itself, It perisheth not when the body is destroyed.

How can that man who knoweth It to be indestructible, changeless, without birth, and immutable, how can he, Arjuna, either slay or cause the slaying of another?

As a man casteth off an old garment and putteth on another which is new, so the Self casteth off its outworn embodiment and entereth into a new form.

This Self, weapons cut not; This, fire burneth not; This, water wetteth not; and This, the winds dry not up.

This Self cannot be cut, it cannot be burnt, it cannot be wetted, it cannot be dried. Changeless, all-pervading, unmoving, Eternal, it is the Unalterable Self.

This Self is invisible, inconceivable, and changeless. Knowing that It is such, cease, therefore, to grieve!

But whether thou believest this Self of eternal duration or subjected constantly to birth and death, yet Mighty-armèd One, hast thou no cause to grieve.

For, to that which is born, death is certain; to that which dieth, birth is certain, and the unavoidable, giveth not occasion for grief.

Nothing may be perceived in its beginning; in its middle state only is it known, and its end again is undisclosed. What herein, Arjuna, is cause for grief?

One man perceiveth the Self as a thing of wonder; another speaketh of It as a wonder; others hear of It as a wonder, but though seeing, speaking, hearing, none comprehendeth It at all.

This, which is the Indweller in all beings, is forever beyond harm. Then, for no creature, Arjuna, hast thou any cause to grieve.

Examine thy duty and falter not, for there is no better thing for a warrior than to wage righteous war.

Fortunate indeed are the soldiers, Arjuna, who, fighting in such a battle, reach this unsought, open gate to heaven.

But to refuse this just fight and forgo thine own duty and honour, is to incur sin.

By so doing the world will also hold thee ever in despite. To the honourable, dishonour is surely worse than death.

The great charioteer warriors will believe that through fear thou hast withdrawn from the battle. Then shalt thou fall from their esteem, who hast hitherto been highly regarded.

Thine enemies moreover, cavilling at thy great prowess, will say of thee that which is not to be uttered. What fate, indeed, could be more unbearable than this?

Dying thou gainest heaven; victorious, thou enjoyest the earth. Therefore, Arjuna, arise, resolved to do battle.

Look upon pain and pleasure, gain and loss, conquest and defeat, as the same, and prepare to fight; thus shalt thou incur no evil.

Now hath been declared unto thee the understanding of the Self. Hearken thou moreover to the Way,[1] following which, O son of Kings, thou shalt break through the fateful bondage of thine act.[2]

On this Way nothing that is begun is lost, nor are there any obstacles, and even a very little progress thereon bringeth security against great fear.

Devotion to God

But those who adore Me, and Me alone, and all beings who are steadfast and supremely dedicated in their worship, I augment in their fullness and fill them up in their emptiness.

Even those who devotedly worship other gods because of their love, worship Me; but the path they follow is not My path.

For I alone am the Deity of all sacrifices, and those who worship other gods than Me reach the end of merit and return to the world, where they must set forth anew upon the way.

One pursueth the gods and attaineth the sphere of the gods suitable to the merit of his works; another worshippeth the Fathers and yet another worshippeth attributes and incarnations, each attaining unto his own place; but he who worshippeth Me cometh unto Me.

Whosoever with devotion offereth Me leaf, flower, fruit, or water, I accept it from him as the devout gift of the pure-minded.

Whatsoever thou doest, Arjuna, whatsoever thou eatest, whatsoever thou givest away, whatsoever thou offerest up as sacrifice, and whatsoever austerity thou shalt practice, do it as an offering unto Me.

Thus shalt thou be released from the fateful bonds of thine acts, and the cage of good and evil. Thine heart shall renounce itself, and being liberated, shall come unto Me.

To Me none is hateful, none dear; but those who worship Me with devotion dwell in Me, and I also in them.

Even a very wicked man who worshippeth Me, eschewing all else in his devotion to Me, shall be regarded as worthy of merit, for great is his faith.

He shall attain righteousness in a short time, Arjuna, and compel everlasting Peace; therefore, proclaim it aloud that no one of My devotees is destroyed.

They also who might be considered of inferior birth, women, tradesmen, as well as day-laborers, even they shall master this world and attain Me, Arjuna, if they seek Me with single mind.

---

[1]Yoga. The exact meaning of Yoga depends on its context. It signifies any consistent way of spiritual life.
[2]"The bondage of thine act," Karma. "The doctrine of true knowledge and of emancipation by means of it."

What need, then, to describe priests and kings who have attained holiness? Therefore, Arjuna, in this transient, joyless world, worship thou Me!

Make thy mind My dwelling place; consecrate thyself to Me; sacrifice unto Me, bow down unto Me, make thy heart steadfast in Me thy Supreme Destination, and thou too shalt assuredly come unto Me.

The Buddhist Tradition

Buddhism represents one of the few truly unifying threads in the diverse cultures of Asia. From its origins in Northeast India around 500 B.C., this religion spread throughout the subcontinent and beyond, into Sri Lanka and Southeast Asia. The patronage of missionary activity by the Indian king of the Mauryan dynasty, Ashoka (269–232 B.C.), particularly promoted the dissemination of Buddhism. Around the beginning of the Christian Era, this religion was introduced into China, and from there it passed via Korea into Japan by A.D. the sixth century. By the seventh century, Buddhism had become the dominant religion of Tibet.

The Buddha's teaching emphasized that life in the endless cycle of transmigration *(samsara)* is inherently fraught with suffering and frustration. The cause of this suffering is our desire for material things and our ignorance of the fact that there is no "self." Our false notions prompt us to action in search of satisfaction for our "selves"; and all of these actions (which the Buddhists and Hindus call *karma*) produce good or bad consequences, depending on whether they involve good or evil deeds. The results push us into another life in the cycle of transmigration, where we will receive our due rewards. However, the Buddha believed that we are only heaps of *skandhas,* material components, which obey natural laws of causation and which eventually disintegrate like all matter. So, the Buddha reasoned, if people could only abandon the false notion of self and give up all desire, they would be liberated from the effects of actions and, therefore, from the cycle of transmigration. Once liberated, people would achieve a condition of absolute peace and tranquility, which the Buddhists call *nirvana.* To achieve this state, the Buddha provided an Eightfold Path for living a disciplined life of calm detachment.

Only monks and nuns, who constitute the Sangha, completely follow this path to reach nirvana. These rare men—and a few women—totally give up their worldly possessions and ways. Historically, most monks lived in monasteries where they spent their time learning and discussing the Buddha's teaching and meditating in order to achieve a deep, inner calm. The Buddhist laypersons (that is, those who lived normal lives outside the monastery) greatly respected the monks and gained merit by providing them food for their one meal a day. This religious practice still prevails in Sri Lanka and Southeast Asia.

Reading 21 shows a new ideal that came to prominence about 500 years after the Buddha, called the Bodhisattva (or Buddha-to-be). Rather than emphasizing the calm reflection on reality that allowed the Buddha, and the community of monks following him, to achieve the total dispassion of nirvana, the Bodhisattva strove for perfection in compassion. The Bodhisattva was dedicated to selflessly helping as many other creatures as possible and delayed achieving nirvana and becoming a Buddha. Guanyin is one of the most popular Bodhisattvas. This form of Buddhism, in which the Bodhisattva predominates, is called the *Mahayana* or Greater Vehicle, since it provides more people with easier access to liberation than the older form of Buddhism (called the *Hinayana,* Lesser Vehicle, or *Theravada,* Doctrine of the Elders), in which the monks were the central element.

20

Enlightenment of the Buddha

This selection is from the best-known biography of the Buddha, called the *Buddhacarita* and written by the Indian poet Ashvaghosha before A.D. 200. The reading begins with Prince Gautama already having abandoned family and home, intent on conquering the cause of human suffering. This Buddha-to-be decides to sit alone under a tree until an answer to his problem is clear. The episode ends with his achieving enlightenment—insight into the cause of suffering and the way to overcome it. This experience turns him into a Buddha, an Enlightened One.

QUESTIONS TO CONSIDER

1. Compare the achievements of the Buddha with those of Jesus, Muhammad, and Confucius.
2. How important is meditation in achieving enlightenment in Buddhism? Why?

The Bodhisattva [Buddha-to-be], possessed of great skill in Transic meditation, put himself into trance, intent on discerning both the ultimate reality of things and the final goal of existence. After he had gained complete mastery over all the degrees and kinds of trance:

1. In the *first watch* of the night he recollected the successive series of his former births. "There was I so and so; that was my name; deceased from there I came here"—in this way he remembered thousands of births, as though living them over again. When he had recalled his own births and deaths in all these various lives of his, the Sage, full of pity, turned his compassionate mind towards other living beings, and he thought to himself: "Again and again they must leave the people they regard as their own, and must go on elsewhere, and that without ever stopping. Surely this world is unprotected and helpless, and like a wheel it turns round and round." As he continued steadily to recollect the past thus, he came to the definite conviction that this world of Samsara is as unsubstantial as the pith of a plantain tree.

2. Second to none in valour, he then, in the *second watch* of the night, acquired the supreme heavenly eye, for he himself was the best of all those who have sight. Thereupon

From E. Conze, trans. and ed., *Buddhist Scriptures* (Baltimore: Penguin, 1959), pp. 49–51 and 186–87. Copyright © Edward Conze, 1959. Reproduced by permission of Penguin Books Ltd.

with the perfectly pure heavenly eye he looked upon the entire world, which appeared to him as though reflected in a spotless mirror. He saw that the decease and rebirth of beings depend on whether they have done superior or inferior deeds. And his compassionateness grew still further. It became clear to him that no security can be found in this flood of Samsaric existence, and that the threat of death is ever-present. Beset on all sides, creatures can find no resting place. In this way he surveyed the five places of rebirth with his heavenly eye. And he found nothing substantial in the world of becoming, just as no core of heartwood is found in a plantain tree when its layers are peeled off one by one.

3. Then, as the *third watch* of that night drew on, the supreme master of trance turned his meditation to the real and essential nature of this world: "Alas, living beings wear themselves out in vain! Over and over again they are born, they age, die, pass on to a new life, and are reborn! What is more, greed and dark delusion obscure their sight, and they are blind from birth. Greatly apprehensive, they yet do not know how to get out of this great mass of ill." He then surveyed the twelve links of conditioned co-production, and saw that, beginning with ignorance, they lead to old age and death, and, beginning with the cessation of ignorance, they lead to the cessation of birth, old age, death, and all kinds of ill.

When the great seer had comprehended that where there is no ignorance whatever, there also the karma-formations are stopped—then he had achieved a correct knowledge of all there is to be known, and he stood out in the world as a Buddha. He passed through the eight stages of Transic insight, and quickly reached their highest point. From the summit of the world downwards he could detect no self anywhere. Like the fire, when its fuel is burnt up, he became tranquil. He had reached perfection, and he thought to himself: "This is the authentic Way on which in the past so many great seers, who also knew all higher and all lower things, have travelled on to ultimate and real truth. And now I have obtained it!"

4. At that moment, in the *fourth watch* of the night, when dawn broke and all the ghosts that move and those that move not went to rest, the great seer took up the position which knows no more alteration, and the leader of all reached the state of all-knowledge. When, through his Buddhahood, he had cognized this fact, the earth swayed like a woman drunken with wine, the sky shone bright with the Siddhas who appeared in crowds in all the directions, and the mighty drums of thunder resounded through the air. Pleasant breezes blew softly, rain fell from a cloudless sky, flowers and fruits dropped from the trees out of season—in an effort, as it were, to show reverence for him. Mandarava flowers and lotus blossoms, and also water lilies made of gold and beryl, fell from the sky on to the ground near the Shakya sage, so that it looked like a place in the world of the gods. At that moment no one anywhere was angry, ill, or sad; no one did evil, none was proud; the world became quite quiet, as though it had reached full perfection. Joy spread through the ranks of those gods who longed for salvation; joy also spread among those who lived in the regions below. Everywhere the virtuous were strengthened, the influence of Dharma increased, and the world rose from the dirt of the passions and the darkness of ignorance. Filled with joy and wonder at the Sage's work, the seers of the solar race who had been protectors of men, who had been royal seers, who had been great seers, stood in their mansions in the heavens and showed him their reverence. The great seers among the hosts of invisible beings could be heard widely proclaiming his fame. All living things rejoiced and sensed that things went well.

The Four Holy Truths

What then is the Holy Truth of Ill? Birth is ill, decay is ill, sickness is ill, death is ill. To be conjoined with what one dislikes means suffering. To be disjoined from what one likes means suffering. Not to get what one wants, also that means suffering. In short, all grasping at any of the five Skandhas involves suffering.

What then is the Holy Truth of the Origination of Ill? It is that craving which leads to rebirth, accompanied by delight and greed, seeking its delight now here, now there, i.e., craving for sensuous experience, craving to perpetuate oneself, craving for extinction.

What then is the Holy Truth of the Stopping of Ill? It is the complete stopping of that craving, the withdrawal from it, the renouncing of it, throwing it back, liberation from it, non-attachment to it.

What then is the Holy Truth of the steps which lead to the stopping of Ill? It is this holy eightfold Path, which consists of right views, right intentions, right speech, right conduct, right livelihood, right effort, right mindfulness, right concentration.

21

Kuan-yin [Guanyin]: Compassion of the Bodhisattva[1]

Guanyin is one of the most popular Bodhisattvas in the Far East. Guanyin means "the one who hears the cry" or "The Regarder of the Cries of the World." Guanyin is believed to be infinitely compassionate and able to deliver all beings from any sort of danger or misfortune. Guanyin appears in many different forms. In early iconography, he appears in male form, but the female form is more popular. As the Goddess of Mercy, she is believed to protect women and children. For example, it is widely believed that women who desire to become mothers and invoke her name will have their prayers answered. Legends and stories about miracles as a result of the intervention by this protectress abound in East Asia; temples and statues in honor of Guanyin are found throughout this part of the world. The following selection from *The Lotus Sutra* tells how compassionate and merciful this Bodhisattva is.

QUESTIONS TO CONSIDER

1. How do you compare the concept of compassion expressed in this selection with the Christian teachings given in the sections from St. Francis (see Reading 70)?
2. Why do you think Guanyin's role is so relevant to Mahayanistic Buddhism?

Thereafter the Bodhisattva Mahasattva Akshayamati rose from his seat, put his upper robe upon one shoulder, stretched his joined hands towards the Lord, and said: For what reason, O Lord, is the Bodhisattva Mahasattva Avalokitesvara called Avalokitesvara [Guanyin]? So he asked, and the Lord answered to the Bodhisattva Mahasattva Akshayamati: All the hun-

---

[1]Also spelled as Kuan Yin or Kwan-shi-yin in Chinese, Kannon in Japanese, and Avalokitesvara in Sanskrit.

H. Kern, trans., *Saddharma-Pundarika or The Lotus of the True Law* (Oxford: Clarendon Press, 1984), pp. 406–09.

dred thousands of myriads of kotis[1] of creatures, young man of good family, who in this world are suffering troubles will, if they hear the name of the Bodhisattva Mahasattva Avalokitesvara, be released from that mass of troubles. Those who shall keep the name of this Bodhisattva Mahasattva Avalokitesvara, young man of good family, will, if they fall into a great mass of fire, be delivered therefrom by virtue of the lustre of the Bodhisattva Mahasattva. In case, young man of good family, creatures, carried off by the current of river, should implore the Bodhisattva Mahasattva Avalokitesvara all rivers will afford them a ford. In case, young man of good family, many hundred thousand myriads of kotis of creatures, sailing in a ship on the ocean, should see their bullion, gold, gems, pearls, lapis lazuli, conch shells, stones, corals, emeralds, Musaragalvas,[2] and other goods lost, and the ship by a vehement, untimely gale case on the island of Giantesses,[3] and if in that ship a single being implores Avalokitesvara, all will be saved from that island of Giantesses. For that reason, young man of good family, the Bodhisattva Mahasattva Avalokitesvara is named Avalokitesvara.

If a man given up to capital punishment implore Avalokitesvara, young man of good family, the swords of the executioners shall snap asunder. Further, young man of good family, if the whole triple chiliocosm[4] were teeming with goblins and giants, they would by virtue of the name of the Bodhisattva Mahasattva Avalokitesvara being pronounced lose the faculty of sight in their wicked designs. If some creature, young man of good family, shall be bound in wooden or iron manacles, chains, or fetters, be he guilty or innocent, then those manacles, chains, or fetters shall give way as soon as the name of the Bodhisattva Mahasattva Avalokitesvara is pronounced. Such, young man of good family, is the power of the Bodhisattva Mahasattva Avalokitesvara. If this whole triple chiliocosm, young man of good family, were teeming with knaves, enemies, and robbers armed with swords, and if a merchant leader of a caravan marched with a caravan rich in jewels; if then they perceived those robbers, knaves, and enemies armed with swords, and in their anxiety and fright thought themselves helpless; if, further, that leading merchant spoke to the caravan in this strain: Be not afraid, young gentlemen, be not frightened; invoke, all of you, with one voice the Bodhisattva Mahasattva Avalokitesvara, the giver of safety; then you shall be delivered from this danger by which you are threatened at the hands of robbers and enemies; if then, the whole caravan with one voice invoked Avalokitesvara with the words: Adoration, adoration be to the giver of safety, to Avalokitesvara Bodhisattva Mahasattva! then by the mere act of pronouncing the name, the caravan would be released from all danger. Such, young man of good family, is the power of the Bodhisattva Mahasattva Avalokitesvara. In case creatures act under the impulse of impure passion, young man of good family, they will, after adoring the Bodhisattva Mahasattva Avalokitesvara, be freed from passion. Those who act under the impulse of hatred will, after adoring the Bodhisattva Mahasattva Avalokitesvara, be freed from hatred. Those who act under the impulse of infatuation will, after adoring the Bodhisattva Mahasattva Avalokitesvara, be freed from infatuation. So mighty, young man of good family, is the Bodhisattva Mahasattva Avalokitesvara. If a woman, desirous of male offspring, young man of good family, adores Bodhisattva Mahasattva Avalokitesvara, she shall get a son, nice, handsome, and beautiful; one possessed of the characteristics of a male child, generally beloved and winning, who has planted good roots. If a woman is de-

---

[1]A figure varying from 100,000 to 10,000,000,000.
[2]It is believed to be a kind of precious stone.
[3]Modern day Ceylon or Sri Lanka.
[4]The triple world is supposed to consist of the Realm of Desire, the Realm of Form, and the Formless Realm.

sirous of getting a daughter, a nice, handsome, beautiful girl shall be born to her; one possessed of the (good) characteristics of a girl, generally beloved and winning, who has planted good roots. Such, young man of good family, is the power of the Bodhisattva Mahasattva Avalokitesvara.

The State and Society in Classical India

The acquisition and retention of material wealth *(artha)* remained a legitimate goal for Hindus, who frequently linked artha to the subject of power necessary for the secure enjoyment of wealth and to discussions of the proper allocation of resources by those in power. The most famous Hindu text on artha is the *Artha Shastra,* a work originally intended as a handbook for kings at the outset of the Mauryan Empire, although the surviving version is now believed to have been copied with many alterations over the centuries and to date from the early Gupta Empire.

The last great period of Hindu state and civilization in India before the arrival of Islam came during the Gupta rule (A.D. 320–ca. 540) and the reign of Harsha Vardhana (A.D. 606–647). During this classical age (A.D. 320–ca. 700), Indian art, literature, sculpture, mathematics, medicine, astronomy, and astrology attained new levels of brilliance. Hinduism developed into popular forms while Buddhism gradually withered away in the land of its birth. This happened in spite of the fact that the most detailed and readable description of the workings of the Indian state and society during the late classical period comes from a Chinese Buddhist, who came to visit India as the land where Gautama was born and where he first taught.

22

Duties of a King, *Artha Shastra*

The original (lost) version of this manual on kingship is ascribed to Kautilya, Chandragupta's Prime Minister. What follows is a much later version, still bearing Kautilya's name, possibly adapted for the founders of the Gupta Empire. Its guidelines are not high-minded with any consistency: the writer(s) stress that in the real world "the law of the fishes" prevails—that is, the big fish eat the little ones.

QUESTIONS TO CONSIDER

1. How does this selection compare with Niccolo Machiavelli's *The Prince* and *The Discourses on Titus Livy* (see Reading 89)?

2. Are these guidelines and advice consistent with Hindu-Buddhist religious precepts? How?

Only if a king is himself energetically active, do his officers follow him energetically. If he is sluggish, they too remain sluggish. And, besides, they eat up his works. He is thereby easily overpowered by his enemies. Therefore, he should ever dedicate himself energetically to activity.

He should divide the day as well as the night into eight parts. . . . During the first one-eighth part of the day, he should listen to reports pertaining to the organization of law and order and to income and expenditure. During the second, he should attend to the affairs of the urban and the rural population. During the third, he should take his bath and meal and devote himself to study. During the fourth, he should receive gold and the department heads. During the fifth, he should hold consultations with the council of ministers through correspondence and also keep himself informed of the secret reports brought by spies. During the sixth, he should devote himself freely to amusement or listen to the counsel of the ministers. During the seventh, he should inspect the military formations of elephants, cavalry, chariots, and infantry. During the eighth, he, together with the commander-in-chief of the army, should make plans for the campaigns of conquest. When the day has come to an end he should offer the evening prayers.

During the first one-eighth part of the night, he should meet with the officers of the secret service. During the second, he should take his bath and meals and also devote himself to study. During the third, at the sounding of the trumpets, he should enter the bed chamber and should sleep through the fourth and fifth. Waking up at the sound of the trumpets, he should, during the sixth part, ponder over the teachings of the sciences and his urgent duties for the day. During the seventh, he should hold consultations and send out officers of the secret service for their operations. During the eighth, accompanied by sacrificial priests, preceptors, and the chaplain, he should receive benedictions; he should also have interviews with a physician, the kitchen superintendent, and the astrologer. Thereafter, he should circumambulate by the right a cow with a calf and an ox and then proceed to the reception hall. Or he should divide the day and the night into parts in accordance with his own capacities and thereby attend to his duties.

When he has gone to the reception hall, he should not allow such persons, as have come for business, to remain sticking to the doors of the hall [i.e., waiting in vain]. For, a king, with whom it is difficult for the people to have an audience, is made to confuse between right action and wrong action by his close entourage. Thereby he suffers from the disaffection of his own subjects or falls prey to the enemy. Therefore he should attend to the affairs relating to gods, hermitages, heretics, learned brahmans, cattle, and holy places as also those of minors, the aged, the sick, those in difficulty, the helpless, and women—in the order of their enumeration or in accordance with the importance or the urgency of the affairs.

A king should attend to all urgent business, he should not put it off. For what has been thus put off becomes either difficult or altogether impossible to accomplish. . . .

In the happiness of the subjects lies the happiness of the king; in their welfare, his own welfare. The welfare of the king does not lie in the fulfillment of what is dear to him; whatever is dear to the subjects constitutes his welfare.

[In foreign affairs, observe] the sixfold policy: peace, war, marking time, attack, seeking refuge, and duplicity. . . . "There are only two forms of policy," says Vatavyadhi, "for the sixfold policy is actually accomplished through peace and war." Kautilya says: "The forms of policy are, verily, six in number, for conditions are different in different cases."

Of these six forms: binding through pledges means peace; offensive operation means war; apparent indifference means marking time; strengthening one's position means attack; giving oneself to another [as a subordinate ally or vassal] means seeking refuge; keeping oneself engaged simultaneously in peace and war with the same state means duplicity. These are the six forms of policy.

When one king [the would-be conquerer] is weaker than the other [i.e., his immediate neighbor, the enemy], he should make peace with him. When he is stronger than the other, he should make war with him. When he thinks: "The other is not capable of putting me down nor am I capable of putting him down," he should mark time. When he possesses an excess of the necessary means, he should attack. When he is devoid of strength, he should seek refuge with another. When his end can be achieved only through the help of an ally, he should practice duplicity.

23

Hsuan-tsang [Xuanzang], The Land and People of India

During the reign of Harsha Vardhana, Hsuan-tsang [Xuanzang], the most famous of the Chinese Buddhist scholars and pilgrims renowned for translating Indian Sanskrit Buddhist scriptures into Chinese, visited India. In search of answers to questions on Chinese versions of Buddhist scriptures, Xuanzang set out westward in 629 from Changan [Zhangan], the capital of T'ang China, along the silk routes via Central Asia. After a difficult journey passing through Turfan, Tashkent, Samarkand, and crossing the Hindu Kush, he entered northwest India. In the following sixteen years, he visited many kingdoms, including Harsha's Kanauji kingdom (area around present-day Lucknow); sites sacred to Buddhism; and Nalanda Monastery, the famous Buddhist center of learning. He studied there and returned to China in 645. Upon his return, he translated seventy-three Buddhist works, mainly scriptures, totaling more than one thousand rolls. In addition, Xuanzang left behind voluminous records of his eyewitness accounts of the land, people, government, and society of In-tu (India) known as *Records of Western Regions (Si-yu-ki),* which provide an invaluable source for reconstructing the history of India's classical age. The following selection is from these records, providing the descriptions of the land, education, military, trial by ordeal, and funeral customs.

QUESTIONS TO CONSIDER

1. How does Xuanzang react to Hindu (as opposed to Buddhist) practices?
2. What does Xuanzang find noteworthy about Buddhism in India? Does he give any indication that Buddhism is in relative decline in India?

3. In what other societies have you heard of trial by ordeal? What is the likely justification for the way it is supposed to work?
4. What aspects of Indian society appear to impress Xuanzang as good or bad?

Adopting a general name that is the most acceptable to the people, we shall call the country "In-tu," which signifies "moon." The moon has many designations, In-tu being one of
them. It is said that all living creatures unceasingly transmigrate, revolving through mortal
existences in the long darkness of ignorance without having a guiding star. It is like the night
after the setting of the bright sun, when, although people get light by candles and have the
shining light of the stars, these are not comparable with the brightness of the serene moon.
For this reason the spiritual condition of India is allegorically compared with the shining
moon. The sages and the wise teachers of this country followed the norm (of the Buddha)
in succession, guided the people, and exercised rule, as the moon sheds its bright influences—on this account this country is called In-tu.

The towns and villages of India have gates; the surrounding walls are broad and high;
the streets and lanes are narrow and crooked. The thoroughfares are dirty and the stalls are
arranged on both sides of the road with appropriate signs. Butchers, fishermen, actors, executioners, scavengers, and so on, have their dwellings outside of the city. In coming and
going these persons are bound to keep on the left side of the road till they arrive at their
homes. As to the construction of houses and the enclosing walls, the land being low and
moist, the walls of the towns are mostly built of bricks or tiles, and the enclosures of the
houses are matted bamboo or wood. The houses have balconies made of wood, as well as
flat roofs with a coating of lime, and are covered with burnt or unburnt tiles. The buildings
are very high, and in style of construction they are like those in China. Branches or common grasses or tiles or boards are used for covering them. The walls are covered with lime,
the floor is smeared with cow's dung as means of purity, and it is strewn with flowers of the
season. In such matters they differ from us.

Many Samgharamas (Buddhist monasteries) are constructed with extraordinary skill.
A three-storied tower is erected at each of the four angles. The beams and the projecting
heads are carved with strange figures. The doors, the windows, and the walls are painted in
many colors; the houses of the ordinary people are luxurious on the inside but plain on the
outside. The interior and central rooms vary in height and width. As to the form and construction of the tiers of terraces and the series of salons, there is no fixed rule. The doors
open toward the east; the royal throne also faces the east.

When the Hindus sit or rest they all use corded benches; the royal family, great per-
sonages, the officials, and the gentry use benches variously ornamented, but in size they are
exactly the same. The throne of the reigning sovereign is exceedingly high and broad, and
it is set with pearls and precious gems; it is called the "lion-throne." It is covered with extremely fine drapery; the footstool is adorned with gems. The ordinary officials carve their
seats in various ways and decorate them beautifully according to their taste.

To educate and encourage the young, they first teach them to study the book of
"Twelve Chapters." After arriving at the age of seven years, the young are instructed in the
great treatises of the "Five Sciences." The first is called Grammar, the elucidation of sounds.
This treatise explains the meaning of words and their derivation.

From A.V. Williams Jackson, ed., *History of India,* Vol. IX (London: The Grolier Society, 1906), pp. 122–49,
passim; condensed by Chong-kun Yoon.

The second science is called *Kiau-ming;* it treats of the arts and of mechanics, and it explains the principles of *Yin* and *Yang* (Negative and Positive Principles) of the calendar. The third is called the "Medicinal Treatise"; it illustrates the use of charms, medicinal stones, needles and moxa.[1] The fourth science is called "Logic," which determines the right and wrong and discriminates between the true and the false. The fifth science is called the science of "Inward Knowledge"; it relates to the Five Vehicles, and the doctrine of cause and effect (karma).

The Brahmans study the four Veda treatises. The first is called *Shau* ("longevity," i.e., the Ayur-Veda); it relates to the preservation of life and the regulation of the natural condition. The second is called *Sse* ("worship," i.e., the Yajur-Veda); it relates to sacrifice and prayer. The third is called *Ping* ("peace regulation," i.e., the Sama-Veda); it relates to decorum, casting of lots, military tactics, and warfare. The fourth is called *Shu* ("arts," i.e., the Atharva-Veda); it relates to various branches of science, incantations, medicine.

The doctrines of the Tathagata (Buddha) may be comprehended by men of different qualities; but, as the time is now remote since the Holy One lived, his doctrine is presented in a changed form, and is therefore understood orthodoxly or heterodoxly, according to the intelligence of those who inquire into it. The different schools are constantly at variance, and their contending utterances rise like the angry waves of the sea. The different schools have their separate masters, but they aim to reach one and the same end, though by different ways.

There are eighteen schools, each claiming pre-eminence. The tenets of the Great and the Little Vehicle [Mahayana and Hinayana] differ widely. There are some of the followers who give themselves up to meditation, and devote themselves, whether walking, standing still, or sitting down, to the acquirement of wisdom and insight. Others, on the contrary, differ from these in raising noisy contentions about their faith. According to their fraternity, they are governed by distinctive rules and regulations, which we need not name.

The chief soldiers of the country are selected from the bravest of the people, and as the sons follow the profession of their fathers, they soon acquire a knowledge of the art of war. These dwell in garrison around the palace (during times of peace), but when on an expedition they march in front as an advance guard. There are four divisions of the army, the infantry, the cavalry, the chariots, and the elephants. The elephants are covered with strong armour, and their tusks are provided with sharp spurs. The commander-in-chief rides on an elephant, with two soldiers on the right and left to manage the animal. The ordinary officer rides in a chariot drawn by four horses; he is surrounded by a file of guards, who keep close to his chariot wheels.

The cavalry spread themselves in front to resist an attack, and in case of defeat they carry orders hither and thither. The infantry by their quick movements contribute to the defence. These men are chosen for their courage and strength. They carry a great shield and a long spear; sometimes they hold a sword or sabre, and advance to the front with impetuosity. All their weapons of war are sharp and pointed. Some of them are these—spears, shields, bows, arrows, swords, sabres, battle-axes, lances, halberds, long javelins, and various kinds of slings. All these they have used for ages.

The law of the state is sometimes violated by base persons, and plots are made against the ruler. When the matter has been fully sifted, the offenders are imprisoned for life. There is no infliction of corporal punishment; they are simply left to live or die, and are not counted among men. When the rules of propriety or justice are violated, or when a man fails in loy-

---

[1]Moxa = Japanese *mogusa:* mixtures of wormwood leaves, to be dried and ignited on the skin to counter infections, inflamations, and tumors.

alty or filial piety, they cut off his nose or his ears, or his hands and feet, or expel him from the country, or drive him out into the desert wilds. For other faults, except these, a small payment of money will commute the punishment. In the investigation of criminal cases there is no use of rod or staff to obtain proofs (of guilt). In questioning an accused person, if he replies with frankness, the punishment is proportioned accordingly; but if the accused obstinately denies his fault, or in spite of it attempts to excuse himself, then in searching out the truth to the bottom, when it is necessary to pass sentence, there are four kinds of ordeal used—ordeal by water, by fire, by weighing, and by poison.

When the ordeal is by water, the accused is placed in a sack connected with a stone vessel and thrown into deep water. They then judge of his innocence or guilt in this way— if the man sinks and the stone floats, he is guilty; but if the man floats and the stone sinks, he is pronounced innocent.

Secondly, by fire. They heat some iron and make the accused kneel on it and then tread on it, and apply it to the palms of his hands; moreover, he is made to pass his tongue over it; if no scars result, he is innocent; if there are scars, his guilt is proved. In the case of timid and weak persons who cannot endure such a horrible ordeal, they take a flower-bud and cast it toward the fire; it if opens, he is innocent; if the flower is burned, he is guilty.

Ordeal by weight is this: A man and a stone are placed in a balance evenly, then they judge according to lightness or weight. If the accused is innocent, then the man weighs down the stone, which rises in the balance; if he is guilty, the man rises and the stone falls.

Ordeal by poison is this: They take a ram, cut off its right hind leg, and put poison upon the portion of flesh that is assigned to the accused to eat; if the man is guilty, the poison takes effect and he dies; if the man is innocent, the poison has no effect and he survives.

Every one who falls sick fasts for seven days. During this interval many recover, but if the sickness lasts they take medicine. The character of these medicines is different, and their names also vary. The doctors differ in their modes of examination and treatment. If a person dies, those who attend the funeral raise lamentable cries and weep together. They rend their garments and tear their hair; they strike their heads, and beat their breasts. There are no regulations as to dress for mourning, nor any fixed period for observing it. There are three methods of paying the last tribute to the dead: first, by cremation—wood being made into a pyre, the body is burnt; second, by water—the body is thrown into a stream to float and fall into dissolution; third, by desertion, in which case the body is cast into some forest-wild to be devoured by beasts.

When the king dies, his successor is first appointed, that he may preside at the funeral rites and fix the different points of precedence. Whilst living they give their rulers titles of merit according to their character; when dead there are no posthumous titles.

In a house where there has been a death there is no eating allowed; but after the funeral they resume their usual habits. There are no anniversaries (of the death) observed. Those who have attended a funeral are regarded as unclean; they all bathe outside the town and then enter their houses.

The old and infirm who are approaching death, or those who are suffering from some incurable disease, who fear to linger to the end of their days, and through disgust at life wish to escape from its troubles, or those who, condemning mortal existence, desire release from the affairs of the world and its concerns—these persons after receiving a farewell meal at the hands of their relatives and friends, they place, amid the sounds of music, on a boat which they propel into the midst of the Ganges, and there these persons drown themselves. They think in this way to secure a birth in Heaven. Hardly one out of ten will not carry out his foolish idea.

The Buddhist brethren are not allowed to lament or weep for the dead; when the father or mother of a monk dies, they recite prayers, recounting their obligations to them and recalling the past, and they carefully attend to them being now dead. They expect by this to increase the happiness of the departed.

The Golden Age
of Chinese Thought

The Eastern Chou [Eastern Zhou] dynasty ruled China from 770 to 249 B.C. During the dynasty's last centuries, however, the land was beset by political and social disintegration and bitter civil war. Ironically, despite the chaotic conditions, this time was the most remarkable golden age of Chinese thought. Many of the philosophies developed during this period had a lasting influence on the cultures of East Asia, similar to the influence Classical Greece had on European civilization. This great age of intellectual ferment is also known as the age of "The Hundred Schools."

During this period, many philosophical schools such as the Naturalists, Logicians, Mohists, Taoists [Daoists], Confucianists, and Legalists evolved in China. They questioned old values and institutions and sought new meaning and purpose in life and society. The following selections represent the three most important schools of philosophy that emerged during this period.

24

Confucius, *Analects*

Perhaps the one individual who was most responsible for molding Chinese mind and institutions was Confucius (551–479 B.C.). The name "Confucius" is the Latinized version of K'ung Fu-tzu [Kong Fuzi] (or Master Kung). His family name was K'ung [Kong], and his given name was Chiu [Jiu]. As a transmitter of the wisdom of the past and a creator of new ideas, his primary concern was the fundamental issue of creating utopia. He believed in the perfectability of all people and used the word "chün-tzu," [junzi] literally meaning "ruler's son," to describe a perfect or morally superior person. This individual possessed among other qualities the five inner virtues of (1) integrity, *chih* [zhi]; (2) righteousness, *i* [yi]; (3) loyalty and conscientiousness toward others, *chung* [chong]; (4) altruism and reciprocity, *shu;* and (5) virtue, love, and human heartedness, *jen* [ren]. The chün-tzu also possessed culture or polish, *wen,* and ritual or proper etiquette, *li.* Confucius' ideal of a well-ordered society was one based on mutual moral obligations in the five basic human relationships. These bonds were between ruler and subject, husband and wife, father and son, elder and younger brother, and friend and friend. All had assigned roles to play in hierarchical society.

The teachings of Confucius were not accepted widely during his lifetime; for the ensuing few centuries, the Confucian school remained only one among many Chinese schools of philosophy. But for more than two thousand years, from around the second century B.C. to the twentieth century, Confucianism was the official creed of the Chinese Empire. The great influence of this philosophy on the civilizations of the East Asian peoples was unmatched by any other body of thinking.

Among the Confucian classics, the most important work is the *Analects (Lun Yü)* [Lunyu], a collection of sayings by Confucius and his disciples. These sayings were selected and compiled, perhaps in the fourth century B.C., long after Confucius' death, by his disciples' followers. The *Analects* consist of twenty chapters (or "books") with 497 proverbial-style verses.

QUESTIONS TO CONSIDER

1. Compare and contrast the tenets of Confucianism with those of Taoism (Reading 25) and Legalism (Reading 26).
2. How do you compare the ideas of Confucius with those developed during the golden age of Greek philosophy (Readings 30 and 31)?
3. What kind of person is "superior" in the Confucian sense?

The Superior Man

1. Tsze-kung [Zigong] asked what constituted the superior man. The Master said, "He acts before he speaks, and afterwards speaks according to his actions."

2. The Master said, "The superior man is catholic and no partizan. The mean man is a partizan and not catholic."

3. (a) The Master said, "Riches and honours are what men desire. If it cannot be obtained in the proper way, they should not be held. Poverty and meanness are what men dislike. If it cannot be obtained in the proper way, they should not be avoided."

(b) "If a superior man abandons virtue, how can he fulfil the requirements of that name?"

(c) "The superior man does not, even for the space of a single meal, act contrary to virtue. In moments of haste, he cleaves to it. In seasons of danger, he cleaves to it."

4. The Master said, "The superior man, in the world, does not set his mind either for anything, or against anything; what is right he will follow."

5. The Master said, "The superior man thinks of virtue; the small man thinks of comfort. The superior man thinks of the sanctions of law; the small man thinks of favours which he may receive."

6. The Master said, "The mind of the superior man is conversant with righteousness; the mind of the mean man is conversant with gain."

7. The Master said, "The superior man wishes to be slow in his speech and earnest in his conduct."

From James Legge, trans., *The Chinese Classics,* Vol. 1 (Taipei: Wen-she-che, 1971), pp. 139, 146, 150, 152, 165, 166, 168, 169, 172, 173, 190, 193, 207, 250, 251, 252, 254, 262, 266, 273, 274, 292, 299, 314, 320, 352–54.

8. The Master said of Tsze-ch'an [Zichan] that he had four of the characteristics of a superior man:—in his conduct of himself, he was humble; in serving his superiors, he was respectful; in nourishing the people, he was kind; in ordering the people, he was just."

9. The Master said, "The superior man, extensively studying all learning, and keeping himself under the restraint of the rules of propriety, may thus likewise not overstep what is right."

10. The Master said, "The superior man is satisfied and composed; the mean man is always full of distress."

11. (a) Sze-ma Niu [Sima Niu] asked about the superior man. The Master said, "The superior man has neither anxiety nor fear."

(b) "Being without anxiety or fear!" said Niu;—"does this constitute what we call the superior man?"

(c) The Master said, "When internal examination discovers nothing wrong, what is there to be anxious about, what is there to fear?"

12. The Master said, "The superior man is affable, but not adulatory; the mean man is adulatory, but not affable."

13. The Master said, "The superior man has a dignified ease without pride. The mean man has pride without a dignified ease."

14. Tsze-lu [Zilu] asked what constituted the superior man. The Master said, "The cultivation of himself in reverential carefulness." "And is this all?" said Tsze-lu. "He cultivates himself so as to give rest to others," was the reply. "And is this all?" again asked Tsze-lu. The Master said, "He cultivates himself so as to give rest to all the people. He cultivates himself so as to give rest to all the people:—even Yao and Shun were still solicitous about this."

15. Confucius said, "The superior man has nine things which are subjects with him of thoughtful consideration. In regard to the use of his eyes, he is anxious to see clearly. In regard to the use of his ears, he is anxious to hear distinctly. In regard to his countenance, he is anxious that it should be benign. In regard to his demeanour, he is anxious that it should be respectful. In regard to his speech, he is anxious that it should be sincere. In regard to his doing business, he is anxious that it should be reverently careful. In regard to what he doubts about, he is anxious to question others. When he is angry, he thinks of the difficulties (his anger may involve him in). When he sees gain to be got, he thinks of righteousness."

Virtue

16. The Master said, "Fine words and an insinuating appearance are seldom associated with true virtue."

17. The Master said, "Those who are without virtue cannot abide long either in a condition of poverty and hardship, or in a condition of enjoyment. The virtuous rest in virtue; the wise desire virtue."

18. The Master said, "It is only the (truly) virtuous man, who can love, or who can hate, others."

19. The Master said, "Virtue is not left to stand alone. He who practises it will have neighbours."

20. (a) Yen Yuan asked about perfect virtue. The Master said, "To subdue one's self and return to propriety, is perfect virtue. If a man can for one day subdue himself and re-

turn to propriety, all under heaven will ascribe perfect virtue to him. Is the practice of perfect virtue from a man himself, or is it from others?"

(b) Yen Yuan said, "I beg to ask the steps of that process." The Master replied, "Look not at what is contrary to propriety; listen not to what is contrary to propriety; speak not what is contrary to propriety; make no movement which is contrary to propriety." Yen Yuan then said, "Though I am deficient in intelligence and vigour, I will make it my business to practise this lesson."

21. Chung-kung [Zonggong] asked about perfect virtue. The Master said, "It is, when you go abroad, to behave to every one as if you were receiving a great guest; to employ the people as if you were assisting at a great sacrifice; not to do to others as you would not wish done to yourself; to have no murmuring against you in the country, and none in the family." Chung-kung said, "Though I am deficient in intelligence and vigour, I will make it my business to practise this lesson."

22. Tsze-chang [Zizhang] asked Confucius about perfect virtue. Confucius said, "To be able to practise five things everywhere under heaven constitutes perfect virtue." He begged to ask what they were, and was told, "Gravity, generosity of soul, sincerity, earnestness, and kindness. If you are grave, you will not be treated with disrespect. If you are generous, you will win all. If you are sincere, people will repose trust in you. If you are earnest, you will accomplish much. If you are kind, this will enable you to employ the services of others."

Virtuous Government

23. The Master said, "He who exercises government by means of his virtue may be compared to the north polar star, which keeps its place and all the stars turn towards it."

24. (a) The Master said, "If the people be led by laws, and uniformity sought to be given them by punishments, they will try to avoid the punishment, but have no sense of shame."

(b) "If they be led by virtue, and uniformity sought to be given them by the rules of propriety, they will have the sense of shame and moreover will become good."

25. The duke Ai asked, saying, "What should be done in order to secure the submission of the people?" Confucius replied, "Advance the upright and set aside the crooked, then the people will submit. Advance the crooked and set aside the upright, then the people will not submit."

26. Chi K'ang [Ji Kang] asked how to cause the people to reverence their ruler, to be faithful to him and to go on to nerve themselves to virtue. The Master said, "Let him preside over them with gravity;—then they will reverence him. Let him be filial and kind to all;—then they will be faithful to him. Let him advance the good and teach the incompetent;—then they will eagerly seek to be virtuous."

27. The Master said, "Is a prince able to govern his kingdom with the complaisance proper to the rules of propriety, what difficulty will he have? If he cannot govern it with that complaisance, what has he to do with the rules of propriety?"

28. (a) Tsze-kung [Zigong] asked about government. The Master said, "The requisites of government are that there be sufficiency of food, sufficiency of military equipment, and the confidence of the people in their ruler."

(b) Tsze-kung said, "If it cannot be helped, and one of these must be dispensed with, which of the three should be foregone first?" "The military equipment," said the Master.

(c) Tsze-kung again asked, "If it cannot be helped, and one of the remaining two must be dispensed with, which of them should be foregone?" The Master answered, "Part with the food. From of old, death has been the lot of all men; but if the people have no faith in their rulers, there is no standing for the State."

29. The Master said, "When a prince's personal conduct is correct, his government is effective without the issuing of orders. If his personal conduct is not correct, he may issue orders, but they will not be followed."

30. (a) Tsze-chang [Zizhang] asked Confucius, saying, "In what way should a person in authority act in order that he may conduct government properly?" The Master replied, "Let him honour the five excellent, and banish away the four bad, things;—then may he conduct government properly." Tsze-chang said, "What are meant by the five excellent things?" The Master said, "When the person in authority is beneficent without great expenditure; when he lays tasks on the people without their repining; when he pursues what he desires without being covetous; when he maintains a dignified ease without being proud; when he is majestic without being fierce."

(b) Tsze-chang said, "What is meant by being beneficent without great expenditure?" The Master replied, "When the person in authority makes more beneficial to the people the things from which they naturally derive benefit;—is not this being beneficent without great expenditure? When he chooses the labours which are proper, makes them labour on them, who will repine? When his desires are set on benevolent government, and he secures it, who will accuse him of covetousness? Whether he has to do with many people or few, or with things great or small, he does not dare to indicate any disrespect;—is not this to maintain a dignified ease without any pride? He adjusts his clothes and cap, and throws a dignity into his looks, so that, thus dignified, he is looked at with awe;—is not this to be majestic without being fierce?"

(c) Tsze-chang then asked, "What are meant by the four bad things?" The Master said, "To put the people to death without having instructed them;—this is called cruelty. To require from them, suddenly, the full tale of work, without having given them warning;—this is called oppression. To issue orders as if without urgency, at first, and, when the time comes, to insist on them with severity;—this is called injury. And, generally, in the giving pay or rewards to men, to do it in a stingy way;—this is called acting the part of a mere official."

25

Taoism [Daoism]: *Lao Tzu* [Lao Zi]

Taoism was probably the second most important and influential philosophy after Confucianism in traditional China. It was antithetical to Confucianism. Taoism emphasized individual life, tranquility, nonconformity, and transcendental spirit, whereas Confucianism taught the importance of regulated social order, an active life, conformity, and worldliness. Taoism had two famous founders: Lao Tzu (meaning "Venerable Master"), a sixth-century B.C. mythical sage whose historicity is questioned, and Chuang-tzu [Zhuang Zi] (369–286 B.C.). The two most important Taoist texts are *Lao Tzu* or *Tao-te-ching* [Dao de Jing]

(Classics of the Way and Its Virtue) and *Chuang Tzu,* probably written in the third century B.C.

Taoism attacked moral idealism and political realism, encouraging people to merge with Tao [Dao], meaning "the Way." Tao was conceived as a natural process, the universal force in the natural world. Tao, which could be sensed only intuitively, was the source of everything—all life, both human and natural.

The way to merge with Tao was through nonaction *(wu-wei).* This concept did not mean complete inaction but rather taking no action contrary to nature. It meant: "Do nothing and nothing will be not done."

According to this theory, human effort to reform morals or to improve nature was a waste of time and destroyed the harmonies of the universe. Taoism taught that the universe was amoral and operated on its own harmonious principles, which ignored human desires or standards of conduct. This philosophy also stressed passivity, simplicity, and a laissez-faire attitude for the individual. Taoism advised the ruler that "the least government is the best government."

The following selections are from *Lao Tzu* or *Tao-te-ching,* a small classic of about 5,250 words. No other Chinese book of this size has had so much influence on the Chinese mind, and no other Chinese book has been translated into English more often than this one. This Chinese classic is a combination of poetry, philosophical speculation, and mystical reflection written in vague, subtle, and cryptic language.

QUESTIONS TO CONSIDER

1. What is the Taoist view of the universe? How do Taoists define human happiness?
2. Why is Taoism considered to be antithetical to Confucian philosophy?
3. Does the Taoist way of life have modern-day relevance? How?

Tao, The Way

> The Way is a void.
> Used but never filled:
> An abyss it is,
> Like an ancestor
> From which all things come.
>
> It blunts sharpness,
> Resolves tangles;
> It tempers light,
> Subdues turmoil.

A deep pool it is,
Never to run dry!
Whose offspring it may be
I do not know:
It is like a preface to God.

The Way begot one,
And the one, two;
Then the two begot three
And three, all else.

All things bear the shade on their backs
And the sun in their arms;
By the blending of breath
From the sun and the shade,
Equilibrium comes to the world.

Orphaned, or needy, or desolate, these
Are conditions much feared and disliked;
Yet in public address, the king
And the nobles account themselves thus.
So a loss sometimes benefits one
Or a benefit proves to be loss.

What others have taught
I also shall teach:
If a violent man does not come
To a violent death,
I shall choose him to teach me.

Wu Wei (Non-Action)

The Way is always still, at rest,
And yet does everything that's done.
If then the king and nobles could
Retain its potency for good,
The creatures all would be transformed.

But if, the change once made in them,
They still inclined to do their work,
I should restrain them then
By means of that unique
Original simplicity
Found in the Virgin Block,
Which brings disinterest,
With stillness in its train,
And so, an ordered world.

The softest of stuff in the world
Penetrates quickly the hardest;
Insubstantial, it enters
Where no room is.

By this I know the benefit
Of something done by quiet being;
In all the world but few can know
Accomplishment apart from work,
Instruction when no words are used.

Government

If those who are excellent find no preferment,
The people will cease to contend for promotion.
If goods that are hard to obtain are not favored,
The people will cease to turn robbers or bandits.
If things much desired are kept under cover,
Disturbance will cease in the minds of the people.

The Wise Man's policy, accordingly,
Will be to empty people's hearts and minds,
To fill their bellies, weaken their ambition,
Give them sturdy frames and always so,
To keep them uninformed, without desire,
And knowing ones not venturing to act.

Be still while you work
And keep full control
Over all.

The ideal land is small
Its people very few,
Where tools abound
Ten times or yet
A hundred-fold
Beyond their use;
Where people die
And die again
But never emigrate;
Have boats and carts
Which no one rides.
Weapons have they
And armor too,
But none displayed.
The folk returns
To use again

The knotted cords.
Their meat is sweet;
Their clothes adorned,
Their homes at peace,
Their customs charm.

And neighbor lands
Are juxtaposed
So each may hear
The barking dogs,
The crowing cocks
Across the way;
Where folks grow old
And folks will die
And never once
Exchange a call.

26

Legalism: The Writings of Han Fei Tzu (Han Feizi)

During the warring state period (403–221 B.C.) in ancient China, the most radical school of philosophy—and the one with the most influence on political
life—was Legalism *(Fa-chia)* [Fajia]. Legalism became the state ideology of the
feudal state of Ch'in [Qin] (221–206 B.C.), which overthrew the Chou [Zhou]
dynasty and created the first unified Chinese empire (221 B.C.).

Two leading Legalists were Kung-sun Yang [Gongsun Yang] (d. 300 B.C.),
also called Wei Yang or Shang Yang (Lord Shang), and Han Fei Tzu [Han Fei Zi]
(d. 223 B.C.). Both served in the government of Ch'in and were political strategists rather than philosophers. These Legalists, rejecting the moral and ethical
basis of human conduct and society, accepted Hsün-tzu's [Xun Zi] (300–237
B.C.) view that human nature was basically evil but potentially improvable. They
advocated rule by force rather than persuasion and favored a strong centralized
government under an absolute ruler.

The main concern of this philosophy was how to make the state a powerful instrument in achieving whatever the ruler desired. The Legalists encouraged war, aggression, and regimentation to strengthen the power of the ruler. To
make people obedient and loyal, the Legalists advised the ruler to manipulate
two presumably basic human drives: greed and fear. Han Fei Tzu proposed the
principle of the "Two Handles" by which the ruler could control others: pro-
portional rewards and harsh punishments. According to this theory, propor-
tional rewards would encourage what was beneficial to the state, and harsh
punishments would restrain evil. Because Legalists viewed human nature as basically evil and selfish, and officials as self-seeking and untrustworthy, they advised the ruler to draw up an exhaustive set of laws and regulations to define
everyone's duties and responsibilities clearly. Any slight infraction was to be

dealt with severely. Thus, they strictly regulated the life and thought of the Chinese people. In the following excerpts, Han Fei Tzu provides a summary of Legalist doctrines.

QUESTIONS TO CONSIDER

1. Why did Legalism gain influence among the rulers of China during the last phase of the Chou period, a politically chaotic time?
2. How does the Legalistic philosophy compare with modern-day totalitarian ideologies?

The Way of the Ruler

The Way is the beginning of all beings and the measure of right and wrong. Therefore the enlightened ruler holds fast to the beginning in order to understand the wellspring of all beings, and minds the measure in order to know the source of good and bad. He waits, empty and still, letting names define themselves and affairs reach their own settlement. Being empty, he can comprehend the true aspect of fullness; being still, he can correct the mover. Those whose duty it is to speak will come forward to name themselves; those whose duty it is to act will produce results. When names and results match, the ruler need do nothing more and the true aspect of all things will be revealed.

Hence it is said: The ruler must not reveal his desires; for if he reveals his desires his ministers will put on the mask that pleases him. He must not reveal his will; for if he does so his ministers will show a different face. So it is said: Discard likes and dislikes and the ministers will show their true form; discard wisdom and wile and the ministers will watch their step. Hence, though the ruler is wise, he hatches no schemes from his wisdom, but causes all men to know their place. Though he has worth, he does not display it in his deeds, but observes the motives of his ministers. Though he is brave, he does not flaunt his bravery in shows of indignation, but allows his subordinates to display their valor to the full. Thus, though he discards wisdom, his rule is enlightened; though he discards worth, he achieves merit; and though he discards bravery, his state grows powerful. When the ministers stick to their posts, the hundred officials have their regular duties, and the ruler employs each according to his particular ability, this is known as the state of manifold constancy.

Hence it is said: "So still he seems to dwell nowhere at all; so empty no one can seek him out." The enlightened ruler reposes in nonaction above, and below his ministers tremble with fear.

This is the way of the enlightened ruler: he causes the wise to bring forth all their schemes, and he decides his affairs accordingly; hence his own wisdom is never exhausted. He causes the worthy to display their talents, and he employs them accordingly; hence his own worth never comes to an end. Where there are accomplishments, the ruler takes credit for their worth; where there are errors, the ministers are held responsible for the blame; hence the ruler's name never suffers. Thus, though the ruler is not worthy himself, he is the leader of the worthy; though he is not wise himself, he is the corrector of the wise. The ministers have the labor; the ruler enjoys the success. This is called the maxim of the worthy ruler.

From Burton Watson, trans., *Basic Writings of Mo Tzu, Hsün Tzu, and Han Fei Tzu.* Copyright © 1964 by Columbia University Press. Reprinted with permission of the publisher.

The Way lies in what cannot be seen, its function in what cannot be known. Be empty, still, and idle, and from your place of darkness observe the defects of others. See but do not appear to see; listen but do not seem to listen; know but do not let it be known that you know. When you perceive the trend of a man's words, do not change them, do not correct them, but examine them and compare them with the results. Assign one man to each office and do not let men talk to each other, and then all will do their utmost. Hide your tracks, conceal your sources, so that your subordinates cannot trace the springs of your action. Discard wisdom, forswear ability, so that your subordinates cannot guess what you are about. Stick to your objectives and examine the results to see how they match; take hold of the handles of government carefully and grip them tightly. Destroy all hope, smash all intention of wresting them from you; allow no man to covet them.

If you do not guard the door, if you do not make fast the gate, then tigers will lurk there. If you are not cautious in your undertakings, if you do not hide their true aspect, then traitors will arise. They murder their sovereign and usurp his place, and all men in fear make common cause with them: hence they are called tigers. They sit by the ruler's side and, in the service of evil ministers, spy into his secrets: hence they are called traitors. Smash their cliques, arrest their backers, shut the gate, deprive them of all hope of support, and the nation will be free of tigers. Be immeasurably great, be unfathomably deep; make certain that names and results tally, examine laws and customs, punish those who act willfully, and the state will be without traitors.

The ruler of men stands in danger of being blocked in five ways. When the ministers shut out their ruler, this is one kind of block. When they get control of the wealth and resources of the state, this is a second kind of block. When they are free to issue orders as they please, this is a third kind. When they are able to do righteous deeds in their own name, this is a fourth kind. When they are able to build up their own cliques, this is a fifth kind. If the ministers shut out the ruler, then he loses the effectiveness of his position. If they control wealth and resources, he loses the means of dispensing bounty to others. If they issue orders as they please, he loses the means of command. If they are able to carry out righteous deeds in their own name, he loses his claim to enlightenment. And if they can build up cliques of their own, he loses his supporters. All these are rights that should be exercised by the ruler alone; they should never pass into the hands of his ministers.

The way of the ruler of men is to treasure stillness and reserve. Without handling affairs himself, he can recognize clumsiness or skill in others; without laying plans of his own, he knows what will bring fortune or misfortune. Hence he need speak no word, but good answers will be given him; he need exact no promises, but good works will increase. When proposals have been brought before him, he takes careful note of their content; when undertakings are well on their way, he takes careful note of the result; and from the degree to which proposals and results tally, rewards and punishments are born. Thus the ruler assigns undertakings to his various ministers on the basis of the words they speak, and assesses their accomplishments according to the way they have carried out the undertaking. When accomplishments match the undertaking, and the undertaking matches what was said about it, then he rewards the man; when these things do not match, he punishes the man. It is the way of the enlightened ruler never to allow his ministers to speak words that cannot be matched by results.

The enlightened ruler in bestowing rewards is as benign as the seasonable rain; the dew of his bounty profits all men. But in doling out punishment he is as terrible as the thunder; even the holy sages cannot assuage him. The enlightened ruler is never overliberal in his rewards, never overlenient in his punishments. If his rewards are too liberal, then ministers who have won merit in the past will grow lax in their duties; and if his punishments are too lenient, then evil ministers will find it easy to do wrong. Thus if a man has truly won merit, no matter how humble and far removed he may be, he must be rewarded; and if he has truly committed error, no matter how close and dear to the ruler he may be, he must be punished. If those who are humble and far removed can be sure of reward, and those close and dear to the ruler can be sure of punishment, then the former will not stint in their efforts and the latter will not grow proud.

The Two Handles

The enlightened ruler controls his ministers by means of two handles alone. The two handles are punishment and favor. What do I mean by punishment and favor? To inflict mutilation and death on men is called punishment; to bestow honor and reward is called favor. Those who act as ministers fear the penalties and hope to profit by the rewards. Hence, if the ruler wields his punishments and favors, the ministers will fear his sternness and flock to receive his benefits. But the evil ministers of the age are different. They cajole the ruler into letting them inflict punishment themselves on men they hate and bestow rewards on men they like. Now if the ruler of men does not insist upon reserving to himself the right to dispense profit in the form of rewards and show his sternness in punishments, but instead hands them out on the advice of his ministers, then the people of the state will all fear the ministers and hold the ruler in contempt, will flock to the ministers and desert the ruler. This is the danger that arises when the ruler loses control of punishments and favors.

The tiger is able to overpower the dog because of his claws and teeth, but if he discards his claws and teeth and lets the dog use them, then on the contrary he will be overpowered by the dog. In the same way the ruler of men uses punishments and favors to control his ministers, but if he discards his punishments and favors and lets his ministers employ them, then on the contrary he will find himself in the control of his ministers.

T'ien Ch'ang [Tian Chang] petitioned the ruler for various titles and stipends, which he then dispensed to the other ministers, and used an extra large measure in doling out grain to the common people. In this way the ruler, Duke Chien [Jian], lost the exclusive right to dispense favors, and it passed into T'ien Ch'ang's hands instead. That was how Duke Chien came to be assassinated.

Tzu-han [Zihan] said to the ruler of Sung [Song], "Since the people all delight in rewards and gifts, you should bestow them yourself; but since they hate punishments and death sentences, I beg to be allowed to dispense these for you." Thereupon the ruler of Sung gave up the exclusive right to hand out penalties and it passed into the hands of Tzu-han. That was how the ruler of Sung came to be intimidated.

T'ien Ch'ang got to bestow favors as he pleased, and Duke Chien was assassinated; Tzu-han got to hand out punishments as he pleased, and the ruler of Sung was intimidated. Hence, if the ministers of the present age are permitted to share in the right to hand out punishments and favors, the rulers of the time will put themselves in greater peril than Duke Chien and the lord of Sung. Invariably when rulers are intimidated, assassinated, obstructed, or forced into the shade, it has always come about because they relinquished the rights to administer punishment and favor to their ministers, and thus brought about their own peril and downfall.

If the ruler of men wishes to put an end to evil-doing, then he must be careful to match up names and results, that is to say, words and deeds. The ministers come forward to present their proposals; the ruler assigns them tasks on the basis of their words, and then concentrates on demanding the accomplishment of the task. If the accomplishment fits the task, and the task fits the words, then he bestows reward; but if they do not match, he doles out punishment. Hence, if one of the ministers comes forward with big words but produces only small accomplishments, the ruler punishes him, not because the accomplishments are small, but because they do not match the name that was given to the undertaking. Likewise, if one of the ministers comes forward with small words but produces great accomplishments, he too is punished, not because the ruler is displeased at great accomplishments, but because he considers the discrepancy in the name given to the undertaking to be a fault too serious to be outweighed by great accomplishments.

Once in the past Marquis Chao [Zhao] of Han got drunk and fell asleep. The keeper of the royal hat, seeing that the marquis was cold, laid a robe over him. When the marquis awoke, he was pleased and asked his attendants, "Who covered me with a robe?" "The keeper of the hat," they replied. The marquis thereupon punished both the keeper of the royal hat and the keeper of the royal robe. He punished the keeper of the robe for failing to do his duty, and the keeper of the hat for overstepping his office. It was not that he did not dislike the cold, but he considered the trespass of one official upon the duties of another to be a greater danger than cold.

Hence an enlightened ruler, in handling his ministers, does not permit them to gain merit by overstepping their offices, or to speak words that do not tally with their actions. Those who overstep their offices are condemned to die; those whose words and actions do not tally are punished. If the ministers are made to stick to their proper duties and speak only what is just, then they will be unable to band together in cliques to work for each other's benefit.

The ruler of men has two worries: if he employs only worthy men, then his ministers will use the appeal to worthiness as a means to intimidate him; on the other hand, if he promotes men in an arbitrary manner, then state affairs will be bungled and will never reach a successful conclusion. Hence, if the ruler shows a fondness for worth, his ministers will all strive to put a pleasing façade on their actions in order to satisfy his desires. In such a case, they will never show their true colors, and if they never show their true colors, then the ruler will have no way to distinguish the able from the worthless. Because the king of Yüeh [Yue] admired valor, many of his subjects defied death; because King Ling of Ch'u [Chu] liked slim waists, his state was full of half-starved people on diets. Because Duke Huan of Ch'i [Chi] was jealous and loved his ladies in waiting, Shu-tiao [Shudiao] castrated himself in order to be put in charge of the harem; because the duke was fond of unusual food, Yi-ya [Yiya] steamed his son's head and offered it to the duke. Because Tzu-k'uai [Zikuai] of Yen admired worthy men, Tzu-chih [Zizhi] insisted that he would not accept the throne even if it were offered to him.

Thus, if the ruler reveals what he dislikes, his ministers will be careful to disguise their motives; if he shows what he likes, his ministers will feign abilities they do not have. In short, if he lets his desires be known, he gives his ministers a clue as to what attitude they had best assume.

Hence Tzu-chih, by playing the part of a worthy, was able to snatch power from his sovereign; Shu-tiao [Shudiao] and Yi-ya, by catering to the ruler's desires, were able to invade his authority. As a result, Tzu-k'uai died in the chaos that ensued, and Duke Huan was left unburied for so long that maggots came crawling out the door of his death chamber.

What caused this? It is an example of the calamity that comes when the ruler reveals his feelings to his ministers. As far as the feelings of the ministers go, they do not necessarily love their ruler; they serve him only in the hope of substantial gain. Now if the ruler of men does not hide his feelings and conceal his motives, but instead gives his ministers a foothold by which they may invade his rights, then they will have no difficulty in doing what Tzu-chih and T'ien Ch'ang did. Hence it is said: Do away with likes, do away with hates, and the ministers will show their true colors. And when the ministers have shown their true colors, the ruler of men will never be deceived.

Classical Greece

The most interesting political and literary developments of classical Greece—roughly those of the fifth century B.C.—were centered in Athens. Athenian democracy reached its fullest development in the half century following the Persian Wars. The success of Pericles (ca. 495–429 B.C.) in centering the Delian League's treasury and judicial system in Athens brought added income and power. The Athenians used the new wealth well: The classical works of architecture, sculpture, and drama set standards for ages to come.

Three great playwrights—Aeschylus (525–456 B.C.), Sophocles (496–406 B.C.), and Euripides (485–406 B.C.)—developed the art of composing tragedies to be performed at Athenian religious festivals. Periclean Athens also produced the first writing of history as we use the term: In his *Histories,* Herodotus (ca. 485–430 B.C.) gave an account of major events in the history of the world accessible to him, events culminating in the great conflict to defend Greek freedom against the Persian threat. The Age of Pericles ended in the great Peloponnesian War, fought between groups of city-states headed by Athens and Sparta from 431 to 404 B.C., although it was interrupted by truces. All modern accounts of that war still rely heavily on the classic work of Thucydides (ca. 455–400 B.C.) as their principal source. His *Peloponnesian War* is far more critical and fact-oriented than is Herodotus' work, and his style conveys the impression of total objectivity in his descriptions. At the same time, his frequent use of speeches and dialogue makes his narrative colorful and readable.

The high point of Greek philosophy came after art, architecture, and drama had reached their peak in the Age of Pericles. Socrates (ca. 469–399 B.C.), his student Plato (427–347 B.C.), and Plato's student Aristotle (384–322 B.C.) are the three greatest philosophers of classical Greece. Philosophy to the Greeks simply meant "love of wisdom," and a philosopher was someone who seriously pursued knowledge relating to human concerns or cosmic matters.

27

Herodotus, *Persian Dialogue*

Herodotus (ca. 485–ca. 425 B.C.) has at least three major claims to fame. Often called "The Father of History," he is also the first writer of prose and the first Western political scientist whose work survives. Greeks before him all wrote in verse, since lines in poetic meter are easier to memorize than ordinary sentences. Although Herodotus is known to have read his *Histories* aloud to audiences, the scope of his work and his striving for factual accuracy led him to abandon the poetic form for prose. A great cultural geographer along with everything else, he stated his intention of writing about the varied cultural achievements and the great men among the Greeks as well as the "barbarians" (Asians and Africans).

In his *Histories,* Herodotus presents all earlier world history as funneling into the great conflict between Europe and Asia in the form of the Persian attempts to conquer Greece; so we usually entitle his sweeping *Histories,* "The Persian Wars." This source focuses on stories of how the freedom-loving Greeks feared the despotic system of the Persians enough to undergo great sacrifices and to defeat many times their own number of invading forces. Writing in the afterglow of the historic Persian Wars, Herodotus felt positive about democracy, which he tended to equate with Greek freedom. While he shared the prejudice of his ethnocentric countrymen that Greeks had higher ideals than the less-than-free Asians (represented by the Persians), he still had abiding respect for foreign things such as the antiquity of Egyptian civilization and the strength with order preserved by Persian society. His basically democratic political philosophy includes the notion that what works best for one people does not necessarily work best for all peoples.

In the following selection, Herodotus records an episode from Persian history, in which, after a break in monarchical rule, three leading Persians—Otanes, Megabyzos, and Darius, who overthrew Magi usurpers—debate rather much like stereotypical Greeks before deciding on the best form of government for Persia. The three forms of government described here, monarchy, aristocracy (oligarchy), and democracy remained as the basic options in speculative political thought through the eighteenth century.

QUESTIONS TO CONSIDER

1. In your view, which of the three advocates, Otanes, Megabyzos, or Darius, defends "his" system with the strongest arguments? Which with the weakest? Why?
2. Do the twentieth-century terms *dictatorship, elite rule,* and *democracy* mean about the same thing to us that *monarchy, aristocracy,* and *democracy* meant to the ancient Greeks? Why or why not?

Otanes advised putting governmental power in the hands of the Persian people, saying: "I cannot think about one of us becoming a sole monarch with any pleasure or optimism. You can all see how far Cambyses' arrogance of power drove him. You also had to suffer the same thing under the Magi. How can absolute monarchy be compatible with ethical behavior when it allows the king to do whatever he wants with no accountability? Even the very best man picked for this position would abandon the character traits which made us choose him. Envy is something everyone is born with. Limit-breaking pride will overwhelm him from the very fullness of his power and wealth. Envy heightened by pride will implant all other vices in him. Overwhelming pride and envy will lead him into commit-

Herodotus, *Histories,* Book III, ed. H. Stein (Berlin: Weidmann, 1856), pp. 76–82. Translated by Henry A. Myers.

ting foolish crimes. Logically, of course, an absolute monarch should be free of all malice; after all, he owns all the goods in his realm. The truth of the matter, however, is that he will behave in the very opposite way towards citizens. He will envy the very best people for the very fact that they are better than he. He will be attracted to the worst people and eager to listen to slander. The most contradictory thing about him is that he will be annoyed when people admire him in moderation, since they are not showing him enough humility in doing so. But if you express really strong admiration for him, then he will be put off by your flattery. Now I have been saving the worst for last: He will trample traditional laws into the ground. He will have our women seized for his own pleasure and men killed without trials.

"When the people rule, on the other hand, first of all their regime is called 'equality before the law,' and there can be no more pleasant sounding name than that. Secondly, democracy is free of all the vices of absolute monarchy. It assigns offices by lot and keeps office-holders responsible. All decisions are put before the whole people. And so I am of the opinion that we should abolish monarchy and give the people power, for the people and the state really should be thought of as the same thing."

That was the case made by Otanes. Megabyzos, however, advocated oligarchy, saying: "I support Otanes in opposing one-man rule; however, he is wrong in advising us to make the multitude into a ruler. There is really nothing less reasonable or more arrogant than the blind masses: It would be unbearable to flee the deadly whims of a sole ruler only to end up with the conceit of a mob, who recognizes no limits. A king at least knows what he is doing, but a mob does not. Where are common people supposed to get reasoning power from? They are not born with it, nor have they met up with it in their experiences. Instead the multitude hurls itself like a mountain stream into politics and washes everything away before it. We should form a government by giving the very best men power: We will be among them ourselves. The best men will make the best decisions as a matter of course." That opinion was presented by Megabyzos.

Darius was the third to speak, saying: "I concur with what Megabyzos just said about the masses, but not what he says about oligarchy. There are three possible constitutional forms. If we examine them in their purest forms, that is, the purest democracy, the purest oligarchy and the purest monarchy, the last one towers over the other two in my opinion. There is obviously nothing better than sole government by the best man: Nothing will keep him from looking after his people. Decisions against enemies of the people are best kept secret by a single ruler. In an oligarchy on the other hand, violent personal feuds arise when a good number of men compete for distinction. Everybody tries to force himself ahead. That way, real enemies are made. Out of this, factional conflicts arise, leading to assassinations. It will all end up with a return to monarchy again, and so you can see how much better monarchy is than any other form of government. When the people rule, it is impossible to prevent corruption. When conspiracies occur in a democracy, it is not a matter of hostility among the worst elements but the wrong kind of friendships: Those who work against the common good will do so in cooperation with each other, putting their heads together. That will go on until a leader of the people puts an end to their abuses. The people will admire him for that, and the admired man will lead you back again to one-man rule. Again we see monarchy emerge as the best constitution. To sum it all up briefly: How did the Persian Empire become free? Who gave Persia her freedom: the people, an oligarchy, or the monarchy? The answer certainly convinces me, and we must stick with that system. Anyway, we would be very foolish to discard our ancient and traditional laws, when they have served us so well, since any change is bound to be for the worse."

28

Sophocles, *Antigone*

In modern times, Athenian tragedies have enjoyed substantial revivals—remarkable given the fact that they were intended to be performed only once. What keeps them in modern repertoires is their concern with conflicts having universal interest. Some themes appear much more frequently than others, to be sure. For example, the Greek tragic hero is typically hounded by a fate inherited from the misdeeds of his forebears. Very often, too, he brings doom upon himself with *hubris,* a mortal's false pride leading to acts that no mortal can get away with.

In Greek drama, the Chorus often recites or chants odes. These relate events on stage to the will of the gods, punishments for those guilty of hubris, the implacability of fate, or similar cosmic concerns. The Chorus leader (or *Choragos*) enters the dialogue with questions and observations.

Sophocles' *Antigone,* from which the following selection is taken, remains a twentieth-century favorite. Along with the themes of implacable fate and punishment for hubris, this excerpt stresses the recurring conflict—truly global in the history of civilization—between the official, promulgated laws of a governing body and the laws believed by an individual to outweigh the claims of the governing body. Athenians saw this problem as a conflict between nature and convention. Later ages would label the conflict as natural law versus positive law (that is, law set down by people) or, returning close to Sophocles' own phrasing, God-made law versus man-made law.

In the play, Creon, King of Thebes, has declared that Polyneices, a member of the royal family, should not be buried. Polyneices—with considerable justification—had led an attack to take Thebes and was killed in single combat by his own brother, Eteocles. In popular Greek belief, the unburied dead found no rest; therefore, Antigone, sister of Polyneices and Eteocles, violates Creon's decree by giving Polyneices burial rites. Ismene, her sister, had shown sympathy for Antigone but lacked the courage to join her in the deed. The guard who appears in this selection is one of a group sent earlier to guard the unburied body; they had failed the first time to stop Antigone as she slipped by them unnoticed.

QUESTIONS TO CONSIDER

1. What is Antigone's attitude toward her "crime" and the death penalty she is facing?
2. How does Creon bring male/female relations into the heated discussion with Antigone?
3. Is Creon guilty of hubris (the crime of overweening pride)? Could Antigone be accused of hubris as well?
4. Was Odysseus guilty of hubris in shouting taunts at Polyphemus as he sailed away from the land of the Cyclopes (see Reading 14)?

5. When have you heard similar arguments in our own time concerning the existence of laws higher than those humans make?

Chorus: But I know her. . . ! Antigone, the ill-fated daughter of the ill-fated Oedipus: why is she under arrest?

Guard: We have the culprit here! We seized her right when she was burying him. Now where is the king?

Chorus: Coming from the palace right now. *(Creon enters.)*

Creon: What is all this. . . ?

Guard: Sire, no man should ever swear he'll never do a thing. After all your threats, I swore you'd never see me return. But being so surprised and so very glad when we captured the one who did it just made a liar out of me . . . I am bringing you the woman we caught in the very act of burying him. Take her and judge her guilt any way you like. I've done my part and ought to be relieved of any further responsibility.

Creon: Just what was she doing when you arrested her? Tell me.

Guard: Burying him. It's that simple. . . .

Creon: You there, standing with your head bowed, do you admit the truth of what he charges you with or not?

Antigone: I did it. I don't deny it.

Creon (to Guard): Feel free to go. . . . *(Guard exits.)*

   (to Antigone): Did you know that I gave the order that he should not be buried? Just tell me yes or no.

 Antigone: I knew your order just as everyone else knew it.

Creon: Then you knowingly broke the law?

Antigone: I knew what I was doing. Zeus would not have approved such an order. Diké [goddess of justice], whose justice rules the world, has other decrees than such laws of men. I did not feel that your royal strength was enough to nullify the unwritten but eternal laws of the gods, laws which were not declared today or yesterday but have kept their living force from origins no mortal can trace or question. . . .

Creon: This girl has outdone herself in insolence: she broke the law, and now she's boasting about breaking it. If she can get away with that, she is the man, not I.

Antigone: Do you want something else besides my execution?

Creon: No, that will be enough for me.

Antigone: Then why wait? Have me killed. Your words are having no effect on me, and you must be getting tired of mine, although you shouldn't be. I deserve all honor for burying my brother. These men right here would all congratulate me for my courage if their fear of you did not keep them quiet. Kings are really fortunate in being able to adjust laws so that whatever they want to do or say is covered by them.

Creon: Not one single Theban thinks that way but you.

From Sophokles, *Antigone* (Gothae: F.A. Perthes, 1883), lines 382–768, *passim.* Translated by Martha B. Caldwell and Henry A. Myers.

Antigone: They think as I do, but you intimidate them.

Creon: Aren't you ashamed to be the only one talking like that?

Antigone: To show respect for a dead kinsman is nothing to be ashamed of. . . . Be what may, Hades requires the rite of burial.

Creon: Not so that good and bad men will be treated equally.

Antigone: Why do you think you know how the gods below will judge this?

Creon: An enemy does not become a friend by dying.

Antigone: Nature inclines me to love, not to hate.

Creon: Go ahead and die then! Love the dead in the world below if you must!

Chorus: Will you really steal your own son's bride from him?

Creon: Hades will take her, not I.

Chorus: Then she really is to die. . . . Now here comes Haemon, your last surviving son. Isn't it grief bringing him here? He's sad and bitter over Antigone's doom. *(Haemon enters.)*

Creon: We'll find out soon enough. . . . Son, have you heard about your bride's death sentence? Have you come here raving mad, or will you accept my decision as an act of love?

Haemon: Father, I belong to you. Your good judgment will steer me, and I will obey. No marriage will mean more to me than your loving guidance.

Creon: That's the right way to act, recognizing your father's authority like a proper son. Men pray for dutiful sons, each one harming his father's enemies and doing good to his father's friends. . . . So you have made the right choice, not to let this woman cloud your mind. You would find her embraces turning cold, Haemon, and then you'd be left with a hateful armful. What is worse than a false love? Let Hades find her a husband! I will not go back on my word to the state, since she alone among my people disobeyed my law. . . . She must surely die. Let her sing her appeal to Zeus who helps guard family ties. If I let my own family rebel, I would be encouraging lawlessness on a grand scale. The man who heads an orderly household is the right one to help with administering the city-state. I will not put up with anyone who wants to bend the law and dictate to his rulers. The ruler entrusted with the power of the state must be obeyed, whether he happens to be right or wrong. . . . There is no greater evil than disrespect for authority, which destroys homes and city-states alike, demoralizing and defeating armies. Discipline makes life orderly and good. With it we will preserve authority and not be led astray by a woman. If I am overthrown, I want it said at least that I was beaten by a man rather than outmaneuvered by a woman.

Chorus: Unless old age is taking its toll, my mind tells me you are speaking sensibly and justly.

Haemon: Father, reason is the greatest gift of the gods to mankind. It's not my place to say you are not using your share of it; however, there are other men around who reason well, and as your son I feel responsible for telling you their thoughts when they pertain to you. The people are afraid of making you angry and will not let you know what they really think, but I have overheard them whispering their complaints and their grief over this girl's fate. You should know how the people are mourning, saying she is doomed to die a shameful death for a glorious deed. They say she refused to leave her brother's body unburied for the vultures and dogs, and they ask: "Doesn't she deserve a prize of gold?" That's what the people are really saying. . . .

Withdraw your anger, and reverse your decree! Young as I am, I do know this: The ideal would be to have absolute wisdom at all times, but since nature doesn't work like that the next best thing is to pay attention to wisdom and reason in good advice.

Chorus: Sire, if what he says makes sense, you would do well to listen. Haemon, you in turn should consider your father's words. Both of you have spoken well.

Creon: You think it's right for a man to take instruction from a boy?

Haemon: Not if I did not have right on my side, but if I do you shouldn't hold my age against me.

Creon: Are you asking me to condone lawlessness?

Haemon: I'm not asking you to protect lawbreakers.

Creon: Isn't that just what this girl is?

Haemon: The people of Thebes don't think so.

Creon: And so the citizens are going to dictate my decrees?

Haemon: It is you now who are talking like a youngster.

Creon: Am I to rule or let others do it?

Haemon: No true city-state obeys one man alone.

Creon: A city-state belongs to its ruler.

Haemon: You might rule well alone in a desert.

Creon: I can tell this boy is under the woman's influence.

Haemon: That's true if you're a woman. I am thinking of your own interests.

Creon: Good for nothing! Getting into a fight of words with your father. . . ! All your arguing is for her sake!

Haemon: For yours and mine, too, and for the sake of the gods below.

Creon: You will never marry her while she's alive.

Haemon: She must die then, but another death will follow hers.

Creon: Another? Are you going so far as to make threats?

Haemon: I'm only trying to keep you from carrying out your vain plan.

Creon: You vain fool: you'll regret condescending talk like that.

Haemon: If you weren't my father, I'd say you were crazy. . . .

Creon: That's enough! I swear by Olympus you will not get away with your raving insults! Bring out the hateful creature: She will die this moment before her bridegroom's very eyes, right close to him.

Haemon: Don't deceive yourself. She will not die with me looking on, and you will never see my face again. Keep on raving as long as you think you have a friend to listen. *(Haemon exits.)*

Chorus: He's gone, Sire. A young man made furious can do great harm.

29

Thucydides, *Peloponnesian War*

As Athenian commerce began to dominate the Aegean Sea trade, Athenian naval power kept member states from leaving the Delian League. Trouble came with increasing discontent over this Athenian domination. There was also a perceived (perhaps real, perhaps imagined) Athenian threat to the freedom of the remaining independent Greek city-states. Many of those city-states allied with Sparta in the Peloponnesian League.

Thucydides, whose *Peloponnesian War* is the classic account of the ensuing conflict, was an Athenian general who failed to carry out his mission of relieving the city of Amphipolis from a Peloponnesian siege; in harmony with Athenian democratic principles and practice, he was relieved of his duties by authority of the people. In his history, Thucydides gives detailed information on troop numbers, types of equipment used, and other data in year-by-year accounts of battles until 411 B.C., when his book breaks off unfinished. He makes his work more vivid with speeches by leading figures on both sides. Although Thucydides was not present to hear many of the speeches, which are presented as extended verbatim quotations, he claims to give their approximate content accurately.

In the first excerpt following, we find Pericles highlighting the greatness of Athenian democracy in a funeral oration after the first battle casualties. But, two years later, Pericles died in a plague, and Athenian democracy became more extreme. As Thucydides saw it, the Athenian people began to suppose that whatever they said was law. In the second excerpt following, Thucydides writes about a confrontation with the Melians in the sixteenth year of the war. In this account, the Athenians seem to believe that might makes right, and that the Athenian Empire is mighty enough to enforce its policies—even genocidal ones—on all would-be enemies.

QUESTIONS TO CONSIDER

1. What does "democracy" appear to mean to Pericles apart from broad participation in government?
2. Does Pericles state or imply that the rights of nonconformists or dissenters in Athens are protected under Athenian democracy?
3. What does Pericles appear to have in mind when he speaks of Athens as a model for all of Greece?
4. These selections contrast Athens as an educational model for Greece (in the first excerpt) and as a state demanding compliance through deadly force (in the second excerpt). Do you think the contrast is too neat to be true?
5. Does Thucydides—the fired Athenian general—give the impression of writing more as dramatist than as historian when stressing evils in the system that rejected him? Or does he convey the image of a realistic historian regretfully documenting the twisting of democratic ideals?

Pericles' Funeral Oration

Pericles . . . was chosen to give the funeral oration for the first who had fallen. When the proper time arrived, he advanced from the tomb . . . and spoke as follows:

"I shall begin with our ancestors. . . . They dwelt in this country without interruption from generation to generation, and handed it down to the present time by their bravery. . . .

"Our constitution does not copy the laws of neighboring states; we are rather a model for others than imitators ourselves. Its administration favors the many instead of the few; this is why it is called a democracy. If we look at the laws, they afford equal justice to all in settling private differences. As for prestige, advancement in public life goes to men with reputations for ability: class considerations are not allowed to interfere with merit, nor again does poverty bar the way. If a man is able to serve the state, he is not hindered by obscure origins or poverty. The freedom we enjoy in our government extends also to our private life. There . . . we do not feel called upon to be angry with our neighbor for doing what he likes, or even to indulge in those injurious looks which cannot fail to be offensive, although they inflict no actual harm. But all this ease in our private relations does not make us lawless as citizens. . . . We obey the magistrates and the laws, particularly those for the protection of the injured, whether they are actually on the statute book, or belong to that code which, although unwritten, yet cannot be broken without acknowledged disgrace.

"Further, we provide plenty of means for the mind to refresh itself from business. We celebrate games and sacrifices all the year round, and the elegance of our private establishments forms a daily source of pleasure and helps to banish our cares. Then, too, the magnitude of our city draws the produce of the world into our harbor, so that to the Athenian the products of other countries are as familiar a luxury as those of his own.

"If we turn to our military policy, there also we differ from our antagonists. We throw open our city to the world, and never pass laws to exclude foreigners from any opportunity of learning or observing, although the eyes of the enemy may occasionally profit from our liberality. We rely less on secrecy than on the native spirit of our citizens. In education, where our rivals from their very cradles seek after manliness through a very painful discipline, at Athens we live as we please, and yet are just as ready to encounter every legitimate danger. . . . And yet if with habits not of labor but of ease, and with courage which is not artificial but real, we are still willing to encounter danger, we have the double advantage of escaping the experience of hardships in anticipation and of facing them in the hour of need as fearlessly as those who are never free from them.

"We cultivate refinement without extravagance and knowledge without effeminacy; wealth we employ more for use than for show, and place the real disgrace of poverty not in admitting the fact of it but in declining the struggle against it. Our public men have, besides politics, their private affairs to tend to, and our ordinary citizens, though occupied with the pursuits of industry, are still fair judges of public matters. Unlike any other nation, we regard a man who takes no part in these duties not as unambitious but as useless. . . . Instead of looking on discussion as a stumbling block in the way of action, we Athenians consider it an indispensable preliminary to any wise action at all.

"In generosity we are equally singular, acquiring our friends by conferring, not receiving, favors. Yet, of course, the doer of the favor is the firmer friend of the two, in order by continued kindness to keep the recipient in his debt; while the debtor feels less keenly

From Thucydides, *Peloponnesian War,* trans. Richard Crawley (London: J.M. Dent & Co., 1903), Vol. 1, pp. 120–128, Vol. II, pp. 59–67; language modernized.

from the very consciousness that the return he makes will be a repayment, not a free gift, and it is only the Athenians who, fearless of consequences, confer their benefits not from calculations of expediency, but in the confidence of liberality.

"In short, I say that as a city we are the school of Hellas; while I doubt if the world can produce a man who is equal to so many emergencies where he has only himself to depend upon, and who is graced by so happy a versatility as the Athenian. . . . For Athens alone of her contemporaries is found when tested to be greater than her reputation, and alone gives no occasion to her assailants to blush at the antagonist by whom they have been worsted, or to her subjects to question her title by merit to rule. Rather, the admiration of the present and succeeding ages will be ours, since we have not left our power without witness, but have shown it by mighty proofs; and far from needing a Homer for our panegyrist, or another poet whose verses might charm for the moment only for the impression which they gave, to melt at the touch of fact, we have forced every sea and land to be the highway of our daring, and everywhere, whether for evil or for good, have left imperishable monuments behind us. Such is the Athens for which these men, in the assertion of their resolve not to lose her, nobly fought and died; and well may every one of their survivors be ready to suffer in her cause.

"If I have dwelt at some length upon the character of our country, it has been to show that our stake in the struggle is not the same as theirs who have no such blessings to lose, and also that the praise of the men over whom I am now speaking might be confirmed by definite proofs. My speech is now largely complete; for the Athens that I have celebrated is only what the heroism of these and others like them have made her, men whose fame, unlike that of most Hellenes, will be found to be only proportionate to what they deserve. And if a test of worth be wanted, it is to be found in their last scene, and this not only in the cases in which it set the final seal upon their merit, but also in those in which it gave the first intimation of their having any. For there is justice in the claim that steadfastness in his country's battles should be as a cloak to cover a man's other imperfections, since the good more than outweighed his demerits as an individual. . . . And while committing to hope the uncertainty of final success, in the business before them they thought fit to act boldly and trust in themselves. Thus choosing to die resisting, rather than to live submitting.

"So died these men as became Athenians. You, their survivors, must be determined to have as unfaltering a resolution in the field, though you may pray that it may have a happier outcome. . . . You must yourselves realise the power of Athens, and feed your eyes upon her from day to day, till the love of her fills your hearts; and then when all her greatness shall break upon you, you must reflect that it was by courage, sense of duty, and a keen feeling of honor in action that men were enabled to win all this, and that no personal failure in an enterprise could make them consent to deprive their country of their bravery except as a sacrifice of the most serious contribution they could offer. For this offering of their lives made in common by them all, each of them individually receives that renown which never grows old, and for a tomb, not so much that in which their bones have been deposited, but that noblest of shrines wherein their glory is laid up to be eternally remembered upon every occasion on which deed or story shall call for its commemoration. . . . Take these as your model, and recognize that happiness comes from freedom and freedom comes from courage; never decline the dangers of war. For it is not the miserable who have the most reason to risk their lives; they have nothing to hope for: instead, it is they to whom continued life may bring reverses as yet unknown, and to whom a fall, if it came, would be most tremendous in its consequences. Surely, to a man of spirit, the degradation of cowardice must be immeasurably more grievous than the unfelt death which strikes him in the midst of his strength and patriotism.

"Comfort, therefore, not condolence, is what I have to offer to the parents of the dead who may be here. Numberless are the chances to which, as they know, the life of man is subject; but fortunate indeed are they who draw their lot a death so glorious as that which has caused your mourning, and to whom life has been so exactly measured as to terminate in the happiness in which it has been passed. . . . If I must say anything on the subject of female excellence to those of you who will now be in widowhood, it will all be comprised in this brief exhortation: great will be your glory in not falling short of your natural character; and greatest will be hers who is least talked of among the men whether for good or bad. My task is now finished. I have performed it to the best of my ability, and in words at least the requirements of the law are now satisfied. If deeds be in question, those who are here interred have received part of their honors already, and for the rest, their children will be brought up till manhood at the public expense: thus the state offers a valuable prize as the garland of victory in this race of valor, for the reward both of those who have fallen and their survivors. And where the rewards for merit are greatest, there the best citizens are found.

"And now that you have brought to a close your lamentations for your relatives, you may depart."

The Melian Conference

The Melians are a colony of Lacedæmon that would not submit to the Athenians like the other islanders, and at first remained neutral and took no part in the struggle, but afterwards upon the Athenians using violence and plundering their territory, assumed an attitude of open hostility. . . . The generals, encamping in their territory . . . before doing any harm to their land, sent envoys to negotiate. These the Melians did not bring before the people, but bade them state the object of their mission to the magistrates and the few; upon which the Athenian envoys spoke as follows: . . .

Athenians: "For ourselves, we shall not trouble you with specious pretences—either of how we have a right to our empire because we overthrew the Mede, or are now attacking you because of wrong that you have done us—and make a long speech which would not be believed; and in return we hope that you, instead of thinking to influence us by saying that you did not join the Lacedæmonians, although their colonists, or that you have done us no wrong, will aim at what is feasible, holding in view the real sentiments of us both; since you know as well as we do that right, as the world goes, is only in question between equals in power, while the strong do what they can and the weak suffer what they must."

Melians: "As we think, at any rate, it is expedient—we speak as we are obliged, since you enjoin us to let right alone and talk only of interest—that you should not destroy what is our common protection, the privilege of being allowed in danger to invoke what is fair and right, and even to profit by arguments not strictly valid if they can be got to pass current. And you are as much interested in this as any, as your fall would be a signal for the heaviest vengeance and an example for the world to meditate upon."

Athenians: "The end of our empire, if end it should, does not frighten us: a rival empire like Lacedæmon, even if Lacedæmon was our real antagonist, is not so terrible to the vanquished as subjects who by themselves attack and overpower their rulers. . . . We will now proceed to show you that we are come here in the interest of our empire, and that we shall say what we are now going to say for the preservation of your country; as we would fain exercise that empire over you without trouble, and see you preserved for the good of us both."

Melians: "And how, pray, could it turn out as good for us to serve as for you to rule?"

Athenians: "Because you would have the advantage of submitting before suffering the worst, and we should gain by not destroying you."

Melians: "So that you would not consent to our being neutral, friends instead of enemies, but allies of neither side."

Athenians: "No; for your hostility cannot so much hurt us as your friendship will be an argument to our subjects of our weakness, and your enmity of our power."

Melians: "Is that your subjects' idea of equity, to put those who have nothing to do with you in the same category with peoples that are most of them your own colonists, and some conquered rebels?"

Athenians: "As far as right goes they think one has as much of it as the other, and that if any maintain their independence it is because they are strong, and that if we do not molest them it is because we are afraid; so that besides extending our empire we should gain in security by your subjection; the fact that you are islanders and weaker than others rendering it all the more important that you should not succeed in baffling the masters of the sea." . . .

Melians: "Well then, if you risk so much to retain your empire, and your subjects to get rid of it, it were surely great baseness and cowardice in us who are still free not to try everything that can be tried, before submitting to your yoke."

Athenians: "Not if you are well advised, the contest not being an equal one, with honour as the prize and shame as the penalty, but a question of self-preservation and of not resisting those who are far stronger than you are."

Melians: "But we know that the fortune of war is sometimes more impartial than the disproportion of numbers might lead one to suppose; to submit is to give ourselves over to despair, while action still preserves for us a hope that we may stand erect."

Athenians: "Hope, danger's comforter, may be indulged in by those who have abundant resources, if not without loss at all events without ruin; but its nature is to be extravagant, and those who go so far as to put their all upon the venture see it in its true colours only when they are ruined. . . ."

Melians: "You may be sure that we are as well aware as you of the difficulty of contending against your power and fortune, unless the terms be equal. But we trust that the gods may grant us fortune as good as yours, since we are just men fighting against unjust, and that what we want in power will be made up by the alliance of the Lacedæmonians. . . ."

Athenians: "When you speak of the favour of the gods, we may as fairly hope for that as yourselves; neither our pretensions nor our conduct being in any way contrary to what men believe of the gods, or practise among themselves. Of the gods we believe, and of men we know, that by a necessary law of their nature they rule wherever they can. . . . But when we come to your notion about the Lacedæmonians, which leads you to believe that shame will make them help you, here we bless your simplicity but do not envy your folly. The Lacedæmonians, when their own interests or their country's laws are in question, are the worthiest men alive; of their conduct towards others much might be said, but no clearer idea of it could be given than by shortly saying that of all the men we know they are most conspicuous in considering what is agreeable honourable, and what is expedient just. Such a way of thinking does not promise much for the safety which you now unreasonably count upon."

Melians: "But it is for this very reason that we now trust to their respect for expediency to prevent them from betraying the Melians, their colonists, and thereby losing the confidence of their friends in Hellas and helping their enemies." . . .

Athenians: "Yes, but what an intending ally trusts to, is not the goodwill of those who ask his aid, but a decided superiority of power for action; and the Lacedæmonians look to this even more than others. At least, such is their distrust of their home resources that it is only with numerous allies that they attack a neighbour; now is it likely that while we are masters of the sea they will cross over to an island? . . . Your strongest arguments depend upon hope and the future, and your actual resources are too scanty, as compared with those arrayed against you, for you to come out victorious. You will therefore show great blindness of judgment, unless, after allowing us to retire, you can find some counsel more prudent than this. You will surely not be caught by that idea of disgrace, which in dangers that are disgraceful, and at the same time too plain to be mistaken, proves so fatal to mankind. . . . You will not think it dishonourable to submit to the greatest city in Hellas, when it makes you the moderate offer of becoming its tributary ally, without ceasing to enjoy the country that belongs to you; nor when you have the choice given you between war and security, will you be so blinded as to choose the worse. And it is certain that those who do not yield to their equals, who keep terms with their superiors, and are moderate towards their inferiors, on the whole succeed best. Think over the matter, therefore, after our withdrawal, and reflect once and again that it is for your country that you are consulting, that you have not more than one, and that upon this one deliberation depends its prosperity or ruin."

The Athenians now withdrew from the conference; and the Melians, left to themselves, came to a decision corresponding with what they had maintained in the discussion, and answered, "Our resolution, Athenians, is the same as it was at first. We will not in a moment deprive of freedom a city that has been inhabited these seven hundred years; but we put our trust in the fortune by which the gods have preserved it until now, and in the help of men, that is, of the Lacedæmonians; and so we will try and save ourselves. Meanwhile we invite you to allow us to be friends to you and foes to neither party, and to retire from our country after making such a treaty as shall seem fit to us both."

Such was the answer of the Melians. The Athenians now departing from the conference said, "Well, you alone, as it seems to us, judging from these resolutions, regard what is future as more certain than what is before your eyes, and what is out of sight, in your eagerness, as already coming to pass; and as you have staked most on, and trusted most in, the Lacedæmonians, your fortune, and your hopes, so will you be most completely deceived."

The Athenian envoys now returned to the army; and the Melians showing no signs of yielding, the generals at once betook themselves to hostilities. . . . Subsequently the Athenians returned with most of their army, leaving behind them a certain number of their own citizens and of the allies to keep guard by land and sea. The force thus left stayed on and besieged the place. . . .

Summer was now over. The next winter the Lacedæmonians intended to invade the Argive territory, but arriving at the frontier found the sacrifices for crossing unfavourable, and went back again. . . . About the same time the Melians again took another part of the Athenian lines which were but feebly garrisoned. Reinforcements afterwards arriving from Athens, . . . the siege was now pressed vigorously; and some treachery taking place inside, the Melians surrendered at discretion to the Athenians, who put to death all the grown men whom they took, and sold the women and children for slaves, and subsequently sent out five hundred colonists and inhabited the place themselves.

30

Plato, *The Republic*

Socrates wrote nothing himself but devoted much of his later life to disputations in which he sought to define the eternal "forms" of items of human interest, such as beauty, love, and immortality. Socrates was a master of the "dialectic," defined then as the art of posing and answering questions to separate error and half-truths from reality. Plato wrote many dialogues in which Socrates is the main speaker and practitioner of the dialectic; however, it is impossible to know whether the statements attributed to Socrates were actually his own or Plato's. But because Plato was such a devoted admirer of Socrates, it seems likely that most of his summaries of Socrates' ideas were accurate.

Five years after the end of the Peloponnesian War (431–404 B.C.), Socrates was convicted by an Athenian court of denying the existence of Greek gods and of corrupting the youth of Athens. The trial and ensuing death sentence were probably the results of Socrates' having antagonized too many prominent Athenians for too long. The charge that he rejected the Greek gods was not altogether false, however: Although Socrates deeply believed in divine beings, these seldom resembled traditional Greek gods.

In the following selections from Plato's *The Republic,* Socrates (the main speaker) attempts to lead his respondents to the discovery of true justice. These excerpts demonstrate the range of subject matter and style that Plato, inspired by Socrates, was able to use in his dialogues. The first selection exemplifies the dialectical pursuit of human excellence (or "virtue" in this and most other translations). The second selection uses forceful arguments for the political equality of women, an idea completely rejected by Aristotle, whose unabashed male chauvinism was much more in keeping with the times. The third selection presents an allegory or parable, which attempts to show the real meaning of Socrates' death by contrasting the actual position of philosophers in society with the position they deserve to have in an ideal world.

Plato's *Republic* has nothing to do with a "republic" in the modern sense of the word. *Politeia* or "Polity," Plato's own name for this work, is the abstract term for *polis* or "city-state." His polity (crudely "polis-ship") relates to polis as "kingship" does to "king." It features the set of ideals arrived at by the dialectic, including a stress on collective ownership in economics and a monopolization of power by a philosophic elite.

QUESTIONS TO CONSIDER

1. What are the four main aspects of human excellence (or cardinal virtues) for Socrates/Plato?
2. What does the example about bleaching and dyeing cloth illustrate?

3. Does Socrates/Plato define justice as you would? Why or why not?
4. How does Socrates/Plato attempt to prove the basic equality of women and men?
5. How does "The Allegory of the Cave" illustrate the story of Socrates? How does this allegory show the role of public opinion in a democracy?
6. How would you compare the concept of *virtue* in the *Analects* of Confucius (see Reading 24) with that in Plato's work?

The Search for the Four Cardinal Virtues

[T]he city we have founded—if we have built rightly—will be good in the fullest sense of the word.

The city is wise, courageous, temperate, and just. Of these virtues, wisdom is evidently the first. The city is certainly wise, for it abounds in good counsel, but there are many diverse skills in the city and many proficiencies. Consider those practiced by carpenters, smiths, and farmers. Are these the skills that produce wisdom and prudence in governing?

No. They could only serve to produce and teach excellence in cabinetry, ironworking, and agriculture.

Is there any form of skill or knowledge possessed by some of the citizens that attends not to particular interests but to the general interest, to the city as a whole? Yes. It is the art of guardianship practiced by the city's rulers.

What description will fit the city possessing this kind of knowledge?

A city that is prudent and truly wise. . . .

If we follow the same approach, I think we can discover the nature of courage. Now whoever calls a city brave or cowardly will think first about its armed forces. The character of the city is not determined by the bravery or cowardice of the citizenry as a whole, but by the part of it that is steadfast in its convictions about what is to be feared and what is not to be feared.

Courage is a preservative. Courage makes a man hold fast to convictions no matter whether he is threatened by danger or lured by desire. I shall try to illustrate what I mean with a comparison.

Consider dyers. When they wish to dye wool so that it will hold fast the true sea-purple color, they choose a white wool. Then they prepare the wool with great care so that the white may perfectly absorb the purple. What is dyed in this way is color-fast, and neither soap nor lye can dull the color's brilliance. But if these procedures are neglected, you know what purple or any other color will look like.

Yes, it will be faded and ugly.

So we make this comparison with the dyers to illustrate the results we were trying to achieve in selecting our soldiers and educating them in music and gymnastics. We were contriving influences that would lead them to take on the colors of our institutions like a dye. With the right temperament and the right education their convictions about danger would be indelibly fixed. They would refuse to yield their convictions because of sorrow, fear, or desire. The quality I call courage, then, is the strength to hold fast to the proper convictions about what is worth fearing and what is not. . . .

[A]fter wisdom and courage we wanted to search out two further virtues in the city. One is temperance—or moderation. . . .

Temperance is the ordering or controlling of certain pleasures and desires. There is both good and bad in the soul of man. When the good part governs the bad, a man is praised for being master of himself. But if bad education or bad company subjects the good to the bad, a man will be blamed for being unprincipled and a slave of self.

If temperance and self-mastery are in charge, if the better part rules the worse, we may well say that the city is master of itself. We may properly call our city temperate.

Now we have inquired into three of the four chief qualities of our city. The fourth and final quality is justice. You remember the original principle we laid down at the founding of the city: each citizen should perform that work or function for which his nature best suits him. This is the principle, or some variation of it, that we may call justice.

We often said that.

We also said that justice was tending to one's own business and not meddling in others'.

Yes.

So minding one's own business really appears, in one sense, at least, to be justice. Do you know how I reached this conclusion?

No.

You remember we were inquiring into the four cardinal virtues of a city. We examined temperance, courage, and wisdom; now justice remains the one still to be considered. What we will find is that justice sustains and perfects the other three; justice is the ultimate cause and condition of their existence.

Which of the four virtues effectually contributes most to the excellence of the city? Is it the harmony existing between rulers and subjects? Is it the soldier's fidelity to what he has learned about real and fictitious dangers? Or wisdom and watchfulness in the rulers? Or, finally, is it the virtue that is found in everyone which leads them each to do his own work and not to interfere with others?

We can at least accept the conclusion that the fourth virtue of minding one's own business rivals the other three virtues in contributing to the city's excellence. That is to say that justice is at least the equal of wisdom, courage, and temperance.

Position of Women in the Ideal State

[I]t is time to speak of women. . . . Let us assume that the birth and education of women will be governed by the same guidelines we prescribed for the man. We can decide later whether or not this procedure seems appropriate.

What do you mean?

This. Do we separate off male and female dogs from one another, or do we expect both to share equally in standing guard and in going out to hunt? Should all activities be shared, or do we expect the females to remain indoors on the grounds that bearing and nursing the pups incapacitate them for anything else, leaving to the males the exclusive care and guarding of the flocks?

There should be no such differentiation. The only distinction between them is that we consider males to be stronger and females weaker.

Now then, can one get any animal to perform the same functions as another without giving both the same guidance and training?

No.

Then if women are to do the same things as men, we must also teach them the same things.

Yes.

The men were taught music and gymnastics, were they not?

Yes.

It follows that we must teach the women the same two arts, as well as learning and practice in the art of war.

From what you have said I suppose it does follow.

Perhaps conventional wisdom would ridicule some of these proposals if we tried to put them into practice.

It surely would.

Well, what do you think would be the most obvious target for ridicule? Perhaps the idea of women attending the wrestling schools and exercising naked with the men, especially when they are no longer young? The whole scene would resemble the behavior of those zealous old men who still persist in going off to exercise in the gymnasium despite all their wrinkles and ugliness.

Our present notions would call the whole thing absurd.

Yet we have vowed to speak our minds. Therefore we must not be daunted by all the wisecracks that will greet such innovations. Nor must we mind what the resident wits say about women studying music and gymnastics, about women bearing arms, nor, above all, what they say about women riding astride horses.

You are right. . . .

The basic question concerns the nature of women: can a woman perform all or none of the tasks a man performs? Can she manage some but not others? Is she really capable of waging war? . . .

We can clarify our meaning by observing, for example, that a man and a woman who both have the qualifications to be a physician have the same nature. Do you agree?

Yes.

But two men, one a physician and one a carpenter, have different natures?

Oh, entirely different.

So, then, those men and women who display distinct aptitudes for any given kind of work will be assigned to do that work. If a critic can do no more than bring up the one distinction between man and woman—that the one begets and the other bears children—we shall say that for our purposes he has offered no proof of difference at all. . . .

And we shall be right in doing so. . . .

Then we must conclude that sex cannot be the criterion in appointments to government positions. No office should be reserved for a man just because he is a man or for a woman just because she is a woman. All the capabilities with which nature endows us are distributed among men and women alike. Hence women will have the rightful opportunity to share in every task, and so will men, even though women are the weaker of the two sexes.

Agreed. . . .

The Allegory of the Cave

Here allegory may show us best how education—or the lack of it—affects our nature. Imagine men living in a cave. Imagine further that since childhood the cave dwellers have had their legs and necks shackled so as to prevent them from turning their heads; they can see only directly in front of them. Next, imagine a light from a fire some distance behind them. Between the prisoners and the fire is a raised path along whose edge there is a low wall.

Imagine, further, men behind the wall carrying all sorts of objects along its length and holding them above it. Presumably, those who carry them sometimes speak and are sometimes silent.

Do you not think those men would see only the shadows cast by the fire on the wall of the cave? Would they have seen anything of themselves or of one another?

How could they if they couldn't move their heads their whole life long?

Could they see the objects held above the wall behind them or only the shadows cast in front?

Only the shadows.

Don't you think they would impute reality to the passing shadows?

Necessarily.

Imagine an echo in their prison, bouncing off the wall toward which the prisoners were turned. Should one of those behind the wall speak, would the prisoners not think that the sound came from the shadows in front of them?

No doubt of it.

By every measure, then, reality for the prisoners would be nothing but shadows.

It could be nothing else.

Imagine how their liberation from bondage and error would come about if something like the following happened. One prisoner is freed from his shackles. He is suddenly compelled to stand up, turn around, walk, and look toward the light. He suffers pain and distress from the glare of the light. So dazzled is he that he cannot even discern the very objects whose shadows he used to be able to see. Now what do you suppose he would answer if he were told that all he had seen before was illusion but that now he was observing real things and therefore seeing more truly? Would he not be at a loss? Would he not regard those things he saw formerly as more real than the things now being shown him?

He would.

Again, let him be compelled to look directly at the light. Would his eyes not feel pain? Would he not flee, turning back to those things he was able to discern before, convinced that they are in every truth clearer and more exact than anything he has seen since?

He would.

Then let him be dragged away by force up the rough and steep incline of the cave's passageway, held fast until he is hauled out into the light of the sun. Would not such a rough passage be painful? Would he not resent the experience? And would he not be able to see what he calls realities?

He could not see even one of them, at least not immediately.

Habituation, then, is evidently required in order to see things higher up. In the beginning he would most easily see shadows; next, reflections in the water. Then he would see the objects themselves. Finally, I suppose, he would be able to look on the sun itself and be able to see what it is really like.

Yes.

It is at this stage that he would be able to conclude that the sun is the cause of the seasons and of the year's turning, that it governs all the visible world and is in some sense also the cause of all visible things.

This is surely the next step he would take.

Now, supposing he recalled where he came from. Supposing he thought of his fellow prisoners and of what passed for wisdom in the cave. Don't you think he would feel pity for all that and rejoice in his own change of circumstance?

He surely would.

Suppose there had been honors and citations those below bestowed upon one another. Suppose prizes were offered for the one quickest to identify the shadows as they go by. Do you think he would covet such rewards?

I think he would prefer anything to such a life.

Consider, further, if he should go back down again into the cave and return to the place he was before, would not his eyes now go dark after so abruptly leaving the sunlight behind?

They would.

Suppose he should then have to compete once more in shadow watching with those who never left the cave. Would he not be laughed at? Would it not be said that he had made the journey above only to come back with his eyes ruined and that it is futile even to attempt the ascent?

Of course.

Now, we must apply the allegory as a whole to all that has been said so far. The prisoners' cave is the counterpart of our own visible order. If you liken the ascent and exploration of things above to the soul's journey through the intelligible order, you will have understood my thinking. In the intelligible world the last thing to be seen—and then only dimly—is the idea of the good. Once seen, however, the conclusion becomes irresistible that it is the cause of all things right and good, that in the visible world it gives birth to light and its sovereign source, that in the intelligible world it is itself sovereign and the author of truth and reason, and that the man who will act wisely in private and public life must have seen it. . . .

31

Aristotle, *Politics*

Aristotle studied with Plato for some twenty years, but in his philosophy he reacted against many of the teachings of Socrates/Plato. Aristotle did not believe in a separate, transcendent world of "forms" that could be reached through the dialectic, but rather in gathering knowledge by observing specifics, leading to general conclusions. He shared the very strong interest of Socrates/Plato in examining the ideal state, but his own findings were very different from those in Plato's *Republic*. In contrast with his teacher, Aristotle did not believe that extensive collective ownership would benefit society, and he looked to the middle class, rather than to philosophers, as the mainstay of the best possible government. "Polity" for Aristotle became the form of government with the best record in providing for stability and human happiness. He uses it, as in the reading that follows, as a synonym for "constitutional government" or "mixed government," containing both aristocratic and democratic elements.

QUESTIONS TO CONSIDER

1. Why does Aristotle consider political science to be the highest field of study? Do you agree with him?
2. What is Aristotle's view of holding property in common as opposed to private property?
3. On the basis of what Aristotle writes about polity or constitutional government, is it possible to see in him an early advocate of the theory of checks and balances?

Ethics as the Search for the Good of Mankind

Every art or systematic inquiry—in reality, every action and goal—seems to aim at some good, so that *the good* is correctly defined as the end at which all things aim. . . . Still, ends differ: some are actions, others are results, rather than the actions which bring them about. In the latter case, it is natural for the results to be valued higher than the actions. . . .

If we find something desirable for its own sake and find also that everything else seems desirable for the sake of this one thing . . . , then clearly we have found *the good,* meaning "the supreme good." Will knowledge of it not be a main determining factor in our lives? Will it not give us, like archers, a proper target to aim at? If there be such a thing, we must try to ascertain what it is and which arts and sciences search for it. It would have to be the object of the most sovereign and comprehensive study.

We find that political study meets the requirements of this master art and science: politics determines what other studies should be pursued in the city-states, what each class of people should learn and how much. We find that politics controls education in the most respected fields of study, such as military strategy, economics and rhetoric. Since it uses the other branches of knowledge and controls what people should and should not do, the goals of political science subsume the goals of the others, making the ends of politics the general ends of mankind. . . .

Origins of the State

Every state is a community of some kind, and every community is established with a view to some good, for mankind always acts in order to obtain what is thought good. But if all communities aim at some good, the state or political community, which is the highest of all, and which embraces the rest, aims at the highest good in greater degree than any other. . . .

Before a state can exist, there must first be a union of those who cannot exist without each other; for example, of male and female, that the race may continue. This is a union which is formed with no deliberate purpose, but because, in common with other animals and even plants, people have a natural desire to leave behind them an image of themselves. Secondly, there must be a union of natural ruler and subject, that both may be preserved. For those who can foresee with their minds are by nature intended to be lords and masters, and those who work with their bodies are subjects and natural slaves; hence master and slave have the same interest. . . .

Of these two relationships, between man and woman, master and slave, the family arises first. . . . The family is the association established by nature for the supply of men's everyday wants. . . . But when several families are united, and the association aims at something more than the supply of daily needs, the village then comes into existence. . . . When several villages are united into a single, complete community, large enough to be nearly or totally self-sufficing, the city-state comes into existence, originating in the bare needs of life and continuing its existence for the sake of a good life. And therefore, if the earlier forms of society are natural, so is the state, for it is the culmination of them. . . . Hence it is evident that the state is a creation of nature and that man is by nature a political animal. He

First section from Aristotelis *Ethica Nicomachea,* ed. Franciscus Susemihl (Leipzig: B.G. Teubner, 1903), I, i, 1094a–1094b; trans. Henry A. Myers. Remaining sections from *The Politics of Aristotle,* trans. Benjamin Jowett, rev. ed. (New York: Colonial Press, 1899), I,1., 1252a–1253a; II, v, 1262b–1263b; IV, vii, 1294a–b; IV, xi, 1295b; V, ix, 1309b; language slightly modernized; condensed by Marcella A. Smith.

who by nature and not by mere accident is without a state is either above or below human-ity. . . . It is a characteristic of man that he alone has any sense of good and evil, of just or unjust, and the like, and the association of living beings who have this sense makes a fam-ily and a state. . . .

Private versus Community Held Property

. . .What should be our arrangements concerning property: should the citizens of the per-fect state have their possessions in common or not? . . . When farmers farm their land, ques-tions arising from common ownership will give a world of trouble. If they do not share equally in enjoyments and toils, those who labor much and get little will necessarily com-plain to those who labor little and receive or consume much. Indeed there is always a dif-ficulty in men living together and having all human relations in common, but especially in their having common property. . . .

In one sense property should be common, but, as a general rule, private. When every-one has a separate interest, men will not complain about one another, and they will make more progress, because each one will be attending to his own business. And yet, by reason of goodness and in matters of use, "Friends," as the proverb says, "have all things in com-mon." Even now there are traces of this principle, showing that it is not impossible, but in well-ordered states, exists already to a certain extent and may be carried further. For al-though a man has his own property, some things he will place at the disposal of friends, while he will share the use of them with others. The Spartans, for example, use one another's slaves, horses and dogs, as if they were their own; and when they lack provisions on a jour-ney they appropriate what they find in the fields throughout the country. It is clearly better that property should be private, but the use of it common. . . .

The Best Possible State in This Imperfect World

Now let us consider how by the side of oligarchy and democracy, the so-called "polity" or constitutional government springs up and how it should be organized. The nature of it will be at once understood from a comparison of oligarchy and democracy: we must ascertain their different characteristics and, taking a portion from each, put the two together. . . . There are three systems by which fusions of government may be brought about. Using the first, we must combine the laws made by both governments, say concerning the administration of justice. In oligarchies they impose a fine on the rich if they do not serve on juries, and to the poor they give no pay when they do serve, but in democracies they give pay to the poor and do not fine the rich. Now combining these two approaches would achieve a middle ground between them, a characteristic of constitutional government, for it is a union of both. A second way is to take a mean between the enactments of the two: democracies require no property qualification, or only a small one, for serving in the assembly, oligarchies a high one, and here a mean or middle ground can be located between them. There is a third way, in which something is borrowed from the oligarchic and something from the democratic principle. For example, the appointment of magistrates by lot is perceived as democratic and the election of them oligarchic; democratic again when there is no property qualifica-tion and oligarchic when there is. In the . . . constitutional state, one element will be taken from each: from oligarchy the principle of electing officials, from democracy the absence of any property qualification to serve. Such are the various modes of combination. There is a true union of oligarchy and democracy when the same state may be termed either a democracy or an oligarchy: those who use both names feel that fusion is complete. . . . Oligarchy or democracy, although a departure from the most perfect form, may yet be a good enough government, but if anyone attempts to push the principle of either to an extreme, he will begin by spoiling the government and end up having none at all. For neither form can begin or continue existence unless both rich and poor are included in it. . . .

We now have to inquire what is the best constitution for most states, and the best life for most men, neither assuming a standard of virtue which is above ordinary persons, nor an education which is exceptionally favored by nature and circumstances . . . , but having regard to the life in which the majority are able to share, and to the form of government which states in general can attain. . . .

Now in all states there are three elements: one class is very rich, another very poor, and a third in a mean. It is well known that moderation and the mean are best, and therefore it will clearly be best to possess the gifts of fortune in moderation; for in that condition of life men are most ready to follow rational principles. But he who greatly excels in good looks, strength, birth or wealth, or on the other hand who is very poor or very weak, or very much disgraced, finds it difficult to follow rational principles. Men of the first sort grow into violent and great criminals, those of the second into rogues and petty rascals. . . . The middle class is least likely to resent rule, or to be over-ambitious for it, both of which are injurious to the state. The evil begins at home: when they are boys, by reason of the luxury in which they are brought up, they never learn the habit of obedience, even at school. On the other hand, the very poor, who are in the opposite extreme, are too degraded. The result is that one class cannot obey, and can only rule despotically; the other does not know how to command and must be ruled like slaves. Thus a city-state arises, not of free men but of masters and slaves, the one despising, the other envying. Nothing can be more fatal to friendship and good fellowship in states than this, for good fellowship springs from friendship, while when men are hostile to one another they would rather not even share the same path. A city-state ought to be composed, as far as possible, of equals and similars, and these are generally the middle classes. Wherefore the city which is composed of middle-class citizens is necessarily best constituted from the elements of which we say the fabric of the state naturally consists. This is the class of citizens which is most secure in a state, for they do not, like the poor, covet their neighbors' goods; nor do others covet theirs, as the poor covet the goods of the rich. As they neither plot against others, nor are themselves plotted against, they pass through life safely. . . . Thus it is obvious that the best political community is formed by citizens of the middle class and that those states are likely to be well-administered, in which the middle class is large, and stronger if possible than both the other classes. . . .

Roman Contributions to Ideologies of Government and Law

Although the Romans were not particularly interested in abstract thought about political matters, they contributed political ideas of lasting significance to succeeding civilizations. They imparted these ideas in large part through stories about heroes and villains who served Rome well or badly and through commentaries on law in many forms.

The Roman Republic (ca. 509–31 B.C.) became the model of "mixed government," or a government of checks and balances. Since it lasted a long time and led Rome on its successful rise to world-power status, it presented a viable alternative to monarchy; however, it is characteristic of the Roman indifference to theory making that the first systematic explanation of why the Roman form of government was so successful came to them from a Greek hostage, Polybius.

Along with the Roman concept of a Republic, Roman law helped to shape the legal systems of future civilizations in Europe and later the New World. The underlying philosophic basis was fairly simple: that laws made by man should be in harmony with Natural Law or, particularly after the triumph of Christianity, with God's Eternal Law. When it came to divisions of man-made law, the Romans refined a lasting distinction between (1) civil law, involving private disputes among citizens, and (2) criminal law, involving the public interest (see the Justinian Code, Reading 47). Later, the Germanic tribes began with a primitive system, in which all disputes were private, but, partly on the basis of the model Roman law codes, they eventually separated "private" from "public" law (see the Code of the Visigoths, Reading 54).

32

Titus Livy, *Early History of Rome*

Titus Livy (59 B.C.–A.D. 17) gave the Western world a panorama of patriotic heroes with an inspirational force well beyond that given by essays in political philosophy. His *History from the Founding of the City* (Rome since 753 B.C.) is much more comprehensive than that of Polybius, beginning with the arrival of the fabled Trojan Prince Aeneas in Rome. It continues in 142 books, of which 35 survive, down to the time of Augustus Caesar, Livy's patron. In the absence of reliable written sources for the early part of his work, Livy was forced to use oral legends that had been recorded much later, but he gave his sketches of people and events in realistic detail.

Livy's subsequent influence was immense. The realistic and cynical Machiavelli was moved by Livy's portrayal of the citizen-soldier-leader Cincinnatus (see Reading 89), and "Horatio at the Bridge" served as a model for patriotic fearlessness into the twentieth century. Almost every educated American of the seventeenth and eighteenth centuries knew Titus Livy stories. Thomas Jefferson thought he had wasted his time laboring through Plato's *Republic,* but he considered Titus Livy's work so valuable that he insisted that his daughter Martha learn to read it with ease enough not to have to ask her tutor for help with it. Livy's story of Tarquin and Lucretia articulated the Roman aversion to kings as potential tyrants and the need to have a government without them. Somewhat as Americans were to consider George III bad enough to make them swear off monarchy forever, many Romans believed that the Tarquins discredited kingship so thoroughly that likely claimants to a crown were public enemies, guilty of high treason and deserving death.

QUESTIONS TO CONSIDER

1. What sort of bet did Collatinus make with the younger Tarquin?
2. How does Lucretia embody a particular type of female virtue?
3. Why does Titus Livy assume that a republic has no place for monarchy in it? Does he differ with Polybius on that subject?
4. How did Horatio Cocles and Caius Mucius Scaevola contribute to the defense of Rome?
5. What made Porsinna abandon his attempt to reestablish the Tarquins as kings of Rome?

While . . . the young princes . . . were drinking in the camp quarters of Sextus Tarquin, they began discussing their wives, with each one showering praise upon his own. When the competitive praise really began to heat up, Collatinus said that there was no reason to settle for verbal displays and that in a few hours they could see how much better than the others his wife Lucretia was: "Why don't we—since we are young and full of energy—get on our horses and see for ourselves what our wives are doing? Let us all agree that the award of 'best wife' will be determined by what she does when her husband comes home unexpected."

"Agreed!" they all shouted, heated with wine, and soon they were urging their horses on towards Rome. It was just beginning to get dark when they arrived there. . . . [Later] they made their way to Collatia, where they discovered Lucretia occupied very differently from the daughters-in-law of the king: they had found *them* spending their time with their friends at a luxurious banquet. Lucretia, however, even though it was well into the night by then was busy working with her wool; her maids were working by lamplight around her as she sat in the great hall. There was no question then but what Lucretia won the "best wife" competition. The leading contenders were cordially received, and Collatinus, the victor, courteously offered refreshments to the young princes. Then and there wicked lust seized Sextus Tarquin: not only her beauty but her confirmed chastity lit flames of passion within him; however, for the time being they all treated what had happened as youthful sport and rode back to camp.

A few days later, Sextus Tarquin took one servant to Collatia without letting Collatinus know. He was graciously welcomed there, since no one knew what was on his mind. After dinner, he was led to a guest room. Burning with desire, he waited until he was sure that everyone around was asleep, and with sword drawn he entered the room of the sleeping Lucretia. He held her down with his left hand on her breast and told her: "Keep quiet, Lucretia. I am Sextus Tarquin; my sword is in my hand. One sound out of you, and you die!" The woman woke up with a start and saw no help at hand, only the threat of imminent death. Then Tarquin declared his love for her, pleading and threatening together, bringing pressure to bear from every angle on the woman's soul. When he saw she was stubborn and not going to be swayed by fear of death, he added the threat of shame. He said he would kill his slave and drag him naked to lie by her own corpse so that she could be reported killed in adultery with a low-born fellow. With this horrible threat, his lust finally overran her steadfast chastity, and Tarquin left in triumph over his conquest of her woman's honor.

Despairing at her fate, Lucretia sent the same message to her father at Rome and her husband at Ardea, asking each to come with a trustworthy friend and to come quickly for a

From *Titi Livi ab urbe condita libri*, ed. Wilhelm Weissenborn (Leipzig: B.G. Teubner, 1926), Part one, I, lvii; II, xv, pp. 64–86, *passim;* trans. Henry A. Myers.

terrible thing had happened. [With their friends, Valerius and Brutus] the men arrived and found Lucretia sitting sadly in her room. The presence of those dear to her brought tears to her eyes. When her husband asked, "Is everything all right?" she answered:

"Not by far. It can never be 'all right' for a woman whose honor has been stolen. The imprint of a stranger, Collatinus, is on your bed. To be sure, only my body has been violated, not my spirit. Death will be my witness for that. But raise your right hands and swear that the criminal will not escape punishment. It was Sextus Tarquin last night who repaid hospitality with the armed force of hostility to ruin me—and himself if you are men—with his perverted, fatal pleasure-taking."

One after the other each takes a solemn oath. They try to console her, by coaxing the poisonous affliction out of her and onto the perpetrator, telling her that the mind sins but not the body, and where there is no consent there is no guilt. "You will decide what is to happen to him. As for me, I absolve myself of sin but not of the need to suffer the fate which must follow. In time to come, let no defiled woman use Lucretia as an excuse to keep on living." Pulling out a knife she had concealed in her dress, she plunged it into her heart and fell forward upon her wound. . . .

While the others were still overcome by grief, Brutus pulled the knife from Lucretia's wound, and as the blood dripped from it spoke: "I swear by this blood—innocent until polluted by royalty—and you, O gods, I call to witness that I will use sword, fire and every other means of force I can apply to bring down Lucius Tarquin with his evil wife and all his children and that I will not allow any of them, nor anyone else, to rule as king in Rome!" The others swore as he told them to swear. Anger devoured their grief, and they followed Brutus as leader when he called upon them to get rid of the rule of kings. . . .

The reaction to this atrocity was every bit as furious in Rome as at Collatia. People streamed to the Forum from all parts of the city. . . . The city gates were closed to keep out Tarquin [who was at the campsite] and he was banished. . . . Rule by kings had lasted two hundred and forty years at Rome. . . . The new liberty was welcomed by the Romans so enthusiastically because of the wretched tyranny of the last king. . . . [A little later, as first consul] Brutus, for his first act of office, while the people were still jealous of their new freedom, required them to swear never to allow any man to be king in Rome. . . .

By that time the Tarquins had fled to Lars Porsena, King of Clusium, and appealed to him with both pleas and advice. Sometimes they would beg him not to permit them, his fellow Etruscans, who shared blood and family names with him, to languish in exile; sometimes they would warn him not to let this growing practice of expelling kings go unpunished. . . . Porsena, convinced that there was safety in having a king rule Rome, particularly an Etruscan king honoring his people, sent an invading army towards Rome.

Never before had such terror seized the Senators—so great was Clusium's reputation for power and Porsena's own prestige. They worried not only about the invaders but also about their own common people's being seized by such fear as to allow the royal forces into the city and accept servitude as the price of peace. To gain popular support, the Senate passed some measures favoring them: . . . the poor were excused from many obligations and taxes. These burdens were assumed by wealthier people who could afford them, and the Senate justified this with the thought that the poor paid enough by raising children for Rome. And so, with these concessions by the City Fathers, harmony within the city held firm under the suffering which was to come when the city was besieged and hunger reigned—so united were the upper and lower classes in rejecting the name of king in disgust. . . .

When the enemy approached, all the Romans left their farms for the city and surrounded it with armed men. Most of Rome seemed protected by the walls, the rest by the

Tiber, but the river bridge almost furnished the enemy a roadway or lane into Rome and would, in fact, have done so had it not been for one man: Horatio Cocles. That day he protected the fortunes of Rome himself. He was on guard at the bridge when a sudden enemy assault overran Janiculum Hill [on the other side of the Tiber from the strongly defended parts of the city]. He saw the invaders coming down the hill from there, with his own people turning into a frightened mob, dropping their weapons behind them as they broke ranks and ran. Confronting them individually, blocking their way and making them listen to him, he told them in the name of gods and men that if they deserted their posts there was no place left to flee to: if they gave up the bridge there would soon be more enemy forces on Palatine Hill and Capitol Hill than on Janiculum. Thus he warned them and ordered them to destroy the bridge with steel, fire or whatever they could find to work with and promised that he would hold back the enemy's charge to the extent that one man's body could block it. Then he walked to the far end of the bridge, his lone figure standing out against the sight of those fleeing from the fight. With his sword and shield ready for single combat, his daring made the invaders pause in amazement. Shame did keep two men from leaving him there alone. . . . With them he withstood the first, most violent onslaught but after a short time he made them retreat to safety, for little support remained under the bridge, and its demolishers were shouting for them to come back. Then, with threatening glances he looked around at the Etruscan elite. Challenging them individually to do combat with him and ridiculing them all as a group, he taunted them for accepting slavery under royal arrogance . . . while coming to take away the liberty of others. The Etruscans looked around at each other, each waiting for his comrade to start fighting with Horatio. Shame finally moved them to attack, and with a loud shout they hurled their spears against their lone enemy. He deflected all these with his shield and, determined as ever, planted his feet in the center of the far end of the bridge. The Etruscans began to advance with a charge to dislodge him, when the crash of falling bridge timbers and the simultaneous roar of joy from the Romans, who saw their work finished in time, stopped them fearfully in their tracks.

"Father Tiber," Horatio began, "I pray reverently that you will receive these arms and this soldier with a kindly current!" The he jumped, fully armed, into the Tiber and with a shower of spears striking the water around him swam unhurt across the river to his people. . . .

Porsinna responded to this defeat in his attempt to conquer Rome by ordering a siege. . . . [After the blockade had been in place for a while], grain supplies were depleted and what remained was selling at very high prices, so that Porsinna began to hope that just by sitting still he could take the city. At that point Caius Mucius, a young noble, brooded over the fact that the Roman people had never been blockaded by enemies in the days of their servitude under kings, but now, when they were free, they were being blockaded by the same Etruscans whose armies they had so often defeated, and so he made up his mind to avenge this indignity with some great and daring deed. . . . [Letting the Senate know only that he was leaving], he set out with a dagger concealed in his clothing. Arriving at the Etruscan camp, he wedged himself into a dense crowd near the platform on which the king was sitting. It was payday for his soldiers and a paymaster was sitting by the king, dressed almost the same way as he, and very busy since most of the soldiers transacted their business with him. Mucius was afraid to ask which of the two was the king, lest his ignorance of who the king was give away who *he* was. Trusting to Fortune, he stabbed the paymaster instead of the king. As he tried to carve a path back through the crowd with his bloody blade, shouts resounded and royal bodyguards surrounded him and led him back to the platform. Yet completely alone and seemingly abandoned by Fortune, his face stayed grim and threatening as befit a man to be feared rather than one afraid: "I am a Roman citizen," he began, "named Caius Mucius. As your enemy, I wanted to kill you, but I am just as ready to die as I was to kill. It is the Roman way to act and to suffer bravely. Nor am I the only one determined to assassinate you. A long line of men behind me will seek the same honor. Get ready if you want for the coming struggle in which you will try to save your life from hour to hour, having one enemy with a dagger after another on your doorstep. This is the kind of war we young men of Rome declare on you. You need fear neither marching ranks nor pitched battles: it will be all between your own self and us, one at a time."

The king, enraged but also very anxious about the danger to himself, ordered the prisoner to be burned alive unless he would give him the details of the plot he had just outlined. "So that you may see how cheap our men who have their eyes fixed on glory consider their bodies—" said Mucius, and with that he shoved his right hand into the altar-fire which had been lit for sacrificing. When he let his hand burn as if his spirit removed any sensation of pain, the king jumped from his seat in astonishment and ordered the young man removed from the altar. "Go free, you who dare injure yourself more than me! I would pray that your bravery be rewarded with success if it were bravery on behalf of my country; at least I am releasing you with no charges of crime and no painful penalties from me."

As if responding to the king's generosity, Mucius answered: "Since you honor bravery, I will give you information in gratitude which you could not have tortured out of me: three hundred young men from Rome's leading families are members of this conspiracy to finish you off by violent means. I drew the first lot. Whoever draws the next and the next after that will seek you out in turn, until Fortune gives one of us an opportunity to get you."

Emissaries from Porsinna arrived in Rome following the release of Mucius, who was afterwards known as "Scaevola" (Lefty) because of his missing right hand. . . . The king had been so disturbed . . . that he sent peace proposals to the Romans. . . .

Peace was concluded, but later Porsinna sought to open negotiations for the restoration of the Tarquins, and the Romans sent their most distinguished Senators to reply, saying they were in hopes of closing discussion on that issue once and for all and that they wanted to remove any hindrance to mutually beneficial relations—the hindrance being royal requests for something incompatible with Roman liberty, asking them to give up something essential for the sake of being agreeable, requiring the Romans to keep on denying his request to a man to whom they did not wish to deny anything. Rome was not to be a kingdom but was to remain in freedom. The Romans were determined to open their gates to enemies sooner than to kings. The Romans were all united in a single prayer—that the city could come to an end when its liberty ended.

33

Polybius, "Why Romans and Not Greeks Govern the World"

The Romans sent men of prominence or from prominent families from those Greek city-states with a recent history of resistance to Rome as hostages in order to ensure the good behavior of the Greek leaders now subject to Rome. In this role, Polybius (ca. 205–125 B.C.), who had been a cavalry general and ambassador to Egypt for the Achaean League (of Greek city-states) arrived in Rome around 170 B.C.

Polybius got along splendidly with the Roman leaders he met and seems to have noted a cavernous gap in Roman historiography and political philosophy that he could fill with his Greek erudition. After some twenty years in Rome, the surviving hostages of his group were allowed to return to Greece, but Polybius stayed and wrote *Universal History* in forty books, which is largely the history of Rome during the hundred years up to his own time and an interpretation of why Rome had become the world power it was. In the following selection, he analyzes the governmental system of the Roman Republic.

QUESTIONS TO CONSIDER

1. Why does Polybius think that checks and balances have given lasting stability to the Roman political system?
2. How does Polybius divide the Roman government into branches? How is his tripartite division both similar to and different from the system outlined in the U.S. Constitution?
3. How does aristocracy fit into the Roman system, according to Polybius? Does the concept of aristocracy play any part in the U.S. Constitution?

With those Greek states which have often risen to greatness and then experienced a complete change of fortune, it is easy to describe their past and to predict their future. For there is no difficulty in reporting the known facts, and it is not hard to foretell the future by inference from the past. But it is no simple matter to explain the present state of the Roman constitution, nor to predict its future owing to our ignorance of the peculiar features of Roman life in the past. Particular attention and study are therefore required if one wishes to survey clearly the distinctive qualities of Rome's constitution.

Most writers distinguish three kinds of constitutions: kingship, aristocracy, and democracy. One might ask them whether these three are the sole varieties or rather the best. In either case they are wrong. It is evident that the best constitution is one combining all three varieties, since we have had proof of this not only theoretically but by actual experience, Lycurgus having organized the Spartan state under a constitution based upon this principle. Nor can we agree that these three are the only kinds of states. We have witnessed monarchical and tyrannical governments, which differ sharply from true kingship, yet bear a certain resemblance to it. Several oligarchical constitutions also seem to resemble aristocratic ones. The same applies to democracies.

We must not apply the title of kingship to every monarchy, but must reserve it for one voluntarily accepted by willing subjects who are ruled by good judgment and not by terror and violence. Nor can we call every oligarchy an aristocracy, but only one where the government is in the hands of a selected body of the justest and wisest men. Similarly the name of democracy cannot be applied to a state in which the masses are free to do whatever they wish, but only to a community where it is traditional and customary to reverence the gods, honor one's parents, respect one's elders, and obey the laws. Such states, provided the will of the greater number prevails, are to be called democracies.

From Polybius, *Historiarum reliquiae* (Paris: Didot, 1839), VI, iii–xvii, pp. 338–48, *passim;* trans. and condensed by Henry A. Myers.

We should therefore recognize six kinds of governments: the three above mentioned, kingship, aristocracy, and democracy, and the three which are naturally related to them, monarchy, oligarchy, and ochlocracy (mob-rule). The first to arise was monarchy, its growth being natural and unaided; the next is true kingship born from monarchy by planning and reforms. Kingship is transformed into its vicious related form, tyranny; and next, the abolishment of both gives birth to aristocracy. Aristocracy by its very nature degenerates into oligarchy; and when the masses take vengeance on this government for its unjust rule, democracy is born; and in due course the arrogance and lawlessness of this form of government produces mob-rule to complete the cycle. Such is the recurring cycle of constitutions; such is the system devised by nature.

Rome, foreseeing the dangers presented by such a cycle, did not organize her government according to any one type, but rather tried to combine all the good features of the best constitutions. All three kinds of government shared in the control of the Roman state. Such fairness and propriety was shown in the use of these three types in drawing up the constitution, that it was impossible to say with certainty if the whole system was aristocratic, democratic, or monarchical. If one looked at the power of the Consuls, the constitution seemed completely monarchical; if at that of the Senate, it seemed aristocratic; and if at the power of the masses, it seemed clearly to be a democracy.

Roman Consuls exercise authority over all public affairs. All other magistrates except the tribunes are under them and bound to obey them, and they introduce embassies to the Senate. They consult the Senate on matters of urgency, they carry out in detail the provisions of its decrees, they summon assemblies, introduce measures, and preside over the execution of popular decrees. In war their power is almost uncontrolled; for they are empowered to make demands on allies, to appoint military tribunes, and to select soldiers. They also have the right of inflicting punishment on anyone under their command, and spending any sum they decide upon from the public funds. If one looks at this part of the administration alone, one may reasonably pronounce the constitution to be a pure monarchy or kingship.

To pass to the Senate: in the first place it has the control of the treasury, all revenue and expenditure being regulated by it; with the exception of payments made to the consuls, no disbursements are made without a decree of the Senate. Public works, whether constructions or repairs, are under the control of the Senate. Crimes such as treason, conspiracy, poisoning, and assassination, as well as civil disputes, are under the jurisdiction of the Senate. The Senate also sends all embassies to foreign countries to settle differences, impose demands, receive submission, or declare war; and with respect to embassies arriving in Rome it decides what reception and what answer should be given to them. All these matters are in the hands of the Senate, so that in these respects the constitution appears to be entirely aristocratic.

After this we are naturally inclined to ask what part in the constitution is left for the people. The Senate controls all the particular matters I mentioned and manages all finances, and the Consuls have uncontrolled authority as regards armaments and operations in the field. But there is a very important part left for the people. For the people alone have the right to confer honors and inflict punishment, the only bonds by which human society is held together. For where the distinction between rewards and punishment is overlooked, or is observed but badly applied, no affairs can be properly administered. For how can one expect rational administration when good and evil men are held in equal estimation? The people judge cases punishable by a fine, especially when the accused have held high office. In capital cases they are the sole judges. It is the people who bestow office on the deserving, the noblest reward of virtue in a state; the people have the power of approving or rejecting laws, and what is most important of all, they deliberate on questions of war and peace. Further in the case of alliances, terms of peace, and treaties, it is the people who ratify all these. Thus one might plausibly say that the people's share in the government is the greatest, and that the constitution is a democratic one.

Having stated how political power is distributed among the three constitutional forms, I will now explain how each of the three parts is enabled, if they wish, to oppose or cooperate with the other parts. The Consul, when he leaves with his army, appears to have absolute authority in all matters necessary for carrying out his purpose; however, in fact he really requires the support of the people and the Senate. For the legions require constant supplies, and without the consent of the Senate, neither grain, clothing, nor pay can be provided; so that the commander's plans come to nothing, if the Senate chooses to impede them. As for the people it is indispensable for the Consuls to conciliate them, however far away from home they may be; for it is the people who ratify or annul treaties, and what is most important, the Consuls are obliged to account for their actions to the people. So it is not safe for the Consuls to underestimate the importance of the good will of either the Senate or the people.

The Senate, which possesses such great power, is obliged to respect the wishes of the people, and it cannot carry out inquiries into the most grave offenses against the state, unless confirmed by the people. The people alone have the power of passing or rejecting any law meant to deprive the Senate of some of its traditional authority. Therefore the Senate is afraid of the masses and must pay due attention to the popular will.

Similarly, the people are dependent on the Senate and must respect its members both in public and in private. Through the whole of Italy a vast number of contracts, which it would not be easy to enumerate, are given out by the Senate for the construction and repair of public buildings, and besides this there are many things which are farmed out, such as navigable rivers, harbors, gardens, mines, lands, in fact everything that forms part of the Roman domains. Now all these matters are undertaken by the people, and everyone is interested in these contracts and the work they involve. Certain people are the actual purchasers of the contracts, others are the partners of these first, others guarantee them, others pledge their own fortunes to the state for this purpose. In all these matters the Senate is supreme. It can grant extension of time; it can relieve the contractor if any accident occurs; and if the work proves to be absolutely impossible to carry out it can liberate him from his contract. There are many ways in which the Senate can either benefit or injure those who manage public property. What is even more important is that the judges in most civil trials are appointed from the Senate. As a result of the fact that all citizens are at the mercy of the Senate, and look forward with alarm to the uncertainty of litigation, they are very shy of obstructing or resisting its decisions. Similarly anyone is reluctant to oppose the projects of the Consuls as all are generally and individually under their authority when in the field.

Such being the power that each part has of hampering the others or cooperating with them, their union is adequate to all emergencies, so that it is impossible to find a better political system than this. Whenever the menace of some common danger from abroad compels them to act in concord and support each other, the strength of the state becomes great, as all are zealously competing in devising means of meeting the need of the hour. Consequently, this peculiar form of constitution possesses an irresistible power of attaining every object upon which it is resolved. When they are freed from external menace, and reap the harvest of good fortune and affluence which is the result of their success, and in the enjoyment of this prosperity are corrupted by flattery and idleness and become insolent and overbearing, as indeed happens often enough, it is then especially that we see the state providing itself a remedy for the evil from which it suffers. For when one part having grown out of proportion to the others aims at supremacy and tends to become too predominant, it is evident that none of the three is absolute. The purpose of one can be offset and resisted by the others, and none of them will excessively outgrow the others or treat them with contempt. All parts abide by the traditional constitutional practices because any aggressive impulse is sure to be checked and because they fear from the outset the possibility of being interfered with by the others. . . .

34

Marcus Tullius Cicero, *The Laws*

The idea of a higher law than men could make had been a familiar one to the Greeks of the Classical Age. It had been well articulated by Sophocles in *Antigone* (see Reading 28). Consequently, it is a matter of some debate how original the Stoics of the Hellenistic Age were in stressing Natural Law as the body of (obviously unwritten) laws governing both the world of nature and the proper conduct of humankind. Be that as it may, the idea of a law based on nature as the proper model for human law appealed to many Roman commentators on law: Ideally man-made law, called *lex positiva* or "positive law"[1] by the Romans, was to reflect and implement the *lex naturalis* or "law of nature." If it did not, it did not deserve to be called "law." In the following selection, Marcus Tullius Cicero (106–43 B.C.), the Roman orator and political ideologue of the Republic, defends this relationship.

Placing higher value on Greek authority than on a claim to originality, Cicero used Plato's titles *The Republic* and *The Laws* to present his political ideas. In his *Republic*, he gives a short summary of the relationship between natural and positive law:

> There is in fact a true law—namely, right reason—which is in accordance with nature, applies to all men, and is unchangeable and eternal. By its commands this law summons men to the performance of their duties; by its prohibitions it restrains them from doing wrong. Its commands and prohibitions always influence good men, but are without effect upon the bad. To invalidate this law by human legislation is never morally right, nor is it permissible ever to restrict its operation, and to annul it wholly is impossible. Neither the Senate nor the people can absolve us from our obligation to obey this law. . . . It will not lay down one rule at Rome and another at Athens, nor will it be one rule today and another tomorrow. But there will be one law, eternal and unchangeable, binding at all times upon all peoples; and there will be, as it were, one common master and ruler of men, namely God, who is the author of this law, its interpreter, and its sponsor. The man who will not obey it will abandon his better self, and,

---

[1]This was not in the sense of "positive" versus "negative," but rather in the no longer common usage of "set down" or "recorded," as in our common words: "de*posit*" and "re*pository*."

in denying the true nature of a man, will thereby suffer the severest of penalties, though he has escaped all the other consequences which men call punishment.[2]

In his *Laws,* this connection is defended at much greater length.

QUESTIONS TO CONSIDER

1. Why does Cicero consider Natural Law to have greater power than man-made law? Do you? Why?
2. Why do you suppose that most twentieth-century lawyers prefer not to argue their cases in terms of Natural Law? Can you think of some cases in which Natural Law argumentation has won out?

Those learned men appear to be right who say that law is the highest reason implanted in Nature, which commands what should be done and prohibits what should not be: when this same reason takes root and develops in the human mind it is law. Thus they consider law to be intelligence which has the power to command people to do what is right and to refrain from what is wrong. . . . The way Nature has made us lets us share the concept of justice with each other and pass it on to all men. . . . Those human beings to whom Nature gave reason were also given *right* reason in matters of command and prohibition. . . .

From the time we were children, we have been calling rules that begin: "If a man makes a complaint in court" and similar things by the name "laws." It would be good now if we could establish that with commands to do things or refrain from doing them nations apply the power to steer people towards doing the right things and away from committing crimes; however, this power is not only older than peoples and governments but is of the same age as the God who protects and rules both Heaven and earth. You see, the divine mind cannot exist without reason, and divine reason must have the power to sanction what is right and wrong.

Nothing was ever written to say that one man alone on a bridge should face massed, armed forces of enemies and command the bridge behind him to be destroyed, but that fact should not mislead us into thinking that [Horatio] Cocles was not following to the utmost the law which summons us to deeds of bravery. If there has been no written law in Rome against rape back when Lucius Tarquin ruled as king, that would not mean that Sextus Tarquin was not breaking that eternal law when he took Lucretia by force. . . . The fact is that reason did exist, a gift of Nature, calling upon man to do right and abstain from wrong. It did not begin to be law when it first came into being, which it did at the same time as the divine mind. . . . The varied ordinances formulated for momentary needs of the peoples bear the name "laws" through being so favored by conventional usage rather than because they are really *laws.* . . . Men introduced such laws to insure the protection of citizens and states, as well as the peaceful and happy lot of mankind. Those who originated these sanctions persuaded their people that what they were writing down and putting into effect would—if the

[2]Marcus Tullius Cicero, *On the Commonwealth,* ed. and trans. George H. Sabine and Stanley B. Smith (Columbus: Ohio State University Press, 1929), III, xxii, pp. 215–16.

From Marcus Tullius Cicero, *De legibus libri,* ed. J. Vahlen (Berlin: F. Vahlenum, 1883; I, vi, 18–19; I, xi, 33; II, iv, 9-v, 13) trans. Henry A. Myers. Dialogue-personage names omitted.

people lived by them—give them happiness and honor. When these sanctions were formulated and went into effect they were indeed called "laws."

How about all the pernicious and pestilential bits of legislation which nations have been known to enact? These no more deserve the name "laws" than the agreements that gangs of robbers might make among themselves. We know that if ignorant and inexperienced men should recommend poisons instead of medicines with the power to heal these would not be called "physicians' prescriptions." In the same way, nothing causing injury should be called a "law," no matter how it may have been enacted by a state or how the people may accept it. Thus we find that law reflects justice, distinct from injustice, and comes from that most ancient and rightfully dominant of all things: Nature, which all human laws reflect when they punish evildoers while defending and protecting good people.

Science in the Greco-Roman and Chinese Worlds

Greeks and Romans made strides toward a comprehensive philosophy of science with their understanding of cause and effect in the world of nature as a system of regularities functioning without any supernatural causes needed to make things happen. This served them well in medicine as in engineering. They prayed, of course, for divine intervention to ward off and cure diseases and occasionally were not above invoking supernatural aid to curse individuals, families, or projects, but in general they separated their study of the workings of nature from theology.

In astronomy, they inherited considerable data, particularly information related to devising calendars, from Egyptian and Babylonian predecessors, and went on to observe with increasing exactness regularities with which planets and stars appeared in the sky, collating the patterns into a basis for more accurately predicting their reoccurrence. With few exceptions, their observations led them to confirm the geocentric theory, according to which the heavenly bodies revolved around the earth, which remained the focal point of the universe in their cosmography.

In general, it was the judgment of the educated Greek, Hellenistic, and Roman worlds that the study of nature should be pursued by observing natural phenomena through sense perception and reflecting upon the data so obtained through reason. This mindset was to surface much later as the formula for scientific—and consequently human—progress sporadically in the Western European Renaissance and as a powerful force in the Enlightenment of the eighteenth century.

The Chinese, on the other hand, pursued scientific cause and effect to the point of developing valuable treatises, particularly on medicine, but Chinese science was always strongly influenced by cosmology. The concept of yin and yang as mutually complementary and balancing regulators of the universe remained the constant point of reference in Chinese medicine until very recent times.

35

Hippocrates, *On the Sacred Disease*

Hippocrates of Cos [460 (?)–375 (?) B.C.] practiced and taught medicine roughly in the days of Socrates and Plato. He forcefully advocated collecting objective data concerning cause and effect in diseases and cautioned against ascribing supernatural causes to any particular category of disease. At the medical school at Cos and then at the much larger one in Greek Alexandria, his writings were copied and new ones ascribed to him long after his death, so that it is impossible to know just which pieces he wrote; however, all the writings that bear his name show the rational, systematic, and secular approach to medicine for which he is known. The famed "Hippocratic Oath" ascribed to him, which physicians in the Western world have taken over the centuries, promising among other things to supply neither a means for abortion nor poison for a physician-assisted suicide, may well reflect some of his concern for ethics in the practice of medicine, but it appears to have been written some four centuries after his death.

The following article deals with epilepsy. Probably because no physician had had any clue as to its cause—understandably, since its cause is still unknown—and its convulsions appeared to come out of nowhere and strike the afflicted, it had been called "the sacred disease."

QUESTIONS TO CONSIDER

1. What sort of people, according to Hippocrates, were first inclined to call this disease "the sacred one"?
2. Why does Hippocrates believe that those who stress the "sacred" nature of the disease are less, rather than more, religious than other people?
3. How does Hippocrates go about refuting the claim that this disease is specially sacred?

It is thus with regard to the disease called Sacred: it appears to me to be nowise more divine nor more sacred than other diseases, but has a natural cause from which it originates like other affections. Men regard its nature and cause as divine from ignorance and wonder, because it is not at all like to other diseases. And this notion of its divinity is kept up by their inability to comprehend it, and the simplicity of the mode by which it is cured, for men are freed from it by purifications and incantations. But if it is reckoned divine because it is wonderful, instead of one there are many diseases which would be sacred; for, as I will show, there are others no less wonderful and prodigious, which nobody imagines to be sacred. The quotidian, tertian, and quartan fevers, seem to me no less sacred and divine in their origin than this disease, although they are not reckoned so wonderful. And I see men become mad and demented from no manifest cause, and at the same time doing many things

From Hippocrates, *On the Sacred Disease*, trans. Francis Adams. Reprinted from *Great Books of the Western World* © 1952, 1990, Encyclopaedia Britannica, Inc.

out of place; and I have known many persons in sleep groaning and crying out, some in a state of suffocation, some jumping up and fleeing out of doors, and deprived of their reason until they awaken, and afterward becoming well and rational as before, although they be pale and weak; and this will happen not once but frequently. And there are many and various things of the like kind, which it would be tedious to state particularly.

They who first referred this malady to the gods appear to me to have been just such persons as the conjurors, purificators, mountebanks, and charlatans now are, who give themselves out for being excessively religious, and as knowing more than other people. Such persons, then, using the divinity as a pretext and screen of their own inability to afford any assistance, have given out that the disease is sacred, adding suitable reasons for this opinion, they have instituted a mode of treatment which is safe for themselves, namely, by applying purifications and incantations, and enforcing abstinence from baths and many articles of food which are unwholesome to men in diseases. Of sea substances, the surmullet, the blacktail, the mullet, and the eel; for these are the fishes most to be guarded against. And of fleshes, those of the goat, the stag, the sow, and the dog: for these are the kinds of flesh which are aptest to disorder the bowels. Of fowls, the cock, the turtle, and the bustard, and such others as are reckoned to be particularly strong. And of potherbs, mint, garlic, and onions; for what is acrid does not agree with a weak person. And they forbid to have a black robe, because black is expressive of death; and to sleep on a goat's skin, or to wear it, and to put one foot upon another, or one hand upon another; for all these things are held to be hindrances to the cure. All these they enjoin with reference to its divinity, as if possessed of more knowledge, and announcing beforehand other causes so that if the person should recover, theirs would be the honor and credit; and if he should die, they would have a certain defense, as if the gods, and not they, were to blame, seeing they had administered nothing either to eat or drink as medicines, nor had overheated him with baths, so as to prove the cause of what had happened. But I am of opinion that (if this were true) none of the Libyans, who live in the interior, would be free from this disease, since they all sleep on goats' skins, and live upon goats' flesh; neither have they couch, robe, nor shoe that is not made of goat's skin, for they have no other herds but goats and oxen. But if these things, when administered in food, aggravate the disease, and if it be cured by abstinence from them, godhead is not the cause at all; nor will purifications be of any avail, but it is the food which is beneficial and prejudicial, and the influence of the divinity vanishes.

Thus, they who try to cure these maladies in this way, appear to me neither to reckon them sacred nor divine. For when they are removed by such purifications, and this method of cure, what is to prevent them from being brought upon men and induced by other devices similar to these? So that the cause is no longer divine, but human. For whoever is able, by purifications and conjurations, to drive away such an affection, will be able, by other practices, to excite it; and, according to this view, its divine nature is entirely done away with. By such sayings and doings, they profess to be possessed of superior knowledge, and deceive mankind by enjoining lustrations and purifications upon them, while their discourse turns upon the divinity and the godhead. And yet it would appear to me that their discourse savors not of piety, as they suppose, but rather of impiety, and as if there were no gods, and that what they hold to be holy and divine, were impious and unholy. This I will now explain.

For, if they profess to know how to bring down the moon, darken the sun, induce storms and fine weather, and rains and droughts, and make the sea and land unproductive, and so forth, whether they arrogate this power as being derived from mysteries or any other knowledge or consideration, they appear to me to practice impiety, and either to fancy that there are no gods, or, if there are, that they have no ability to ward off any of the greatest evils. How, then, are they not enemies to the gods? For if a man by magical arts and sacrifices will bring down the moon, and darken the sun, and induce storms, or fine weather, I should not believe that there was anything divine, but human, in these things, provided the power of the divine were overpowered by human knowledge and subjected to it. But perhaps it will be said, these things are not so, but, men being in want of the means of life, invent many and various things, and devise many contrivances for all other things, and for this disease, in every phase of the disease, assigning the cause to a god. Nor do they remember the same things once, but frequently. For, if they imitate a goat, or grind their teeth, or if their right side be convulsed, they say that the mother of the gods is the cause. But if they speak in a sharper and more intense tone, they resemble this state to a horse, and say that Poseidon is the cause. Or if any excrement be passed, which is often the case, owing to the violence of the disease, the appellation of Enodia is adhibited; or, if it be passed in smaller and denser masses, like bird's, it is said to be from Apollo Nomius. But if foam be emitted by the mouth, and the patient kick with his feet, Ares then gets the blame. But terrors which happen during the night, and fevers, and delirium, and jumpings out of bed, and frightful apparitions, and fleeing away—all these they hold to be the plots of Hecate, and the invasions of the Heroes, and use purifications and incantations, and, as appears to me, make the divinity to be most wicked and most impious. For they purify those laboring under this disease, with the same sorts of blood and the other means that are used in the case of those who are stained with crimes, and of malefactors, or who have been enchanted by men, or who have done any wicked act; who ought to do the very reverse, namely, sacrifice and pray, and, bringing gifts to the temples, supplicate the gods. But now they do none of these things, but purify; and some of the purifications they conceal in the earth, and some they throw into the sea, and some they carry to the mountains where no one can touch or tread upon them. But these they ought to take to the temples and present to the god, if a god be the cause of the disease. Neither truly do I count it a worthy opinion to hold that the body of man is polluted by god, the most impure by the most holy; for were it defiled, or did it suffer from any other thing, it would be like to be purified and sanctified rather than polluted by god. For it is the divinity which purifies and sanctifies the greatest of offenses and the most wicked, and which proves our protection from them. And we mark out the boundaries of the temples and the groves of the gods, so that no one may pass them unless he be pure, and when we enter them we are sprinkled with holy water, not as being polluted, but as laying aside any other pollution which we formerly had. And thus it appears to me to hold, with regard to purifications.

But this disease seems to me to be no more divine that others; but it has its nature such as other diseases have, and a cause whence it originates, and its nature and cause are divine only just as much as all others are.

36

Pliny the Elder, *The Nature Story*

Pliny the Elder (A.D. 23–79) ranked high among Romans as a scientist largely on the basis of his *Naturalis Historia,* roughly *The Nature Story* (not *history* in the sense of a chronological narration). Always a busy man, Pliny studied at Rome for an official career, commanded a cavalry squadron in Germany, returned to Rome, and although he kept a low profile during most of Nero's reign, eventually became governor of Spain, a naval commander, and then adviser to Emperor Vespasian, with whom he had served in Germany. He constantly read and took notes on natural phenomena, and two years before his death presented Emperor Titus with *The Nature Story,* containing, as he put it, "twenty thousand things well worth knowing" (none evidently more important than the rest), gathered from research in two thousand volumes by one hundred authors, and enriched by many of his own observations. His was more of a science-hero's death in the line of duty than was the demise of most scientists, when he went to observe what was happening with Mount Vesuvius as it erupted and directed molten lava toward Pompeii. Before Pompeii was wiped out by the volcano, Pliny was overcome by poisonous fumes and died.

Pliny was convinced of the existence of a World Soul, which made and directed the earth, world, and/or universe (he uses the same word, *mundus,* for all three). He saw the World Soul as a living being and consequently as God. The World Soul is central in his scheme of things, and he refers to it in determining what is natural and unnatural. But in the great bulk of his work, he is content to compile a wealth of factual information about places, things, and events on the basis of his observations or those of authors whom he trusts. In this selection, he discusses the world at large and the basic elements. The four elements, as he describes them, were *the* elements until modern times, and his description of them may serve to explain why neither ancient Greeks nor Romans nor early Arabs nor Western medieval people got very far with the science of chemistry.

QUESTIONS TO CONSIDER

1. Can you relate Pliny's "World Soul" to "the One" in the Hindu creation story (see Reading 16) or to "the Way" in Taoism (see Reading 25)? What are the similarities and differences?
2. What are the four elements? Why do you suppose Greeks and Romans settled on one of them as "the highest"?
3. What is distinctive about humans, as opposed to other animals, in Pliny's description of the effects of lightning?

The World

The world, and whatever that be which we otherwise call the heavens, by the vault of which all things are enclosed, we must conceive to be a Deity, to be eternal, without bounds, neither created, nor subject, at any time, to destruction. To inquire what is beyond it is no concern of man, nor can the human mind form any conjecture respecting it. It is sacred, eternal, and without bounds, all in all; indeed including everything in itself; finite, yet like what is infinite; the most certain of all things, yet like what is uncertain, externally and internally embracing all things in itself; it is the work of nature, and itself constitutes nature.

The Natural History of Pliny, trans. and ed. John Bostock and H.T. Riley (London: Henry G. Bohn, 1855), Vol. I, pp. 13–20, 84–86 *passim.*

It is madness to harass the mind, as some have done, with attempts to measure the world, and to publish these attempts; or, like others, to argue from what they have made out, that there are innumerable other worlds, and that we must believe there to be so many other natures, or that, if only one nature produced the whole, there will be so many suns and so many moons, and that each of them will have immense trains of other heavenly bodies. As if the same question would not recur at every step of our inquiry, anxious as we must be to arrive at some termination; or, as if this infinity, which we ascribe to nature, the former of all things, cannot be more easily comprehended by one single formation, especially when that is so extensive. It is madness, perfect madness, to go out of this world and to search for what is beyond it, as if one who is ignorant of his own dimensions could ascertain the measure of anything else, or as if the human mind could see what the world itself cannot contain.

That it has the form of a perfect globe we learn from the name which has been uniformly given to it, as well as from numerous natural arguments. For not only does a figure of this kind return everywhere into itself and sustain itself, also including itself, requiring no adjustments, not sensible of either end or beginning in any of its parts, and is best fitted for that motion, with which, as will appear hereafter, it is continually turning round; but still more, because we perceive it, by the evidence of sight, to be, in every part, convex and central, which could not be the case were it of any other figure.

The rising and setting of the sun clearly prove that this globe is carried round in the space of twenty-four hours, in an eternal and never-ceasing circuit, and with incredible swiftness. I am not able to say, whether the sound caused by the whirling about of so great a mass be excessive, and therefore, far beyond what our ears can perceive, nor, indeed, whether the resounding of so many stars, all carried along at the same time and revolving in their orbits, may not produce a kind of delightful harmony of incredible sweetness. To us, who are in the interior, the world appears to glide gently along, both by day and by night.

Various circumstances in nature prove to us, that there are impressed on the heavens innumerable figures of animals and of all kinds of objects, and that its surface is not perfectly polished like the eggs of birds, as some celebrated authors assert. For we find that the seeds of all bodies fall down from it, principally into the ocean, and, being mixed together, that a variety of monstrous forms are in this way frequently produced. And, indeed, this is evident to the eye; for, in one part, we have the figure of a wain, in another of a bear, of a bull, and of a letter; while, in the middle of them, over our heads, there is a white circle.

The Elements and Planets

I do not find that any one has doubted that there are four elements. The highest of these is supposed to be fire, and hence proceed the eyes of so many glittering stars. The next is that spirit, which both the Greeks and ourselves call by the same name, air. It is by the force of this vital principle, pervading all things and mingling with all, that the earth, together with the fourth element, water, is balanced in the middle of space. These are mutually bound together, the lighter being restrained by the heavier, so that they cannot fly off; while, on the contrary, from the lighter tending upwards, the heavier are so suspended, that they cannot fall down. Thus, by an equal tendency in the opposite direction, each of them remains in its appropriate place, bound together by the never-ceasing revolution of the world, which always turning on itself, the earth falls to the lowest part and is in the middle of the whole, while it remains suspended in the center, and, as it were, balancing this center, in which it is suspended. So that it alone remains immoveable, whilst all things revolve round it, being connected with every other part, whilst they all rest upon it.

Between this body and the heavens there are suspended, in this aerial spirit, seven stars, separated by determinate spaces, which, on account of their motion, we call wandering, although, in reality, none are less so. The sun is carried along in the midst of these, a body of great size and power, the ruler, not only of the seasons and of the different climates, but also of the stars themselves and of the heavens. When we consider his operations, we must regard him as the life, or rather the mind of the universe, the chief regulator and the God of nature; he also lends his light to the other stars. He is most illustrious and excellent, beholding all things and hearing all things, which, I perceive, is ascribed to him exclusively by the prince of poets, Homer.

The Laws of Lightning

It is certain that the lightning is seen before the thunder is heard, although they both take place at the same time. Nor is this wonderful, since light has a greater velocity than sound. Nature so regulates it, that the stroke and the sound coincide; the sound is, however, produced by the discharge of the thunder, not by its stroke. But the air is impelled quicker than the lightning, on which account it is that everything is shaken and blown up before it is struck, and that a person is never injured when he has seen the lightning and heard the thunder. Thunder on the left hand is supposed to be lucky, because the east is on the left side of the heavens. We do not regard so much the mode in which it comes to us, as that in which it leaves us, whether the fire rebounds after the stroke, or whether the current of air returns when the operation is concluded and the fire is consumed. In relation to this object the Etruscans have divided the heavens into sixteen parts. The first great division is from north to east; the second to the south; the third to the west; and the fourth occupies what remains from west to north. Each of these has been subdivided into four parts, of which the eight on the east have been called the left, and those on the west the right divisions. Those which extend from the west to the north have been considered the most unpropitious. It becomes therefore very important to ascertain from what quarter the thunder proceeds, and in what direction it falls. It is considered a very favorable omen when it returns into the eastern divisions. But it prognosticates the greatest felicity when the thunder proceeds from the first-mentioned part of the heavens and falls back into it; it was an omen of this kind which, as we have heard, was given to Sulla, the Dictator. The remaining quarters of the heavens are less propitious, and also less to be dreaded. There are some kinds of thunder which it is not thought right to speak of, or even listen to, unless when they have been disclosed to the master of a family or to a parent. But the futility of this observation was detected when the temple of Juno was struck at Rome, during the consulship of Scaurus, he who was afterwards the Prince of the Senate.

It lightens without thunder more frequently in the night than in the day. Man is the only animal that is not always killed by it, all other animals being killed instantly, nature having granted to him this mark of distinction, while so many other animals excel him in strength. All animals fall down on the opposite side to that which has been struck; man, unless he be thrown down on the parts that are struck, does not expire. Those who are struck directly from above sink down immediately. When a man is struck while he is awake, he is found with his eyes closed; when asleep, with them open. It is not considered proper that a man killed in this way should be burnt on the funeral pile; our religion enjoins us to bury the body in the earth. No animal is consumed by lightning unless after having been previously killed. The parts of the animal that have been wounded by lightning are colder than the rest of the body.

37

The Yellow Emperor, *Nei-ching [Neijing]* (Canon of Medicine)

The Yellow Emperor's Classic of Medicine (*Huangdi Neijing Suwen,* abbreviated *Neijing*) is one of the world's oldest medical classics. It remained for more than two thousand years the most basic and influential reference on internal medicine in China, Japan, and Korea in premodern times. Although the authorship of this extraordinary classic is attributed to the Yellow Emperor, one of the most famous legendary rulers of ancient China who reigned from 2696–2598 B.C., the earliest mention of this work is found in the *History of Former Han* (206 B.C.–A.D. 25) by Ban Gu (A.D. 32–92), the great historian of the first century A.D. Various dates for the origin of this classic have been suggested, ranging from 1000 B.C. to the end of the fourth century B.C. It is also difficult to determine who the real author was. Whoever the original author may be, it is highly likely that the Yellow Emperor's name was used to enhance the authoritativeness of this classic of medicine. This classic is written in the form of dialogue between the Yellow Emperor (Huangdi) and his minister Qi Bo.

The *Neijing* in its currently available form consists of eighty-one chapters. It covers wide-ranging topics such as a cosmological view of humans and health, etiology, diagnoses of various diseases, pulse analysis, methods of treatment, the art of acupuncture, pathology, psychiatry, and admonitions for physicians. The recurring themes that underlie this medical canon are cosmological concepts of yin and yang and the five elements. This philosophy explains that the universe is basically evolved from yin and yang, the mutually complementary and balancing cosmic regulators. Yang stands for sun, day, light, male, hot, active, and life and yin for moon, night, dark, female, cold, passive, and death. Yin and yang are interdependent. Yang grows or fades into yin and vice versa. The concept of the five elements explains that all nature is made up of varying combinations of the five elements, which are wood, fire, earth, metal, and water. These five elements interact with one another and produce a constant state of internal motion. Such a pattern of motion is similarly extended to the human body. Since humans are very much a part of nature and the universe, traditional Chinese medicine extensively applies the concepts of yin and yang and the five elements to the understanding of the human body and mind, etiology, physiology, pathology, and treatment.

The following excerpts are from Chapter 5, "The Manifestation of Yin and Yang from Macrocosm to the Microcosm"; and Chapter 54, "The Art of Acupuncture" in *The Yellow Emperor's Classic of Medicine.*

QUESTIONS TO CONSIDER

1. How similar and how different was traditional Chinese medicine from Hellenic and Hellenistic medicine? Did cosmology play any role in Western medicine in premodern times?
2. What are the reasons behind the growing interest in acupuncture in the West in recent years?
3. How are the concepts of yin and yang and the five elements reflected in the art of acupuncture?

Manifestation of Yin and Yang

Huang Di said, "The law of yin and yang is the natural order of the universe, the foundation of all things, mother of all changes, the root of life and death. In healing, one must grasp the root of the disharmony, which is always subject to the law of yin and yang.

"In the universe, the pure yang qi energy ascends to converge and form heaven, while the turbid yin qi descends and condenses to form the earth. Yin is passive and quiet, while the nature of yang is active and noisy. Yang is responsible for expanding and yin is responsible for contracting, becoming astringent, and consolidating. Yang is the energy, the vital force, the potential, while, yin is the substance, the foundation, the mother that gives rise to all this potential. . . .

"In nature, the clear yang forms heaven and the turbid yin qi descends to form earth. The earthly qi evaporates to become clouds, and when the clouds meet with the heavenly qi, rain is produced. Similarly, in the body, pure yang qi reaches the sensory orifices, allowing one to see, hear, smell, taste, feel, and decipher all information so that the shen/spirit can remain clear and centered. The turbid yin qi descends to the lower orifices. The clear yang qi disperses over the surface of the body; the turbid yin qi flows and nourishes the five zang visceral organs. The pure yang qi expands and strengthens the four extremities, and the turbid yin qi fills the six fu organs.[1]

"The elements of fire and water are categorized into yang and yin, the fire being yang and the water being yin. The functional aspect of the body is yang and the nutritive or substantive aspect is yin. While food can be used to strengthen and nourish the body, the body's ability to transform it is dependent on qi. The functional part of qi is derived from the jing/essence. Food is refined into jing/essence, which supports the qi, and the qi is required for both transformation and bodily functions. For this reason, when the diet is improper, the body may be injured, or if activities are excessive, the jing/essence can be exhausted.

"The yin and yang in the body should be in balance with one another. If the yang qi dominates, the yin will be deprived, and vice versa. Excess yang will manifest as febrile disease, whereas excess yin will manifest as cold disease. When yang is extreme, however, it can turn into cold disease, and vice versa.

"Cold can injure the physical body, and heat can damage the qi or energetic aspect of the body. When there is injury to the physical body there will be swelling, but if the qi level is damaged, it can cause pain because of the qi blockage. In an injury that has two aspects,

[1]The *fu* organs are those of digestion and excretion; *zang* and *fu* together comprise the internal organs.

Maoshing Ni, trans., *The Yellow Emperor's Classic of Medicine* (Boston: Shambhala, 1995), pp. 17–26, 192–94. Reprinted by permission.

such as swelling (yin) and pain (yang), treatment may consist of pungent herbs to disperse swelling and cooling herbs to subdue the pain. If a patient complains of pain first and swelling afterward, this means the qi level was injured first. But if a patient complains of swelling first followed by pain, the trauma occurred at the physical level initially."

* * *

"In the human body there are the zang organs of the liver, heart, spleen, lung, and kidneys. The qi of the five zang organs forms the five spirits and gives rise to the five emotions. The spirit of the heart is known as the shen, which rules mental and creative functions. The spirit of the liver, the hun, rules the nervous system and gives rise to extrasensory perception. The spirit of the spleen, of yi, rules logic or reasoning power. The spirit of the lungs, or po, rules the animalistic instincts, physical strength and stamina. The spirit of the kidneys, the zhi, rules the will, drive, ambition, and survival instinct.

"Overindulgence in the five emotions—happiness, anger, sadness, worry or fear, and fright—can create imbalances. Emotions can injure the qi, while seasonal elements can attack the body. Sudden anger damages the yin qi; becoming easily excited or overjoyed will damage the yang qi. This causes the qi to rebel and rise up to the head, squeezing the shen out of the heart and allowing it to float away. Failing to regulate one's emotions can be likened to summer and winter failing to regulate each other, threatening life itself."

* * *

Then Huang Di inquired, "What are the methods to balance yin and yang?"

Qi Bo answered, "If one understands the methods or Tao of maintaining health and the causes of depletion, then one can readily master the balance of yin and yang and stay healthy. Normally, by the age of forty, people have exhausted fifty percent of their yin qi, and their vitality is weakened. At age fifty the body is heavy, the vision and the hearing deteriorated; by age sixty the yin qi is further diminished, the kidneys drained; the sensory organs and the nine orifices, including the excretory organs, have all become functionally impaired. Conditions will manifest such as prostatitis, vision loss, deficiency in the lower jiao (viscera cavity) and excess in the upper jiao, tearing, and nasal drainage problems.

"Thus, the body of one who understands the Tao will remain strong and healthy. The one who does not understand the Tao will age. One who is careless will often feel deficient, while one who knows will have an abundance of energy. Those who are knowledgeable have clear orifices, perceptions, hearing, vision, smell, and taste, and are light and strong. Even though their bodies are old, they can perform most of life's activities."

The Art of Acupuncture

Huang Di said, "Will you please explain to me the nine different needles? And will you also please discuss the methods of tonification and sedation in excess and in deficiency?"

Qi Bo answered, "When acupuncturing deficient conditions one should elicit heat sensation with the needle. Only when the qi is strong will it be able to produce heat. In treating excess conditions one should elicit a cooling sensation. When the pathogenic qi is weakening one will experience a cooling feeling. When there is stagnation in the blood caused by the accumulation of a pathogen, one should promote bloodletting to rid the bad blood. In withdrawing the needle on patients with an excess condition, withdraw the needle quickly. Allow the hole to remain open in order to disperse the pathogen. In deficiency, withdraw the needle slowly and close the hole to prevent loss of qi. . . .

"In order to master the techniques one must be able to use the nine needles with equal ease. Each of the nine has a specific indication. In terms of the timing in tonifying or sedating, one must coordinate the technique with the opening and closing of the hole, and the arrival and departure of the qi. When the qi arrives, we call this opening. At this point, one can sedate. When the qi leaves, we call this closing. Now one can tonify.

"The nine needles are of different size, shape, and use. When acupuncturing excess, one must sedate. Insert the needles and await the arrival of yin qi. When one feels a cooling sensation under the needle, remove the needles. In deficiency, one must tonify. After needle insertion, await the arrival of yang qi. When there is a warming sensation, remove the needles. Once you grasp the qi with the needle, be very attentive and listen so as not to lose the opportunity to manipulate the effects. Treat disease according to where it is located; determine whether to insert deeply or shallowly. When the disease is located deep, insert deeply. When the disease is superficial, needle shallowly. Although there is a difference in depth of penetration, the principle of awaiting the qi is the same.

"When acupuncturing, one should be prepared and careful, as if one is facing a deep abyss. Move carefully so as not to fall. In handling the needle, hold it as if holding the tiger—firmly grasped and in control. One needs a calm mind to observe the patient. Concentrate clearly on the patient and do not become scattered. Upon inserting the needle, be accurate and precise. It should not be crooked or miss the target. When the needle enters the body, the physician should observe the patient closely in order to help guide the patient's attention. This allows the qi in the channels to move more easily, and the results are more effective."

Huang Di said, "I've heard that the nine types of needles have a relationship to yin and yang and the four seasonal energies. Can you please explain this so it may be passed on to later generations as a principle of healing?"

Qi Bo answered, "In Taoist cosmology the number one corresponds to heaven; two to earth; three to man; four to the seasons; five to sounds; six to rhythms; seven to the stars; eight to wind; nine to the continents. People have physical form and connect to nature. The various shapes and forms of the nine needles conform to different types of conditions. The skin of human beings envelops and protects the body, just as heaven envelops and protects the myriad things. Muscles are soft, pliable, and calm, just as earth, which contains the myriad things.

"People move about and also sleep. The pulse mirrors this with excess and deficiency. The tendons that strap together the whole body have differing uses at different locations. This is similar to the seasons of the year, which have their unique uses and purposes too.

"People's voices correspond to the five sounds. People's six zang and six fu organs are yin-yang couples, similar to the six rhythms and scales. People's sensory organs and their positions, as well as their teeth, are similar to the positions of the stars. People's breath is like the wind of nature. The nine orifices and three hundred and sixty-five luo [channel points] collaterals spreading throughout the body are like the rivers and tributaries spreading over the earth; they feed the oceans, which in turn surround the nine continents.

"Therefore, we have the nine needles. The first, called chan zhen, superficially punctures the skin. The second needle, called yuan zhen, does not penetrate but instead massages the acupoints on the flesh and muscles. The third needle, ti zhen, punctures the vessels. The fourth needle, feng zhen, punctures and draws blood from capillaries and small veins. The fifth needle, fei pi zhen, lances the skin to drain pus. The sixth needle, yuan li zhen, punctures the joints for bi conditions. The seventh needle, hao zhen, punctures the acupoints on the flesh. The eighth needle, chang zhen, punctures deep fleshy locations. The ninth needle, da zhen, punctures the abdomen to relieve edema or masses. Choose these needles wisely for the appropriate occasion."

* * *

"The blood and qi within the body circulate throughout the channels and vessels, balancing yin and yang, just as water in rivers and lakes circulates endlessly. The qi of the liver connects with the eyes, and the eyes are part of the nine orifices."

CHRISTIANITY TO ISLAM

The Rise of Christianity

In the last century of the Roman Republic, religious and civil conflicts made Palestine vulnerable to Roman intervention in Jewish affairs. Pompey the Great stormed Jerusalem in 63 B.C. and aided an Idumean named Antipater in being named foreign minister to the temple state. Thereafter, Antipater's son, Herod, became friends with Julius Caesar, Mark Antony, and Augustus Caesar. In return for his loyalty and obedience, the Romans permitted Herod to resurrect the monarchy (37–4 B.C.).

Herod's reign was a prosperous one: He was able to rebuild Jerusalem with a great palace, the Second Temple, and to add many forts throughout the kingdom. Nonetheless, many Jews hated Herod because they saw him as pro-Roman, a murderer of his family, and—above all—not wholly Jewish.

Factions also dominated Judea, where Jesus was born. There were the Sadducees, supported by the upper classes, who controlled the Temple priesthood and were strict supporters of the Torah. Their opponents were the Pharisees, who were seen as more liberal. They supported public education, believed in personal immortality, and sponsored scribal commentaries on the Laws. Other groups, such as the Essenes, had withdrawn from secular life completely and became ascetics in desert communities. One of these latter, the New Covenanters, expected an end to the wicked age and the establishment of a new kingdom of righteousness.

Jesus was born some time near the end of Herod's rule—not, as the later Christians believed, in the year A.D. 1. Although we cannot establish a true date, his parents, Joseph and Mary, had to leave their village of Nazareth and proceed to Bethlehem. They were displaced because Augustus Caesar had ordered a census of the empire, requiring that everyone register in the city of his or her family. In the Gospels, Jesus' lineage is traced back to Bethlehem, the home of David, from whose line the Hebrew prophets had predicted a Messiah would come.

Little information is recorded in the Gospels about the middle years of Jesus' life. Not until he was baptized by his cousin, John the Baptist, would Jesus begin his public ministry. From that time until his crucifixion three years later, Jesus gathered his apostles, preached a new religious message, and worked his miracles.

As Jesus' fame increased in Galilee and Judea, the religious authorities feared disturbances. The Sadducees accused him of religious blasphemy, arrested him, and handed him over to the Roman governor of Judea, Pontius Pilate. Jesus was tried and executed for sedition against Rome.

Within a short period, the apostles announced that Jesus had risen from the grave and would shortly return in the Second Coming, which would inaugurate the Messianic Kingdom. In order to amplify this theology, the Apostle Paul identified Jesus as the son of God, or God-made flesh, whose sacrifice on the Cross made salvation from sin possible for all humanity. The apostles traveled from city to city with these messages, appealing first to the Jews and then to the Gentiles. This was the true foundation of the Christian religion.

38

The Golden Rule and God's Will

In this passage, Jesus explains that the person who hears and does God's will is fulfilling the Law.

QUESTIONS TO CONSIDER

1. What are the Lord's requirements of a true believer?
2. Why are not all prophets acceptable?
3. Compare Jesus' Sermon on the Mount and other teachings with those of Moses and the Hebrews (see Readings 1 and 7), Buddha (see Readings 20 and 21), and Hindu sources (see Readings 17 to 19) touching on the same subjects.

Judge not, that ye be not judged.

For with what judgment ye judge, ye shall be judged: and with what measure ye mete, it shall be measured to you again.

And why beholdest thou the mote that is in thy brother's eye, but considerest not the beam that is in thine own eye?

Or how wilt thou say to thy brother, Let me pull out the mote out of thine eye: and, behold, a beam is in thine own eye?

Thou hypocrite, first cast out the beam out of thine own eye; and then shalt thou see clearly to cast out the mote out of thy brother's eye.

Give not that which is holy unto the dogs, neither cast ye your pearls before swine, lest they trample them under their feet, and turn again and rend you.

Ask, and it shall be given you: seek, and ye shall find: knock, and it shall be opened unto you:

For every one that asketh receiveth: and he that seeketh findeth: and to him that knocketh it shall be opened.

Or what man is there of you, whom if his son ask bread, will he give him a stone?

Or if he ask a fish, will he give him a serpent?

If ye then, being evil, know how to give good gifts unto your children, how much more shall your Father which is in heaven give good things to them that ask him?

From Matthew 7:1–29 (King James Version); slightly modernized.

Therefore all things whatsoever ye would that men should do to you, do ye even so to them: for this is the law and the prophets.

Enter ye in at the strait gate: for wide is the gate, and broad is the way, that leadeth to destruction, and many there be which go in there:

Because strait is the gate, and narrow is the way, which leadeth unto life, and few there be that find it.

Beware of false prophets, which come to you in sheep's clothing, but inwardly they are ravening wolves.

Ye shall know them by their fruits. Do men gather grapes of thorns, or figs of thistles?

Even so every good tree bringeth forth good fruit; but a corrupt tree bringeth forth evil fruit.

A good tree cannot bring forth evil fruit, neither can a corrupt tree bring forth good fruit.

Every tree that bringeth not forth good fruit is hewn down, and cast into the fire.

Wherefore by their fruits ye shall know them.

Not every one that saith unto me, Lord, Lord, shall enter into the kingdom of heaven; but he that doeth the will of my Father which is in heaven.

Many will say to me in that day, Lord, Lord, have we not prophesied in thy name? and in thy name have cast out devils? and in thy name done many wonderful works?

And then will I profess unto them, I never knew you: depart from me, ye that work iniquity.

Therefore whosoever heareth these sayings of mine, and doeth them, I will liken him unto a wise man, which built his house upon a rock:

And the rain descended, and the floods came, and the winds blew, and beat upon that house; and it fell not: for it was founded upon a rock.

And every one that heareth these sayings of mine, and doeth them not, shall be likened unto a foolish man, which built his house upon the sand:

And the rain descended, and the floods came, and the winds blew, and beat upon that house; and it fell: and great was the fall of it.

And it came to pass, when Jesus had ended these sayings, the people were astonished at his doctrine:

For he taught them as one having authority, and not as the scribes.

39

The Writings of St. Paul on Women

Women in many ancient societies were subordinate to men in legal, political, and religious rights. And at first glance, this might appear to be the case in the Old and New Testaments where woman (Eve) is depicted as the source of "Original Sin" or compared to Israel, God's unfaithful wife; however, woman is also viewed in the Old Testament as the faithful companion of God and in the Gospels as the way to salvation through the New Eve, Mary.

When all the Gospel accounts are taken as a whole, they seem to reflect a significant change in human relations and an increased importance for women. Jesus' teachings emphasize the idea that men and women have equal duties in marriage; just as divorce is forbidden for both, so adultery is not limited to women. Women such as Mary Magdalene were attracted to Jesus' ministry, and it was to women that Jesus appeared at his tomb. They were also important as helpers (deaconesses) or patrons in the newly established Christian communities.

The ideas of St. Paul reflect both the Old Testament and the Gospel views of women. Born into a Jewish family that had acquired Roman citizenship, Saul of Tarsus (Paul) at first rejected Christianity and joined in the persecution of early Christians. Later, according to his own account, a blinding light appeared to him on the road to Damascus, where God commanded him to stop harming Christians and to begin preaching the Gospel. Under his Roman name of Paul, he became such an effective Christian preacher and teacher that he was listed among the Apostles. His letters became an important part of Christian theology.

St. Paul changed the course of Christianity as he preached to the gentile communities of the Roman world instead of concentrating exclusively on Jews. When doctrinal disputes arose within Christian groups, Paul attempted to settle these problems in his letters through interpretation and application of Jesus' teachings.

St. Paul was frequently in trouble with Jewish leaders, who saw him as a traitor. Roman authorities at first had nothing against Christians but later took a dim view of religious figures, such as Paul, whose speeches provoked an uproar. When some confusion resulted in Paul's being arrested in Palestine, he used his Roman citizenship to appeal his case to the emperor. According to Church tradition, he was sent to the capital and released after several years of captivity. Some seven or eight years later, however, he was one of the Christians executed during Nero's persecution.

The following excerpts from Paul's letters to the Galatians and Corinthians illustrate some of his teachings. These include the equality of men and women in Christ through baptism but their inequality in marriage and sexuality.

QUESTIONS TO CONSIDER

1. What was life like for women in the ancient world? Are there any exceptions?
2. How did the Hebrew religion influence the Christian view of women (see Reading 1)?
3. How does St. Paul argue for equality for all persons?
4. Does St. Paul address himself only to men in the area of freedom and responsibilities in marriage?
5. Many authors say that St. Paul subordinates women to men in 1 Corinthians 11:2–16. Could his statements express his view of a "natural law" governing men and women?

Baptism and Faith

Wherefore the law was our schoolmaster to bring us unto Christ, that we might be justified by faith.

But after that faith is come, we are no longer under a schoolmaster.

The first section is from Galatians 3:24–28. The second is from 1 Corinthians 7:1–17, 25–28, 32–40. The third section is from 1 Corinthians 11:2–16. (King James Version; slightly modernized.)

For you are all the children of God by faith in Christ Jesus.

For as many of you as have been baptized into Christ have put on Christ.

There is neither Jew nor Greek, there is neither bond [slave] nor free, there is neither male nor female: for you are all one in Christ Jesus.

Marriage

Now concerning the things whereof you wrote unto me: It is good for a man not to touch a woman.

Nevertheless, to avoid fornication, let every man have his own wife, and let every woman have her own husband.

Let the husband render unto the wife due benevolence: and likewise also the wife unto the husband.

The wife has no power of her own body, but the husband: and likewise also the husband has not power of his own body, but the wife.

Do not refuse one another except by agreement for a time, that you may give yourselves to fasting and prayer; and come together again, lest that Satan tempt you through lack of self-control.

But I speak this by permission, and not of commandment.

For I wish that all men were even as I myself. But every man has his proper gift of God, one after this manner, another after that.

I say therefore to the unmarried and widows, it is good for them if they remain even as I.

But if they cannot contain, let them marry: for it is better to marry than to burn.

And to the married I command, yet not I, but the Lord, Let not the wife depart from her husband:

But and if she depart, let her remain unmarried, or be reconciled to her husband: and let not the husband put away his wife.

But to the rest I speak, not the Lord: If any brother has an unbelieving wife, and she is pleased to live with him, let him not put her away.

And the woman who has an unbelieving husband, and if he is pleased to live with her, let her not leave him.

For the unbelieving husband is sanctified by the wife, and the unbelieving wife is sanctified by the husband: otherwise your children were unclean; but now they are holy.

But if the unbelieving departs, let him depart. A brother or sister is not under bondage in such cases: but God has called us to peace.

For what do you know, Oh wife, whether you shall save your husband? or how do you know, Oh man, whether you shall save your wife?

But as God has distributed to every man, as the Lord has called every one, so let him walk. And so I ordain in all churches. . . .

Now concerning virgins I have no commandment of the Lord: yet I give my judgment, as one that has obtained mercy of the Lord to be faithful.

I suppose therefore that this is good for the present distress, I say, that it is good for a man so to be.

Art you bound to a wife? seek not to be freed. Art you freed from a wife? seek not a wife.

But if you marry, you have not sinned; and if a virgin marry, she has not sinned. Nevertheless such shall have trouble in the flesh: but I spare you.

But this I say, brothers, the time is short: it remains that both they who have wives be as though they had none; . . .

But I would have you without carefulness. He that is unmarried cares for the things that belong to the Lord, how he may please the Lord:

But he that is married cares for the things that are of the world, how he may please his wife.

There is difference also between a wife and a virgin. The unmarried woman cares for the things of the Lord, that she may be holy both in body and in spirit: but she who is married cares for the things of the world, how she may please her husband.

And this I speak for your own profit; not that I may cast a snare on you, but for that which is proper, and that you may attend upon the Lord without distraction.

But if any man thinks that he behaves improperly toward his virgin, if she is passed the flower of her age, and need requires it, let him do what he will, he does not sin; let them marry.

Nevertheless he that stands steadfast in his heart, having no necessity, but has power over his own will, and has so decreed in his heart that he will keep his virgin, does well.

So then he that gives her in marriage does well; but he that does not give her in marriage does better.

The wife is bound by the law as long as her husband lives; but if her husband is dead, she is at liberty to be married to whomever she will; only in the Lord.

But she is happier if she so abide, after my judgment: and I think also that I have the Spirit of God.

Physical Differences of Sexes

Now I praise you, brothers, that you remember me in all things, and keep the ordinances, as I delivered them to you.

But I would have you know, that the head of every man is Christ; and the head of the woman is the man; and the head of Christ is God.

Every man praying or prophesying, having his head covered, dishonors his head.

But every woman who prays or prophesies with her head uncovered dishonors her head: for that is even all one as if she were shaven.

For if the woman is not covered, let her be shorn: but if it is a shame for a woman to be shorn or shaven, let her be covered.

For a man indeed ought not to cover his head, as he is the image and glory of God: but the woman is the glory of man.

For the man is not of the woman; but the woman of the man.

Neither was the man created for the woman; but the woman for the man.

For this cause ought the woman to have power on her head because of the angels.

Nevertheless neither is the man without the woman, neither the woman without the man, in the Lord.

For as the woman is of the man, even so is the man also by the woman; but all things of God.

Judge in yourselves: is it seemly that a woman pray unto God uncovered?

Does not even nature itself teach you, that, if a man has long hair, it is his shame?

But if a woman has long hair, it is a glory to her: for her hair is given her for a covering.

But if any man seems to be quarrelsome, we have no such custom, neither the churches of God.

Rome and the Christians

For three hundred years, the Roman government showed an unusual tolerance in the area of personal religion. In rare instances, such as during the Great Fire of A.D. 64, the Christians were persecuted; however, the persecution occurred not only for their religious practices. The Emperor Nero needed scapegoats to stop the rumors that he had started the fire. Most persecutions took place in the provinces and were sporadic. They were undertaken by local governors who saw the Christians as unlicensed groups, practicing barbaric rites and refusing to make public sacrifices to the emperors. In the second century, the official government position was established by Emperor Trajan who decreed that only conspicuous and defiant Christians were to be punished; the rest would be tolerated. As the empire crumbled in the last half of the third century, Emperor Diocletian viewed the Christians as a danger to the unity of the empire and began the Great Persecution (A.D. 303–311). After Constantine (306–337) conquered the western half of the Roman empire, however, he issued a declaration of religious toleration in 313 that became the governmental policy until 392 when Emperor Theodosius I made Christianity the sole religion.

The first two selections concerning the Roman treatment of Christians come from Tacitus' *Annals* and Pliny the Younger's *Letters*. Tacitus (A.D. 55–117?), who wrote such works as *Agricola, Germania,* and the *Histories,* is considered the greatest historian of the empire. In the *Annals,* his purpose was to depict the imperial court from Tiberius through Nero in a series of vivid, unforgettable character sketches. As a moralist, he depicted those vices that led to Rome's decline. This is evident when he described the Great Fire in A.D. 64 that Nero was rumored to have started because he wished to renovate the city of Rome. Nero's subsequent treatment of Christians earned Tacitus' disapproval.

The second selection is from Pliny the Younger (A.D. 62–113), whose ten books of *Letters* illustrate travel, court, and daily life, and politics at the turn of the first century. About A.D. 110, Emperor Trajan appointed Pliny proconsul or special imperial representative in the province of Bithynia, which lay along the south coast of the Black Sea. Pliny's task was to deal with irregularities in politics and public finances and to maintain public order. When he began to have a problem with Christians in his province, Pliny immediately wrote to Emperor Trajan, asking if he had acted in accord with the emperor's wishes. The emperor's response demonstrated a great deal of humanity.

The next two selections, from St. Augustine's *Twenty-Two Books on the City of God* and Orosius' *Seven Books of History Against the Pagans,* date from the late Western Roman Empire when the Christian Church emerged as the only stable institution amidst the defunct governmental, social, and religious traditions of the past. St. Augustine of Hippo (354–430) was educated by his parents in Africa and Milan to be a teacher of rhetoric. He was not a Christian until after 384, when he listened to the sermons of St. Ambrose, Bishop of Milan. Augustine became a priest and returned to Africa, where he was made the Bishop of Hippo in 390.

Augustine began to write against various Christian heresies and developed explanations on predestination, grace, and free will that became the primary

Christian doctrines. His most famous work, *City of God,* was an attempt to create a philosophy of history with the belief that citizens should place their trust in God, or the Heavenly City, and not on the City of Man.

The last selection concerns monasticism as formulated by St. Benedict (480–545). In contrast to the East, where monks often led solitary lives filled with extreme fasts or self-inflicted torments, Benedict's rule prescribed moderation. Each monk took the vows of poverty, chastity, and obedience, but the rule also provided for simple meals, clothing, recreation, and adequate sleep. The most important of a monk's duties was prayer, but manual labor was instituted, as all monasteries were to be self-sufficient.

40

Tacitus, *The Annals*

In the late summer of A.D. 64, a fire began and burned for six days, devastating the heart of Rome. Tacitus describes Emperor Nero's persecution of Christians as an attempt to dispel the rumor that he had set the fire himself.

QUESTIONS TO CONSIDER

1. From a historical viewpoint, why is Tacitus' report important to Christianity?
2. Why did Tacitus disapprove of Nero's actions?
3. What does Tacitus think is the real reason that Nero persecuted the Christians?
4. What is the contrast between the actions of Nero and Emperor Trajan (see Reading 41) on the treatment of Christians?

The Great Fire

38 There followed a catastrophe, whether through accident or the design of the emperor is not sure, as there are authorities for both views, but it was the most disastrous and appalling of all the calamities brought on this city through the violence of fire. It had its beginning in the part of the Circus[1] next to the Palatine and Caelian hills among the shops where inflammable merchandise is sold. Here the fire broke out and, immediately gaining strength, was fanned by the wind and swept through the length of the Circus. No houses surrounded by enclosures or temples girded by walls or any other obstruction served as a check. First the blaze, as it rushed ahead, overran the level stretches, then rose to higher ground and

[1]Circus Maximus.

From Leon, Harry J., trans., "Selections from Tacitus" in MacKendrick, Paul and Herbert M. Howe, *Classics in Translation, Vol. II: Latin Literature,* © 1952 (Madison: The University of Wisconsin Press). Reprinted by permission of the University of Wisconsin Press.

again descended to devastate the low-lying areas, moving so swiftly in its destructive path as to outstrip all efforts to fight it, and aided by the fact that the city was vulnerable to fire because of the narrow streets winding in every direction and the irregular blocks of houses, such as old Rome had. . . .

39 During this time Nero was at Antium and did not come back to Rome until the fire approached his palace, with which he had joined the Palatine. . . . Even so the fire could not be stopped until the Palatine and the palace and everything in the area were devastated. To relieve the homeless refugees he opened up the Campus Martius and the public buildings of Agrippa and even his own gardens, and he built temporary structures to shelter the helpless multitude. Supplies were brought up from Ostia and the neighboring towns and the price of wheat was reduced. . . . These measures, though in the public interest, were wasted, because a rumor had spread abroad that at the very time when the city was burning, Nero had mounted on his private stage and sung of the destruction of Troy, comparing the present disaster with that ancient catastrophe. . . .

But no amount of human effort, no acts of generosity on the part of the emperor or appeasement of the gods could save Nero's reputation from the general belief that the fire had been set at his command.

In order to put an end to these rumors Nero provided scapegoats and visited most fearful punishments on those popularly called Christians, a group hated because of their outrageous practices. The founder of this sect, Christus, was executed in the reign of Tiberius by the procurator Pontius Pilatus. Thus the pernicious superstition was suppressed for the while, but it broke out again not only in Judaea, where this evil had its origin, but even in Rome, to which all obnoxious and disgraceful elements flow from everywhere in the world and receive a large following. The first ones to be seized were those who confessed; then on their information a vast multitude was convicted, not so much on the charge of incendiarism as because of their hatred of humanity. Their executions were made into a sport in that they were covered with skins of wild beasts and torn to pieces by dogs, or they were fastened to crosses or wrapped with inflammable materials, so that when the daylight waned, they could be burned to serve as torches in the night. Nero, who had offered his own gardens for this spectacle, gave a chariot racing exhibition in which he mingled with the crowd dressed as a charioteer or drove a chariot. The result was that despite the fact that these people were criminals worthy of the worst kind of punishment, a feeling of sympathy arose for them, since they were being destroyed not for the public good but to satisfy the cruelty of one man.

41

Pliny the Younger, *Letters to Emperor Trajan*

After a senatorial career and consulship, Pliny the Younger was sent by Emperor Trajan as a special representative to the Roman province of Bithynia in Asia Minor. His task was to keep the peace. When he had trouble dealing with the Christians, Pliny wrote to the emperor asking how he should proceed against them. The emperor replied with a surprisingly humanitarian approach.

QUESTIONS TO CONSIDER

1. What caused Pliny to write to Emperor Trajan for advice?
2. How was Emperor Trajan's approach to dealing with Christians different from that of Nero (see Reading 40)?
3. Why did a misunderstanding of Christian rites lead Roman authorities to accuse the Christians of outlandish practices (see Reading 40)?
4. Why did the Christian religion appeal to all classes and sexes?

The Official Treatment of the Christians

It is my custom, Sire, to refer to you all matters in which I am in doubt. For who can better guide my hesitancy or instruct my ignorance? I have never been present at trials of Christians; therefore I do not know what is sought and punished, nor to what extent. I have been puzzled in no small degree as to whether there is any difference in the treatment of ages or if the young, no matter how young, are treated just like more mature defendants; whether pardon is given to those who repent or it avails not at all to have given up the aberration if one has once been a Christian; whether the name itself, if free from criminal practices, is punished or only the abominations that are associated with the name.

For the present I have followed this procedure in the case of those who were denounced to me as Christians: I asked the defendants in person whether they were Christians. If they admitted it I asked them for a second and third time, threatening punishment: if they persisted, I ordered them to be executed. For I had no doubt that whatever it was they were confessing, their persistence and unbending stubbornness deserved to be punished. There were others of similar folly whom I sent to Rome, since they were Roman citizens. Soon the accusation became common, as usual, from the very fact that cases were being tried, and several variations appeared. An anonymous information was lodged listing a number of names. If defendants who denied that they were now Christians or had been in the past would, following my example, pray to the gods and offer incense and wine to your statue, which I had had placed beside those of the gods for this purpose, and if they would curse Christ, they should, I thought, be dismissed; for it is declared that real Christians cannot be compelled to do any of these acts. Others, named by an informer, said that they were Christians but later denied it; they had indeed been, but had given up the practice, some of them several years ago, one even twenty years ago. All of these also worshipped your image and the statues of the gods, and cursed Christ. However, they asserted that their guilt or mistake had amounted to no more than this, that they had been accustomed on a set day to gather before dawn and to chant in antiphonal form a hymn to Christ as if to a god, and to bind themselves by a pledge, not for the commission of any crime, but rather that they would not commit theft nor robbery nor adultery nor break their promises, nor refuse to return on demand any treasure that had been entrusted to their care; when this ceremony had been completed, they would go away, to reassemble later for a feast, but an ordinary and innocent one. They had abandoned even this custom after my edict in which, following your instruction, I had forbidden the existence of fellowships. So I thought it the more necessary to extract the truth even by torture from two maidservants who were called deaconesses. I found nothing save a vile superstition carried to an immoderate length.

From Heironimus, John Paul, trans., "Selected Letters of the Younger Pliny," in MacKendrick, Paul and Herbert M. Howe, *Classics in Translation, Vol. II: Latin Literature,* © 1952 (Madison: The University of Wisconsin Press). Reprinted by permission of the University of Wisconsin Press.

So, postponing further trials, I have resorted to consulting you. For it seemed to me a subject worthy of consultation, especially because of the number of people charged. For many of every age and rank, and of both sexes, are being brought to trial, and will be. The contagion of the superstition has pervaded not only the cities but the villages and country districts as well. Yet it seems that it can be halted and cured. It is well agreed that temples almost desolate have begun to be thronged again, and stated rites that had long been abandoned are revived; and a sale is found for the fodder of sacrificial victims, though hitherto buyers were rare. So it is easy to conjecture what a great number of offenders may be reformed, if a chance to repent is given.

The Emperor's Answer About the Christians

You have followed the proper course, my friend, in examining the cases of those who have been denounced to you as Christians. It is impossible to establish a hard and fast procedure for general use. They are not to be sought out; if they are accused, and the case is proved, they are to be punished, with the restriction, however, that if one denies that he is a Christian and makes it manifest in very deed, that is, by offering sacrifice to our gods, he shall be pardoned because of his repentance, however suspicious his past conduct was. Information lodged anonymously ought not to be regarded in dealing with any charge; it is of an abominable tendency, and not consonant with our enlightened age.

42

St. Augustine of Hippo, *The City of God*

In A.D. 410, the Visigothic armies of Alaric sacked Rome. Not only was this a major military defeat for the Empire in the West, but the victory of Arian Goths also undermined a basic doctrine widely held in Church circles since the time of Constantine: that people of the wrong religion could not prevail against orthodox Christian rulers.

St. Augustine (A.D. 354–430) of Hippo in North Africa began the task of explaining the Roman debacle in the first of what were to become twenty-two books of *The City of God*. At the outset, he attempted to refute pagan claims that Rome had done better under its old gods than under the Christian God by recalling positive experiences for the Empire under its Christian rulers and arguing that Christian morality led these emperors, with God's aid and direction, to provide a happier life for Romans than their pagan predecessors had achieved. At the same time, he stressed that true Christians lose nothing of value in worldly calamities, which, of course, rendered the havoc of barbarian invasions relatively unimportant.

For St. Augustine, the City of God, or the Heavenly City, includes God, the angels, and mortals predestined for salvation among its citizens. Those citizens of the Heavenly City who are making their way through earthly life pay no attention to material interests. Consequently, if churchgoers show too much concern about loss of property and physical suffering, they are probably citizens of the Earthly City in this life and doomed to hell in the hereafter. Citizens of the Earthly City are identified through their interests, which are limited to those earthly concerns that are insignificant to saved Christians.

St. Augustine worked on *The City of God* for thirteen years. Early in the project, he seems to have realized that comprehensive proof of the relative happiness of Christian times should be presented more systematically than he was doing, and so he entrusted that part of his work to Paulus Orosius, a young priest from Spain who had come to serve him and study with him (see Reading 43).

The first selections that follow are from the early books of *The City of God;* the last two from the much later Book XIX. Two different and influential Christian theories of history emerge in the work of St. Augustine and Orosius. In the early books of *The City of God* and consistently in *Seven Books of History Against the Pagans,* God rewards Christian emperors and peoples for faith and good works, rather much as Jahweh rewarded the Children of Israel for the same thing. Then, in *The City of God* as a whole, particularly the later books, a theory unfolds more consistent with New Testament values: The Christian kingdom is not of this world, and true Christians should not worry much about even such momentous, earthly happenings as lost wars and falling empires.

QUESTIONS TO CONSIDER

1. Why does St. Augustine view the sack of Rome as a cause for heightened, rather than diminished, respect for Christianity?
2. Compare Kautilya's statement from the *Duties of a King* (see Reading 22): "In the happiness of the subjects lies the happiness of the king . . ." with St. Augustine's statement on the happiness of Christian emperors.
3. Why is a temporary peace observable between the City of God and the Earthly City?
4. Why does St. Augustine say that the City of God or the Heavenly City is in a state of pilgrimage on earth?
5. What was going on in the years A.D. 410–423, in which St. Augustine was writing *The City of God,* that might well have led him to modify his original stance that people enjoyed a better quality of peace under Christian emperors than under their predecessors?

Elements of Christian Emperors' Real Happiness

We call the Christian emperors happy if they rule justly; if they are not carried away by conceit in the midst of voices praising them extravagantly and by men hailing them with a debasing show of excess humility, but remember that they are men; if they turn their power to the service of the Divine Majesty, by using it to spread the worship of God as far as they

De civitate Dei libri xxii, ed. Emanuel Hoffman (Vienna: F. Tempsky, 1899–1900), extracts from Books I–V and Book XIX, *passim,* trans. Henry A. Myers.

can; and if they fear love, and worship God. We call them happy if they are relatively slow with punishments, inflicting them only when pressed by the requirements of governing and defending the state, but are all the more quick with pardons, not to let crimes go unpunished but in the hope of rehabilitating the offenders; and if they make up for often necessarily harsh decrees with kindness and mercy and with sweeping generosity. We call them happy if they restrict their luxury all the more as their wealth lets them afford it; if they prefer ruling over low desires within themselves to ruling over any nation at all; and if they do all this not out of a passion for vain glory but out of a love for eternal happiness, without failing to offer the sacrifice of humility, mercy and prayer for their sins to their own true God.

The Prosperity God Granted Emperor Constantine

On Emperor Constantine . . . God bestowed such an abundance of earthly favors as no man would dare wish for. He permitted him to found a city to share in the imperial rule of Rome, a daughter, so to speak, of Rome herself but without any temples or images of the demons.[1] He reigned for a long time, maintaining the whole Roman world as sole emperor. He was most victorious in directing and waging wars, and he was always successful in putting down usurpers. He was very old when he died of sickness and age, and he left sons to rule after him.

The Faith and Piety of Emperor Theodosius [I]

Theodosius . . . put down the usurper Eugenius, who had illegally installed himself in that emperor's place, prevailing against his very powerful army more by prayer than by the sword. Some soldiers who were there have told me that all the spears they were throwing were snatched from their hands by a very strong wind, which blew away from Theodosius' side in the enemy's direction, and that it not only gave greater force to whatever they threw against them but even turned back the spears which the enemy soldiers were throwing into their own bodies. . . .

About the War in Which King Radagais of the Goths, a Worshipper of Demons, Was Defeated with His Huge Army in a Single Day

When Radagais, King of the Goths, was already threatening the Romans' very necks with his huge and savage army encamped near the city, he was beaten in one day with such speed and in such a way that not one single Roman was wounded, let alone killed, while well over a hundred thousand of his soldiers were struck down, and he was captured and soon put to a deserved death. For if such a godless man with such equally godless troops had entered Rome, who would have been spared by him? What shrines of the martyrs would he have respected? In dealing with what person would the fear of God have restrained him? Whose blood would he have wanted to leave unshed and whose chastity unravaged?

[1]Reference is to Constantinople, founded by Constantine upon the site of Byzantium, which, of course, had previously contained pagan temples, although Constantine tried to make the new capital a purely Christian city.

Whether the Sweep of Imperial Command . . . Is Among Things of Value for Wise and Happy Men

It makes sense that if the true God is worshipped and served with true rites and good morals, it is a benefit for good men to have long reigns over great territories. This is actually not of so much use to themselves as it is to their subjects, because as far as they themselves are concerned their own true faith and righteousness, which are great gifts from God, are enough to give them the true happiness that lets them live this life well and attain eternal life afterwards. Thus the reign of good men here on earth does not serve their own good so much as it does human concerns.

The Harsh Brutality in the Sack of Rome Corresponded with Established Customs of War, Whereas the Mercy Shown Revealed the Power of Christ's Name

All the destruction, killing, looting, burning, and suffering which took place in the recent sack of Rome happened in accordance with the customs of waging war. What was altogether new and previously unheard of, however, was that the barbarian brutality [of the Goths] was so tamed that they picked the largest of the basilicas and allowed them to remain sanctuaries, where no one could be struck down and from which no one could be dragged away. Many people were led there to freedom and safety by soldiers showing sympathy for them. . . . Anyone who does not see fit to credit this to the name of Christ—yes, to Christian times—is blind. Anyone who sees this new turn of events but fails to praise it is most ungrateful.

The Saints Lose Nothing of Value in Losing Material Goods

In the sack of Rome faithful and godly men . . . "lost everything they had." How about their faith? How about their godliness? How about the goods of the inner being which make a person rich before God? Listen to what the Apostle Paul says about the riches of Christianity: ". . .Godliness with contentment is great gain, for we brought nothing into this world and certainly we can carry nothing out. If we have food and clothing, let us be content with them. People who want to be rich fall into temptations and traps. They fall into foolish and harmful desires which drown men in destruction and perdition."[2]

The Universal Peace, Which the Law of Nature Preserves Through All Disturbances, and the Condition Which Each Person Deserves to Find Himself in, According to the Way He Has Used His Will and According to the Decision of the Just Judge

Domestic peace is a harmonious arrangement in matters of command and obedience among those of the same household, and the peace of a [normal] city is a similar one among its citizens. The peace of the Heavenly City is the most perfectly and harmoniously designed com-

[2]*I Timothy* 6:6–10.

munal relationship in the enjoyment of God and in the fellowship resulting from union with God. Peace for all beings is tranquility within order. Order is the arrangement of equal and unequal things, with each assigned its proper place.

And so we see that miserable people [lacking faith and godliness] . . . in the very fact that they justly deserve their misery are confined to a condition of misery by the principle of order. This keeps them from being united with saved people. When they live without obvious disturbances they adapt to their bondage, and so there is a bit of tranquil order among them, and so they enjoy a peace of sorts. They still remain miserable, however, since, in spite of not suffering constantly from a total lack of security, they are not within that realm where there is no cause to worry about either suffering or security. . . .

Where Peace and Discord Between the Heavenly and Earthly Cities Come From

The Earthly City, which does not live by faith, desires an earthly peace, seeking to bring it about through harmony of command and obedience among citizens, even though its scope is limited to uniting people's wills on matters pertaining to this mortal life.

The Heavenly City, however, or, to be more precise, those of its members who are living by faith during their mortal pilgrimages, must make use of this peace, although only until they are through with their transient status on earth, which requires it. For this reason, the Heavenly City sojourning either as a captive or a wandering stranger in the Earthly City does not hesitate to obey earthly authority in matters required by the communal life of mortals. With mortal life common to the people of both Cities, a certain harmony between them may be maintained in relation to its requirements.

While the Heavenly City sojourns on earth, it recruits members from all peoples and forms a pilgrim society of men and women speaking all different languages, which pays no attention to the diversity of customs, laws, and institutions among them, by which earthly peace is established and maintained.

43

Paulus Orosius, *History Against the Pagans*

In writing his dissertation for St. Augustine (see Reading 42), which took him a full seven years, young Paulus Orosius became the first Christian graduate student on record. His work, entitled without the slightest pretense of objectivity, *Seven Books of History Against the Pagans,* became *the* Christian textbook of world history, as opposed to plain church history, from creation to A.D. 417. In it, Orosius sought to demonstrate once and for all that Christian times were better than pagan times. It was one of the most widely copied and cited books in the Middle Ages and sold so well in the first centuries of printed books that four-hundred-year-old copies of *History Against the Pagans* are not really rare books today. Actually, St. Augustine did not think highly of the finished work of Orosius, but that fact did not become known until the late 1950s, and for some fifteen hundred years Orosius was viewed as having written what the great St. Augustine would have written if he had not given young Paulus this assignment to ease the burdens on his own time.

Orosius selectively rewrites history to make "pagan times," including those periods such as the Age of Pericles and Rome in the Early Republic, which the usual narrative, world-history textbook presents as enjoyable times to have lived in, as characterized by misery and uncertainty of existence. For him, times became happier with the birth of Christ, not only spiritually for those who accepted the Christian faith, but in terms of worldly peace and greater earthly happiness. In stressing this, he has God bestow divine approval on the Empire founded by Augustus Caeser, which, give or take thirty years, came into being when Christ was born. Predictably, times become even better with the reigns of Constantine and Theodosius, who turn the Empire into a Christian one. Proving this involves selecting the best aspects of an Empire, which, in fact, was crumbling all around him. The Roman Empire in the West had only a scant sixty years of life left in it when Orosius wound up his research, but you would never guess from what follows that its weaknesses were severe. Orosius treated the barbarian invasions that rocked his own fifth century as minor inconveniences, ordained by God to facilitate the spread of the Catholic faith to the invaders and to civilize them through their contacts with Roman Christians. Orosius is faithful enough to earlier Christian doctrine to state his love of the City of God, but by an odd quirk of fate and conviction his commitment to it made him a much more avid spokesman for the outgoing *Pax Romana* than any subsequent pagan writer or orator.

QUESTIONS TO CONSIDER

1. In spite of the great optimism of Orosius, he does give a few hints that the Roman Empire in the West is coming apart at the seams. Can you find one or more of them?
2. Comparing the excerpts from St. Augustine and Orosius, what similarities do you find? Where is the emphasis different?

Let us assume there is no doubt about the fact that it was under Augustus Caesar, following the peace treaty with the Parthians, that for the first time the entire world laid down its arms and overcame its disagreements under an all-encompassing peace and new tranquility in obedience of Roman laws. Foreign peoples preferred relying on Roman laws to relying on their own arms. All races, all provinces, innumerable city-states, infinite populations—in fact, the whole world—finally united with a single will in freely and honestly serving the cause of peace, ever mindful of the common good. In earlier days, not even one city-state, nor one group of citizens, nor even (more significantly) one household of brothers could get along with another indefinitely. If we confirm that all this came to pass under Augustus as ruler, it is quite clear that in the same empire of Augustus the birth of our Lord Jesus Christ was beginning to light up the world in a most certain manifestation of His approval.

Historiarum adversum paganos libri VII, ed. Karl Zangemeister (Vienna: C. Gerold, 1882), excerpts from Books III, viii, 5–8, and V, i, 10–13, ii, 1–8; trans. Allen C. Myers.

Although it will be against their will, those driven to blasphemy by jealousy will be forced to admit and acknowledge that this worldwide peace and most tranquil serenity was made possible not by the greatness of Augustus Caesar, but by the Son of God, who appeared at the time of Caesar and who came not just to be the ruler of one city-state but rather as the Creator of the universe, to be recognized by everyone, in order to unite the world. In the same way as the rising sun fills the day with light, upon His arrival he mercifully adorned the world with peace.

We need to take a look at ourselves and the lifestyles we have chosen and gotten used to, in order to get our bearings. Our ancestors waged wars until, exhausted by wars, they sought peace by offering to pay tribute. Tribute is the price of peace: we pay tribute to avoid the suffering of war, and we stop and wait in the same harbor (of tribute-paying) where our ancestors sheltered themselves from storms of evils.

It is in this light that we should judge whether our times are happy ones: surely we find them happier than those of old because we continually enjoy the peace they arrived at only late in their game. We are strangers to the violence of wars which exhausted them. In fact, we are able to enjoy that carefree existence from birth to old age, which they could enjoy only in part after the coming of Augustus Caesar's empire and Christ's birth. What we contribute freely for our defense was simply taken from them earlier, as what they owed in their slave-like status. How different modern times are from past ones can be seen when we compare the way Rome extorted money by force of arms from its subject peoples, in order to support Roman luxury, with the way Rome now allocates funds for the general good of all our communities.

For me my native land is everywhere. I can get away to a safe place at the first hint of any sort of disturbance. Right now Africa has taken me in with a hospitality commensurate with my confidence in approaching her. *Now* Africa receives me into its own community with its carefree enjoyment of peace under laws common to us all. That same Africa, of which it was said in olden days and truly said,

> We dare not ask for refuge on her sand:
> The wars they stir up keep us from this land[1]

now opens wide the doors to her hearths for weary bodies and keeps them warm and welcome. The huge expanse of the East, the abundance produced in the North, the expansive diversity of the South, the great and secure strongholds on our large islands now have my law and name because I come to Christians and Romans as a Christian and Roman. I do not fear any gods of my host. I do not fear that his religion will mean my death. I have none of that fear of strange lands where a native gets away with whatever he wants and a traveller cannot tend to his own business in peace or even of lands where the law of foreigners is not mine. One God, loved and feared by all, established this unity of the kingdom at the time He chose to reveal Himself among men: those same laws under one God now rule everywhere. Whenever I arrive unknown, I need not fear sudden violence as if I were alone and deserted. Among Romans, as I was saying, I am a Roman; among Christians, a Christian; among men, a man. I can appeal to the state on the basis of its laws, to the consciences of men on the basis of religion, and to nature on the basis of our common sharing of it. I enjoy time spent in each country, as though it were my own fatherland—keeping in mind that

---

[1] Vergil, *The Aeneid,* Book I, lines 540–541.

the true fatherland I love most does not have its roots on earth. I have lost nothing where I loved nothing, and I have everything when He whom I do love is with me, particularly since He is the same among all men. He not only gives me an introduction to all men but helps me become a friend of theirs. Nor does He desert me when I am in need, for "The earth is His and the fullness thereof." He instructs that all things from this abundance be made available to all people in common. These are the benefits of our *own* time, and our ancestors did *not* enjoy them fully, whether we refer to our present tranquility, or to hope for the future, or to places of refuge for all. Lacking these, they waged wars without end. Since they were not free to move as groups from place to place, they had to cling to their old homes when warfare came and face miserable death or the disgrace of enslavement.

44

Monastic Life: The Rule of St. Benedict

In the midst of a disorderly world, medieval monasteries established communities devoted to achieving salvation. St. Benedict of Nursia (A.D. 480–543), the most influential figure in Western European monastic history, came from a wealthy Italian family; but at age twenty, he renounced all worldly temptations and withdrew to the mountains to live as a hermit. His reputation for holiness led others to seek him out, and in time they became his devoted disciples.

St. Benedict eventually decided that a communal setting was a better environment for most men trying to lead a life pleasing to God. He founded twelve monasteries in Italy before he and his followers built a large one at Monte Cassino around 529, where he applied his "Rule" and lived the rest of his life. Requiring vows of chastity, poverty, and obedience, St. Benedict's Rule became the basis for monastic life in the West.

Unlike the stricter Celtic monasticism of St. Columban, the strength of St. Benedict's Rule lies in its combination of religious commitment, encouragement of good works along with faith, and common-sense moderation in discipline. In contrast, the more extreme Celtic rules required severe punishment for even unintentional lapses. The Benedictine model is the family, with the abbot in the role of a strict, but patient and loving father. Other members of the community overcome un-Christian willfulness through continual acts of humility; they complete their tasks in a mutually supportive fashion as brothers. In the year before St. Benedict died, his sister, Scholastica, founded a convent near Monte Cassino. With appropriate modifications, the Benedictine Rule guided nuns as well as monks in the medieval West.

QUESTIONS TO CONSIDER

1. What should the monk do in order to achieve progressively greater degrees of humility?
2. What are St. Benedict's guidelines for correcting the faults of those who commit offenses?

3. What is St. Benedict's basic attitude toward providing food, drink, and other necessities of life for the monks?

What Kind of Man the Abbot Ought to Be

An abbot who is worthy to rule over the monastery ought always to remember what he is called, and correspond to his name of superior by his deeds. For he is believed to hold the place of Christ in the monastery, since he is called by his name, as the apostle says: "You have received the spirit of the adoption of children, in which we cry Abba, Father." And, therefore, the abbot ought not (God forbid) to teach, or ordain, or command anything contrary to the law of the Lord; but let his bidding and his doctrine be infused into the minds of his disciples like the leaven of divine justice.

Let the abbot be ever mindful that at the dreadful judgment of God an account will have to be given both of his own teaching and of the obedience of his disciples. And let him know that to the fault of the shepherd shall be imputed any lack of profit which the father of the household may find in his sheep. Only then shall he be acquitted, if he shall have bestowed all pastoral diligence on his unquiet and disobedient flock, and employed all his care to amend their corrupt manner of life: then shall he be absolved in the judgment of the Lord.

For the abbot in his doctrine ought always to observe the bidding of the apostle, wherein he says: "Reprove, entreat, rebuke"; mingling, as occasions may require, gentleness with severity; showing now the rigor of a master, now the loving affection of a father, so as sternly to rebuke the undisciplined and restless, and to exhort the obedient, mild, and patient to advance in virtue. And such as are negligent and haughty we charge him to reprove and correct. Let him not shut his eyes to the faults of offenders; but as soon as they appear, let him strive with all his might to root them out, remembering the fate of Eli, the priest of Shiloh. Those of good disposition and understanding let him, for the first or second time, correct only with words; but such as are forward and hard of heart, and proud, or disobedient, let him chastise with bodily stripes at the very first offence, knowing that it is written: "The fool is not corrected with words." . . .

Of Obedience

The first degree of humility is obedience without delay. This becomes those who hold nothing dearer to them than Christ, and who on account of the holy servitude which they have taken upon them, either for fear of hell or for the glory of life everlasting, as soon as anything is ordered by the superior, suffer no more delay in doing it than if it had been commanded by God himself. It is of these that the Lord says: "At the hearing of the ear he has obeyed me." And again, to teachers he says: "He that hears you hears me."

Such as these, therefore, leaving immediately their own occupations and forsaking their own will, with their hands disengaged, and leaving unfinished what they were about, with the speedy step of obedience follow by their deeds the voice of him who commands; and so as it were at the same instant the bidding of the master and the perfect fulfilment of

From "The Rule of Saint Benedict," trans. Dom Oswald Hunter Blair, in Emmanuel Heufelder, *The Way to God According to the Rule of St. Benedict* (Kalamazoo, MI: Cistercian Publications, 1983), pp. 224–266, *passim.* Reprinted by permission of Fort Augustus Abbey.

the disciple are joined together in the swiftness of the fear of God by those who are moved with the desire of attaining eternal life.

Of the Practice of Silence

Let us do as says the prophet: "I said, I will take heed to my ways, that I sin not with my tongue, I have placed a watch over my mouth; I became dumb and was silent, and held my peace even from good things." Here the prophet shows that if we ought at times to refrain even from good words for the sake of silence, how much more ought we to abstain from evil words, on account of the punishment due to sin. Therefore, on account of the importance of silence, let leave to speak be seldom granted even to perfect disciples, although their conversation be good and holy and tending to edification; because it is written: "In much speaking you shall not avoid sin." . . . But as for buffoonery or idle words, such as move to laughter, we utterly condemn them in every place, nor do we allow the disciple to open his mouth in such discourse. . . .

Of Humility

The Holy Scripture cries out to us, brothers, saying: "Every one that exalts himself shall be humbled, and he who humbles himself shall be exalted." . . .

The first degree of humility, then, is that a man, always keeping the fear of God before his eyes, avoid all forgetfulness; and that he be ever mindful of all that God has commanded, bethinking himself that those who despise God will be consumed in hell for their sins, and that life everlasting is prepared for them that fear him. . . .

The second degree of humility is, that a man love not his own will, nor delight in fulfilling his own desires; but carry out in his deeds that saying of the Lord: "I came not to do mine own will, but the will of him who sent me." And again Scripture says: "Self-will has punishment, but necessity wins the crown."

The third degree of humility is, that a man for the love of God submit himself to his superior in all obedience; imitating the Lord, of whom the apostle says: "He was made obedient even unto death."

The fourth degree of humility is, that if in this very obedience hard and contrary things, nay even injuries, are done to him, he should embrace them patiently with a quiet conscience, and not grow weary or give in, as the Scripture says: "He that shall persevere to the end shall be saved." And again: "Let your heart be comforted, and wait for the Lord."

The fifth degree of humility is, not to hide from one's abbot any of the evil thoughts that beset one's heart, or the sins committed in secret, but humbly to confess them. Concerning which the Scripture exhorts us, saying: "Make known your way unto the Lord, and hope in him." . . .

The sixth degree of humility is for a monk to be contented with the meanest and worst of everything, and in all that is enjoined him to esteem himself a bad and worthless laborer, saying with the prophet: "I have been brought to nothing, and I knew it not: I am become as a beast before you, yet I am always with you."

The seventh degree of humility is that he should not only call himself with his tongue lower and viler than all, but also believe himself in his inmost heart to be so, humbling himself, and saying with the prophet: "I am a worm and no man, the shame of men and the outcast of the people: I have been exalted, and cast down, and confounded." . . .

The eighth degree of humility is for a monk to do nothing except what is authorized by the common rule of the monastery, or the example of the seniors.

The ninth degree of humility is, that a monk refrain his tongue from speaking, keeping silence until a question be asked him, as the Scripture shows: "In much talking you shall not avoid sin," and, "The talkative man shall not be directed upon the earth."

The tenth degree of humility is, that he be not easily moved and prompt to laughter; because it is written: "The fool lifts up his voice in laughter." . . .

Having, therefore, ascended all these degrees of humility, the monk will presently arrive at that love of God which, being perfect, casts out fear. . . .

Of Those Who, Being Often Corrected, Do Not Amend

If any brother who has been frequently corrected for some fault, or even excommunicated, does not amend, let a more severe chastisement be applied: that is, let the punishment of stripes be administered to him. But if even then he does not correct himself, or perchance (which God forbid), puffed up with pride, even wishes to defend his deeds, then let the abbot act like a wise physician. If he has applied fomentations and the unction of his admonitions, the medicine of the Holy Scriptures, and the last remedy of excommunication or corporal chastisement, and if he see that his labors are of no avail, let him add what is still more powerful, his own prayers and those of all the brothers for him, that God, who is all-powerful, may work the cure of the sick brother. But if he be not healed even by this means, then at length let the abbot use the sword of separation, as the apostle says: "Put away the evil one from you." And again: "If the faithless one depart, let him depart," lest one diseased sheep should taint the whole flock. . . .

What Kind of Man the Cellarer of the Monastery Is to Be

Let there be chosen out of the community, as cellarer of the monastery, a man wise and of mature character, temperate, not a great eater, not haughty, nor headstrong, nor arrogant, not slothful, nor wasteful, but a Godfearing man, who may be like a father to the whole community. Let him have the care of everything, but do nothing without leave of the abbot. Let him take heed to what is commanded him, and not sadden his brothers. If a brother ask him for anything unreasonably, let him not treat him with contempt and so grieve him, but reasonably and with all humility refuse what he asks for amiss. Let him be watchful over his own soul, remembering always that saying of the apostle, that "he that has ministered well, purchases to himself a good degree." Let him have special care of the sick, of the children, of guests and of the poor, knowing without doubt that he will have to render an account of them all on the day of judgment. . . .

Whether Monks Ought to Have Anything of Their Own

The vice of private ownership is above all to be cut off from the monastery by the roots. Let none presume to give or receive anything without leave of the abbot, nor to keep anything as their own, either book or writing-tablet or pen, or anything whatsoever; since they are permitted to have neither body nor will in their own power. But all that is necessary they may hope to receive from the father of the monastery; nor are they allowed to keep anything which the abbot has not given, or at least permitted them to have. Let all things be common to all, as it is written: "Neither did anyone say that anything which he possessed was his own." But if anyone should be found to indulge in this most baneful vice, and after one or two admonitions does not amend, let him be subjected to correction. . . .

Whether All Ought Alike to Receive What Is Needful

As it is written: "Distribution was made to every man, according as he had need." Herein we do not say that there should be respecting of persons—God forbid—but consideration for infirmities. Let him, therefore, that has need of less give thanks to God and not be grieved; and let him who requires more be humbled for his infirmity and not made proud by the kindness shown to him; and so all members of the family shall be at peace. Above all, let not the evil of murmuring show itself by the slightest word or sign on any account whatever. If anyone be found guilty herein, let him be subjected to severe punishment. . . .

Of the Weekly Servers in the Kitchen

Let the brothers wait on one another in turn, so that none be excused from the work of the kitchen, except he be prevented by sickness or by some more necessary employment; for thus is gained a greater reward and an increase of charity. But let assistance be given to the weak, that they may not do their work with sadness; and let all have help according to the number of the community and the situation of the place. If the community be large, let the cellarer be excused from work in the kitchen, and also those, as already mentioned, who are occupied in more urgent business. Let the rest serve each other in turn with all charity. Let him who ends his week in the kitchen make all things clean on Saturday and wash the towels with which the brothers dry their hands and feet. Let both him who goes out and him who is coming in wash the feet of all. Let him hand over to the cellarer the vessels of his office, clean and whole; and let the cellarer deliver the same to him who enters, that he may know what he gives and what he receives.

   Let the weekly servers each take a cup of drink and a piece of bread over and above the appointed portion, one hour before the time for reflection, that so they may serve their brothers when the hour comes without murmuring or great labor. . . .

Of Old Men and Children

Although human nature is of itself drawn to feel pity for these two times of life, namely, old age and infancy, yet the authority of the Rule should also provide for them. Let their weakness be always taken into account, and the strictness of the Rule respecting food be by no means kept in their regard; but let a kind consideration be shown for them, and let them eat before the regular hours. . . .

Of the Measure of Food

We think it sufficient for the daily meal, whether at the sixth or the ninth hour, that there be at all seasons of the year two dishes of cooked food, because of the weakness of different people; so that he who perchance cannot eat the one may make his meal of the other. Let two dishes, then, suffice for all the brothers; and if there be any fruit or young vegetables, let a third be added. Let one pound weight of bread suffice for the day, whether there be but one meal or both dinner and supper.

Of the Measure of Drink

Everyone has his proper gift from God, one after this manner, another after that. And, therefore, it is with some misgiving that we appoint the measure of other men's living. Yet, considering the infirmity of the weak, we think that one pint of wine a day is sufficient for each; but let those to whom God gives the endurance of abstinence know that they shall have their proper reward. If, however, the situation of the place, the work, or the heat of summer require more, let it be in the power of the superior to grant it, taking care in every thing that surfeit or drunkenness creep not in. And although we read that wine ought by no means to be the drink of monks, yet since in our times monks cannot be persuaded of this, let us at least agree to drink not to satiety, but sparingly; because "wine makes even the wise to fall away." But where the necessity of the place allows not even the aforesaid measure, but much less, or none at all, let those who dwell there bless God and not murmur. This above all we admonish, that there be no murmuring among them.

The Reign of Emperor Justinian

Upon the death of his uncle Justin I, Justinian (A.D. 527–565) became Roman Emperor and immediately had his wife, Theodora (a former prostitute), crowned Empress. Together they worked hard to meet the challenges of imperial rule. In A.D. 532, Theodora's timely advice helped Justinian successfully suppress the Nika tax riots in Constantinople.

Justinian's central policy was to reunite the Western Roman Empire, which had fallen to various barbarian Germanic peoples, with the East. This goal was accomplished with the aid of many great generals; for example, Belisarius conquered Vandal-held Africa and led the first invasions of Ostrogothic Italy. In addition to the Western reunification, there were a series of confrontations with the Sassanid Persian Empire in Syria-Palestine and Armenia. In these latter engagements, Justinian sent his armies but preferred to reach a series of very expensive truces with Persia rather than any definitive conclusion. Justinian is remembered in considerable part for the great codification of Roman Law (*Codex Iuris Civilis*), which took place during his reign. In centuries to come, the *Justinian Code* would become the foundation of law in continental Europe and, to a lesser extent, the British Isles.

Another imperial objective was peace within the Christian Church, which was disturbed by heretics called Monophysites. These Christians rejected the orthodox view that Christ had two natures, human and divine; they rejected Christ's humanity and stressed only his divine nature. After attempting a series of compromises, Justinian finally resorted to religious persecution that only increased the dissatisfaction of orthodox and heretics alike.

Our major source for Justinian's reign is Procopius of Caesarea. Born about A.D. 500, he went to Constantinople, where he became the private secretary (ca. 527) to General Belisarius. From his pen came three known works: *History of the Wars, On the Buildings,* and the *Secret History.* The first book details the events concerning Justinian's wars in Africa, Italy, and Persia. The second work praises the emperor for his architectural contributions such as the rebuilding of Santa Sophia, which had been destroyed in the Nika riots. Yet it is Procopius' third and smallest book—the *Secret History* or *Anecdota*—that has given him the most fame. It records in vitriolic splendor the "crimes," vices, and scandals of Justinian, Theodora, General Belisarius, and his wife Antonina.

45

Procopius, *History of the Wars*

In A.D. 532, citizens of Constantinople revolted against the tax policies of Emperor Justinian. The following selection reveals Empress Theodora's part in controlling this uprising.

QUESTIONS TO CONSIDER

1. Why was Empress Theodora one of the most influential women in Byzantine history?
2. Compare Procopius' description of Theodora's early life with the present selection (see Reading 46). What are the most significant differences in his views?
3. What other women in history had so much influence?

At this same time an insurrection broke out unexpectedly in Byzantium among the populace, and, contrary to expectation, it proved to be a very serious affair, and ended in great harm to the people and to the senate, as the following account will show. In every city the population has been divided for a long time past into the Blue and the Green factions; but within comparatively recent times it has come about that, for the sake of these names and the seats which the rival factions occupy in watching the games, they spend their money and abandon their bodies to the most cruel tortures, and even do not think it unworthy to die a most shameful death. And they fight against their opponents knowing not for what end they imperil themselves, but knowing well that, even if they overcome their enemy in the fight, the conclusion of the matter for them will be to be carried off straightway to the prison, and finally, after suffering extreme torture, to be destroyed. So there grows up in them against their fellow men a hostility which has no cause, and at no time does it cease or disappear, for it gives place neither to the ties of marriage nor of relationship nor of friendship,

Reprinted by permission of the publishers and the Loeb Classical Library from Procopius, *History of the Wars,* Book I, trans. H.B. Dewing (Cambridge, MA: Harvard University Press, 1914/1961), pp. 219, 223, 231, 233.

and the case is the same even though those who differ with respect to these colours be brothers or any other kin. They care neither for things divine nor human in comparison with conquering in these struggles; and it matters not whether a sacrilege is committed by anyone at all against God, or whether the laws and the constitution are violated by friend or by foe; nay even when they are perhaps ill supplied with the necessities of life, and when their fatherland is in the most pressing need and suffering unjustly, they pay no need if only it is likely to go well with their "faction"; for so they name the bands of partisans. And even women join with them in this unholy strife, and they not only follow the men, but even resist them if opportunity offers, although they neither go to the public exhibitions at all, nor are they impelled by any other cause; so that I, for my part, am unable to call this anything except a disease of the soul. This, then, is pretty well how matters stand among the people of each and every city.

But at this time the officers of the city administration in Byzantium were leading away to death some of the rioters. But the members of the two factions, conspiring together and declaring a truce with each other, seized the prisoners and then straightway entered the prison and released all those who were in confinement there, whether they had been condemned on a charge of stirring up sedition, or for any other unlawful act. And all the attendants in the service of the city government were killed indiscriminately; meanwhile, all of the citizens who were sane-minded were fleeing to the opposite mainland, and fire was applied to the city as if it had fallen under the hand of an enemy. The sanctuary of Sophia and the baths of Zeuxippus, and the portion of the imperial residence from the propylaea as far as the so-called House of Ares were destroyed by fire, and besides these both the great colonnades which extended as far as the market place which bears the name of Constantine, in addition to many houses of wealthy men and a vast amount of treasure. During this time the emperor and his consort with a few members of the senate shut themselves up in the palace and remained quietly there. Now the watchword which the populace passed around to one another was Nika,[1] and the insurrection has been called by this name up to the present time. . . .

Now the emperor and his court were deliberating as to whether it would be better for them if they remained or if they took to flight in the ships. And many opinions were expressed favouring either course. And the Empress Theodora also spoke to the following effect: "As to the belief that a woman ought not to be daring among men or to assert herself boldly among those who are holding back from fear, I consider that the present crisis most certainly does not permit us to discuss whether the matter should be regarded in this or in some other way. For in the case of those whose interests have come into the greatest danger nothing else seems best except to settle the issue immediately before them in the best possible way. My opinion then is that the present time, above all others, is inopportune for flight, even though it brings safety. For while it is impossible for a man who has seen the light not also to die, for one who has been an emperor it is unendurable to be a fugitive. May I never be separated from this purple, and may I not live that day on which those who meet me shall not address me as mistress. If, now, it is your wish to save yourself, O Emperor, there is no difficulty. For we have much money, and there is the sea, here the boats. However consider whether it will not come about after you have been saved that you would gladly exchange that safety for death. For as for myself, I approve a certain ancient saying that royalty is a good burial-shroud." When the queen had spoken thus, all were filled with boldness, and, turning their thoughts towards resistance, they began to consider how they might be able to defend themselves if any hostile force should come against them.

[1]Conquest or victory.

46

Procopius, *The Secret History*

Belisarius was Justinian's most important general. Procopius relates, however, how easily Belisarius was deceived by his unscrupulous wife Antonina.

QUESTIONS TO CONSIDER

1. Why would Procopius not want his *Secret History* published in his lifetime?
2. How were the depictions of Belisarius and Justinian less than flattering?
3. Compare Procopius' views of women in *The Secret History* with those in *History of the Wars.*

Belisarius had a wife, whom I have had occasion to mention in the previous books; her father and grandfather were charioteers who had given exhibitions of their skill in both Byzantium and Thessalonica, and her mother was one of the prostitutes attached to the theatre. This woman, having in her early years lived a lewd sort of a life and having become dissolute in character, not only having consorted much with the cheap sorcerers who surrounded her parents, but also having thus acquired the knowledge of what she needed to know, later became the wedded wife of Belisarius, after having already been the mother of many children. Straightway, therefore, she decided upon being an adulteress from the very start, but she was very careful to conceal this business, not because she was ashamed of her own practices, nor because she entertained any fear so far as her husband was concerned (for she never experienced the slightest feeling of shame for any action whatsoever and she had gained complete control of her husband by means of many tricks of magic), but because she dreaded the punishment the Empress might inflict. . . .

There was a certain youth from Thrace in the household of Belisarius, Theodosius by name. . . . Now when Belisarius was about to embark on the voyage to Libya, he bathed this youth in the sacred bath, from which he lifted him with his own hands, thus making him the adopted child of himself and his wife, as is customary for Christians to make adoptions, and consequently Antonina loved Theodosius, as she naturally would, as being her son through the sacred word, and with very particular solicitude she kept him near herself. And straightway she fell extraordinarily in love with him in the course of this voyage, and having become insatiate in her passion, she shook off both fear and respect for everything both divine and human and had intercourse with him, at first in secret, but finally even in the presence of servants of both sexes. For being by now possessed by this passion and manifestly smitten with love, she could see no longer any obstacle to the deed. And on one occasion Belisarius caught them in the very act in Carthage, yet he willingly allowed himself to be deceived by his wife. For though he found them both in an underground chamber and was transported with rage, she, without either playing the coward or attempting to conceal the deed, remarked "I came down here in order to hide with the aid of the boy the most valu-

Reprinted by permission of the publishers and the Loeb Classical Library from Procopius, *The Secret History or Anecdota*, Vol. 6, trans. H.B. Dewing (Cambridge, MA: Harvard University Press, 1935/1960), pp. 7, 13, 95, 107, 111.

able of our booty, so that it may not get to the knowledge of the Emperor." Now she said this as a mere pretext, but he, appearing to be satisfied, dropped the matter, though he could see that the belt which supported the drawers of Theodosius, covering his private parts, had been loosened. For under compulsion of love for the woman, he would have it that the testimony of his own eyes was absolutely untrustworthy.

[In another section of *The Secret History,* Procopius describes the nature and moral character of the emperor.]

And I think it not inappropriate to describe the appearance of this man. He was neither tall in stature nor particularly short, but of a medium height, yet not thin but slightly fleshy, and his face was round and not uncomely; for his complexion remained ruddy even after two days of fasting. But that I may describe his appearance as a whole in few words, I would say that he resembled Domitian, son of Vespasian, very closely, an Emperor who so impressed the Romans who suffered under him that even after they had chopped his whole body into pieces they felt that they had not satisfied their rage against him. . . .

Such was Justinian in appearance; but his character I could not accurately describe. For this man was both an evil-doer and easily led into evil, the sort of a person whom they call a moral pervert, never of his own accord speaking the truth to those with whom he conversed, but having a deceitful and crafty intent behind every word and action, and at the same time exposing himself, an easy prey, to those who wished to deceive him. . . .

This Emperor was insincere, crafty, hypocritical, dissembling his anger, double-dealing, clever, a perfect artist in acting out an opinion which he pretended to hold, and even able to produce tears, not from joy or sorrow, but contriving them for the occasion according to the need of the moment, always playing false, yet not carelessly but adding both his signature and the most terrible oaths to bind his agreements, and that too in dealing with his own subjects. But he departed straightway from his agreements and his oaths, just like the vilest slaves, who, through fear of the tortures hanging over them, are induced to make confession of acts which they had denied on oath. He was a fickle friend, a truceless enemy, an ardent devotee of assassination and of robbery, quarrelsome and an inveterate innovator, easily led astray into wrong, but influenced by no counsel to adopt the right, keen to conceive and to execute base designs, but looking upon even the hearing about good things as distasteful. How could any man be competent to describe adequately the character of Justinian? These faults and many others still greater he manifestly possessed to a degree not in accord with human nature. On the contrary, Nature seemed to have removed all baseness from the rest of mankind and to have concentrated it in the soul of this man. And in addition to his other shortcomings, while he was very easy-going as to lending an ear to slanders, yet he was severe as to inflicting punishment. For he never paused for a thorough investigation before reaching a decision, but straightway upon hearing what the slanderer said, he would make his decision and order it published. And he did not hesitate to write orders that called for the capture of towns and the burning of cities and the enslavement of whole peoples, for no reason whatever. Consequently, if one should care to estimate all the misfortunes which have befallen the Romans from the earliest times and then to balance against them those of the present day, it seems to me that he would find a greater slaughter of human beings to have been perpetrated by this man than has come to pass in all the preceding time. And while he had no scruples whatever against the quiet acquisition of other men's money—for he never even made any excuse, putting forward justice as a screen in trespassing upon things which did not belong to him—yet when once these had become his own, he was perfectly ready to shew his contempt for the money, with a prodigality in which there was no trace of calculation, and for no reason at all to fling it away to the barbarians. And, to sum up the whole matter, he neither had any money himself, nor would he allow anyone else in the world to have it, as though he were not a victim of avarice, but simply consumed by envy of those who possessed money. Consequently he lightly banished wealth from the Roman world and became the creator of poverty for all.

[In the following section of *The Secret History*, Procopius describes Theodora's unsavory life before she met and married Justinian.]

The traits, then, of Justinian's character, as far as we are able to state them, were roughly these. And he married a wife concerning whom I shall now relate how she was born and reared and how, after being joined to this man in marriage, she overturned the Roman State to its very foundations. There was in Byzantium a certain Acacius, keeper of the animals used in the circus, an adherent of the Green Faction, a man whom they called Master of the Bears. This man had died a natural death during the reign of Anastasius, leaving three girls, Comito, Theodora and Anastasia, the eldest of whom was not yet seven years of age. And the woman, now reduced to utter distress, entered into marriage with another husband, who, she thought, would later on assist her in both the care of the household and in her first husband's occupation. But the Dancing Master of the Greens, a man named Asterius, was bribed by another man to remove these persons from that office and to make no difficulty about putting in the position the man who had given him the money. For the Dancing Masters had authority to administer such matters as they wished. But when the woman saw the whole populace gathered in the Circus, she put garlands on the heads and in both hands of the three girls and caused them to sit as suppliants. And though the Greens were by no means favourable to receiving the supplication, the Blues conferred this position of honour upon them, since their Master of the Bears also had recently died. And when these children came of age, the mother immediately put them on the stage there—since they were fair to look upon—not all three at the same time, but as each one seemed to her to be ripe for this calling. Now Comito, the first one, had already scored a brilliant success among the harlots of her age; and Theodora, the next in order, clothed in a little sleeved frock suitable to a slave girl, would follow her about, performing various services and in particular always carrying on her shoulders the stool on which her sister was accustomed to sit in the assemblies. Now for a time Theodora, being immature, was quite unable to sleep with a man or to have a woman's kind of intercourse with one, yet she did engage in intercourse of a masculine type of lewdness with the wretches, slaves though they were, who, following their masters to the theatre, incidentally took advantage of the opportunity afforded them to carry on this monstrous business, and she spent much time in the brothel in this unnatural traffic of the body. But as soon as she came of age and was at last mature, she joined the women of the stage and straightway became a courtesan, of the sort whom men of ancient times used to call "infantry." For she was neither a flute-player nor a harpist, nay, she had not even acquired skill in the dance, but she sold her youthful beauty to those who chanced to come along, plying her trade with practically her whole body. Later on she was associated with the actors in all the work of the theatre, and she shared their performances with them, playing up to their buffoonish acts intended to raise a laugh. For she was unusually clever and full of gibes, and she immediately became admired for this sort of thing. For the girl had not a particle of modesty, nor did any man ever see her embarrassed, but she undertook shameless services without the least hesitation, and she was the sort of a person who, for instance, when being flogged or beaten over the head, would crack a joke over it and burst into a loud laugh; and she would undress and exhibit to any who chanced along both her front and her rear naked, parts which rightly should be unseen by men and hidden from them.

And as she wantoned with her lovers, she always kept bantering them, and by toying with new devices in intercourse, she always succeeded in winning the hearts of the licentious to her; for she did not even expect that the approach should be made by the man she was with, but on the contrary she herself, with wanton jests and with clownish posturing with her hips, would tempt all who came along, especially if they were beardless youths. Indeed there was never anyone such a slave to pleasure in all forms; for many a time she would go to a community dinner with ten youths or even more, all of exceptional bodily vigour who had made a business of fornication, and she would lie with all her banquet companions the whole night long, and when they were too exhausted to go on, she would go to their attendants, thirty perhaps in number, and pair off with each one of them; yet even so she could not get enough of this wantonness.

On one occasion she entered the house of one of the notables during the drinking, and they say that in the sight of all the banqueters she mounted to the projecting part of the banqueting couch where their feet lay, and there drew up her clothing in a shameless way, not hesitating to display her licentiousness. And though she made use of three openings, she used to take Nature to task, complaining that it had not pierced her breasts with larger holes so that it might be possible for her to contrive another method of copulation there. And though she was pregnant many times, yet practically always she was able to contrive to bring about an abortion immediately.

And often even in the theatre, before the eyes of the whole people, she stripped off her clothing and moved about naked through their midst, having only a girdle about her private parts and her groins, not, however, that she was ashamed to display these too to the populace, but because no person is permitted to enter there entirely naked, but must have at least a girdle about the groins. Clothed in this manner, she sprawled out and lay on her back on the ground. And some slaves, whose duty this was, sprinkled grains of barley over her private parts, and geese, which happened to have been provided for this very purpose, picked them off with their beaks, one by one, and ate them. And when she got up, she not only did not blush, but even acted as if she took pride in this strange performance. For she was not merely shameless herself, but also a contriver of shameless deeds above all others. . . .

47

The Institutes of Justinian from the *Corpus Iuris Civilis*

In 528, Justinian entrusted "twelve civilians" with putting together the disjointed fragments of law governing the Roman Empire, ostensibly updating and refining the Theodosian Code begun but not completed under Theodosius II. The resulting *Corpus Iuris Civilis,* literally the "Body of Civil Law," is divided into four parts from which excerpts of the first, called *The Institutes of Justinian,* follow. The *Institutes* were intended to instruct students in the law: They generally paraphrase the laws, but in that form they had the force of law, at least in the Eastern (Byzantine) Empire.

QUESTIONS TO CONSIDER

1. In the excerpts from Justinian's *Institutes,* deterrence is obviously the overriding consideration. How much of a part does deterrence play in philosophies of law today? What other considerations influence the way our own society attempts to cope with the offenses indicated?
2. Why do you suppose Justinian, like the Visigoths later (see Reading 54) considered parricide the worst of all possible crimes? Would you agree?

Institutes and Code

Public prosecutions bear no resemblance to the other legal remedies of which we have been speaking. There is a great difference between them both in the mode in which they are begun and in that in which they are carried on.

They are called public, because generally any citizen may institute them.

Some public prosecutions are capital, some are not. We term capital those which involve the extreme punishment of the law, or the interdiction from fire and water, or deportation, or the mines. Those which carry with them infamy and a pecuniary penalty are public, but not capital.

Public prosecutions are instituted under the following laws. The Julian Treason Law, which subjects to its severe provisions all who attempt anything against the emperor or State. The penalty it inflicts is the loss of life, and the memory of the guilty is condemned even after his death.

Also the Julian Adultery Law, which punishes with death not only those who are guilty of adultery, but those who give themselves up to works of lewdness with their own sex. The same law also punishes the seduction without violence of a virgin, or of a widow of honest character. The penalty upon offenders of honorable condition is the confiscation of half their fortune, upon those of low condition, corporal punishment and relegation.

Also the Cornelian Murder and Lethal Weapons Law, which strikes with the sword of vengeance murderers and those who for the purpose of killing a man go armed with a lethal weapon. By the same law, poisoners are capitally condemned who by hateful arts use poisons or magic charms to kill men, or publically sell hurtful drugs.

Another law, the Pompeian Intrafamily Murder Law, inflicts upon the most horrible of crimes an unusual punishment. It provides, that anyone who has hastened the death of a parent or child, or of any other relation whose murder is legally termed parricide, whether he acts openly or secretly, and whoever instigates or is an accomplice in the commission of a crime, although a stranger, shall undergo the penalty of parricide. He will be punished, not by the sword, nor by fire, nor by any ordinary mode of punishment, but he is to be sewed up in a sack with a dog, a cock, a viper, and an ape, and enclosed in this horrible prison he is to be, according to the nature of the place, thrown into the sea, or into a river, that even in his lifetime he may begin to be deprived of the use of the elements, and that the air may be denied to him while he lives, and earth when he dies.[1]

[1]The fact that the dog could not see for ten days or so after birth symbolized the parricide's blindness to natural decency; the rooster's crowing symbolized arrogant pride; the viper symbolized treachery; the monkey's semi-human appearance symbolized having human attributes but not the right ones

From *The Institutes of Justinian* with English introduction, trans. and notes by C. Sandars (London: Longmans Green and Co., 6th ed., 1878). Book IV Title xviii, pp. 503–06, *passim.*

The Rise of Islam

Arabia in the sixth century A.D. was inhabited primarily in the southern area of Yemen, along the western slopes of the Hejaz Mountains, and along scattered desert oases. Large-scale international trade in dates and imported spices from Africa and India was made possible through the use of camel caravans. Religion was well developed; the people worshipped the moon, planets, spirits, stone idols, and rocks.

The major center of religious worship and pilgrimage, however, was the city of Mecca. Within the city there was a sacred precinct containing a well, called the Zamzam, and the holy shrine, referred to as the Kaaba. A great variety of religions were connected with the Kaaba, which housed approximately 300 idols, including statues of Jesus.

Politically, the Byzantines and Persians, each of whom had launched several invasions to gain control of Arabia, were fierce competitors. Yet, despite these struggles, no major power had secured total domination of the independent peoples.

Muhammad (A.D. 570?–632) was born into the Kuraysh clan, which was one of the leading camel-caravan trading groups in Mecca. Unfortunately, before Muhammad's birth his father died. The child was left in the care of his mother until she, too, died when he was six. At this time, he was placed under the protection of his paternal uncle.

There is little information about Muhammad's life until 595, when he became an overseer for a wealthy, older caravan owner, a woman named Khadija. Muhammad did so well at his job that soon Khadija asked him to marry her; this marriage of convenience turned to true affection and lasted until Khadija's death in 619. After her death, Muhammad married many times, in each case to bind new converts to his religion. Despite his numerous marriages, Muhammad never had a son who lived beyond infancy; however, he later adopted a cousin as a foster son.

During the month of Ramadan (Fasting) in the year 610, Muhammad said he was called by God (Allah) to become his prophet. Through the messages of the Archangel Gabriel, which Muhammad received for the rest of his life, he formed the religion called Islam (meaning submission to the Will of God). Muhammad was instructed to preach the message of Allah to the Meccans. At first he was able to convert only members of his family and some young men in the city, while most Meccans resisted his teachings.

Persecution of Muhammad and his small group of followers intensified. When he finally decided to leave Mecca, his Hegira (migration) took him to a small date-palm oasis called Yathrib (Medina), some 250 miles north. Once in Yathrib, Muhammad became a political as well as a religious leader for his Muslims; as such, he resorted to the time-honored tradition of raiding caravans that passed near Yathrib. These actions brought swift retaliation from Mecca, but the Meccans were never able to defeat Muhammad, whose prestige continually increased. Finally, the Meccans ended their opposition to Muhammad and allowed him into the city to perform the act of "pilgrimage" (or Hajj). Once inside Mecca, he cleansed the Kaaba of idolatry and rededicated it to the sole worship of Allah.

48

The Koran

The Koran is the Holy Scripture and basis of the Islamic religion. The work comprises 114 chapters (or suras) arranged according to their length, running from the longest to the shortest. The Koran is believed to be the word of God, transmitted by the Archangel Gabriel to the prophet Muhammad. The prophet, in turn, preached these messages, first in Mecca, then in Medina, to his small group of converts (Muslims). Only after Muhammad's death were the messages gathered together and given their final arrangement by the third caliph,[1] Othman.

The basic beliefs of Islam are drawn from contacts with both Jews and Christians and then adapted for the Arab peoples. Essential to the religion is the need for each person to submit to the one and only god, Allah. According to this religion, Allah knows and sees everything. He has determined each person's fate; however, lest one fall into fatalism, each person must account for his or her actions on the Day of Last Judgment.

Drawing upon the scriptures of the "Peoples of the Book" (Jews and Christians), Muhammad preached that Allah had described to his twenty-eight prophets—including Adam, Noah, Moses, John the Baptist, and Jesus—the method in which He was to be worshipped. However, Muhammad thought that the Jews and Christians had deliberately distorted the original messages. Muhammad claimed that the Koran was the most perfect guide for worshipping Allah, and that he was the final prophet or "Seal."

In the following Koranic selections, note the descriptions of Muhammad's call to God's Word, the Last Judgment, the Islamic view of the "Peoples of the Book," and the duties that each Muslim must follow. Today the Koran governs approximately 800 million lives.

QUESTIONS TO CONSIDER

1. What are some of the basic beliefs and duties in Islam?
2. What are significant similarities and differences among Islam, Judaism, and Christianity?
3. Why was the description of Paradise so appealing in Arabia?
4. How were women to be treated according to the Koran?

---

[1] *Caliph* means "Successor of the Apostle of God (Muhammad)." A caliph was the head of state, a judge, leader in worship, and commander of the army.

The Clot

In the Name of Allah, the Beneficent, the Merciful

1. Read in the name of your Lord Who created.
2. He created man from a clot.
3. Read and your Lord is Most Honorable,
4. Who taught (to write) with the pen,
5. Taught man what he knew not.
6. Nay! man is most surely inordinate,
7. Because he sees himself free from want.

The Food

In the Name of Allah, the Beneficent, the Merciful

97. Allah has made the Kaaba, the sacred house, a maintenance for the people, and the sacred month and the offerings and the sacrificial animals with garlands; this is that you may know that Allah knows whatever is in the heavens and whatever is in the earth, and that Allah is the Knower of all things.

The Great Event

In the Name of Allah, the Beneficent, the Merciful

1. When the great event comes to pass,
2. There is no belying its coming to pass—
3. Abasing (one party), exalting (the other),
4. When the earth shall be shaken with a (severe) shaking,
5. And the mountains shall be made to crumble with (an awful) crumbling,
6. So that they shall be as scattered dust.
7. And you shall be three sorts.
8. Then (as to) the companions of the right hand; how happy are the companions of the right hand!
9. And (as to) the companions of the left hand; how wretched are the companions of the left hand!
10. And the foremost are the foremost,
11. These are they who are drawn nigh (to Allah),
12. In the gardens of bliss.
13. A numerous company from among the first,
14. And a few from among the latter.

From *Holy Qur'an,* trans. M.H. Shakir (Elmhurst, NY: Tahrike Tarsile Qur'an, 1985), Surahs 96:1–7, 5:97, 56:1–44, 62:1–9, 3:45–71, 4:34, 24:31–32, 2:174–185, 187, 196–197, 219–220. Reprinted by permission of Tahrike Tarsile Qur'an, Inc.

15. On thrones decorated,
16. Reclining on them, facing one another.
17. Round about them shall go youths never altering in age,
18. With goblets and ewers and a cup of pure drink;
19. They shall not be affected with headache thereby, nor shall they get exhausted;
20. And fruits such as they choose,
21. And the flesh of fowl such as they desire.
22. And pure, beautiful ones,
23. The like of the hidden pearls:
24. A reward for what they used to do.
25. They shall not hear therein vain or sinful discourse,
26. Except the word peace, peace.
27. And the companions of the right hand; how happy are the companions of the right hand!

Friday

In the Name of Allah, the Beneficent, the Merciful

9. O you who believe! when the call is made for prayer on Friday, then hasten to the remembrance of Allah and leave off trading; that is better for you, if you know. . . .

The Family of Imram

In the Name of Allah, the Beneficent, the Merciful

45. When the angels said: O Mary, surely Allah gives you good news with a Word from Him (of one) whose name is the Messiah, Jesus son of Mary, worthy of regard in this world and the hereafter and of those who are made near (to Allah).
46. And he shall speak to the people when in the cradle and when of old age, and (he shall be) one of the good ones.
47. She said: My Lord! when shall there be a son (born) to me, and man has not touched me? He said: Even so, Allah creates what He pleases; when He has decreed a matter, He only says to it, Be, and it is.
48. And He will teach him the Book and the wisdom and the Torah and the Gospel.
49. And (make him) an apostle to the children of Israel: That I have come to you with a sign from your Lord, that I determine for you out of dust like the form of a bird, then I breathe into it and it becomes a bird with Allah's permission and I heal the blind and the leprous, and bring the dead to life with Allah's permission and I inform you of what you should eat and what you should store in your houses; most surely there is a sign in this for you, if you are believers.
50. And a verifier of that which is before me of the Torah, and that I may allow you part of that which has been forbidden you, and I have come to you with a sign from your Lord, therefore be careful of (your duty to) Allah and obey me.
51. Surely Allah is my Lord and your Lord, therefore serve Him; this is the right path.
52. But when Jesus perceived unbelief on their part, he said: Who will be my helpers in Allah's way? The disciples said: We are helpers (in the way) of Allah: We believe in Allah and bear witness that we are submitting ones.

53. Our Lord! we believe in what Thou hast revealed and we follow the apostle, so write us down with those who bear witness.

54. And they planned and Allah (also) planned, and Allah is the best of planners.

55. And when Allah said: O Jesus I am going to terminate the period of your stay (on earth) and cause you to ascend unto Me and purify you of those who disbelieve and make those who follow you above those who disbelieve to the day of resurrection; then to Me shall be your return, so I will decide between you concerning that in which you differed.

56. Then as to those who disbelieve, I will chastise them with severe chastisement in this world and the hereafter, and they shall have no helpers.

57. And as to those who believe and do good deeds, He will pay them fully their rewards; and Allah does not love the unjust.

58. This We recite to you of the communications and the wise reminder.

59. Surely the likeness of Jesus is with Allah as the likeness of Adam; He created him from dust, then said to him, Be, and he was.

65. O followers of the Book! why do you dispute about Abraham, when the Torah and the Gospel were not revealed till after him; do you not then understand?

66. Behold! you are they who disputed about that of which you had knowledge; why then do you dispute about that of which you have no knowledge? And Allah knows while you do not know.

67. Abraham was not a Jew nor a Christian but he was (an) upright (man), a Muslim, and he was not one of the polytheists.

68. Most surely the nearest of people to Abraham are those who followed him and this Prophet and those who believe and Allah is the guardian of the believers.

69. A party of the followers of the Book desire that they should lead you astray, and they lead not astray but themselves, and they do not perceive.

70. O followers of the Book! Why do you disbelieve in the communications of Allah while you witness (them)?

Women

In the Name of Allah, the Beneficent, the Merciful

34. Men are the maintainers of women because Allah has made some of them to excel others and because they spend out of their property; the good women are therefore obedient, guarding the unseen as Allah has guarded; and (as to) those on whose part you fear desertion, admonish them, and leave them alone in the sleeping-places and beat them; then if they obey you, do not seek a way against them; surely Allah is High, Great.

The Light

In the Name of Allah, the Beneficent, the Merciful

31. And say to the believing women that they cast down their looks and guard their private parts and do not display their ornaments except what appears thereof, and let them wear their head-coverings over their bosoms, and not display their ornaments except

to their husbands or their fathers, or the fathers of their husbands, or their sons, or the sons of their husbands, or their brothers, or their brothers' sons, or their sisters' sons, or their women, or those whom their right hands possess, or the male servants not having need (of women), or the children who have not attained knowledge of what is hidden of women; and let them not strike their feet so that what they hide of their ornaments may be known; and turn to Allah all of you, O believers! so that you may be successful.

32. And marry those among you who are single and those who are fit among your male slaves and your female slaves; if they are needy, Allah will make them free from want out of His grace; and Allah is Ample-giving, Knowing.

The Cow

In the Name of Allah, the Beneficent, the Merciful

174. Surely those who conceal any part of the Book that Allah has revealed and take for it a small price, they eat nothing but fire into their bellies, and Allah will not speak to them on the day of resurrection, nor will He purify them, and they shall have a painful chastisement.

177. It is not righteousness that you turn your faces towards the East and the West, but righteousness is this that one should believe in Allah and the last day and the angels and the Book and the prophets, and give away wealth out of love for Him to the near of kin and the orphans and the needy and the wayfarer and the beggars and for (the emancipation of) the captives, and keep up prayer and pay the poor-rate; and the performers of their promise when they make a promise, and the patient in distress and affliction and in time of conflicts—these are they who are true (to themselves) and these are they who guard (against evil).

178. O you who believe! retaliation is prescribed for you in the matter of the slain; the free for the free, and the slave for the slave, and the female for the female, but if any remission is made to any one by his (aggrieved) brother, then prosecution (for the blood-wit) should be made according to usage, and payment should be made to him in a good manner; this is an alleviation from your Lord and a mercy; so whoever exceeds the limit after this, he shall have a painful chastisement.

183. O you who believe! fasting is prescribed for you, as it was prescribed for those before you, so that you may guard (against evil).

184. For a certain number of days; but whoever among you is sick or on a journey, then (he shall fast) a (like) number of other days; and those who are not able to do it may effect a redemption by feeding a poor man; so whoever does good spontaneously it is better for him; and that you fast is better for you if you know.

185. The month of Ramadan is that in which the Quran was revealed, a guidance to men and clear proofs of the guidance and the distinction; therefore whoever of you is present in the month, he shall fast therein, and whoever is sick or upon a journey, then (he shall fast) a (like) number of other days;

187. It is made lawful to you to go into your wives on the night of the fast; they are an apparel for you and you are an apparel for them; Allah knew that you acted unfaithfully to yourselves, so He has turned to you (mercifully) and removed from you (this burden); so now be in contact with them and seek what Allah has ordained for you, and

eat and drink until the whiteness of the day becomes distinct from the blackness of the night at dawn, then complete the fast till night, and have not contact with them while you keep to the mosques;

196. And accomplish the pilgrimage and the visit for Allah, but if you are prevented, (send) whatever offering is easy to obtain, and do not shave your heads until the offering reaches its destination; but whoever among you is sick or has an ailment of the head, he (should effect) a compensation by fasting or alms or sacrificing; then when you are secure, whoever profits by combining the visit with the pilgrimage (should take) what offering is easy to obtain; but he who cannot find (any offering) should fast for three days during the pilgrimage and for seven days when you return; these (make) ten (days) complete; this is for him whose family is not present in the Sacred Mosque, and be careful (of your duty) to Allah, and know that Allah is severe in requiting (evil).

219. They ask you about intoxicants and games of chance. Say: In both of them there is a great sin and means of profit for men, and their sin is greater than their profit. And they ask you as to what they should spend. Say: What you can spare. Thus does Allah make clear to you the communicants, that you may ponder.

220. On this world and the hereafter. And they ask you concerning the orphans. Say: To set right for them (their affairs) is good, and if you become co-partners with them, they are your brethren; and Allah knows the mischief-maker and the peacemaker; and if Allah had pleased, He would certainly have caused you to fall into a difficulty; surely Allah is Mighty, Wise.

49

Sayings *(Hadith)* Ascribed to the Prophet: Holy War

The *hadith,* or sayings, are one source of Islamic law. They are stories or sayings connected with Muhammad's life, which were, and are, used to justify actions in the past and present. Each of the hadith is connected with the Prophet or one of his Companions through a narrative story that passed from one person to another over the centuries.

The following selection concerns the undertaking of a *Jihad,* or Holy War, in which every *amir* (a political-military leader) should participate. It describes the motivations for the undertaking, the duties and actions of a good warrior, and prohibitions against certain unacceptable actions in warfare.

QUESTIONS TO CONSIDER

1. What will be the rewards for a warrior of the faith?
2. How are polytheists, women, and children to be treated and why?
3. Compare a Jihad with a Christian Crusade. What are the similarities and differences?

Jihad is incumbent upon you with every amir, whether he be godly or wicked and even if he commit major sins. Prayer is incumbent upon you behind every Muslim, be he godly or wicked and even if he commit major sins. Prayer is incumbent upon you for every Muslim who dies, be he godly or wicked and even if he commit major sins.

Paradise is under the shadow of swords.

Where the believer's heart shakes on the path of God, his sins fall away from him as the fruit falls off a date palm.

If anyone shoots an arrow at the enemy on the path of God and his arrow reaches his enemy, whether it hits him or misses, it is accounted equal in merit to liberating a slave.

He who draws his sword in the path of God has sworn allegiance to God.

If anyone ransoms a prisoner from the hands of the enemy, I am that prisoner.

He who fights so that the word of God may prevail is on the path of God.

He who dies fighting on the frontier in the path of God, God protects him from the testing of the tomb.

The unbeliever and the one who kills him will never meet in Hell.

God sent me as a mercy and a portent; He did not send me as a trader or as a cultivator. The worst of the community on the Day of Resurrection are the traders and the cultivators, except for those who are niggardly with their religion.

A day and a night of fighting on the frontier is better than a month of fasting and prayer.

The best thing a Muslim can earn is an arrow in the path of God.

He who equips a warrior in the Holy War for God has the same reward as he, while the warrior's reward is not diminished.

He who when he dies has never campaigned or even intended to campaign dies in a kind of hypocrisy.

Fight against the polytheists with your property, your persons, and your tongues.

Swords are the keys of Paradise.

A sword is sufficient witness.

God wonders at people who are led to Heaven in chains.

A campaign by sea is like ten campaigns by land, and he who loses his bearings at sea is like one who sheds his blood in the path of God.

Every prophet has his monasticism, and the monasticism of this community is the Holy War in the path of God.

If a campaigner by sea is seasick, he has the reward of a martyr; if drowned, of two martyrs.

In Islam there are three dwellings, the lower, the upper, and the uppermost. The lower is the Islam of the generality of Muslims. If you ask any one of them he will answer, "I am a Muslim." In the upper their merits differ, some of the Muslims being better than others. The uppermost is the *jihad* in the cause of God, which only the best of them attain.

Will you not ask me why I laugh? I have seen people of my community who are dragged to Paradise against their will. They asked, "O Prophet of God, who are they?" He said, "They are non-Arab people whom the warriors in the Holy War have captured and made to enter Islam."

Shoot and ride! Of the two, I would rather have you shoot than ride. Anything in which a man passes his time is vain except for shooting with his bow, training his horse, or dallying with his wife. These three things are right. He who abandons archery after having learned it is ungrateful to the one who taught him.

Accursed be he who carries the Persian bow. Keep to the Arab bow and to the lances by which God gives you power in these lands and gives you victory over your enemy.

Learn to shoot, for what lies between the two marks is one of the gardens of Paradise.

Warfare is deception.

The Muslims are bound by their stipulations.

The Muslims are bound by their stipulations as long as these are lawful.

Of any village that you come to and stay in, you have a share, but of any village that is disobedient to God and His Prophet, one-fifth of it belongs to God and His Prophet and the rest is yours.

Treat an Arab as an Arab and a half-breed as a half-breed. The Arab has two shares and the half-breed one.

Kill the old polytheists, but spare the young ones.

If you find a tithe collector, kill him.

Go in the name of God and in God and in the religion of the Prophet of God! Do not kill the very old, the infant, the child, or the woman. Bring all the booty, holding back no part of it. Maintain order and do good, for God loves those who do good.

Why are some people so bent on killing today that they even kill children? Are not the best of you the sons of idolators? Do not kill children! Do not kill children! Every soul is born with a natural disposition [to the true religion] and remains so until their tongue gives them the powers of expression. Then their parents make Jews or Christians of them.

Expel the Jews and the Christians from the Arabian peninsula.

Accept advice to treat prisoners well.

Looting is no more lawful than carrion.

He who loots is not one of us.

He has forbidden looting and mutilation.

He has forbidden the killing of women and children.

He who flees is not one of us.

The bite of an ant is more painful to the martyr than the thrust of a weapon, which is more desirable to him than sweet, cold water on a hot summer day.

Commentaries on Islamic Law and Culture

Islam developed during the lifetime of the Prophet Muhammad not only as a religion in the sense of a way of worship and a systematic elaboration of the relationship between man and his creator; through the circumstances of its incubation, it also evolved as a social and political institution that claimed divine authority for the regulation of relations between man and man, believer and nonbeliever. The Koran, the revealed word of God, was the prime and unchanging authority. The early generations of Muslims could also recall decisions made by the Prophet, whose teachings were considered a supplement to and commentary on the divine text. Soon, however, as the community of Islam expanded and embraced former subjects of Byzantium, Sassanid Iran, and others as far west as Spain and as far east as India that belonged to many different nations and cultures, the need arose to formalize the social teachings of Islam and to unify its rituals.

50

Wills, Slave Emancipation, and Clientship

The evolution of Islamic law took place largely in the second and third centuries of Islam (ca. A.D. 750–950), and a number of distinct systems emerged based on the teachings of various scholars. By a self-selecting process, these were eventually reduced (among Sunni Muslims) to four law schools, each of which was considered to be equally authoritative. To the Koran and the sayings of the Prophet—the Ḥadīth (diligently amassed in written collections)—were added a number of other subsidiary principles—notably analogical reasoning—and by the fourth century of Islam (A.D. tenth century), we see the appearance of manuals enunciating agreed positions on all the main issues in ritual, personal status (marriage, divorce, inheritance, etc.), commercial transactions, and criminal and moral law (e.g., theft, adultery, drinking intoxicating liquors). The *Risāla* of Ibn Abī Zayd, a jurisprudent of Qayrawan (modern Tunisia) who died in A.D. 996 is one such manual. It reflects the views of the law school of Malik ibn Anas (d. 797) which is dominant in North and West Africa and the upper Nile valley. As with the Jewish Talmud, the Islamic law manuals have been commented upon by later generations of scholars, and the commentaries themselves have been further elucidated by other scholars. This is reflected in the first selection by the use of square brackets [ ]. In the second selection, the brackets reflect explanatory words of the translator, who thus, in effect, becomes yet another commentator.

Slavery was an ancient institution in the Middle East, and Islam acknowledged its validity while mitigating its effects. Neither the Koran nor the law speaks about enslavement as such, although it came to be agreed that prisoners taken in a war waged on behalf of the faith—a *jihād*—could be made slaves. The Koran stresses kind treatment to slaves and enumerates ways for their emancipation, and this is echoed in the Prophetic *Hadith* (see Reading 49). The law books devote a section to emancipation and to clientship—the lingering bonds of attachment of a slave to the master's family after emancipation—but otherwise deal with slaves' rights and disabilities only incidentally under appropriate sections, such as marriage, pilgrimage, punishments, and so on, the slave generally having only half the rights of a free people and, often, suffering only half the penalties.

QUESTIONS TO CONSIDER

1. In what ways might a slave have gained his or her freedom?
2. Did slaves have any legal rights under Islamic law?
3. Was it possible for slaves to acquire property?

It is fitting that he who has something to bequeath should draw up a will. There can be no bequest in favor of an heir. Bequests come out of the disposable one-third of the estate. Any bequests exceeding the one-third should be given back [to the designated heirs], unless they authorize otherwise. The specified emancipation of a slave is to be dealt with before proceeding to bequests. [A declaration that] a slave is to be emancipated on the owner's death made when the owner was in good health takes precedence over a declaration made when he was [gravely] ill referring to emancipation or other [dispositions regarding the slave such as being given as a gift or a charitable donation]. It also takes precedence over the payment of outstanding alms-tax (*zakāt*) which a man decides to pay off from his estate. Such latter payments come out of the disposable third and take precedence over other bequests. A declaration of emancipation on the owner's death made when the owner was in good health, however, takes precedence.

If the disposable one-third is insufficient [to cover all the bequests made], the legatees whose bequests have no precedence the one over the other, take proportionate shares. A man may annul a legacy, whether it involves emancipation or any other matter.

The formula for declaring a slave free upon the master's death is: "You are *mudabbar*." or "You are free after my demise." After this the master cannot sell him or give him away. The master may make use of the slave's services until he dies, at which point the slave is free. The master may confiscate his slave's possessions, so long as the slave is not [gravely] ill. The master may have sexual relations with his female slave, but he may not do so with one to whom emancipation has been promised after a stated lapse of time, nor can he sell her. However, he may enjoy her labor and he has the right to confiscate her possessions, provided the time of her emancipation is not close.

When a master dies the value of his *mudabbar* slave is considered part of the disposable one-third, whereas the value of a slave to be emancipated after a fixed lapse of time is reckoned as a part of the total estate. The slave with whom a contract of emancipation has been agreed remains a slave while he owes any portion [of the agreed price of his freedom]. A contract may be drawn up stipulating any sum of money agreed upon by the master and the slave, to be paid in installments, either few or many. If the slave becomes unable to pay, he becomes a simple slave again. What the master has taken from him [by way of installments] may lawfully be retained [by the master]. If a slave refuses [to acknowledge his insolvency] only the civil authority has the power to declare him insolvent [unilaterally] after first granting him a respite [during which he might become solvent].

The offspring of a woman [other than by her master] assume her status, whether she is a slave with whom a contract of manumission has been drawn up, a *mudabbar* slave, or one to be emancipated after a fixed lapse of time, or one who has been given as a pledge. The child born to an *umm walad* (i.e., a slave woman who has already borne her master's child) fathered by some one other than her master shares his mother's rights and disabilities [if born after she became *umm walad*].

A slave's possessions belong to him, unless the master confiscates them from him. If the master frees him unconditionally or contractually and does not exclude the slave's possessions [from such emancipation], then the master cannot confiscate them.

A master may have sexual relations with a female slave under contract of manumission. Any offspring fathered by a male or born to a female slave under contract of manumission partakes in the contract with them and becomes free at the time of their emancipation.

From the *Risāla* of Ibn Abī Zayd al-Qayrawānī with the commentary of Abū 'l-Ḥasan al-Mālikī and the supercommentary of ʿAlī al-Ṣaʿidī al-ʿAdawī, Cairo: Muṣṭafā al-Bābī al-Ḥalabī, 1937, ii, 177–99. Edited and translated by John O. Hunwick, professor of History, Northwestern University.

It is permissible to draw up a contract of emancipation with a group [of slaves], but none of them becomes free until all have paid [the price of] their freedom. A slave under contract of emancipation cannot free his own slave or dissipate his wealth until he attains freedom; neither may he marry or travel to a distant destination without his master's permission. Should he die [before paying for his freedom in full], having a child, the child takes his place and pays from the [dead slave's] wealth whatever sum remains outstanding [in the emancipation contract], this now being considered a debt whose repayment has fallen due. [If anything remains], those of his sons conjoined with him [in contractual freedom] inherit the surplus. If the wealth the slave leaves is insufficient to pay off the contractual debt of emancipation, the slave's offspring, if they are adult, should work to pay off the debt by installments. If they are minors and the legacy of their deceased slave father is insufficient to pay the installments up to the time when they will be old enough to work, they are immediately returned to unconditional slavery. If [the slave under contract of emancipation dies] having no offspring conjoined with him in the contract, his master inherits him [even if his estate is greater than his debt].

Whoever fathers a child from his female slave has the right to continue having sexual relations with her for the rest of his life and she is freed out of his total estate after his death. She cannot be sold, nor can her master demand service from her, nor can he hire out her services to others, though he may demand service and hire out the services of a child of hers from another man [born after she became *umm walad*]. Such a child shares its mother's status and becomes free when she does. Whatever she aborts which is recognized to be a child [by the testimony of midwives] causes her thereby to become *umm walad.* The master's protestations of *coitus interruptus* shall be of no avail if he denies paternity but admits having had sexual relations with her. If he claims that he had her declared free of pregnancy [before purchasing her] and did not thereafter have sexual relations with her, then the offspring to which she gives birth will not be considered his.

A man so deeply in debt [that he has no inheritance to leave] may not free a slave. If a man partially frees his slave [either a fraction of him or a particular limb, for example], the slave's freedom is to be made complete [by judicial decree]. If another person has a share in the slave, the one who freed a portion of his half shall pay the price of his partner's share according to the value of the slave on the day he took the action and [both halves of the slave having been emancipated] the slave shall be free. If a man who freed a part of his half of the slave does not have the means to pay his partner's share, the partner's half of the slave remains enslaved.

Whoever punishes his slave by disfiguring him in an obvious fashion, e.g., by amputating a limb, is compelled to free the slave.

If any of the following relatives of a man come into his possession as a slave, they are to be freed without compensation: one or both parents, a son or daughter, the child of a son or daughter, a grandfather or a grandmother, a full brother or a half-brother. If a pregnant woman is emancipated her foetus is emancipated along with her.

The following categories of slave are not to be freed when emancipation is a religious obligation [in expiation of unintentional homicide]: one who is already a *mudabbar;* one who is already in a contract of emancipation; anyone who belongs to a similar category, such as an *umm walad* or a slave to be freed at the expiry of a fixed term; a blind slave, a slave with an amputated hand [or leg, or finger or toe]; any slave in a similar condition [e.g., paralysed or disfigured]; a non-Muslim slave. It is not permissible for a minor to emancipate a slave, nor for anyone who is a ward [by reason of mental illness] to do so.

Patronage belongs to the one who emancipates and it cannot be sold or given away. If a man frees the slave of another, patronage devolves upon the owner of the slave [not the one who emancipated him]. Patronage does not go to the man at whose hands a slave converts to Islam; it goes to the [community of] Muslims. If a woman emancipates a slave she becomes that slave's patron. She is also the patron of those attracted to this status, such as the child [of the freed slave] or [the slave's] slave. A woman does not inherit from a slave whom her father, her son or her husband, etc. freed. The inheritance of a slave [who is emancipated with the formula; "You are like a camel] set free to roam" belongs to the community of Muslims. Patronage goes to the closest of the agnates of the dead man. If he leaves two sons they jointly inherit patronage of a client of their father. If one of these sons dies leaving two sons, the patronage goes back to the other brother rather than to the sons. If one of the two sons dies and leaves a male child, then the other dies leaving two children, the patronage is shared by these three equally.

51

Kai Kaus, "Scientific Physiognomy and the Purchase of Slaves"

Slavery was a part of most ancient and many modern societies until the nineteenth century. Slaves inherited their status and were regularly bought and sold on the domestic market, although war captives frequently became slaves, and a fair amount of kidnapping by professionals, who could easily sell their human wares to dealers in foreign countries, introduced new slaves to the markets. Slaves were common in Islamic society, where they were used as domestic servants, guardians of harem women, or as specially trained soldiers. They were sometimes used as field workers, but much less frequently than the victims of the later Atlantic/West African slave trade, who were later taken, at its height, by the hundreds of thousands annually to labor on the plantations and in the mines of the New World.

The following selection is by an eleventh-century ruler of several provinces on the south shore of the Caspian Sea, Kai Kaus, from his guidebook for princes, considered a classic of Persian literature. In it he gives advice on subjects as diverse as love, astrology, and polo. Here he suggests the qualities a buyer should look for in purchasing both black and white and male and female slaves.

QUESTIONS TO CONSIDER

1. What were the qualities a person should look for when buying slaves?
2. How is this article an example of racial or ethnic stereotyping?
3. From the author's description of how to apply it, what does physiognomy involve? Do people occasionally use something like it in our own day in making statements about types of humans?
4. Both this writer and St. Thomas Aquinas (see Reading 71) use the term "science" generally in a way we probably would not. How is our modern notion of "science" different from theirs?

When you set out to buy slaves, be cautious. The buying of men is a difficult art; because many a slave may appear to be good, who, when regarded with knowledge, turns out to be the opposite. Most people imagine that buying slaves is like any other form of trading, not understanding that the buying of slaves, or the art of doing so, is a branch of philosophy. Anyone who buys goods of which he has no competent understanding can be defrauded over them, and the most difficult form of knowledge is that which deals with human beings. There are so many blemishes and good points in the human kind, and a single blemish may conceal a myriad good points, while a single good point may conceal a myriad faults.

Human beings cannot be known except by the science of physiognomy and by experience, and the science of physiognomy in its entirety is a branch of prophecy that is not acquired to perfection except by the divinely directed apostle. The reason is that by physiognomy the inward goodness or wickedness of man can be ascertained.

Now let me describe to the best of my ability what is essential in the purchasing of slaves, both white and black, and what their good and bad points are, so that they may be known to you. Understand then that there are three essentials in the buying of slaves; first is the recognition of their good and bad qualities, whether external or internal, by means of physiognomy; second is the awareness of diseases, whether latent or apparent, by their symptoms; third is the knowledge of the various classes and the defects and merits of each.

With regard to the first requirement, that of physiognomy, it consists of close observation when buying slaves. Whoever it may be that inspects the slave must first look at the face, which is always open to view, whereas the body can only be seen as occasion offers. Then look at eyes and eyebrows, followed by nose, lips and teeth, and lastly at the hair. The reason for this is that God placed the beauty of human beings in eyebrows, delicacy in the nose, sweetness in the lips and teeth and freshness in the skin. To all these the hair of the head has been made to lend adornment, since [God] created the hair for adornment.

You must, consequently, inspect everything. When you see beauty in the eyes and eyebrows, delicacy in the nose, sweetness in the lips and teeth and freshness in the skin, then buy the slave possessing them without concerning yourself over the extremities of the body. If all of these qualities are not present, then the slave must possess delicacy; because, in my opinion, one that is delicate without having beauty is preferable to one that is beautiful but not possessed of delicacy.

The learned say that one must know the indications and signs by which to buy the slaves suited for particular duties. The slave that you buy for your private service and conviviality should be of middle proportions, neither tall nor short, fat nor lean, pale nor florid, thickset nor slender, curly-haired nor with hair overstraight. When you see a slave soft-fleshed, fine-skinned, with regular bones and wine-coloured hair, black eyelashes, dark eyes, black eyebrows, open-eyed, long-nosed, slender-waisted, round-chinned, red-lipped, with white regular teeth, and all his members such as I have described, such a slave will be decorative and companionable, loyal, of delicate character, and dignified.

The mark of the slave who is clever and may be expected to improve is this: he must be of erect stature, medium in hair and flesh, broad of hand and with the middle of the fingers lengthy, in complexion dark though ruddy, dark-eyed, open-faced and unsmiling. A slave of this kind would be competent to acquire learning, to act as treasurer or for any other [such] employment.

The slave suited to play musical instruments is marked out by being soft-fleshed

From Qabus-nameh, *The Book of Kaus,* trans. Reuben Levy, in *Anthology of Islamic Literature from the Rise of Islam to Modern Times,* pp. 160–66, slightly condensed. Copyright © 1964 by Holt, Rinehart and Winston, Inc.

(though his flesh must not be over-abundant, especially on the back), with his fingers slender, neither lean nor fat. (A slave whose face is over-fleshy, incidentally, is one incapable of learning.) His hands must be soft, with the middles of the fingers lengthy. He must be bright-visaged, having the skin tight; his hair must not be too long, too short or too black. A slave of this kind will swiftly acquire a delicate art of whatever kind, particularly that of the instrumentalist.

The mark of the slave suited for arms-bearing is that his hair is thick, his body tall and erect, his build powerful, his flesh hard, his bones thick, his skin coarse and his limbs straight, the joints being firm. Shoulders must be broad, the chest deep, the neck thick and the head round; also for preference he should be bald. The belly should be concave, the buttocks drawn in and the legs in walking well extended. And the eyes should be black. Any slave who possesses these qualities will be a champion in single combat, brave and successful.

The mark of a slave suited for employment in the women's apartments is that he should be dark-skinned and sour-visaged and have withered limbs, scanty hair, a shrill voice, little [slender] feet, thick lips, a flat nose, stubby fingers, a bowed figure, and a thin neck. A slave with these qualities will be suitable for service in the women's quarters. He must not have a white skin nor a fair complexion; and beware of a ruddy-complexioned man, particularly if his hair is limp. His eyes, further, should not be languorous or moist; a man having such qualities is either over-fond of women or prone to act as a go-between.

The mark of a slave who is callous [insensitive] and suited to be a herdsman or groom is that he should be open-browed and wide-eyed, and his eyelids should be flecked with red. He should, further, be long in lips and teeth and his mouth should be wide. A slave with these qualities is extremely callous, fearless and uncivilized.

The mark of the slave suited for domestic service and cookery is that he should be clean in face and body, round-faced, with hands and feet slender, his eyes dark inclining to blue, sound in body, silent, the hair of his head wine-colored and falling forward limply. A slave with these qualities is suitable for the occupations mentioned.

Each then, should have the essential characteristics which I have recounted. But I will also mention the defects and virtues which should be known in respect of each separate race. You must understand that Turks are not all of one race, and each has its own nature and essential character. Amongst them the most ill-tempered are the Ghuzz and the Qipchaqs; the best-tempered and most willing are the Khutanese, the Khallukhis, and the Tibetans; the most active are the Tatars and the Yaghma, whereas the laziest of all are the Chigil.

It is a fact well-known to all that beauty or ugliness in the Turks is the opposite of that in the Indians. If you observe the Turk feature by feature [he has] a large head, a broad face, narrow eyes, a flat nose, and unpleasing lips and teeth. Regarded individually the features are not handsome, yet the whole is handsome. The Indian's face is the opposite of this; each individual feature regarded by itself appears handsome, yet looked at as a whole the face does not create the same impression as that of the Turk. To begin with, the Turk has a personal freshness and clearness of complexion not possessed by the Indian; indeed the Turks win for freshness against all other races.

Without any doubt, what is fine in the Turks is present in a superlative degree, but so also is what is ugly in them. Their faults in general are that they are blunt-witted, ignorant, boastful, turbulent, discontented, and without a sense of justice. Without any excuse they will create trouble and utter foul language, and at night they are poor-hearted. Their merit is that they are brave, free from pretense, open in enmity, and zealous in any task allotted to them. For the [domestic] establishment there is no better race.

Slavs, Russians, and Alans are near in their temperament to the Turks, but are more patient. The Alans are more courageous than the Turks at night and more friendly disposed towards their masters. Although in their craftsmanship they are nearer to the Byzantines, being artistic, yet there are faults in them of various kinds; for example, they are prone to theft, disobedience, betrayal of secrets, impatience, stupidity, indolence, hostility to their masters, and escaping. Their virtues are that they are soft-natured, agreeable, and quick of understanding. Further, they are deliberate in action, direct in speech, brave, good road-guides, and possessed of good memory.

The defect of the Byzantines is that they are foul-tongued, evil-hearted, cowardly, indolent, quick-tempered, covetous, and greedy for worldly things. Their merits are that they are cautious, affectionate, happy, economically-minded, successful in their undertakings, and careful to prevent loss.

The defect of the Armenians is that they are mischievous, foul-mouthed, thieving, impudent, prone to fight, disobedient, babblers, liars, friendly to misbelief, and hostile to their masters. From head to foot, indeed, they incline rather towards defects than to merits. Yet they are quick of understanding and learn their tasks well.

The defect of the Hindu is that he is evil-tongued and in the house no slave-girl is safe from him. But the various classes of the Hindus are unlike those that prevail amongst other peoples, because in other peoples the classes mingle with each other, whereas the Hindus, ever since the time of Adam (Upon whom be peace!), have practiced the following custom: namely, no trade will form an alliance with any outside it. Thus, grocers will give their daughters only to grocers, butchers to butchers, bakers to bakers, and soldiers to soldiers.

Each of these groups therefore has its own special character, which I cannot describe one by one because that would entail a book in itself.

However, the best of them, people benevolent, brave or skilled in commerce, are [respectively] the Brahman, the Rawat and the Kirar. The Brahman is clever, the Rawat brave, and the Kirar skilled in commerce, each class being superior to the one after. The Nubian and the Abyssinian are freer of faults, and the Abyssinian is better than the Nubian because many things were said by the Prophet in praise of the former.

These then are the facts concerning each race and the merits and defects of each.

When you buy a slave, you must take and lay him down, press him on both sides and watch closely that he has no pain or swelling. If he has, it will be in the liver or spleen. Having looked for such hidden defects, seek further for the open ones, such as smells from the mouth and nose, hardness of hearing, hesitation in utterance, irregularity of speech, walking off the road, coarseness of the joints, and hardness at the base of the teeth, to prevent any trickery being practiced on you.

When you have seen all that I have mentioned and have made certain, then if you should buy, do so from honest people, and so secure a person who will be of advantage to your household. As long as you can find a non-Arab do not buy an Arabic-speaking slave. You can mould a non-Arab to your ways, but never the one whose tongue is Arabic. Further, do not have a slave-girl brought before you when your appetite is strong upon you; when desire is strong, it makes what is ugly appear good in your eyes. First abate your desires and then engage in the business of purchasing.

Never buy a slave who has been treated with affection in another place. If you do not hold him dear, he will show ingratitude to you, or will flee, or will demand to be sold, or will nourish hatred in his heart for you. Even if you regard him with affection, he will show you no gratitude, in view of what he has experienced elsewhere. Buy your slave from a house in which he has been badly treated, so that he will be grateful for the least kindness on your part and will hold you in affection. From time to time make your slaves a gift of something; do not allow them to be constantly in need of money in such a way that they are compelled to go out seeking it.

Buy slaves of a good price, for each one's value is in accordance with his price. Do not buy a slave who has had numerous masters; a woman who has had many husbands and a slave who has had many masters are held in no esteem. Let those you buy be well-favored. And when a slave truly desires to be sold, do not dispute with him, but sell; when a slave demands to be sold or a wife to be divorced, then sell or divorce, because you will have no pleasure from either.

If a slave is deliberately (and not through inadvertence or mistake) lazy or neglectful in his work, do not teach him under compulsion to improve; have no expectation of that, for he will in no wise become industrious or capable of improvement. Sell him quickly; you may rouse a sleeping man without a shout, but a dead body cannot be roused by the sound of a hundred trumpets and drums.

Provide for your slaves in such fashion that they will not escape, and treat them that you would have well, as benefits your dignity; if you have one person in good condition it is better than having two in ill condition. Do not permit your male slave to take to himself in your household someone whom he calls "brother," nor permit slave-girls to claim sisterhood with each other; it leads to great trouble. On bond and free impose the burdens which they are able to bear, that they may not be disobedient through sheer weakness. Keep yourself ever adorned with justice, that you may be included amongst them that are honored as such.

The slave must recognize your brother, sister, mother or father as his master. Set no store by the slave who always, when called to any work, demands to be sold and never has any fears with regard to being bought and sold; you will gain nothing good from him. Change him quickly for another, seeking out one such as I have described. Thus you will achieve your purpose and suffer no troubles.

52

Circumcision of Men and Women

This reading—on circumcision—reflects Muslims' concern with ritual purity and conformity to Prophetic practice. The attitude displayed toward excision for women, however, seems more centered in male chauvinism than in a concern for ritual purity. Though it is less obligatory than male circumcision, it continues to be widely practiced in the Muslim world and—at least in Africa—in many non-Muslim cultures.

QUESTIONS TO CONSIDER

1. Why is circumcision practiced in Islam?
2. Why do other civilizations practice circumcision?

Text: Circumcision is a *sunna*—Prophetic practice—obligatory for men, while excision for women is an ennoblement.

Commentary: *"Obligatory"*—that is "confirmed" because of the saying of the Prophet in the two Authentic Collections [of al-Bukhārī and Muslim]: The natural state [of a man comprises] five things: circumcision, shaving of the pubic hair, clipping the mustache and plucking the hair of the armpits. Circumcising on the day of birth or on the seventh day is disapproved unless there is fear for the child's health, since that is the custom of the Jews. It may be done [prematurely] if the child is sick and it is feared he may die. There are conflicting views over whether a boy who is born without a foreskin should be operated upon.

Supercommentary: *"The natural state . . . five things."* i.e., the qualities whereby a man is perfected so that he displays the finest characteristics. His statement: *"should be operated upon"*: one view is that whatever there is to be cut should be cut. Others said not.

Commentary: There are conflicting views over whether an adult who becomes a Muslim should be circumcised, if he fears this might be injurious to his health. Whoever fails to be circumcised without any excuse or reason is not permitted to be an imam—leader of communal prayer—or to give formal testimony.

Supercommentary: One of the commentators said: "It is forbidden to look at the genitals of an adult, or an adolescent or a boy who has attained puberty and no forbidden act should be committed in order to carry out a sunna." It would appear, therefore, that [the adult convert to Islam] should circumcise himself, since the man who has attained the age of legal responsibility is bound to do what will make his Islam complete. You are aware that circumcision makes a man's Islam complete. The same applies to a slave who is purchased after he attains puberty or who is adolescent. His statement *"is not permitted to be an imam"* lacks authority since [the accepted view of] the law school is that for an uncircumcised man to be imam is [merely] disapproved of [not forbidden].

Commentary: Excision is removal of excess [flesh] from the woman's vulva.

Supercommentary: Ibn ʿUmar said: "Excision is taking away some part of the protuberance [which lies] between the two labia."

Commentary: *"An ennoblement"*—that is to say, a Sunna like the circumcision of men. It brings back fluid to a woman's face and makes intercourse more pleasant for the husband.

Supercommentary: His statement: *"That is to say, a Sunna"* lacks authority. The reliable view is that it is [merely] "preferred." His statement: *"It brings back fluid to a woman's face"* appears to mean that fluid was in the face and then disappeared and was brought back by excision. However, this is not so. The meaning of its bringing back fluid to the face is that [excision] gives rise to a glamorous appearance in the face, to its glowing and shining.

Final Remark: Should an hermaphrodite be circumcised or not? Ibn Nājī said not, since on principle it is better to forbid something than to allow it, i.e., the hermaphrodite should not have either or both of its genitals operated upon.

From the *Risāla* of Ibn Abī Zayd al-Qayrawānī with the commentary of Abū 'l-Ḥasan al-Mālikī and the supercommentary of ʿAlī al-Ṣaʿidī al-ʿAdawī, Cairo: Muṣṭafā al-Bābī al-Ḥalabī, 1937, ii, 177–99. Edited and translated by John O. Hunwick, professor of History, Northwestern University.

MEDIEVAL EUROPE, AFRICA, AND THE EAST

The Germanic Tribes Succeed the Romans in the West

In the declining centuries of the Roman Empire in the West, Roman leaders increasingly relied on Germanic barbarian tribes to do their fighting for them, with the eventual result that more military power was in Germanic hands than in Roman ones. A broad array of Germanic tribes assumed a rather shapeless hegemony in Italy when the last Roman Emperor in the West, Romulus Augustulus, was eased out in favor of Odoakar, king of the Scirians, a rather small tribe, in 476. Odoakar called himself *rex* (king) on his coinage but could not decide for the life of him *what* he was king of. He was, in fact, king of the Germanic tribes in Italy, which would have made a poor title. The Romans probably would not have stood for his styling himself "King of Italy" or "King of the Romans," let alone "Roman Emperor," and so he had himself referred to as "Odoakar the King" and let it go at that.

Soon, however, King Theoderic of the Ostrogoths, the most advanced and best organized of the Germanic tribes, invaded Italy, killed Odoakar in 493, and established Ostrogothic rule in Italy. Theoderic ran Italy roughly by keeping military affairs in the hands of his fellow Goths, but entrusting much civilian administration to cooperative Romans. His long reign until 526 was a peaceful and prosperous one, which enabled considerable economic recovery in Italy. Apart from being barbarians in the eyes of the Romans, however, the Goths had a more serious flaw: Like most of the other Germanic tribes, they had accepted Arianism as their version of Christianity. The Arians believed that if the terms "God the Father" and "God the Son" were accurate, there must have been a time when there was a Father and no Son, and consequently the powers of Jesus, the Son, were derivative from God the Father. This meant that they rejected the equality of the persons of the Trinity and were consequently heretics from the Trinitarian or Catholic standpoint, which prevailed in Roman Italy. Consequently, most Roman Italians applauded the forces serving the Eastern Emperor Justinian when they invaded Italy in the early 550s and nearly wiped out the Ostrogoths.

Meanwhile the Franks, who had remained pagan until the end of the fifth century, accepted Trinitarian Christianity under Clovis. Their resulting religious identification with Rome meant that they immediately enjoyed the support of the Catholic Church. Partly through Clovis's victories and partly through general Catholic Church support, the Franks became the dominant Germanic tribe and in their own minds at least inherited the governance of Western Europe from the Romans. Three centuries after Clovis, the great Frankish king Charlemagne would be acclaimed as Roman Emperor and crowned as such by the pope.

Georgius Florentinus Gregorius (538/9–594) came from a Roman family of the senatorial class, which held governing and high church positions in Gaul and worked with the Frankish conquerors there. As Gregory, Bishop of Tours, he distinguished himself by writing the first substantial work of history in and about that earliest part of the medieval world, often called the "Dark Ages." Although very conscious of his Roman roots, he shows no resentment at all toward the Franks, although he casually refers to them as "barbarians," probably because their native language is not Latin, as is his. His work, which he calls simply *Ten Books of History,* begins as a world history of sorts with the creation and relevant Hebrew history, funneling into church, Roman, and Gallic history but becoming expansive only with the story of the Franks and how the church fared under them.

An important aspect of Gregory's work is his portrayal of early medieval kingship. Students frequently assume that because of the superstitious nature of the Dark Ages monarchs could exploit their ignorant, gullible people without hindrance through a claim to rule divinely. Gregory's stories make it clear that this was not the case at all. Kings and queens had about the same totality of power as did chiefs among the Native Americans before the arrival of Europeans, although, taking one with the other, they seem to have been much more ambitious to consolidate their personal power than were the North American chiefs of old. Consequently, they had to bestir themselves, often using deception and violence, when they really wanted to have their way.

People in Gregory's accounts invoke laws, written and unwritten—often to highlight the lawlessness of powerful figures—and there is an underlying consensus that willingness to be law-abiding is a great virtue. The Franks, like other Germanic tribes, had their law codes. At first, Germanic tribal law was not at all severe and resembled that of the Hittites considerably more than *The Institutes of Justinian* (see Readings 6 and 47). In time, as the Germanic peoples grew more settled, they began to favor the harsh deterrent laws of the Romans, a trend that accelerated as they became more city-oriented.

53

Gregory of Tours, *History of the Franks*

The first selections that follow present Clovis (ca. 466–511), who made Catholic Christians out of his Franks and greatly extended Frankish rule. He is easily the greatest secular hero of Gregory's work and remains for him an enduring model. Although Clovis is scarcely a Christian model at all by later standards, for Gregory his Christian commitment is shown by the fact that once he was well established, he defended the lands and property of churches and monasteries and never let his Franks take anything from them.

Clovis's domains were divided upon his death: the pieces were combined and redivided throughout the sixth century with Austrasia, Neustria, and Burgundy emerging as the most prominent Frankish kingdoms. The last selections feature Queen Fredegunde of Neustria, who spent much of her life in a feud with Queen Brunhilde of Austrasia. It is difficult to say who got the better of it. Fredegunde died before Brunhilde, but she did succeed in raising her own son to rule as Chlothar II, King of Neustria—no mean achievement in view of the number and strength of her enemies. According to the seventh-century "Chronicle of Fredegar," Chlothar charged Brunhilde, when she was about eighty years old, with the death of ten Frankish kings, including two he had ordered killed himself. Then, after three days of diverse tortures, he consigned her "to be tied by her hair, one leg and one arm to the tail of a very wild horse, so that his hooves and speed tore her limb from limb."

The murderous rivalry between the two queens lived on in medieval legend and was probably one of the inspirations for the lethal conflict between Queens Brunhilde and Kriemhilde in the *Nibelungenlied* (see Reading 55).

QUESTIONS TO CONSIDER

1. How would you rate Clovis on his handling of the valued-vessel incident in Soissons? Did he have any better options or did he do essentially the right thing?
2. What were Clovis's motives in accepting Christianity? How compatible were his motives with the basic teachings of Christianity in the New Testament (see Reading 38)?
3. Do you think Fredegunde behaved much differently in dealing with her enemies than a male figure, such as Clovis, would have?
4. Some perhaps turf-conscious medieval historians become defensive when confronted with the term "Dark Ages" for the early medieval centuries. One remarks that the period is "dark" only because we have failed to shed light on it. Do you have the feeling that if you knew more about Clovis and Fredegunde you would not consider their period a particularly "dark" one? Why?

1. The Vessel of Soissons

In the fifth year of his reign, Clovis advanced against Syagrius, a Roman king whose power was centered in the city of Soissons. The two waged a battle against each other, and when Syagrius saw his troops being pushed back he fled.

In those days Clovis's army plundered many churches, for he was still entrapped by the perverse superstition of unbelievers. And so, his Franks took with them a vessel of great size and beauty, along with other treasured pieces used in church services. The Bishop of the church they had robbed then sent a messenger to King Clovis and asked that his church might at least have that pitcher back, even if the Franks kept all the other pieces of value. The King listened to the messenger and said: "Follow us to Soissons, for there everything taken as booty must be divided up. If I draw that vessel by lot, I will do as the Bishop desires."

From Gregorius Turonensis, *Historiarum Libri Decem*, ed. Bruno Krusch and Rudolf Buchner (Darmstadt: Wissenschaftliche Buchgesellschaft, 1967), II, 27; IV, 27–28; VIII, 31; trans. Henry A. Myers.

Afterwards they reached Soissons, where all the loot was spread out for display. "Bravest of warriors," the King began, "I am going to ask you to do me a special favor." He pointed to this pitcher: "Let me have that pitcher, not counting it in the lot-drawing."

When the King spoke, the warriors of a healthier mind responded: "Everything we see here is yours, glorious King; we, too, belong under your authority. Do now whatever you like, for no one can withstand your power."

As they said this, however, one impulsive, envious, and thoughtless man struck his battle-ax into the pitcher with a loud shout: "You are not going to get anything except what you get rightfully by lot!"

This upset everyone, but the King took this insult patiently in stride, giving the broken pitcher to the Bishop's messenger, but the shame inflicted on him burned secretly in his heart.

The following year at the annual inspection of arms and gear on March 1, Clovis had all his warriors display their weapons, to show how well they were polished and cared for. As he made his rounds among them, he came to the man who had struck the pitcher and said to him: "No one carries such shabby weapons as you do. Your spear, your sword and your battle-ax are all worthless!" Then he threw the man's battle-ax on the ground, but when its owner leaned over to pick it up, the King raised his own ax with both hands and drove it into the man's head.

"That is what you did with the pitcher at Soissons," said Clovis. When the man was dead, the King told the rest to go home, and his deed seized them with mighty dread. He went on to wage many wars and win many victories.

2. Baptism of Clovis

[Chrodichilde, his Queen] kept imploring Clovis to renounce the false gods and recognize the one true God, but he could not be converted to the faith until he found himself in a war with the Alamanni. Naked need forced him to confess what his heart had previously denied. When the two armies collided, the result was a terrible bloodbath, with Clovis's army coming close to annihilation. When he realized that, he raised his eyes to Heaven, his heart was moved, his eyes filled with tears, and he spoke: "Jesus Christ, Chrodichilde has revealed to me that Thou art the Son of the living God. They say Thou givest help to the hard-pressed and victory to those who have faith in Thee. I humbly plea for Thy mighty assistance. If Thou grantest me victory over these enemies of mine and I experience that might which Thy followers claim to have tested, then I will believe in Thee and have myself baptized in Thy name. For I have called upon my gods, only to find that they are a long ways from helping me. I believe they are powerless, since they don't help those who serve them. Just deliver me from the hands of mine enemies!" When he spoke these words, the Alamanni turned and began to flee. Then when they saw their own king lying there dead they surrendered to Clovis, saying: "Do not let any more people be killed, we plead with you. We belong to you now." Then Clovis stopped the fighting, gave instructions to the people, and they went home in peace. He told the Queen how he had called upon the name of Christ and thus won the victory. . . .

The Queen then had Saint Remigius summoned and asked him to bring the word of salvation to the King's heart. . . .

"Holy Father, I would be glad to obey you, but one thing bothers me: the people who follow me will not stand for my deserting their gods. But I will still go and speak with them, as you ask me to do."

As he met with his people, the whole crowd shouted in unison, even before he could open his mouth: "We renounce the mortal gods, gracious King, and are prepared to follow the immortal God, Whom Remigius preaches."

The King asked Remigius to baptize him first, and so he went, a new Constantine, to the baptismal bath, to wash himself pure of the old leprosy and to cleanse himself of the dirty spots on his past. . . .

And so the King recognized the Almighty God as the Trinitarian One and had himself baptized in the name of the Father, the Son, and the Holy Ghost. Then he was anointed with holy oil under the sign of the cross of Christ. From his army, more than three thousand were baptized.

3. Brunhilde and Fredegunde

When King Sigbert saw that his brothers were marrying wives unworthy of them and were even lowering themselves to the point of marrying servant women, he sent a delegation to Spain with many gifts and asked for [the Visigothic] King Athanagild's daughter, Brunhilde. She was a maiden of noble bearing, beautiful to behold, intelligent and charming to talk with. Her father did not turn down the request but sent her to the King with many treasures. The King assembled his chief nobles, prepared a great banquet for the ceremony and with great rejoicing and merriment all around he married her. She came as an Arian, but the bishop's teaching and the king's own encouragement converted her to believe in the blessed Trinity. . . .

When King Chilperic saw all this, he sent—although he already had several wives— to Spain for Galswintha, Brunhilde's sister. Through his messengers he promised to put away his other wives if he could have her, the daughter of a king and thus his own equal. The father believed these promises and sent off his daughter, as he had the previous one, with a great wealth of riches. . . . When Galswintha arrived at King Chilperic's court she was received with great honors, and she married him. He treated her very lovingly: she had brought *really* splendid treasures with her, but his scandalous love for Fredegunde, now one of his ex-wives, caused great friction between them. . . . Galswintha complained to the king about the insults she constantly had to endure, insisting that she must not really be important to him. She told him to go ahead and keep the treasures she had brought but to let her return free to her homeland. The king would not agree to this, but cleverly reassured her with soft words. Finally, however, he had a servant strangle her and "found" her dead on her bed.

Upon her death, God worked a great miracle: the cord holding the lamp which hung and burned at her tomb broke, although no one touched it, and the lamp fell upon the cement floor. The hard cement yielded to it, and the lamp sank into it as if it had been a soft mass until it was half covered by it but not damaged in the least. Those who saw this recognized it as an awesome miracle. The king mourned her death but after a few days took Fredegunde back as his wife.

4. Fredegunde and Her Enemies

Fredegunde was staying in Rouen. In a bitter tirade against Bishop Praetestatus she said that the time would return when he would see the exile he had been through before. He replied, "Exiled or not, I remained a bishop, and I will continue to be one. You, however, will not always have your royal power. Through God's grace those such as I may ascend from exile to God's kingdom. You, however, will be cast down to hell from this kingdom. Still, it would be better for you to renounce your stupid and wicked ways and start behaving better: that way you could gain salvation and also succeed in raising the little son you bore to maturity. . . ."

When Sunday dawned, the bishop went to his church early and began, as was his custom, to sing responses to the antiphones of the choir. He knelt during the singing, and a cursed murderer came up, drew a dagger from his belt and stabbed him through his armpit. He shouted to the clergy there to come and help him, but none of those there would come right away. Then he stretched out his bloody hands towards the altar, saying prayers and still giving thanks to God, until finally faithful hands carried him to his room and laid him on his bed. Right away, Queen Fredegunde appeared with Dukes Beppolen and Ansovald and said: "O holy bishop, this really should not have happened to you or your congregation, particularly while you were worshipping! If only we could find out who dared commit such a crime as this, so that he might suffer the punishment he deserves!"

The bishop, however, knew full well how treacherously she was speaking and answered: "And *who* did this? None other than the one who has murdered kings and who often has spilled innocent blood and unleashed all kinds of evil in this kingdom."

The woman replied: "I have very experienced doctors, who can cure your wound. . . ."

"God is summoning me from this world, but you, who have instigated these wicked acts, are cursed in this world, and God will avenge my blood on your head."

She left then, and the bishop ordered his affairs put in order and breathed his last. Bishop Romachard of Coutances came to his funeral. Grief prevailed among all the people of Rouen, but particularly among the aristocratic Franks of that city. One of these lords came to Fredegunde and spoke: "You have caused a great deal of evil in this world, but you never did anything worse than this—having a priest of God murdered. May God take vengeance upon you for his innocent blood. All of us want to track this evil to its source, so that you will no longer be free to carry out such crimes."

When he had said this, he left the Queen, but she sent someone to him to invite him to join her for a merry meal. When he declined the messenger asked him—since he would not accept the dinner invitation—would he at least drink a cup of wine so that he would not be leaving the royal palace without accepting some hospitality. He did stay and drink a cup of vermouth mixed with honey . . . , but this wine was poisoned. . . . Things turned black before his eyes. He mounted his horse, but when he had ridden about six hundred yards he fell from his horse and died.

Afterwards, Bishop Leudowald sent messengers to all other bishops around Rouen and, after getting their approval, closed all Rouen's churches: the people were not to expect any divine services until those responsible for this crime had been identified; everyone was to join the search. He had several men detained, and when they were tortured they confessed that Fredegunde had ordered these crimes. She denied everything, however, so he could not follow up on what they had said. People were saying that murderers came after him, too, since he was quite determined to resume the investigation, but since he was bravely guarded by his own men they could not do him any harm.

54

Law Code of the Visigoths

In matters of robbery and homicide, although not in matters of angering gods, relatively primitive law codes have tended to be mild even by modern standards. Their aim is less to do absolute justice than to reestablish "peace," placating the victims or his survivors with money, sheep, pigs, or whatever it takes to keep them from unleashing blood feuds. For them, there is little, if any, idea of the "state" that is obliged to punish criminals because fraud and violence are threats to public safety. Each tribal member is considered valuable, and no lives should be taken if offenders can pay compensation enough to aggrieved families in order to pacify them.

At the onset of the Middle Ages, the Franks were less settled than the Goths and retained this sort of tribal thinking in their laws, even when they began recording them in Latin. The Visigoths, who had more contact with the Roman world than did the Franks, had already absorbed something of a Roman outlook in their earliest surviving Latin law code, which specifically brings in deterrence (*ad aliorum terrorum*—"for the terror of others") as an aim. In the following excerpt from their law code, the "state" is already playing a role through judges and courts.

QUESTIONS TO CONSIDER

1. Can you see the institutions of manorialism and strict class differentiation in the Visigothic Code? Where in particular?
2. Compare the punishment of parricides in the last article cited from the *Visigothic Code* with the same item from *The Institutes of Justinian* (see Reading 47). Do you suppose one was a more effective deterrent than the other? Why?

Attacks

1. Only the master or lord is to be considered guilty when a common man or a serf commits [these] crimes at his command.
2. When someone in possession of a place is driven from it by another who fails to get a court order for what he intends to do, that latter person will lose his case even if right is otherwise mostly on his side. The man who is attacked and displaced should receive back everything which he possessed in the condition it was in when he had it before and should retain it in assured safety. Moreover, if the guilty man should have taken possession of a property in a way which he cannot justify before a court, he shall lose his case and give to the man he attacked as much of this property as is equal to the value of the one he tried to take over. . . .

From *Leges Visigothorum antiquiores,* ed. Karl Zeumer (Hanover and Leipzig: Hahn, 1894), pp. 58–59, 66, 103; trans. Henry A. Myers.

3. If someone assembles a gang (*turba*) for the purpose of committing murder, or has instigated some disruptive activity with the intent of doing someone bodily harm, of if he has committed people for this purpose, the judge shall have him seized as soon as he learns of the misdeed. The ringleader shall lose his good name and receive sixty lashes before the judge; he must name all those who assembled at his instigation so that they—provided they are free men and not legally obedient to him—shall receive fifty lashes. Serfs, however, who belong to another lord but who took part in this crime, shall, as a deterrent to others, be stretched out before the judge and receive two hundred lashes. . . .

Inducement to Robbery

If a man has induced another to commit robbery, to destroy someone's goods, or to steal his sheep or other animals, he must pay to the person eleven times the value of what he stole. His free accomplices shall be fined five solidi each or shall, if they do not have enough money to pay this fine, receive fifty lashes. If serfs have committed such a crime without the approval of their lord they shall receive 150 lashes. All goods shall be returned on the spot.

(Robbery in a Lord's Absence)

While a lord is away or on a public military expedition no one shall disturb the peace of his estate. Let no one force entrance into the house of anyone who is away or taking part in a public military expedition. If during such an absence anyone takes possession of an item he might have sued to get legally, he shall replace it with double its value. If, however, he takes something to which he had absolutely no legal claim, he shall replace it with triple its value.

Concerning the Murderers of Relatives or Concerning their Property

Concerning those who have killed their next of kin, when a son kills his father or a father kills his son, or a husband kills his wife or the wife her husband, or a mother her daughter or a daughter her mother, or a brother his brother, a sister her sister [the list goes on] . . . that person shall be condemned to death. A murderer, however, who flees to a church or to any holy altars and whose life is spared by the order of a ruler or judge must live in perpetual exile. All of his (or her) property shall be given to the heirs in the sequence provided by law or to the treasury in case the murdered person has left no heirs. For the murderer should not enjoy this property in freedom, even if he escapes with his life.

Feudalism and Chivalry, West and East

The feudal system began to take shape in Western Europe in the early eighth century when Charles Martel, Charlemagne's grandfather, first made the practice of *benefice*—giving land in return for services, previously in the form of grants to monasteries, in return for masses or other Church services—into a secular institution. He entrusted land in a form that would later be called a *fief* to leaders among the Frankish warrior nobility in return for their pledge of military service against the Moors. Owing service for the lands entrusted to them, the Frankish nobles thus functioned as Charles's *vassals.* Under Charlemagne's own, fairly strong central regime, these relationships were not decisive, but with the breakup of the Carolingian Empire and the onset of the second wave of Dark Ages, feudal relations became the dominant way of upholding something like law and order in much of Western Europe.

The term "chivalry" originally meant cavalry, but under feudalism the warrior nobility fighting on horseback developed a value system all its own. Chivalry, as an ideology, stressed courageous loyalty for good reasons: In the centuries when feudalism prevailed, the "state" (in the sense of an independent entity with a legal monopoly on the use of force) did not exist. Dukes, counts, and others in the feudal hierarchy were supposed to keep a semblance of law and order in their territories and assist their liege lords in doing the same, but the responsibilities were a matter of individual contract. For example, a lord promised to uphold his vassal's rights in his fief, and the vassal promised to give "aids" and counsel to his lord. For the system to work properly, it was necessary—in the absence of readily available enforcing power—for both sides to feel a strong sense of honor in carrying out their commitments. Consequently, the utmost value was attached to having sufficient loyalty and courage to stand by the feudal contract despite overwhelming threats.

The ideas of chivalry were conveyed in epics known by their French generic name, *chansons de geste* (songs of deeds), of which the *Song of Roland* is easily the most famous, but chivalric epics were written in many parts of Europe. The first selection that follows, the *Nibelungenlied* (*Song of the Nibelungs*), written anonymously in Germany around 1200, mixes elements of the older epic; emphasis is on detailed and bloody battles with elements of the new "courtly" style, in which refinement, good manners, and fine clothing come into their own. In this new courtly style, women play active roles.

The second epic selection, taken from the anonymous *Book of Emperors and Kings,* illustrates among other things the feudal-chivalric theme in having Charlemagne function as vassal of his feudal lord, St. Peter. It displays the ideology of the Holy Roman Empire in which the Church, secular monarchy, and the feudal nobility were supposed to function in a unity of mutual support.

Absolute monarchy was destined to win out over feudalism as the Middle Ages waned, but until this happened, the feudal nobility along with the clergy exercised its own restraints against overly ambitious monarchs. Only when the resistance of the feudal nobility and clergy was overcome could kings become absolute rulers.

Feudalism in Japan had very different origins from feudalism in the West.

In Japan, leaders of armed groups in the provinces began to challenge the aristocrats who controlled the central government in the ninth century, and by the twelfth century these *bushi* or *samurai* were effectively in control of Japan. Thus, they replaced one kind of aristocratic rule with another, whereas in Europe from the eighth through the thirteenth century all the nobility who counted were real or imagined descendants of a warrior elite. The samurai culture of Japan developed an ethical system similar to that of European chivalry, which is illustrated by both the *Bushido Code* or *Way of the Samurai* and the tale of self-sacrificing heroism for the honor of a feudal lord, *The Forty-Seven Ronin.*

55

The *Nibelungenlied*

The following excerpts from this epic sample both the violence-loving older emphasis of the genre and the (by 1200 contemporary but still fairly new) emphasis on what is polite and fashionable. Siegfried, the most heroic among the male figures, is a master of both helmet-splitting combat and the courtly arts. He knows just what to do, just what to say, and just what to wear to cut a fine chivalric picture.

To understand the second and third excerpts, it is necessary to know that Brunhilde, Queen of Iceland, was a beautiful but Amazonian figure who offered her hand in marriage to any aspiring knight who would attempt to defeat her in sports but who would be killed if he lost to her. Gunther, King of Burgundy, was no match for Brunhilde and knew it, but he enlisted the aid of Siegfried by giving him a magic helmet that gave supernatural strength and invisibility to the wearer. In return for his help, Siegfried would have the beautiful Princess Kriemhilde, Gunther's sister, as his wife. Gunther went through the motions of throwing the required spear and a huge stone, but it was the invisible Siegfried who really won the games for him. Later, on their wedding night, Brunhilde refused to yield to Gunther's embraces but rather tied him up and hung him on the wall until dawn. Gunther then enlisted Siegfried's aid again: The next night, the invisible Siegfried physically overcame Brunhilde but then turned her over to Gunther for the consummation of their marriage, after which her Amazonian features left her and she became simply the "home queen" of Burgundy. Siegfried's fatal mistake was in taking a ring and valuable belt from Brunhilde as souvenirs of his adventure and then—an even worse judgment call—giving them to his own bride, Kriemhilde.

Eventually, rivalry between the two women led Kriemhilde to tell Brunhilde that Siegfried was the first man to possess her, and Brunhilde's longing for vengeance led her to persuading Hagen, one of Gunther's vassals who was trusted by Siegfried, to murder Siegfried. Much, much later Kriemhilde got her own revenge by bringing about the bloody deaths of Hagen and other traitors, even though she had to marry Attila the Hun to do so and lost her own life in the process of carrying out the demands of justice as she saw them.

QUESTIONS TO CONSIDER

1. How does the author go about making Siegfried an appealing figure for his audience?
2. Why do you suppose the author starts the conflict with the Danes and the Saxons with a description of single combat and ends it with one combining single combat and mass fray?
3. Where do you suppose the author got the idea of a man risking his life on a wager on his athletic performance for the hand of a desirable woman? Have you met up with a roughly similar story in one or more earlier cultures?
4. The author of this epic announces early on that he intends to tell of disaster brought on "by the conflicts between two noble women." Do you think the story of Brunhilde and Fredegunde (see Reading 53) furnished the inspiration for his stories after centuries of retelling? Why or why not?
5. What does the feudal structure have to do with the rivalry between Brunhilde and Kriemhilde?

I

In the Netherlands, a son of the mighty King Siegmund and Queen Sieglinde grew up. There, downstream on the Rhine, the royal castle with the city called Xanten was known far and wide for its splendor. The bold young prince was named Siegfried. His manly courage was to lead him on tests of his warrior's skill into many kingdoms; his bold strength kept him riding through the lands. . . . He was of an age now to take his own place at the royal court. The people loved to watch him ride by. Many ladies and many girls hoped that his desires might pull him in their direction. Many loved him. . . . Siegmund and Sieglinde kept him very well dressed, and wise men who knew what honor was all about instructed him in winning lands and people to rule. . . .

[Hearing tales of the great beauty and charm of the Burgundian princess, Kriemhilde, Siegfried makes a knightly journey to Worms, the Burgundian capital. While he is there, messengers of the hostile kings of Saxony and Denmark approach her brother, King Gunther:] "If you will permit us, Sire, there is no reason for us to delay in giving you our message: It is that Ludgast and Ludger, the rulers who sent us, declare the feud you have caused by kindling great hatred in them, as we have been told, as reason for marauding your land. They plan an expedition to Worms on the Rhine, and there should be no doubt that many bold knights will follow them here. . . . They will start out in twelve weeks; that is, unless you want to negotiate with them: Then offer what you can. If you choose that course, the vast armies of your mighty enemies will not ride so close to Worms, bringing conflict that will cause you sorrow because so many of your good knights will be killed."

"Give me a little time," the good king said, "until I can think all this over. I will let you know what I decide later. If I indeed have loyal vassals, I will not want to keep this from them. Such a harsh message calls for the advice of my friends."

The best of his men who could be located came to him, and he said: "Ludgast and Ludger intend to invade our lands with strong forces: Just think about the grief that this will bring us."

From *Das Nibelungenlied*, ed. Friedrich Zarncke (Halle: M. Niemeyer, 1905), verses 20–843. Translated by Henry A. Myers.

"Let's defend with swords," said Gernot. "He will die whose lot it is to fall. I will not forget my honor in the fight: Let us welcome our enemies to do battle here."

Then Hagen of Tronya spoke up: "That does not seem like a good idea. Ludgast and Ludger are too full of themselves. We can't get a decent army together in such a short time. Why don't you tell Siegfried about this?"

Gunther directed men to see that the messengers were given lodgings in his city. Even though they were enemies, he had them very well taken care of. His act was generous, and he was doing the right thing until he could find friends who would support him.

But then the boldest of knights [Siegfried] saw how something terrible was depressing the king. He had no way of knowing what had gone on, and so he asked King Gunther to let him know what had happened. . . .

"I don't want to tell everybody about the troubles I have to bear secretly, but there is nothing wrong with opening your heart to your real friends."

At this, Siegfried turned both pale and red and said to the king: "I have never turned you down in anything yet, and I will help you deal with everything that is worrying you. If you need the help of friends, count on me. Trust me to support you through it all with honor until my own end comes."

"May God reward you, Lord Siegfried! I like the way you talk. Even if you don't actually fight in my cause, I'm glad to hear that you are so supportive. If I live through all this, I will see that you are well rewarded. And so, I will let you in on what troubles me so much right now. I just learned from my enemies' messengers that they are going to invade my lands, which no knights have ever done before."

"Don't pay too much attention to that threat," said Siegfried, "and don't let it worry you. Just do what I ask you to. Send for your vassals to come to your aid, but let me win honor and victories for you. If your mighty enemies can enlist thirty thousand knights, I would still beat them even if I had only a thousand. You can count on that."

"If you do, I will see that you receive lasting rewards," said King Gunther. . . .

When the news reached Denmark [that Gunther was going to fight and that the renowned Siegfried was supporting him], the king's men hurried to assemble more and more forces until Ludgast had twenty thousand knights ready to ride under his banner. King Ludger kept recruiting in Saxony until forty thousand and more had pledged to ride against the Burgundians.

[A little later at Gunther's court] "Let your Royal Highness stay at home," said Siegfried, "since your knights are willing to follow me. Look after the ladies and be of good cheer because I will prevent those invaders from attacking you at Worms on the Rhine. They will wish they had stayed at home because we will ride so far back into their own lands that their arrogance will be turned to grief." . . .

From the Rhine, the Burgundian forces rode through Hesse toward Saxony, where the battle was soon to be fought. . . . Never had the Saxons experienced such a devastating attack as this was to be. . . . "I will ride out myself," said Siegfried the hero, "and do some reconnaissance in our enemies' direction until I can establish where their knights are." He rode directly into Saxony . . . , and there he caught sight of a great army encamped in the field. From the forward sentries' position, one noble warrior soon rode out ready for combat. That bold man had seen Siegfried, and Siegfried saw him now.

I'll tell you who that was, riding now from the vanguard and holding a light shield of gold: It was King Ludgast himself, who had come to lead his army in person! Siegfried galloped toward him in all his glory, and Ludgast sought his noble "guest" for single combat as well. . . . Spurred on, their horses bore the two royal warriors, who had lowered their lances to rest on their shields for the charge, toward each other with such lightness that the wind itself appeared to be carrying them.

[The impact did not dislodge either of them, however, and] each grim and determined foe turned his steed around and sought the other with his sword. The field echoed the sounds of clanging metal, as Siegfried struck heavy blows. Under his hero's hand, great red sparks of fire sprayed from Ludgast's helmet. For a while, each of them found the other his equal, for Ludgast struck Siegfried many severe blows, too: Gashes made by the other's sword soon marked both their shields. Thirty of Ludgast's men saw what was going on, but before they reached him, Siegfried won the combat with three deep wounds he dealt the king through his light armor: They were decisive. The cutting edge of his sword drew blood from Ludgast's wounds and destroyed his will to continue. He asked for his life and, letting Siegfried know that he was Ludgast, offered him his lands.

But then his knights, who had seen from the outpost what was happening rode up and attacked Siegfried, all thirty of them, while he was leading Ludgast away. But Siegfried's strong arm let him keep his valuable hostage for himself: That wonderful knight inflicted still more destruction on his foes. Of the thirty, he killed all but one, leaving him to ride back to tell the news of what had happened with the red on his helmet bearing testimony. Denmark's warriors were sad and grim to learn that their ruler had been captured. When his brother, Ludger, heard the news, he went into convulsions of rage and grief.

[After turning Ludgast over to Hagen at the Burgundian camp,] Siegfried told the knights there to tie their flags on their lances: "There is much more to be done on the field of battle," he said. "If I stay alive, the wife of many a fine knight will be grieving in Saxony before sundown. . . . I can lead you to Ludger's forces. There your strong arms will split many helmets before we return." . . .

They led no more than one thousand knights and the twelve brought by Siegfried. Clouds of dust began to rise on the road as they rode over the land, but many an ornamented shield rim still gleamed from their midst.

By then the full army of the Saxons was on the march. With their well-sharpened swords . . . , the Saxons hoped to defend their towns and lands from the stranger. . . . The Danes, too, gave their hands a good try. [When the battle began,] you could hear the clang of blows on many shield rims, while the sharp swords struck many wounds. Eager for combat, the Saxons did plenty of damage, but the Burgundians pressed into the fray, slashing wide wounds everywhere. You could watch the blood flowing over the saddles as those bold and good warriors competed for honor. Yes, you could hear their sharp weapons ring loud and far as they wielded them. Those who had followed Siegfried from the Netherlands pushed forward behind their lord into the thickest combat. You could see a bloody brook flowing through the gleaming helmets split by Siegfried's strong hand until he confronted King Ludger before his comrades at arms. . . .

When brave Ludger caught sight of Siegfried swinging his wonderful sword . . . high and low and slaughtering so many of his men, rage welled up in him. Both kings' followers rushed at each other with loud sword blows, as their leaders tested each other. Hate was seething all around, but then the Saxons began to back off a little. The Saxon king was told that his brother had been captured, and this gave him sad cause to grieve. . . . Siegfried soon took such blows from Ludger's sword that he felt his horse falter under his saddle. . . . In the press of battle, many knights dismounted, as did Siegfried and Ludger, who charged each other on foot. Siegfried's blows sent the rim clasps holding Ludger's shield together flying off, and the hero from the Netherlands felt sure of winning victory. . . . King Ludger recognized the crown painted on Siegfried's shield, and, realizing that the peerless hero must be its owner, began shouting loudly to his followers: "Give up fighting, all you on my side; I now see Siegmund's son before me. Yes, I recognize that strongest of men: The devil himself sent him against us Saxons!"

And so the Saxons lowered their battle flags. Ludger sought peace, and this was granted him with the stipulation that he must go to King Gunther's country as a hostage. Brave Siegfried's strong hand had made him a prisoner.

II

"I want to sail over the North Sea to Brunhilde," said Gunther, the king from the Rhineland. "I don't care what happens to me: I am going to put my life on the line to win her love and die if I fail to win her as my wife."

"I would advise against that," said Siegfried. "That queen has introduced a savage custom at her court: The man who seeks her love will pay dearly for it. You really should find out more what *that* trip involves."

"If you insist on going," said Hagen, "I would advise you to take Siegfried along to help you with the grave dangers there, since he seems to know so much about the ways of Brunhilde's court."

"Noble Siegfried, will you help me to win my beloved? If you do what I ask and help me win that most desirable of women for my wife, I will risk my own honor and life to repay you."

"If you give me your sister to be my queen, I will do it," answered Siegfried. "I would not want any other reward for my trouble than that exalted princess, the beautiful Kriemhilde."

"I promise!" said Gunther. "Siegfried, let me shake your hand and swear that if the beautiful Brunhilde comes here to my kingdom I will give you my sister as your wife and you shall live happily ever after with your own beautiful bride." And so those bold knights confirmed their promises with oaths.

[A little later, Gunther spoke to Kriemhilde:] "My dearest sister, we cannot make good on what we plan without your help. We are going to undertake real challenges in Brunhilde's country, and for that we will need truly magnificent clothing to wear when we appear before the women there."

The maiden answered him: "My dearest brother, rest assured that I will surely do everything in my power to help you. Kriemhilde would be very sorry indeed if someone else were to let you down. In fact, noble knight that you are, I would rather that you didn't make requests of me as if it worried you to do so. Act confident in letting me know what you would like me to do for you. You will find me not only willing but eager to carry out your wishes. . . ."

"My dear sister, we want to go there wearing the best of clothes. Your own white hands can well see to our needs, but your serving women should help you, too, so that we look splendid for this trip. We wouldn't know where to begin otherwise."

The maiden answered: "I'm glad to let you know that I have just the silk for the task. See that we get a couple of shields full of gems. When we have sewn the gems on the silks, every combination you wear will do you honor before that prized princess. But who is going along to her court with you and will need fine clothes?"

"Four of us," he said. "Siegfried and two of my vassals, Dankwart and Hagen, are going to her court with me. Now pay close attention, sister, to what I am requesting: I would like each of us to have three changes of clothes per day for four days, outfits nice enough that when we leave Brunhilde's kingdom there will be no negative comments."

With cheerful words of parting, the royal lords left her. Princess Kriemhilde then had thirty of her ladies-in-waiting come from their chambers, those who had a keen sense of craftsmanship for the work at hand. They set gems on Arabian silks, white as snow, and the fine silks from Zazamanc, green as clover. Out of these they made fine garments with that wonderful young lady, Kriemhilde, cutting the cloth herself.

They also took some hides from exotic creatures of the deep[1] to serve as bottom layers, sewing the silk on top of them and mounting gold on top of both layers to catch the eyes of their hosts in that foreign land. You can just imagine what comments of amazement those glittering outfits later received! Kriemhilde certainly demonstrated her willing support of the project. She had an abundance of the very best silks that royalty had ever heard of from Morocco and some from Libya, too. Since this was the most exalted of all kinds of expeditions, they would have considered mere ermine furs unworthy. They did use ermine, but they mounted pieces of velvet, black as coals, on it so fine and costly that it would make bold heroes even of our own day stand out at ceremonies. The ladies took great pains with their work, and within seven weeks they had completed the wardrobe, which included garments with gems set in a background of Arabian gold. . . .

III

Kriemhilde and Brunhilde, the two exalted queens, were sitting next to each other [at a palace window, looking on] as outside many knights took part in jousting. They began to speak of two very special heroes who deserved the highest praise. "I have a husband," said the lovely Kriemhilde, "who deserves control over all these domains."

"How could that come about?" Brunhilde responded. "If no other royal kin were still living but you and Siegfried, then the lands could owe allegiance to him, but as long as Gunther is alive they never will."

"Just look at him out there," said Kriemhilde, "riding so nobly and so handsomely in front of the other knights. He displays the moon's radiance dominantly in front of the milder glow of the stars. I have to admit that I derive pleasure from that fact."

"I don't care how well-outfitted your husband is," said Brunhilde, "or how well-mannered or how good-looking, you will still have to concede a higher place to your royal brother, the noble Gunther. You know very well that he must take his place before all other kings."

"My husband is so great," said Kriemhilde, "that I did not exaggerate with my praise of him. He deserves the very highest respect in a good many areas. Take it from me, Brunhilde: He is Gunther's equal and maybe more than that."

[The verbal exchanges escalated in sharpness until] "You are ranking yourself too high," said Brunhilde: "I am just waiting to see if people show you as much respect in public as they do me." Both of the ladies were really getting angry. . . .

[Later the two queens confronted each other upon approaching the door of the cathedral.] The home queen could not suppress her rage and rudely told Kriemhilde to stand where she was, saying: "No vassal's woman has a right to enter before a ruling king's wife."

---

[1]Probably sharkskin.

That infuriated Kriemhilde: "You had better learn to hold your tongue. You brought disgrace on your own lovely body. How do you think another man's mistress can ever hope to be a real queen?"

"Who are you calling 'mistress'?" asked the king's wife.

"That is my name for you," said Kriemhilde, "because it was *my* dear husband, Siegfried, who first possessed that beautiful body of yours. It just wasn't my brother that you lost your virginity to. What are you so mad about? Or are you just pretending to be hurt? Why did you let him be your lover if he is supposed to be your vassal?"

Brunhilde began to cry. Kriemhilde waited no longer before the home king's wife but strode into the cathedral followed by her retinue.

56

The Book of Emperors and Kings, "Charlemagne and Pope Leo III"

In the mid-twelfth century, one or more anonymous clerics in the German city of Regensburg made the first attempt since ancient times to present history to a broad—in fact, largely illiterate—audience in its own vernacular language. *The Book of Emperors and Kings,* now referred to with greater frequency and less accuracy as *The Imperial Chronicle,* was composed for reading or chanting aloud. Although it retains the outward form of a rhymed epic, the main author states his intention of telling the true history of the Roman Empire (meaning the Holy Roman Empire as well as the ancient one) from its beginning to the present day. He makes it plain that, unlike other "songs," his will refute lies instead of spreading them.

In the following excerpt, we see this author's idea of truth. He is more concerned throughout with true models of Christian rulership and contrasting examples of falsity than with mere "facticity." For example, he is intent on portraying Charlemagne as a monumental figure of stern faith and courage who collaborated with Pope Leo III in giving new life to the Roman Empire after the Byzantine Greeks, "the preceding house," had let the Empire's fortunes slide. To explain the motivation behind their mutual support, the author makes Pope Leo III into Charlemagne's brother.

The episode in which Charlemagne threatens Saint Peter may seem extreme by modern standards, but it reminds us that ideas of contract and loyalty thoroughly permeated the religious as well as the secular value system of the feudal world. Charlemagne has kept his part of the feudal contract; when he is convinced that Saint Peter has not kept his, he acts accordingly. Saint Peter responds like a liege lord who has been late in relieving his vassal's distress.

The selection also demonstrates the ambivalence of medieval people in northern Europe toward Rome and the Romans. All of them acknowledged the Bishop of Rome, the pope, as head of the Church, whereas the descent of their Empire from Rome was stressed in the German-speaking lands. Still, those loyal to the Empire regarded the current inhabitants of Rome as a frequently treacherous group who had to be controlled from time to time by "right-thinking" rulers with armies from the "uncorrupted" countries to the north of Italy.

By the twelfth century, the tradition that electoral princes (ranking members of the nobility and clergy) chose the German king (who officially became Roman emperor when consecrated by the pope) had become established. In describing Charlemagne's ascension to these positions, the author of *The Book of Emperors and Kings* drifts between historical accounts from learned sources and traditional accounts from his own day.

The Saint Pancras episode reflects the legal view that people of different tribes or nations were entitled to be tried according to their own native laws. At the same time, this account heightens the author's ethnic stereotypes: The brave Germanic peoples settle their disputes through trial by combat, whereas the less courageous Romans settle legal disputes by raising two fingers and swearing oaths. According to legend, Pancras was a youth of fourteen who was martyred during Diocletian's (A.D. 284–305) persecution of Christians. As a reward for his courage in the face of death, God gave him the power to inflict a wasting, terminal illness on any who swore a false oath at his grave.

QUESTIONS TO CONSIDER

1. How does the author establish Charlemagne as a model Christian ruler?
2. What motivates the Romans to attack the pope? Why is Charlemagne ultimately to blame for this conflict?
3. Why is the pope's requesting mercy for his assailants unacceptable to Charlemagne?
4. Does *The Book of Emperors and Kings* give any justification for identifying most of the inhabitants of Arles as "heathens"?
5. How does Charlemagne finally win his struggle in Spain?

The Empire remained without a head. The lords of Rome set the crown on Saint Peter's Altar. Meeting all together, they swore before the people that never again would they choose a king—nor judge, nor anyone else to rule them—from the kin of the preceding house, which had proven unable to maintain faith and honor with them. They wanted kings from other lands. . . .

According to a custom of those days, young princes from all over the Empire were raised and instructed with great care at the court in Rome. The Romans gave them the sword of knighthood when the time came. . . , sending the young heirs back to their homelands. This helped keep all the dominions mindful of serving Rome.

It came to pass that Pippin, a mighty king of Karlingen,[1] had two fine sons. One of them named Leo came to hold Saint Peter's throne after being raised in Rome, while Charles, the other, stayed home.

[1]"Karlingen," the name given by several medieval German writers to the domain of Charlemagne and his ancestors, is probably a derivation by analogy on the assumption that the name of the great Charles (Karl) was given to his whole family domain. Similarly, his grandson Lothar's name was applied to Lorraine (Lotharingen).

From *The Book of Emperors and Kings (Der keiser und der kunige buoch)*. Trans. Henry A. Myers from text published as *Die Kaiserchronik eines Regensburger Geistlichen*, ed. Eduard Schröder, in *Monumenta Germaniae Historica, Deutsche Chroniken* (Hannover: Hahn, 1892), vol. 1, pp. 339–53, *passim*.

One night when Charles fell asleep, a voice called out to him three times: "Arise, beloved Charles, and hurry to Rome! Your brother Leo needs you!" And quickly Charles made ready, saying nothing to anyone about what he intended to do until he asked leave of the King to go. . . .

When the young Prince asked for leave, his father granted it to him gladly and bestowed gifts upon his son in a manner worthy of a mighty king. . . .

Charles really undertook his journey more for [the chance to pray at the tombs of] the divine Apostles than for his brother's sake. Early and late in the day his thoughts, which he revealed to no one, were filled with love of God. . . .

When Charles arrived in Rome, he was given a fine reception by old and young. . . . Pope Leo sang a mass then in honor of the Holy Ghost and to strengthen the Prince's spirit. Then he received God's Body. All who were there praised God, finding Charles so worthy and to their liking that the law should make him their ruler.

Charles did not listen to what was being said: He had made his journey for the sake of prayer, and he let no commotion distract him. He entered churches barefoot and, imploring God's mercy, he prayed for his soul. This steadfast devotion brought him every worldly honor, too. . . .

Thus he spent four weeks so wrapped in prayer and meditation that no one could approach him to speak, until once his brother, Pope Leo, and all the people fell at his feet. Charles pointed out to God in Heaven that if he were to prove unworthy he never should have made his journey. Then he received the royal emblems, and they set a magnificent crown on his head. All those there in Rome rejoiced that day, and all said, "Amen."

Then the King sat in judgment, and the Pope made complaint before him that church properties and the collection of tithes, entrusted to him by his predecessors for his use in the saving of souls, were being granted away from his jurisdiction, and that his benefices had been taken from him. His complaint angered a number of the nobles.

Then Charles spoke these true ruler's words: "Never in this world, I feel sure, did anyone make a gift to honor God in order that another might take it. That would clearly be robbery. . . . Whoever would take anything away from gifts bestowed on God's houses, through which God's work is furthered, would be despised of God and could not remain a good Christian. . . ." Then those nobles departed, full of resentment. Charles also had no desire to remain there any longer.

Charles returned to Ripuaria.[2] The Romans realized very well that he was their rightful judge, but stupid men among them ridiculed the others for ever having proclaimed him ruler. . . . In Saint Peter's Cathedral they caught the Pope and pushed his eyes out of their sockets . . . , and sent him blind to the King in Ripuaria.

Nothing remained for the Pope to do but set out on the journey in his hapless condition. He rode on a donkey and took with him two of his chaplains, desiring no other escort. . . .

The Pope arrived in Ingelheim with his two chaplains and rode into the King's courtyard. When the King saw him coming, he said to one of his men: "Someone has attacked this pilgrim, and we shall do justice in his cause if we can. He seems badly injured. Someone must have robbed him. . . ."

The King strode quickly across the courtyard . . . and said: "Good pilgrim, if you wish to stay here with me, I will gladly take you in. Tell me if your misfortune is such that I can help you with it. Why don't you dismount?"

---

[2]Territorial home of one historic group of the Franks on the Rhine River; for the author, this location is sometimes synonymous with "Karlingen," sometimes one of its provinces.

The noble Pope wanted to draw closer to the King. His head hung at a strange angle, and his eyes stared askew. "That God should have granted me your presence!" he began. . . . "It has not been long since I sang a mass for you at Rome, when I could still see." As he spoke these words, the noble King recognized him and was so shocked that he could neither see nor hear. . . . His body went limp and he could not speak. . . .

When the Emperor had recovered, the Pope told him sorrowfully: "I have come here that you may take pity on me. It was because of you that I lost my eyes: they blinded me to get even with you. Still, Brother, you must pull yourself together, and weep no more. . . ."

The Emperor himself lifted him down and carried him across the courtyard into his private chamber. There they sat together, and Charles told his men to go outside. "Brother," he said, "how did this happen to you? Let me hear your complaint, and then my forces of justice will right the wrong."

Pope Leo answered the King: "Brother, after you left Rome, the Romans very soon betrayed their loyalty to me in a conspiracy. They caught me in the Cathedral and committed this terrible crime upon me. Brother, we must bear this patiently: I seek vengeance only in Heaven, and you must not injure any of them for this."

"It would be doing God a dishonor to spare those murderers!" the noble King replied. "Ah! How sorely that would injure Christendom. I am called 'Judge' and 'Ruler': and this means I have the duty of judging over the peoples. . . . I must defend Christendom with the sword. You will have them sorely regret their crime against you. I will avenge your eyes, or I will renounce my sword."

Then he dispatched messengers to King Pippin to tell him of his great need and let the nobles of Karlingen know that if they ever wanted to render God a loving service they should hurry to him. And there were none in Karlingen but who proclaimed all with one voice: "Woe to the fatal hour that Rome was ever founded!" . . .

The messengers galloped ceaselessly from land to land and from lord to vassal: all men were willing to come to the cause of Charles. Farmers and merchants, too—no one could hold them back. They left all their belongings and set out to join Charles. The mourning and grief over the news traveled through Christendom from people to people, and the streams of warriors converged like clouds over the Great Saint Bernard Pass. . . . The book does not give a number for the total army, but it was the greatest military expedition that ever descended on Rome.

When the army had advanced to within sight of the Aventine Hill in Rome, the worthy King asked three days and nights for himself. This annoyed his great lords, who went to him to say that it ill became his office to pause there, now that they had come so close that they could see the city which had aggrieved them.

"First we must pray to God, for we must gain His leave to carry through," answered the King. "Then we shall fight with ease. . . ."

Early one morning the voice of God spoke to him: "God in Heaven commands you, King, to remain here no longer. Ride on to Rome: God has rendered judgment, and just vengeance shall overtake them."

And so the King's banner was raised, and Charles let word pass through his whole army that when the knights were prepared for battle they should keep their eyes upon the banner and ride in close formation. Hearts swelling with high spirits, Charles's men swarmed over the hill. . . .

Owî, what an army this was that besieged Rome and the Lateran for seven days and seven nights, so menacingly that no one would fight against it! On the eighth day—this is the truth I am telling you—the Romans ordered the city gates opened and offered to let the King enter with this condition: that any man who could prove himself innocent of committing, aiding, or advising the crime would remain in the King's favor, while the King would deal with the guilty ones after deciding on a just sentence. . . .

As the Emperor sat in judgment and the document naming the guilty men was read, the accused all fervently denied their guilt when they were called forward. The King ordered them to submit to trial by combat for their unwillingness to confess. But then the Romans objected that this was not according to their law, and that no Emperor had ever forced such treatment on them before; instead, they should prove their innocence by swearing with their two fingers.

Then King Charles spoke: "I doubt that any crime so great was ever committed before. Don't be overhasty now: I imagine my brother saw at the time who did it." Still, when so very many of the accused offered their oaths in the Cathedral, the King said: I will not deprive you of recourse to your own law any longer; however, I know of a youth here named Pancras. If you are willing to swear an oath at his grave and if he tolerates it, then I will be willing to believe you."

Icy fear seized the Romans at the mention of this test. As they came to the place sacred to Saint Pancras and were supposed to hold up their fingers and to keep asserting their innocence under oath, one man was overcome, and panic gripped all the rest. They retreated in fear and fled back over the bridge although a fair number went back to Saint Peter's Cathedral.

Charles hesitated no longer but rode after them angrily. For three days, he and his men struck them down, and for three days they carried them out. Then they washed down the floor stones. . . . Charles fell on his knees before Saint Peter's tomb and made his plea to Christ: "Lord God in Heaven, how can I be any good to You as King when You let such shame befall me? Sinner that I may be, I do make every attempt to judge the people in a manner worthy of You. The Romans swore allegiance to a Pope, and You granted him a portion of Your power that he might loose the people from their sins and bind them. I [ask] . . . that you give the evil people of Rome something to recognize Your hidden power by: then they will know for certain that You are a true God. Grant me this, Holy Christ!"

A second time Charles, the noble King, fell to the ground and said: "Hail noble Saint Peter! You are really a divine stalwart of God, a watchman of Christendom. Think now, my lord, what I am going through! You are a summoner of the Kingdom of Heaven. Just look at your Pope! I left him sound of body in your care. Blinded was how I found him, and if you do not heal the blind man today I shall destroy your Cathedral and ruin the buildings and grounds donated to you, and then I shall leave him for you blind as he is, and go back again to Ripuaria."

Quickly the noble Pope Leo made himself ready and said his confession. As he spoke the last word, he saw a heavenly light with both his eyes. Great are the hidden powers of God.

The Pope turned around and spoke to the multitude: "My dearest children gathered from afar, be glad of heart, for the Kingdom of God is drawing near to you. God has heard you and because of your holy prayer has turned His face toward you. Here, at this very place, you are called to be public witnesses that a great miracle has happened. . . . I can see with both eyes better than I ever saw in this world." . . .

The Pope consecrated him as Emperor and granted absolution to all his comrades in arms. Owî, what joy there was in Rome then! The whole people rejoiced then and sang: *"Gloria in excelsis Deo."*

Then Charles laid down the Imperial Law, as an angel recited the true words of God to him. . . . And so the mighty Emperor left us many good laws, which God caused to be spoken before him. . . .

The very first laws the Emperor established dealt with what seemed to him to be the most exalted matters, those concerning bishops and priests, for the Imperial Law of Constantine had been sadly neglected. At the same time, he established laws governing tithes and gifts of property to the Church. . . .

Now I shall tell you about what the peasant is to wear according to the Imperial Law: his clothes may be black or gray, and he is allowed no other. . . . He is to have shoes of cow leather only and seven yards of towcloth for his shirt and breeches. He is to spend six days at the plow and doing plenty of other work; on Sunday he is to go to Church, carrying his animal goad openly in his hand. If a sword is found on a peasant, he is to be led bound to the churchyard fence, where he is to be tied and his skin and hair are to be flayed. If he is threatened by enemies, however, let him defend himself with a pitchfork. This law King Charles established for the peasants. . . .

Emperor Charles besieged a walled city called Arles [France], which actually took him more than seven years. The inhabitants had considered him unworthy of his office. By way of an underground canal, wine was conveyed to them in plentiful supply, but finally Charles's cunning succeeded in cutting off their source. When the inhabitants could not hold out any longer, they threw open the city gates and fought fiercely, offering no terms at all. So many were slain on both sides that there is no man who can tell another how many of either the Christians or the heathens were lying there dead after the battle. No one could tell the dead apart until the Emperor solved the problem with God's help: He found the Christians lying separately in well adorned coffins. Now that is a wonder really worth telling about. . . .

The Emperor and his men turned toward Galicia [in Spain], where the king of the heathens inflicted great losses upon them. The Christian soldiers were all slain, and Charles barely escaped from the battle. Today the stone stays wet on which Charles sat afterwards, weeping passionately as he lamented his sins, saying: "Hail to You, God sublime! Grant me mercy for my poor soul. Take me out of this world, so that my people will no longer be punished because of me. I can never be consoled again."

Then an angel comforted him, saying: "Charles, beloved of God, your joy will come to you quickly. Bid your messengers make haste to summon virgin women—leave the married ones at home—for God will reveal His power through them. If you will fear and love God, the maidens will win your honor back again for you."

The messengers made haste and thoroughly searched through all the lands. They gathered together the maidens and brought them together . . . where the Emperor was waiting for them. Many a young maid came to join the host, fifty-three thousand—I am telling you this as a fact—and sixty-six more. . . .

When all the maidens arrived in a valley since named for Charles, they readied themselves for battle in formations just like men. . . .

Each heathen sentry was struck by wonder as to who this people could be, for it all seemed very strange to them. They hurried back, and one of them said to their king: "Sire, even though we slew the old ones, we must tell you for a fact that the young ones have followed them here. I have the feeling they want to slake their thirst for vengeance. They are big around the chest. Sire, if you fight with them, it will not come to any good end. Their hair is long, and their gait is very graceful: They are fine knights indeed. They are a terrifying lot. . . . No force could ever be assembled on this earth to defeat them. . . ."

At the advice of his experienced counsellors, their king turned over hostages to the Emperor. The king then had himself baptized—how well he suddenly believed in God!—and all his people with him. . . . Thus God made Charles victorious without the thrust of a spear or the blow of a sword, and the maidens well realized that God in Heaven was with them.

Charles and his heroines returned to their own homes back in the Empire. On the way, the worthy maidens came to a green meadow. Tired from the expedition, the heroines stuck their spearshafts into the ground and stretched out their arms in the form of a cross, sleeping on the ground after praising God for the goodness which He had shown them. They stayed there overnight, and a great miracle occurred. Their spearshafts had turned green and had sent forth leaves and blossoms. That is why the place is called "Woods of the Spearshafts"; it can be seen to this day.

Charles, the rich and powerful, built a mighty and beautiful church for the praise of Holy Christ, the honor of Saint Mary and all God's maidens, and the solace of Christendom. Since through chastity and spiritual purity the maids achieved their victory, the church is called *Domini Sanctitas.*[3]

57

Tsunetomo Yamamoto, *Hagakure* (The Way of the Samurai)

In the ninth century, as the aristocracy-dominated central government of Japan weakened and lost control of the provinces, the local gentry began to fortify its own armed constabulary forces. The leaders of these armed groups were called "the bushi" or "samurai," and they were largely descendants of the old provincial uji (clan) aristocracy. The bushi were mounted; armored; armed with bows, arrows, and curbed swords; and accompanied by supporting foot soldiers. By the twelfth century, they had begun to emerge as a dominant social class, providing the key values that permeated life in medieval Japan. They became rulers and guardians of peace as well as fighters.

As clashes among the local armed groups became more frequent, the smaller ones were absorbed into larger and more powerful ones. These groups were eventually consolidated into two powerful rival military clans, one under Minamoto in eastern Japan and the other under Taira in the west. In 1156, a dispute over the imperial succession pitted them against each other in a series of struggles that continued until 1185. At this time, Minamoto Yoritomo (1147–1199) emerged as the unchallenged military master of Japan. In 1192, the court bestowed upon Minamoto Yoritomo the title of Seii-tai-shogun ("Barbarian-Subduing Generalissimo"). This title was once given to generals in charge of expeditions against the Ainu (old proto-Caucasoid inhabitants of Japan), but henceforth it was used in the shortened form of "Shogun" to denote supreme military commander. The country was governed from Minamoto's military headquarters at Kamakura. For the next 700 years, until the Meiji Restoration in 1868, Japan was ruled by the men of the sword. The samurai culture rooted in *Bushido* (meaning "the way of the warrior") flourished.

Bushido was roughly equivalent to medieval European chivalry or the noblesse oblige of the warrior class. Although it did not evolve into an articulated code of conduct for the ruling samurai class until the late seventeenth century,

[3]This church is the Emperor's Chapel, the main and oldest part of the Aachen Cathedral, also called Saint Mary's.

the incipient stage goes back to about the tenth century. The principles of Bushi-do were to be observed by the warrior in his daily life as well as in his vocation. An unwritten code consisting of a few maxims, Bushido was primarily transmitted orally or through the pen of some well-known warrior or savant. The principles of Bushido were drawn from Zen Buddhism, Shintoism, and the Confucian moral precepts. They stressed justice, honor, duty, loyalty, courage, self-control, and a transcendent fearlessness in the face of death.

The following excerpt is from *Hagakure* (*In the Shadow of Leaves*), which is one of the best-known classics on Bushido. This book contains the teachings of Tsunetomo Yamamoto (1659–1719), who was a samurai turned Zen monk. Written and compiled in 1716 by Yamamoto's student Tsuramoto Tashiro, the *Hagakure* emphasizes the samurai philosophy of dying.

QUESTIONS TO CONSIDER

1. Compare and contrast Bushido with the medieval European chivalric code. How were they similar? How were they different? (See Readings 55 and 56.)
2. What aspects of Bushido were drawn from Confucianism and from Buddhism?

The Way of the Samurai is found in death. When it comes to either/or, there is only the quick choice of death. It is not particularly difficult. Be determined and advance. To say that dying without reaching one's aim is to die a dog's death is the frivolous way of sophisticates. When pressed with the choice of life or death, it is not necessary to gain one's aim.

We all want to live. And in large part we make our logic according to what we like. But not having attained our aim and continuing to live is cowardice. This is a thin dangerous line. To die without gaining one's aim *is* a dog's death and fanaticism. But there is no shame in this. This is the substance of the Way of the Samurai. If by setting one's heart right every morning and evening, one is able to live as though his body were already dead, he gains freedom in the Way. His whole life will be without blame, and he will succeed in his calling. . . .

Being a retainer is nothing other than being a supporter of one's lord, entrusting matters of good and evil to him, and renouncing self-interest. If there are but two or three men of this type, the fief will be secure.

If one looks at the world when affairs are going smoothly, there are many who go about putting in their appearance, being useful by their wisdom, discrimination and artfulness. However, if the lord should retire or go into seclusion, there are many who will quickly turn their backs on him and ingratiate themselves to the man of the day. Such a thing is unpleasant even to think about. Men of high position, low position, deep wisdom and artfulness all feel that *they* are the ones who are working righteously, but when it comes to the point of throwing away one's life for his lord, all get weak in the knees. This is rather disgraceful. The fact that a useless person often becomes a matchless warrior at such times is because he has already given up his life and has become one with his lord. At the time of Mitsushige's death there was an example of this. His one resolved attendant was I alone.

The others followed in my wake. Always the pretentious, self-asserting notables turn their backs on the man just as his eyes are closing in death.

Loyalty is said to be important in the pledge between lord and retainer. Though it may seem unobtainable, it is right before your eyes. If you once set yourself to it, you will become a superb retainer at that very moment. . . .

Every morning, the samurai of fifty or sixty years ago would bathe, shave their foreheads, put lotion in their hair, cut their fingernails and toenails rubbing them with pumice and then with wood sorrel, and without fail pay attention to their personal appearance. It goes without saying that their armor in general was kept free from rust, that it was dusted, shined, and arranged.

Although it seems that taking special care of one's appearance is similar to showiness, it is nothing akin to elegance. Even if you are aware that you may be struck down today and are firmly resolved to an inevitable death, if you are slain with an unseemly appearance, you will show your lack of previous resolve, will be despised by your enemy, and will appear unclean. For this reason it is said that both old and young should take care of their appearance.

Although you say that this is troublesome and time-consuming, a samurai's work is in such things. It is neither busy-work nor time-consuming. In constantly hardening one's resolution to die in battle, deliberately becoming as one already dead, and working at one's job and dealing with military affairs, there should be no shame. But when the time comes, a person will be shamed if he is not conscious of these things even in his dreams, and rather passes his days in self-interest and self-indulgence. And if he thinks that this is not shameful, and feels that nothing else matters as long as he is comfortable, then his dissipate and discourteous actions will be repeatedly regrettable.

The person without previous resolution to inevitable death makes certain that his death will be in bad form. But if one is resolved to death beforehand, in what way can he be despicable? One should be especially diligent in this concern.

Furthermore, during the last thirty years customs have changed; now when young samurai get together, if there is not just talk about money matters, loss and gain, secrets, clothing styles or matters of sex, there is no reason to gather together at all. Customs are going to pieces. One can say that formerly when a man reached the age of twenty or thirty, he did not carry despicable things in his heart, and thus neither did such words appear. If an elder unwittingly said something of that sort, he thought of it as a sort of injury. This new custom probably appears because people attach importance to being beautiful before society and to household finances. What things a person should be able to accomplish if he had no haughtiness concerning his place in society!

It is a wretched thing that the young men of today are so contriving and so proud of their material possessions. Men with contriving hearts are lacking in duty. Lacking in duty, they will have no self-respect. . . .

If one were to say in a word what the condition of being a samurai is, its basis lies first in seriously devoting one's body and soul to his master. And if one is asked what to do beyond this, it would be to fit oneself inwardly with intelligence, humanity and courage. The combining of these three virtues may seem unobtainable to the ordinary person, but it is easy. Intelligence is nothing more than discussing things with others. Limitless wisdom comes from this. Humanity is something done for the sake of others, simply comparing oneself with them and putting them in the fore. Courage is gritting one's teeth; it is simply doing that and pushing ahead, paying no attention to the circumstances. Anything that seems above these three is not necessary to be known.

As for outward aspects, there are personal appearance, one's way of speaking and calligraphy. And as all of these are daily matters, they improve by constant practice. Basically, one should perceive their nature to be one of quiet strength. If one has accomplished all these things, then he should have a knowledge of our area's history and customs. After that he may study the various arts as recreation. If you think it over, being a retainer is simple. And these days, if you observe people who are even a bit useful, you will see that they have accomplished these three outward aspects.

58

The Forty-Seven Ronin

One of the most celebrated episodes in Japanese history is the vendetta of the forty-seven Ronin.[1] This story of the samurai ideals of loyalty and honor has been told innumerable times, on the stage and in literature, and has become an important part of the heritage of the Japanese people. Although its origins can be dated to the early eighteenth century, when the warrior class reigned supreme under the Tokugawa shogunate (1600–1867), the chivalric ideals it expresses were the essence of the samurai culture of feudal Japan. In the spring of 1701, Asano Naganori, lord of the small fief of Ako in western Japan, was charged by the shogunal government with the reception of an imperial envoy from Kyoto. He was put under the guidance of Kira Yoshinaka, the shogun's chief of protocol, to prepare for this event. Lord Asano, who was inexperienced in the fine details of protocol, was ridiculed by Kira, who was reputed to be arrogant and corrupt. Pushed to the limits of his patience, Lord Asano drew his sword and wounded Kira in violation of the law prohibiting the drawing of a sword in the shogun's castle. For this offense, Lord Asano was ordered to commit suicide, and his domain was confiscated. His retainers suddenly found themselves masterless. Believing that Asano was a victim of Kira's arrogance and wrongdoing, forty-seven of Asano's most single-mindedly royal retainers, led by the senior retainer Oishi Kuranosuke, vowed to avenge their lord's death. After long and careful planning, forty-six conspirators[2] burst into Kira's mansion in Edo[3] and killed Kira Yoshinaka. They carried Kira's head to the Sengakuji temple outside Edo and offered it to their Lord Asano's grave. Their vendetta was thus completed. In February 1703, after much controversy surrounding the case, the Ronin were finally punished by the shogunal government, not for the murder of Kira but for their contempt of authority, and were ordered to commit harakiri—ritual disembowelment. The bodies of the samurai, ranging in age from fifteen to seventy-seven, were interred in the Sengakuji temple near their master's grave. The following two letters, the first of which was allegedly found on the person of each of the forty-seven men and the second of which was laid upon

---

[1] Masterless samurai or warriors.

[2] One of the forty-seven did not participate in the final act of the vendetta but remains as an honorary member.

[3] Present-day Tokyo.

the tomb of their master, together with the head of Kira, reflect the fanatical devotion of these samurai to the ideals of the feudal warrior in Japan.

QUESTIONS TO CONSIDER

1. If you were the judge assigned to this case, how would you rule? How would you reconcile the conflict between private morality and public law? Should the forty-seven Ronin have been acquitted? Why?
2. How would you compare the issues raised in this reading with the issues suggested in *Antigone* (see Reading 28)?

Last year in the third month, Asano Takumi no Kami (Lord Asano), upon the occasion of the entertainment of the Imperial ambassador, was driven, by the force of the circumstances, to attack and wound my Lord Kotsuke no Suke (Kira Yoshinaka) in the castle, in order to avenge an insult offered to him. Having done this without considering the dignity of the place, and having thus disregarded all rules of propriety, he was condemned to hara kiri, and his property and castle of Ako were forfeited to the State, and were delivered up by his retainers to the officers deputed by the Shogun to receive them. After this his followers were all dispersed. At the time of the quarrel, the high officials prevented [Lord Asano] from carrying out his intention of killing his enemy, my Lord Kotsuke no Suke [Kira]. So Asano Takumi no Kami [Lord Asano] died without having avenged himself, and this was more than his retainers could endure. It is impossible to remain under the same heaven with the enemy of lord or father; for this reason we have dared to declare enmity against a personage of so exalted rank. This day we shall attack Kira Kotsuke no Suke, in order to finish the deed of vengeance which was begun by our dead lord. If any honorable person should find our bodies after death, he is respectfully requested to open and read this document.

15th year of Genroku, 12th month[1]

Signed, Oishi Kuranosuke, Retainer of Asano
Takumino no Kami, and forty-six others

The 15th year of Genroku, the 12th month, and the 15th day. We have come this day to do homage here, forty-seven men in all, from Oishi Kuranosuke down to the foot-soldier Terasaka Kichiemon, all cheerfully about to lay down our lives on your behalf. We reverently announce this to the honored spirit of our dead master. On the 14th day of the third month of last year our honored master was pleased to attack Kira Kotsuke no Suke, for what reason we know not. Our honored master put an end to his own life, but Kira Kotsuke no Suke lived. Although we fear that after the decree issued by the Government this plot of ours will be displeasing to our honored master, still we, who have eaten of your food, could not without blushing repeat the verse, "Thou shall not live under the same heaven, nor tread the same earth with the enemy of thy father or lord," nor could we have dared to leave hell and present ourselves before you in paradise, unless we had carried out the vengeance which you began. Every day that we waited seemed as three autumns to us. Verily, we have trod-

---

[1]1702.

From Donald Keene, trans., *Chushingura (The Treasury of Loyal Retainers)*. Copyright © 1971 by Columbia University Press. Reprinted with permission of the publisher.

den the snow for one day, nay, for two days, and have tasted food but once. The old and decrepit, the sick and ailing, have come forth gladly to lay down lives. Men might laugh at us, as at grasshoppers trusting in the strength of their arms, and thus shame our honored lord; but we could not halt in our deed of vengeance. Having taken counsel together last night, we have escorted my Lord Kotsuke no Suke hither to your tomb. This dirk[2] by which our honored lord set great store last year, and entrusted to our care, we now bring back. If your noble spirit be now present before this tomb, we pray you, as a sign, to take the dirk, and, striking the head of your enemy with it a second time, to dispel your hatred for ever. This is the respectful statement of forty-seven men.

East-West Images and Realities

At present, most historians agree that they should attempt to write as impartially and factually as possible, even though each is a product of his or her own culture. This was not the case, however, with the historians of the distant past.

The first three selections that follow substantiate the xenophobic stance common in early historical accounts. They reflect an aversion to alien things, supported by a view that the writer's own culture is somehow morally or culturally superior to that of the strange and barbaric or decadent peoples with whom he or she has had some contact. Ibn Fadlan's account of the Vikings depicts them as a filthy race, whereas the Vikings believed that their funeral rites were superior to those of the Arabs. Liutprand's *A Mission to Constantinople* describes nothing that is good about the Byzantines (e.g., their food, clothing, or entertainments) compared with people at the German court. Christian Crusaders were seen by most Muslim authors as ruthless, unbelieving barbarians who carved out their feudal states in the Near East at the expense of the native population.

The fourth selection, from *The Travels of Sir John Mandeville,* illustrates the opposite extreme of stereotyping: the portrayal of faraway places as utopian, abounding in riches and harmonious relationships among their peoples. Generally in the medieval West, the not-to-distant East populated by Byzantines and Arabs was viewed with suspicion, whereas what their writers called "the Far East" tended to be viewed much more favorably. Marco Polo's report on his stay in China strikes about the right balance from a modern viewpoint. He writes as an understanding and appreciative sojourner in Mongol China, indicating that his European contemporaries could learn something from East Asians, but the images he conveys to entertain his readers are fairly well grounded in the realities he has observed. Oddly enough, Marco Polo is the only one of the five writers featured in this section whose work evoked widespread disbelief when it circulated among his own countrymen.

---

[2]A dirk is a dagger. The dirk with which Lord Asano disemboweled himself, and with which Oishi Kuranosuke cut off Kira's head.

59

Ibn Fadlan's Account of Vikings in Early Russia

In 921, Al-Muktadir, the Caliph of Baghdad, sent his ambassador, Ahmed ibn Fadlan, to the King of Bulgaria to arrange for the sending of Muslim missionaries to Bulgaria. Ahmed ibn Fadlan's roundabout journey, north from Baghdad and then west to Bulgaria, took him through southeastern Russia where, near the Volga River in 922, he encountered a Viking settlement and recorded these impressions of the "Northmen."

QUESTIONS TO CONSIDER

1. How does Ibn Fadlan's account of this funeral suggest Viking religious beliefs?
2. Why do you suppose the Vikings killed animals to throw them into the dead man's boat?
3. What are the main things Ibn Fadlan finds revolting about the Vikings?

They are the filthiest race that God ever created. They do not wipe themselves after going to stool, nor wash themselves after a nocturnal pollution, any more than if they were wild asses.

They come from their own country, anchor their ships in the Volga, which is a great river, and build large wooden houses on its banks. In every such house there live ten or twenty, more or fewer. Each man has a couch, where he sits with the beautiful girls he has for sale. Here he is as likely as not to enjoy one of them while a friend looks on. At times several of them will be thus engaged at the same moment, each in full view of the others. Now and again a merchant will resort to a house to purchase a girl, and find her master thus embracing her, and not giving over until he has full had his will.

Every morning a girl comes and brings a tub of water, and places it before her master. In this he proceeds to wash his face and hands, and then his hair, combing it out over the vessel. Thereupon he blows his nose, and spits into the tub, and leaving no dirt behind, conveys it all into this water. When he has finished, the girl carries the tub to the man next to him, who does the same. Thus she continues carrying the tub from one to another till each of those who are in the house has blown his nose and spit into the tub, and washed his face and hair. . . .

I was told that the least of what they do for their chiefs when they die, is to consume them with fire. When I was finally informed of the death of one of their magnates, I sought to witness what befell. First they laid him in his grave—over which a roof was erected—for the space of ten days, until they had completed the cutting and sewing of his clothes. In the case of a poor man, however, they merely build for him a boat, in which they place him, and consume it with fire. At the death of a rich man, they bring together his goods, and divide them into three parts. The first of these is for his family; the second is expended for

From Albert Stanburrough Cook, "Ibn Fadlan's Account of Scandinavian Merchants on the Volga in 922," *Journal of English and Germanic Philology* 22(1923):54–63.

the garments they make; and with the third they purchase strong drink, against the day when the girl resigns herself to death, and is burned with her master. To the use of wine they abandon themselves in mad fashion, drinking it day and night; and not seldom does one die with the cup in his hand.

When one of their chiefs dies, his family asks his girls and pages, "Which one of you will die with him?" Then one of them answers, "I." From the time that he utters this word, he is no longer free: should he wish to draw back, he is not permitted. For the most part, however, it is the girls that offer themselves. So, when the man of whom I spoke had died, they asked his girls, "Who will die with him?" One of them answered, "I." She was then committed to two girls, who were to keep watch over her, accompany her wherever she went, and even, on occasion, wash her feet. The people now began to occupy themselves with the dead man—to cut out the clothes for him, and to prepare whatever else was needful. During the whole of this period, the girl gave herself over to drinking and singing, and was cheerful and gay.

When the day was now come that the dead man and the girl were to be committed to the flames, I went to the river in which his ship lay, but found that it had already been drawn ashore. Four corner-blocks of birch and other woods had been placed in position for it, while around were stationed large wooden figures in the semblance of human beings. Thereupon the ship was brought up, and placed on the timbers above-mentioned. In the meantime the people began to walk to and fro, uttering words which I did not understand. The dead man, meanwhile, lay at a distance in his grave, from which they had not yet removed him. Next they brought a couch, placed it in the ship, and covered it with Greek cloth of gold, wadded and quilted, with pillows of the same material. There came an old crone, whom they call the angel of death, and spread the articles mentioned on the couch. It was she who attended to the sewing of the garments, and to all the equipment; it was she, also, who was to slay the girl. I saw her; she was dark, thick-set, with a lowering countenance.

When they came to the grave, they removed the earth from the wooden roof, set the latter aside, and drew out the dead man in the loose wrapper in which he had died. Then I saw that he had turned quite black, by reason of the coldness of that country. Near him in the grave they had placed strong drink, fruits, and a lute; and these they now took out. Except for his colour, the dead man had not changed. They now clothed him in drawers, leggings, boots, and a *kurtak* and *chaftan* of cloth of gold, with golden buttons, placing on his head a cap made of cloth of gold, trimmed with sable. Then they carried him into a tent placed in the ship, seated him on the wadded and quilted covering, supported him with the pillows, and, bringing strong drink, fruits, and basil, placed them all beside him. Then they brought a dog, which they cut in two, and threw into the ship; laid all his weapons beside him; and led up two horses, which they chased until they were dripping with sweat, whereupon they cut them in pieces with their swords, and threw the flesh into the ship. Two oxen were then brought forward, cut in pieces, and flung into the ship. Finally they brought a cock and a hen, killed them, and threw them in also.

The girl who had devoted herself to death meanwhile walked to and fro, entering one after another of the tents which they had there. The occupant of each tent lay with her, saying, "Tell your master, 'I [the man] did this only for love of you.'"

When it was now Friday afternoon, they led the girl to an object which they had constructed, and which looked like the framework of a door. She then placed her feet on the extended hands of the men, was raised up above the framework, and uttered something in her language, whereupon they let her down. Then again they raised her, and she did as at first. Once more they let her down, and then lifted her a third time, while she did as at the previous times. They then handed her a hen, whose head she cut off and threw away; but the hen itself they cast into the ship. I inquired of the interpreter what it was that she had done. He replied: "The first time she said, 'Lo, I see here my father and mother'; the second time, 'Lo, now I see all my deceased relatives sitting'; the third time, 'Lo, there is my master, who is sitting in Paradise. Paradise is so beautiful, so green. With him are his men and boys. He calls me, so bring me to him.'" Then they led her away to the ship.

Here she took off her two bracelets, and gave them to the old woman who was called the angel of death, and who was to murder her. She also drew off her two anklets, and passed them to the two serving-maids, who were the daughters of the so-called angel of death. Then they lifted her into the ship, but did not yet admit her to the tent. Now men came up with shields and staves, and handed her a cup of strong drink. This she took, sang over it, and emptied it. "With this," so the interpreter told me, "she is taking leave of those who are dear to her." Then another cup was handed her, which she also took, and began a lengthy song. The crone admonished her to drain the cup without lingering, and to enter the tent where her master lay. By this time, as it seemed to me, the girl had become dazed; she made as though she would enter the tent, and had brought her head forward between the tent and the ship, when the hag seized her by the head, and dragged her in. At this moment the men began to beat upon their shields with the staves, in order to drown the noise of her outcries, which might have terrified the other girls, and deterred them from seeking death with their masters in the future. Then six men followed into the tent, and each and every one had carnal companionship with her. Then they laid her down by her master's side, while two of the men seized her by the feet, and two by the hands. The old woman known as the angel of death now knotted a rope around her neck, and handed the ends to two of the men to pull. Then with a broad-bladed dagger she smote her between the ribs, and drew the blade forth, while the two men strangled her with the rope till she died.

The next of kin to the dead man now drew near, and, taking a piece of wood, lighted it, and walked backwards towards the ship, holding the stick in one hand, with the other placed upon his buttocks (he being naked), until the wood which had been piled under the ship was ignited. Then the others came up with staves and firewood, each one carrying a stick already lighted at the upper end, and threw it all on the pyre. The pile was soon aflame, then the ship, finally the tent, the man, and the girl, and everything else in the ship. A terrible storm began to blow up, and this intensified the flames, and gave wings to the blaze.

At my side stood one of the Northmen, and I heard him talking with the interpreter, who stood near him. I asked the interpreter what the Northman had said, and received this answer: "You Arabs," he said, "must be a stupid set! You take him who is to you the most revered and beloved of men, and cast him into the ground, to be devoured by creeping things and worms. We, on the other hand, burn him in a twinkling, so that he instantly, without a moment's delay enters into Paradise." At this he burst out into uncontrollable laughter, and then continued: "It is the love of the Master [God] that causes the wind to blow and snatch him away in an instant." And, in very truth, before an hour had passed, ship, wood, and girl had, with the man, turned to ashes.

60

Liutprand, Bishop of Cremona, *A Mission to Constantinople*

In theory, all medieval Christians recognized the leadership within a single church until 1054, when the leaders of what we know as the Roman Catholic Church in the West and the Greek Orthodox Church in the East broke with each other and remain separate to this day. In reality, differences in style and theology had come to alienate the Greek-oriented Easterners from their counterparts in the West well before 1054. The self-image of the Easterners was one of pride in continuing Roman civilization with sophistication and refinement; Westerners appeared rough and savage by contrast. The self-image of Westerners was one of being honest and straightforward, as well as fearless in facing enemies; Easterners appeared devious and decadent by contrast.

In 968, the Western or Holy Roman Emperor Otto I sent Bishop Liutprand of Cremona, Italy, to the court of the Eastern Emperor Nicephorus Phocas to negotiate a marriage between his son, Otto II, whom he had made his co-ruler, and Princess Theophano, the daughter of Romanus II, Byzantine emperor between 959 and 963. His hope was that the marriage would help overcome strife between Greeks and Saxons over territories in Italy claimed by both empires. Liutprand's account of his stay in Constantinople, a much-condensed version of which follows, conveys the conflict of cultural images vividly. In reporting to the Ottos, he is determined *not* to let Easterners get away with their boasts of living on a higher plane of civilization. (Some of his complaints were also reported by Western crusaders in the following centuries.) His complaints range from an emphatic rejection of the most common Greek wine to indignation over Greek attempts to overcharge him for everything. (Even today, Western travelers in Greece are likely to remark that retsina, the resinated wine that Greeks favor above all others, "tastes a little like turpentine" or, more kindly, "is going to take a little getting used to.") Like many Westerners then and later, Liutprand found the eunuchs at the Eastern capital to be proof of the degraded and effeminate nature of Byzantine society. Wearing apparel was another source of conflict. The fur-trimmed leather garments, in which Germanic Europeans took much pride, seem to have been harshly criticized by their southern and eastern counterparts since the days of the great migrations. In the selection that follows, Liutprand is very defensive on this score. In a section not included in the reading, he refers to the long-sleeved, silky garments of the East as of a type "that only street-walkers and sorcerers wear" in the West.

Still, both East and West were moved by the feeling that they should pull toward unity, particularly in the face of the Muslim threat. Liutprand's mission foundered at the time on the shoals of mutual dislike, but the following year Nicephorus was assassinated by his nephew, John Zimisces, who became emperor; and in 972, under this new Eastern regime, Otto II did, in fact, marry the Princess Theophano, whom Liutprand had attempted to secure for him as a bride. From the perspective of centuries, however, Theophano's genteel influence scarcely put a dent in East-West ethnic prejudices. The mutual excommunications of 1054 and the sacking of Constantinople by Western crusaders a hundred and fifty years after that attest to the fragile nature of East-West medieval Christian harmony.

QUESTIONS TO CONSIDER

1. How does Liutprand mentally cope with the wealth and scope of the Byzantine Empire?
2. What main elements in the Westerners' self-image emerge in Liutprand's account?
3. Nearly a thousand years after Liutprand's mission, we find *Webster's Biographical Dictionary,* which we generally recognize as a fairly dispassionate source of information, noting that when Princess Theophano married Otto and came to the West, she "had great influence at his court, introducing much of the refinement of Constantinople."[1] Liutprand died in 972 or thereabouts, but if he had lived another ten or fifteen years, how do you suppose he would have judged the efforts of a Byzantine-born empress to upgrade the culture of the Saxon court?

When we arrived in Constantinople on June 4, we were received very shabbily as a sign of disrespect to you, and afterwards treated the same way. They shut us up in a palace of sorts, which was big enough, all right, but had no roof to keep out heat or cold. Armed soldiers stood guard outside, to keep any of my companions from going out or anyone else from coming in. We were located so far away from the palace of Nicephorus that we were always out of breath from the long walk up to it whenever we went. We found the Greek wine, which is mixed with tar, resin, and plaster unfit to drink, but we could not even *buy* water to quench our thirst. No earthly being, but only one from hell, could be compared to the warden assigned to look after our daily needs. Like a drenching cloudburst, his inventiveness soaked us with misfortunes, extortions, torture, and grief for a hundred and twenty days.

On June 7, I was led before Nicephorus, a human freak with a very wide head and eyes as small as a mole's. He is thoroughly repulsive to look at with a thick neck less than an inch in length, long and bristly hair, Ethiopian skin color, drooping paunch and short stature. He is of a type you would hope not to meet up with after dark. And his clothes! They are very costly but ancient, faded, and bad-smelling. I always thought of my own august lords and emperors as handsome, but this horrible sight made me appreciate your handsome qualities all the more. In the same way, I was always aware of your great magnificence, power, kindness, and virtue: How much more did being with Nicephorus make me appreciate these even more!

Both these rulers . . . , the King of the Greeks and the King of the Franks[1] are men . . . , but they are as different from each other—I would exaggerate only a little if I said: as species of animals differ from each other—as people of a sound mind differ from the insane. The King of the Greeks wears long hair and a tunic with long sleeves and a hood. He is lying, scheming, without mercy, fox-like, proud, insincerely humble, stingy, and greedy. He eats garlic, onions, and leeks, and he drinks bathwater. By way of contrast, the King of the Franks wears his hair tastefully trimmed, his clothing is altogether different from a

[1]*Webster's Biographical Dictionary* (Springfield, MA: G. & C. Merriam, 1960), p. 1131.

[1]By Liutprand's time, the term "Frank" no longer applied simply to the original ethnic group of that name, but to any people associated with running the Germanic or Holy Roman Empire. By the time of the Crusades, it had become a rather generic term for Westerners as opposed to inhabitants of the East, and Asians from Arabia to China called all Western peoples "Franks."

"Legatio," in *Liudprandi episcopi Cremonensis opera omnia* (Hannover: Hahn, 1877), chs. i–xl, *passim.* Translated and condensed by Henry A. Myers; calendar usage modernized.

woman's, and he wears a hat. He is truthful, straightforward, merciful when this is appropriate but severe when it is not. He is always sincerely humble and never stingy. He does not live on garlic, onions, and leeks, nor does he pile up money by saving animals to sell rather than having them to eat. . . .

[Liutprand was defending the Western imperial position on governing areas in Italy claimed by the Byzantines, when Nicephorus interrupted him:][2] "It is time for the solemn procession to the church. Let us attend to the needs of the hour, and when I have some time I will take up your requests again."

And what a procession it was indeed, with craftsmen and base-born people lining both sides of the road in masses thick as walls from the palace to Saint Sophia's. They were made even uglier than they already were by the thin little shields and flimsy spears which many of them carried. The fact that they came barefooted, which I think was to honor Nicephorus, made them more disgusting than ever to look at. The nobles who passed through that multitude of low-lifes were wearing tunics that were really old. Their grandfathers must have worn those self-same garments, which were very, very old even when their grandfathers wore them. None of them was wearing any gold, not even jewels, except Nicephorus himself; however, the symbols of imperial majesty which had been made for his imperial predecessors simply made him all the more loathsome to look at. I swear by your very salvation, which I value more than my own, that one precious garment of any of your nobles is worth more than a hundred of the things his were wearing. I had to take part in this procession and ended up on a platform next to the singers.

When Nicephorus, like a slithering reptile, reached the cathedral's interior, the singers chanted loudly: "Behold the Morning Star as he approaches. His glances do reflect the sun's own rays: Nicephorus, our ruler, who brings swift death to Muslims." They kept on like that: "A long life to our ruler, Nicephorus! Worship him, O people, adore him; bow your heads to him alone." It would have been much more appropriate if they had sung: "Come to us, burnt-out wood-ember that you are, fool who looks like an evil spirit of the forest and walks like an old woman; you double-jointed rebel, scaly-headed, bristly of hide, totally rural, barbarian, rude serf-by-nature, most at home in filthy places!" And so, blown up by the lying chants of dunces, he entered Saint Sophia's.

That day he asked me to dinner, but, acting as if I were unworthy to be placed above any of his nobles, he assigned me a seat fifteen places away from him without even a tablecloth in front of me. The meal was completely disgusting; everything smelt bad. All the food was soaked in oil, and they washed it all down with a perfectly awful kind of spicy fish juice. During that meal he asked me many questions about you, the lands you rule, and the forces which serve you. Then when I had given him true and straightforward answers, he accused me of lying.

Eight days later, he invited me back again, thinking no doubt that I would appreciate the food and drink he served. Many bishops were there, including the Patriarch of Constantinople. He asked me many Bible questions, which I answered eloquently enough, but then he tried to make fun of us by comparing the great church councils which have been held in the East with the lack of them in the West. [The Patriarch implied that the dearth of councils held in Western cities showed that the Christian faith there was not mature; for Liutprand, however, councils had the function of coping with heresies, so that a lack of them meant a lack of heresy in the region.] I answered: "It is the member of the body which is afflicted that must be cauterized with a hot iron. All heresies have come from your territory. We of the Western nations have strangled them and put an end to them. The Saxon people

---

[2]Material in brackets is the editor's condensed summary of Liutprand's writing.

have produced no heresies from the time they first received baptism and the knowledge of God. With no errors of doctrine among them, they had no need of holding church councils. I am willing to agree with you that faith among the Saxons is young: Faith in Christ is *always* young, not old, in people who actually live according to it. Where people do not live according to the faith, where people scorn it and throw it away like worn-out clothes—that is where faith is old. But let me add that I do know for sure of one council held by Saxons: It determined that it is better to fight with swords than with pens and to submit to death than run from the enemy. Your own army has learned the truth confirmed by *that* council." And to myself I said: "May the Saxons soon have a chance to show what they can do in war!"

I just hope you believe me—and, of course, I know that you will believe me—when I tell you that [if war reoccurs in Italy] four hundred of your fighting men can slay the whole army dispatched by Nicephorus, unless they survive by hiding behind ditches and walls. It seems to me that it is as if to show his scorn of you that he has given the command of this army to a kind of man—I say "kind of" because he has ceased to be a male and has not yet been able to become a female.

[By mid-September, the outcome of Liutprand's mission seemed very much in doubt. When Nicephorus appeared reluctant to let him leave, Liutprand indicated to a group of Byzantine nobles that Emperor Otto might consider taking vengeance on the Greeks for having detained his messenger so long.] "If he tries it," they said, "neither Italy, nor the poor region of Saxony, land of his birth, where the natives go around in wild animal skins, will be able to protect him. Our money gives us power, and with it we will rally all manner of peoples against him. We will break him like a clay pot, which, once shattered, cannot be put back together again." [These nobles also seized some purple garments from Liutprand and his companions in a forced purchase, saying that they were too good for people from the West.] How totally inappropriate it is that these soft, effeminate, lying, neutered, idle creatures with their long sleeves, hoods, and veils should go around in purple, while heroes representing you, strong warriors that they are, experienced in the military arts, possessing love and the true faith—men who hold God in real reverence and are full of virtues—may not. What is this, if not horrendous vanity!

Those who seek God upon false paths shall never find Him!

61

Memoirs of Usamah Ibn-Munqidh

By the mid-tenth century, the once mighty Abbasid caliphs [the head of state] of Baghdad were puppets of their own bodyguards. About a century later, Turkish nomads, the Seljuks, who had come from central Asia into Iran and had converted to Islam, rescued the caliphs. These Seljuk sultans slowly extended their political power from Iran-Iraq through Syria and Palestine. In 1071, the Byzantine emperor, Romanus IV Diogenes, tried to stop Seljuk raids into Anatolia (modern Turkey), but he was defeated at Manzikert. The Seljuks soon took over most of Anatolia from the Byzantine government.

Soon, however, the Seljuk sultanate broke up into quarreling petty states. This situation, plus appeals from the Byzantines and the Seljuk restrictions on the number of Christian pilgrims to the Holy Land, led Pope Urban II in 1095 to call for the First Crusade (1096–1099). The Crusaders, or Franks, as Muslim authors refer to them, were able to create a series of western states along the Mediterranean coast from Anatolia to Egypt. These states did not last. The Turkish lord of Mosul, Zangi, and the Kurdish warrior Saladin became the anti-Crusading champions as they recaptured northern Syria and then Jerusalem by 1187.

One Arab-Syrian who lived through this period was Usamah Ibn Munqidh. He was born in 1095 to one of the most important families of the area who controlled the Castle of Shayzar on the Orontes river, which guarded routes into northern Syria or south into Lebanon. Usamah was given such a well-rounded education by his father that he not only gained military fame in fighting the Franks but was also considered a world traveler, poet, and scholar. His fame was so great that Saladin appointed him a lecturer on Islamic law and tutor in rhetoric in one of the academies in Damascus.

The following selections from Usamah's *Memoirs* relate a personal view of the Franks. Although the Crusaders are referred to as "devils" or "infidels" whose morals were both shocking or amusing to a conservative Muslim, Usamah developed a friendship with and respect for some of the Christians.

QUESTIONS TO CONSIDER

1. Compare the culture and society of Western Europe to that of the Near East. Why did the Franks seem barbaric to the Muslims?
2. Why would the sexual customs of the Franks shock Usamah?
3. How did Western Europe and Islamic society treat women?
4. Is there any indication that relations between the Franks and Muslims were not solely as enemies?
5. Compare the present selection with the Portuguese and Spanish relations with Africa and the New World (see Readings 94, 95, 96, and 98). What are some similar or different attitudes?

Their curious medication.—A case illustrating their curious medicine is the following:

The lord of al-Munaytirah[1] wrote to my uncle asking him to dispatch a physician to treat certain sick persons among his people. My uncle sent him a Christian physician named Thābit. Thābit was absent but ten days when he returned. So we said to him, "How quickly hast thou healed thy patients!" He said:

They brought before me a knight in whose leg an abscess had grown; and a woman afflicted with imbecility.[2] To the knight I applied a small poultice until the abscess

[1] In Lebanon near Afqah, the source of Nahr-Ibrāhīm, i.e., ancient Adonis.
[2] Ar. *nashāf*, "dryness," is not used as a name of a disease. I take the word therefore to be Persian *nishāf*—"imbecility."

opened and became well; and the woman I put on diet and made her humor wet. Then a Frankish physician came to them and said, "This man knows nothing about treating them." He then said to the knight, "Which wouldst thou prefer, living with one leg or dying with two?" The latter replied, "Living with one leg." The physician said, "Bring me a strong knight and a sharp ax." A knight came with the ax. And I was standing by. Then the physician laid the leg of the patient on a block of wood and bade the knight strike his leg with the ax and chop it off at one blow. Accordingly he struck it—while I was looking on—one blow, but the leg was not severed. He dealt another blow, upon which the marrow of the leg flowed out and the patient died on the spot. He then examined the woman and said, "This is a woman in whose head there is a devil which has possessed her. Shave off her hair." Accordingly they shaved it off and the woman began once more to eat their ordinary diet—garlic and mustard. Her imbecility took a turn for the worse. The physician then said, "The devil has penetrated through her head." He therefore took a razor, made a deep cruciform [cross-shaped] incision on it, peeled off the skin at the middle of the incision until the bone of the skull was exposed and rubbed it with salt. The woman also expired instantly. Thereupon I asked them whether my services were needed any longer, and when they replied in the negative I returned home, having learned of their medicine what I knew not before.

Newly arrived Franks are especially rough: One insists that Usāmah should pray eastward.—Everyone who is a fresh emigrant from the Frankish lands is ruder in character than those who have become acclimatized and have held long association with the Moslems. Here is an illustration of their rude character.

Whenever I visited Jerusalem I always entered the Aqṣa Mosque, beside which stood a small mosque which the Franks had converted into a church. When I used to enter the Aqṣa Mosque, which was occupied by the Templars,[3] who were my friends, the Templars would evacuate the little adjoining mosque so that I might pray in it. One day[4] I entered this mosque, repeated the first formula, "Allah is great," and stood up in the act of praying, upon which one of the Franks rushed on me, got hold of me and turned my face eastward saying, "This is the way thou shouldst pray!" A group of Templars hastened to him, seized him and repelled him from me. I resumed my prayer. The same man, while the others were otherwise busy, rushed once more on me and turned my face eastward, saying, "This is the way thou shouldst pray!" The Templars again came in to him and expelled him. They apologized to me, saying, "This is a stranger who has only recently arrived from the land of the Franks and he has never before seen anyone praying except eastward." Thereupon I said to myself, "I have had enough prayer." So I went out and have ever been surprised at the conduct of this devil of a man, at the change in the color of his face, his trembling and his sentiment at the sight of one praying towards the *qiblah.*[5]

Another wants to show to a Moslem God as a child.—I saw one of the Franks come to al-Amīr [chieftain] Mu'īn-al-Dīn (may Allah's mercy rest upon his soul!) when he was in the Dome of the Rock[6] and say to him, "Dost thou want to see God as a child?" Mu'īn-al-Din said, "Yes." The Frank walked ahead of us until he showed us the picture of Mary

[3]Knights Templars were members of a military religious order called the Knights of the Temple of Solomon, named from their house in Jerusalem.
[4]About 1140.
[5]The direction of the Ka'bah in the holy city, Mecca.
[6]The mosque standing near al-Aqṣa in Jerusalem.

with Christ (may peace be upon him!) as an infant in her lap. He then said, "This is God as a child." But Allah is exalted far above what the infidels say about him!

Franks lack jealousy in sex affairs.—The Franks are void of all zeal and jealousy. One of them may be walking along with his wife. He meets another man who takes the wife by the hand and steps aside to converse with her while the husband is standing on one side waiting for his wife to conclude the conversation. If she lingers too long for him, he leaves her alone with the conversant and goes away. . . .

We had with us a bath-keeper named Sālim, originally an inhabitant of al-Ma'arrah,[7] who had charge of the bath of my father (may Allah's mercy rest upon his soul!). This man related the following story:

> I once opened a bath in al-Ma'arrah in order to earn my living. To this bath there came a Frankish knight. The Franks disapprove of girding a cover around one's waist while in the bath. So this Frank stretched out his arm and pulled off my cover from my waist and threw it away. He looked and saw that I had recently shaved off my pubes. So he shouted, "Sālim!" As I drew near him he stretched his hand over my pubes and said, "Sālim, good! By the truth of my religion, do the same for me." Saying this, he lay on his back and I found that in that place the hair was like his beard. So I shaved it off. Then he passed his hand over the place and, finding it smooth, he said, "Sālim, by the truth of my religion, do the same to madame" (*al-dāma* in their language means the lady), referring to his wife. He then said to a servant of his, "Tell madame to come here." Accordingly the servant went and brought her and made her enter the bath. She also lay on her back. The knight repeated, "Do what thou has done to me." So I shaved all that hair while her husband was sitting looking at me. At last he thanked me and handed me the pay for my service.

Consider now this great contradiction! They have neither jealousy nor zeal but they have great courage, although courage is nothing but the product of zeal and of ambition to be above ill repute.

Their judicial trials: A duel.—I attended one day a duel in Nāblus between two Franks. The reason for this was that certain Moslem thieves took by surprise one of the villages of Nāblus. One of the peasants of that village was charged with having acted as guide for the thieves when they fell upon the village. So he fled away. The king[8] sent and arrested his children. The peasant thereupon came back to the king and said, "Let justice be done in my case. I challenge to a duel the man who claimed that I guided the thieves to the village." The king then said to the tenant who held the village in fief, "Bring forth someone to fight the duel with him." The tenant went to his village, where a blacksmith lived, took hold of him and ordered him to fight the duel. The tenant became thus sure of the safety of his own peasants, none of whom would be killed and his estate ruined.

I saw this blacksmith. He was a physically strong young man, but his heart failed him. He would walk a few steps and then sit down and ask for a drink. The one who had made the challenge was an old man, but he was strong in spirit and he would rub the nail of his thumb against that of the forefinger in defiance, as if he was not worrying over the duel. Then came the viscount, i.e., the seignior of the town, and gave each one of the two contestants a cudgel and a shield and arranged the people in a circle around them.

The two met. The old man would press the blacksmith backward until he would get

[7]Ma'arrah-al-Nu'mān, between Ḥamāh and Aleppo.
[8]Fulk of Anjou, king of Jerusalem (1131–1142).

him as far as the circle, then he would come back to the middle of the arena. They went on exchanging blows until they looked like pillars smeared with blood. The contest was prolonged and the viscount began to urge them to hurry, saying, "Hurry on." The fact that the smith was given to the use of the hammer proved now of great advantage to him. The old man was worn out and the smith gave him a blow which made him fall. His cudgel fell under his back. The smith knelt down over him and tried to stick his fingers into the eyes of his adversary, but could not do it because of the great quantity of blood flowing out. Then he rose up and hit his head with the cudgel until he killed him. They then fastened a rope around the neck of the dead person, dragged him away and hanged him. The lord who brought the smith now came, gave the smith his own mantle, made him mount the horse behind him and rode off with him. This case illustrates the kind of jurisprudence and legal decisions the Franks have—may Allah's curse be upon them!

Ordeal by water.—I once went in the company of al-Amīr Muʿīn-al-Dīn (may Allah's mercy rest upon his soul!) to Jerusalem. We stopped at Nāblus. There a blind man, a Moslem, who was still young and was well dressed, presented himself before al-amīr carrying fruits for him and asked permission to be admitted into his service in Damascus. The amīr consented. I inquired about this man and was informed that his mother had been married to a Frank whom she had killed. Her son used to practice ruses against the Frankish pilgrims and coöperate with his mother in assassinating them. They finally brought charges against him and tried his case according to the Frankish way of procedure.

They installed a huge cask and filled it with water. Across it they set a board of wood. They then bound the arms of the man charged with the act, tied a rope around his shoulders and dropped him into the cask, their idea being that in case he was innocent, he would sink in the water and they would then lift him up with the rope so that he might not die in the water; and in case he was guilty, he would not sink in the water. This man did his best to sink when they dropped him into the water, but he could not do it. So he had to submit to their sentence against him—may Allah's curse be upon them! They pierced his eyeballs with red-hot awls [drills].

62

Sir John Mandeville, "The Land of Prester John"

One of the most widely read accounts of travel to the East in the centuries preceding those of the Age of Exploration was *The Travels of Sir John Mandeville.* Nothing of significance is known of the author: it is now generally doubted that he was a knight, and what scanty evidence there is points to an Englishman who fled to France after committing a crime in his homeland and took this name as a pseudonym. Whoever he was, his stories of the fabulous East fascinated audiences in England, France, Spain, and Portugal and helped to strengthen the image of the East as a land of untold riches.

Medieval people had been captivated since the twelfth century by the story of the (fictional) Prester John, who ruled a great Christian kingdom to the East. "Prester" is an English contraction of the Latin *presbyter* (priest), and the man was supposed to combine kingship with priesthood, ruling over vast domains as a benign leader of peoples living in perfect Christian harmony. The earliest accounts of Prester John put him somewhere east of India. Mandeville's geography is problematic when he writes of Prester John. On one hand, he describes his main capital as Susa, which was in the Persian Empire, but elsewhere his lands appear to be not only east of India but farther away than "Cathay" (China). In the minds of Europeans interested in geography, the locale of Prester John's kingdom shifted from (very roughly) Mongolia to India, and from there to Africa, where the Portuguese were still looking for Prester John in the fifteenth century. Mandeville claimed to have set out on his journey at dates given in the various surviving manuscripts from 1322 to 1332. There is some factuality in his accounts of Arab and Ottoman-controlled territory, including Egypt, which he may well have visited, but it seems doubtful that he actually traveled farther east than that.

QUESTIONS TO CONSIDER

1. What does Mandeville find most striking about Prester John and his kingdom?
2. Some modern commentators believe that Mandeville's attitude toward religion in Prester John's land hints that he may be a heretic, perhaps sympathetic to pre-Reformation criticism of the Roman Catholic Church. Do you get this impression? Why or why not?
3. What impression do Mandeville's pointed assurances that his experiences in Asia are to be trusted make on you?

This emperor Prester John has many diverse countries under his empire, in which are many noble cities and fair towns and many islands great and large. For this land of India is separated into islands because of the great floods that come out of Paradise and run through and divide it. And also in the sea he has many great islands. . . .

This very royal king Prester John and the great Caan of Tartary are evermore allied together through marriage; for each of them weds the daughter or sister of the other one. In the land of Prester John are a great plenty of precious stones of diverse kinds, some of them so great and so large that they make vessels out of them: dishes, bowls, cups and so many other kinds it would take a long time to list them all.

Now I will speak of some of the principal islands of Prester John's land, and of the royalty of his state and what law and belief his people hold. This emperor Prester John is a Christian man, and the most part of his land is also, even if it be so that they do not have all of the articles of our belief so clearly as we have. Not for nought do they trust in God, Father and Son and Holy Ghost, and full devout men they are and true, one to the other, and there is no fraud or guile among them. The emperor has under his subjection seventy-two provinces, and in each one of them is a king. And these kings have other kings under them, and all are tributaries to the emperor Prester John. In the land of Prester John are many marvels. Among them is a great sea all of gravel and sand and no drop of water therein. And it ebbs and flows as the great sea does in other countries with great waves and nevermore

From *The Voyage and Travaile of Sir John Ma(u)ndeville, Knight, Which Treateth of the Way to Hierusalem [Jerusalem], and of Marvayles of Inde [India] with Other Islands and Countries,* ed. J.O. Halliwell (London: F.S. Ellis, 1866), 121–22, 187–93, *passim;* language modernized.

stands still without moving. That sea no man may pass, neither by ship nor otherwise; and therefore it is unknown to any man what kind of land or country is on the other side of that sea. And although there be no water in that sea, nevertheless there is a great plenty of good fishes taken at its seabanks. They are right savory in the mouth, but they are of a different shape from the fishes of other waters. I, John Mandeville, ate of them: therefore, trust me, for surely it is so.

Three days' journey from that sea are great hills, out of which flows a great river that comes from Paradise; and it is full of precious stones but not a drop of water. It runs with great waves into the Gravelly Sea, and then the waves are seen no more. Three days out of every week this river runs so fast that no man dare step into it, but on all the other days men may go into it whenever they will and gather precious stones.

Beyond that river towards the wilderness is a great plain among hills, all sandy and gravelly. On this plain are trees, as it seems, which begin to grow at the rising of the sun and fruit begins to spring out of them. They grow so until it be mid-day, and then they begin to dwindle and turn again into the earth, so that by sunset there is nothing to be seen of them, and they keep doing this every day. . . .

In the aforesaid wilderness are many wild men with horns upon their heads. They dwell in the woods as beasts and do not speak but grunt as swine do. Also in some woods of that land are wild hounds that never will come to men, anymore than foxes will do in this country. And there are fowls who speak in their own way, and they will hail men who come through the deserts, speaking as openly as if they were men. These fowls have large tongues and five nails on each foot. There are others that have only three nails on each foot, and they speak neither so well nor so openly.

When this very great king and emperor Prester John marches into battle against his enemies, he has no banner borne before him, but instead of a banner three crosses of fine gold are borne before him. These are great and high and are well studded with precious stones. Then a thousand knights and more than a hundred thousand men on foot are assigned to guard each cross, in the same way that men guard a banner or a standard in other places. This number of men is always assigned to guard the aforesaid crosses when the emperor sets off for battle: it does not include his principal army, or those of his nobles with their own men—those who are actually to fight the battle—nor does it include wings of troops that are assigned to foraging for provisions.

When he rides forth in peacetime with his personal company of men, a cross of wood is borne before him, with no gold or painting or precious stones on it, in remembrance of Christ's suffering on a cross of wood. Also he has borne before him a plate of gold full of earth, as a token of the fact that he came from the earth and to the earth he shall return. And there is borne before him another vessel full of gold and of such precious stones as rubies, diamonds, sapphires, emeralds, topazes, olivines and many others as a token of his great nobility, lordship and might.

Now I will tell you of the adornment of Prester John's palace, where he commonly resides, at the city of Susa. That palace is so rich, so delightful and so noble, that it is a wonder to tell. For above the principal tower are two large balls of gold, and in each of these are two glowing rubies, great and fair, which shine right clear upon the night. The principal gates of the palace are of those precious stones that men call "sardonyxes"[1] and their bars are of ivory. The windows of the hall and the chambers are of crystal. All the tables on which they eat are of emeralds, amethysts and some of gold set full of precious stones; and the pillars that bear the tables are of the same manner of precious stones. The steps on which the

---

[1]Onyxes with parallel layers of sard, a deep-orange variety of chalcedony.

emperor goes up to his throne where he sets at the meal are: one of onyx, another of crystal, another of jasper, another of amethyst, another of sardony, and another of coral; the highest step, on which he sets his feet at the meal, is of olivine. All these steps are bordered with fine gold, set full of precious stones. The pillars in his chamber are of fine gold, set full of precious stones, of which many are glowing rubies, which give great light at night. Nevertheless, in his chamber he also has twelve crystal vessels full of balm, burning to give off a good and sweet smell and to drive away wicked air. The frame of his bed is all of sapphires, well bound with gold, for to make him sleep well and for to destroy lechery; for he will not lie with wives except four times a year and then only to beget children. . . .

Ye shall understand that every day at his court Prester John has more than thirty thousand people eating, not counting comers and goers. . . . This emperor has seven kings in his court to serve him, and when they have served him a month they return home and another seven kings come and serve another month. And with these kings seventy-two dukes and three hundred and sixty earls are always serving, along with many other lords and knights. Every day twelve archbishops and twenty bishops eat at his court. All archbishops, bishops and abbots there are kings and are great lords over fiefs. And the Patriarch of Saint Thomas is there, as it were, pope. . . .

At the foot of a mountain [in a nearby land] is a well, noble and fair, and the water thereof has a sweet savor and pungent, as it were, of a diverse manner of spicery. And every hour of the day the water changes diversely its savor and smell. And whosoever, fasting, drinks thrice of that well, he shall be whole of whatever manner of malady he has. And thus those who live nearby drink the other therefrom, and therefore they nevermore have sickness, but evermore they seem young. I, John Mandeville, saw this well and drank thereof thrice, and all my fellows, and evermore since that time I feel me the better and the wholer. . . .

It is four months' journey across the width of his land, and its length is beyond measuring. Trust me in all this, for surely I saw it with my own eyes and much more than I have told you. For my fellows and I were dwelling with him in his court a long time and saw all that I have told you and much more than I have leisure for to tell.

63

Marco Polo in China

The creation of a huge Eurasian Empire by the Mongols in the thirteenth century again opened the overland routes—the roads once used by the ancient silk traders and Buddhist pilgrims—that had been blocked since the eleventh century by the expansion of Islam. Caravans of traders and pilgrims were again able to move to and from the East. Many European missionaries and merchants made overland journeys to the court of the Mongol Khans. Perhaps the best-known European traveler to the court of Kublai Khan in Cambaluc (Peking) was Marco Polo (1254–1324), the son of a Venetian merchant.

In about 1264, young Marco's adventurous father Nicolo and uncle Maffeo reached the Grand Khan's court after a long and difficult journey through southern Russia, Bukhara, and Chinese Turkestan. They aroused much curiosity in Kublai's mind about Europe and the papacy. In 1266, they were sent back to Europe as Kublai's ambassadors to ask the pope to send one hundred well-schooled missionaries and scholars to China. The Holy See failed to take Kublai's request seriously and sent two priests who made it only as far east as Armenia. Had the Pope sent one hundred dedicated and well-trained missionaries, the course of history might have been altered.

In 1271, Marco Polo joined his father and uncle in their second journey to the court of the Kublai Khan. After three and a half years of difficult, overland journey, they reached Shang-Tu (Xandu), the summer residence of Kublai Khan. The Grand Khan was delighted to see them and grew particularly fond of Marco, whom he appointed as his personal, roving administrator for important missions in several distant provinces. In 1292, after seventeen years of service at Kublai Khan's court, the three Polos set out for Europe. This time they went by ship and took with them a young princess whom Kublai was sending as a bride to the Mongol Khan of Persia. In 1295, the Polos returned to Venice, where the Venetians lionized Marco with the nickname "Il milione" (the million).

Shortly after Marco Polo's return, a war broke out between Venice and Genoa. While serving as a Venetian naval commander in this war, Marco was captured and sent to a Genoese prison for three years. During this time, Marco Polo dictated the account of his adventures and travels in China to a fellow prisoner. His book, printed in Italian, Latin, French, and other languages, introduced Asia to Renaissance Europe and also inspired the great explorers, such as Christopher Columbus, to begin the Age of Discovery in the fifteenth century.

The following excerpts are Marco Polo's eyewitness accounts of the Grand Khan and the capital city of Cambaluc.

QUESTIONS TO CONSIDER

1. Compare and contrast the Kublai Khan's power and palace with those of one of the powerful medieval kings of Europe (see Reading 56).
2. From a historical perspective, what do you think are the most important contributions made by Marco Polo?
3. How would you compare Marco Polo's views on China with Ibn Battuta's views on Africa (see Reading 64)?

Concerning the Person of the Great Kaan

The personal appearance of the Great Kaan [Khan], Lord of Lords, whose name is Cublay, is such as I shall now tell you. He is of good stature, neither tall nor short, but of a middle height. He has a becoming amount of flesh, and is very shapely in all his limbs. His complexion is white and red, the eyes black and fine; the nose well formed and well set on. He has four wives, whom he retains permanently as his legitimate consorts; and the eldest of his sons by those four wives ought by rights to be emperor;—I mean when his father dies. Those four ladies are called empresses, but each is distinguished also by her proper name.

From Henry Yule, trans. and ed., *The Book of Ser Marco Polo*, Vols. 1 and 2 (London: John Murray, 1903), pp. 356–58, 362–64, 374–75.

And each of them has a special court of her own, very grand and ample; no one of them having fewer than 300 fair and charming damsels. They have also many pages and eunuchs, and a number of other attendants of both sexes; so that each of these ladies has not less than 10,000 persons attached to her court.

When the Emperor desires the society of one of these four consorts, he will sometimes send for the lady to his apartment and sometimes visit her at her own. He has also a great number of concubines, and I will tell you how he obtains them.

You must know that there is a tribe of Tartars called Ungrat, who are noted for their beauty. Now every year an hundred of the most beautiful maidens of this tribe are sent to the Great Kaan, who commits them to the charge of certain elderly ladies dwelling in his palace. And these old ladies make the girls sleep with them, in order to ascertain if they have sweet breath [and do not snore], and are sound in all their limbs. Then such of them as are of approved beauty, and are good and sound in all respects, are appointed to attend on the Emperor by turns. Thus six of these damsels take their turn for three days and nights, and wait on him when he is in his chamber and when he is in his bed, to serve him in any way, and to be entirely at his orders. At the end of the three days and nights they are relieved by other six. And so throughout the year, there are reliefs of maidens by six and six, changing every three days and nights.

Concerning the Palace of the Great Kaan

You must know that for three months of the year, to wit December, January, and February, the Great Kaan resides in the capital city of Cathay, which is called Cambaluc [Peking]. . . . In that city stands his great Palace, and now I will tell you what it is like.

It is enclosed all round by a great wall forming a square, each side of which is a mile in length; that is to say, the whole compass thereof is four miles. This you may depend on; it is also very thick, and a good ten paces in height, whitewashed and loop-holed all around. At each angle of the wall there is a very fine and rich palace in which the war-harness of the Emperor is kept, such as bows and quivers, saddles and bridles, and bowstrings, and everything needful for an army. Also midway between every two of these Corner Palaces there is another of the like; so that taking the whole compass of the enclosure you find eight vast Palaces stored with the Great Lord's harness of war. And you must understand that each Palace is assigned to only one kind of article; thus one is stored with bows, a second with saddles, a third with bridles, and so on in succession right round.

The great wall has five gates on its southern face, the middle one being the great gate which is never opened on any occasion except when the Great Kaan himself goes forth or enters. Close on either side of this great gate is a smaller one by which all other people pass; and then towards each angle is another great gate; also open to people in general; so that on that side there are five gates in all.

Inside of this wall there is a second, enclosing a space that is somewhat greater in length than in breadth. This enclosure also has eight palaces corresponding to those of the outer wall, and stored like them with the Lord's harness of war. This wall also hath five gates on the southern face, corresponding to those in the outer wall, and hath one gate on each of the other faces, as the outer wall hath also. In the middle of the second enclosure is the Lord's Great Palace, and I will tell you what it is like.

You must know that it is the greatest Palace that ever was. [Towards the north it is in contact with the outer wall, whilst towards the south there is a vacant space which the Barons and the soldiers are constantly traversing. The Palace itself] hath no upper story, but is all on the ground floor, only the basement is raised some ten palms above the surrounding soil [and this elevation is retained by a wall of marble raised to the level of the pavement, two paces in width and projecting beyond the base of the Palace so as to form a kind of terrace-walk, by which people can pass round the building, and which is exposed to view, whilst on the outer edge of the wall there is a very fine pillared balustrade; and up to this the people are allowed to come]. The roof is very lofty, and the walls of the Palace are all covered with gold and silver. They are also adorned with representations of dragons [sculptured and gilt], beasts and birds, knights and idols, and sundry other subjects. And on the ceiling too you see nothing but gold and silver and painting. [On each of the four sides there is a great marble staircase leading to the top of the marble wall, and forming the approach to the Palace.]

The Hall of the Palace is so large that it could easily dine 6000 people; and it is quite a marvel to see how many rooms there are besides. The building is altogether so vast, so rich, and so beautiful, that no man on earth could design anything superior to it. The outside of the roof also is all coloured with vermilion and yellow and green and blue and other hues, which are fixed with a varnish so fine and exquisite that they shine like crystal, and lend a resplendent lustre to the Palace as seen for a great way round. This roof is made too with such strength and solidity that it is fit to last for ever.

[On the interior side of the Palace are large buildings with halls and chambers, where the Emperor's private property is placed, such as his treasures of gold, silver, gems, pearls, and gold plate, and in which reside the ladies and concubines. There he occupies himself at his own convenience, and no one else has access.] . . .

Concerning the City of Cambaluc

Now there was on that spot in old times a great and noble city called Cambaluc, which is as much as to say in our tongue "The city of the Emperor." But the Great Kaan was informed by his Astrologers that this city would prove rebellious, and raise great disorders against his imperial authority. So he caused the present city to be built close beside the old one, with only a river between them. And he caused the people of the old city to be removed to the new town that he had founded; and this is called Taidu. . . .

As regards the size of this (new) city you must know that it has a compass of 24 miles, for each side of it hath a length of 6 miles, and it is four-square. And it is all walled round with walls of earth which have a thickness of full ten paces at bottom, and a height of more than 10 paces; but they are not so thick at top, for they diminish in thickness as they rise, so that at top they are only about 3 paces thick. And they are provided throughout with loop-holed battlements, which are all whitewashed.

There are 12 gates, and over each gate there is a great and handsome palace, so that there are on each side of the square three gates and five palaces; for (I ought to mention) there is at each angle also a great and handsome palace. In those palaces are vast halls in which are kept the arms of the city garrison.

The streets are so straight and wide that you can see right along them from end to end and from one gate to the other. And up and down the city there are beautiful palaces, and many great and fine hostelries, and fine houses in great numbers. [All the plots of ground on which the houses of the city are built are four-square, and laid out with straight lines; all the plots being occupied by great and spacious palaces, with courts and gardens of proportionate size. All these plots were assigned to different heads of families. Each square plot is encompassed by handsome streets for traffic; and thus the whole city is arranged in squares just like a chess-board, and disposed in a manner so perfect and masterly that it is impossible to give a description that should do it justice.]

Moreover, in the middle of the city there is a great clock—that is to say, a bell—which is struck at night. And after it has struck three times no one must go out in the city, unless it be for the needs of a woman in labour, or of the sick. And those who go about on such errands are bound to carry lanterns with them. Moreover, the established guard at each gate of the city is 1000 armed men; not that you are to imagine this guard is kept up for fear of any attack, but only as a guard of honour for the Sovereign, who resides there, and to prevent thieves from doing mischief in the town.

Perceptions of Africa

For most of the history of civilization, North Africa has developed with links to one or more dominant Mediterranean civilizations—Egyptian, Carthaginian, Hellenistic, Roman, and Islamic-Arab—rather than to the rest of Africa south of the Sahara. To this day, except near the Indian Ocean coast, the Sahara Desert remains a basic dividing line between North Africa and "Black Africa." Only with the spread of Islam into Black Africa were lasting, culturally significant contacts formed across the great desert.

Islamic missionaries, traders, and other travelers provide us with the first written observations of the great African kingdoms of Ghana and Mali, which flourished during the Western Middle Ages. Islamic observers were much impressed by the wealth and splendor of both societies, although, like the Islamic judge and cultural geographer Ibn Battuta, they were sometimes put off by the compromises made with strict Islam in the practices of African Muslims south of the Sahara.

Ethiopia stood out as an exception among African kingdoms for several reasons: It was the home base for several empires with histories as old as the Roman Empire. Although assigned by outside observers to Black Africa, it had an ethnically diverse population; and the fact that its ruler and most of the population accepted Christianity in the fourth century meant that it maintained a distinctive identity in the Islamic tide that flowed over most of North Africa and much of the Indian Ocean coastal region of Africa. Its Coptic-Christian Church promoted Ethiopian national identity. The fact that it had a Christian ruler led the Portuguese to claim they had located the long-sought kingdom of Prester John there (see Reading 62). Somewhat in the fashion of earlier Islamic observers reporting on the great wealth and power of kings such as Mansa Musa of Mali, Portuguese sojourners gave expansive reports on the splendor of their Ethiopian Prester John.

In the later Middle Ages, the Spanish and Portuguese were intent on driving the Islamic Moors out of Iberia, which meant, in their perceptions, driving them back to the Africa from which they had come long ago. The Iberian *Reconquista* was complete in 1492, but the Portuguese had no problem with continuing the conflict by fighting Islamic Africans in Africa itself during the course of their exploration and expansion from the late fifteenth into the seventeenth centuries.

64

Ibn Battuta in Mali

Born in Algiers, Ibn Battuta (1304–1368) was the premier world traveler of the Middle Ages. Although Marco Polo's adventures are better known in the West, never did Polo travel as far or see as many different countries as this indefatigable Berber did. In 1325, Ibn Battuta made the first of four visits to the Holy City of Mecca, thereby beginning an itinerary of 75,000 miles. Later in life, this devout Muslim would dictate to a Moroccan scribe an account of his journeys.

For nearly thirty years, Ibn Battuta traveled continuously throughout Africa, the Middle East, Persia, Russia, India, China, and Spain. He made it a rule, if possible, never to travel the same road twice, and he frequently paid the price of taking the less-traveled road. He often was stranded or overcome by disease. His African editors note: "He seems to have experienced most travellers' diseases from Lahore sore to Delhi belly. Only the fact that the New World had not been discovered saved him from Montezuma's revenge."[1]

The following selection illustrates the range of Ibn Battuta's travels and also suggests that, by the fourteenth century, Islamic civilization, spanning four continents, was truly the "world" civilization. In 1344, Ibn Battuta left the Malabar coast of India and sailed south to the Maldive Islands, where for eighteen months he served as a judge of Islamic sacred law.

Later, after journeys to Ceylon, China, and Syria, he returned to Algiers. In 1352, on his last journey, he set off on foot across the Sahara to visit the African kingdoms of the Niger basin. His account of this experience is one of the primary records of the social customs in the Kingdom of Mali, particularly the city of Iwalatan (Walata).

In reporting on Black Africa, Ibn Battuta's accounts are basically favorable, but his enthusiasm over the devout acceptance of Islam is offset by reservations about non-Islamic elements in living customs.

QUESTIONS TO CONSIDER

1. Why was Ibn Battuta so troubled by his African hosts' methods of tracing genealogy? Are there political implications of this genealogical system?
2. How would you compare Ibn Battuta's observations of Africa with those of Gomes Eannes de Azurara (see Reading 94)?

The condition of these people [of Iwalatan] is strange and their manners are bizarre. As for their men, there is no sexual jealousy about them. None of them is named after his father,

---

[1]Said Hamdun and Noel King, eds. and trans., *Ibn Battuta in Black Africa* (London: Rex Collings, 1975), p. 4.

From Ibn Battuta, *Voyages D'Ibn Batoutah*, trans. from the Arabic by C. Defrémery and B.R. Sanguinétti (Paris: Imprimerie Impériale, 1858), IV, 387–90, 421–24. Trans. Philip F. Riley.

but each traces his genealogy from his maternal uncle. A man's inheritance is not passed to his own sons but to the sons of his sister. I have never seen such a thing in any other part of the world except among the infidels who live on the Malabar coast of India. These people are Muslims who follow exactly the prescribed laws for prayer, study the laws of Islam, and know the Koran by heart. Their women are not modest in the presence of men; despite reciting their prayers punctually, they do not veil their faces. Any male who wishes to marry one of them can do so very easily, but the women do not travel with their husbands for her family would not allow it. In this country, the women are permitted to have male friends and companions among men who are not members of her family. So too for men; they are permitted to have female companions among women who are not members of his family. It happens quite often that a man would enter his own house and find his wife with one of her own friends and would not rebuke her.

Anecdote

One day I entered the home of a judge in Iwalatan after he had given his permission, and I found him with a very young and beautiful woman. Immediately I thought it best to leave, but she laughed at me and was not at all embarrassed. The judge asked me "Why would you want to leave? She is my friend." I was astonished at the conduct of these two. He was a judge and had made a pilgrimage to Mecca. Later I learned that he has asked permission of the Sultan to go on a pilgrimage to Mecca that year with his female friend. Whether it was this one or another I do not know, but the Sultan refused to let him go.

A Similar Anecdote

One day I entered the home of Aboû Mohammed Yandecán, a man of the Mesoûfah tribe. He was sitting on a rug while in the middle of his house was a bed covered with a canopy. On it was his wife in conversation with another man sitting at her side. I said to Aboû Mohammed "Who is this woman?"—"She is my wife," he responded—"And who is the man with her?" I asked. "He is her friend," replied the judge. I asked how he, who knew the divine law on such matters, could permit such a thing. He replied that "The companionship of women with men in this country is proper and honorable: It does not inspire suspicion. Our women are not like the women of your country." I was shocked at his stupid answer and immediately left his home and never returned. . . .

Good and Bad Qualities

Among their good qualities we can cite the following:

1. There is a small amount of crime, for these people obey the law. Their sultan does not pardon criminals.
2. Travelers and natives alike are safe from brigands, robbers, and thieves.
3. The natives do not confiscate the property of white men who die in this country, even if they are very wealthy; instead they entrust it to another, respected white man to dispose of it properly.

4. The prayers are offered punctually and with fervor. Children who neglect their prayers are beaten. If you do not come to the mosque early on a Friday you cannot find a place to pray because the crowds are so large. Quite often they send their slaves to the mosque with a prayer rug to find and hold a place for their masters. These prayer rugs are made from the leaves of trees similar to palm trees, but one that bears no fruit.
5. White garments are worn on Fridays. If by chance one does not have a proper white garment, regular clothing is washed and cleaned to wear for public prayer.
6. They are committed to learn by heart the sublime Koran. Children who fail to learn the Koran by heart have their feet shackled and these shackles are not removed until they memorize the Koran. On a feast day I visited a judge who had his children in chains. I said to him "Why don't you release them?" He said "I will not do so until they know the Koran by heart." Another day I passed a handsome young black man dressed superbly, but shackled by a heavy chain on his feet. I asked my companion, "What has this young man done? Is he a murderer?" The handsome young black man laughed and my companion told me, "He has been chained so that he will learn the Koran by heart."

Among their bad qualities we can cite the following:

1. Their female servants, slave women and small daughters appear before men completely naked, exposing their private parts. Even during the month of Ramadan [a period of fast], military commanders broke their fast in the palace of the Sultan. Twenty or more naked servant girls served them food.
2. Nude women without veils on their faces enter the palace of the Sultan. On the twenty-seventh night of Ramadan, I saw about a hundred naked female slaves coming out of the palace of the Sultan with food. Two of the Sultan's daughters, who have large breasts, were with them and they were naked.
3. These natives put dust and ashes on their head to show their education and as a sign of respect.
4. They laugh when poets recite their verse before the Sultan.
5. Finally, they eat impure meat such as dogs and donkeys.

65

Martín Fernández de Figueroa, Confronting the Moors in Somalia

Martín Fernández de Figueroa was from Castile, but in 1505 he went to Lisbon where he joined a Portuguese fleet bound for "the Indies," a rather expansive concept at the time, including in its Eastern sweep alone territories from Ethiopia through what today is Indonesia. Figueroa spent six years traveling with the Portuguese in Africa and Asia and participated in the initial Portuguese seizure of Goa in India in 1510. A year later, he returned home and published an account of his travels. Figueroa's narrative was one of the earliest attempts to bring to the attention of Spain the world of the East that the Portuguese were discovering and conquering.

QUESTIONS TO CONSIDER

1. Why does Figueroa seem to think it is normal enough for the Portuguese to attack the inhabitants of Brava and Mogadishu in Somalia? For what acts does he reproach them as exceeding acceptable limits in the behavior of victors?
2. Why do the Portuguese and Spanish seem to get along so well with most of the people of Socotra, the large island about equally far east of Somalia and south of the Arabian peninsula?
3. What sort of limited community of interests and harmony of action among the Portuguese and Spanish does Figueroa's account bear testimony to? What do you suppose the Africans and Arabians they encountered thought of the Iberians coming to their shores?

Afonso de Albuquerque had set out for the Strait of Mecca as captain major of six ships. He then informed them of his arrival at a city on the mainland called Brava. The Portuguese entered it by force of arms, killed many Moors, and carried off great riches which their owners had not thought to save, thinking they could defend the city. Nor could they save their women, very rich and handsome with seven and eight bracelets on each arm, and just as many, thick and valuable, on their legs. This occasioned severe cruelty, for the men, blinded by avarice rather than enlightened by mercy, so as not to lose a moment's time, cut off the arms, the legs, and the ears which bore the jewelry, without a trace of pity. Good men would never do such a thing, if only because women are "vessels of generation" and of tender, delicate flesh and gentle condition. What man would not have been moved to pity contemplating their beauty! What man would not have cast down his sword before bloodying it on a woman! Worthy of reprimand are such cruel victors and their cruel deeds, but you may be sure that the ones who did such foul things were not the ordinary nor the best of men. The women all ran crying through the streets, covered with blood. Some went fleeing with children in their arms but could find no haven. Quite a few of them were defended and sheltered by the virtuous men who were there.

The city was finally ordered burned, which was done, whereupon they set out for another city, Mogadishu, which was nearby. There, although the army was sore afraid, the ferocity of contrary winds kept the Christians from waiting and attacking, and thus hostile weather frustrated their good and worthy goal. They left that place and went to Socotra,[1] whose inhabitants consider themselves Christians. They fast during Lent and Advent, eating neither meat nor fish. They have churches and altars with crosses on them. They observe most of the principal feast days, as well as those of the Apostles, whose names they take. They give alms. Every day they hear Matins, Vespers, and Compline. They hold the Cross in such veneration that he who wears it goes about without fear of harm from the enemies or the authorities. So states at length the King Manuel letter written in Portuguese that I had in hand. . . . This land is completely surrounded by water. They anchored opposite the castle, and as soon as it was realized that they were Portuguese, mortars were hauled out and a stout defense made ready. They did not want peace or even to let the Portuguese take on Socotran water. There the Christians killed a Socotran captain. The battle was very

---

[1] An island in the Indian Ocean off Cape Guardafui, at the horn of Africa.

Reprinted by permission of the publishers and the Loeb Classical Library from James B. McKenna, *A Spaniard in the Portuguese Indies: The Narrative of Martín Fernández de Figueroa.* Cambridge, Mass.: Harvard University Press, © 1967.

rough, and a captain named Leonel Coutinho proved himself unflinchingly courageous. With the fierce blows he dealt them, he sorely pressed the castle defenders. As he drove the Moors back from the walls, he put up scaling ladders. Thus, the first Christians who succeeded in entering opened the castle gates, and the Christians entered and captured the fort. No Moor survived, because, rather than surrender and live without their patrimony, they chose to die. Then the conquerers consolidated the land. Although these people were defeated, they died courageously. When winter passed, the men of Hispania attacked the city of Hormuz under the orders of Captain Afonso de Albuquerque. They conquered and took possession of it. The Moors rose up against the Christians, so they went to Socotra again and from there to Cape Guardafui to lie in wait for infidel ships.

During their voyage, the captains came upon Mogadishu, of which we have already spoken. They sighted a Moorish ship and drove it ashore. When they reached it, they saw that everyone was gone, so they set it afire along with its entire rich cargo. Without stopping, they journeyed to Afonso de Albuquerque, by whom they were honorably welcomed. Cape Guardafui is called a cape because there the seacoast comes to an end. There is another cape there, called Fartak, and between these two enters the sea they call the Strait of Mecca. Arabia is a wretched land; the airs are torrid. Its inhabitants are Arabs, cattle-raisers. Fresh water is far away and is brought there in leather gourds to be sold. From there they went to Socotra to spend the winter.

The captains, and Martín Fernández de Figueroa with them, spent the entire winter (which out there runs from the month of April through the middle of August) on the island of Socotra. On this island one finds good-natured men. Their churches do not have statues of men or women saints, only crosses. They sound for Mass with wooden tablets. The men enter church by one door and the women by another, and this practice never varies. On solemn occasions they anoint the cross with lard. The women dearly love the Christians of Hispania. Some of these people know Arabic, but they have their own language. The men go about naked except for their shameful parts. The women wear Moorish tunics; they wear their hair long and comb it down their backs. Women are held in common, which is an abominable custom. Thus the husband will invite you to sleep with his wife, and fathers and mothers with their daughters. They are a libidinous people. In that land it rarely rains except for the dew. No wheat grows there, nor rice, millet, nor barley. There are lots of cattle and palm groves. A pitcher of wine there costs sixteen hundred maravedis, a needle twenty maravedis, and similar pieces must be paid for many other necessary things.

A knight from Captain Major Afonso de Albuquerque's company scrupulously related to the captains of the other coast the conquest of Hormuz. He told how, after they had seized the fort from the Fartaks, who fight like Swiss mercenaries, they left it strongly garrisoned and set out in search of provisions. Sailing along the Arabian coast, they came to Kalhat, a rich port city, and the Captain Major was delighted to have come upon a land of good supplies. They entered the harbor, although with difficulty, for it was occupied by many handsome ships and ringed by elegant buildings along the shore. They gave a thunderous artillery display to frighten the inhabitants. They took the supplies the Moors had provided, and the Captain did not harm them, because he had given them a guarantee and one of his rings as token thereof. Kalhat, later destroyed when Hormuz revolted, was more populated outside the city than within. Afonso de Albuquerque departed the next day, and they went to a port named Quryat, which also belongs to the King of Hormuz. It is a very wealthy town located at the water's edge, well stocked with mortars. The Captain Major requested provisions, but the Moors paid no attention. So the next day Afonso de Albuquerque organized his men and the captains of the rear guard and commenced the attack. He destroyed the enemy, and, with Moors fleeing and Christians killing, the ships were well stocked with the riches and supplies they found ashore, namely an abundance of wheat, flour, rice, dates, fish, lard, and honey. They rested there for three days. In all this said encounter or battle no Christian was killed, only one of the Captain Major's Negroes who had strayed off. After this victory, they boarded their ships. They had burned and razed the mosque, the land, and the ships; nothing remained. They sailed forth to Masqat, which belongs to the King of Hormuz. Larger than Kalhat, it had a good port and stout defenses. However, the Moors met with the Captain Major (who truly awed and terrified them) under a flag of truce, whereupon they did as he directed and became vassals of the King of Portugal. There the Christians secured very fresh and rich provisions, but first they had to fight a fierce and cruel battle, for the Moors broke their promise of peace. The city was sacked, the ruler killed, and one Christian captain wounded. The city, its ships and riches were burned and reduced to ashes. With this victory they returned to the ships; the battle had taken place on a Sunday morning and lasted three hours. From there Afonso de Albuquerque and his men moved along the coast to a town called Suhar, where there was a fort garrisoned by a captain and men of the King of Hormuz. As soon as they saw the Christian ships, the captain and his men were terrified, so Suhar and its Moors became vassals of King Manuel of Portugal. Great celebrations were held, and the Portuguese banner was raised over the fort, with Moors and Christians shouting: "Portugal and Spain!"

Byzantium: The Later Period of Triumph and Tragedy

After the glorious reign of Emperor Basil II (976–1025) during which the Byzantine Empire subdued the Russians, Bulgars, Muslims, and powerful Byzantine nobles, it began to decline. Among the reasons for this disintegration were disinterested leadership of later emperors, a reemergence of the powerful nobility, the baleful influence of certain empresses, the coming of Seljuk Turks, and a competition for the imperial throne, which ultimately led to the disasters of the Fourth Crusade for the Empire.

Two selections illustrate the triumphs and tragedies of this period. The first is about the restoration of the empire, resulting from the efforts of Emperor Alexius I Comenus (1081–1118), as reported by his daughter Anna Comnena in her *Alexiad.* The second selection, however, marks the permanent decay of the empire. It is a report by Robert de Clari of the Fourth Crusade, which left the empire a mere shadow of its former glory.

66

Anna Comnena, *The Alexiad*

By the mid-tenth century, the once mighty Abbasid caliphs (the head of state) of Baghdad were puppets of their own bodyguards. About a century later, Turkish nomads, the Seljuks, who had come from Central Asia into Iran and had converted to Islam, rescued the caliphs. These Seljuk sultans slowly extended their political power from Iran-Iraq through Syria and Palestine. In 1071, the Byzantine emperor Romanus IV Diogenes tried to stop Seljuk raids into Anatolia (modern Turkey), but he was defeated and captured at Manzikert. The Seljuks soon took over most of Anatolia from the Byzantine government.

When the Seljuk sultanate broke up into quarreling petty states, the Byzantine emperor Alexius I Comnenus appealed to the West for a body of knights to aid him in recapturing Anatolia. This appeal, plus Seljuk restrictions on the number of Christian pilgrims to the Holy Land, led Pope Urban II in 1095 to call for the First Crusade (1096–1099).

The first people to answer the pope's request, however, were not those whom he had envisioned as going to the East, nor those whom the Byzantines had wanted, but a religiously inspired group of peasants led by popular preachers, such as the Frenchman called Peter the Hermit. When these unwanted peasants arrived at Constantinople, the emperor quickly transported them to Anatolia where they were soon massacred by the Turks.

On the heels of this disaster, in October 1096, the first of the crusaders reached Constantinople. The Franks, as the Byzantines called them, were not exactly what Alexius I had hoped for either; they were not a band of knights who were to fight solely for the return of Anatolian lands, but a vast horde of quarrelsome knights who seemed interested only in plundering the suburbs of the city. After much negotiation, the knights agreed to return any lands they might win from the Seljuks of Anatolia in return for which the emperor agreed to supply them with any equipment needed.

QUESTIONS TO CONSIDER

1. Why did Emperor Alexius fear the coming of the crusaders?
2. What caused the Turkish massacre of the Peasant's Crusade?
3. Can you find any errors in Anna's description relating to Peter the Hermit or to Islam?

Before he had enjoyed even a short rest, the emperor heard a report of the approach of innumerable Frankish armies. Now he dreaded their arrival for he knew their irresistible manner of attack, their unstable and mobile character and all the peculiar natural and concomitant characteristics which the Frank retains throughout; and he also knew that they were always agape for money, and seemed to disregard their truces readily for any reason that cropped up. For he had always heard this reported of them, and found it very true. However, he did not lose heart, but prepared himself in every way so that, when the occasion called, he would be ready for battle. And indeed the actual facts were far greater and more terrible than rumour made them. For the whole of the West and all the barbarian tribes which dwell between the further side of the Adriatic and the pillars of Heracles, had all migrated in a body and were marching into Asia through the intervening Europe, and were making the journey with all their household. The reason of this upheaval was more or less the following. A certain Frank, Peter by name, nicknamed Cucupeter, had gone to worship at the

The Alexiad of the Princess Anna Comnena, trans. Elizabeth A.S. Dawes (London: Kegan Paul, Trench, Trubner & Co. Ltd, 1928; reprint, Ann Arbor, MI: Xerox University Microfilms, 1976), pp. 248–52. Copyright © 1928 by Elizabeth A.S. Dawes.

Holy Sepulchre and after suffering many things at the hands of the Turks and Saracens who were ravaging Asia, he got back to his own country with difficulty. But he was angry at having failed in his object, and wanted to undertake the same journey again. However, he saw that he ought not to make the journey to the Holy Sepulchre alone again, lest worse things befall him, so he worked out a cunning plan. This was to preach in all the Latin countries that "the voice of God bids me announce to all the Counts in France that they should all leave their homes and set out to worship at the Holy Sepulchre, and to endeavour wholeheartedly with hand and mind to deliver Jerusalem from the hand of the Hagarenes." And he really succeeded. For after inspiring the souls of all with this quasi-divine command he contrived to assemble the Franks from all sides, one after the other, with arms, horses and all the other paraphernalia of war. And they were all so zealous and eager that every highroad was full of them. And those Frankish soldiers were accompanied by an unarmed host more numerous than the sand or the stars, carrying palms and crosses on their shoulders; women and children, too, came away from their countries. And the sight of them was like many rivers streaming from all sides, and they were advancing towards us through Dacia generally with all their hosts. Now the coming of these many peoples was preceded by a locust which did not touch the wheat, but made a terrible attack on the vines. This was really a presage as the diviners of the time interpreted it, and meant that this enormous Frankish army would, when it came, refrain from interference in Christian affairs, but fall very heavily upon the barbarian Ishmaelites who were slaves to drunkenness, wine, and Dionysus. For this race is under the sway of Dionysus and Eros, rushes headlong into all kind of sexual intercourse, and is not circumcised either in the flesh or in their passions.[1] It is nothing but a slave, nay triply enslaved, to the ills wrought by Aphrodite. For this reason they worship and adore Astarte and Ashtaroth too and value above all the image of the moon, and the golden figure of Hobar in their country. Now in these symbols Christianity was taken to be the corn because of its wineless and very nutritive qualities; in this manner the diviners interpreted the vines and the wheat. However let the matter of the prophecy rest.

The incidents of the barbarians' approach followed in the order I have described, and persons of intelligence could feel that they were witnessing a strange occurrence. The arrival of these multitudes did not take place at the same time nor by the same road (for how indeed could such masses starting from different places have crossed the straits of Lombardy all together?). Some first, some next, others after them and thus successively all accomplished the transit, and then marched through the Continent. Each army was preceded, as we said, by an unspeakable number of locusts; and all who saw this more than once recognized them as forerunners of the Frankish armies. When the first of them began crossing the straits of Lombardy sporadically the Emperor summoned certain leaders of the Roman forces, and sent them to the parts of Dyrrachium and Valona with instructions to offer a courteous welcome to the Franks who had crossed, and to collect abundant supplies from all the countries along their route; then to follow and watch them covertly all the time, and if they saw them making any foraging-excursions, they were to come out from under cover and check them by light skirmishing. These captains were accompanied by some men who knew the Latin tongue, so that they might settle any disputes that arose between them.

Let me, however, give an account of this subject more clearly and in due order. According to universal rumour Godfrey, who had sold his country, was the first to start on the appointed road; this man was very rich and very proud of his bravery, courage and con-

---

[1] In the Middle Ages, Arabs were often referred to as "Hagarenes" or "Ishmaelites," with the thought that they were descendents of Abraham and Hagar (Abraham's Egyptian maid) on the basis of Chapter 16 of Genesis. Notice that Anna is passing on a wealth of misinformation about Arab customs and Islam.

spicuous lineage; for every Frank is anxious to outdo the others. And such an upheaval of both men and women took place then as had never occurred within human memory, the simpler-minded were urged on by the real desire of worshipping at our Lord's Sepulchre, and visiting the sacred places; but the more astute, especially men like Bohemund and those of like mind, had another secret reason, namely, the hope that while on their travels they might by some means be able to seize the capital itself, looking upon this as a kind of corollary. And Bohemund disturbed the minds of many nobler men by thus cherishing his old grudge against the Emperor. Meanwhile Peter, after he had delivered his message, crossed the straits of Lombardy before anybody else with eighty thousand men on foot, and one hundred thousand on horseback, and reached the capital by way of Hungary. For the Frankish race, as one may conjecture, is always very hotheaded and eager, but when once it has espoused a cause, it is uncontrollable.

The Emperor, knowing what Peter had suffered before from the Turks, advised him to wait for the arrival of the other Counts, but Peter would not listen for he trusted to the multitude of his followers, so crossed and pitched his camp near a small town called Helenopolis. After him followed the Normans numbering ten thousand, who separated themselves from the rest of the army and devastated the country round Nicæa, and behaved most cruelly to all. For they dismembered some of the children and fixed others on wooden spits and roasted them at the fire, and on persons advanced in age they inflicted every kind of torture. But when the inhabitants of Nicæa became aware of these doings, they threw open their gates and marched out upon them, and after a violent conflict had taken place they had to dash back inside their citadel as the Normans fought so bravely. And thus the latter recovered all the booty and returned to Helenopolis. Then a dispute arose between them and the others who had not gone out with them, as is usual in such cases, for the minds of those who had stayed behind were aflame with envy, and thus caused a skirmish after which the headstrong Normans drew apart again, marched to Xerigordus and took it by assault. When the Sultan heard what had happened, he dispatched Elchanes against them with a substantial force. He came, and recaptured Xerigordus and sacrificed some of the Normans to the sword, and took others captive, at the same time laid plans to catch those who had remained behind with Cucupeter. He placed ambushes in suitable spots so that any coming from the camp in the direction of Nicæa would fall into them unexpectedly and be killed. Besides this, as he knew the Franks' love of money, he sent for two active-minded men and ordered them to go to Cucupeter's camp and proclaim there that the Normans had gained possession of Nicæa, and were now dividing everything in it. When this report was circulated among Peter's followers, it upset them terribly. Directly they heard the words "partition" and "money" they started in a disorderly crowd along the road to Nicæa, all but unmindful of their military experience and the discipline which is essential for those starting out to battle. For, as I remarked above, the Latin race is always very fond of money, but more especially when it is bent on raiding a country; it then loses its reason and gets beyond control. As they journeyed neither in ranks nor in squadrons, they fell foul of the Turkish ambuscades near the river Dracon and perished miserably. And such a large number of Franks and Normans were the victims of the Ishmaelite sword, that when they piled up the corpses of the slaughtered men which were lying on either side they formed, I say, not a very large hill or mound or a peak, but a high mountain as it were, of very considerable depth and breadth—so great was the pyramid of bones. And later men of the same tribe as the slaughtered barbarians built a wall and used the bones of the dead to fill the interstices as if they were pebbles, and thus made the city their tomb in a way. This fortified city is still standing to-day with its walls built of a mixture of stones and bones. When they had all in this way fallen a prey to the sword, Peter alone with a few others escaped and re-entered Helenopolis; and the Turks who wanted to capture him, set fresh ambushes for him. But when the Emperor received reliable information of all this, and the terrible massacre, he was very worried lest Peter should have been captured. He therefore summoned Constantine Cat- acalon Euphorbenus (who has already been mentioned many times in this history), and gave him a large force which was embarked on ships of war and sent him across the straits to Pe- ter's succour. Directly the Turks saw him land they fled. Constantine, without the slightest delay, picked up Peter and his followers, who were but few, and brought them safe and sound to the Emperor. On the Emperor's reminding him of his original thoughtlessness and saying that it was due to his not having obeyed his, the Emperor's, advice that he had in- curred such disasters, Peter, being a haughty Latin, would not admit that he himself was the cause of the trouble, but said it was the others who did not listen to him, but followed their own wills, and he denounced them as robbers and plunderers who, for that reason, were not allowed by the Saviour to worship at His Holy Sepulchre. Others of the Latins, such as Bo- hemund and men of like mind, who had long cherished a desire for the Roman Empire, and wished to win it for themselves, found a pretext in Peter's preaching, as I have said, de- ceived the more single-minded, caused this great upheaval and were selling their own es- tates under the pretence that they were marching against the Turks to redeem the Holy Sepulchre.

67

Robert of Clari, *The Conquest of Constantinople*

The purpose of the Fourth Crusade (1202–1204), as envisioned by Pope Inno- cent III, was to continue the Western attack on the Muslim-held holy places in the Near East. The French Norman crusaders were diverted from their original task, however, because of the Venetian desire to control the trade routes to the Near East coupled with a plea for aid from Alexius Angelus. Angelus was the son of the imprisoned, blinded, and dethroned Byzantine emperor, Isaac.

Although the crusaders were able to restore Isaac and his son to their right- ful positions, the Byzantine emperors were not able to fulfill their bargain to pay the Normans for the restoration. As a result, tensions between the natives and the crusaders eventually led to the usurpation of the Byzantine throne as well as to the deaths of Isaac and his son. In 1204, the crusaders decided to attack Constantinople, which fell amid scenes of violence and rapacity on the part of the Normans. In the period from 1204 to 1261, a Latin kingdom, ruled by Franks, arose in the East. The crusade also forcibly instituted Roman Catholi- cism in place of the Eastern Orthodox Church. These actions left a lasting reli- gious bitterness and an Eastern empire that never recovered from the devasta- tion.

Robert of Clari, who was among the Fourth Crusaders, left an eyewitness account from the perspective of a simple soldier. After returning home in 1205, Robert dictated his memoirs, adding one last piece concerning the death of the second Latin emperor, Henry I, in 1216.

This chronicle is the best single Western source describing the motivations and actions of the crusaders. Robert, with great accuracy, describes the Great

Palace, Santa Sophia, and the Golden Gate; he also offers diversions concerning miracle cures and sacred relics such as the True Cross, the head of John the Baptist, and perhaps the Shroud of Turin, thought by many to be the burial cloth of Jesus.

QUESTIONS TO CONSIDER

1. Why was the Fourth Crusade a perversion of the crusading spirit?
2. What was the cause of the religious problems between Rome and Constantinople?
3. What caused the crusaders to sack the city?
4. What miraculous objects or places impressed the crusaders?
5. What comparison can you make between Robert of Clari's description and the Spanish conquest of Mexico (see Reading 98)?

In the meantime, while the crusaders and the Venetians were staying there [on the Dalmation coast] that winter, the crusaders bethought them that they had spent a great deal. And they talked with one another and said that they could not go to Babylon or to Alexandria or to Syria, because they had neither provisions nor money for going there. For they had spent nearly everything, on the long delay they had made as well as on the great price they had given for the hire of the fleet. . . .

The doge of Venice saw right well that the pilgrims were in sore straits, and he spoke to them and said: "Lords, in Greece there is a land that is very rich and plenteous in all good things. If we could have a reasonable excuse for going there and taking provisions and other things in the land until we were well restored, it would seem to me a good plan. Then we should be well able to go oversea." . . .

Now you have heard how Isaac arose and how he became emperor and how his son went to Germany—he for whom the crusaders and the Venetians were going to send, on the advice of the marquis of Montferrat, their leader, . . . so that they might have an excuse for going to the country of Constantinople. And now we shall tell you about this youth and the crusaders, how the crusaders sent for him and how they went to Constantinople and how they conquered it. . . .

Then all the barons of the host were summoned and the Venetians. And when they were all assembled, the doge of Venice rose and spoke to them. "Lords," said the doge, "now we have a good excuse for going to Constantinople, if you approve of it, for we have the rightful heir." Now there were some who did not at all approve of going to Constantinople. Instead they said: "Bah! what shall we be doing in Constantinople? We have our pilgrimage to make, and also our plan of going to Babylon or Alexandria. Moreover, our navy is to follow us for only a year, and half of the year is already past." And the others said in answer: "What shall we do in Babylon or Alexandria, when we have neither provisions nor money to enable us to go there? Better for us before we go there to secure provisions and money by some good excuse than to go there and die of hunger. Then we shall be able to accomplish something. Moreover, he offers to come with us and to maintain our navy and our fleet a year longer at his own cost." . . . When they of Constantinople saw this fleet which was so finely arrayed, they gazed at it in wonder, and they were mounted on the walls

From Robert of Clari, *The Conquest of Constantinople*, trans. Edgar Holmes McNeal. Copyright © 1936 Columbia University Press. Reprinted by permission of the publisher.

and on the houses to look upon this marvel. And they of the fleet also regarded the great size of the city, which was so long and so wide, and they marveled at it exceedingly.

When the emperor of Constantinople learned of it, he sent good envoys to ask them what they sought there and why they were come there, and he sent word to them that if they wanted any of his gold or his silver, he would right gladly send it to them. When the high men heard this, they answered the envoys that they did not want any of his gold or his silver, but rather they wanted the emperor to surrender the empire, for he held it neither rightfully nor loyally, and they sent word to him that they had the rightful heir with them, Alexius, the son of Isaac the emperor. Thereupon the envoys answered and said that the emperor would do nothing of the sort, and with that they went away. . . .

While the French and the Venetians were talking together, there arose a great clamor in the city, for they of the city told the emperor that he ought to deliver them from the French who were besieging them, and that if he did not fight with them they would seek out the youth whom the French had brought and make him emperor and lord over them.

When the emperor heard this, he gave them his word that he would fight them on the morrow. But when it came near midnight, the emperor fled from the city with as many people as he could take with him.

When the morning was come on the morrow and they of the city knew that the emperor was fled, what do they do but go to the gates and open them and issue forth and come to the camp of the French and ask and inquire for Alexius, the son of Isaac. And they were told that they would find him at the tent of the marquis. When they came there, they found him, and his friends did him great honor and made great rejoicing over him. And they thanked the barons right heartily and said that they who had done this thing had done right well and had done a great deed of baronage. And they said that the emperor had fled, and that they [the crusaders] should come into the city and into the palace as if it all belonged to them. Then all the high barons of the host assembled, and they took Alexius, the son of Isaac, and they led him to the palace with great joy and much rejoicing. And when they were come to the palace, they had Isaac, his father, brought out of prison, and his wife also. This was the one who had been imprisoned by his brother, the recent emperor. When Isaac was out of prison, he made great rejoicing over his son and embraced and kissed him, and he gave great thanks to the barons who were there and said that it was by the help of God first and next by theirs that he was out of prison. Then they brought two golden chairs and seated Isaac on one and Alexius his son on the other beside him, and to Isaac was given the imperial seat. . . .

Afterwards the emperor sought out the barons and said to them that he had nothing save Constantinople and that this was worth little to him by itself, for his uncle held all the cities and castles that ought to be his. So he asked the barons to help him conquer some of the land around, and he would right gladly give them still more of his wealth. Then they answered that they would be very glad to do it, and that anyone who wanted to profit by this could go. Then a good half of the host went with Alexius and the other half stayed in Constantinople to receive the payment, and Isaac stayed behind to make the payment to the barons. So Alexius went with all his host and conquered full twenty cities and full forty castles or more of the land, and Alexius, the other emperor, his uncle, fled always before him. . . .

When this respite was past and the French saw that the emperor was not going to pay them anything, all the counts and the high men of the host came together, and they went to the palace of the emperor and asked again for their payment. Then the emperor answered them that he could not pay them anything, and the barons answered that if he did not pay them they would seize enough of his possessions to pay themselves. . . .

While these things were going on, those of the Greeks who were traitors toward the emperor and this Murzuphlus whom the emperor had freed from prison came together and plotted a great treason. For they wanted to make someone else emperor, someone who would deliver them from the French, because Alexius did not seem good to them any longer. And finally Murzuphlus said: "If you will leave it to me," said he, "and will make me emperor, I will deliver you from the French and from this emperor, so that you will never have any more trouble from them." And they said that if he would deliver them they would make him emperor, and Murzuphlus vowed to free them within a week, and they agreed to make him emperor.

Then Murzuphlus went and lost no time. He took sergeants with him and entered by night into the chamber where his lord the emperor, who had freed him from prison, was sleeping, and he had them tie a cord around his neck and strangle him and his father Isaac also. . . . It was not long afterwards that Murzuphlus sent word to the count of Flanders, to Count Louis, to the marquis, and to all the other high barons, telling them to go away and vacate his land, and letting them know that he was emperor and that if he came on them there a week from then he would slay them all. When the barons heard the message that Murzuphlus had sent, they replied: "What?" said they, "He who has treacherously murdered his lord by night has sent this word to us?" And they sent back word to him that they defied him and let him now beware of them, for they would not abandon the siege until they had avenged him whom he had murdered and had taken Constantinople again and had secured in full the payment which Alexius had promised them. . . .

Then it came about on a Friday, about ten days before Palm Sunday, that the pilgrims and the Venetians got their ships and their engines ready and prepared for the assault. So they ranged their ships side by side, and the French had their engines loaded on barges and galleys, and they set out to go toward the city, and the navy extended fully a good league along its front. . . .

When the navy was about to make land, they took strong cables and drew their ships as close as they could to the walls, and the French had their engines set up, their "cats" and "carts" and "sows," to mine the walls. And the Venetians mounted on the bridges of their ships and hardily assailed the walls and the French likewise assailed them with their engines. When the Greeks saw the French attacking them thus, they set to hurling huge blocks of stone, more than enough, onto the engines of the French, and they began to crush and break to pieces and destroy all these engines, so that no one dared to remain inside or under them. And the Venetians on their part were not able to reach the walls or the towers, they were so high. Nor ever that day were the Venetians or the French able to accomplish anything at the walls or at the city. When they saw that they could not do anything, they were greatly disheartened and drew off. When the Greeks saw them withdrawing, they began to hoot and to call out more lustily than a great deal, and they mounted on the walls and let down their clouts and showed them their backsides. . . .

Then when the bishops had preached and had shown the pilgrims that the battle was a righteous one, they all confessed themselves right well and were given communion. When it came to Monday morning, the pilgrims all made themselves ready and armed themselves right well, and the Venetians also. Then they repaired the bridges on their ships and got ready their transports and their galleys and ranged them side by side for the assault, and the navy had fully a good league of front. When they reached the shore and had drawn up as close as they could to the walls, they cast anchor. And when they were at anchor, they began to attack vigorously and to shoot and hurl stones and throw Greek fire on the towers, but the fire could not take hold on them because of the hides with which they were covered. And those within the city defended themselves right hardily, and they had fully sixty petraries [medieval military engines for discharging stones] hurling missiles, and at each cast they hit the ships, but the ships were so well covered with planks and with grapevines that they did not do them any harm, and the stones were so large that a man could not lift one of them from the ground. . . . When my lord Pierre of Amiens saw that those who were in the towers were not advancing and saw the condition of the Greeks, what does he do but descend to the land on foot, he and his people with him, on a little piece of ground that was between the sea and the wall. When they were on land, they looked ahead and saw a false postern, the door of which had been removed and it had been walled up again. . . .

When they were come to this postern, they began to attack it hardily with their picks, and the quarrels of the crossbows were flying so thick and they were hurling so many stones down on them from the walls, that it seemed as if they would be buried under them, so many were thrown. And those below had shields and targes with which they covered those who were picking at the postern. And the others hurled down on them pots full of boiling pitch and Greek fire and immense stones, so that it was a miracle of God they were not all crushed. And my lord Pierre of Amiens and his people endured there labors and difficulties more than a great deal. So they picked away at this postern with axes and with good swords, with pieces of wood, with bars and with picks, until they made a great hole in it. . . .

When those who were defending the towers and the walls saw that the French were entered into the city and their emperor had fled away, they did not dare remain there but fled away each one as best he could. Thus was the city taken. When the city was taken in this way and the French were inside, they stayed right where they were. Then the high barons assembled and took counsel among them as to what they should do. And finally it was cried through the host that no one should dare to go on into the city, for it was a great peril to go there, lest they should cast stones on them from the palaces, which were very large and high, or lest they should slay them in the streets, which were so narrow that they would not be able to defend themselves, or lest the city should be set on fire behind them and they be burned. Because of these dangers and perils, they did not dare seek quarters or disperse, but remained there right where they were. . . .

When morning came on the morrow, what do they do, the priests and clergy in their vestments, the English, Danes, and people of other countries, but come in procession to the camp of the French and cry them mercy and tell them all that the Greeks had done, and they said that all the Greeks had fled and no one was left in the city but the poor people. When the French heard this, they were mightily glad. Then they had it cried through the host that no one should take possession of a house until it had been decided how they should be divided. Then the high men, the rich men, came together and agreed among themselves to take the best houses of the city, without the common people or the poor knights of the host knowing anything about it. And from that time on they began to betray the common people and to keep bad faith and bad comradeship with them. . . .

So they sent to seize all the best houses and the richest of the city, and they had them all taken before the poor knights and the common people of the host were aware of it. And when the poor people were aware of it, they went each one as best he could and took what they could get. . . .

When the city was captured and the pilgrims were quartered, . . . and the palaces were taken over, then they found in the palaces riches more than a great deal. And the palace of Boukoleon was very rich and was made in such a way as I shall tell you. Within this palace, . . . there were fully five hundred halls, all connected with one another and all made with gold mosaic.[1] And in it there were fully thirty chapels, great and small, and there was one

---

[1]In these terms Robert attempts to describe the great complex of buildings lying between the Hippodrome and the sea walls, which was known as the Great Palace. . . .

of them which was called the Holy Chapel. . . .[2] Within this chapel were found many rich relics. One found there two pieces of the True Cross as large as the leg of a man and as long as half a *toise,* and one found there also the iron of the lance with which Our Lord had His side pierced and two of the nails which were driven through His hands and feet, and one found there in a crystal phial quite a little of His blood, and one found there the tunic which He wore and which was taken from Him when they led Him to the Mount of Calvary, and one found there the blessed crown with which He was crowned, which was made of reeds with thorns as sharp as the points of daggers. And one found there a part of the robe of Our Lady and the head of my lord St. John the Baptist and so many other rich relics that I could not recount them to you or tell you all the truth. . . .

Now I will tell you about the church of Saint Sophia, how it was made. Saint Sophia in Greek means Sainte Trinité ["Holy Trinity"] in French [*sic*.] The church of Saint Sophia was entirely round, and within the church there were domes, round all about, which were borne by great and very rich columns, and there was no column which was not of jasper or porphyry or some other precious stone, nor was there one of these columns that did not work cures. There was one that cured sickness of the reins when it was rubbed against, and another that cured sickness of the side, and others that cured other ills. . . . On the ring of the great door of the church, which was all of silver, there hung a tube, of what material no one knew; it was the size of a pipe such as shepherds play on. This tube had such virtue as I shall tell you. When an infirm man who had some sickness in his body like the bloat, so that he was bloated in his belly, put it in his mouth, however little he put it in, when this tube took hold it sucked out all the sickness and it made the poison run out of his mouth and it held him so fast that it made his eyes roll and turn in his head, and he could not get away until the tube had sucked all of this sickness out of him. And the sicker a man was the longer it held him, and if a man who was not sick put it in his mouth, it would not hold him at all, much or little. . . .

And among the rest, there was another of the churches which they called My Lady Saint Mary of Blachernae, where was kept the *sydoine* in which Our Lord had been wrapped, which stood up straight every Friday so that the features of Our Lord could be plainly seen there.[3] And no one, either Greek or French, ever knew what became of this *sydoine* after the city was taken. . . .

Afterwards it came about that all the counts and all the high men came together one day at the palace of Boukoleon, which belonged to the marquis, and they said to one another that they ought to decide on an emperor and ought to choose their ten electors, and they told the doge of Venice to choose his ten. When the marquis heard this, he wanted to put in his own men and those who he thought would choose him as emperor, and he wanted to be emperor forthwith. . . . This discord lasted a good fortnight without their ever being able to agree. And there was no day on which they did not assemble for this affair, until at length they agreed that the clergy of the host, the bishops and abbots who were there, should be the electors. . . .

When the mass was chanted, the electors assembled and took counsel together, and they talked of one and of another, until the Venetians and the bishops and abbots, all twenty electors, agreed all together that it should be the count of Flanders, nor was there one of them who was against it. . . .

[2]This is the celebrated church of the Blessed Virgin of the Pharos (lighthouse). . . .
[3]Robert seems to have confused the *sudarium* (the sweat cloth or napkin, the True Image of St. Veronica) with the *sindon* (the grave cloth in which the body of Jesus was wrapped for entombment). Both relics were in the church of the Blessed Virgin in the Great Palace, and not in the church in the palace of Blachernae, as Robert says.

Scholasticism, Spirituality, and Mysticism

A great deal of reading and copying went on in medieval monasteries and nunneries, as did occasional writing of letters and longer original works. Monks and nuns not only read godly works themselves but at mealtimes a reader would often read to them, usually from Scripture, commentary, or saints' lives. Improving literacy among the clergy and encouraging the copying of religious books had been a main aim of the Carolingian Renaissance, but in the later ninth century a second wave of Dark Ages swept over Europe with the invasions of Norsemen and Magyars, among others, causing the erosion of what modest central government Charlemagne and his family had established on the continent. Sometime after 1050, however, new stirrings of revived learning led to the Renaissance of the Twelfth Century.

In the twelfth century, some clerics pursued their studies beyond the Scriptures and works of the Church Fathers into writings from pagan antiquity in search of better sources of philosophy. Philosophy included all subjects not medical, legal, nor strictly theological, but its devotees often focused particularly on questions of being and reality. Two schools of medieval philosophy picked up this part of philosophy where the ancients had left off: The Realists, following Socrates and Plato, taught that reality existed only in the eternal essences or ideal forms of things, but not in actual, observable things in this world, while the Nominalists, following the Sophists and some ambiguous statements of Aristotle, taught that general ideas reflect only the names of things that are agreed upon by human convention, with basic reality residing in the things named. In the early twelfth century, Pierre (Peter) Abelard rose to youthful distinction by reconciling the two positions to his own satisfaction and that of his students. In modern times, to be sure, Abelard is less known for his philosophical achievements than for his calamitous personal history, which, apart from its enduring romantic content, highlights some of the mindsets of the twelfth century concerning fame, academics, and the clergy.

Most nonacademic clergymen of the twelfth century harbored at least a mild dislike for Realism, Nominalism, *or* Abelard's new Conceptualism, preferring good old Revelation and traditional teaching as the source of knowledge. Mysticism, in the sense of a person's longing for nearness to God through pious living, prayer, and revelations flourished right along with the study of critical philosophies revived from the Greek and Roman worlds. In the twelfth century, the mystics' search for God included more of an attempt to understand the total unity of creation than was later typical of Western European mysticism, with all parts of creation fitted together through explanations of visions and the words of heavenly voices. In writing vivid, easily communicated visions, in which all parts of the universe fall into their sanctioned places, St. Hildegard of Bingen knows no equal. A younger contemporary of Abelard, she actually shared his underlying (Dualistic) conviction that the spirit is good and the flesh is evil, but she was content to relate to the struggle between the two forces as a recorder and interpreter of revelations—rather than participate in the struggle as he had—and certainly came away from it much better off than he did.

The Church's acquisition of early wealth and power produced a variety of reactions among faithful medieval Christians. Some groups voiced open criticism of Church worldliness and demanded that churchmen return to the simple lifestyle of the Apostles, but overt condemnation of Church practices was likely to lead to charges of heresy and an untimely end for the critics. In the early thirteenth century, the Franciscan Order offered a living model of Apostolic poverty without attacking Church leaders for their non-Apostolic riches and political influence. St. Francis of Assisi personified personal sacrifices and total commitment to spiritual endeavors; however, he did not advocate rejection of the world by seclusion from it, as was the practice of the more austere religious orders. Instead, he and his followers went boldly and joyfully into the world with the Gospel message. The Franciscans flourished in Europe and soon sent many of the more successful missionaries abroad.

Although the Renaissance of the Twelfth Century furthered a great revival of interest in the ancient Greek and Roman classics, Church leaders in the West occasionally expressed reservations about this enthusiastic propagation of secular learning. They were all the more concerned because many Greek philosophical and scientific works had reached Europe through the new universities in Arab works on alchemy, astronomy, mathematics, and medicine. The most comprehensive commentary on Aristotle before 1200 was that of the Spanish Muslim Averroes.

The reservations of Church authorities concerning pagan or Muslim learning influenced Scholasticism toward attempts to harmonize useful pagan learning with Christian teachings. During the earlier Carolingian Renaissance, teachers of the liberal arts had been called "scholastics," or "school-men"; as a loose and general term, the earlier Scholasticism had signified the teaching of theology and philosophy, particularly at points where the two overlapped. During the thirteenth century, however, Scholasticism became the systematic defense of approved dogma with a combination of secular philosophy and scriptural authority.

The censoring aspect of Scholasticism had stifled some of the open inquisitiveness of the Renaissance of the Twelfth Century. Soon, however, the great Italian Renaissance would develop a still more independent attitude toward science and philosophy. Meanwhile, the type of mysticism of St. Hildegard's, with its concern for explaining the totality of existence, was giving way to more nearly exclusive searches on the part of mystics for unions of their souls with God. They placed less stress on identifying analogies to relate the workings of nature to the human condition, leaving that sort of study to "natural philosophers." The later mystics conveyed their revelations as more personal, less easily describable experiences than was true of their predecessors. Paradoxically, however, the highly individual nature of their experiences sometimes led them to quite radical conclusions about God and the cosmos. In this connection, we encounter the revelation by Julian or Juliana of Norwich that Jesus was essentially a mother.

68

Peter Abelard, *The Story of My Misfortunes*

Peter Abelard (1079–1142), son of a Breton nobleman, felt drawn to philosophy early in life and came to the cathedral school at Paris, where his energy and insights gained him a following among its students. He soon aroused suspicion with a book, *Sic et Non (Yes and No),* featuring statements of the Church Fathers contradicting each other and leaving them unreconciled, remarking in his preface that this was to stimulate students into a search for truth on their own. His own "Conceptualism" opposed the notion of the Realists that only eternal essences, ideas, and ideals have reality but rejected the Nominalist conviction that names of things were mere conventions. He sought to prove that those general concepts we arrive at by extracting the common features from particular phenomena have an existence of their own once they are formulated. Such concepts are necessary for human discourse, and what is necessary has a good claim to being real.

Abelard's life was full of controversy. His questioning of doctrine brought him into conflict with St. Bernard of Clairvaux, a great mystic, ascetic, and church reformer. St. Bernard succeeded in having a Church council condemn some of Abelard's writings, and Abelard set off for Rome to appeal his condemnation but died on the way. The following excerpt from his autobiography has the form of a long letter written to an anonymous friend.

QUESTIONS TO CONSIDER

1. One modern reaction to Abelard's story is: Why in the world did that man become a clergyman, since he obviously did not have the personality for it? What do you think? Would he have been better adjusted in a different medieval occupation, or did he probably sense no other option?
2. Why did Abelard think—or at least say that he thought—that he deserved his severe punishment?

Now there dwelt in that same city of Paris a certain young girl named Heloise, the niece of a canon who was called Fulbert. Her uncle's love for her was equalled only by his desire that she should have the best education which he could possibly procure for her. Of no mean beauty, she stood out above by reason of her abundant knowledge of letters. Now this virtue is rare among women, and for that very reason it doubly graced the maiden, and made her the most worthy of renown in the entire kingdom. It was this young girl whom I, after carefully considering all those qualities which are wont to attract lovers, determined to unite with myself in the bonds of love, and indeed the thing seemed to me very easy to be done. So distinguished was my name, and I possessed such advantages of youth and comeliness, that no matter what woman I might favor with my love, I dreaded rejection of none.

From *The Story of My Misfortunes: The Autobiography of Peter Abelard,* trans. Henry Adams Bellows. Reprinted with the permission of The Free Press, a division of Simon & Schuster.

Thus, utterly aflame with passion for this maiden, I sought to discover means whereby I might have daily and familiar speech with her, thereby the more easily to win her consent. For this purpose I persuaded the girl's uncle to take me into his household in return for the payment of a small sum. My pretext for this was that the care of my own household was a serious handicap to my studies, and likewise burdened me with an expense far greater than I could afford. Now, he was a man keen in avarice, and likewise he was most desirous for his niece that her study of letters should ever go forward, so, for these reasons, I easily won his consent to the fulfillment of my wish, for he was fairly agape for my money, and at the same time believed that his niece would vastly benefit by my teaching. He entrusted her wholly to my guidance, begging me to give her instruction whensoever I might be free from the duties of my school, and to punish her sternly if ever I should find her negligent of her tasks. In all this the man's simplicity was nothing short of astounding to me; I should not have been more smitten with wonder if he had entrusted a tender lamb to the care of a ravenous wolf. What had he done save to give free scope to my desires, and to offer me every opportunity to bend her to my will?

Why should I say more? Under the pretext of study we spent our hours in the happiness of love, and learning held out to us the secret opportunities that our passion craved. Our speech was more of love than of books which lay open before us; our kisses far outnumbered our reasoned words. Our hands sought less the book than each other's bosoms; love drew our eyes together far more than the lesson drew them to the pages of our text.

In measure as this passionate rapture absorbed me more and more, I devoted ever less time to philosophy and to the work of school. My lecturing became utterly careless and lukewarm; I did nothing because of inspiration, but everything merely as a matter of habit. I had become nothing more than a reciter of my former discoveries, and though I still wrote poems, they dealt with love, not with the secrets of philosophy. Of these songs you yourself well know how some have become widely known and have been sung in many lands.

A thing so manifest could deceive only a few, no one, methinks, save him whose shame it chiefly bespoke, the girl's uncle, Fulbert. The truth was often enough hinted to him, and by many persons, but he could not believe it. But no matter how slow a matter may be in disclosing itself, it is sure to come forth at last, nor is it easy to hide from one what is known to all. So, after the lapse of several months, did it happen to us. Oh, how great was the uncle's grief when he learned the truth, and how bitter was the sorrow of the lovers when we were forced to part! Each grieved most, not for himself, but for the other. Each sought to allay, not his own sufferings, but those of the one he loved. Once the first wildness of shame had passed, it left us more shameless than before, and as shame died within us the cause of it seemed to us ever more desirable. And so it chanced with us as, in the stories that the poets tell, it once happened with Mars and Venus when they were caught together.

It was not long after this that Heloise found that she was pregnant, and of this she wrote to me in the utmost exultation, at the same time asking me to consider what had best be done. Accordingly, I stole her secretly away from her uncle's house, sending her without delay to my own country. She remained there with my sister until she gave birth to a son, whom she named Astrolabe. Meanwhile her uncle, after his return, was almost mad with grief, only one who had seen him could rightly guess the burning agony of his sorrow and the bitterness of his shame. What steps to take against me, or what snares to set for me, he did not know. If he should kill me or do me some bodily hurt, he feared greatly lest his dear-loved niece should be made to suffer for it among my kinsfolk.

At length, however, in pity for his boundless grief, and bitterly blaming myself for the suffering which my love had brought upon him through the baseness of the deception I had practiced, I went to him to entreat his forgiveness, promising to make any amends that he himself might decree. I pointed out that what had happened could not seem incredible to any one who had ever felt the power of love, or who remembered how, from the very beginning of the human race, women had cast down even the noblest men to utter ruin. And in order to make amends even beyond his extremest hope, I offered to marry her whom I had seduced, provided only the thing could be kept secret, so that I might suffer no loss of reputation thereby. To this he gladly assented, pledging his own faith and that of his kindred.

Forthwith I repaired to my own country, and brought back thence my mistress, that I might make her my wife. She, however, most violently disapproved of this, and for two chief reasons: the danger thereof, and the disgrace which it would bring upon me. She swore that her uncle would never be appeased by such satisfaction as this, as, indeed, afterwards proved only too true. She asked how she could ever glory in me if she should make me thus inglorious, and should shame herself along with me. What penalties, she said, would the world rightly demand of her if she should rob it of so shining a light! What curses would follow such a loss to the Church, what tears among the philosophers would result from such a marriage! How unfitting, how lamentable it would be for me, whom nature had made for the whole world, to devote myself to such humiliation!

Her final argument was that it would be dangerous for me to take her back to Paris, and that it would be far sweeter for her to be called my mistress than to be known as my wife; nay, too, that this would be more honorable for me as well. In such case, she said, love alone would hold me to her, and the strength of the marriage chain would not constrain us. Even if we should by chance be parted from time to time, the joy of our meetings would be all the sweeter by reason of its rarity. But when she found that she could not convince me or dissuade me from my folly by these and like arguments, and because she could not bear to offend me, with grievous sighs and tears she made an end of her resistance, saying: "Then there is no more left but this, that in our doom the sorrow yet to come shall be no less than the love we two have already known." Nor in this, as now the whole world knows, did she lack the spirit of prophecy.

So, after our little son was born, we left him in my sister's care, and secretly returned to Paris. A few days later, in the early morning, having kept our nocturnal vigil of prayer unknown to all in a certain church, we were united there in the benediction of wedlock, her uncle and a few friends of his and mine being present. We departed forthwith stealthily and by separate ways, nor thereafter did we see each other save rarely and in private, thus striving our utmost to conceal what we had done. But her uncle and those of his household, seeking solace for their disgrace, began to divulge the story of our marriage, and thereby to violate the pledge they had given me on this point. Heloise, on the contrary, denounced her own kin and swore that they were speaking the most absolute lies. Her uncle, aroused to fury thereby, visited her repeatedly with punishments. No sooner had I learned this than I sent her to a convent of nuns at Argenteuil, not far from Paris, where she herself had been brought up and educated as a young girl. I had them make ready for her all garments of a nun, suitable for the life of a convent, excepting only the veil, and these I bade her put on.

When her uncle and his kinsmen heard of this, they were convinced that now I had completely played them false and had rid myself forever of Heloise by forcing her to become a nun. Violently incensed, they laid a plot against me, and one night, while I, all unsuspecting, was asleep in a secret room in my lodgings, they broke in with the help of one of my servants, whom they had bribed. There they had vengeance on me with a most cruel and most shameful punishment, such as astounded the whole world, for they cut off those parts of my body with which I had done that which was the cause of their sorrow. This done, straightaway they fled, but two of them were captured, and suffered the loss of their eyes and their genital organs. One of these two was the aforesaid servant, who, even while he was still in my service, had been led by his avarice to betray me.

69

St. Hildegard of Bingen, *Know the Ways*

As was true of their male contemporaries, women served in the formative years of the Christian church as deaconesses or later helped to convert relatives or barbarian peoples. A few, such as St. Teresa of Avila and St. Catherine of Siena, became famous for their teaching roles and were sometimes even called "Doctors," but for the most part female mystics remained relatively unknown, although their writings would be gathered and recopied over the centuries. It is only in the twentieth century that their important contributions are being recognized.

A notable exception to the general rule that female mystics received little attention was St. Hildegard (1098–1179), mother superior of a community of Benedictine nuns at Rupertsburg near Bingen on the Rhine. Over a period of many years, she spoke and wrote of experiencing large-scale, highly detailed visions with figures or voices explaining the significance of their related parts. She also wrote on medical subjects and the world of nature; occasionally she brought her natural-scientific observations to bear on the interpretation of her visions. In 1150, she finished recording her visions of the preceding nine years in a book, *Scivias (Sci Vias* means Know the Ways), which enhanced her contemporary recognition. As long as she lived after that, people from all walks of life sought her out for advice and help with prophecy, which she freely gave.

QUESTIONS TO CONSIDER

1. How does St. Hildegard relate body and soul to each other?
2. What are the main attributes of Holy Mother Church, as she appears in a vision?
3. Why does Hildegard refer to secular authority, even in its royal ruling form, as "inferior"?

Body and Soul

The body is a tent and the resting place of all spiritual powers, for the soul, who lives outside the body, works with it—and it with her—for both good and evil. . . . The soul is the lady in charge, the flesh truly is her serving-maid. In what way? The soul rules the body in giving life to it; the body submits to the soul's governance for living, since the body dis-

From *Scivias* in *S. Hildegardis Abbatissae Opera Omnia, Patrologia,* Vol. CXCVII (Paris: J.P. Migne, 1853), columns 427–28, 453–57, 625–33, *passim,* trans. Henry A. Myers.

solves when the soul no longer sustains life in it. When a person does an evil deed with the soul conscious of it, it is as bitter for the soul as if the body knowingly took some poison, but then the soul rejoices at a good deed in the way that the body finds delight in a tasty dish.

The soul flows through the body as sap through a tree. What is that? The sap enables the tree to send forth green leaves, to blossom and to bear fruit. But what makes the fruit of the tree ripen? The weather gives it sunny days with their warmth and rainy ones with water, and so it ripens under the influence of the weather. What does that mean? That, like the sun, the merciful grace of God gives light to man, the breath of the Holy Spirit, like the rain, gives him the water of encouragement and, like the weather elements in turn, they bring good fruit in him to full development.

The soul is thus for the body what the sap is for the tree, applying its powers to the tree as it grows into its ordained form. How so? Gathering knowledge is like unto the greening of the tree's twigs and leaves, directing the will is like unto its blossoming, while feelings resemble the fruit in its early stages and reason the fully developed fruit. Finally, the development of understanding is like unto the spreading growth of the tree to its full dimensions.

And so in this way the soul strengthens and sustains the body. Therefore, o man, recognize what you are in your soul, you who reject the good of knowledge as if wanting to put yourself on the same level as cattle!

Holy Mother Church

After this I saw a female image, so huge that it was like looking at a large city. She wore a wonderfully decorated crown on her head. Bright rays of light, beaming from Heaven to earth, fell from her arms like flowing sleeves. Her lower abdomen resembled a net, full of open spaces through which a great throng of humanity entered. . . . And this image spread her radiance out like a garment and spoke: "I must conceive and bear!"

Then I saw black children swimming through the air, close to the ground, like fish in water. Through the openings they entered the womb of the great figure. She then took a deep breath, drawing them up to her head, from whence they came out of her mouth. She herself was not hurt by all this.

And behold: there appeared a bright light and within it a human figure, surrounded by a fiery red glow. This apparition pulled the black skin off every child and threw it aside, clothed every single one of them with a garment of blinding white and caused a bright light to beam upon them all. "Take off," she said to each of them, "your old clothing of unrighteousness and put on the new garment of holiness, for the gates to your inheritance have been opened. . . ."

And again, I heard the voice from Heaven, saying to me: "The edifice of living souls is built in Heaven to its perfection. It receives the virtues of its sons, which become its building stones of priceless gems, like a huge city absorbs throngs of people and a wide net pulls up great numbers of fish together. . . . The woman you see, so tall that she resembles a large city when you look at her, is my Son's bride, who keeps on giving him new children, those born again from the spirit and the water. The most stout-hearted warrior of all has chosen her to gather in the great throng of His chosen ones . . . and make them perfect. No attacking enemy can storm her towers, for she hurls unbelief into flight, and through the faith of believers she continues to grow. . . .

Her head is crowned with wonderful adornments. When the Church first came into being, awakened in the blood of the Lamb, the apostles and martyrs fittingly crowned her the true bride wed to my Son with their deeds. From the blood of His wounds she went through faith into the world, where she builds her own structure with hallowed souls. For this reason, bright rays of light descend from her arms like flowing sleeves. This signifies the working of divine power in the priests, who present the holiest of sacrifices at the consecrated altar in the mystery of the flesh and blood of their Redeemer. . . .

Like a net, the lower abdomen of the woman is open in many places through which a great crowd of people enter: this is her maternal love, opening for a catch of believing souls. . . . You see black children swimming through the air close to the ground, like fish in water. Through the openings they enter the figure's womb. . . . Their blackness signifies the foolishness of people who are not yet washed in the bath of redemption. Although they love earthly things, run about in the world and set up their dwellings in it, they have finally succeeded in reaching the mother of holiness. . . .

It is for this reason that the figure takes a deep breath, drawing them up inside her head, where they come out through her mouth. The process does not hurt her in the least. As often as a baptism is carried out . . . the Holy Mother [Church] takes a deep breath—her breath is the Holy Spirit—so that the human being is drawn up to the highest bestower of blessedness, the Head of all, and becomes a member of Christ[1] when he is born again, this time to salvation, calling upon the Holy Trinity through the mouth of the Holy Mother. . . .

The human figure shimmering in the fiery red glow . . . pulls the black skin off each individual child and casts it aside, then clothes all of them in garments of blinding white and reveals a brightly shining light to them with words of salvation bringing admonition. The divine power, which looks into the hearts of men, mercifully takes away all sinful unbelief with the bath of baptism, for in Christ there is no death but rather life through the righteous acknowledgment of Him and the washing away of sins.

The Walls of Authority

And then I was looking from inside the great building between the north and west corners out at the surrounding walls. The inner wall was one of arches filled with lattice work, but filled in solidity and not with any empty space in the usual fashion of lattice work. . . . Out from this inner wall, I saw two lesser walls running parallel to it from the north corner to the west corner. . . . On both ends they turned towards the inner wall, joining at the top in the way that plates on a turtle's shell come together. Both of these walls were a yard and a half high. Half a yard's distance separated the middle wall from the inner one with only the width of a child's palm between it and the outer one. . . .

While I was attentively observing, He who was sitting on the throne spoke to me again: "Let no believer who wants to serve God humbly withhold in doubt his submission to earthly authority. For the Holy Spirit has established government over the people, to further the people's wellbeing. . . .

"These two outer walls, each a yard and a half high, signify that, following the division into two estates on earth—those situated high and those low[2]—three groups make up

---

[1]Her meaning here is not exactly "church member" as we would understand it. She is using the organic analogy of Christian tradition in which the Church is a living body with believing Christians functioning as its members in the sense of arms, legs, and the like, and with Christ functioning as the body's head.

[2]For Hildegard, the difference in authority that really counts is between the spiritual authority of clergymen, making up the first order or estate, and the rest of mankind, making up the second order of laymen. In stressing this, she plays down the importance of divisions among laymen, paying no attention to the distinction between serfs and free townspeople nor to the distinction between townspeople and the nobility; the categories of free townspeople and serfs thus appear as subdivisions of the second state.

the second estate: those leaders with exalted ruling powers, those who are free and not bound in [manorial] service, and those who are obedient to lords to whom they owe [manorial] services. And so the reason that there is a distance of half a yard from the middle wall to the inner one of arches is that this signifies the distance in dignity between those who rank higher because of their spiritual office and those who are assigned lesser titles because their occupations are earthly ones. They enjoy one faith together, but the differentiation still exists according to God's will until the final gathering together of His subjects. But between the outer and middle wall the space is only the width of a child's palm, because between the power of secular rulership, with its inferior ranking, and those who are bound to serve their higher-ups the distance—justly considered—is very limited, so that with the single-minded, simple devotion of innocent children they can touch each other and carry out the chores hand in hand.

70

St. Francis of Assisi, "The Rule of St. Francis"

Francis of Assisi (1182–1226), founder of the Franciscan Order, is one of the most celebrated saints of medieval Europe. As the son of a prosperous merchant, young Francis enjoyed a carefree life of pleasure and paid little attention to religion. But in 1206, he underwent a conversion experience and committed the rest of his life to ministering to the poorest of the poor living in the burgeoning cities of his native Italy. In imitation of the first apostles, Francis accepted a life of absolute poverty. He gave away all of his property and made his way by begging. Francis was an open, joyful man who loved animals and loved to laugh. Despite the hardships of his ministry, he naturally drew people to him. Francis was loath to establish detailed regulations for his followers, but by 1210, so many people had joined in his work that he was compelled to organize a rule for his followers. To underscore the virtue of humility, Francis called his followers the Order of Friars Minor. Unlike monks, who retreated from the world to live in monasteries, his "little brothers" or friars were to live among the people.

The Franciscan Friars, and the women's order of the Poor Clare nuns that he inspired, were to own nothing. Like Francis, they were to earn their way by manual labor or by begging. The focus of their ministry was the poor of the inner cities. Soon the Franciscans had established hospitals for lepers, orphanages for abandoned children, and shelters for the homeless. By 1217, Franciscan missionaries had been sent to France, Germany, Hungary, Spain, and North Africa and would soon be in China and Japan (see Reading 93). By the end of the thirteenth century, fourteen hundred Franciscan convents and friaries had been established. Because of the tremendous growth of the Franciscan movement, Francis was forced to revise his rule of 1210, and in 1223, three years before his death, he produced a more detailed rule to guide his Franciscans.

QUESTIONS TO CONSIDER

1. Why would the Rule of St. Francis be so attractive to thousands of men and women throughout medieval Europe?
2. Why did Francis exempt his followers from certain periods of fasting and permit them to "eat whatever food is set before them"?
3. What does the success of the Franciscan order suggest about social conditions in thirteenth-century Europe?
4. How would you compare the life of a Franciscan with that of a Benedictine (see Reading 44)?
5. Why would the Franciscans excel as foreign missionaries (see Reading 78)?

1. This is the rule and life of the Minor Brothers, namely, to observe the holy gospel of our Lord Jesus Christ by living in obedience, in poverty, and in chastity. Brother Francis promises obedience and reverence to pope Honorius and to his successors who shall be canonically elected, and to the Roman Church. The other brothers are bound to obey brother Francis, and his successors.

2. If any, wishing to adopt this life, come to our brothers [to ask admission], they shall be sent to the provincial ministers, who alone have the right to receive others into the order. The provincial ministers shall carefully examine them in the catholic faith and the sacraments of the church. And if they believe all these and faithfully confess them and promise to observe them to the end of life, and if they have no wives, or if they have wives, and the wives have either already entered a monastery, or have received permission to do so, and they have already taken the vow of chastity with the permission of the bishop of the diocese [in which they live], and their wives are of such an age that no suspicion can rise against them, let the provincial ministers repeat to them the word of the holy gospel, to go and sell all their goods and give to the poor [Matt. 19:21]. But if they are not able to do so, their good will is sufficient for them. And the brothers and provincial ministers shall not be solicitous about the temporal possessions of those who wish to enter the order; but let them do with their possessions whatever the Lord may put into their minds to do. Nevertheless, if they ask the advice of the brothers, the provincial ministers may send them to God-fearing men, at whose advice they may give their possessions to the poor. Then the ministers shall give them the dress of a novice, namely: two robes without a hood, a girdle, trousers, a hood with a cape reaching to the girdle. But the ministers may add to these if they think it necessary. After the year of probation is ended they shall be received into obedience [that is, into the order], by promising to observe this rule and life forever. And according to the command of the pope they shall never be permitted to leave the order and give up this life and form of religion. For according to the holy gospel no one who puts his hand to the plough and looks back is fit for the kingdom of God [Luke 9:62]. And after they have promised obedience, those who wish may have one robe with a hood and one without a hood. Those who must may wear shoes, and all the brothers shall wear common clothes, and they shall have God's blessing if they patch them with coarse cloth and pieces of other kinds of cloth. But I warn and exhort them not to despise nor judge other men who wear fine and gay clothing, and have delicious foods and drinks. But rather let each one judge and despise himself.

From Oliver J. Thatcher and Edgar J. McNeal, eds., *A Source Book for Medieval History: Selected Documents* (New York: Charles Scribner's Sons, 1905), pp. 499–504.

3. The clerical brothers shall perform the divine office according to the rite of the holy Roman church, except the psalter, from which they may have breviaries. The lay brothers shall say 24 Paternosters at matins, 5 at lauds, 7 each at primes, terces, sexts, and nones, 12 at vespers, 7 at completorium, and prayers for the dead. And they shall fast for All Saints' day [November 1] to Christmas. They may observe or not, as they choose, the holy Lent which begins at epiphany [January 6] and lasts for 40 days, and which our Lord consecrated by his holy fasts. Those who keep it shall be blessed of the Lord, but those who do not wish to keep it are not bound to do so. But they shall all observe the other Lent [that is, from Ash-Wednesday to Easter]. The rest of the time the brothers are bound to fast only on Fridays. But in times of manifest necessity they shall not fast. But I counsel, warn, and exhort my brothers in the Lord Jesus Christ that when they go out into the world they shall not be quarrelsome or contentious, nor judge others. But they shall be gentle, peaceable, and kind, mild and humble, and virtuous in speech, as is becoming to all. They shall not ride on horseback unless compelled by manifest necessity or infirmity to do so. When they enter a house they shall say, "Peace be to this house." According to the holy gospel, they may eat of whatever food is set before them.

4. I strictly forbid all the brothers to accept money or property either in person or through another. Nevertheless, for the needs of the sick, and for clothing the other brothers, the ministers and guardians may, as they see that necessity requires, provide through spiritual friends, according to the locality, season, and the degree of cold which may be expected in the region where they live. But, as has been said, they shall never receive money or property.

5. Those brothers to whom the Lord has given the ability to work shall work faithfully and devotedly, so that idleness, which is the enemy of the soul, may be excluded and not extinguish the spirit of prayer and devotion to which all temporal things should be subservient. As the price of their labors they may receive things that are necessary for themselves and the brothers, but not money or property. And they shall humbly receive what is given them, as is becoming to the servants of God and to those who practise the most holy poverty.

6. The brothers shall have nothing of their own, neither house, nor land, nor anything, but as pilgrims and strangers in this world, serving the Lord in poverty and humility, let them confidently go asking alms. Nor let them be ashamed of this, for the Lord made himself poor for us in this world. This is that highest pitch of poverty which has made you, my dearest brothers, heirs and kings of the kingdom of heaven, which has made you poor in goods, and exalted you in virtues. Let this be your portion, which leads into the land of the living. Cling wholly to this, my most beloved brothers, and you shall wish to have in this world nothing else than the name of the Lord Jesus Christ. And wherever they are, if they find brothers, let them show themselves to be of the same household, and each one may securely make known to the other his need. For if a mother loves and nourishes her child, how much more diligently should one nourish and love one's spiritual brother? And if any of them fall ill, the other brothers should serve them as they would wish to be served.

7. If any brother is tempted by the devil and commits a mortal sin, he should go as quickly as possible to the provincial minister, as the brothers have determined that recourse shall be had to the provincial ministers for such sins. If the provincial minister is a priest, he shall mercifully prescribe the penance for him. If he is not a priest, he shall, as may seem best to him, have some priest of the order prescribe the penance. And they shall guard against being angry or irritated about it, because anger and irritation hinder love in themselves and in others.

8. All the brothers must have one of their number as their general minister and ser-

vant of the whole brotherhood, and they must obey him. At his death the provincial ministers and guardians shall elect his successor at the chapter held at Pentecost, at which time all the provincial ministers must always come together at whatever place the general minister may order. And this chapter must be held once every three years, or more or less frequently, as the general minister may think best. And if at any time it shall be clear to the provincial ministers and guardians that the general minister is not able to perform the duties of his office and does not serve the best interests of the brothers, the aforesaid brothers, to whom the right of election is given, must, in the name of the Lord, elect another as general minister. After the chapter at Pentecost, the provincial ministers and guardians may, each in his own province, if it seems best to them, once in the same year, convoke the brothers to a provincial chapter.

9. If a bishop forbids the brothers to preach in his diocese, they shall obey him. And no brother shall preach to the people unless the general minister of the brotherhood has examined and approved him and given him the right to preach. I also warn the brothers that in their sermons their words shall be chaste and well chosen for the profit and edification of the people. They shall speak to them of vices and virtues, punishment and glory, with brevity of speech, because the Lord made the word shortened over the earth [Rom. 9:28].

10. The ministers and servants shall visit and admonish their brothers and humbly and lovingly correct them. They shall not put any command upon them that would be against their soul and this rule. And the brothers who are subject must remember that for God's sake they have given up their own wills. Wherefore I command them to obey their ministers in all the things which they have promised the Lord to observe and which shall not be contrary to their souls and this rule. And whenever brothers know and recognize that they cannot observe this rule, let them go to their ministers, and the ministers shall lovingly and kindly receive them and treat them in such a way that the brothers may speak to them freely and treat them as lords speak to, and treat, their servants. For the ministers ought to be the servants of all the brothers. I warn and exhort the brothers in the Lord Jesus Christ to guard against all arrogance, pride, envy, avarice, care, and solicitude for this world, detraction, and murmuring. And those who cannot read need not be anxious to learn. But above all things let them desire to have the spirit of the Lord and his holy works, to pray always to God with a pure heart, and to have humility, and patience in persecution and in infirmity, and to love those who persecute us and reproach us and blame us. For the Lord says, "Love your enemies, and pray for those who persecute and speak evil of you" [cf. Matt. 5:44]. "Blessed are they who suffer persecution for righteousness' sake, for theirs is the kingdom of heaven" [Matt. 5:10]. He that endureth to the end shall be saved [Matt. 10:22].

11. I strictly forbid all the brothers to have any association or conversation with women that may cause suspicion. And let them not enter nunneries, except those which the pope has given them special permission to enter. Let them not be intimate friends of men or women, lest on this account scandal arise among the brothers or about brothers.

12. If any of the brothers shall be divinely inspired to go among Saracens and other infidels they must get the permission to go from their provincial minister, who shall give his consent only to those who he sees are suitable to be sent. In addition, I command the ministers to ask the pope to assign them a cardinal of the holy Roman church, who shall be the guide, protector, and corrector of the brotherhood, in order that, being always in subjection and at the feet of the holy church, and steadfast in the catholic faith, they may observe poverty, humility, and the holy gospel of our Lord Jesus Christ, as we have firmly promised to do. Let no man dare act contrary to this confirmation. If anyone should, and so on.

71

St. Thomas Aquinas, "The Existence of God"

St. Thomas Aquinas (ca. 1225–1274), a Dominican monk, was easily the greatest of the Scholastic writers. His *Summa Theologica* uses human reason and ancient philosophy, particularly that of Aristotle, to confirm revealed religious propositions, especially those found in the letters of St. Paul. In Thomas's work, like that of many other Scholastics, Aristotle is simply called the "Philosopher" and St. Paul the "Apostle."

In the following selection from the *Treatise on God,* part of the *Summa Theologica,* St. Thomas employs the dialectic, the ancient Greek form of argumentation so effectively used by Plato in his dialogues (see Reading 30). By the thirteenth century, the dialectic no longer had separate speakers designated in it. It had come to mean presenting a bit of theory as a question; examining all the arguments for it, if it was a false proposition, or against it, if it was a true one; and finally, answering these wrong arguments with reason and evidence.

QUESTIONS TO CONSIDER

1. Why does St. Thomas find it useful to dispute the proposition that the existence of God is self-evident?
2. What does motion have to do with St. Thomas's proof of the existence of God?
3. How do we know, according to St. Thomas, that one can *demonstrate* (as opposed to *believe*) that God exists?
4. The "efficient cause" for Aristotle involved the maker of a thing, such as the sculptor of a statue, who *causes* the object to be his or her handiwork. How does St. Thomas introduce the idea of "efficient cause" among his proofs for the existence of God?
5. What are the similarities and differences between the ways St. Thomas and Plato (see Reading 30) use the dialectic? Which approach seems more effective?

Is the Existence of God Self-Evident?

Objection 1. It seems so; for those things are said to be "self-evident to us" the knowledge of which exists naturally in us, as is clear in the case of first principles. But as Damascene says in the beginning of his book, "the knowledge of God's existence is naturally implanted in all." Therefore the existence of God *is* self-evident.

Objection 2. Moreover, those things are said to be "self-evident" which are known as soon as the terms are grasped; this, the Philosopher says in Book I of the *Posterior Analytics,* is true of the first principles of demonstration. Thus, when the nature of a whole and of

From St. Thomas Aquinas, *Treatise on God,* texts selected and translated by James F. Anderson (Englewood Cliffs, NJ: Prentice Hall, 1963), pp. 6–12. Reprinted by permission of Prentice Hall. Footnotes omitted.

a part is known, it is at once recognized that every whole is greater than its part. But as soon as the meaning of the word *God* is understood, it is at once seen that God exists. For by this term is signified a reality than which nothing greater can be signified. But that which exists both actually and mentally is greater than that which exists only mentally. Hence, since as soon as the name "God" is understood He exists mentally, it also follows that He exists actually. Therefore the existence of God *is* self-evident.

Objection 3. Then, too, the existence of truth is self-evident. For he who denies the existence of truth, concedes its existence. For if truth does not exist, then the proposition "Truth does not exist" is true; and if there is anything true, there must be truth. But God is truth itself: "I am the way, the truth, and the life" (*John 14:6*). Therefore God's existence is self-evident.

On the contrary: No one can think the opposite of what is self-evident, as the Philosopher makes clear in Book IV of the *Metaphysics* and in Book I of the *Posterior Analytics,* in regard to the first principles of demonstration. But the opposite of the proposition "God is" can be thought: "The fool said in his heart, There is no God" (*Psalm 52:1*). Hence God's existence is not self-evident.

I answer that: A thing can be self-evident in two ways: on the one hand, self-evident in itself, though not to us; on the other, self-evident in itself, and to us. A proposition is *self-evident* because the predicate is included in the meaning of the subject: e.g., "Man is an animal"; for *animal* is contained in the concept of *man.* So if the meaning of the predicate and subject be known to all, the proposition will be self-evident to all: as is clear regarding the first principles of demonstrations, whose terms are certain common notions that all are acquainted with, such as being and not-being, whole and part, and the like. But if there are some to whom the meaning of the predicate and subject is unknown, the proposition will be self-evident in itself, but not to those who do not know the meaning of its predicate and subject. And so it happens, as Boethius says in his *De Hebdomadibus,* that there are some conceptions which are common and self-evident only to the learned, as that "incorporeal substances are not in space." Therefore I say that this proposition, "God exists," of itself is self-evident, for the predicate is the same as the subject, because God *is* His own existence, as will be shown presently. But because we do not know the essence of God, the proposition is not self-evident to us, but needs to be demonstrated through things that are more known to us, though less known in their nature, viz., through effects.

Reply Objection 1. To know that God exists in a general and indeterminate way is implanted in us by nature, in that God is indeed man's beatitude. For man naturally desires happiness, and what is naturally desired by man is naturally known by him. This, however, is not to know precisely that *God* exists; just as to know that *someone* is approaching is not the same as to know that *Peter* is approaching, even though it is Peter who is approaching. For there are many who suppose that man's perfect good, which is happiness, consists in riches, and others in pleasures, and others in something else.

Reply Objection 2. It may be that one who hears this name "God" does not understand it to signify something than which nothing greater can be thought; for some have believed God to be a body. But even if it be supposed that everyone understands that by this name *God* is signified something than which nothing greater can be thought, it does not follow that he understands that what the name signifies exists actually, but only that it exists mentally. Nor can it be argued that it actually exists, unless it be admitted that there actually exists something than which nothing greater can be thought. And this is just what is not admitted by those who hold that God does not exist.

Reply Objection 3. The existence of truth-in-general is self-evident, but the existence of a Primal Truth is not self-evident to us.

Can It Be Demonstrated That God Exists?

Objection 1. It seems not; for it is an article of faith that God exists. But what is of faith cannot be demonstrated, because a demonstration produces scientific knowledge, whereas faith is of the unseen, as is clear from the Apostle (*Hebrews 11:1*). So it cannot be demonstrated that God exists.

Objection 2. Moreover, what-a-thing-is, is the middle term of demonstration. But we cannot know what God is, but only what He is not, as Damascene says. Therefore we cannot demonstrate that God exists.

Objection 3. Then too, if the existence of God were demonstrated, this could only be from His effects. But His effects are not proportioned to Him because He is infinite and His effects are finite; and between the finite and infinite there is no proportion. So, since a cause cannot be demonstrated through an effect not proportioned to it, it seems that the existence of God cannot be demonstrated.

On the contrary: The Apostle says: "The invisible things of God are clearly seen, being understood by the things that are made" (*Romans 1:20*). But this would not be unless the existence of God could be demonstrated through the things that are made. For the first thing that must be known of anything is whether it exists.

I answer that: Demonstration is twofold: One type is through the cause, and is called *"propter quid";* and this is through what is prior simply. The other is through the effect, and is called a demonstration *"quia";* this is through what is prior relatively to us. When an effect is more manifest to us than its cause, from the effect we proceed to the knowledge of the cause. And from every effect the existence of its proper cause can be demonstrated, so long as its effects are better known to us. For, since every effect depends upon its cause, if the effect exists, the cause must pre-exist. Hence the existence of God, being not self-evident to us, can be demonstrated through effects which are known to us.

Reply Objection 1. The existence of God and other similar truths about God, which, as is said (*Romans 1:19*), can be known by natural reason, are not articles of faith, but are preambles to the articles. For faith presupposes natural knowledge, just as grace presupposes nature, and perfection the perfectible. But there is nothing to prevent a man, who does not grasp the demonstration, from accepting as a matter of faith something which in itself is capable of being demonstrated and scientifically known.

Reply Objection 2. When the existence of a cause is demonstrated from an effect, the latter must take the place of the definition of the cause in proving the cause's existence; and this is pre-eminently the case in regard to God. For in order to prove the existence of anything, it is necessary to accept as middle term the meaning of the name, and not what the thing is, because the question of *what* it is follows on the question of *whether* it is. Now the names given to God are derived from His effects, as will be later shown. Hence, in demonstrating the existence of God from His effects, we can take for the middle term the meaning of the name *God.*

Reply Objection 3. From effects not proportioned to the cause no perfect knowledge of that cause can be obtained. Yet, as we have said, from any effect manifest to us the existence of the cause can be demonstrated. And so we can demonstrate the existence of God from His effects; though from them we cannot know Him perfectly according to His essence.

Does God Exist?

Objection 1. It seems not; because if one of two contraries be infinite, the other would be wholly eliminated. But the very word *God* implies infinite goodness. So if God existed, there would be no evil discovered. But evil is found in the world. Therefore God does not exist.

Objection 2. Moreover, that which can be brought about through fewer causes has not been produced by many. But it seems that everything we see in the world can be brought about through other causes, supposing God did not exist. For all natural things can be traced to one cause, which is nature; and all voluntary things can be traced to one cause, which is human reason, or will. So there is no need to suppose *God's* existence.

On the contrary: It is said in the person of God: "I am Who am" (*Exodus 3:14*). *I answer that:* The existence of God can be proved in five ways.

The *first* and more manifest *way* is taken from motion. It is certain, and evident to our senses, that in the world some things are in motion. Now, whatever is being moved is being moved by another, for nothing is *moved* except insofar as it is in potency to that toward which it is moved; whereas a thing *moves* insofar as it is in act. For "to move" is nothing else than to reduce something from potency to act. But nothing can be reduced from potency to act except by something existing in act. Thus, that which is actually hot—such as fire—makes wood, which is potentially hot, to be actually hot, and thereby "moves" and alters it. Now it is not possible that the same thing should be at once in act and in potency in the same respect, but only in different respects: what is actually hot cannot simultaneously be potentially hot; rather, it is simultaneously potentially cold. So it is impossible that in the same respect and in the same way a thing should be both *moving* and *moved;* in other words, that it should *move itself.* Therefore, whatever is *being moved* must be moved by another. If that by which it is being moved be itself moved, then this also must be moved by another, and that by another again. But this cannot go on to infinity, because then there would be no *first* mover and, consequently, no other mover. For secondary movers move only because they are themselves moved by the primary one; even as the staff moves only because it is moved by the hand. That is why it is necessary to conclude to a First Mover—which is moved by nothing else whatever. And this all understand as being "God."

The *second way* is from the nature of the efficient cause. Among sensible things in our world we find an order of efficient causes. There is no case of a thing's being the efficient cause of itself; nor is such a thing possible, for then it would be prior to itself; which is impossible. Now in efficient causes it is not possible to proceed to infinity, because in all efficient causes following in order, the first is the cause of the intermediate, and the intermediate is the cause of the ultimate, whether the intermediate be several or only one. Now to remove the cause is to remove the effect. So, if there be no *first* in efficient causes, there will be no last, nor any intermediate, term. But if it is possible to proceed to infinity in efficient causes, there will be no first efficient cause; and so there will be no terminal effect, nor any intermediate efficient causes. But this is patently false. Therefore it is necessary to admit a *first* efficient cause, which all call "God."

The *third way* is taken from the possible and the necessary; and it is this. We find in things some which are possible of being and of not-being, since they are found to be generated, and to be corrupted and, consequently, to be possible of being and of not-being. But it is impossible for all such things always to exist, for that which can not-be at some time is not. So if everything can not-be, then at one time there was nothing. But if this were true, even now there would be nothing, because that which is not does not begin to be except by something which is. So, if at one time nothing existed, it would have been impossible for anything to have begun to exist; and thus even now nothing would be in existence—which is patently false. Therefore, not all beings are possibles, but there must be something whose existence is necessary. But every necessary entity either has its necessity caused by another, or not. Now it is impossible to proceed to infinity in necessary things whose necessity is caused, as has been already proved in regard to efficient causes. It is therefore necessary to admit the existence of a being having its necessity through itself, and not receiving it from another, but rather causing in others their necessity. This all men call "God."

The *fourth way* is taken from the grades [of perfection] found in things. Among beings there are some more and some less good, true, and noble; and so in the case of other perfections of this kind. But "more" and "less" are predicated of diverse things according as they approach in diverse measures something which is the maximum, as a thing is hotter the more it approaches that which is hottest. There is, then, something which is truest and best and noblest and, consequently, something which is maximally a being. For those things that are greatest in truth are greatest in being, as Aristotle says in Book II of the *Metaphysics*. Now that which is predicated maximally in a genus is the cause of all in that genus; e.g., fire, which is maximally hot, is the cause of all hot things, as is said in the same book. Hence there is a reality which is for all things the cause of their being, goodness, and every other perfection; and this we call "God."

The *fifth way* is taken from the governance of things. For we see that certain beings devoid of knowledge, namely, natural bodies, act for an end; and this is evident from their acting always, or almost always, in the same way, in order to obtain the best result. Hence it is clear that they achieve their end, not fortuitously, but purposefully. Now whatever lacks knowledge does not tend toward an end unless it be directed by some being endowed with knowledge and intelligence, even as the arrow is directed by the archer. It follows that some intelligent being exists by whom all natural things are directed to their end. This being we call "God."

Reply Objection 1. As Augustine says in the Enchiridion: "Since God is the highest good, He would not allow any evil to exist in His works, unless His omnipotence and goodness were such as to bring good even out of evil." This, therefore, belongs to the infinite goodness of God: that He permits evil to exist, and out of them draw goods.

Reply Objection 2. Since nature works for a determinate end under the direction of a higher agent, whatever is done by nature must be traced back to God as to its first cause. So too, whatever is done voluntarily must be traced back to a higher cause than human reason and will, since these can change and fail. For all things that are changeable and capable of defect must be traced back to an immutable and self-necessary primal source, as has been shown.

72

Julian(a) of Norwich, *Showings*

Julian (or Juliana) of Norwich (ca. 1334–1416) is more typical of medieval female mystics than is St. Hildegard. We know very little about her life, family, or how she acquired her writing skills. She lived a solitary life in a cell that adjoined the parish church of St. Julian in Conisford at Norwich, opposite the house of the Augustinian Friars.

These two selections are from her writings called the *Showings:* Through sixteen Revelations we come to know her thoughts on sin and redemption. This reconciliation with God through mercy and grace comes in her description from the second person of the Trinity whose dual personality has attracted the attention of modern feminists.

QUESTIONS TO CONSIDER

1. Why was the medieval church suspicious of some mystics?
2. What are the Revelations of Julian?
3. Why is her description of Christ's roles innovative?
4. What are points of comparison and contrast between the writings of Julian and St. Hildegard (see Reading 69)?

But now I should say a little more about this penetration, as I understood our Lord to mean: How we are brought back by the motherhood of mercy and grace into our natural place, in which we were created by the motherhood of love, a mother's love which never leaves us.

Our Mother in nature, our Mother in grace, because he wanted altogether to become our Mother in all things, made the foundation of his work most humbly and most mildly in the maiden's womb. And he revealed that in the first revelation, when he brought that meek maiden before the eye of my understanding in the simple stature which she had when she conceived; that is to say that our great God, the supreme wisdom of all things, arrayed and prepared himself in this humble place, all ready in our poor flesh, himself to do the service and the office of motherhood in everything. The mother's service is nearest, readiest and surest: nearest because it is most natural, readiest because it is most loving, and surest because it is truest. No one ever might or could perform this office fully, except only him. We know that all our mothers bear us for pain and for death. O, what is that? But our true Mother Jesus, he alone bears us for joy and for endless life, blessed may he be. So he carries us within him in love and travail, until the full time when he wanted to suffer the sharpest thorns and cruelest pains that ever were or will be, and at the last he died. And when he had finished, and had borne us so for bliss, still all this could not satisfy his wonderful love. And he revealed this in these great surpassing words of love: If I could suffer more, I would suffer more. He could not die any more, but he did not want to cease working; therefore he must needs nourish us, for the precious love of motherhood had made him our debtor.

The mother can give her child to suck of her milk, but our precious Mother Jesus can feed us with himself, and does, most courteously and most tenderly, with the blessed sacrament, which is the precious food of true life; and with all the sweet sacraments he sustains us most mercifully and graciously, and so he meant in these blessed words, where he said: I am he whom Holy Church preaches and teaches to you. That is to say: All the health and the life of the sacraments, all the power and the grace of my word, all the goodness which is ordained in Holy Church for you, I am he.

God the blessed Trinity, who is everlasting being, just as he is eternal from without beginning, just so was it in his eternal purpose to create human nature, which fair nature was first prepared for his own Son, the second person; and when he wished, by full agreement of the whole Trinity he created us all once. And in our creating he joined and united us to himself, and through this union we are kept as pure and as noble as we were created. By the power of that same precious union we love our Creator and delight in him, praise

From Julian of Norwich, *Showings,* trans. Edmund Colledge, O.S.A., and James Walsh, S.J. (New York: Paulist Press, 1978), pp. 175–77, 295–97. Copyright © 1978 The Missionary Society of St. Paul the Apostle in the State of New York. Reprinted by permission.

him and thank him and endlessly rejoice in him. And this is the work which is constantly performed in every soul which will be saved, and this is the godly will mentioned before.

And so in our making, God almighty is our loving Father, and God all wisdom is our loving Mother, with the love and the goodness of the Holy Spirit, which is all one God, one Lord. And in the joining and the union he is our very true spouse and we his beloved wife and his fair maiden, with which wife he was never displeased; for he says: I love you and you love me, and our love will never divide in two.

I contemplated the work of all the blessed Trinity, in which contemplation I saw and understood these three properties; the property of the fatherhood, and the property of the motherhood, and the property of the lordship in one God. In our almighty Father we have our protection and our bliss, as regards our natural substance, which is ours by our creation from without beginning; and in the second person, in knowledge and wisdom we have our perfection, as regards our sensuality, our restoration and our salvation, for he is our Mother, brother and saviour; and in our good Lord the Holy Spirit we have our reward and our gift for our living and our labour, endlessly surpassing all that we desire in his marvellous courtesy, out of his great plentiful grace. For all our life consists of three: In the first we have our being, and in the second we have our increasing, and in the third we have our fulfillment. The first is nature, the second is mercy, the third is grace.

As to the first, I saw and understood that the high might of the Trinity is our Father, and the deep wisdom of the Trinity is our Mother, and the great love of the Trinity is our Lord; and all these we have in nature and in our substantial creation. And furthermore I saw that the second person, who is our Mother, substantially the same beloved person, has now become our mother sensually, because we are double by God's creating, that is to say substantial and sensual. Our substance is the higher part, which we have in our Father, God almighty; and the second person of the Trinity is our Mother in nature in our substantial creation, in whom we are founded and rooted, and he is our Mother of mercy in taking our sensuality. And so our Mother is working on us in various ways, in whom our parts are kept undivided; for in our Mother Christ we profit and increase, and in mercy he reforms and restores us, and by the power of his Passion, his death and his Resurrection he unites us to our substance. So our Mother works in mercy on all his beloved children who are docile and obedient to him, and grace works with mercy, and especially in two properties, as it was shown, which working belongs to the third person, the Holy Spirit. He works, rewarding and giving. Rewarding is a gift for our confidence which the Lord makes to those who have laboured; and giving is a courteous act which he does freely, by grace, fulfilling and surpassing all that creatures deserve.

Thus in our Father, God almighty, we have our being, and in our Mother of mercy we have our reforming and our restoring, in whom our parts are united and all made perfect man, and through the rewards and the gifts of grace of the Holy Spirit we are fulfilled. And our substance is in our Father, God almighty, and our substance is in our Mother, God all wisdom, and our substance is in our Lord God, the Holy Spirit, all goodness, for our substance is whole in each person of the Trinity, who is one God. And our sensuality is only in the second person, Christ Jesus, in whom is the Father and the Holy Spirit; and in him and by him we are powerfully taken out of hell and out of the wretchedness on earth, and gloriously brought up into heaven, and blessedly united to our substance, increased in riches and nobility by all the power of Christ and by the grace and operation of the Holy Spirit.

Medieval Domestic Life in Western and Eastern Europe

Domestic life in early modern France and Russia centered on relations between husbands and wives, the preparation of food, cleaning of the living quarters, the disciplining of children and servants, and the smooth running of the household. Although separated by two hundred years, the following two accounts provide useful insights into domestic life in fourteenth-century Paris and sixteenth-century Moscow. Both were capital cities with burgeoning populations, replete with muddy, insect-infested streets and foul drinking water that ensured frequent outbreaks of disease, especially cholera and dysentery. Although public-health measures were virtually unknown at the time, both readings emphasize that cleanliness was of high priority. But a smooth-running household involved much more than clean rooms, a well-swept foyer, and a clean-burning, smoke-less chimney fire. Domestic harmony could be achieved only if husbands and especially wives understood their place within the household and discharged their responsibilities properly. In different but revealing ways, each reading tells us much about gender relations and the importance of love, obedience, piety, affection, and discipline in ensuring domestic harmony in early modern France and Russia.

73

The Goodman of Paris

Written late in the fourteenth century by an elderly, anonymous author ("The Goodman of Paris") to his much younger new wife, these instructions center on the importance of a tidy house and good relations between husband and wife. In this communication to her, the Goodman of Paris indicates that he loves his young wife so much that he not only wants her to manage his house efficiently but, after his death, if she should marry again, he wants her to please her new husband by performing properly all of her domestic responsibilities.

QUESTIONS TO CONSIDER

1. What does this reading tell you about the character and quality of domestic life in fourteenth-century Parisian homes?
2. According to the Goodman of Paris, how should a wife keep the love of her husband and of her children? What does the author mean when he urges wives to "bewitch and bewitch again your husband"? Do you agree with his advice?
3. How would the Goodman of Paris react to the *Domostroi*'s advice about the proper method of disciplining wives (see Reading 74)?

Indeed fair sister, certain services make a man love and want to return home to see his good wife, and keep away from others. Therefore I advise you to comfort your husband all the while, persevere and be at peace with him. Remember the rustic proverb that says there are three things that drive a goodman from home: a leaking roof, a smoking chimney, and a scolding woman.

Dear sister I beg you, if you want to keep the love and good will of your husband, be gentle, loving, and sweet. Do for him what the good, simple women of our country say other people have done to their own sons, when these sons give their love elsewhere, and their own mothers cannot win them back. For it is certain that when fathers and mothers are dead and stepfathers and stepmothers scold their stepsons, rebuke them, or pay no attention to where they sleep, what they eat or drink, to their stockings, to their shirts, or other needs, these children will find a good home and counsel with some other woman, one who gives them warm shelter, soup, a bed, keeps them clean, mends their stockings, breeches, shirts, and other clothes. These children follow her, they want to be with her and to sleep and be cradled between her breasts. Soon they will be completely estranged from their step parents who neglected them, but now want them back.

But it is too late, for now these children prefer the company of strangers who care for them, rather than their own relatives who cared so little for them. These step parents lament and cry and say that these women have bewitched their children and have used spells to turn their children against them. But, no matter what they say, this is not witchcraft. For it is done for the sake of the love, the care, the intimacies, the joys and pleasures that these women have shown them in all things and, on my soul, there is no witchcraft. For whoever gives pleasure to a bear, a wolf, or a lion, that same bear, wolf, or lion will follow them. And so the other beasts might say, if they could speak, that those tamed animals must be bewitched. And, by my soul, I believe that this is not witchcraft; it is simply doing good. One does not bewitch a man by doing what pleases him.

Therefore dear sister, I ask that you bewitch and bewitch again your husband. Protect him from a poorly roofed house, a smoky chimney, and do not scold him, but be sweet, gentle, amiable and peaceable. See to it that in winter he has a good, smokeless fire. Be certain that he rests well between your breasts, and bewitch him there!

And in summer ensure that there be no fleas in your room nor in your bed. I have heard you may do this in six ways. Some suggest that if the room be strewn with alder leaves, the fleas will be caught on them. Also I have heard that at night if you set out in your room one or two slices of bread spread with glue or turpentine, along with a lighted candle, the fleas will come stick to the bread. Another way I have tried that works, is to take a rough cloth: spread it about your room and over your bed; then all the fleas that land on it will be caught, and you can whisk them away with the cloth. Also sheepskins or white wool set on the straw or on the bed works well, for when the black fleas land on this white background they can be seen and killed. But the best way is to be mindful that there are fleas in the coverlets, the furs, and the clothing you wear. One way I have tried to get rid of fleas is to take the infested coverlets, furs, or dresses, fold them and shut them tightly up in a chest, that is cinched tightly with straps. Another way is to put all the clothing in an air-tight bag so that the fleas will not have any light or air and will eventually die. Occasionally I have seen rooms full of mosquitoes, which were attracted by the sleeper's breath, so that they sat on their face, stung them so hard, that they were forced to awake, light a fire of hay to make a

From Jérôme Pichon, ed., *Le Ménagier de Paris: Traité de Morale et d'Économie domestique composé vers 1393 par un Bourgeois Parisien.* 2 vols. (Paris: Imprimerie Crapelet, 1847), 1:169–76. Translated by Philip F. Riley.

smoke to drive the mosquitoes away. Certainly this can be done in daytime as well. Also, if you have a mosquito net use it.

If you have a chamber or a passage where there are many flies, take little cuttings of fern and tie them together and hang them up in the evening so that the flies will land on them; then take down the cuttings and throw them out. In the evening close off all your room save a little opening in the wall towards the east. At first light, all the flies will go through this opening; afterwards close the opening.

Take a bowl of milk and a hare's gall;[1] mix them together and then set out two or three bowls in places where the flies light so that all the flies that drink this mixture will die.

Tie a piece of linen to the bottom of a pot with an opening in its neck, and set that pot in the place where the flies gather and smear it within with honey, apples, or pears; when it is full of flies, cover it and shake it.

Take raw red onions, dice them and pour the juice into a bowl and set it where the flies are so that when they drink it they will die. Have fly swatters to kill them by hand. Have little twigs covered with glue in a bowl of water. Shut your windows tightly with oil cloth, parchment or something else, so that no fly can enter, and those that do can be killed with a fly swatter. Soak a string in honey, and after the flies land on it, gather them up each evening in a bag. Remember that flies will not stop in a room where there are no standing tables, dressers or other things they can light on and rest. For if they have nothing but broad, flat surfaces to settle and cling to, they will not settle. Nor will they light in a place that is watered and shut up. Therefore, it seems to me that if the room is well watered, closed and sealed, and if nothing is left on the floor, no fly will settle there.

Protect your husband from all discomforts, give him all the comforts you can think of, serve him and have him well served in your house. You can expect him to take care of matters outside the home, for if he is good, he will do even more than you could wish. Do what I have said and he will treasure you and give his heart to you. He will avoid all other houses, all other women, and all other services and households. None of these will interest him, but follow the example of horsemen who as soon as they return from a journey give their horses fresh bedding up to their bellies. These horses are unharnessed and made comfortable. They are given hay and oats, and they are well cared for in their own stables. If the horses are treated this way, the same should be done for persons, especially the masters when they return home. Upon returning from the woods and from hunting, the master gives his dogs fresh litter and a place before the fire. Their feet are greased with soft cream, they are given treats and are made as comfortable as possible.

Wives should do at least as much for their husbands as men do for their horses, dogs, asses, mules, and other beasts. If this is the case, all other houses, where their husbands have been served, will seem like dark prisons and strange places, when compared to their own home, which will be a restful haven for them. And so, when traveling, husbands will think only of their wives. No burden will be too heavy, for they will think only of their wives, whom they want to see again, just as the poor hermits and penitents wish to see the face of Jesus Christ. If cared for in this way, these husbands will never be content to live elsewhere. For all other places will seem to them to be a bed of stones compared to their home. Never stop loving: do it honestly and with a good heart.

[1]Hare's gall refers to a rabbit's gallbladder.

74

The Domostroi, Rules for Russian Households in the Time of Ivan the Terrible

Although *The Domostroi* (which means "house order") has no clearly identified author, it is most often attributed to a Russian Orthodox priest, Sil'vester, who lived in Moscow in the late sixteenth century. Like *The Goodman of Paris, The Domostroi* is a complete set of domestic instructions on piety, entertaining, needlework, food preparation, the rearing of children, dress for formal occasions, the disciplining of servants, and the proper conduct between husbands and wives.

QUESTIONS TO CONSIDER

1. What does this reading tell you about the character and tone of family life in the households of sixteenth-century Moscow?
2. How does the author of *The Domostroi* suggest a Russian husband love, instruct, and discipline his wife and servants? Is it possible for a husband to bring "understanding with the lash"? Why must a Russian housewife, but not her husband, grieve over their servants' punishments? Would the Goodman of Paris (see Reading 73) agree?

Husbands should instruct their wives lovingly and with due consideration. A wife should ask her husband every day about matters of piety, so she will know how to save her soul, please her husband, and structure her house well. She must obey her husband in everything. Whatever her husband orders, she must accept with love; she must fulfill his every command. Above all, she must fear God and keep her chastity as decreed above.

When she rises from her bed, she should first wash herself, then complete her prayers. Then she should order the daily work for women and maids: telling each which embroidery to work, which food to cook that day, which breads to bake of finely sifted wheat flour. . . .

Wash the table, dishes, jars, spoons, ladles, and goblets. Rinse them off and dry them. Do the same after dinner and in the evening. Wash the pails, trays, kneading troughs, sieves, colanders, clay pots, pitchers, and metal saucepans as well. Rinse them, dry them, and put them in a clean suitable place. Every dish and every utensil should always be clean and accounted for.

Dishes should not be carried about the shop, the courtyard, or the house. Dishes, goblets, ladles, and spoons should not be scattered about the shop. They should be arranged somewhere in a clean place. They should be turned upside down. Any dish that contains food or drink should be covered, even inside the house. Tie the cover down to protect the contents from cockroaches and other unclean things.

Jars, dishes, spoons, goblets, ladles, and all the best dishes—silver, pewter, and

From *The Domostroi: Rules for Russian Households in the Time of Ivan the Terrible,* ed. and trans. Carolyn Johnston Pouncy (Ithaca and London: Cornell University Press, 1994), pp. 124–25, 141–44. Reprinted by permission.

wood—should be kept under lock and key in a safe place. When you have guests or a celebration with respectable people, bring them out to the table. After the feast, look them over, have them washed and counted. Then lock them up again. Treat the everyday dishes as described above.

Inside the house, wash the walls, benches, floors, windows, doors, storerooms, and porches. Rinse them, sweep them, and scrape off the dirt. A house should always be clean; so should the staircases and the entranceway. Everything should be washed, raked out, rinsed, and swept.

Put straw in front of the entranceway for wiping muddy feet, so the staircase will not be muddied. Before the doors of the warehouses and granaries, put a bast mat, an old piece of felt, or a towel for wiping muddy feet so they will not dirty the pavement. In muddy weather change the hay or straw in the entranceway and change the bast mat or the piece of felt at the doors. Either put down a clean mat or rinse the dirty mat and dry it; then it will be ready to put down under people's feet again.

By doing these things, an orderly woman will always have a clean and well-arranged house.

Your servants should always sweep in the courtyard, and in the street before your gates, and should rake when it is muddy. They should shovel snow in the winter as well. They should pile up the kindling, the wood, and the lumber. Then everything will be neat and clean.

In the stables, the bakery and all the workrooms, all should be in order, everything put away in some appropriate place, clean and swept. To enter such order is like entering Paradise.

The wife should supervise all this and should teach her servants and children in goodly and valiant fashion. If someone fails to heed her scoldings, she must strike him. If the husband sees something amiss for which his wife or her servants are responsible, or notices that all is not in accord with what is written in this document, he should reason with his wife and correct her. If she heeds him and does everything according to this book, he should love her and reward her.

But if your wife does not live according to this teaching and instruction, does not do all that is recommended here, if she does not teach her servants, then the husband should punish his wife. Beat her when you are alone together; then forgive her and remonstrate with her. But when you beat her, do not do it in hatred, do not lose control. A husband must never get angry with his wife; a wife must live with her husband in love and purity of heart.

You should discipline servants and children the same way. Punish them according to the extent of their guilt and the severity of their deed. Lay stripes upon them but, when you have punished them, forgive them.

The housewife must grieve over her servants' punishment, insofar as that is reasonable, for that gives the servants hope.

Only if his wife or son or daughter will not pay attention to scoldings, if they show no respect and refuse to do what they were told to do, should a husband or father bring understanding with the lash. But do not beat the culprit before others; punish him alone, then talk to him and grant him forgiveness.

A wife should not get angry at her husband about anything, nor a husband at his wife.

Do not box anyone's ears for any fault. Do not hit them about the eyes or with your fist below the heart. Do not strike anyone with a stick or staff or beat anyone with anything made of iron or wood. From such a beating, administered in passion or anguish, many misfortunes can result: blindness or deafness, dislocation of an arm, leg or finger, head injury, or injury to a tooth. With pregnant women or children, damage to the stomach could result, so beat them only with the lash, in a careful and controlled way, albeit painfully and fearsomely. Do not endanger anyone's health; beat someone only for a grave fault.

When you must whip someone, take off the culprit's shirt. Beat him in a controlled way with the lash, holding him by the hands while you think of his fault. When you have punished him, you must talk with him; there should be no anger between you. Your people should know nothing of it.

There should be no fights among your people that stem from past quarrels or rumors unsupported by direct investigation. Whenever you discover signs of bad feeling or unkind words, question the offender alone, kindly. If he sincerely repents, punish him lightly and forgive him. If the person is innocent, do not connive with the slanderer. To prevent enmity henceforth, punish appropriately and only after personal investigation. If an offender does not repent, punish him severely. Otherwise the guilty remain guilty and only the righteous learn righteousness.

Chinese Culture Under the T'ang and Sung [Song] Dynasties

After nearly four centuries of disruption and disunity following the end of the first great imperial period under the Ch'in [Qin] (221–206 B.C.) and Han (206 B.C.–A.D. 220) dynasties, China, reunified by the short-lived Sui dynasty (589–618), rejuvenated itself and entered into the second great imperial period under the T'ang (618–907) and Sung (960–1279) dynasties. The Han and the T'ang periods are often viewed as the two golden ages of the Chinese empire, but the T'ang exceeded the Han in material splendor, cultural refinement, and international influence. Its empire was vast; its military was powerful and feared; its bureaucracy was elaborate and dependable; its laws were codified; its art and literature, especially its poetry, achieved new heights of sophistication. Changan, its capital, was large and cosmopolitan; it attracted scholars, diplomats, missionaries, and merchants from surrounding lands and as far away as Persia and Arabia. The religious life of this period was rich in diversity. Although Confucianism strengthened its hold on China, Buddhism and Taoism [Daoism] grew to maturity, and several foreign cults such as Zoroastrianism, Manichaeism, Judaism, Islam, and Nestorian Christianity entered China. Also, the Chinese invention of printing greatly stimulated intellectual life. The world's oldest extant printed book, a whole Buddhist *sutra,* printed in 868, can be traced to this period. Thus T'ang China furnished the models of advanced institutions and a way of life for neighboring countries to emulate. The foundation of this brilliant civilization was initially laid by the second ruler and co-founder of this dynasty, EmperorT'ai-tsung [Taizong]. A heroic warrior and an ardent Confucianist, he was firm but willing to be guided by the counsel of his ministers on matters of state (see Reading 76).

The Sung dynasty came into existence in 960 after more than a half century of disruptions and fragmentation of the empire and remained in power until the Mongols overran the whole empire in 1279. By 1127, the Sung had lost the northern half of its empire to the Tungusic tribal people of Manchuria. Although it was militarily feeble, Sung China fostered great social and cultural development and economic prosperity. The advanced state of its material civilization was unmatched by any other civilization. Trade and industry flourished; urbanization spread, and the inventive genius of the Sung craftsmen was unexcelled in the technical perfection of their silk, lacquer, and porcelain. Gunpowder, an earlier Chinese invention, was now employed for the first time in warfare. Socially, the institution of concubinage grew, and the practice of footbinding among the upper-class women can be dated to the Sung period (see Reading 77). To run their large imperial bureaucracy efficiently, the Sung government relied heavily upon the imperial examination system, which had been reinaugurated by the Sui and reinvigorated by the T'ang (see Reading 75). The widespread use of the imperial examination system contributed to a revival of interest in Confucianism (see Reading 24) and the development of a neo-Confucian movement during the Sung period.

75

Imperial Examination System

One of the unique features of the Imperial Government of China was the imperial examination system. Through it, the Chinese government recruited the members of its bureaucracy from the general populace, rather than leaving the imperial administration to the hereditary nobles. This system evolved gradually, starting in the second century B.C. during the Former Han dynasty (206 B.C.–A.D. 8), becoming more elaborate and institutionalized during the early part of the Sung [Song] dynasty (960–1279), and continuing with only slight modifications down to the early years of this century. The last imperial examinations were held in 1905.

Millions of young men in China during the imperial period invested their time, energy, money, and passion in an effort to pass the examination, since this was the road to power and wealth. Aspirants for imperial bureaucratic posts usually spent ten or more years preparing for the examination, primarily by reading, analyzing, and memorizing the voluminous Confucian classics. During the Sung period, prospective candidates for imperial administrative posts were expected to pass three levels of highly competitive examinations—prefectural, metropolitan, and palace—and attain the Presented Scholar (Chin-shih [Jinshi]) degree, which was the most coveted degree, roughly comparable to a Ph.D. in the West. The candidates in the palace examination were ranked in order of their achievements in the examination. The higher the rank the candidates achieved, the better the chances were that they would receive more powerful and prestigious imperial appointments. The candidate for the Chin-shih degree was required to produce, among other things, poems in various styles, a rhyme prose piece, a policy essay, answers to five policy questions, and answers to ten "written elucidation" questions on Confucian classics such as the *Spring and Autumn Annals* and the *Book of Rites.* The following selection is an example of an essay question on policy matters.

QUESTIONS TO CONSIDER

1. What do you think are the merits and demerits of the Chinese Imperial Examination System?
2. How does this system compare with the way the Ottoman Empire recruited Janissaries (see Reading 83)?

It is stated in the Book of Kuan-tzu [Guan Zi][1]: "the method by which a sage rules the world is this: he does not let the four classes of people live together. Therefore, there are no complaints, and things run smoothly. As a result, scholars know how to spend their leisure, laborers abide with the orders of officials, merchants go to the marketplaces and farmers go to the fields. Everyone goes to his appropriate place and lives there satisfactorily. Young children are sent to study; their wills are satisfied and they do not change their minds when they see strange things." The *Kuan-tzu* Book further states: "Children of scholars and farmers must always be scholars and farmers and children of merchants and laborers must also always be merchants and laborers, so that a scholar can give instructions and take care of his proper status, and a farmer can work attentively in cultivating his crops to feed the people. Everyone is satisfied with his occupation and does not seek to change. This is truly good! Otherwise, hundreds of laborers might all go to the marketplaces and ten thousand merchants might all try to work in the same [most profitable] business; they would all become cunning, deceitful, eager to play tricks, and they would also become capricious, greedy and seek only profits."

Now, to fit people in their occupations is not to improve morals. To see something better and change—what harm is there in this? Take the example of Tuan-mu [Duanmu] who became a merchant [after being a disciple of Confucius], Chiao Li [Jiao Li] who became a fisherman [after being an important official] and Wang Meng who went to sell dustbaskets [after being a prime minister]; these men responded to their times and changed in a myriad ways, why should they have been restricted to their fixed occupations? Similarly, Huang Hsien [Huang Xian] was originally a lowly veterinarian, Sang Hung-yang [Sang Hongyang] a merchant, Sun Shu-ao a wood-cutter, and yet they all were able to preserve their intelligence and help strengthen their states. How can we accuse them of responding to their times and of going to take up responsibilities other than their own occupations! We now have a regulation keeping the descendants of those in despised occupations from taking the civil service examinations. Although this rule has been in force for some time, I consider that it still is a good time to examine this regulation. You candidates have excelled yourselves in knowledge of the past, and in debating various problems; I would like you to spend time considering the issue I have just outlined above.

---

[1]Kuan-tzu or Master Kuan [Guan], who lived in the middle of the seventh century B.C., is regarded in Chinese history as one of the most innovative government reformers in ancient China. He was a great supporter of a centralized form of government.

76

Emperor T'ai-tsung [Taizong]: "On the Art of Government"

China under the T'ang [Tang] dynasty (618–907), which was contemporaneous with Charlemagne's empire in Western Europe, marked one of the most brilliant eras of Chinese history. At the height of its power, the empire stretched from Korea in the east to Central Asia in the west, and Siberia in the north to Annam (Vietnam) in the south. Its culture was sophisticated and cosmopolitan. Although Confucianism was the state cult, other religions were tolerated, and its art, architecture, and literature reached new levels of excellence. Changan, the capital of the empire, was one of the finest in the world, with two million people—including hundreds of foreign students who were eagerly seeking a model of civilized life.

The foundation of this great T'ang empire was largely laid by Emperor T'ai-tsung (also known as Li Shimin, 626–649) who had helped his father Kao-tsu [Gao Zu] (also known as Li Yuan) found the T'ang dynasty by overthrowing the Sui dynasty. Ambitious, energetic, and versatile, Emperor T'ai-tsung created an elaborate system of imperial bureaucracy, rebuilt palaces, constructed more canals, tolerated foreign religions, established publicly supported state colleges in provincial capitals and a university in Changan, and compiled extensive law codes. Externally, he pursued an aggressive foreign policy and expanded the empire. His extraordinary reign was thus the first high point of the three-century-long T'ang period. The following article by Emperor T'ai-tsung reflects his thoughts on the good ruler and good government.

QUESTIONS TO CONSIDER

1. How do you compare Emperor T'ai-tsung with Charlemagne? How similar and how different are these two rulers (see Reading 56)?
2. What aspects of Emperor T'ai-tsung's essay reflect his being a great ruler? Why?

As a young man, I loved archery and prided myself as an expert in the evaluation of bows and arrows. Recently I came into possession of a dozen bows, the quality of which was the best I had ever observed. I showed them to the bow makers and was surprised to hear that they were not as good as they looked. "Why?" I asked.

"The center of the wood is not located at the center of the bow; consequently all the wood grain moves in a bizarre fashion," replied the bow makers. "Though the bow is strong and durable, an arrow released from it cannot travel straight for a long distance."

I used a countless number of bows and arrows in unifying the country; yet I still do

"On the Art of Government" by T'ang T'ai-tsung, *Chen-kuan Cheng-yao* (Politics in Brief: The Chen-kuan Period, 627–49), ed. Wu Ching (669–749), in Dun J. Li, trans. and intro., *The Civilization of China, From the Formative Period to the Coming of the West* (New York: Charles Scribner's Sons, 1975), pp. 161–64. Copyright © by Dun J. Li. Reprinted with permission.

not know enough about them. Now that I have the country for only a short time, how can I say that I know enough about it to govern it successfully, taking into consideration the fact that my knowledge of it is certainly inferior to my knowledge of bows which I have used throughout my life? . . .

Lately the draft decrees that originate from the First Secretariat are often contradictory and in some cases correct one another. To clarify this point, let me say that the purpose of having both the First and the Second Secretariats is for them to check and balance each other, so that the error of one will be corrected by the other and that an error, whoever commits it, will not remain undetected for a long time and thus cause irreparable damage.

Different people are bound to have different opinions; the important thing is that differences in opinion should not degenerate into personal antagonism. Sometimes to avoid the possibility of creating personal grievances or causing embarrassment to a colleague, an official might decide to go ahead with the implementation of a policy even though he knows that the policy is wrong. Let us remember that the preservation of a colleague's prestige, or the avoidance of embarrassment to him, cannot be compared with the welfare of the nation in importance, and to place personal consideration above the well-being of the multitude will lead to defeat for the government as a whole. I want all of you to understand this point and act accordingly.

During the Sui dynasty all officials, in the central as well as the local governments, adopted an attitude of conformity to the general trend in order to be amiable and agreeable with one another. The result was disaster as all of you well know. Most of them did not understand the importance of dissent and comforted themselves by saying that as long as they did not disagree, they could forestall harm to themselves that might otherwise cross their path. When the government, as well as their families, finally collapsed in a massive upheaval, they were severely but justifiably criticized by their contemporaries for their complacency and inertia, even if they themselves may have been fortunate enough to escape death through a combination of circumstances. This is the reason that I want all of you to place public welfare above private interest and hold steadfastly the principle of righteousness, so that all problems, whatever they are, will be resolved in such a way as to bring about a most beneficial result. Under no circumstances are you allowed to agree with one another for the sake of agreement. . . .

As for Sui Wen-ti [Wendi], I would say that he was politically inquisitive but mentally closed. Being close-minded, he could not see truth even if it were spotlighted for him; being overinquisitive, he was suspicious even when there was no valid reason for his suspicion. He rose to power by trampling on the rights of orphans and widows[1] and was consequently not so sure that he had the unanimous support of his own ministers. Being suspicious of his own ministers, he naturally did not trust them and had to make a decision on every matter himself. He became a hard worker out of necessity and, having overworked, could not make the right decision every time. Knowing the kind of man he was, all his ministers, including the prime minister, did not speak as candidly as they should have and unanimously uttered "Yes, sir" when they should have registered strong dissent.

I want all of you to know that I am different. The empire is large and its population enormous. There are thousands of matters to be taken care of, each of which has to be closely coordinated with the others in order to bring about maximum benefit. Each matter must be thoroughly investigated and thought out before a recommendation is submitted to the prime

---

[1]In 581 Sui Wen-ti forced Chou Ching-ti [Zhou Jingdi], aged seven, to abdicate the throne on his behalf. The boy's father had died only one year earlier; his mother was a young widow at the time of the abdication. Four months after his abdication, the boy died under suspicious circumstances.

minister, who, having consulted all the men knowledgeable in this matter, will then present the recommendation, modified if necessary, to the emperor for approval and implementation. It is impossible for one person, however intelligent and capable, to be able to make wise decisions by himself. Acting alone, he may be able, if he is fortunate, to make five right decisions out of ten each day. While we congratulate him for the five right decisions he has made that bring benefit to the country, we tend to forget the enormous harm that results from the implementation of the other five decisions that prove to be wrong. How many wrong decisions will he accumulate in a period of days, months, and years if he makes five such decisions every day? How, in that case, can he not lose his country or throne? Instead he should delegate authority to the most able and virtuous men he can find and supervise their work from above most diligently. When he makes clear to them that he will not tolerate any violation of the law, it is doubtful that they will abuse the authority with which they have been entrusted.

I want all of you to know that whenever an imperial decree is handed down you should carefully study its content and decide for yourselves whether all or part of it is or is not wise or feasible. If you have any reservations, postpone the enforcement and petition me immediately. You can do no less as my loyal ministers. . . .

Governing a country is like taking care of a patient. The better the patient feels, the more he should be looked after, lest in a moment of complacency and neglect one irrevocably reverse the recovery process and send him to death. Likewise, when a country has only recently recovered from chaos and war, those responsible for running the country should be extremely diligent in their work, for false pride and self-indulgence will inevitably return the country to where it used to be and perhaps make it worse.

I realize that the safety of this nation relies to a great extent on what I can or may do and consequently I have not relaxed for a moment in doing the best I can. But I cannot do it alone. You gentlemen are my eyes and ears, legs and arms, and should do your best to assist me. If anything goes wrong anywhere in the empire, you should let me know immediately. If there is less than total trust between you and me and consequently you and I cannot do the best we can, the nation will suffer enormous damage. . . .

As the ancients say, a friend in need is a friend indeed. If mutual assistance governs the relations between two friends, how can it not do so between a king and his ministers? Whenever I read of Chieh's [Jie] execution of Kuan Lung-feng [Guan Lung feng] and Han Chingti's [Han Jingdi] execution of Ch'ao Ts'o [Chao Cuo],[2] I cannot but feel deeply about the mistakes these monarchs made. Contrary to these monarchs, I am asking you gentlemen to speak candidly on matters that you believe are most important to the well-being of the nation, even though the opinion you express may not coincide with my own. Needless to say, there will be no penalty of any kind, let alone execution, for opinions honestly held.

Recently I have made several decisions that are clear violations of the law, even though such violations were not apparent to me at the time when the decisions were made. You gentlemen obviously thought that these violations were inconsequential and therefore abstained from speaking about them. The truth is that the most consequential acts are usually an accumulation of acts of less consequence and in order to prevent the greatest harm, one has to make sure that even the smallest harm does not occur. It will be too late to reverse the course after small disasters have coalesced to become a great one. Keep in mind

---

[2]Kuan Lung-feng was a loyal but outspoken minister under King Chieh (r. 1818–1765 B.C.), last ruler of the Hsia [Xia] dynasty. He was executed because of his criticism of the king's policies and personal behavior. Han Ching-ti (ca. 156–141 B.C.) ordered the execution of Ch'ao Ts'o (d. 154 B.C.) to appease some of the feudal lords who were then in rebellion. Previously Ch'ao Ts'o had recommended breaking up large feudal domains into smaller ones, a recommendation that angered the lords.

that a government does not fall because of the occurrence of a major catastrophe; rather, its demise usually results from an accumulation of small misfortunes.

It enlightens one to note that not a single person expressed regret when Sui Yang-ti [Sui Yangdi], a brutal and merciless tyrant, met his death at the hands of a group of assassins. If you gentlemen keep in mind the reason why I have been able to overthrow the Sui regime, I, on my part, will constantly remind myself of the injustice suffered by Kuan Lung-feng and Ch'ao Ts'o. Only in this way can you and I be permanently secure.

77

Chinese Footbinding

One of the most bizarre and painful customs of old China was the binding of women's feet. It is difficult to determine precisely when and how this custom came to be, but historical records seem to indicate that it began with the dancers of the imperial harem of the Southern T'ang [Tang] dynasty (937–975), sometime in the tenth century. In the beginning, the custom was practiced only by fashionable women of the upper class, but footbinding gradually spread down to the rest of the female population and persisted well into the twentieth century. The custom persisted even after the end of the last imperial dynasty (1644–1912), despite a series of official efforts to end it, beginning with an antifootbinding edict issued by Empress Dowager Tz'u-hsi [Ci Xi] in 1902. In the following selection, a middle-aged maidservant named Chang, probably born around the turn of the century, recalls her painful footbinding experience for her master. The story is told sometime in the early 1930s.

QUESTIONS TO CONSIDER

1. Compare the footbinding custom of old China with a comparable custom from another society.
2. Why did such a painful custom continue for so long in China?

I was born in a certain district in western Honan Province, at the end of the Manchu dynasty. In accordance with custom, at the age of seven I began binding. I had witnessed the pain of my cousins, and in the year it was to begin was very much frightened. That autumn, distress befell me. One day prior my mother told me: "You are now seven, just at the right age for binding. If we wait, your foot will harden, increasing the pain. You should have started in the spring, but because you were weak we waited till now. Girls in other families have already completed the process. We start tomorrow. I will do this for you lightly and so that it won't hurt; what daughter doesn't go through this difficulty?" She then gave me fruit to eat, showed me a new pair of phoenix-tip shoes, and beguiled me with these words: "Only

Howard S. Levy, *Chinese Footbinding: The History of a Curious Erotic Custom* (New York: Walton Rawls Publisher, 1966), pp. 224–27. Reprinted by permission.

with bound feet can you wear such beautiful shoes. Otherwise, you'll become a large-footed barbarian and everyone will laugh at and feel ashamed of you." I felt moved by a desire to be beautiful and became steadfast in determination, staying awake all night.

I got up early the next morning. Everything had already been prepared. Mother had me sit on a stool by the bed. She threaded a needle and placed it in my hair, cut off a piece of alum and put it alongside the binding cloth and the flowered shoes. She then turned and closed the bedroom door. She first soaked my feet in a pan of hot water, then wiped them, and cut the toenails with a small scissors. She then took my right foot in her hands and repeatedly massaged it in the direction of the plantar.[1] She also sprinkled alum between my toes. She gave me a pen point to hold in my hands because of the belief that my feet might then become as pointed as it was. Later she took a cloth three feet long and two inches wide, grasped my right foot, and pressed down the four smaller toes in the direction of the plantar. She joined them together, bound them once, and passed the binding from the heel to the foot surface and then to the plantar. She did this five times and then sewed the binding together with thread. To prevent it from getting loosened, she tied a slender cotton thread from the tip of the foot to its center.

She did the same thing with the left foot and forced my feet into flowered shoes which were slightly smaller than the feet were. The tips of the shoes were adorned with threads in the shape of grain. There was a ribbon affixed to the mouth of the shoe and fastened on the heel. She ordered me to get down from the bed and walk, saying that if I didn't the crooked-shaped foot would be seriously injured. When I first touched the ground, I felt complete loss of movement; after a few trials, only the toes hurt greatly. Both feet became feverish at night and hurt from the swelling. Except for walking, I sat by the *k'ang* [Kang].[2] Mother rebound my feet weekly, each time more tightly than the last. I became more and more afraid. I tried to avoid the binding by hiding in a neighbor's house. If I loosened the bandage, mother would scold me for not wanting to look nice. After half a year, the tightly bound toes began to uniformly face the plantar. The foot became more pointed daily; after a year, the toes began to putrefy. Corns began to appear and thicken, and for a long time no improvement was visible. Mother would remove the bindings and lance the corns with a needle to get rid of the hard core. I feared this, but mother grasped my legs so that I couldn't move. Father betrothed me at the age of nine to a neighbor named Chao, and I went to their house to serve as a daughter-in-law in the home of my future husband. My mother-in-law bound my feet much more tightly than mother ever had, saying that I still hadn't achieved the standard. She beat me severely if I cried; if I unloosened the binding, I was beaten until my body was covered with bruises. Also, because my feet were somewhat fleshy, my mother-in-law insisted that the foot must become inflamed to get the proper results. Day and night, my feet were washed in a medicinal water; within a few washings I felt special pain. Looking down, I saw that every toe but the big one was inflamed and deteriorated. Mother-in-law said that this was all to the good. I had to be beaten with fists before I could bear to remove the bindings, which were congealed with pus and blood. To get them loose, such force had to be used that the skin often peeled off, causing further bleeding. The stench was hard to bear, while I felt the pain in my very insides. My body trembled with agitation. Mother-in-law was not only unmoved but she placed tiles inside the binding in order to hasten the inflammation process. She was deaf to my childish cries. Every other day, the binding was made tighter and sewn up, and each time slightly smaller shoes had to be worn. The sides of the shoes were hard, and I could only get into them by

[1]Relating to the sole of the foot.
[2]A brick-bed warmed by a fire.

using force. I was compelled to walk on them in the courtyard; they were called distance-walking shoes. I strove to cling to life, suffering indescribable pain. Being in an average family, I had to go to the well and pound the mortar unaided. Faulty blood circulation caused my feet to become insensible in winter. At night, I tried to warm them by the *k'ang,* but this caused extreme pain. The alternation between frost and thawing caused me to lose one toe on my right foot. Deterioration of the flesh was such that within a year my feet had become as pointed as new bamboo shoots, pointing upwards like a red chestnut. The foot surface was slightly convex, while the four bean-sized toes were deeply imbedded in the plantar like a string of cowry shells.[3] They were only a slight distance from the heel of the foot. The plantar was so deep that several coins could be placed in it without difficulty. The large toes faced upwards, while the place on the right foot where the little toe had deteriorated away pained at irregular intervals. It left an ineffacable scar.

My feet were only three inches long, at the most. Relatives and friends praised them, little realizing the cisterns of tears and blood which they had caused. My husband was delighted with them, but two years ago he departed this world. The family wealth was dissipated, and I had to wander about, looking for work. That was how I came down to my present circumstances. I envy the modern woman. If I too had been born just a decade or so later, all of this pain could have been avoided. The lot of the natural-footed woman and mine is like that of heaven and hell.

Mongols and the West

Until reports from Franciscan friars and Venetian merchant-travelers reached Europe in the thirteenth century, people in the West were only dimly aware of anything in the world east of India. The Romans became aware of the existence of China more by logic than by knowledge. Silk was greatly prized by the Romans, so much so that in some periods ounces of silk were sold for the same weight in gold. The ancient Greeks had noted a people around eastern India called "the Seres," and the Romans picked up on the fact that *sericos* in both Greek and Latin meant "silk." Given the existence of *sericos* cloth, there must have been people out there in the furthest Orient whose lives revolved around making it: Ergo, "the Seres" were the Silk People. The natural assumption that the Silk People must have a land of their own led geographers to designate one for them, and so the land of Serica or Sericum was born. Any country worthy of the name had to have a capital city, and so by the time we get to the great Greco-Roman geographer, Ptolemy (A.D. 127–151), the Seres had one, called ever so logically Sera Metropolis or Great Silk City. Ancient and medieval geographers ascribed both utopian and monstrous elements to the inhabitants of Asia east of India. The thought of total peace and harmony prevailing among some of the tribes there was a constant element in Western perceptions. On the other hand, several Greco-Roman sources described the Seres as towering 20 feet tall and having life expectancies of over 200 years; yet, even they were not thought to be the most unusual East Asians.

[3]A type of shell somewhat resembling the female sex organ; it was used as a sort of primitive money in prehistoric times in China.

Contacts with the Mongols were to lead Westerners to China. Islamic *jihads* and Western crusades gave rise to a different sort of Western interest in East Asia. The notion of a great Christian kingdom to the East, headed by one Prester (Priest) John, secular and clerical ruler in one, spread rapidly throughout Western Europe after the mid-twelfth century. The accompanying hope was that Prester John's forces would make excellent allies against the Muslims. In the early thirteenth century, rumors reached the camps of crusaders in North Africa that Christian forces from the Far East were on the march, slaughtering Muslims left and right as they came to aid Western fighters in the liberation of the Holy Land. The reports of massive slaughter of Muslims turned out to be true in 1219, but the perpetrators were the armies of Jenghiz Khan [Chinghiz Khan], a distinctly non-Christian leader who did not resemble Prester John (or "King David," another hoped-for but fictional Christian king from the East). Jenghiz Khan's Mongol-led hordes soon acquired the name "Tartars," derived from Tartary, the infernal region below Hades in Greco-Roman mythology, for they killed off Slavic and Hungarian Christians with as much enthusiasm as they annihilated Muslims. By the 1240s, Matthew of Paris described the Mongols as "a monstrous and inhuman branch of mankind."

In spite of what we might call "a bad press," some Church leaders in the West still found the ongoing Mongol hostility to Turks, Persians, and Arabs an enduring and consoling fact. They were proven anti-Saracens, and if peace and friendship could be established with them, perhaps they could be converted to Christianity, after which they could be counted on as genuine allies against Islam. In 1245, Pope Innocent IV dispatched the first of a series of Franciscan missionary-explorers to negotiate with the great Khan of the Mongols. Friar John Pian del Carpini did, in fact, reach the court of Jenghiz's grandson, Kuyuk Khan, with a message from the pope.

78

John Pian del Carpini, *The Tartars*

John (Giovanni) del Carpini (1182?–1252) had been a companion and disciple of St. Francis of Assisi (see Reading 70). He led the Franciscan expedition sent by Pope Innocent IV to Kuyuk Khan and wrote extensively of his travels and experiences at the Mongol court. It is not known how he entitled his work, which is often called the *History of the Mongols,* even though there is relatively little *history* in it. One of the surviving manuscripts has the simple title *A Book About the Tartars,* which seems more accurate. The following excerpts from it are fairly typical in showing his admiration for the hardiness and capacity for cooperation the Mongols exhibited among themselves, coupled with his revulsion at their ferocity and lack of scruples in dealing with foreign peoples. John was less hopeful of converting the Mongols to Christianity than most of the explorer-missionaries who followed him; both his travel book and the letter he brought to the pope from Kuyuk Khan indicate why. His Franciscan successors who visited China under Mongol conquest had better experiences, however; they and

Venetian traders, particularly the very observant Marco Polo, who became a Mongol administrator in China, were beginning to acquaint Europe with some of the real East Asia.

QUESTIONS TO CONSIDER

1. Why does John consider the Mongol threat a real one?
2. What does John think Westerners could learn from the Mongols?

The Tartars have a very different appearance from other peoples. There is more space between their eyes and between their cheekbones than is true of other men. . . . They have flat noses and rather small eyes. . . . Almost all of them are of medium height. Their men have only sparce growths of beard, some letting their wispy moustaches droop long. . . .

I will tell something of their good characteristics and then of their bad ones. . . . They show greater respect to their superiors than any other people in the world. . . . They deceive their own masters rarely or never with words and never at all with deeds. . . . They do not fight among themselves: Internal warfare, brawls and assaults do not occur. . . . If a large animal strays, whoever finds it either lets it go or leads it to men of authority from whom the owner can get it back with no difficulty at all simply by asking for it. They respect each other quite well enough and . . . throw frequent banquets in spite of the scarcity of good things to eat among them. At the same time, they are so hardy that they can go a day or even two without eating and still sing and joke around as if they had had plenty to eat. . . . Tartar women are chaste: There are not even rumors of immodest female behavior among them, although the women do sometimes use filthy language. . . . Even though the Tartars get quite drunk often, this does not lead to hostile words or actions among them.

Having said this much about their good side, let me go on to their bad one. Their pride is terrible when they confront non-Tartars—nobles and commoners alike—whom they are apt to despise. . . . They show their angry and totally condescending natures to foreigners, to whom they habitually lie. When Tartars speak to non-Tartars the truth is seldom in them. When they start off, their conversation is nice enough, but they sting like scorpions before they are through talking. They are cunning, crafty, and very elusive with their falsehoods. When they have hostile plans toward foreigners, they are experts in concealing them so that the foreigners will not know to be on guard. . . . They are very greedy and shameless with their outrageous demands, while they hold fast to what is theirs and are unbelievably stingy givers. Killing off foreign peoples simply does not bother them.

Chinghiz Khan arranged their order of battle by putting ten men under the command of a squad leader, ten squad leaders under one centurion, ten centurions under a battalion commander, thus giving him a thousand men, ten battalion commanders under a colonel and the whole army under two or three generals, but with one of them clearly the theater commander. If in battle, one, two, or three—any number—of men flee from a squad, the whole squad is executed; if the whole squad flees, then the hundred soldiers with the centurion over them are all executed; and, to summarize this point briefly, units with men in them who flee are wiped out. . . . If members of a squad are captured and not rescued by the rest, the rest are executed. The minimum arms they are required to carry are: two bows

Historia Mongalorum, in *Studi Italiani di Filologia Indo-Iranica*, Vol. IX (Firenze: Carnesecchi e Figli, 1913), pp. 54–101, *passim*. Translated by Henry A. Myers.

..., three quivers full of arrows, one ax, and ropes to pull along machines of war. To be sure, their nobles carry . . . slightly curved swords with sharp points, and their horses wear armor of multiple thickness of leather shaped to fit their bodies. . . .

Some of them have a hook attached to the necks of their lances with which they will pull a rider off his saddle if they can. Their arrows are about two feet, eight inches long . . . and each man carries a file in his quiver to sharpen their heads. . . .

When they come to a river, they cross it with the higher ups using large, lightweight leather bags with loops and drawstrings to seal up their clothes and necessary equipment for the crossing. The resulting pack floats. Tied to the tails of their horses, who swim over, the pack serves as a sort of boat. . . . Even the common soldiers have nearly waterproof leather bags, into which they stuff their things . . . and then hang them securely on the bases of their horses' tails before crossing.

You should know that the Tartar emperor told me in person that he wanted to send his armies into Livonia [on the Baltic Sea] and Prussia and that he intended to destroy the whole countryside or reduce it to servitude. They enslave people in a way which we find intolerable. . . . Their tactics include using captives from lands just conquered to fight against a province still holding out against them. They put these captives in the front ranks: If they fight poorly, they kill them; if they fight well, they encourage them with cheering words and promise to make them great lords so that they will not escape. However, once the dangers of battle are passed, they keep these people in line by making hapless serfs out of them, while taking the women they want for serving maids and concubines. Their use of men from one defeated country after another against the next country makes it impossible for any single country to resist them, unless God chooses to fight for them. . . .

Thus, if Christians wish to defend themselves, their countries, and Christianity, it will be necessary for kings, princes, barons, and other chiefs of the lands to cooperate as one and to send men under a consolidated command into battle against them before they have so drained the earth of men that there will be nowhere to draw aid from. . . . This army should be ordered as *they* do it, from officers commanding a thousand through officers commanding a hundred and overall commanders of the army. These generals should never enter the fighting themselves, just as Tartar commanders do not enter it, but they should be able to observe the army's action and direct it. Our people should make it a regulation that the soldiers advance into battle together or elsewhere in the order established.

79

Kuyuk Khan, Letter to Pope Innocent IV

Kuyuk Khan, who ruled the Mongols for a brief period beginning in 1246, participated in the Mongol invasion of Europe in the 1230s and quite possibly was planning another invasion at the time he died in 1248.

QUESTIONS TO CONSIDER

1. How did Kuyuk Khan assess the relationship between Mongols and the Christian world?

Courage. Kuyuk Khan, Emperor of all men, whose courage is God-given, sends a letter of his own to the great Pope in reply to the message sent to us in which you express your desire to have peace and friendship with us, as we have understood from your emissary.

Your letter to us contains a number of things we must do: We must be baptized and must become Christians. To this we answer that we do not understand how you seek to require us to do anything. Then, as for what you have in your letter showing great surprise at such thorough slaughter of men, for the most part Hungarian Christians, as well as some Polish or Moravian ones, we have not heard of anything that would require us to answer you about that either; however, so that you will not think that we wish to lull you through our silence [into feeling secure], we will answer you in this way:

No khan can heed more apt advice than comes from the command of God and the recorded words of Jenghiz Khan. Khans have been inspired to do some killing all right, because—once God has decided upon the destruction of men—what God does not do Himself He will enable man to do to man. Consequently, with our God-inspired courage we have wrought massive destruction on every land from the East to the West.

You Christians do worship God, but then—believing yourselves to be the only true ones—you despise nations other than those you consider worthy of having your grace bestowed upon them.

You now, Pope: If you want to have peace and friendship with us, come with all the kings and potentates who serve you to our court. You should listen to this response of ours: Subject your will to us and bring us tribute, for if you do not obey our instructions and do not journey to us we are certain that you will have war with us. After that, to be sure, we do not know what the future holds. Only God knows that.

80

The Yuan Code: Homicide

In 1279, for the first time in Chinese history, all of China fell under an alien rule—that of the Mongols who invaded from across the Great Wall. The Mongol conquerors, who remained in control of the Chinese empire for less than a century (until 1368), adopted the dynastic name "Yuan," according to Chinese custom. Once in the seat of power, the Mongols, who were disdained by the Chinese as nomadic barbarians, sought to establish their supremacy as new masters by implementing systematic discriminatory policies against the Chinese, who constituted more than 90 percent of the Mongol empire's population. For instance, the Mongol rulers patronized Lamaism, a Buddhist sect which had originated in Tibet, in order to undercut the pervasive influence of Confucianism and Taoism. The Mongols stratified the population of the empire in such a way that the Chinese were placed at the bottom of the social ladder, even below the foreigners. The Chinese suffered from administrative and judicial discrimination and were also forced to carry a heavy burden in taxes and forced labor. The following excerpts from the Yuan penal code show, for instance, that

From "Lettere del Gran Can al Sommo Pontefece," appended to Friar John's *Historia Mongalorum,* in *Studi Italiani di Filologia Indo-Iranica,* Vol. IX (Firenze: Carnesecchi e Figli, 1913), p. 125. Translated by Henry A. Myers.

the murder of a Mongol by a Chinese invoked the death penalty, whereas the murder of a Chinese by a Mongol was punished by exile to an expeditionary army. Interestingly, the code also seems to reflect the Mongol's nomadic background in that it shows a preference for corporal punishment over imprisonment.

QUESTIONS TO CONSIDER

1. Compare the punishments for homicides provided in the Yuan Code with that of the Visigoths (see Reading 54).
2. How differently were the cases involving involuntary manslaughter and premeditated murders treated in the Yuan Code? What seemed to be the criteria for the differences?

1. A person who kills another person is punishable by death. The family of the victim is entitled to receive from the family of the killer fifty taels of silver for funeral expenses. The amount could be reduced if the family of the killer is too poor, but under no circumstances should it be less than ten taels of silver in paper currency. If a general clemency is declared before the death sentence is carried out, the payment to the injured family will be doubled.
2. When more than one person conspire to kill an official and succeed in their attempt, all persons involved, the leader or leaders who plan the killing as well as their followers who execute the killing, are punishable by death. If injury rather than death is the result, all persons involved are to be punished by 107 blows and then be exiled to a distant region. The families of the guilty must pay funeral expenses for the dead official.
3. A person who, after having killed another person, chooses to commit suicide but fails in his attempt is punishable by death nevertheless.
4. A person who kills another person is eligible for clemency if he has accumulated good deeds after the killing, provided that the killing is accidental rather than intentional.
5. In a physical fight between two persons, the person who has no intention to kill at the beginning but acquires such intention during the process of fighting is regarded as having harbored the intention to kill, if the physical fight ends with the death of the other person.
6. In a physical fight between two or more persons, the person who has used a weapon, such as a knife, in the fight and thus caused the death of a person or persons against whom he has been fighting is regarded as having harbored the intention to kill. . . .
8. If a person wielding a knife intends to kill another person but is unsuccessful in his attempt after his intended victim has managed to escape and if, subsequent to this escape, he shifts his anger to those bystanders who have tried to stop him, he is regarded as having harbored the intention to kill, if he kills one or more of these bystanders.
9. A person who kills a tax collector is regarded as having harbored the intention to kill, even though the tax collector has used high-pressure methods to collect the taxes due and the taxpayer, out of desperation, decides to kill him.
10. If a man while intoxicated with liquor attempts to kill his wife and, having failed in his

From Dun J. Li, trans., *The Civilization of China* (New York: Charles Scribner's Sons, 1975), pp. 259–69.Reprinted by permission of Charles Scribner's Sons, a division of Simon & Schuster. Copyright © 1975 by Dun J. Li.

attempt, shifts his anger to those bystanders who have tried to stop him, the man is regarded as having harbored the intention to kill and will be sentenced to death if he kills one or more of these bystanders.

11. If a man kills a prostitute who has refused to elope with him, the man will be regarded as guilty as if he had killed a person other than a prostitute. . . .

13. A person who beats to death the person who has killed his father is regarded as guiltless. The family of the person who has killed his father is responsible for the payment of fifty taels of silver for his father's funeral expenses.

14. If a Mongol, in a physical fight or in a state of drunkenness, kills a Chinese, the Mongol will be punished by exile to an expeditionary army, in addition to the payment of funeral expenses for the dead person. . . .

16. If a man beats to death another man who has been flirting with his wife, he will receive a punishment one degree lower than the death sentence. He will be responsible for the dead man's funeral expenses.

17. If a person beats to death a notorious outlaw who would have been sentenced to death if captured by governmental authorities, he is guiltless. He is not responsible for the dead man's funeral expenses.

18. If a person with an object other than a knife causes injury to another person who subsequently dies as a result of this injury, he will receive a punishment three degrees lower than the death sentence.

19. In a quarrel between two persons, if one person smashes his head into the chest of the other and, in the process of falling down, accidentally causes death by damaging the other person's heart with his elbow, the offending person will be punished by 107 blows, in addition to the payment of the dead person's funeral expenses. . . .

21. In a physical fight resulting from one person's violent response to another person's joke, the person who causes injury and subsequent death to the other person will be punished by 107 blows.

22. The man who marries a widow becomes the foster father of the widow's offspring by her first marriage. He will not be responsible, however, for any crime committed by any of his adopted sons if the latter has been evicted by him from his house and lives in a separate residence. In this case the son alone is responsible for any injury he causes to others.

23. A convicted criminal who kills another convicted criminal will be punished in the same manner as if he had killed any other person. A tax collector who beats a person to death in the process of exacting tax payment will be sentenced to death.

24. If an official beats to death a civilian who has accused him in the court of justice of having accepted bribery, the official will be regarded as having harbored the intention to kill and be punished accordingly. . . .

28. A father who inexcusably kills his son with a knife will be punished by 77 blows.

29. A father is guiltless if the son he kills has been undutiful toward him. However, any of his brothers or nephews who have collaborated in, or given assistance to, this killing will be punished by 107 blows.

30. If a father kills his married daughter after having discovered a serious offense committed by her, the father will be punished by 57 blows. The husband of his deceased daughter is entitled to receive from him the full amount of money which he paid for his daughter, so the husband can marry someone else.

31. If a father, with valid reason, beats a son or daughter of his and accidentally causes his or her death, the father is guiltless.

32. A man who kills the son of his wife by her first marriage is punishable by death.

33. A wife who kills a son of her husband's concubine will be punished by 97 blows. Her husband can either marry her off or sell her as a slave.
34. A man or woman who mistreats his or her daughter-in-law and causes her death will be punished by 107 blows, despite the fact that the woman, before her death, has not been a good daughter-in-law.
35. If a man kills not only his son who has been undutiful toward him but also his daughter-in-law, for no other reason than the fact that she happens to be his son's wife, the man will be punished by 77 blows. Her dowry and all of her other belongings shall be returned to her parents.
36. A man who, for flimsy reasons, kills his younger brother is punishable by death. . . .
38. If a man kills his younger brother who has struck him first, the man will be regarded as having killed a guilty person. He will not be punished in the same manner as a murderer would be.
39. If a man, in a quarrel, accidentally kills his younger brother who has lived in a separate residence, the man will be punished by 77 blows. He shall pay half of his younger brother's funeral expenses.
40. A man who kills his cousin in a quarrel will be punished in a manner as if he had killed an unrelated person.
41. If a man kills his younger sister who, though a nun, has had illicit sexual relations with some other man, the man is regarded as having killed a guilty person and will not be punished in the same manner as a murderer would be, provided that before the killing he has warned her about her improper conduct and that his sister, instead of heeding his advice, has verbally abused him in return and physically wrestled with him. . . .
47. A man who kills his wife for flimsy reasons will be punished by death.
48. If a man hates his wife and subsequently causes her death by poisoning, the man will be regarded as having killed an unrelated person.
49. If a man beats his wife and subsequently causes her death for her arrogant attitude toward his parents, the man will be punished by 77 blows.
50. If a man beats his wife and accidentally causes her death after his wife has refused to attend to his needs during his illness and if, in the meantime, she has been verbally abusing his parents and has caused him to lose all affection for her, the man is guiltless.
51. If a man who hates his wife and loves his concubine chooses to kill his wife by citing some minor faults of hers, the man will be punished by death.
52. If a man, having heard some rumor of a derogatory nature about his fiancée, kills her, the man will be regarded as having killed an unrelated person.
53. A woman who cruelly beats to death her husband's concubine will be punished by 107 blows. She shall be stripped before the beatings are inflicted upon her body. . . .
56. If a man beats to death his slave who has verbally and physically abused him, the man is guiltless.
57. If a person kills his or her slave who has been faultless, he or she will be punished by 87 blows. If he or she is in a state of drunkenness when the killing takes place, the punishment will be reduced by one degree [i.e., 77 blows].
58. If a person beats to death a slave who is about to gain his or her freedom, the offending person will be punished by 77 blows.
59. If a person plans and then carries out the killing of a former slave, he or she will be regarded as having killed a free person. . . .
71. A killer under the age of fourteen is guiltless if the killing is accidental rather than intentional. However, the killer and his family are responsible for the dead person's funeral expenses.

73. If a blind person beats another person who subsequently dies as a result of injury, the blind person will be punished by 107 blows. He is responsible for the dead person's funeral expenses.

74. If a person in a state of insanity beats another person who subsequently dies as a result of injury, the person is guiltless. He is responsible, however, for the dead person's funeral expenses.

75. If a physician, because of his insufficient knowledge, kills a patient with his needle or medicine, the physician will be punished by 107 blows. He shall pay for the dead person's funeral expenses.

The Black Death: Christian and Muslim Views

The outbreak of the Black Death in the fourteenth century is an example of how cross-cultural disease contacts can dramatically change the course of history for millions of people. The Black Death was a combination of three disease strains: a bubonic strain (so called because of buboes, or swelling of the victim's glands) that attacked the lymphatic system, a pneumonic strain that invaded the lungs, and a septicemic strain that was lethal upon entering the bloodstream. In all likelihood, Mongol horsemen carried these disease bacilli westward out of Asia so that by the 1340s, the disease had spread from the Gobi Desert to the Black Sea. In 1347, Genoese traders, returning from the Crimea, brought the disease to Italy. Because of a vigorous and hearty flea and rat population, it spread quickly throughout most of Europe and parts of the Middle East, killing at least twenty million people by 1350. Once a victim was infected, death was certain, usually coming within four days. Certain groups of people, such as bakers, suffered particularly heavy losses because their warm ovens were the choice nests for infected rats. Monasteries, too, seemed to have suffered high mortality rates, as did virtually all the large urban areas.

What is certain is that after the first outbreak of plague, the Black Death recurred at regular intervals. Over time, the huge population losses were restored, not because Europe or the Middle East ever fully conquered the plague, but because the population slowly developed a greater tolerance for the disease. By the eighteenth century, the Black Death had lost much of its lethal effect.

Although these facts are clear, there is no way to determine the degree to which the disease contributed to political, religious, and social change after 1350. Postplague European art, for example, showed a fascination with themes of death, decay, and suffering. Popular culture soon developed new rituals celebrating death, such as the dance of death (the word "macabre" describing this dance appeared first in 1376) and the processional liturgy of flagellants seeking deliverance while scourging themselves. High society's rituals changed as well. Postplague nobility now often hired musicians to play at elaborate funerals. In Paris, polite society now sought the cemetery of the Holy Innocents for its Sunday promenades and amorous rendezvous.

81

The Chronicle of Jean de Venette

The following account is by Jean de Venette (died ca. 1368). A Carmelite monk who witnessed the ravages of death in France, he wrote this account in the late 1350s.

QUESTIONS TO CONSIDER

1. How does Jean de Venette's account explain the origins of the Black Death?
2. What does the account reveal about the character and assumptions of fourteenth-century medicine?
3. What does the account suggest about medieval attitudes of anti-Semitism?
4. What were some of the plague's aftereffects in France?

In A.D. 1348, the people of France and of almost the whole world were struck by a blow other than war. For in addition to the famine . . . and to the wars . . . pestilence and its attendant tribulations appeared again in various parts of the world. In the month of August, 1348, after Vespers when the sun was beginning to set, a big and very bright star appeared above Paris, toward the west. It did not seem, as stars usually do, to be very high above our hemisphere but rather very near. As the sun set and night came on, this star did not seem to me or to many other friars who were watching it to move from one place. At length, when night had come, this big star, to the amazement of all of us who were watching, broke into many different rays and, as it shed these rays over Paris toward the east, totally disappeared and was completely annihilated. Whether it was a comet or not, whether it was composed of airy exhalations and was finally resolved into vapor, I leave to the decision of astronomers. It is, however, possible that it was a presage of the amazing pestilence to come, which, in fact, followed very shortly in Paris and throughout France and elsewhere, as I shall tell. All this year and the next, the mortality of men and women, of the young even more than of the old, in Paris and in the kingdom of France, and also, it is said, in other parts of the world, was so great that it was almost impossible to bury the dead. People lay ill little more than two or three days and died suddenly, as it were in full health. He who was well one day was dead the next and being carried to his grave. Swellings appeared suddenly in the armpit or in the groin—in many cases both—and they were infallible signs of death. This sickness or pestilence was called an epidemic by the doctors. Nothing like the great numbers who died in the years 1348 and 1349 has been heard of or seen or read of in times past. This plague and disease came from *ymaginatione* or association and contagion, for if a well man visited the sick he only rarely evaded the risk of death. Wherefore in many towns timid priests withdrew, leaving the exercise of their ministry to such of the religious as were more daring. In many places not two out of twenty remained alive. So high was the mortality at the Hôtel-Dieu in Paris that for a long time, more than five hundred dead were car-

From Richard A. Newhall, ed., *The Chronicle of Jean de Venette*, trans. Jean Birdsall, Records of Civilization, Sources and Studies, no. 50. Copyright © 1953 by Columbia University Press. Reprinted by permission of the publisher.

ried daily with great devotion in carts to the cemetery of the Holy Innocents in Paris for burial. A very great number of the saintly sisters of the Hôtel-Dieu who, not fearing to die, nursed the sick in all sweetness and humility, with no thought of honor, a number too often renewed by death, rest in peace with Christ, as we may piously believe.

This plague, it is said, began among the unbelievers, came to Italy, and then crossing the Alps reached Avignon, where it attacked several cardinals and took from them their whole household. Then it spread, unforeseen, to France, through Gascony and Spain, little by little, from town to town, from village to village, from house to house, and finally from person to person. It even crossed over to Germany, though it was not so bad there as with us. During the epidemic, God of His accustomed goodness deigned to grant this grace, that however suddenly men died, almost all awaited death joyfully. Nor was there anyone who died without confessing his sins and receiving the holy viaticum. To the even greater benefit of the dying, Pope Clement VI through their confessors mercifully gave and granted absolution from penalty to the dying in many cities and fortified towns. Men died the more willingly for this and left many inheritances and temporal goods to churches and monastic orders, for in many cases they had seen their close heirs and children die before them.

Some said that this pestilence was caused by infection of the air and waters, since there was at this time no famine nor lack of food supplies, but on the contrary great abundance. As a result of this theory of infected water and air as the source of the plague the Jews were suddenly and violently charged with infecting wells and water and corrupting the air. The whole world rose up against them cruelly on this account. In Germany and other parts of the world where Jews lived, they were massacred and slaughtered by Christians, and many thousands were burned everywhere, indiscriminately. The unshaken, if fatuous, constancy of the men and their wives was remarkable. For mothers hurled their children first into the fire that they might not be baptized and then leaped in after them to burn with their husbands and children. It is said that many bad Christians were found who in a like manner put poison into wells. But in truth, such poisonings, granted that they actually were perpetrated, could not have caused so great a plague nor have infected so many people. There were other causes; for example, the will of God and the corrupt humors and evil inherent in air and earth. Perhaps the poisonings, if they actually took place in some localities, reenforced these causes. The plague lasted in France for the greater part of the years 1348 and 1349 and then ceased. Many country villages and many houses in good towns remained empty and deserted. Many houses, including some splendid dwellings, very soon fell into ruins. Even in Paris several houses were thus ruined, though fewer here than elsewhere.

After the cessation of the epidemic, pestilence, or plague, the men and women who survived married each other. There was no sterility among the women, but on the contrary fertility beyond the ordinary. Pregnant women were seen on every side. Many twins were born and even three children at once. But the most surprising fact is that children born after the plague, when they became of an age for teeth, had only twenty or twenty-two teeth, though before that time men commonly had thirty-two in their upper and lower jaws together. What this diminution in the number of teeth signified I wonder greatly, unless it be a new era resulting from the destruction of one human generation by the plague and its replacement by another. But woe is me! the world was not changed for the better but for the worse by this renewal of population. For men were more avaricious and grasping than before, even though they had far greater possessions. They were more covetous and disturbed each other more frequently with suits, brawls, disputes, and pleas. Nor by the mortality resulting from this terrible plague inflicted by God was peace between kings and lords established. On the contrary, the enemies of the king of France and of the Church were stronger and wickeder than before and stirred up wars on sea and on land. Greater evils than before pullulated everywhere in the world. And this fact was very remarkable. Although there was an abundance of all goods, yet everything was twice as dear, whether it were utensils, victuals, or merchandise, hired helpers or peasants and serfs, except for some hereditary domains which remained abundantly stocked with everything. Charity began to cool, and iniquity with ignorance and sin to abound, for few could be found in the good towns and castles who knew how or were willing to instruct children in the rudiments of grammar. . . .

In the year 1349, while the plague was still active and spreading from town to town, men in Germany, Flanders, Hainaut, and Lorraine uprose and began a new sect on their own authority. Stripped to the waist, they gathered in large groups and bands and marched in procession through the crossroads and squares of cities and good towns. There they formed circles and beat upon their backs with weighted scourges, rejoicing as they did so in loud voices and singing hymns suitable to their rite and newly composed for it. Thus for thirty-three days they marched through many towns doing their penance and affording a great spectacle to the wondering people. They flogged their shoulders and arms with scourges tipped with iron points so zealously as to draw blood. But they did not come to Paris nor to any part of France, for they were forbidden to do so by the king of France, who did not want them. He acted on the advice of the masters of theology of the University of Paris, who said that this new sect had been formed contrary to the will of God, to the rites of Holy Mother Church, and to the salvation of all their souls. That indeed this was and is true appeared shortly. For Pope Clement VI was fully informed concerning this fatuous new rite by the masters of Paris through emissaries reverently sent to him and, on the grounds that it had been damnably formed, contrary to law, he forbade the Flagellants under threat of anathema to practise in the future the public penance which they had do presumptuously undertaken. His prohibition was just, for the Flagellants, supported by certain fatuous priests and monks, were enunciating doctrines and opinions which were beyond measure evil, erroneous, and fallacious. For example, they said that their blood thus drawn by the scourge and poured out was mingled with the blood of Christ. Their many errors showed how little they knew of the Catholic faith. Wherefore, as they had begun fatuously of themselves and not of God, so in a short time they were reduced to nothing. On being warned, they desisted and humbly received absolution and penance at the hands of their prelates as the pope's representatives. Many honorable women and devout matrons, it must be added, had done this penance with scourges, marching and singing through towns and churches like the men, but after a little like the others they desisted.

82

Ibn al-wardī, *An Essay on the Report of the Pestilence*

Ibn al-Wardī's account of the Black Death, written at the same time as Jean de Venette's, describes the infestation of the plague in Aleppo, a city in northwestern Syria near the Turkish border, where this author died of the plague in 1349. His account parallels Jean de Venette's by attributing the plague's origins and deadly consequences to God's wrath but, as a Muslim scholar, he incorporates the teachings of Islam to explain the Black Death.

QUESTIONS TO CONSIDER

1. Why would Ibn al-Wardī advise his readers that the Black Death for Muslims could be a "martyrdom and a reward," but for the infidel it is strictly a punishment? Would Jean de Venette agree with this assessment?
2. According to this author, the Black Death was not caused by infection, but came directly from God; therefore a Muslim should not enter nor flee from a plague-stricken land. Would Jean de Venette agree with his diagnosis and advice?
3. What are the major differences between the explanations of Jean de Venette and Ibn al-Wardī? Are there areas of agreement between these two observers of the plague?
4. How would you compare the literary styles of Ibn al-Wardī and Jean de Venette? Which of the two styles gives a more powerful description of the plague? Why?
5. Are there any parallels between these two explanations of the Black Death and those offered for modern epidemics?

God is my security in every adversity. My sufficiency is in God alone. Is not God sufficient protection for His servant? Oh God, pray for our master, Muhammad, and give him peace. Save us for his sake from the attacks of the plague and give us shelter.

The plague frightened and killed. It began in the land of darkness. Oh, what a visitor! It has been current for fifteen years. China was not preserved from it nor could the strongest fortress hinder it. The plague afflicted the Indians in India. It weighed upon the Sind. It seized with its hand and ensnared even the lands of the Uzbeks. How many backs did it break in what is Transoxiana![1] The plague increased and spread further. It attacked the Persians, extended its steps toward the land of the Khitai, and gnawed away at the Crimea. It pelted Rūm with live coals and led the outrage to Cyprus and the islands. The plague destroyed mankind in Cairo. Its eye was cast upon Egypt, and behold, the people were wide-awake. It stilled all movement in Alexandria. The plague did its work like a silkworm. . . .

Then, the plague turned to Upper Egypt. It, also, sent forth its storm to Barqah. The plague attacked Gaza, and it shook 'Asqalān severely. The plague oppressed Acre. The scourge came to Jerusalem and paid the *zakāt*[2] [with the souls of men]. It overtook those people who fled to the al-'Aqsā Mosque, which stands beside the Dome of the Rock. If the door of mercy had not been opened, the end of the world would have occurred in a moment. It then hastened its pace and attacked the entire maritime plain. The plague trapped Sidon and descended unexpectedly upon Beirut, cunningly. Next, it directed the shooting of its arrows to Damascus. There the plague sat like a king on a throne and swayed the power, killing daily one thousand or more and decimating the population. It destroyed mankind with its pustules.[3] May God the Most High spare Damascus to pursue its own path and extinguish the plague's fires so that they do not come close to her fragrant orchards. . . .

The plague and its poison spread to Sarmīn. It reviled the Sunnī and the Shī'ī.[4] It

[1]Sind is a province in northwestern India. The Uzbeks were the Mongol tribes east and southeast of the Ural River. Transoxiana is in central Asia, south and east of the Aral Sea.
[2]*Zakāt* is an annual charitable tax each Muslim was expected to pay.
[3]Pustules are swelling of the skin similar to a blister and were an early sign of the plague.
[4]Sunnī and Shī'ī are two major religious divisions within Islam.

From Michael Dols, *"IBN Al-WARDĪ's RISĀLHA AL-NABA"* An Al-Waba, "A Translation of Major Source for the History of the Black Death in the Middle East," in Dickran K. Kouymjian, ed., *Near Eastern Numismatics, Iconography, Epigraphy and History: Studies in Honor of George C. Miles* (Beirut: American University of Beirut, 1974), pp. 443–55, *passim*. Reprinted by permission.

sharpened its spearheads for the Sunnī and advanced like an army. The plague was spread in the land of the Shī'ī with a ruinous effect. To Antioch the plague gave its share. Then, it left there quickly with a shyness like a man who has forgotten the memory of his beloved. Next, it said to Shayzar and to al-Hārim: "Do not fear me. Before I come and after I go, you can easily disregard me because of your wretchedness. And the ruined places will recover from the time of the plague." Afterward, the plague humbled 'Azāz and took from the people of al-Bāb its men of learning. It ravished Tel Bāshar. The plague subjected Dhulūl and went straight through the lowlands and mountains. It uprooted many people from their homes.

Then, the plague sought Aleppo, but it did not succeed. By God's mercy the plague was the lightest oppression. I would not say that plants must grow from their seeds. . . .

How amazingly does it pursue the people of each house! One of them spits blood, and everyone in the household is certain of death.[5] It brings the entire family to their graves after two or three nights.

Oh God, it is acting by Your command. Lift this from us. It happens where You wish; keep the plague from us. Who will defend us against this horror other than You the Almighty?

How many places has the plague entered? It swore not to leave the houses without its inhabitants. It searched them out with a lamp. The pestilence caused the people of Aleppo the same disturbance. It sent out its snake and crept along. It was named the "Plague of the Ansāb." It was the sixth plague to strike in Islam.[6] To me it is the death of which our Prophet warned, on him be the best prayers and peace.

Oh, if you could see the nobles of Aleppo studying their inscrutable books of medicine. They multiply its remedies by eating dried and sour foods. The buboes which disturb men's healthy lives are smeared with Armenian clay.[7] Each man treated his humours and made life more comfortable.[8] They perfumed their homes with ambergris and camphor, cyperus and sandal.[9] They wore ruby rings and put onions, vinegar, and sardines together with the daily meal. They ate less broth and fruit but ate the citron and similar things.

If you see many biers and their carriers and hear in every quarter of Aleppo the announcements of death and cries, you run from them and refuse to stay with them. In Aleppo the profits of the undertakers have greatly increased. Oh God, do not profit them. Those who sweat from carrying the coffins enjoy this plague-time. Oh God, do not let them sweat and enjoy this. They are happy and play. When they are called by a customer, they do not even go immediately.

> The Grey [i.e., Aleppo] became blackened in my eyes because of the anxiety and deceit. The sons of the coffins [i.e., the undertakers] are themselves about to follow death.

[5]Spitting of blood probably refers to the pneumonic form of plague, which is infectious and quite fatal.

[6]Ibn al-Wardī is referring to the fact that Islamic chroniclers recorded five great plagues before the Black Death's arrival in the fourteenth century.

[7]Buboes are an inflamed swelling of the lymphatic glands, especially in the area of the armpit or groin. The ancient Greek medical authority, Galen, recommended the use of Armenian clay as an astringent for wounds and, because of its abundant iron oxide, he also recommended it for the prevention and treatment of the plague.

[8]Humours refers to the fourteenth-century's physiology of the four body fluids (humours) of blood, phlegm, choler, and black bile. Medieval medical authorities believed that illness resulted when the humours were not in proper equilibrium.

[9]Ambergris is a waxlike substance often found floating on tropical seas; camphor is a white, crystalline solid with a pungent odor and taste; cyperus is an aromatic marsh plant; and sandal probably refers to a medicinal ointment derived from sandalwood.

We ask God's forgiveness for our souls' bad inclination; the plague is surely part of His punishment. We take refuge from His wrath in His pleasure and from His chastisement in His restoring.

They said: the air's corruption kills. I said: the love of corruption kills. How many sins and how many offenses does the crier call our attention to!

Among the things which exasperated the Muslims and brought suffering is that our enemy, the damned people of Sis, are pleased by our trial.[10] They act as if they are safe from the plague—that there is a treaty so that it will not approach them or that they have triumphed over it. Our Lord does not create us as an enticement for those who disbelieve.

The dwellers of Sis are happy with what afflicts us, and this is what you can expect from the enemies of the true religion. God will spread it to them soon so that He will put plague upon plague.

This plague is for the Muslims a martyrdom and a reward, and for the disbelievers a punishment and a rebuke. When the Muslim endures misfortune, then patience is his worship. It has been established by our Prophet: God bless him and give him peace, that the plague-stricken are martyrs. This noble tradition is true and assures martyrdom. And this secret should be pleasing to the true believer. If someone says it causes infection and destruction, say: God creates and recreates. If the liar disputes the matter of infection and tries to find an explanation, I say that the Prophet, on him be peace, said: who infected the first? If we acknowledge the plague's devastation of the people, it is the will of the Chosen Doer. So it happened again and again.

I take refuge in God from the yoke of the plague. Its high explosion has burst into all countries and was an examiner of astonishing things. Its sudden attacks perplex the people. The plague chases the screaming without pity and does not accept a treasure for ransom. Its engine is far-reaching. The plague enters into the house and swears it will not leave except with all of its inhabitants. "I have an order from the *qadi* [a judge] to arrest all those in the house." Among the benefits of this order is the removal of one's hopes and the improvement of his earthly works. It awakens men from their indifference for the provisioning of their final journey.

Nothing prevented us from running away from the plague except our devotion to the noble tradition. Come then, seek the aid of God Almighty for raising the plague, for He is the best helper. Oh God, we call You better than anyone did before. We call You to raise from us the pestilence and plague. We do not take refuge in its removal other than with You. We do not depend on our good health against the plague but on You. We seek Your protection, Oh Lord of creation, from the blows of this stick. We ask for Your mercy which is wider than our sins even as they are the number of the sands and pebbles. We plead with You, by the most honored of the advocates, Muhammad, the Prophet of mercy, that You take away from us this distress. Protect us from the evil and the torture and preserve us. For You are our soul support; what a perfect trustee!

[10]Sis was the ancient capital of the Cilician Armenian kingdom and is reported to have suffered from the Black Death after Aleppo.

A WORLD IN CHANGE

The Rise of the Ottoman Empire

Osman, after whom the Ottomans were named, was the son of Ertogrul, who had led a small group of Turks out of Asia in advance of the Mongols during the second half of the thirteenth century. Ertogrul eventually received a small fief in northeastern Anatolia and became a frontier warrior against the Byzantines.

When Osman succeeded his father, the Ottomans had converted to Islam, which only served to reinforce their military ambitions. The territory expanded slowly until 1354, when a descendant of Osman crossed into Europe (Thrace) and began to attack Byzantine lands as well as other Balkan states.

In 1366, Sultan Murad I decided to move the Ottoman capital from Anatolia to Europe. The emphasis of Ottoman policy for the next century was to be on Christian Europe with the ultimate goal of Constantinople. This was achieved by Mehmed II in 1453, when he captured the former Byzantine capital and made it the center of Ottoman government.

Having eliminated the Byzantine Empire, which had been the chief opposing force to Ottoman expansion toward the West, the Turks moved up the Balkan peninsula and reduced many of the peoples of (the then "future," now "former") Yugoslavia to subjection. In the Balkans, only the Bosnians were willing to accept Islam in any numbers. Most Balkan peoples accepted Turkish occupation passively, but on the northern edge of the Balkans the Wallachians, under their colorful but probably psychopathic leader Dracula, continued to make life difficult for Sultan Mehmed.

83

Konstantin Mihailovic, *Memoirs of a Janissary*

After Mehmed II The Conqueror (1451–1481) had captured Constantinople in 1453 and made it the capital of the Ottoman Empire, he eliminated the last remnants of the Byzantine royal family in Trebizond, on the Black Sea, and in Greece. Thereafter, his Ottoman armies engaged in a series of battles to reduce Albania, Serbia (except for the city of Belgrade), Croatia, and Montenegro to complete subjection. Mehmed frequently sent his raiders across the Danube into the Christian provinces of Moldavia and Wallachia, ruled by the kings of

Hungary, and forced a few of the local princes to become allies. His last action was to begin an invasion of Italy, which was stopped when it was learned by his troops that the Conqueror had died.

These military victories were gained by a very large and well-trained Ottoman army. At the core of the army was the Janissary Corps (*Yeni Cheri* or New Army), whose origins dated to the fourteenth century. The Ottoman sultans decided to create a loyal slave army who would have no ties to family or land from their Christian subjects. At irregular intervals, special commissioners traveled through Albania, Bosnia, and Bulgaria—though any area was subject—and collected a number of Christian boys between ten and fifteen years old. This practice was called *devshirme*. The boys were toughened, converted to Islam, and Turkified and then given out to high Ottoman officials who trained them in the art of war. A very small number were sent to the sultan's palace (Grand Seraglio) in Constantinople, where they were trained to hold the highest governmental positions.

The following selections come from the *Memoirs* of a Serb named Konstantin Mihailovic (1430s?–?), who was captured in 1455 when Mehmed II tried to take the city of Belgrade. Without the necessary education or training, Konstantin acquired some function in the Janissary Corps as he was engaged in 1456 in Mehmed's siege of Belgrade. He later went with the sultan to fight against Trebizond and to participate in raids against Vlad Tsepes (Dracula) in Wallachia. He was finally put in charge of a Bosnian fortress in 1463. The Hungarian king, Matthew Corvinus, quickly captured the fortress, and Konstantin reconverted to Christianity. After these experiences, the author traveled through Bohemia, Hungary, and Poland, where he settled to write his memoirs.

The first part of the selection relates how Mehmed II captured Konstantin and how the sultan later punished Serbian (Raskan) youths who had tried to assassinate him. The second describes the gathering, training, organization, and a typical military operation of the Janissaries.

QUESTIONS TO CONSIDER

1. Why did the Ottoman sultans form the Janissary Corps from Christian tribute boys and not from Muslim boys?
2. What were the rewards or punishments for these boys?

And from there the Emperor marched and surrounded a city which they called Novo Brdo, "Mountain of Silver and Gold," and having attacked it, conquered it [June, 1455], but by means of an agreement: he promised to let them keep their possessions and also not to enslave their young women and boys. And when the city of Novo Brdo had surrendered, the Emperor ordered that the gates be closed and that one small gate be left open. Having arrived in the city the Turks ordered all the householders with their families, both males and females, to go out of the city through the small gate to a ditch, leaving their possessions in

Konstantin Mihailovic, *Memoirs of a Janissary*, trans. Benjamin Stolz (Ann Arbor: Michigan Slavic Translations, no. 3, Michigan Slavic Publications, 1975), pp. 99–101, 157–59, 185–87. Published under the auspices of the Joint Committee on Eastern Europe, American Council of Learned Societies by the Department of Slavic Languages and Literatures. Reprinted by permission.

the houses. And so it happened that they went one after another, and the Emperor himself standing before the small gate sorted out the boys on one side and the females on the other, and the men along the ditch on one side and the women on the other side. All those among the men who were the most important and distinguished he ordered decapitated. The remainder he ordered released to the city. As for their possessions, nothing of theirs was harmed. The boys were 320 in number and the females 74. The females he distributed among the heathens, but he took the boys for himself into the Janissaries, and sent them beyond the sea to Anatolia, where their preserve is.

I was also taken in that city with my two brothers, and wherever the Turks to whom we were entrusted drove us in a band, and wherever we came to forests or mountains, there we always thought about killing the Turks and running away by ourselves among the mountains, but our youth did not permit us to do that; for I myself with nineteen others ran away from them in the night from a village called Samokovo. Then the whole region pursued us, and having caught and bound us, they beat us and tortured us and dragged us behind horses. It is a wonder that our soul remained in us. Then others vouched for us, and my two brothers, that we would not permit this anymore, and so they peacefully led us across the sea.

Then the Emperor, having arrived at Adrianople, took eight youths of this same group among the chamberlains. These youths agreed to kill the Emperor on night watch, saying among themselves, "If we kill this Turkish dog, then all of Christendom will be freed; but if we are caught, then we will become martyrs before God with the others."

And when the night watch came, they had made preparations, each having a knife on himself. And when the Emperor was to go to his bedchamber, then one of them named Dmitar Tomašić left them as an ignoble traitor and told the Emperor what was to happen. Then the Emperor ordered them seized and brought before him. The Emperor, having seen a knife on each one, asked them: "Who led you to this, that you dared attempt this?" Their reply was in a word: "None other than our great sorrow for our fathers and dear friends."

Then the Emperor ordered that hens' eggs be brought and ordered that they be placed in hot ashes so that they would be baked as hard as possible. And having taken them from the ashes, he had a hot egg fastened under each one's knee so that their muscles would shrink and burn. Then he ordered that they be carried by wagon to Persia with the eggs [attached], not allowing them to be removed from them until they cooled off by themselves. And after a year he ordered that they be brought back; and seeing that there was nothing to them, he ordered them beheaded, and several of us, having taken the bodies in the night, buried them beside an empty church called "Does Not See the Sun." And so it happened to those youths in Constantinople. And the one who had warned the Emperor he made a great lord at his court, but later such a serious illness—some sort of consumption—befell him, that he dried up to death. And his heathen name was Haydari. And so the Lord God deigned to visit that upon him for his ignobility and faithlessness.

Thereafter Emperor Machomet did not want to have any Raškan boys in his bedchamber. So he took six boys and had all their genital organs cut off to the very abdomen; and so one died and five remained alive. They are called in their language *hadomlar,* which means in our language "eunuchs." And these guard the Emperor's wives.

Whenever the Turks invade foreign lands and capture their people an imperial scribe follows immediately behind them, and whatever boys there are, he takes them all into the Janissaries and gives five gold pieces for each one and sends them across the sea. There are about two thousand of these boys. If, however, the number of them from enemy peoples does not suffice, then he takes from the Christians in every village in his land who have boys, having established what is the most every village can give so that the quota will always be full. And the boys whom he takes in his own land are called *cilik.* Each one of them can leave his property to whomever he wants after his death. And those whom he takes among the enemies are called *pendik.* These latter after their deaths can leave nothing; rather, it goes to the emperor, except that if someone comports himself well and is so deserving that he be freed, he may leave it to whomever he wants. And on the boys who are across the sea the emperor spends nothing; rather, those to whom they are entrusted must maintain them and send them where he orders. Then they take those who are suited for it on ships and there they study and train to skirmish in battle. There the emperor already provides for them and gives them a wage. From there he chooses for his own court those who are trained and then raises their wages. The younger must serve the older, and those who come of age and attain manhood he assigns to the fortress so that they will look after them. . . .

And at the court there are about four thousand Janissaries, and among them there is the following organization. They have over them a senior hetman [military commander] called an *aga,* a great lord. He receives ten gold pieces a day, and his steward, one gold piece a day. To each centurion they give a gold piece every two days, and to their stewards, a gold piece every four days. And all their sons who grow out of boyhood have a wage from the emperor. And no courtier who permits himself something will be punished by the honest ones by fine, but rather by death; they dare not, however, punish any courtier publicly, but secretly, because of the other courtiers, for they would revolt. And no Janissary nor any decurion [cavalry commander] of theirs dare ride a horse, save the hetman himself and the steward. And among them it is so arranged that some are archers who shoot bows, some are gunners who shoot mortars, other muskets, and still others, crossbows. And every day they must appear with their weapons before their hetmans. And he gives each one a gold piece per year for a bow, and in addition a tunic, a shirt, and large trousers made, as is their fashion, of three ells [27–45 inches in length] of cloth, and a shirt of eight ells. And this I myself distributed to them for two years from the imperial court.

Concerning the Organization of a Turkish Assault

The Turkish emperor storms and captures cities and also fortresses at great expense in order not to remain there long with the army. First having battered the city or fortress walls until it seems sufficient to him, and seeing that it is the moment to launch a general assault, he then orders it to be cried throughout the army first that horses and camels and all kinds of stock be brought from pasture to the army; and when that is accomplished, he then orders it to be cried throughout the army second specifying the day of the assault. And they prefer to set the day on Friday. And they crying thus, they name the rewards in this fashion: to the one who carries a banner upon the wall they promise a voivodeship [governorship]; . . . to others, money, naming the sum; and in addition, distributing various garments. And whatever is mentioned then, without fail all of this if fulfilled and carried out whether the city is taken or not taken.

Then they cry in the evening throughout the army that lighted tallow candles be raised profusely throughout the army so that it looks as if the stars are shining profusely above the clouds. And that night and early in the morning the next day they prepare themselves for the assault, right up to evening.

And at night then they go toward the city from all sides silently, slowly approaching the fosse [ditch], carrying before them barricades woven of branches and also strongly-built ladders so that they can climb up and down both sides of the ladder. The Janissaries then in this fashion go to the place where the wall is breached, and having approached the breached place, they wait until day begins to appear. Then first the gunners fire from all the cannon and when they have fired off the cannon, the Janissaries quickly scale the wall, for at this moment the Christians are retreating before the cannon, and when they see that the Janissaries are on the walls, having turned about suddenly, they begin to fight bravely on both sides. And here the Janissaries, urging one another on, climb up. And in addition the shot from bows comes very thick, for they continually bring and replenish their shot, and besides [there is] a great tumult from drums and human outcry. Thus the battle lasts an hour or at most two, and if the Christians overcome the heathens in that time, then little by little the heathens weaken and slack off and the Christians grow stronger. And so this assault lasts until noon and can last no longer, for the ammunition is used up, some men are killed, some are wounded, and some are exhausted.

The emperor, seeing that he cannot take it, orders them to retreat from the city and to pull the cannon and other equipment away from the wall and to load them on wagons. And having picked up all the wounded he orders them sent ahead and himself stays at this place until nightfall, and only in the night departs from there with the whole army so that they will not cry out at them from the fortress. Therefore he always posts a rear guard in case some troops should come out of the fortress in order to seek vengeance upon them somehow. Therefore the men who are in the fortresses must take care not to ride or run out of the fortress haphazardly.

If, then, a certain fortress or city once defends itself against him, he will not make another attempt for a long time.

Now those heathens who are crippled in the arm or leg, each of them is provided by the emperor with a livelihood until he dies. And thus a Turkish general assault is accomplished.

84

Kritovoulos, *History of Mehmed the Conqueror*

Mehmed II (reigned 1451–1481) assumed the throne of the Ottoman Empire on the death of his father, Murad II. The new sultan began at once to plan his greatest achievement—the seizure of Constantinople from the last Byzantine Emperor, Constantine XI. This successful capture would earn Mehmed II the title of "The Conqueror."

In 1452, Mehmed gathered thousands of cavalry, Janissaries (Christian tribute slaves), irregular troops, naval personnel, and military engineers for the undertaking. For 54 days during the months of April and May 1453, the sultan's forces pounded on the eleven-hundred-year-old impenetrable land walls. Finally, on May 29 of that same year, his men, spying an inadvertently unlocked sally port, poured into the capital with a frenzy. That fateful day extinguished Greek independence for almost four centuries.

After taking the city, Sultan Mehmed's troops were not allowed to rest. For almost the next thirty years, they raided and captured land and inhabitants in the Balkans, Wallachia-Moldavia (Romania), and even in the hinterland of Venice.

The *History of Mehmed the Conqueror* is by a contemporary Greek historian named Kritovoulos. Little is known of this writer except that he was not at the fall of Constantinople but soon arrived at that city to record Mehmed's life. Kritovoulos eventually entered the sultan's service and became a governor on the island of Imbros.

QUESTIONS TO CONSIDER

1. Why was Mehmed II successful in his naval attack on the city?
2. Can you find an example that illustrates the superstitious nature of the Byzantines?
3. How would you compare the actions of the Ottoman warriors with those of the sultan when the city had been taken?
4. How did the fall of the Byzantine Empire affect the growth of the Russian monarchy (see Reading 87)?

He also resolved to carry into execution immediately the plan which he had long since studied out and elaborated in his mind and toward which he had bent every purpose from the start, and to wait no longer nor delay. This plan was to make war against the Romans [Byzantines or Greeks] and their Emperor Constantine and to besiege the city. For he thought, as was true, that if he could succeed in capturing it and becoming master of it, there was nothing to hinder him from sallying forth from it in a short time, as from a stronghold for all the environs, and overrunning all and subduing them to himself. For this reason he could no longer be restrained at all. He did not think he ought to stay quiet in his own parts any longer and maintain peace, but believed he should speedily make war and capture the city. . . .

Sultan Mehmed considered it necessary in preparation for his next move to get possession of the harbor and open the Horn for his own ships to sail in. So, since every effort and device of his had failed to force the entrance, he made a wise decision, and one worthy of his intellect and power. It succeeded in accomplishing his purpose and in putting an end to all uncertainties.

He ordered the commanders of the vessels to construct as quickly as possible glideways leading from the outer sea to the inner sea, that is, from the harbor to the Horn, near the place called Diplokion, and to cover them with beams. This road, measured from sea to sea, is just about eight stadia. It is very steep for more than half the way, until you reach the summit of the hill, and from there again it descends to the inner sea of the Horn. And as the glideways were completed sooner than expected, because of the large number of workers, he brought up the ships and placed large cradles under them, with stays against each of their sides to hold them up. And having undergirded them well with ropes, he fastened long cables to the corners and gave them to the soldiers to drag, some of them by hand, and others by certain machines and capstans. . . .

Thus, then, there was assembled in the bay called Cold Waters, a little beyond Galata, a respectable fleet of some sixty-seven vessels. They were moored there.

The Romans, when they saw such an unheard-of-thing actually happen, and warships lying at anchor in the Horn—which they never would have suspected—were astounded at the impossibility of the spectacle, and were overcome by the greatest consternation and perplexity. They did not know what to do now, but were in despair. In fact they had left un-

From Kritovoulos, *History of Mehmed the Conqueror,* trans. Charles T. Riggs (Princeton, NJ: Princeton University Press, 1954), pp. 22–23, 55–59, 66–67, 70–72, 76–77, 82–83. Copyright 1954, © renewed 1982 by Princeton University Press. Reprinted with permission of Princeton University Press.

guarded the walls along the Horn for a distance of about thirty stadia, and even so they did not have enough men for the rest of the walls, either for defense or for attack, whether citizens or men from elsewhere. Instead, two or even three battlements had but a single defender.

And now, when this sea-wall also became open to attack and had to be guarded, they were compelled to strip the other battlements and bring men there. This constituted a manifest danger, since the defenders were taken away from the rest of the wall while those remaining were not enough to guard it, being so few. . . .

During those same days there occurred the following divine signs and portents of the terrors that were very soon to come to the city. Three or four days before the battle, when all the people in the City were holding a religious procession, men and women together, and marching around with the Ikon of the Mother of God, this latter slipped suddenly from the hands of its bearers without any cause or power being apparent, and fell flat on the ground. And when everybody shouted immediately, and rushed to raise up the ikon, it sank down as if weighted with lead, and as if fastened to the ground, and became well-nigh impossible to raise. And so it continued for a considerable time, until, by a great effort and much shouting and prayers by all, the priests and its bearers barely managed to raise it up and place it on the shoulders of the men.

This strange occurrence filled everyone with much terror and very great agony and fear, for they thought this fall was no good omen—as was quite true. Later, when they had gone on but a short distance, immediately after that, at high noon, there was much thunder and lightning with clouds, and a violent rain with severe hail followed, so that they could neither stand against it nor make any progress. The priests and the bearers of the ikon and the crowds that followed were depressed and hindered by the force of the waters that flowed down and by the might of the hail. Many of the children following were in danger of being carried away and drowned by the violent and powerful rush of water, had not some men quickly seized them and with some difficulty dragged them out of the flood. Such was the unheard-of and unprecedented violence of that storm and hail which certainly foreshadowed the imminent loss of all, and that, like a torrent of fiercest waters, it would carry away and annihilate everything. . . .

The hour was already advanced, the day [May 28, 1453] was declining and near evening, and the sun was at the Ottoman's backs but shining in the faces of their enemies. This was just as the Sultan had wished; accordingly he gave the order first for the trumpets to sound the battle-signal, and the other instruments, the pipes and flutes and cymbals too, as loud as they could. All the trumpets of the other divisions, with the other instruments in turn, sounded all together, a great and fearsome sound. Everything shook and quivered at the noise. After that, the standards were displayed.

To begin, the archers and slingers and those in charge of the cannon and the muskets, in accord with the commands given them, advanced against the wall slowly and gradually. When they got within bowshot, they halted to fight. And first they exchanged fire with the heavier weapons, with arrows from the archers, stones from the slingers, and iron and leaden balls from the cannon and muskets. Then, as they closed with battleaxes and javelins and spears, hurling them at each other and being hurled at pitilessly in rage and fierce anger. On both sides there was loud shouting and blasphemy and cursing. Many on each side were wounded, and not a few died. This kept up till sunset, a space of about two or three hours.

Then, with fine insight, the Sultan summoned the shield-bearers, heavy infantry and other troops and said: "Go to it, friends and children mine! It is time now to show yourselves good fighters!" They immediately crossed the moat, with shouts and fearful yells, and attacked the outer wall. All of it, however, had been demolished by the cannon. There were only stockades of great beams instead of a wall, and bundles of vine-branches, and jars full of earth. At that point a fierce battle ensued close in and with the weapons of hand-to-hand fighting. The heavy infantry and shield-bearers fought to overcome the defenders and get over the stockade, while the Romans and Italians tried to fight these off and to guard the stockade. At times the infantry did get over the wall and the stockade, pressing forward bravely and unhesitatingly. And at times they were stoutly forced back and driven off. . . .

Sultan Mehmed, who happened to be fighting quite near by, saw that the palisade and the other part of the wall that had been destroyed were now empty of men and deserted by the defenders. He noted that men were slipping away secretly and that those who remained were fighting feebly because they were so few. Realizing from this that the defenders had fled and that the wall was deserted, he shouted out: "Friends, we have the City! We have it! They are already fleeing from us! They can't stand it any longer! The wall is bare of defenders! It needs just a little more effort and the City is taken! Don't weaken, but on with the work with all your might, and be men and I am with you!"

Capture of the City

So saying, he led them himself. And they, with a shout on the run and with a fearsome yell, went on ahead of the Sultan, pressing on up to the palisade. After a long and bitter struggle they hurled back the Romans from there and climbed by force up the palisade. They dashed some of their foe down into the ditch between the great wall and the palisade, which was deep and hard to get out of, and they killed them there. The rest they drove back to the gate.

Death of Emperor Constantine

He had opened this gate in the great wall, so as to go easily over to the palisade. Now there was a great struggle there and great slaughter among those stationed there, for they were attacked by the heavy infantry and not a few others in irregular formation, who had been attracted from many points by the shouting. There the Emperor Constantine, with all who were with him, fell in gallant combat. . . .

Then a great slaughter occurred of those who happened to be there: some of them were on the streets, for they had already left the houses and were running toward the tumult when they fell unexpectedly on the swords of the soldiers; others were in their own homes and fell victims to the violence of the Janissaries and other soldiers, without any rhyme or reason; others were resisting, relying on their own courage; still others were fleeing to the churches and making supplication—men, women, and children, everyone, for there was no quarter given.

The soldiers fell on them with anger and great wrath. For one thing, they were actuated by the hardships of the siege. For another, some foolish people had hurled taunts and curses at them from the battlements all through the siege. Now, in general they killed so as to frighten all the City, and to terrorize and enslave all by the slaughter. . . .

Other women, sleeping in their beds, had to endure nightmares. Men with swords, their hands bloodstained with murder, breathing out rage, speaking out murder indiscriminate, flushed with all the worst things—this crowd, made up of men from every race and nation, brought together by chance, like wild and ferocious beasts, leaped into the houses, driving them out mercilessly, dragging, rending, forcing, hauling them disgracefully into the public highways, insulting them and doing every evil thing.

They say that many of the maidens, even at the mere unaccustomed sight and sound of these men, were terror-stricken and came near losing their very lives. And there were also honorable old men who were dragged by their white hair, and some of them beaten unmercifully. And well-born and beautiful young boys were carried off. . . .

After this the Sultan entered the City and looked about to see its great size, its situation, its grandeur and beauty, its teeming population, its loveliness, and the costliness of its churches and public buildings and of the private houses and community houses and of those of the officials. He also saw the setting of the harbor and of the arsenals, and how skillfully and ingeniously they had everything arranged in the City—in a word, all the construction and adornment of it. When he saw what a large number had been killed, and the ruin of the buildings, and the wholesale ruin and destruction of the City, he was filled with compassion and repented not a little at the destruction and plundering. Tears fell from his eyes as he groaned deeply and passionately: "What a city we have given over to plunder and destruction!" . . .

The Sultan Mehmed, when he had carefully viewed the City and all its contents, went back to the camp and divided the spoils. First he took the customary toll of the spoils for himself. Then also, as prizes from all the rest, he chose out beautiful virgins and those of the best families, and the handsomest boys, some of whom he even bought from the soldiers. He also chose some of the distinguished men who, he was informed, were above the rest in family and intelligence and valor. . . .

Then, with the notable men, and his courtiers, he went through the City. First he planned how to repopulate it, not merely as it formerly was but more completely, if possible, so that it should be a worthy capital for him, situated, as it was, most favorably by land and by sea. Then he donated to all the grandees, and to those of his household, the magnificent homes of the rich, with gardens and fields and vineyards inside of the City. And to some of them he even gave beautiful churches as their private residences.

For himself, he chose the most beautiful location in the center of the City for the erection of a royal palace. After this, he settled all the captives whom he had taken as his portion, together with their wives and children, along the shores of the city harbor, since they were sea-faring men whom they previously had called Stenites. He gave them houses and freed them from taxes for a specified time.

He also made a proclamation to all those who had paid their own ransom, or who promised to pay it to their masters within a limited time, that they might live in the City, and he granted them, also, freedom from taxes, and gave them houses, either their own or those of others.

He wanted those of the nobility whom he approved of to live there with their wives and children. Accordingly he gave them houses and lands and provisions for living, and tried in every way to help them. This was his intention and purpose, as has been stated.

85

Vlad Tsepes, "The Impaler": The Real Dracula or How the Enemy of the Ottomans Became a Legend

Vlad Tsepes (1431–1476) was born to Vlad Dracul (Order of the Dragon), who was the voivode (governor) of Wallachia (modern Romania). Hemmed between his sovereign, the Christian king of Hungary, and the Ottoman Empire south of the Danube, Vlad Dracul tried to placate both sides in order to keep his power. He was to lose on all accounts. In 1444, Sultan Murad II forced Dracul to give his sons Vlad Tsepes and a younger brother Radu the Handsome as hostages, and three years later King Mathias of Hungary ordered Dracul's assassination for disloyalty.

Vlad Tsepes managed to escape Ottoman captivity in 1448. He set about regaining control of Wallachia through intrigue and invasions. He finally achieved his goal in 1456 and ruled the area until 1462. It was during these years that Dracula engaged in a frenzy of killing; none were immune to his savage nature—the poor, nobles, or Ottoman Turks were killed by impaling, skinning, boiling, or decapitation. Finally, in 1462, Sultan Mehmed II invaded Wallachia, chased Vlad out, and placed Vlad's brother Radu in power.

Vlad fled to Hungary, where he was kept in prison and house arrest under suspicion of disloyalty until 1474. He was able to rehabilitate himself in the eyes of Mathias, with whose aid he tried once more, in 1476, to regain Wallachia from his brother. He was successful for two months. When the Hungarian forces, who had helped him, left the lands, a native uprising cost Vlad his throne and his head.

The following two selections contrast Dracula's personality and actions. The first selection details Dracula's strategy against an invasion of Wallachia by Sultan Mehmed II. The second comes from manuscripts and folktales that were created about Dracula and have passed into legend in Russia, Germany, and Romania. Most of these stories relate Dracula's vicious nature, but some, we might say, contain a sense of "black humor."

QUESTIONS TO CONSIDER

1. How do Dracula's methods compare with those of King Ashurnasirpal of Assyria (Reading 12)?
2. Can you cite similar examples of inhumanity to the present time?
3. Why could Dracula be called a national savior for Wallachia?
4. What constitutes Dracula's "black humor"?

Dracula Defends Wallachia Against Sultan Mehmed II

In the year 6970 [1462] Mehmed dispatched an ambassador to the voivode of Vlachia[1] commanding him to come quickly to make obeisance and to bring with him five hundred boys as well as the annual tribute of ten thousand gold coins. He replied that whereas the gold coins were ready for payment, he was unable to deliver the boys, and moreover, for him to come and make obeisance was completely out of the question. When the tyrant[2] heard this he became wild with rage. He dispatched one of his nobles and one of his secretaries, and told them, "Bring me the tribute, and I myself will give some thought to the rest." When,

---

[1] Vlad Tsepes (Dracula).
[2] "The tyrant" is Mehmed II, not Dracula ("The Vlach").

From Michael Doukas, *Decline and Fall of Byzantium to the Ottoman Turks,* trans. Harry J. Magoulias (Detroit: Wayne State University Press, 1975), pp. 259–61. Copyright © 1975 by Wayne State University Press. Reprinted with permission.

on their arrival, they disclosed the tyrant's message to the Vlach, he impaled them on stakes, condemning them to an inhuman, excruciating, and ignominious death. The Vlach afterward crossed the Danube with his troops and overran the environs of Dristra. He took captive many of the rabble and transported them to Vlachia, after which he took their lives by meting out the same death by impalement.

One of the tyrant's[2] commanders who was stationed along these borders, desiring to display his prowess, crossed into Vlachia with ten thousand Turkish troops. The Vlach engaged them in battle and all those Turks who were not killed but taken alive, he condemned to bitter death by impalement, together with their commander Hamza.

The tyrant, apprised of these events, was distraught. Mustering from all quarters a force of more than one hundred and fifty thousand men, he marched out of Adrianople in the spring and came to the Danube. There he pitched his tents and waited until the entire army was assembled. The Vlach, deploying all his troops along mountain defiles and wooded areas, left the plains deserted. Flocks of all kinds of animals were driven into the interior toward the borders of the Alans and Hunns [Poland and Hungary], while he passed the days with his troops in the dense woodlands and forest areas. The tyrant crossed the Danube and, during a march of over seven days, found nothing whatsoever, neither man nor animal nor food nor drink of any kind. He came upon a meadow where he saw countless stakes planted in the ground, laden not with fruit but with corpses, and on a stake in the middle was transfixed Hamza, still wearing his purple and red garments. When the tyrant beheld this terrible portent, he was panic-stricken. Terrified of the night, he raised trench embankments in the area where he had pitched his tents and lay down between the trenches. The Vlach, rising in the half-light of dawn and drawing up his troops in battle array, descended while it was still dark. He came by chance upon the right side of the camp, and made a sudden charge inside; by morning he had already cut down countless numbers. Until dawn broke, the Turks were killing one another. With the coming of daylight, the Vlachs returned to their bivouacs and bedded down. The tyrant, in disgrace, crossed the Danube and returned to Adrianople.

Folktales about Dracula

There lived in the Wallachian lands a Christian prince of the Greek faith who was called Dracula in the Wallachian language, which means devil in our language, for he was as cruelly clever as was his name and so was his life.

Once some ambassadors from the Turkish sultan came to him. When they entered his palace and bowed to him, as was their custom, they did not take their caps from their heads and Dracula asked them: "Why have you acted so? You ambassadors have come to a great prince and you have shamed me." The ambassadors answered, "Such is the custom which our land has, Lord." And Dracula told them, "Well, I want to strengthen you in your law. Behave bravely." And he ordered that their caps be nailed to their heads with small iron nails. And then he allowed them to go. He said, "Go tell your lord, for he is a cultured man: let him accept this shame from us. For you seem to think that we are not cultured. Let him

From Raymond T. McNally and Radu Florescu, *In search of Dracula a true history of Dracula and vampire legends* (New York: Galahad Books, 1972), pp. 193–94, 196, 198, 207–08. The German stories come from Ms. 806 at the Monastery Library of St. Gall, Switzerland, the Russian stories are from Ms. 11/1088 in the Kirillov-Belozersky Monastery Collection in the Saltykov-Schredin Public Library in St. Petersburg and the Romanian stories are word of mouth. They were all translated by the authors. Copyright 1972 by Raymond T. McNally and Radu Florescu.

not impose his customs on other rulers who will not accept them, but let him keep his customs in his own land."

Once Dracula ordered throughout the land that whoever was old or sick or poor should come to him. And there gathered at the palace a huge multitude of poor and old people, who expected a great act of mercy. And he ordered that all these miserable people be gathered together, in a large palace which was prepared with this idea in mind. And he ordered that they be given food and drink in accordance with their wishes. So they began to eat, and they became happy. Later on Dracula personally came to see them and spoke to them in the following way: "What else do you need?" And they answered him in unison, "Our good lord, God knows how to give, and your highness surely understands the wishes of God." He then said to them, "Do you want me to make you without any further cares, so that you have no other wants in this world?" And they all expected some great gift and they answered, "We wish it so, my lord." Then he ordered that the palace be locked and he set it on fire, and all of them perished within it. Later he told his nobles, "Know that I have done this so that these unfortunate people will have no further burdens, and so that there should be no more poor in my land but only rich people, and in the second place I freed these people so that they no longer suffer in this world either because of poverty, or because of sickness."

If a woman made love with a man who was not her husband Dracula ordered that her vagina be cut and he skinned her alive and tied her skin to a pole. And the skin was usually hanging on the pole in the middle of the city right there in the market place. He did the same thing with young girls who had not preserved their virginity and also widows. In some cases he cut the nipples of their breasts. In other cases he took the skins from their vagina and he placed an iron poker, reddened by fire, up their vaginas so far upwards that the iron bar emerged from their mouths. They remained naked, tied to a pole until the flesh and bones detached themselves or served as food for the birds.

Dracula had a mistress. Her house was located in a dark and isolated suburb of Targoviste. When Dracula went to see her he was oblivious of everything, for this woman unfortunately happened to be to his taste. For her, he had mere physical attraction, nothing else.

The unfortunate woman tried in every way to be pleasing to Dracula. And he reciprocated all the outward manifestations of love which she showed him. One might also say that Dracula expressed a certain gaiety when he was by her side.

One day when she saw his expression somewhat gloomier, she wished in some way to cheer him up and she dared tell him a lie. "Your highness, you will be glad to hear my tidings." "What news can you give me?" answered Dracula. "The little mouse," she answered allegorically, "has entered the milk churn." "What does this mean?" questioned Dracula, grinning. "It means, Your Highness, that I am with child." "Don't you dare prattle such tales." The woman knew Dracula's method of punishing lies and wished to justify her statement. "It is, Your Highness, as I have said." "This will not be," said Dracula, frowning with his eyebrows. "But if it were possible I reckon that Your Highness would be glad," dared she continue. "I told you this will *not* be," retorted Dracula, rudely stamping his foot, "and I will show you it will not happen." Unsheathing his sword, he opened her entrails in order to see for himself whether she had spoken the truth or had lied.

As the woman lay dying, Dracula told her: "You see that it cannot be." He left while she agonized in great pain. She was punished because, hoping to cheer up her lover, she had told a lie.

Dracula caused many other sufferings and such great pain and tortures as all the bloodthirsty persecutors of Christendom, such as Herod, Nero and Diocletian and other pagans had never thought up or made such martyrs as did this bloodthirsty berserker. Once he had humans impaled, usually indiscriminately, young and old, women and men. People also tried to defend themselves with hands and feet and they twisted around and twitched like frogs. After that he had them also impaled and spoke often in this language: "Oh, what great gracefulness they exhibit!" And they were pagans, Jews, Christians, heretics, and Wallachians.

Once he caught a gypsy who had stolen. Then the other gypsies came to him and begged Dracula to release him to them. Dracula said: "He should hang, and you must hang him." They said: "That is not our custom." Dracula had the gypsy boiled in a pot, and when he was cooked, he forced them to eat him, flesh and bone.

Once a nobleman was sent to him, who came to him among the people whom he had impaled. There, Dracula walked under them and gazed upon them, and there were as many as a great forest. And he asked Dracula why he walked around under the stench. Dracula asked: "Do you mind the stink?" The other man said: "Yes." So Dracula immediately had him impaled and hoisted him up high in the air, so that he would not smell the stench.

Once a priest had preached that sins could not be forgiven until one made good the injustice done. Then Dracula had that same priest invited to his house and set him at his table. Then the lord had simmel bread put into his food. The priest took the broken bread up with his tablespoon. Then the lord spoke about how he had preached about sins, etc., etc. The priest said: "Lord, it is true." He said: "Why then do you take from me my bread, which I have broken into the food?" And he immediately had him impaled.

The sultan sent an ambassador once to Dracula, in order that he be given the yearly tribute. Dracula greatly honored this ambassador and showed him the whole treasury which he had. And said, "I not only wish to give the sultan the yearly tax, but I also wish to go in his service with my whole army and with my whole treasury. I shall do as he commands and you shall announce this to your emperor, so that when I shall place myself at his disposal, he will give orders in his whole land that no harm should come to me or to my men. And I shall come to my sultan, my liege, quickly after you get back. And I shall bring him the yearly tribute, and I shall personally place myself at his disposal."

When the sultan heard from his ambassador that Dracula wished to come into his service, he honored the ambassador and gave him gifts, and was happy because at that time the Turkish sultan was at war with many of the eastern countries. Immediately the sultan sent to all his fortresses and towns and throughout his land the message that when Dracula comes, no one should do him any harm. On the contrary, they should honor him. Dracula set out with his whole army. With him were his various yeomen. And he was greeted and greatly honored by the emperor. And he traveled throughout the Turkish empire for about five days. But then suddenly instead of helping the sultan, he began to rob and attack the towns and the villages. And he captured many prisoners whose heads he cut off. Some he impaled, others he cut in two, and others he burned. The whole country which he penetrated was laid to waste. He allowed no one to remain alive, not even the babes in the arms of their mothers. But others, that is, those who were Christian, he spared and set them up in his own lands. After taking much booty, he returned to Wallachia. And he set a few prisoners free and said, "Go and tell your sultan what you have seen. As much as I could, I have served him. If my service was pleasing to him, I shall serve him again with as much power as I can." And the sultan could do nothing against him and fled in shame. [*This episode from 1462 is confirmed by historical documents.*] Dracula so hated evil in his land that if someone stole, lied or committed some injustice, he was not likely to stay alive. Whether he was a nobleman, or a priest or a monk or a common man, and even if he had great wealth, he could not escape death if he were dishonest. And he was so feared that the peasants say that in a certain place, near the source of the river, there was a fountain; at this fountain at the source of this river, there came many travelers from many lands and all these people came to drink at the fountain, because the water was cool and sweet. Dracula had purposely put this fountain in a deserted place, and had set a cup wonderfully wrought in gold and who-ever wished to drink the water, had to drink it from this gold cup and had to put it back in its place. And so long as this cup was there no one dared to steal it. [*Romanian folklore stresses Dracula's maintenance of law and order.*]

The Rise of Russia

The Byzantine Greeks converted the pagan Russians to Orthodox Christianity in the tenth century. With their conversion, the Russians obtained an alphabet, so they might copy religious texts; they also adopted many aspects of Byzantine culture, which merged with their pagan Slavic and Viking culture.

In the thirteenth century, the close ties between Constantinople and Rus-sia—still only a loose confederation of city-states—were broken by the Mongol conquest, which lasted over 200 years. It was not until the fifteenth century that the Moscovite Grand Princes succeeded in casting off the Mongol yoke and uni-fying Russia into a nation-state. Russian ties with Orthodox Christendom were then renewed; but, by coincidence, Constantinople and the eastern Roman Em-pire fell in 1453 to the Ottoman Turks.

86

The Russian Primary Chronicle

The Russian Primary Chronicle is the first written document for Russian history. It is a collection of different texts, written by monks in the twelfth century, about the period 852–1120. Modeled on Greek sources, the Chronicle offers a reli-gious interpretation of past events, incorporating legendary and mythical stories about the early Russian princes and nobles (*boyars*).

QUESTIONS TO CONSIDER

1. Why did the Russians choose Greek Orthodoxy over other religions?
2. How did this choice affect Russia's relations with Western Europe?

Vladimir summoned together his boyars and the city-elders, and said to them, "Behold, the Bulgars came before me urging me to accept their religion. Then came the Germans and praised their own faith; and after them came the Jews. Finally the Greeks appeared, criti-

From *The Russian Primary Chronicle: Laurentian Text,* trans. and ed. Samuel Hazzard Cross and Olgerd P. Sherbowitz-Wetzor (Cambridge, MA: The Medieval Academy of America, 1953), pp. 110–13. Reprinted by per-mission of The Medieval Academy of America. Footnotes omitted.

cizing all other faiths but commending their own, and they spoke at length, telling the history of the whole world from its beginning. Their words were artful, and it was wondrous to listen and pleasant to hear them. They preach the existence of another world. 'Whoever adopts our religion and then dies shall arise and live forever. But whosoever embraces another faith, shall be consumed with fire in the next world.' What is your opinion on this subject, and what do you answer?" The boyars and the elders replied, "You know, oh Prince, that no man condemns his own possessions, but praises them instead. If you desire to make certain, you have servants at your disposal. Send them to inquire about the ritual of each and how he worships God."

Their counsel pleased the prince and all the people, so that they chose good and wise men to the number of ten, and directed them to go first among the Bulgars and inspect their faith. The emissaries went their way, and when they arrived at their destination they beheld the disgraceful actions of the Bulgars and their worship in the mosque; then they returned to their country. Vladimir than instructed them to go likewise among the Germans, and examine their faith, and finally to visit the Greeks. They thus went into Germany, and after viewing the German ceremonial, they proceeded to Tsar'grad, where they appeared before the Emperor. He inquired on what mission they had come, and they reported to him all that had occurred. When the Emperor heard their words, he rejoiced, and did them great honor on that very day.

On the morrow, the Emperor sent a message to the Patriarch to inform him that a Russian delegation had arrived to examine the Greek faith, and directed him to prepare the church and the clergy, and to array himself in his sacerdotal robes, so that the Russes might behold the glory of the God of the Greeks. When the Patriarch received these commands, he bade the clergy assemble, and they performed the customary rites. They burned incense, and the choirs sang hymns. The Emperor accompanied the Russes to the church, and placed them in a wide space, calling their attention to the beauty of the edifice, the chanting, and the pontifical services and the ministry of the deacons, while he explained to them the worship of his God. The Russes were astonished, and in their wonder praised the Greek ceremonial. Then the Emperors Basil and Constantine invited the envoys to their presence, and said, "Go hence to your native country," and dismissed them with valuable presents and great honor.

Thus they returned to their own country, and the Prince called together his boyars and the elders. Vladimir then announced the return of the envoys who had been sent out, and suggested that their report be heard. He thus commanded them to speak out before his retinue. The envoys reported, "When we journeyed among the Bulgars, we beheld how they worship in their temple, called a mosque, while they stand ungirt. The Bulgar bows, sits down, looks hither and thither like one possessed, and there is no happiness among them, but instead only sorrow and a dreadful stench. Their religion is not good. Then we went among the Germans, and saw them performing many ceremonies in their temples; but we beheld no glory there. Then we went to Greece, and the Greeks led us to the edifices where they worship their God, and we knew not whether we were in heaven or on earth. For on earth there is no such splendor or such beauty, and we are at a loss how to describe it. We only know that God dwells there among men, and their service is fairer than the ceremonies of other nations. For we cannot forget that beauty. Every man, after tasting something sweet, is afterward unwilling to accept that which is bitter, and therefore we cannot dwell longer here." Then the boyars spoke and said, "If the Greek faith were evil, it would not have been adopted by your grandmother Olga who was wiser than all other men." Vladimir then inquired where they should all accept baptism, and they replied that the decision rested with him.

After a year had passed, in 6496 (988), Vladimir proceeded with an armed force against Kherson, a Greek city, and the people of Kherson barricaded themselves therein. Vladimir halted at the farther side of the city beside the harbor, a bowshot from the town, and the inhabitants resisted energetically while Vladimir besieged the town. Eventually, however, they became exhausted, and Vladimir warned them that if they did not surrender, he would remain on the spot for three years. When they failed to heed this threat, Vladimir marshalled his troops and ordered the construction of an earthwork in the direction of the city. While this work was under construction, the inhabitants dug a tunnel under the city-wall, stole the heaped-up earth, and carried it into the city, where they piled it up in the center of the town. But the soldiers kept on building, and Vladimir persisted. Then a man of Kherson, Anastasius by name, shot into the Russ camp an arrow on which he had written, "There are springs behind you to the east, from which water flows in pipes. Dig down and cut them off." When Vladimir received this information, he raised his eyes to heaven and vowed that if this hope was realized, he would be baptized. He gave orders straightway to dig down above the pipes, and the water-supply was thus cut off. The inhabitants were accordingly overcome by thirst, and surrendered.

Vladimir and his retinue entered the city, and he sent messages to the Emperors Basil and Constantine, saying, "Behold, I have captured your glorious city. I have also heard that you have an unwedded sister. Unless you give her to me to wife, I shall deal with your own city as I have with Kherson." When the Emperors heard this message they were troubled, and replied, "It is not meet for Christians to give in marriage to pagans. If you are baptized, you shall have her to wife, inherit the kingdom of God, and be our companion in the faith. Unless you do so, however, we cannot give you our sister in marriage." When Vladimir learned their response, he directed the envoys of the Emperors to report to the latter that he was willing to accept baptism, having already given some study to their religion, and that the Greek faith and ritual, as described by the emissaries sent to examine it, had pleased him well. When the Emperors heard this report, they rejoiced, and persuaded their sister Anna to consent to the match. They then requested Vladimir to submit to baptism before they should send their sister to him, but Vladimir desired that the Princess should herself bring priests to baptize him. The Emperors complied with his request, and sent forth their sister, accompanied by some dignitaries and priests. Anna, however, departed with reluctance. "It is as if I were setting out into captivity," she lamented; "better were it for me to die at home." But her brothers protested, "Through your agency God turns the land of Rus' to repentance, and you will relieve Greece from the danger of grievous war. Do you not see how much harm the Russes have already brought upon the Greeks? If you do not set out, they may bring on us the same misfortunes." It was thus that they overcame her hesitation only with great difficulty. The Princess embarked upon a ship, and after tearfully embracing her kinfolk, she set forth across the sea and arrived at Kherson. The natives came forth to greet her, and conducted her into the city, where they settled her in the palace.

By divine agency, Vladimir was suffering at that moment from a disease of the eyes, and could see nothing, being in great distress. The Princess declared to him that if he desired to be relieved of this disease, he should be baptized with all speed, otherwise it could not be cured. When Vladimir heard her message, he said, "If this proves true, then of a surety is the God of the Christians great," and gave order that he should be baptized. The Bishop of Kherson, together with the Princess's priests, after announcing the tidings, baptized Vladimir, and as the Bishop laid his hand upon him, he straightway received his sight. Upon experiencing this miraculous cure, Vladimir glorified God, saying, "I have now perceived the one true God." When his followers beheld this miracle, many of them were also baptized.

Vladimir was baptized in the Church of St. Basil, which stands at Kherson upon a square in the center of the city, where the Khersonians trade. The palace of Vladimir stands beside this church to this day, and the palace of the Princess is behind the altar. After his baptism, Vladimir took the Princess in marriage.

87

A Letter of Monk Philotheos to Grand Prince Vasily III

In this letter of Monk Philotheos to Grand Prince Vasily III (1505–1533), the theory of Moscow as the Third Rome was first elaborated. The Russian Grand Prince was now portrayed as the tsar (caesar), descendant of both Roman emperors and ruler of Orthodoxy. He personified the state and legitimized both state and church.

QUESTIONS TO CONSIDER

1. What were the political and religious implications of the theory of Moscow as the Third Rome?
2. What does this document suggest about the role of the church in Russian politics?

[I write] to you, the Most bright and most highly-throning Sovereign, Grand Prince, orthodox Christian tsar and lord of all, rein-holder of the Holy oecumenical and Apostolic Church of God of the Most Holy Virgin . . . which is shining gloriously instead of the Roman or Constantinopolitan [one]. For the Old Rome fell because of its church's lack of faith, the Apollinarian heresy; and of the second Rome, the city of Constantine, the pagans broke down the doors of the churches with their axes. . . . And now there is the Holy synodal Apostolic church of the reigning third Rome, of your tsardom, which shines like the sun in its orthodox Christian faith throughout the whole universe. And that is your realm, pious tsar, as all the empires [tsardoms] of the orthodox Christian faith have gathered into your single empire . . . you are the only tsar for Christians in the whole world. . . .

Do not break, O tsar, the commandments laid by your ancestors, the Great Constantine and the blessed Vladimir, and the God chosen Iaroslav, and the other blessed saints, of which root you are. . . .

Listen and attend, pious tsar, that all Christian empires are gathered in your single one, that two Romes have fallen, and the third one stands, and a fourth one there shall not be; your empire will not fall to others, according to the great Evangelist.

From a letter of Monk Philotheos to Grand Prince Vasily III, early sixteenth century, translated in Michael Cherniavsky, *Tsar and People: Studies in Russian Myths* (New York: Random House, 1969), p. 38. Reprinted by permission of Mrs. Lucy Cherniavsky.

88

Heinrich von Staden, *The Land and Government of Muscovy*

In 1565, a troubled and perhaps demented Tsar Ivan IV ("Ivan the Terrible," 1533–1584) created a special administrative apparatus, the *oprichnina* (from the Russian word, *oprich,* meaning a part or beside) to govern over one third of the Russian state, leaving the remaining part of his realm, the *zemshchina,* under the control of his traditional imperial officials. Between 1565 and 1572 the *oprichniki,* the servants who administered the *oprichnina,* launched a reign of terror by relentlessly attacking all who opposed the tsar. Dressed in black and bearing special symbols of their authority, the *oprichniki* cruelly inflicted devastation on large parts of Russia. One of these *oprichniki* was Heinrich von Staden, a German who had come to Russia and joined the imperial state service. His account gives us insight into this bleak chapter of Russian history.

QUESTIONS TO CONSIDER

1. Are there any connections between *The Domostroi's* description of domestic life in the time of Ivan the Terrible (see Reading 74) and this account?
2. What does this reading tell us about Ivan IV's approach to governance? Which other periods of Russian history does this description of the *Oprichnina* suggest?

Ivan Vasilievich [Ivan IV], Grand Prince of all Russia, . . . chose from his own and foreign nations a hand-picked order, thus creating the *oprichnina* and the *zemshchina.*

The oprichnina was [composed of] his people; the zemshchina, of the ordinary people. The Grand Prince thus began to inspect one city and region after another. And those who, according to the military muster rolls, had not served [the Grand Prince's] forefathers by fighting the enemy with their [estates] were deprived of their estates, which were given to those in the oprichnina.

The princes and boyars who were taken into the oprichnina were ranked not according to riches but according to birth. They then took an oath not to have anything to do with the *zemskie* people or form any friendships with them. Those in the oprichnina also had to wear black clothes and hats; and in their quivers, where they put their arrows, they carried some kind of brushes or brooms tied on the ends of sticks. The *oprichniki* were recognized in this way.

Because of insurrection [in Moscow in December 1564], the Grand Prince left Moscow for Aleksandrova Sloboda, a two-day trip. He placed guards in this sloboda,[1] and had any nobles that he wanted called to him from Moscow and other cities.

The Grand Prince sent an order to the zemskie people saying that they must judge justly: ". . . Judge justly, ours [the oprichniki] shall not be in the wrong." Because of this

[1]Sloboda: a large village inhabited by free peasants.

order, the zemskie people became despondent. A person from the oprichnina could accuse someone from the zemshchina of owing him a sum of money. And even if the oprichnik had never known nor seen the accused from the zemshchina, the latter had to pay him immediately or he was publicly beaten in the marketplace with knouts or cudgels every day until he paid. No one was spared in this, neither clerics nor laymen. The oprichniki did a number of indescribable things to the zemskie people to get all their money and property. . . .

The Grand Prince arrived in Moscow from Aleksandrova Sloboda and murdered one of the chief men of the zemshchina, Ivan Petrovich Cheliadnin. In the Grand Prince's absence from Moscow, this man was the chief boyar and judge. He willingly helped the poor people find justice quickly, and for a number of years he was governor and commander in Livonia—at Dorpat and at Polotsk. . . .

Prince Andrei Kurbskii was governor and commander after him. When [Kurbskii] became aware of the oprichnina business, he rode off to King Sigismund August in Poland, leaving behind his wife and children. In his place came the boyar Mikhail Morozov. . . .

Afterward [Cheliadnin] was summoned to Moscow. In Moscow he was killed and thrown into a filthy pit near the Neglinna river. The Grand Prince then went with his oprichniki and burned all the [estates] in the country belonging to this Ivan Petrovich. The villages were burned with their churches and everything that was in them, icons and church ornaments. Women and girls were stripped naked and forced in that state to catch chickens in the fields. The oprichniki caused great misery in the country, and many people were secretly murdered.

This was too much for the zemskie people. They began to confer, and they decided to elect as grand prince Vladimir Andreevich [Staritskii]. . . .

Prince Vladimir Andreevich [Staritskii] revealed the compact to the Grand Prince, and revealed everything that the zemskie people had planned and prepared. The Grand Prince . . . returned by post road to Aleksandrova Sloboda, and had someone write down [the names of] those zemskie leaders whom he wanted slaughtered, killed, and executed first. . . .

The Grand Prince continued to have one [zemskii] leader after another seized and killed as it came into his head, one this way, another that way.

Metropolitan Philip could remain silent about this business no longer, and spoke affably to the Grand Prince saying that he ought to live and rule as his forefathers had. The good metropolitan fell into disgrace with these words, and he had to live in very large iron chains until he died. The Grand Prince then chose a metropolitan according to his wishes.

After that the Grand Prince set out from Aleksandrova Sloboda with all his oprichniki. Every city, road, monastery from the sloboda to Livonia was occupied by oprichnina guards, as though it were done because of plague, so that one city or monastery could learn of nothing from another.

The oprichniki came to the *iam*—or post station—at Chernaia and began to plunder. The places where the Grand Prince spent the night were set afire and were burned down the next morning.

All those who came from Moscow to the guard post and wanted to go to the camp of [Ivan's] own hand-picked people, whether they were princes or boyars or their servants, were seized by the guards, bound, and immediately killed. Some were stripped naked in front of the Grand Prince and rolled around in the snow until they died. The same thing happened to those who wanted to leave the camp for Moscow and were caught by the guards.

The Grand Prince then arrived at the city of Tver and had everything plundered, even churches and monasteries. And he had all the prisoners killed, likewise his own people who had befriended or married foreigners. All the bodies had their legs cut off, because of the ice, and were then stuck under the ice of the Volga River. The same occurred in the city of Torzhok. Neither church nor monastery was spared here.

The Grand Prince arrived again outside the city of Great Novgorod. He settled down three furlongs from the city and sent in an army commander with his retinue. He was to spy and reconnoiter. The rumor was that the Grand Prince wanted to march to Livonia. Then the Grand Prince moved into Great Novgorod, into the bishop's palace, and took everything belonging to the bishop. He took the largest bells and whatever he wanted from the churches. The Grand Prince thus left the city alone. He ordered the merchants to buy and sell and to ask a just price from his soldiers, the oprichniki. Every day he arose and moved to another monastery. He indulged his wantonness and had monks tortured, and many of them were killed. There are three hundred monasteries inside and outside the city and not one of these was spared. Then the pillage of the city began. . . .

This distress and misery continued in the city for six weeks without interruption [in January and February 1570]. Every shop and room where money or property were thought to be was sealed. Every day the Grand Prince could also be found in the torture chamber in person. Nothing might remain in the monasteries and the city. Everything that the soldiers could not carry off was thrown into the water or burned. If one of the zemskie people retrieved anything from the water, he was hanged. . . .

The oprichniki ransacked the entire countryside and all the cities and villages of the zemshchina, although the Grand Prince had not given them permission to do that. They drew up instructions themselves, as though the Grand Prince had ordered them to kill this or that merchant or noble—if he was thought to have money—along with his wife and children, and to take his money and property to the Grand Prince's Treasury. In the zemshchina, they thus committed many murders and assassinations, which are beyond description. . . .

When the oprichniki had tortured Russia—the entire zemshchina—according to their will and pleasure so that even the Grand Prince realized it was enough, the oprichniki still had not sated themselves with the money and property of the zemskie people. If one of the zemskie people brought a suit for a thousand rubles, he would accept a hundred rubles or less, but give a receipt [to the oprichniki] for the full amount. All the petitions were set aside together with the records and receipts. [The oprichniki] had sworn to maintain no friendships with the zemskie people and to have nothing to do with them; but then the Grand Prince turned the tables and had all petitions accepted. And when the oprichniki were indebted for a thousand and had a receipt, but had not fully paid, these oprichniki had to pay the zemskie people again. The oprichniki did not at all like this situation. . . .

Then the Grand Prince began to wipe out all the chief people of the oprichnina. Prince Afanasii Viazemskii died in chains in the town of Gorodets. Aleksei [Basmanov] and his son [Fedor], with whom the Grand Prince indulged in lewdness, were killed. Maliuta Skuratov was shot near Weissenstein [Paide] in Livonia. He was the pick of the bunch, and according to the Grand Prince's order, he was remembered in church. Prince Mikhail, the son of the Grand Prince's brother-in-law from the Circassian land, was chopped to death by the harquebusiers [musketeers] with axes or halberds [weapons combining the virtues of the spear and the battle axe]. Prince Vasilii Temkin was drowned. Ivan Saburov was murdered. Peter Seisse was hanged from his own court gate opposite the bedroom. Prince Andrei Ovtsyn was hanged in the Arbatskaia street of the oprichnina. A living sheep was hung next to him [an *ovtsa* is a sheep, thus the murderers played a prank on his name]. The marshal Bulat wanted to marry his sister to the Grand Prince. He was killed and his sister was raped by five hundred harquebusiers. The captain of the harquebusiers, Kuraka Unkovskii, was killed and stuck under the ice. In the previous year [name unclear] was eaten by dogs at the Karinskii guard post of Aleksandrova Sloboda. Grigorii Griaznoi was killed and his son Nikita was burned alive. His brother Vasilii was captured by the Crimean Tatars. The scribe and clerk Posnik Suvorov was killed at the Land Chancellery. Osip Il'in was shamefully executed in the Court Chancellery.

All the chief men of the oprichnina and zemshchina and all those who were to be killed were first publicly whipped in the marketplace until they signed over all their money and property, if they had any, to the Treasury of the Grand Prince. Those who had no money and property were killed in front of churches, in the street, or in their homes, whether asleep or awake, and were thrown into the street. The cause of the death, and whether it was legal or not, was written on a note, which was then pinned to the clothes of the corpse. The body had to lie in the street day and night as a warning to the people.

The Renaissance and Reformation

By 1500, a sharp contrast had developed between Italy and northern Europe. Most northern European states, except the Holy Roman Empire, were evolving toward centralized political authority, whereas in Italy fragmentation became the norm. Italian rulers had none of the feudal loyalties with which they might have ruled their subjects. If rulers wished to succeed, they had to rely solely on what was termed *virtu;* they had only their own political, diplomatic, or military abilities to maintain their position. Constant maneuvering for supremacy among the states led to instability.

Economic prosperity of Italian cities was based on manufacturing and international trade. Individual cities and families were known for wool and silk weaving and for banking and the importation of luxury goods from the Near and Far East. The accumulated wealth was used to patronize artists and writers whose works enhanced the reputations of cities and patrons alike.

Italian scholars returned to a study of antiquity and sought to revive classical education in their own period. These studies or "liberal arts" included grammar, rhetoric, poetry, history, and moral philosophy and produced an educated elite called Renaissance humanists.

Perhaps the most famous Italian civic humanist and politician was Niccolò Machiavelli (1469–1527), who served as a secretary and diplomat to the Florentine Republic (1498–1512). Machiavelli's most famous works include *Discourses on the First Ten Books of Livy* (1518), *Mandragola* (1512–1520?), *The History of Florence* (1525), and *The Prince* (1513).

In northern Europe, feudal traditions and gothic art were the norm. Social change developed slowly, but with the growth of capitalism, scholars and princes came to admire the Italian humanist movement. Kings, princes, emperors, and high Church officials became patrons of humanists. Yet, there was a difference—northern scholars emphasized the need to purify the Christian church.

The greatest northern humanist was Desiderius Erasmus of Rotterdam (1469–1536). He was born and educated for the priesthood in Holland, studied in France, and traveled and taught in England and on the Continent. His

Christian humanism was not based on a search for religious relics, buying indulgences, or doing good works, but rather on a desire to restore Christianity through true piety and a love of Christ. In this last respect, Erasmus hoped for an internal religious reform and refused to break with the Catholic church as Martin Luther did.

Among Erasmus's works were classical Latin quotations or the *Adages* (1500), *The Handbook of a Christian Knight* (1508), and a new translation of the New Testament (1516). Erasmus's most noted work was his satire on European morals, entitled *The Praise of Folly* (1511), whose Latin title was a pun on the name of his English fellow humanist, Sir Thomas More.

Although Christian humanists flourished in every country, those in the Germanies led the general revolt against the Catholic Church. Among the causes of the Reformation were a reaction against the gross abuses in the Church, lack of moral leadership of the popes, textual criticisms of the humanists, and the political disunity within the Holy Roman Empire.

Martin Luther (1483–1546) was to combine the demands for purification of the Church with a new theology. The son of a prosperous mine owner, Luther was educated for the law at Erfurt University until a crisis of conscience made him enter an Augustinian monastery and become a priest. Luther continued his studies and received a doctorate while teaching theology at Wittenberg University in Saxony. It was while lecturing on St. Paul's Letters to the Romans that Luther came to believe that God's salvation comes to each person through faith, not by personal actions or good works.

Luther might have remained a little-noted priest had he not chosen to attack indulgence selling by posting his Ninety-Five Theses on the Castle Church door in Wittenberg in 1517. Almost immediately, he became the center of a controversy that eventually led to his condemnation as a heretic. Luther took up the challenge and in a stream of pamphlets and treatises further elaborated his theology into what has become the Lutheran church.

89

Niccolò Machiavelli, *The Prince* and *The Discourses on Titus Livy*

Niccolò Machiavelli (1469–1527) remains one of the most articulate spokesmen for the Italian Renaissance, marking a shift toward secular or humanistic values, away from the church-oriented values of the Middle Ages. Like most men of the later Renaissance, Machiavelli looked back to the pagan Roman Republic for inspiration in addressing problems of his own times.

In defending a set of political, social, economic, and religious norms, Machiavelli writes as a philosopher in the sense of one who attempts to integrate knowledge from different fields into a coherent world outlook. He would probably not qualify as a philosopher under the more narrow twentieth-century meaning of that term. Machiavelli's Renaissance philosophy typically sets itself apart from that of the Middle Ages by its understanding of *virtu* as human excellence. Based on the Latin word *vir* (man), *virtu* in practice meant making the absolute most of human talents for human ends—as today a *virtuoso* violinist is one who gets the most out of a violin. In the first section of the reading, Pope Alexander VI (Rodrigo Borgia) and his son, Duke Valentine (Cesare Borgia)—who were too much tainted by intrigue and violent crime to qualify as "virtuous" by current standards—are both treated as virtuoso statesmen. Their grand designs may have been thwarted by fortune, but they made the most of their talents nonetheless.

The first two excerpts are from Machiavelli's most notorious work, *The Prince,* in which he appears to justify nearly any measures to gain and keep rulership. For example, he advises princes to break faith and treaties to keep themselves in power. One can interpret Machiavellianism as a cynical combination of the ideas that "Might makes right" and "The end justifies the means." Yet even in *The Prince,* as the second excerpt illustrates, there are limits. The best form of government for Machiavelli, as for most people of the later Renaissance, was a republic—rather than the monarchy (or "princely rule," as Machiavelli calls it) advocated by Dante. Consequently, someone who subverts a successful republic to establish selfish, personal rule is guilty of nothing less than "villainy."

Machiavelli wrote *The Prince* in a short period of time as he attempted to find employment in the service of the Medicis, one of the leading "princely families" of Italy. The Medicis had ruled Florence in the late fifteenth century and had recently come to power again after the overthrow of the republican government of Florence, which Machiavelli had served as an administrator and diplomat.

Machiavelli gives a better presentation of his world outlook in the much longer *Discourses on the First Ten Books of Titus Livy,* from which the second two excerpts are taken. Here, he describes the means for founding and preserving republics, using the early Roman method described by Livy as his primary model. Notice that in the section entitled "The Religion of the Romans," Machiavelli takes a totally humanistic view of religion. The truth or falsity of pagan Roman religion is irrelevant; he is merely interested in illustrating the type of religion that supports a healthy social and political order. In the final excerpts, Machiavelli praises moderate poverty as a positive good, since he believes that small farmers are more likely than rich men to use their political talents for the public benefit.

QUESTIONS TO CONSIDER

1. Why were the activities of Pope Alexander VI contrary to his official position?
2. In modern textbooks, Pope Alexander VI generally gets bad reviews. Why does Machiavelli like him so much?
3. Why was Cesare Borgia an example of *virtu,* and not the villainous Agathocles the Sicilian?
4. Why was L. Quintius Cincinnatus an ideal Roman citizen according to Machiavelli?

Territories Acquired by Virtue or by Fortune

They who from private condition become princes, and, merely by the indulgence of fortune, arrive without much trouble at that dignity, though it costs them dear to maintain it, meet but little difficulty in their passage, being hurried as it were with wings, yet when they come to settle and establish then begins their misery.

. . . About the arrival at this authority, either by virtue or by good fortune, I shall instance two examples that are in our memory; one is Francesco Sforza, the other Caesar Borgia. Sforza, by just means and extraordinary virtue, made himself Duke of Milan, and enjoyed it in great peace, though it was gained with much trouble. Borgia, on the other hand, (called commonly Duke of Valentine), got several fair territories by the fortune of his father, Pope Alexander, and lost them all after his death, though he used all his industry, and employed all the arts that a wise and brave prince ought to use to fix himself in the sphere where the arms and fortune of other people had placed him. . . .

Pope Alexander VI had a desire to make his son Duke Valentine great, but he saw many impediments in the way, both for the present and for the future. First, he could not see any way to advance him to any territory that depended not upon the Church; and to those in his gift he was sure the Duke of Milan and the Venetians would never consent; for Faenza and Riminum had already put themselves under Venetian protection. He was likewise sensible that the forces of Italy, especially those that were capable of assisting him, were in the hands of those that ought to apprehend the greatness of the Pope . . . and therefore could not repose any great confidence in them; besides, the laws and alliances of all the states in Italy must of necessity be disturbed before he could make himself master of any part, which was no hard matter to do, finding the Venetians, upon some private interest of their own, inviting the French to another expedition into Italy, which his Holiness was so far from opposing that he promoted it by dissolution of King Louis's former marriage. Louis therefore passed the Alps by the assistance of the Venetians and Alexander's consent, and was no sooner in Milan than he sent forces to assist the Pope in his enterprise against Romagna, which was immediately surrendered upon the King's reputation. Romagna being in this manner reduced by the Duke, and the Colonnesi defeated, he was ambitious both to keep what he had got, and to advance in his conquests. . . .

When the Duke had possessed himself of Romagna, finding it had been governed by poor and inferior lords, who had rather robbed than corrected their subjects, and given them more occasion of discord than of unity, insomuch as that province was full of robberies, riots, and all manner of disturbances, to reduce them to unanimity and subjection to monarchy, he thought it necessary to provide them a good governor, and thereupon he conferred that office upon Remiro d'Orco, with absolute power, though he was a cruel and passionate man. Orco soon settled it in peace, with no small reputation to himself. Afterward the Duke, apprehending that so large a power might become odious to the people, erected a court of judicature in the center of the province, in which every city had its advocate, and an excellent person was appointed to preside. And as he discovered that his past severity had made him many enemies, to remove that ill opinion, and recover the affections of the people, he had a mind to show that, if any cruelty had been exercised, it proceeded not from him but from the arrogance of his minister; and for their further confirmation he caused the said governor to be apprehended, and his head chopped off one morning in the market-place

First two excerpts from Niccolò Machiavelli, *The Prince,* trans. S.G.W. Benjamin (n.p.: The National Alumni, 1907), pp. 25–39, *passim.* Latter two excerpts from Niccolò Machiavelli, *The Discourses,* in *The Prince and The Discourses,* trans. Luigi Ricci, E.R.P. Vincent, and Christian E. Detmold (New York: Modern Library, 1950), pp. 145–48, 486–88, *passim.*

at Cesena, with a wooden dagger on one side of him and a bloody knife on the other; the ferocity of which spectacle not only appeased but amazed the people for a while.

The Duke, finding himself powerful enough, and secure against present danger, being as strong as he desired, and his neighbors in a manner reduced to an incapacity of hurting him, was willing to go on with his conquests. Nothing remained but jealousy of France, which was without cause, for he knew that King Louis had found his error at last, and would be sure to obstruct him. Hereupon he began to look abroad for new allies, and to hesitate and stagger toward France, as appeared when the French army advanced into the kingdom of Naples against the Spaniards, who had besieged Cajeta. His main design was to secure himself against the French, and he would doubtless have done it if Alexander had lived.

These were his provisions against the dangers that were imminent; but those that were remote were more doubtful and uncertain. The first thing he feared was, lest the next Pope should be his enemy and reassume all that Alexander had given him, to prevent which he considered four ways. The first was by destroying the whole line of those lords whom he had dispossessed, that his Holiness might have no occasion to restore them. The second was to cajole the nobility in Rome, and draw them over to his party, that thereby he might put an awe and restraint upon the Pope. The third was, if possible, to make the College his friends. The fourth was to make himself so strong before the death of his father as to be able to stand upon his own legs and repel the first violence that should be practised against him. Three of these four expedients he had tried before Alexander died, and he was in a fair way for the fourth. . . .

On serious examination, therefore, of the whole conduct of Duke Valentine, I see nothing to be reprehended; it seems rather proper to me to present him, as I have done, as an example for the imitation of all such as by the favor of fortune, or the supplies of other princes, have got into power; for, his mind being so large, and his intentions so high, he could not do otherwise, and nothing could have opposed the greatness and wisdom of his designs but his own infirmity and the death of his father. He, therefore, who thinks it necessary in the minority of his dominion to secure himself against his enemies, to gain himself friends; to overcome, whether by force or by fraud; to make himself beloved or feared by his people; to be followed and reverenced by his soldiers; to destroy and exterminate such as would do him injury; to repeal and suppress old laws, and introduce new; to be severe, grateful, magnanimous, liberal, cashier and disband such of his army as were unfaithful, and put new in their places; manage himself so in his alliances with kings and princes that all should be either obliged to requite him or afraid to offend him—he, I say, cannot find a fresher or better model than the actions of this prince.

Of Such Who Have Arrived at Dominion by Wicked Means

Agathocles, the Sicilian, not only from a private but from a vile and abject condition was made King of Syracuse; and being but the son of a potter, he continued the dissoluteness of his life through all the degrees of his fortune. Nevertheless, his vices were accompanied with such courage and activity that he applied himself to the wars, by which, and his great industry, he came at length to be the Pretor of Syracuse. Being settled in that dignity, and having determined to make himself prince, and hold by violence, without obligation to anybody, that which was conferred upon him by consent, he came to an understanding with Hamilcar the Carthaginian, who was then at the head of an army in Sicily; and, calling the people and the Senate of Syracuse together one morning, as if he intended to consult them on some matter of importance to the state, on a signal appointed he caused his soldiers to kill all the senators and the most wealthy of the people; after whose death he usurped the dominion of that city without any obstruction.

Nevertheless it cannot be called virtue in him to kill his fellow-citizens, betray his friends, and be without faith, pity, or religion; these are ways that may get a man empire, but no glory or reputation. Yet, if the wisdom of Agathocles be considered, his dexterity in encountering and overcoming of dangers, his courage in supporting and surmounting his misfortunes, I do not see why he should be held inferior to the best captains of his time. But his unbounded cruelty and barbarous inhumanity, added to numerous other vices, will not permit him to be numbered among the most excellent men. So, then, that which he performed cannot justly be attributed either to fortune or to virtue. . . .

It may seem wonderful to some that it should come to pass that Agathocles, and such as he, after so many treacheries and acts of inhumanity, should live quietly in their own country so long, defend themselves so well against foreign enemies, and none of their subjects conspire against them at home; since several others, by reason of their cruelty, have not been able, even in time of peace, to maintain their government. I conceive it fell out according as their cruelty was well or ill applied. I say well applied (if that word may be applied to an ill action), and it may be called so when committed but once, and that of necessity for one's own preservation, but never repeated, and even then converted as much as possible to the benefit of the subjects. Ill applied are such cruelties as are but few in the beginning, but in time do rather multiply than decrease. . . .

Whence it is to be observed that he who usurps the government of any State is to execute and put in practice all the cruelties that he thinks material at once, that he may have no occasion to renew them often, but that by his discontinuance he may mollify the people, and by benefits bring them over to his side. He who does otherwise, whether from fear or from ill counsel, is obliged to be always ready with his knife in his hand; for he never can repose any confidence in his subjects, while they, by reason of his fresh and continued inhumanities, cannot be secure against him.

So then injuries are to be committed all at once, that the last being the less, the distaste may be likewise the less; but benefits should be distilled by drops, that the relish may be the greater.

The Religion of the Romans

Although the founder of Rome was Romulus, yet the gods did not judge the laws of this prince sufficient for so great an empire, and therefore inspired the Roman Senate to elect Numa Pompilius as his successor, so that he might regulate all those things that had been omitted by Romulus. Numa, finding a very savage people, and wishing to reduce them to civil obedience by the arts of peace, had recourse to religion as the most necessary and assured support of any civil society; and he established it upon such foundations that for many centuries there was nowhere more fear of the gods than in that republic, which greatly facilitated all the enterprises which the Senate or its great men attempted. Whoever will examine the actions of the people of Rome as a body, or of many individual Romans, will see that these citizens feared much more to break an oath than the laws, like men who esteem the power of the gods more than that of men . . . , which can be ascribed to nothing else than the religious principles which Numa had instilled into the Romans. And whoever reads Roman history attentively will see in how great a degree religion served in the command of the armies, in uniting the people and keeping them well conducted, and in covering the wicked with shame. . . . In truth, there never was any remarkable lawgiver amongst any people who did not resort to divine authority, as otherwise his laws would not have been accepted by the people; for there are many good laws, the importance of which is known to the sagacious lawgiver, but the reasons for which are not sufficiently evident to enable him to persuade others to submit to them; and therefore do wise men, for the purpose of removing this difficulty, resort to divine authority. Thus did Lycurgus and Solon, and many others who aimed at the same thing.

The Roman people, then, admiring the wisdom and goodness of Numa, yielded in all things to his advice. It is true that those were very religious times, and the people with whom Numa had to deal were very untutored and superstitious, which made it easy for him to carry out his designs, being able to impress upon them any new form. And doubtless, if any one wanted to establish a republic at the present time, he would find it much easier with the simple mountaineers, who are almost without any civilization, than with such as are accustomed to live in cities, where civilization is already corrupt; as a sculptor finds it easier to make a fine statue out of a crude block of marble than out of a statue badly begun by another. Considering then, all these things, I conclude that the religion introduced by Numa into Rome was one of the chief causes of the prosperity of that city; for this religion gave rise to good laws, and good laws bring good fortune, and from good fortune results happy success in all enterprises. And as the observance of divine institutions is the cause of the greatness of republics, so the disregard of them produces their ruin; for where the fear of God is wanting, there the country will come to ruin.

Cincinnatus: Illustration of Poverty as Good for Republics

It is of the greatest advantage in a republic to have laws that keep her citizens poor. Although there does not appear to have been any special law to this effect in Rome . . . , yet experience shows that even so late as four hundred years after its foundation there was still great poverty in Rome. We cannot ascribe this fact to any other cause than that poverty never was allowed to stand in the way of the achievement of any rank or honor, and that virtue and merit were sought for under whatever roof they dwelt; it was this system that made riches naturally less desirable. We have a manifest proof of this on the occasion when the Consul Minutius and his army were surrounded by the Equeans, and all Rome was full of apprehensions lest the army should be lost, so that they resorted to the creation of a Dictator, their last remedy in times of difficulty. They appointed L. Quintius Cincinnatus, who at the time was on his little farm, which he cultivated with his own hands. This circumstance is celebrated by Titus Livius in the following golden words: "After this let men not listen to those who prefer riches to everything else in this world, and who think that there is neither honor nor virtue where wealth does not flow." Cincinnatus was engaged in ploughing his fields, which did not exceed four acres, when the messengers of the Senate arrived from Rome to announce his election to the dictatorship, and to point out to him the imminent danger of the Roman republic. He immediately put on his toga, gathered an army, and went to the relief of Minutius; and having crushed and despoiled the enemy, and freed the Consul and his army, he would not permit them to share the spoils, saying, "I will not allow you to participate in the spoils of those to whom you came so near falling a prey." He deprived Minutius of the consulate, and reduced him to the rank of lieutenant, saying to him, "You will remain in this grade until you have learned to be Consul."

Cincinnatus had chosen for his master of cavalry L. Tarquinius whose poverty had obliged him to fight on foot. Let us note here how Rome honored poverty, (as has been said), and how four acres of land sufficed for the support of so good and great a citizen as Cincinnatus. We find also that poverty was still honored in the times of Marcus Regulus, who when commanding an army in Africa asked permission of the Roman Senate to return to look after his farm, which was being spoiled by the laborers in whose charge it had been left by him. These instances suggest two reflections: the one, that these eminent citizens were content to remain in such poverty, and that they were satisfied merely to win honor by their military achievements, and to leave all the profits of them to the public treasury; for if they had thought of enriching themselves by their wars, they would have cared little whether their fields were being spoiled or not; and the other, as to the magnanimity of these citizens, who, when placed at the head of an army, rose above all princes solely by the grandeur of their souls. . . .

I might demonstrate here at length that poverty produces better fruit than riches,—that the first has conferred honor upon cities, countries, and religions, whilst the latter have only served to ruin them,—were it not that this subject has been so often illustrated by other writers.

90

Erasmus, *Julius II Excluded*

Popes generally supported the artistic and literary creativity of the Renaissance. At the same time, humanistic scholars north of Italy felt increasingly inclined to turn their learning and persuasive skills against the worldliness of the papacy as well as the backwardness of monastic orders.

Erasmus of Rotterdam (1469–1536) was a literary genius who thought that he had been unfairly coerced as a youth into taking monastic vows. Believing himself to be a defender of true Christianity while attacking monastic narrowness, he advocated both the study of Scripture and the study of classical, pre-Christian literature. In his words, the proper "weapons" for the struggle of life were "prayer and knowledge."

His major contribution to the Renaissance in Northern Europe was his edition of the Greek New Testament with a Latin translation and commentaries. Printed by a market-oriented publisher in Switzerland, it was a runaway bestseller: One hundred thousand copies were sold in France alone. Erasmus's popular Latin translation and commentaries greatly heightened the debate on the nature of the Church and its function in society.

The following excerpts from a play by Erasmus illustrate sentiments of the coming Reformation. The play was first staged in 1514 for a sympathetic audience, largely composed of students and faculty members, in Paris. Julius II, the pope from 1503 to 1514, had earned Machiavelli's admiration for his military and diplomatic skills. His excellent artistic taste led him to employ both Michelangelo and Raphael as he sought to adorn the Vatican. Yet for Christian humanists, Julius left something to be desired as the spiritual leader of Christendom. In an early version of an enduring story, the play presents Saint Peter dealing with someone with doubtful credentials for entering Heaven. Its serious theme—contrasting the headstrong success of Church leaders in accumulating worldly power with the totally different goals of the early fathers of the Church, or Christ himself—has resurfaced periodically in literary satire; the best-known modern example is perhaps the "Grand Inquisitor" episode in Dostoyevsky's *Brothers Karamazov.*

When he wrote the play, Erasmus was looking to France as the country where leaders were most likely to further Church reform. The play's Julius II calls the French "barbarians," as did Machiavelli and other Italians of the time. But Erasmus sees a connection between the uncorrupted, natural, "barbarian" characteristics of the French and the hope of changing the Church for the better. Within a decade, Martin Luther would make a similar link in relating German national character to his program of reform.

Erasmus, who hated being caught up in the middle of controversies, despite a lifetime of helping to instigate them, disowned the authorship of the play. But the overwhelming similarities in sentiments, observations, and style between *Julius II Excluded* and other works he published make him the only likely candidate for consideration as its author.

QUESTIONS TO CONSIDER

1. Why was Pope Julius II not considered a reforming pope such as Gregory VII and Innocent III?
2. Why would Machiavelli never have written this satire (see Reading 89)?
3. Whom did Erasmus favor, the "barbarians" or the papacy?
4. Why would the Protestant reformers have welcomed this satire?

Scene—Gate of Heaven

Julius: What the devil is this? The gates not opened! Something is wrong with the lock. . . .

Peter: Well that the gates are adamant, or this fellow would have broken in. He must be some giant, or conqueror. Heaven, what a stench! Who are you? What do you want here? . . .

Julius: Enough of this. I am Julius . . . , P.M., as you can see by the letters if you can read.

Peter: P.M.! What is that? Pestis Maxima?

Julius: Pontifex Maximus, you rascal. . . .

Peter: . . . Let me look at you a little closer. Hum! Signs of impiety in plenty . . . not precisely like an apostle. Priest's cassock and bloody armour below it, eyes savage, mouth insolent, forehead brazen, body scarred with sins all over, breath loaded with wine, health broken with debauchery. Ay, threaten as you will, I will tell you what you are for all your bold looks. You are Julius the Emperor come back from hell. . . .

Julius: Make an end, I say, or I will fling a thunderbolt at you. I will excommunicate you. I have done as much to kings before this. . . .

Peter: You must show your merits first; no admission without merits. . . .

Julius: The invincible Julius ought not to answer a beggarly fisherman. However, you shall know who and what I am. First, I am a Ligurian, and not a Jew like you. My mother was

From Erasmus, *Julius II Exclusus: A Dialogue.* Translated and included by J.A. Froude in his *Life and Letters of Erasmus* (New York: Charles Scribner's Sons, 1894), pp. 149–68, *passim.*

the sister of the great Pope Sextus IV. The Pope made me a rich man out of Church property. I became a cardinal. I had my misfortunes. I had the French pox. I was banished, hunted out of my country; but I knew all along that I should come to be pope myself in the end . . . I succeeded. I rose to the top, and I have done more for the Church and Christ than any pope before me.

Peter: What did you do?

Julius: I raised the revenue. I invented new offices and sold them. . . . Then I annexed Bologna to the Holy See. I have torn up treaties, kept great armies in the field. I have covered Rome with palaces, and I have left five millions in the Treasury behind me. . . .

Peter: Invincible warrior! All this is quite new to me. Pardon my simplicity, who are these fair curly-haired boys that you have with you?

Julius: Boys I took into training to improve their minds.

Peter: And those dark ones with the scars?

Julius: Those are my soldiers and generals who were killed fighting for me. They all deserve heaven. I promised it to them under hand and seal if they lost their lives in my service, no matter how wicked they might be. . . .

Peter: My orders are not to admit men who come with Bulls, but to admit those who have clothed the naked, fed the hungry, given the thirsty drink, visited the sick and those in prison. Men have cast out devils and worked miracles in Christ's name and yet have been shut out. . . .

Julius: If I had but known.

Peter: What would you have done? Declared war?

Julius: I would have excommunicated you.

Peter: . . .When I was pope the difficulty was to find men who would be priests or deacons.

Julius: Naturally, when bishops and priests had nothing for their reward but fasts, and vigils, and doctrines, and now and then death. Bishops nowadays are kings and lords, and such positions are worth struggling for. . . .

Peter: Why did you take Bologna . . . ?

Julius: Because I wanted the revenue for my own treasury, and because Bologna was otherwise convenient for me. So I used my thunderbolts, the French helped me, and now Bologna is mine, and every farthing of the taxes goes to Rome for the Church's use. If you had only seen my triumphal entry. . . .

Peter: He who represents Christ ought to try to be like Christ. But, tell me, is there no way of removing a wicked pope?

Julius: Absurd! Who can remove the highest authority of all?

Peter: That the Pope is the highest is a reason why he should be removed if he causes scandal. Bad princes can be removed. The Church is in a bad way if it must put up with a head who is ruining it.

Julius: A Pope can only be corrected by a general council, but no general council can be held without the Pope's consent; otherwise it is a synod, and not a council. Let the council sit, it can determine nothing unless the Pope agrees; and, again, a single pope having absolute power is superior to the council. Thus he cannot be deposed for any crime whatsoever. . . .

Peter: A novel privilege for my successors—to be the wickedest of men, yet be safe from punishment. So much the unhappier the Church which cannot shake such a monster off its shoulders.

Julius: Some say there is one cause for which a Pope can be deposed.

Peter: When he has done a good action, I suppose, since he is not to be punished for his bad actions.

Julius: If he can be convicted publicly of heresy. But this is impossible, too. For he can cancel any canon which he does not like. . . .

Peter: In the name of the papal majesty, who made these fine laws?

Julius: Who? Why, the source of all law, the Pope himself, and the power that makes a law can repeal it.

Peter: What else can you do?

Julius: What else? How do kings levy revenues? They persuade the people that they owe their fortunes to them, and then they ask, and the people give. So we make the people believe that they owe to us their knowledge of God, though we sleep all our lives. Besides, we sell them indulgences in small matters at a cheap rate, dispensations for not much more, and for blessings we charge nothing. . . .

Peter: This is all Greek to me. But why do you hate the barbarians, and move heaven and earth to get rid of them?

Julius: Because barbarians are superstitious, and the French worst of all.

Peter: Do the French worship other gods besides Christ?

Julius: No; but they have precise notions of what is due to Christ. They use hard words about certain things which we have left off.

Peter: Magical words, I presume?

Julius: No, not magical. They talk of simony and blasphemy, sodomy, poisoning, witchcraft, in language expressing abomination of such actions.

Peter: I do not wish to be personal, but can it be that such crimes are to be found among yourselves, professing Christians?

Julius: The barbarians have vices of their own. They censure ours and forget theirs. We tolerate ours and abominate theirs. Poverty, for instance, we look on as so wicked that anything is justifiable to escape from it, while the barbarians scarcely approve of wealth if innocently come by. . . . Barbarians forbid usury; we regard it as a necessary institution. They think looseness with women polluting and disgusting; we—well, we do not think so at all. They are shocked at simony; we never mention it. They stick to old laws and customs; we go for novelty and progress. While our views of life are so different, we don't like to have the barbarians too close to us. They have sharp eyes. They write letters about us to our friends. . . . Thus the Church suffers: we sell fewer dispensations, and get a worse price for them, and we receive less money for bishoprics and abbeys and colleges; worst of all, people are no longer frightened at our thunderbolts. Once let them think that a wicked Pope cannot hurt them, we shall be starved out. So we mean to keep the barbarian at a distance.

Peter: The Church is a community of Christians with Christ's Spirit in them. You have been a subverter of the Church.

Julius: The Church consists of cathedrals, and priests, and the Court of Rome, and myself at the head of it.

Peter: Christ is our Head, and we are His ministers. Are there two Heads? How have you increased the Church?

Julius: I found it poor: I have made it splendid.

Peter: Splendid with what? With faith? . . .

Julius: I have filled Rome with palaces, trains of mules and horses, troops of servants, armies and officers.

Spirit: With scarlet women and the like.

Julius: With purple and gold, with revenues so vast that kings are poor beside the Roman Pontiff. Glory, luxury, hoards of treasure, these are splendours, and these all I have created.

Peter: Pray, inform me. The Church had nothing of all this when it was founded by Christ. Whence came all this splendour, as you call it? . . .

Julius: You are thinking of the old affair, when you starved as Pope, with a handful of poor hunted bishops about you. Time has changed all that, and much for the better. You had only the name of Pope. Look now at our gorgeous churches, our priests by thousands; bishops like kings, with retinues and palaces; cardinals in their purple gloriously attended, horses and mules decked with gold and jewels, and shod with gold and silver. Beyond all, myself, Supreme Pontiff, borne on soldiers' shoulders in a golden chair, and waving my hand majestically to adoring crowds. Hearken to the roar of the cannon, the bugle notes, the boom of the drums. Observe the military engines, the shouting populace, torches blazing in street and square, and the kings of the earth scarce admitted to kiss my Holiness's foot. Behold the Roman Bishop placing the crown on the head of the Emperor, who seems to be made king of kings, yet is but the shadow of a name. Look at all this, and tell me it is not magnificent!

Peter: I look at a very worldly tyrant, an enemy of Christ and a disgrace to the Church.

Julius: Mere envy! You perceive what a poor wretch of a bishop you were compared to me.

Peter: Insolent wretch! Dare you compare your glory with mine?—and mine was Christ's, and not my own. Christ gave to me the keys of the Kingdom of Heaven, trusted His sheep to my feeding and sealed my faith with His approval. Fraud, usury, and cunning made you Pope, if Pope you are to be called. I gained thousands of souls to Christ: you have destroyed as many thousands. I brought heathen Rome to acknowledge Christ: you have made it heathen again. I healed the sick, cast out devils, restored the dead to life, and brought a blessing with me where I went. What blessings have you and your triumphs brought? I used my power for the good of all: you have used yours to crush and vex mankind. . . .

Julius: Do you mean to say I am to give up money, dominion, revenues, pleasures, life? Will you leave me to misery?

Peter: Yes, if you count Christ as miserable. He who was Lord of all became the scorn of all, endured poverty, endured labour, fasting, and hunger, and ended with a death of shame.

Julius: Very admirable, no doubt. But He will not find many imitators in these times of ours.

Peter: To admire is to imitate. Christ takes nothing good from any man. He takes what is falsely called good, to give him instead eternal truth, as soon as he is purged from the taint of the world. Being Himself heavenly, He will have His Church like Him, estranged from the world's corruption, and those who are sunk in pollution can not resemble One who is sitting in heaven. Once for all, fling away your imagined wealth, and receive instead what is far better.

Julius: What, I beseech you?

Peter: The gift of prophecy, the gift of knowledge, the gift of miracles, Christ Himself. The more a man is afflicted in the world the greater his joy in Christ, the poorer in the world the richer in Christ, the more cast down in the world the more exalted in Christ. Christ will have His followers pure, and most of all His ministers, the bishops. The higher in rank they are the more like Christ they are bound to be, and the less entangled in earthly pleasures. Yet you, the bishop next to Christ, who make yourself equal with Christ, think only of money, and arms, and treaties, to say nothing of vicious pleasures, and you abuse His name to support your own vanities. You claim the honour due to Christ, while you are Christ's enemy. You bless others, you are yourself accursed. You pretend to have the keys of heaven, and you are yourself shut out from it. . . .

Julius: Then you won't open the gates?

Peter: Sooner to anyone than to such as you. We are not of your communion in this place. You have an army of sturdy rogues behind you, you have money, and you are a famous architect. Go build a paradise of your own, and fortify it, lest the devils break in on you.

91

Martin Luther at the Diet of Worms, 1521[1]

Although the Holy Roman Emperor Charles V (1500–1558) saw rebellion against the Church as leading to rebellion against the state, he could neither ignore the aroused German nationalism nor Luther's powerful princely support. It is for these reasons that the emperor did not immediately publish the papal bull[2] "Exsurge domine" against Luther but, rather, granted Luther a safe conduct so that he could appear before the Diet of Princes at Worms in order to defend his religious views.

The following excerpt is from Luther's reply to the Diet at Worms on April 18, 1521.

QUESTIONS TO CONSIDER

1. What were Luther's criticisms of the Church?
2. What would have convinced Luther to change his opinions?

[1]The imperial Diet had been created in the fifteenth century; it included three houses: (1) the seven electors who chose the emperors, (2) the House of Princes, and (3) the House of Free Cities. The Diets always tried to stop the emperors from exercising any real authority over them. The emperors had to depend for any moneys or troops on voluntary contributions from the Diet. The imperial free city of Worms, located in Hesse on the Rhine, had been designated as the meeting place of the Emperor Charles V and the Diet in 1520. The emperor had promised the princes that no German should be branded an outlaw before a hearing in the empire; he, therefore, had to follow constitutional practices and give Martin Luther a safe-conduct pass to the meeting of the Diet.

[2]A papal bull [*Bulla*] is the most solemn official pronouncement of a pope. It was sealed with lead or a *Bulla*.

3. Why would the Catholic Church not favor Luther's individual interpretation of the Scriptures?
4. From your general reading, how did the Protestant Reformation affect the political situation during the sixteenth century?

"Most serene emperor, most illustrious princes, concerning those questions proposed to me yesterday on behalf of your serene majesty, whether I acknowledged as mine the books enumerated and published in my name and whether I wished to persevere in their defense or to retract them, I have given to the first question my full and complete answer, in which I still persist and shall persist forever. These books are mine and they have been published in my name by me, unless in the meantime, either through the craft or the mistaken wisdom of my emulators, something in them has been changed or wrongly cut out. For plainly I cannot acknowledge anything except what is mine alone and what has been written by me alone, to the exclusion of all interpretations of anyone at all.

"In replying to the second question, I ask that your most serene majesty and your lordships may deign to note that my books are not all of the same kind.

"For there are some in which I have discussed religious faith and morals simply and evangelically, so that even my enemies themselves are compelled to admit that these are useful, harmless, and clearly worthy to be read by Christians. Even the bull, although harsh and cruel, admits that some of my books are inoffensive, and yet allows these also to be condemned with a judgment which is utterly monstrous. Thus, if I should begin to disavow them, I ask you, what would I be doing? Would not I, alone of all men, be condemning the very truth upon which friends and enemies equally agree, striving alone against the harmonious confession of all?

"Another group of my books attacks the papacy and the affairs of the papists as those who both by their doctrines and very wicked examples have laid waste the Christian world with evil that affects the spirit and the body. For no one can deny or conceal this fact, when the experience of all and the complaints of everyone witness that through the decrees of the pope and the doctrines of men the consciences of the faithful have been most miserably entangled, tortured, and torn to pieces. Also, property and possessions, especially in this illustrious nation of Germany, have been devoured by an unbelievable tyranny and are being devoured to this time without letup and by unworthy means. . . . If, therefore, I should have retracted these writings, I should have done nothing other than to have added strength to this [papal] tyranny and I should have opened not only windows but doors to such great godlessness. It would rage farther and more freely than ever it has dared up to this time. Yes, from the proof of such a revocation on my part, their wholly lawless and unrestrained kingdom of wickedness would become still more intolerable for the already wretched people; and their rule would be further strengthened and established, especially if it should be reported that this evil deed had been done by me by virtue of the authority of your most serene majesty and of the whole Roman Empire. Good God! What a cover for wickedness and tyranny I should have then become.

"I have written a third sort of book against some private and (as they say) distinguished individuals—those, namely, who strive to preserve the Roman tyranny and to destroy the godliness taught by me. Against these I confess I have been more violent than my

Martin Luther, *Luther's Works, Career of the Reformer II,* ed. George W. Forell (Philadelphia: Muhlenberg Press, 1958), pp. XXXII, 109–13.

religion or profession demands. But then, I do not set myself up as a saint; neither am I disputing about my life, but about the teaching of Christ. It is not proper for me to retract these works, because by this retraction it would again happen that tyranny and godlessness would, with my patronage, rule and rage among the people of God more violently than ever before.

"However, because I am a man and not God, I am not able to shield my books with any other protection than that which my Lord Jesus Christ himself offered for his teaching. When questioned before Annas about his teaching and struck by a servant, he said: 'If I have spoken wrongly, bear witness to the wrong.' . . . If the Lord himself, who knew that he could not err, did not refuse to hear testimony against his teaching, even from the lowliest servant, how much more ought I, who am the lowest scum and able to do nothing except err, desire and expect that somebody should want to offer testimony against my teaching! Therefore, I ask by the mercy of God, may your most serene majesty, most illustrious lordships, or anyone at all who is able, either high or low, bear witness, expose my errors, overthrowing them by the writings of the prophets and the evangelists. Once I have been taught I shall be quite ready to renounce every error, and I shall be the first to cast my books into the fire.

"From these remarks I think it is clear that I have sufficiently considered and weighed the hazards and dangers, as well as the excitement and dissensions aroused in the world as a result of my teachings, things about which I was gravely and forcefully warned yesterday. To see excitement and dissension arise because of the Word of God is to me clearly the most joyful aspect of all in these matters. For this is the way, the opportunity, and the result of the Word of God, just as He [Christ] said, 'I have not come to bring peace, but a sword. For I have come to set a man against his father, etc.' . . . Therefore, we ought to think how marvelous and terrible is our God in his counsels, lest by chance what is attempted for settling strife grows rather into an intolerable deluge of evils, if we begin by condemning the Word of God. And concern must be shown lest the reign of this most noble youth, Prince Charles (in whom after God is our great hope), become unhappy and inauspicious. I could illustrate this with abundant examples from Scripture—like Pharaoh, the king of Babylon, and the kings of Israel who, when they endeavored to pacify and strengthen their kingdoms by the wisest counsels, most surely destroyed themselves. For it is He who takes the wise in their own craftiness . . . and overturns mountains before they know it. . . . Therefore we must fear God. I do not say these things because there is a need of either my teachings or my warnings for such leaders as you, but because I must not withhold the allegiance which I owe my Germany. With these words I commend myself to your most serene majesty and to your lordships, humbly asking that I not be allowed through the agitation of my enemies, without cause, to be made hateful to you. I have finished."

When I had finished, the speaker for the emperor said, as if in reproach, that I had not answered the question, that I ought not call into question those things which had been condemned and defined in councils; therefore what was sought from me was not a horned response, but a simple one, whether or not I wished to retract.

Here I answered:

"Since then your serene majesty and your lordships seek a simple answer, I will give it in this manner, neither horned nor toothed: Unless I am convinced by the testimony of the Scriptures or by clear reason (for I do not trust either in the pope or in councils alone, since it is well known that they have often erred and contradicted themselves), I am bound by the Scriptures I have quoted and my conscience is captive to the Word of God. I cannot and I will not retract anything, since it is neither safe nor right to go against conscience.

"I cannot do otherwise, here I stand, may God Help me, Amen."

Age of Exploration and Expansion

Almost a century before Portuguese captain Vasco da Gama successfully rounded the Cape of Good Hope and reached the Malabar coast of India in 1498, in 1405, Emperor Yung-lo (1403–1424) of the Ming dynasty (1308–1644) had launched the first of a series of grand-scale maritime expeditions. Over the next twenty-eight years, the Chinese court dispatched six more large-scale naval expeditions to Southeast Asia, India, Persia, and the east coast of Africa. These gigantic expeditions involved more than 70,000 men and hundreds of vessels and covered thousands of nautical miles. In contrast with the goals of the European adventurers who came to Asia several decades later, the main purpose of these grand undertakings was neither conquest nor trade. The Ming government was mainly interested in spreading and enhancing its dynastic prestige and power as well as winning for China the nominal control of those distant regions. By 1415, nineteen kingdoms had sent tributes to the Ming court; however, after nearly three decades of naval expeditions, not a single permanent overseas Ming colony was established.

Then, in 1433, the great Ming naval expeditions suddenly ceased, never to resume. Although scholars do not know the precise reasons why China refused to embark on her own Age of Exploration, possible explanations might include the high cost of the naval expeditions; China's long-held tradition of anticommercialism; and the ruling Confucian scholars' and officials' prejudice toward the seafaring people, who neglected to observe two important Confucian virtues—namely, filial piety and ancestor worship. Had those Chinese seafarers sustained support from a leader such as Portugal's Prince Henry, the course of world history might have been quite different; certainly China would have "discovered" such distant lands as Spain, England, and France. A little more than six decades after the last Ming naval expedition of 1433, Vasco da Gama opened an era of European domination of the Asian waters. The compass and gunpowder, two important gifts of China to the West, permitted the Europeans to develop empires in Asia.

As the demand for Oriental products increased in Western Europe in the fifteenth century, merchants and monarchs, hoping to break the Italian monopoly of that trade, began their search for an all-water route to the East. Another powerful impetus was a strong sense of Christian duty to convert pagans and infidels. For centuries, Portuguese and Spaniards had struggled to expel the Muslims who occupied their land. That effort generated a religious fervor and missionary zeal and also helped establish a sense of national identity. By the early fifteenth century, Portugal had become a unified state, separate from the expanding Spanish kingdoms of Leon and Castile. The Iberians, with their strategic location facing the Atlantic and with new knowledge of navigation and shipbuilding gained from Italian seafarers on the Mediterranean, initiated the age of European exploration and expansion.

Prince Henry, the third son of King John I of Portugal (1385–1433), focused the small nation's attention on various maritime projects. Under his leadership, Portugal became a center of knowledge for shipbuilding, navigation, and the study of geography. Portugal also was the first European nation to embark on colonial expansion. Prince Henry took the initiative in settling Portuguese adventurers in the Azores, and in 1415 he crossed the Strait of Gibraltar to capture the North African port of Ceuta, the terminal of the caravan routes into Africa. In succeeding years, lured by the potential profits in trading gold, ivory, and slaves, Prince Henry directed Portuguese explorations down the West African coast and established trading centers there. He had also obtained from the papacy a monopoly of missionary activities in the area. When he died in 1460, Prince Henry's economic and religious rights in West Africa passed to the Portuguese monarchs, who continued sending explorers to probe the African coast. They rounded the Cape of Good Hope by 1488 and a decade later arrived in the Indian Ocean, where Muslim states had a monopoly of the trade with India and the Far East. In the New World, Pedro Cabral landed on the east coast of South America in 1500, strengthening Portugal's claim to Brazil.

As a youth, Christopher Columbus (1451–1506) had served as a seaman on various ships in the Mediterranean. He eventually settled in Portugal, where he developed his idea of sailing west to Asia. He was unable to gain financial support from the Portuguese monarchs, who favored opening the sea route to India by way of Africa, but he continued his search for a sponsor in Spain. After the fall of the Muslim stronghold of Granada on January 2, 1492, Queen Isabella finally agreed to his terms. His four voyages established Spanish influence in the Caribbean.

It did not take long, however, for Spain and other European countries to begin conquering the New World that Columbus had stumbled upon. The final reading in this section describes the conquest of Mexico.

92

Cheng Ho [Zheng He]: Ming Maritime Expeditions

Most of the large naval expeditions of the Ming dynasty were led by a Muslim court eunuch named Cheng Ho (1371–1433). The following selection describes China's Columbus and the maritime explorations he led.

QUESTIONS TO CONSIDER

1. What does the size, organization, and nature of the Ming maritime fleet indicate about China's capabilities in the early fifteenth century?
2. What do the Ming Emperor's bans on imperial naval explorations suggest about Chinese views of the world?
3. Compare and contrast the Ming maritime expeditions with the Age of Discovery in Western history. What motives inspired Cheng Ho, Columbus, and Magellan?
4. How might the course of world history have been altered had the Chinese seafarers received sustained support from a leader such as Prince Henry of Portugal?

Cheng Ho (1371–1433), eunuch and commander-in-chief of the Ming expeditionary fleets in the early years of the 15th century, was born into a family named Ma at K'un-yang [Kun-yang] in central Yunnan. His great-grandfather was named Bayan, and his grandfather and father were both named Ḥājjī, which suggests that the two probably visited Mecca and that the family had a long tradition of Islamic faith and may have been of Mongol-Arab origin. At the beginning of the Ming dynasty, a number of generals who fought on the frontier were in charge of recruiting eunuchs for the court. In 1381, when Yunnan was pacified by an army under Fu Yu-de, Cheng Ho, at that time about ten years old, was one of the children selected to be castrated. As a trainee for eunuch service, he was assigned to the retinue of Chu Ti [Zhu Di] [Emperor Yung-lo]. In his early twenties, he accompanied Chu Ti on a series of military campaigns and in the course of them took up a career in the army. As his family records relate, "when he entered adulthood, he reportedly became seven feet tall and had a waist about five feet in circumference. His cheeks and forehead were high but his nose was small. He had glaring eyes and a voice as loud as a huge bell. He knew a great deal about warfare and was well accustomed to battle." . . .

Cheng Ho first achieved official prominence early in 1404 when he was promoted to the position of director of eunuch affairs and granted the surname of Cheng [Zheng]. Shortly afterward he received the appointment of commander-in-chief of the first expedition. Meanwhile local officials of the eastern coastal regions were ordered to build ocean-going vessels. By July, 1405, some 1,180 ships of various sizes and types had been constructed. The large or treasure ships were, according to measures of that time, as much as 440 feet long and 186.2 wide, and those of medium size, or horse ships, 370 feet long and 150 wide. There were supply ships which measured 280 feet in length and 120 in breadth, and billet ships measuring 240 feet by 94. The battleships equipped with cannon were much smaller, measuring only 180 feet by 68. Most of the treasure ships were the product of the Lung-chiang [Long Jiang] shipyard near Nanking [Nanjing]. None of these has survived, but near the site of the shipyard was recently discovered (1957) a large wooden rudder (length 11 meters) thought to have been fashioned for one of the bigger vessels. It is now preserved in the Kiangsu [Jiangsu] provincial museum.

The first voyage began in the summer of 1405 with a 27,800 man crew and 62 (or 63) large and 255 smaller vessels. . . . [In the second voyage, which was launched in late autumn of 1407, the expedition sailed into the Indian Ocean.]

In the summer of 1409 Cheng Ho returned to Nanking to report on his mission to the emperor. Here he built a temple in honor of T'ien-fei [Tianfei], the goddess of the sea, to whose virtue and power he attributed the safe voyages of his fleets. The inscription on the stele erected later (May 3, 1416) has been partly translated into French by Claudine Lombard-Salmon; the complete Chinese text may be found in the book by Louis Gaillard.

After a brief stay in the capital, Cheng Ho was again sent overseas, accompanied by Wang Ching-hung [Wang Jinghong] and Hou Hsien [Hou Xian]. His third voyage was comparable to the first and second in the number of men but with only 48 vessels; it lasted from September, 1409, to June, 1411. This expedition reached the same destination on the Malabar coast of India, but along the way several excursions were made, including brief visits to Siam, Malacca, Sumatra, and Ceylon. It also undertook lumbering operations and gathered fragrant herbs in the Sembilan Islands. . . .

It was the fourth voyage, which began in 1413 and ended in August, 1415, that took the expedition far beyond its earlier destinations. Under the same command but with a crew of 27,670 men and some 63 large vessels, the expedition touched at a number of new places, including the Maldives, Hormuz, the Hadramaut coast, and Aden. In Sumatra the expedition became involved in a local power struggle at Ch'iao-shan [Qiaoshan] (Samudra-Pasai). A usurper by the name of Su-wa-la, after murdering the king, directed his forces against the expedition, but was subsequently defeated and pursued as far as Lambri, where he and his family were captured. The prisoners were taken to Nanking on the return of the fleet. As a result of this voyage, nineteen countries sent envoys and tribute to the Ming court. Chu Ti was so pleased with the results that he rewarded all participants in the expedition according to their ranks.

In December, 1416, Cheng Ho was commissioned to escort home the envoys of the nineteen states, and embarked, possibly in the autumn of 1417, on his fifth voyage, which lasted up to August, 1419. The returning envoys, who had witnessed the delight of the Ming emperor at his first sight of a giraffe, spread the news to other countries. Hence an impressive collection of strange animals, among them lions, leopards, single-humped camels, ostriches, zebras, rhinoceroses, antelopes, and giraffes offered by rulers of several states highlighted this journey.

The spring of 1421 saw the launching of the sixth voyage, but Cheng may not have joined the fleet until later. It returned on September 3, 1422, accompanied by a large number of envoys from such states as Hormuz, Aden, Djofar, La-sa (Al-shsā?), Brawa, Mogadishu, Calicut, Cochin, Cail, Ceylon, the Maldive Islands, Lambri, Sumatra, Aru, Malacca, Kan-pa-li (Coyampadi?), Sulu, Bengal, Borneo, Ku-ma-la (-lang, Cabarruyan Islands?), and Ts'eng-pa (Zanzibar). The number of countries visited on this trip has not been listed, but the expedition reached at least as far as Aden, near the mouth of the Red Sea, and Mogadishu and Brawa on the coast of east Africa. . . .

In the meanwhile Chu Ti had died (August 12, 1424), and almost at once the idea of another maritime expedition came under attack. The emperor designate, Chu Kao-chih [Zhu Gaozhi], promptly (August 28) released from prison Hsia Yüan-chi [Xia Yuanji], perhaps the most outspoken critic of the treasure fleets, and on September 7, the very day of Chu's accession to the throne as the fourth Ming emperor, other voices joined Hsia's in recommending their abolition. This protest seems to have settled the matter, for in the following February Cheng Ho received an appointment as garrison commander of the Nanking district, and was told to maintain order in his own expeditionary forces, and consult with Wang Ching-hung and two other eunuchs. . . .

Only a few months later the fourth emperor died and for several years the plan to launch another expedition lay dormant. Finally in June, 1430, his successor, the fifth emperor, Chu Chan-chi [Zhu Zhanji], issued an order for the seventh (and what proved to be the last) voyage, but it was not to leave the Fukien [Fujian] coast until a year and a half later. It returned in July, 1433. The mission was intended to regenerate the tributary relationships once maintained under Chu Ti, which had significantly weakened since his death. A score of states were revisited, including those along the coasts of the Arabian peninsula and eastern Africa. In this instance too ambassadors returned with the fleet, bringing such gifts as giraffes, elephants, and horses. Cheng Ho, who was already in his sixties, did not perhaps visit all of them in person, and some of the side missions were conducted by his aides. . . .

What happened to Cheng Ho from this point is not clear. It has customarily been said that he died in 1435 or 1436 at the age of sixty-five, no specific date or site of burial being indicated in contemporary sources. A later source, the *T'ung-chih Shang Chiang liang-hsien chih [Tongzhi Shang Jiang liangxian Zhi]* (preface of 1874), 3/39a, however, maintains that Cheng Ho died at Calicut and was buried at Niushoushan outside Nanking. If this be true, he must have passed away early in 1433.

93

St. Francis Xavier on the Japanese:
"The Best People Who Have Yet Been Discovered"

In 1549, St. Francis Xavier (1506–1552), an ethnic Basque from Spain and one of the founding members of the Society of Jesus, introduced Christianity to Japan, the land of Buddhism and Shintoism. As an apostolic nuncio (highest-ranking papal legate permanently accredited to a civil government) for Asia, he left Europe in 1541 for Goa, an important Portuguese outpost located on the west coast of India. He traveled far and wide along the coastal towns of India, Ceylon, and Malaya to proselytize indigenous Asian people. Glowing accounts of Japan by a Japanese fugitive named Anjiro (Yajiro), whom he met in Malacca in 1547, persuaded Xavier to carry his evangelical endeavor to Japan. On August 15, 1549, Xavier, accompanied by two Jesuit priests and Anjiro as an interpreter, reached Kagoshima, Anjiro's native town, located on the southern tip of Japan's Kyushu island. There, Xavier preached Christianity and won approximately one hundred converts. Apparently, many believed that Christianity was just another version of Buddhism. Encouraged by the good reception to his message in Kagoshima, he traveled to Kyoto, then the Imperial capital, in February 1551. There, he explored the possibility of obtaining official approval for expanding evangelical work throughout the country. Xavier probably did not realize that the country he was visiting was in the throes of bloody civil wars among contending feudal daimyo (feudal territorial warlords). Furthermore, he was probably unaware that the Ashikaga shogunate (1336–1573) was in the last phase of its demise. Disappointed by not being able to have an audience with the emperor, Xavier returned to Kyushu. After two years and three months of his proselytizing work in Japan, he left the country for India at the end of 1551.

The following is a letter written by Xavier to fellow Jesuits in Goa, a few months after his arrival in Kagoshima. In this letter he describes the Japanese people as "the best who have yet been discovered."

QUESTIONS TO CONSIDER

1. What aspects of Japanese life and character impressed Xavier to give such high praise?
2. What were the reasons for the more receptive attitudes of the provincial lords and people in western Japan toward Christianity than those in the rest of the country?

By the experience which we have of this land of Japan, I can inform you thereof as follows. Firstly, the people whom we have met so far, are the best who have yet been discovered, and it seems to me that we shall never find among heathens another race to equal the Japanese. It is a people of very good manners, good in general, and not malicious; they are men

From C.R. Boxer, *The Christian Century in Japan, 1549–1650* (Berkeley: University of California Press, 1967), pp. 401–05. Reproduced by permission of Carcent Press Limited.

of honor to a marvel, and prize honor above all else in the world. They are a poor people in general; but their poverty, whether among the gentry or those who are not so, is not considered as a shame. They have one quality which I cannot recall in any people of Christendom; this is that their gentry howsoever poor they may be, and the commoners howsoever rich they may be, render as much honor to a poor gentleman as if he were passing rich. On no account would a poverty-stricken gentleman marry with someone outside the gentry, even if he were given great sums to do so; and this they do because they consider that they would lose their honor by marrying into a lower class. Whence it can clearly be seen that they esteem honor more than riches. They are very courteous in their dealings one with another; they highly regard arms and trust much in them; always carrying sword and dagger, both high and low alike, from the age of fourteen onwards. They are a people who will not submit to any insults or contemptuous words. Those who are not of gentle birth give much honor to the gentry, who in their turn pride themselves on faithfully serving their feudal lord, to whom they are very obedient. It seems to me that they act thus rather because they think that they would lose their honor if they acted contrarily, than for fear of the punishment they would receive if disobedient. They are small eaters albeit somewhat heavy drinkers, and they drink rice wine since there are no ordinary wines in these parts. They are men who never gamble, because they consider it a great dishonor, since those who gamble desire what is not theirs and hence tend to become thieves. They swear but little, and when they do it is by the Sun. There are many persons who can read and write, which is a great help to their learning quickly prayers and religious matters. It is a land where there are but few thieves in some kingdoms, and this by the strict justice which is executed against those that are, for their lives are never spared. They abhor beyond measure this vice of theft. They are a people of very good will, very sociable and very desirous of knowledge; they are very fond of hearing about things of God, chiefly when they understand them. Of all the lands which I have seen in my life, whether those of Christians or of heathens, never yet did I see a people so honest in not thieving. Most of them believe in the men of old, who were (so far as I understand) persons who lived like philosophers; many of them adore the Sun and others the Moon. They like to hear things propounded according to reason; and granted that there are sins and vices among them, when one reasons with them pointing out that what they do is evil, they are convinced by this reasoning. I discerned fewer sins in the laity and found them more obedient to reason, than those whom they regard as fathers and priests, whom they call Bonzes.

Two things have astonished me greatly about this country. The first, to see how lightly they regard great sins; and the reason is because their forebears were accustomed to live in them, from whom those of the present generation take their example; see how continuation in vices which are against nature corrupts the people, in the same manner as continual disregard of imperfections undermines and destroys perfection. The second point is to see that the laity live better in their state than the Bonzes in theirs; and withal this is so manifest, it is astonishing in what esteem the former hold the latter. There are many other errors and evils among these Bonzes, and the more learned are the worst sinners. I spoke many times with some of the wiser, chiefly with one who is highly regarded by all in these parts, both for his letters, life, and dignity, as for his great age, he being eighty years old, and called Ningit [Ninjitsu], which is to say in Japanese "truthful heart"; he is as a bishop amongst them, and if the term could be applied to him, might well be called "blessed." In many talks which I had with him, I found him doubtful, and unable to decide whether our soul is immortal, or whether it dies with the body; sometimes he told me yes, at others no, and I fear that the other learned are alike. This Ningit is so great a friend of mine, that it is a marvel to see. All, both laity and Bonzes like us very much, and are greatly astonished to see how we have come from such distant lands as from Portugal to Japan, which is more than six thousand leagues, only to speak of the things of God, and how people can save their souls by belief in Jesus Christ; saying that our coming to these lands is the work of God. One thing I tell you, for which you may give many thanks to God Our Lord, that this land of Japan is very fit for our holy faith greatly to increase therein; and if we knew how to speak the language, I have no doubt whatsoever that we would make many Christians. May it please Our Lord that we may learn it soon, for already we begin to appreciate it, and we learned to repeat the ten commandments in the space of forty days which we applied ourselves thereto. . . .

God granted us a signal favor in bringing us to these lands which lack such abundancies, so that even if we wished to minister to our bodies with these superfluities, the country does not allow of it. They neither kill nor eat anything which they rear. Sometimes they eat fish; there is rice and corn, albeit little; there are numerous herbs, on which they live, and some fruit but not much. This people live wonderfully healthy lives and there are many aged. The Japanese are a convincing proof of how our nature can subsist on little, even if it is not a pleasing sustenance. We live in this land very healthy in body, God grant that we may be likewise in our souls. A great part of the Japanese are Bonzes, and these are strictly obeyed in the places where they are, even if their sins are manifest to all; and it seems to me that the reason why they are held in such esteem is because of their rigorous abstinence, for they never eat meat, nor fish, but only herbs, fruit, and rice, and this once a day and very strictly, and they are never given wine. There are many Bonzes and their temples are of but little revenue. By reason of their continual abstinence and because they have no intercourse with women (especially those who go dressed in black like clergy) on pain of death, and because they know how to relate some histories or rather fables of the things in which they believe, it seems to me they are held in great veneration. And it may well happen that since they and we feel so differently about God and the method of salvation, that we may be persecuted by them with something stronger than words. What we in these parts endeavor to do, is to bring people to the knowledge of their Creator and Saviour, Jesus Christ Our Lord. We live with great hope and trust in him to give us strength, grace, help, and favor to prosecute this work. It does not seem to me that the laity will oppose or persecute us of their own volition, but only if they are importuned by the Bonzes. We do not seek to quarrel with them, neither for fear of them will we cease to speak of the glory of God, and of the salvation of souls.

It is well that we should give you an account of our stay in Cangoxima [Kagoshima]. We arrived here at a season when the winds were contrary for going to Miaco, [Kyoto] which is the chief city of Japan, where the King and the greatest lords of the Kingdom reside. And there is no wind that will serve us to go thither, save only five months from now, and then we will go with the help of Our Lord. It is three hundred leagues from here to Miaco, according to what they tell us, and we are likewise told great things of that city, which is said to contain more than ninety thousand houses; there is also a great university frequented by students therein, which has six principal colleges and more than two hundred houses of Bonzes, and of others like friars who are called Ieguixu [Zen-shu], and of nuns who are called Hamacata [Amakata]. Besides this university of Miaco, there are five other chief universities whose names are these, Coya [Koya], Nenguru [Negoro], Feizan [Hieizan], Taninomine [Tamu no mine]. These are in the neighborhood of Miaco, and it is said that there are more than 3,500 students in each one of them. There is another university, a great way off, which is called Bandou [Bando, the Ashikaga Gakko] which is the best and biggest in Japan, and more frequented by students than any other. Bandou is a great lordship where there are six dukes, and a chief one among them, whom the others obey.

This chief owes allegiance to the King of Japan who is the great King of Miaco. They tell us such things of the greatness of these lands and universities, that we would prefer to see them before affirming and writing them; and if things be as they tell us, then we will write of our experiences in detail. In addition to these principal universities, they say that there are many other smaller ones throughout the kingdom. During the year 1551, we hope to write you at length concerning the disposition that there is in Miaco and its universities for the knowledge of Jesus Christ Our Lord to be spread therein. This year two Bonzes are going to India who have studied in the universities of Bandou and Miaco, and with them many other Japanese to learn the things of our law. . . .

> From Cangoxima, fifth of November of the year 1549.
> Your most loving brother wholly in Christ,
>
> FRANCISCO

The Portuguese in Africa, Asia, and Brazil

Portugal played a key role in initiating the age of discovery and exploration. Prince Henry "the Navigator" (1394–1460) devoted much of his life to directing explorations along the west coast of Africa and advancing Portuguese commercial interests. A transitional figure, he exhibited the combination of medieval and more modern characteristics that characterized early Portuguese exploration efforts.

We recall that the Portuguese continued the medieval search for Prester John until they finally "found" him in the Christian emperor of Ethiopia (see Reading 62) and that they carried the Iberian struggle against the Moors around the coast of Africa to the Persian Gulf (see Reading 65). Under Afonso Albuquerque (1453–1515), occasionally called "the Portuguese Mars," the Portuguese went on to take Goa, a city-state in India, which became a Portuguese colony and functioned as one of the capitals in their expanding maritime empire. By the 1530s, the Portuguese had established bases at many points in East Asia, including Ning-po on the Chinese mainland near Canton where, as Fernao Mendes Pinto tells us, they confidently built an enclave town of expensive houses, oblivious to the fact that the Chinese Empire was not so weak yet as to allow them to settle in permanently.

94

The Chronicle of Gomes Eannes de Azurara

The following excerpts are from the chronicle of Gomes Eannes de Azurara (1410–1474), who was a friend and contemporary of Prince Henry. The first portrays Henry's personal qualities and character; the second describes the birth of the African slave trade with Portugal.

QUESTIONS TO CONSIDER

1. In what ways did Prince Henry reflect traits of the medieval age combined with more modern characteristics? Do you think he would have understood and been receptive to Machiavelli's advice (see Reading 89)?
2. What physical qualities of the Africans led the writer to describe some of them as a "marvelous sight" and others as "images of a lower hemisphere"? What were the implications and consequences of these reactions?
3. How did the African natives respond to the Portuguese? According to Azurara, in addition to their enslavement, what caused African suffering to increase?
4. How does this selection reflect the importance of religion as a factor in the expansion of Europe?

Prince Henry

The prince was a man of great wisdom and authority, very discreet and of good memory, but in some matters a little tardy, whether it was from the influence of the phlegm in his nature, or from the choice of his will, directed to some certain end not known to men. His bearing was calm and dignified, his speech and address gentle. He was constant in adversity, humble in prosperity. Never was hatred known to him, nor ill-will toward any man, however great the wrong done him; and such was his benignity in this respect, that wiseacres reproached him as wanting in distributive justice. And this they said, because he left unpunished some of his servants who deserted him at the siege of Tangier, which was the most perilous affair in which he ever stood before or after, not only becoming reconciled to them, but even granting them honourable advancement over others who had served him well, which in the judgment of men was far from their deserts, and this is the only shortcoming of his I have to record. The Infant drank wine only for a very small part of his life and that in his youth, but afterwards he abstained entirely from it.

He ever showed great devotion to the public affairs of this kingdom, toiling greatly for their good advancement and he much delighted in the trial of new undertakings for the profit of all, though with great expense of his own substance, and he keenly enjoyed the labour of arms, especially against the enemies of the holy Faith, while he desired peace with all Christians. Thus he was loved by all alike, for he made himself useful to all and hindered no one. His answers were always gentle and he showed great honour to the standing of every one who came to him, without any lessening of his own estate. A base or unchaste word was never heard to issue from his mouth. He was very obedient to the commands of Holy Church and heard all its offices with great devotion; aye and caused the same to be celebrated in his chapel, with no less splendour and ceremony than they could have been in the college of any Cathedral Church. . . . Well-nigh one-half of the year he spent in fasting and the hands of the poor never went away empty from his presence. . . . His heart knew not fear, save the fear of sin. . . .

The African Slave Trade

On the next day, which was the 8th of the month of August, very early in the morning, by reason of the heat, the seamen began to make ready their boats, and to take out their cap-

From Gomes Eannes de Azurara, *The Chronicle of the Discovery and Conquest of Guinea*, Vol. 1, trans. C.R. Beazley and Edgar Prestage (London: Hakluyt Society, 1896), pp. 12–15, 81–83, *passim*.

tives and carry them on shore, as they were commanded. And these, placed altogether in that field, were a marvellous sight, for amongst them were some white enough, fair to look upon and well proportioned, others were less white like mulattoes; others again were as black as Ethiops, and so ugly, both in features and in body, as almost to appear the images of a lower hemisphere. But what heart could be so hard as not to be pierced with piteous feeling to see that company? For some kept their heads low and their faces bathed in tears, looking one upon another; others stood groaning very grievously, looking up to the height of heaven, fixing their eyes upon it, crying out loudly, as if asking help of the Father of Nature; others struck their faces with the palms of their hands, throwing themselves at full length upon the ground; others made their lamentations in the manner of a dirge, after the custom of their country. And though we could not understand the words of their language, the sound of it right well accorded with the measure of their sadness. But to increase their sufferings still more, there now arrived those who had charge of the division of the captives and who began to separate one from another in order to make an equal partition of the fifths; and then it was needful to part fathers from sons, husbands from wives, brothers from brothers. No respect was shewn either to friends or relations, but each fell where his lot took him.

And who could finish that partition without very great toil, for as often as they had placed them in one part, the sons, seeing their fathers in another, rose with great energy and rushed over to them; the mothers clasped their other children in their arms, and threw themselves flat on the ground with them, receiving blows with little pity for their own flesh, if only they might not be torn from them.

The Infant was there, mounted upon a powerful steed, and accompanied by his retinue, making distribution of his favours, as a man who sought to gain but small treasure from his share; for he made a very speedy partition of the forty-six souls that fell to him as his fifth. His chief riches lay in his purpose, and he reflected with great pleasure upon the salvation of those souls that before were lost. And certainly his expectation was not in vain, since, as we said before, as soon as they understood our language, they turned Christians with very little ado; and I who put together this history into the present volume, saw in the town of Lagos boys and girls (the children and grandchildren of those first captives) born in this land, as good and true Christians as if they had directly descended, from the beginning of the dispensation of Christ, from those who were first baptised.

95

Pero Vaz de Caminha and the Brazilian Indians

The following selection comes from a letter written by Pero Vaz de Caminha who was with Pedro Cabral's expedition to Brazil in 1500. It describes the first encounter between the Portuguese and the Brazilian Indians.

QUESTIONS TO CONSIDER

1. What was the Portuguese reaction to the Brazilian Indians? Does the writer appear disturbed by any of the native customs? Which ones? Explain why or why not.

2. Compare Portuguese reactions with those of other world travelers such as Ibn Fad-
    lan (see Reading 59) and Ibn Battuta (see Reading 64).
3. Why did the Brazilian Indians react adversely to the animals, foods, and bever-
    ages the Portuguese showed them?
4. What were the immediate and long-range consequences for the Portuguese of
    these initial encounters? For the Africans and Brazilian Indians?

At the Captain's order Afonso Lopez, our pilot in one of the smaller boats, being a fit and
skillful man for such a task, boarded a skiff to enter and sound the harbor. And he seized
from a canoe two of the young and huskier natives, one of whom was carrying a bow with
six or seven arrows. And many more were standing on the beach with their bows and arrows but did not make use of them. That very night the same two were brought before the
captain, where they were received with great pleasure and festivity.

They are darkish red in appearance with good-looking faces and well-shaped noses.
They go naked without the slightest covering and pay no special attention to showing or not
showing their shameful parts—and in this respect with as much innocence as they have in
showing their faces. The lower lips of both natives were punctured and through each punc-
ture a white bone was inserted: the length of the width of one hand and the thickness of a
cotton spindle and pointed like a bodkin. They insert it from the inside of the lip, and the
part of the bone which remains between lip and teeth is fashioned much like a chess rook.
And they seem to place it somehow so that it never annoys them in any way or prevents
their speaking or eating or drinking. Their hair is straight and they go with heads shaven
nearly to the crown, where the hair grows quite long, and their faces are shaven clean to
above the ears. And one of the two was wearing a kind of headdress, which extended from
both temples around the back of the head and the ears. He had feather after feather stuck to
his hair by means of a kind of smooth concoction, like wax but not; so that he had a very
round and very full and very even headdress which was by no means small and was in fact
a difficult thing to carry upright.

When the two came before the Captain, he was seated in a chair with a carpet at his
feet for a dais and was well dressed with a great gold collar around his neck. And Sancho
de Toar, Simão de Miranda, Nicolao Coelho, Aires Correa, and the rest of us there in the
boat with the Captain were seated upon the carpet on the floor. We lit the torches and the
two entered the cabin, but showed none of the usual courtesies nor spoke to the Captain or
to anyone; but one of them noticed the Captain's collar and began to point with his hand to
land and then to the collar, as if to say to us that there was gold on the land. And he also noticed a silver candleholder and, in the same way as before, pointed to land and then to the
holder, as if there were silver there also. We showed them a gray parrot which belonged to
the Captain; they took it easily in hand and pointed to land, as if they had parrots there. We
showed them a ram, but they made no mention of its being there also. We showed them a
chicken; they were somewhat afraid of it and did not want to put a hand out for it, and they
touched it, fearfully, only after a while. At that point we gave them bread and cooked fish,
sweets, cakes, honey, and dried figs; they did not want to eat most of the foods and tried
only one or two things and threw these down at once. We brought them wine in a cup; they
barely touched it to their lips and did not like what they tasted or want any more of it. We
brought them water in a waterskin; they each took a taste without swallowing any, only to

From *The Borzoi Anthology of Latin American Literature,* ed. Emir Rodríguez Monegal with the assistance of
Thomas Colchie (New York: Alfred A. Knopf, 1987), Vol. I, pp. 12–13.

wash their mouths and spit it out. One of them saw some white rosary beads, made signs for us to give them to him, and with these amused himself for quite a while, putting them around his neck and throwing them up in the air, getting them tangled around his arm. And he pointed to land and then to the beads and the Captain's collar, as if to give gold for the beads. Or rather we took this to be his meaning because we wished it to be so, while he really meant to say that he would take the beads and the collar together for himself; this we did not wish to understand because we did not have it to give. And after that he returned the rosary to the one who had given it, and then he and the other stretched out on their backs to sleep on the carpet without showing the least concern for covering their shameful parts, which were not circumcised and were shaven clean of any hair. The Captain ordered us to place pillows for each one beneath their heads and to be careful with the one's headdress, not to break it, and to throw blankets over both of them. And they consented to this and lay there and fell asleep.

96

The Travels of Mendes Pinto

Fernao Mendes Pinto (1510 ?–1583) was born in Portugal and was in his late twenties when he sailed for India in 1537. He became wealthy as a merchant adventurer and spent many years in China and Japan. His account of his travels became important in Portuguese literature. The following selections describe his adventures on the China coast, where the Portuguese had established Ningpo as an enclave near Canton.

QUESTIONS TO CONSIDER

1. What was the Portuguese motive in attacking Nouday?
2. What were the practices of warfare on both sides that could be seen as making Chinese-Portuguese relations difficult, in spite of the fact that China and Portugal were officially at peace with each other?
3. How does religion enter into Pinto's narrative?

The Sack of Nouday

The following morning, shortly before daybreak, Antonio de Faria sailed up the river with the three junks, the *lorcha,*[1] and the four fishing barges he had seized, and dropped anchor in six and a half fathoms of water right up against the walls of the city. Dispensing with the noisy salvo of artillery, he lowered the sails and hoisted the flag of commerce in keeping

---

[1]A junk is a Chinese sailing vessel distinguished by a high poop, overhanging stem, little or no keel, high pole masts, and a deep rudder. A lorcha is a three-masted sailing vessel combining features of Chinese and European ship building.

From Fernão Mendes Pinto, *The Travels of Mendes Pinto,* ed. and trans. Rebecca D. Catz (Chicago: University of Chicago Press, 1989), pp. 123–27. Reprinted with permission of The University of Chicago Press.

with the Chinese custom, intent upon observing all the outward signs of peace and leaving nothing undone by way of complying with the formalities, though he knew full well, from the way matters stood with the mandarin, that it would do him no good.

From here he sent him another letter which was extremely polite and friendly in tone, offering to raise the ransom for the captives; but it made that dog of a mandarin so angry, that he had the poor Chinese messenger crucified on an X-shaped cross and exhibited from the top of the wall in full view of the fleet. The sight was enough to make Antonio de Faria abandon the last shred of hope to which some of the men still made him cling, and at the same time, it made the soldiers so furious that they told him that, as long as he had decided to go ashore, there was no point in his waiting any longer because he would just be giving the enemies time to increase their strength.

Since this seemed like good advice to him, he embarked immediately with all the men who were determined to go ashore, leaving orders behind for the junks to direct a steady barrage of fire against the enemies and the city, wherever major gatherings were to be seen, provided he was not engaged in a battle with them. And after disembarking at a spot about a culverin[2]-shot's distance below the roadstead, without encountering the slightest opposition, he marched along the shore in the direction of the city where, by this time, many people were stationed on top of the walls, waving an enormous number of silk banners, trying to put on a brave show by shouting and playing their martial music and generally carrying on like people who put more stock in words and outward appearances than in actual deeds.

As our men came within a musket-shot's distance of the moat surrounding the wall, about 1,000 to 1,200 soldiers—a guess hazarded by some—sallied forth from two gates; and of this number, about 100 to 120 were mounted on horseback, or to put it in a better way, they were mounted on some rather sorry looking nags. They began by putting on a fine show of skirmishing, running back and forth just as free and easy as you please, getting in each other's way most of the time, and often colliding and falling down in heaps of three and four, from which it was obvious that they were country bumpkins who were there not so much out of a desire to fight, but because they had been forced to come.

Antonio de Faria gently spurred his men on, and after signalling to the junks, he waited for the enemy out in the field, for he thought that they would want to engage him there, judging by the brave show they were putting on. But instead, they went right on with their skirmishing, running around in circles for a while, as though they were threshing wheat, thinking that this alone would be enough to scare us off. However, when they saw that we would not turn tail and run as they thought or probably hoped we would, they got together in a huddle and remained that way for a while, in a single body, in great disorder, without coming any closer.

Seeing them in that way, our captain ordered all the muskets, which had been silent until then, to fire at once; and, as God willed, they hit the mark so well that more than half of the cavalrymen, who were in the vanguard, were knocked to the ground. Off to a good start, we rushed them all together, calling on the name of Jesus as we went; and he, in his mercy, caused the enemy to abandon the field to us and sent them fleeing so wildly that they were falling on top of each other; and when they reached the bridge spanning the moat, they got themselves jammed in there so tightly that they were unable to move either backward or forward.

At this juncture, the main body of our men caught up to them and handled them so efficiently that, before long, more than three hundred of them were lying on top of each other—a pitiful sight indeed—for not a single one of them ever drew a sword.

[2]A long cannon.

Exhilarated by this victory, we made a dash for the gate, and there in the entrance we found the mandarin, surrounded by nearly six hundred men, mounted astride a fine horse, wearing an old-fashioned gilt-studded breastplate of purple velvet, which we found out later had belonged to a certain Tome Pires, whom King Manuel, of glorious memory, had sent as an ambassador to China. . . . The mandarin and his men tried to stop us at the entrance, where a cruel battle ensued, during which, little by little, in the time it would take to recite four or five Credos, they began to drive us back with a lot less fear than the ones on the bridge had shown, and they would have given us a little difficult time had it not been for one of our slave boys who knocked the mandarin off his horse with a musket ball that struck him right in the chest. At that, the Chinese became so frightened that they all spun around and immediately began retreating through the gates in complete disorder, and we along with them, knocking them down with our lances, while not a single one of them had enough presence of mind to shut the gates. And off we went, chasing them before us like cattle, down a very long road, until at last they swept through another gate that led to the forest where every last one of them disappeared from sight.

Next, to prevent disorder, Antonio de Faria gathered his soldiers together and, in a single corps, marched with them straight to the prison where they were holding our men, who at the sight of us let out such a loud and terrifying cry of "Lord God, have mercy on us!" that it was enough to send the shivers down one's spine. He immediately had the prison doors and bars broken with axes, a task that our men threw themselves into with such great enthusiasm that it took but a moment to smash everything to bits and remove the prisoners' shackles, so that in a very short time all our companions were unfettered and free.

The order was given to our soldiers and the others in our company that each man was to lay hold of as much as he could for himself, because there would be no sharing of the spoils, and everyone was to keep whatever he could carry; but he asked them to be quick about it, for he would allow them no more than the brief space of half an hour in which to do it. And they all answered that they would be perfectly satisfied with that.

And then they all disappeared into the houses, while Antonio de Faria headed straight for the mandarin's, which he had staked out for himself, and there he found eight thousand taels in silver alone, as well as five huge jars of musk, all of which he had gathered up. The rest, which he left for the slaves accompanying him, consisted of large quantities of silk, yarn, satin, damask, and fine-quality porcelain packed in straw, which they carried until they were ready to collapse.

As a result, the four barges and three sampans that had been used as landing craft had to make four trips to transfer the loot to the junks, and there was not a slave or sailor among them who did not speak of his booty in terms of whole cases and bales of piece goods, to say nothing of the secrets each one kept locked in his heart.

When he saw that more than an hour and a half had gone by, Antonio de Faria quickly ordered the men to return to the ships, but there was absolutely no way of getting them to stop their looting, and this was especially true of the men of most account. But with night coming on, he was afraid some disaster might befall them, and he had the torch put to the city in ten or twelve different places, and since most of the buildings were constructed of pine and other woods, the fire spread so fiercely that in less than a quarter of an hour it looked like a blazing inferno.

Withdrawing to the beach with all the men, he embarked, with not a murmur of protest from any of them, for they were all leaving very rich and happy; and they had many pretty girls in tow, which was really pathetic to see, for they were tied up with musket wicks by fours and fives, and they were all crying while our men were laughing and singing.

Pirates at the Gates of Ning-po

Since it was already late when Antonio de Faria and all his men got back to the ship, there was no time left for anything but to attend to the wounded, who numbered fifty—eight of them Portuguese and the rest slaves and sailors—and to bury the dead, who numbered nine, counting one Portuguese.

And after spending the night with a careful lookout on account of the junks up the river, at daybreak he departed for a small town located at water's edge on the opposite bank, and discovered that it was completely deserted, all the inhabitants having fled. But he found the houses filled to overflowing with their goods and enormous quantities of food which Antonio de Faria had loaded on board the junks out of fear that in the ports along the way people would refuse to sell him anything because of what he had done.

After that was decided, since everyone thought it best and advised him to do so, that the three winter months he still had to wait before he could set out on his voyage should be spent on a deserted island called Pulo Hinhor, located out to sea fifteen leagues from Ning-po, where there was fresh water and good anchorage, because he thought that his presence in Ning-po would be detrimental to the commerce of the Portuguese merchants who spent their winters there peacefully carrying on their trade. And everyone praised him highly for this decision and his good intentions.

We departed from the port of Nouday, and after five days of sailing between the mainland and the islands of Comolem, at midday on a Saturday we were attacked by a robber named Premata Gundel, a bitter enemy of the Portuguese people, who had already done them a great deal of harm several times before, not only in Patani but in Sunda and Siam and other places as well, wherever he chanced to meet them in a way that suited his purposes. Mistaking us for Chinese, he attacked us with two huge junks carrying two hundred fighting men, not counting the crew that worked the sails. One of them, after sinking its grappling hooks into Mem Taborda's junk, nearly finished him off. However, when Quiay Panjao, who was a little way out to sea, saw what was happening, he turned back and rammed the enemy junk, going after it under full sail and smashing into its starboard quarter with such force that both of them promptly sank to the bottom, leaving Mem Taborda free of the danger threatening him. Then three of our *lorchas,* which Antonio de Faria had brought from the port of Nouday, came running to the rescue at top speed and—thanks be to God—they saved most of our people while those on the enemy side all drowned.

About this time, Premata Gundel had reached the big junk that Antonio de Faria was on and tackled it with a pair of grappling hooks attached to very long iron chains, immobilizing him fore and aft, and engaging him in a battle that was truly remarkable to see. For more than half an hour the enemy fought so bravely that most of Antonio de Faria's men were wounded, leaving him, on two occasions, in danger of being taken. However, at that point the three *lorchas* and a small junk commanded by Pero da Silva came to his aid, and—as God willed—with their help our men soon regained the ground they had lost. They pressed the enemy so hard that in no time at all the whole business was over, ending with the death of the eighty-six Moors who had boarded Antonio de Faria's junk and given him such a bad time that the only part of the ship still held by our men was the poop deck. And from here, they boarded the pirate's junk and put everyone they found on it to the sword, sparing none, though the crew had already dived into the sea.

However, the price of this victory was not cheap by any means, for it cost us the lives of seventeen men, five of them Portuguese—the best and bravest soldiers in the whole company—and left forty-three badly wounded, one of them Antonio de Faria, who came out of it with a spear injury and two sword cuts.

The battle over, an inventory was taken of what was found on the enemy junk and the booty was appraised at eighty thousand *taels,* the bulk of it in Japanese silver that the pirate had stolen from three merchant junks. That meant that, on this ship alone, the pirate was carrying 120,000 *cruzados;* and they said that he had been carrying almost as much on the junk that went down, which aggrieved many of our men.

With this prize, Antonio de Faria withdrew to a little island called Buncalou, located three or four leagues to the west where there was fresh water and good anchorage. He went ashore and remained there for eighteen days, sleeping in huts that were improvised for the large numbers of wounded men where—as it pleased the Lord—all of them regained their health.

And from there, we proceeded on our determined course with Antonio de Faria on his big junk, Mem Taborda and Antonio Henriques on theirs, Pero da Silva on the small one that had been captured in Nouday, and Quiay Panjao and all his people on the one just taken from the robber, which was given to him to compensate him for the one he had lost, in addition to twenty thousand *taels* from the common funds, with which he felt completely satisfied and well paid for his trouble; and all our men were also pleased with this arrangement because Antonio de Faria had been most adamant about it and had promised to make up for it handsomely in the future.

We went sailing along in this manner, and within six days we reached the Gates of Ning-po, which are actually two islands located three leagues from where the Portuguese traded in those days. It was a town they had built ashore with over a thousand houses that was governed by a city council, a high court magistrate, constables, six or seven judges, and administrative officers of state, where the notaries would sign the legal documents they drew up in the following manner: "I, So-and-So, Notary Public of the Archives and Judiciary of the city of Ning-po, in the name of His Majesty, the King . . . ," as though it were situated between Santarem and Lisbon. And they felt so sure of themselves and were so complacent about it that they had gone so far as to build homes costing between three and four thousand *cruzados,* all of which, from large to small, were later destroyed and completely leveled by the Chinese—for our sins—with not a trace of them left to show for it, as I will explain more fully at the proper time when I come to it. And then it will be plain to see how uncertain things are in China, about which there is such great interest in Portugal and for which some people mistakenly have such high regard, for at every hour of the day they are exposed to all kinds of disasters and misfortunes.

Spain in America

In his eagerness to discover a western sea route to Asia, Christopher Columbus did not anticipate the extent of the Atlantic Ocean when he and his crew set sail from Spain. The following excerpt from Columbus's *Journal* includes an account of the effect on the men of sailing two months without sighting land. After this initial voyage, the Admiral led three additional expeditions that established Spain's base for expansion in the Indies and the Western hemisphere. In February 1519, the Governor of Cuba sent an expedition of some six hundred men led by Hernán Cortés to the mainland of Mexico, where the conquistadors encountered Indian resistance. Bernal Díaz del Castillo, a participant in the battle that ensued, describes the historic confrontation in the second selection.

Throughout these years of conquest, a central problem of Spain's emerging colonial policy was to develop an effective labor system. On the island of Hispaniola (Haiti/Santo Domingo), Columbus had distributed Indians to the colonists, who used their forced labor to deliver a daily tribute of gold; when Indians rebelled and tried to escape, they were hunted down by the colonists who wanted to keep them under control as slaves. This system of labor, approved by the crown, became the *encomienda*. The first voices to be raised condemning this system and its effect on the native population came from a group of Dominican friars who arrived in Hispaniola in 1510. They elected Antonio de Montesinos to serve as their spokesman in raising this issue with the colonists. The effort to protect the Indians from abuse and to abolish the encomienda system intensified with the efforts of Bartolomé de Las Casas (1474–1566). The final readings in this section contain excerpts from Montesinos's fiery sermon to the colonists in Hispaniola, Las Casas's account of the decimation of the Indians in Cuba, and his suggestions for pursuing a different and better method of converting Indians to Christianity.

97

Christopher Columbus, *Journal of First Voyage to America*

Columbus and his crew of ninety sailed from Spain on August 3, 1492, arriving at San Salvador in the Bahamas in October. After three additional voyages exploring the Yucatan peninsula and Central America, he died in poverty and neglect, still believing he had discovered the coast of Asia.

QUESTIONS TO CONSIDER

1. What did Columbus tell his crew in order to pacify and encourage them when they complained and became impatient with the length of the voyage?
2. What was the nature of this initial encounter between Spaniards and the natives? What were the reactions of each?
3. In what ways do these journal notes reveal some of Spain's motives for exploration, conquest, and colonization?
4. Consider how the Age of Exploration and Expansion changed the course of world history.

Monday, Oct. 8th. Steered W.S.W. and sailed day and night eleven or twelve leagues; at times during the night, fifteen miles an hour, if the account can be depended upon. Found the sea like the river at Seville, *"thanks to God,"* says the Admiral. The air soft as that of Seville in April, and so fragrant that it was delicious to breathe it. The weeds appeared very

From Christopher Columbus, *Journal of First Voyage to America* (New York: A. & C. Boni, 1924), pp. 20–26, *passim.*

fresh. Many land birds, one of which they took, flying towards the S.W.; also *grajaos,* ducks, and a pelican were seen.

Tuesday, Oct. 9th. Sailed S.W. five leagues, when the wind changed, and they stood W. by N. four leagues. Sailed in the whole day and night, twenty leagues and a half; reckoned to the crew seventeen. All night heard birds passing.

Wednesday, Oct. 10th. Steered W.S.W. and sailed at time ten miles an hour, at others twelve, and at others, seven; day and night made fifty-nine leagues' progress; reckoned to the crew but forty-four. Here the men lost all patience, and complained of the length of the voyage, but the Admiral encouraged them in the best manner he could, representing the profits they were about to acquire, and adding that it was to no purpose to complain, having come so far, they had nothing to do but continue on to the Indies, till with the help of our Lord, they should arrive there.

Thursday, Oct. 11th. Steered W.S.W.; and encountered a heavier sea than they had met with before in the whole voyage. Saw pardelas and a green rush near the vessel. The crew of the Pinta saw a cane and a log; they also picked up a stick which appeared to have been carved with an iron tool, a piece of cane, a plant which grows on land, and a board. The crew of the Niña saw other signs of land, and a stalk loaded with roseberries. These signs encouraged them, and they all grew cheerful. Sailed this day till sunset, twenty-seven leagues.

After sunset steered their original course W. and sailed twelve miles an hour till two hours after midnight, going ninety miles, which are twenty-two leagues and a half; and as the Pinta was the swiftest sailer, and kept ahead of the Admiral, she discovered land and made the signals which had been ordered. . . . At two o'clock in the morning the land was discovered, at two leagues' distance; they took in sail and remained under the squaresail lying to till day, which was Friday, when they found themselves near a small island, one of the Lucayos, called in the Indian language Guanahani. Presently they descried people, naked, and the Admiral landed in the boat, which was armed, along with Martin Alonzo Pinzon, and Vincent Yañez his brother, captain of the Niña. The Admiral bore the royal standard, and the two captains each a banner of the Green Cross, which all the ships had carried; this contained the initials of the names of the King and Queen each side of the cross, and a crown over each letter. Arrived on shore, they saw trees very green, many streams of water, and divers sorts of fruits. The Admiral called upon the two Captains, and the rest of the crew who landed, as also to Rodrigo de Escovedo, notary of the fleet, and Rodrigo Sánchez, of Segovia, to bear witness that he before all others took possession (as in fact he did) of that island for the King and Queen his sovereigns, making the requisite declarations, which are more at large set down here in writing. Numbers of the people of the island straightway collected together. Here follow the precise words of the Admiral: "As I saw that they were very friendly to us, and perceived that they could be much more easily converted to our holy faith by gentle means than by force, I presented them with some red caps, and strings of beads to wear upon the neck, and many other trifles of small value, wherewith they were much delighted, and became wonderfully attached to us. Afterwards they came swimming to the boats, bringing parrots, balls of cotton thread, javelins and many other things which they exchanged for articles we gave them, such as glass beads, and hawk's bells; which trade was carried on with the utmost good will. But they seemed on the whole to me, to be a very poor people. They all go completely naked, even the women, though I saw but one girl. All whom I saw were young, not above thirty years of age, well made, with fine shapes and faces; their hair short, and coarse like that of a horse's tail, combed toward the forehead, except a small portion which they suffer to hang down behind, and never cut. . . . It appears to me, that the people are ingenious, and would be good servants; and I am of opinion that they would very readily become Christians, as they appear to have no religion.

They very quickly learn such words as are spoken to them. If it please our Lord, I intend at my return to carry home six of them to your Highnesses, that they may learn our language. I saw no beasts in the island, nor any sort of animals except parrots." These are the words of the Admiral.

98

Bernal Díaz del Castillo, The Conquest of Mexico

Bernal Díaz del Castillo, one of the soldiers who fought with Cortés in the conquest of Mexico, wrote a vivid account of that event. In the selection that follows, he describes the battle with the Tlascalan Indians who were traditional enemies of the Aztecs and who, after their defeat by the Spaniards, became the Spaniards' allies after witnessing the superiority of their weapons and fighting ability. This alliance was a major factor in the success of the Spanish conquest.

QUESTIONS TO CONSIDER

1. Why were so few conquistadors able to defeat considerably larger numbers of Indians?
2. How did the Spaniards treat their wounded?
3. Compare this battle with the Ottoman conquest of Constantinople (see Reading 84).

The next morning, the 5th September, 1519, we mustered the horses. There was not one of the wounded men who did not come forward to join the ranks and give as much help as he could. The crossbowmen were warned to use the store of darts very cautiously, some of them loading while the others were shooting, and the musketeers were to act in the same way, and the men with sword and shield were instructed to aim their cuts and thrusts at the bowels [of their enemies] so that they would not dare to come as close to us as they did before. With our banner unfurled, and four of our comrades guarding the standard-bearer, Corral, we set out from our camp. We had not marched half a quarter of a league before we began to see the fields crowded with warriors with great feather crests and distinguishing devices, and to hear the blare of horns and trumpets.

All the plain was swarming with warriors and we stood four hundred men in number, and of those many sick and wounded. And we knew for certain that this time our foe came with the determination to leave none of us alive excepting those who would be sacrificed to their idols.

How they began to charge on us! What a hail of stones sped from their slings! As for

From Bernal Díaz del Castillo, *The True History of the Conquest of New Spain*, trans. and ed. A.P. Maudslay (London: The Hakluyt Society, 1908–1916), 5 vols., I, pp. 237–40, *passim*.

their bowmen, the javelins lay like corn on the threshing floor; all of them barbed and fire-hardened, which would pierce any armour and would reach the vitals where there is no protection; the men with swords and shields and other arms larger than swords, such as broadswords, and lances, how they pressed on us and with what mighty shouts and yells they charged upon us! The steady bearing of our artillery, musketeers, and crossbowmen, was indeed a help to us, and we did the enemy much damage, and those of them who came close to us with their swords and broadswords met with such sword play from us that they were forced back and they did not close in on us so often as in the last battle. The horsemen were so skillful and bore themselves so valiantly that, after God who protected us, they were our bulwark. However, I saw that our troops were in considerable confusion, so that neither the shouts of Cortés nor the other captains availed to make them close up their ranks, and so many Indians charged down on us that it was only by a miracle of sword play that we could make them give way so that our ranks could be reformed. One thing only saved our lives, and that was that the enemy were so numerous and so crowded one on another that the shots wrought havoc among them, and in addition to this they were not well commanded, for all the captains with their forces could not come into action and from what we knew, since the last battle had been fought, there had been disputes and quarrels between the Captain Xicotenga and another captain the son of Chichimecatecle, over what the one had said to the other, that he had not fought well in the previous battle; to this the son of Chichimecatecle replied that he had fought better than Xicotenga, and was ready to prove it by personal combat. So in this battle Chichimecatecle and his men would not help Xicotenga, and we knew for a certainty that he had also called on the company of Huexotzinco to abstain from fighting. Besides this, ever since the last battle they were afraid of the horses and the musketry, and the swords and crossbows, and our hard fighting; above all was the mercy of God which gave us strength to endure. So Xicotenga was not obeyed by two of the commanders, and we were doing great damage to his men, for we were killing many of them, and this they tried to conceal; for as they were so numerous, whenever one of their men was wounded, they immediately bound him up and carried him off on their shoulders, so that in this battle, as in the last, we never saw a dead man.

The enemy was already losing heart, and knowing that the followers of the other two captains whom I have already named, would not come to their assistance, they began to give way. It seems that in that battle we had killed one very important captain, and the enemy began to retreat in good order, our horsemen following them at a hard gallop for a short distance, for they could not sit their horses for fatigue, and when we found ourselves free from that multitude of warriors, we gave thanks to God.

In this engagement, one soldier was killed, and sixty were wounded, and all the horses were wounded as well. They gave me two wounds, one in the head with a stone, and one in the thigh with an arrow; but this did not prevent me from fighting, and keeping watch, and helping our soldiers, and all the soldiers who were wounded did the same; for if the wounds were not very dangerous, we had to fight and keep guard, wounded as we were, for few of us remained unwounded.

Then we returned to our camp, well contented, and giving thanks to God. We buried the dead in one of those houses which the Indians had built underground, so that the enemy should not see that we were mortals, but should believe that, as they said, we were Teules. We threw much earth over the top of the house, so that they should not smell the bodies, then we doctored all the wounded with the fat of an Indian. It was cold comfort to be even without salt or oil with which to cure the wounded. There was another want from which we suffered, and it was a severe one—and that was clothes with which to cover ourselves, for such a cold wind came from the snow mountains, that it made us shiver, for our lances and muskets and crossbows made a poor covering.

99

Antonio de Montesinos: Sermon to Colonists, 1511

Antonio de Montesinos, a Dominican friar, delivered a provocative sermon to Spanish colonists gathered in a small church on the island of Hispaniola on the Sunday before Christmas, 1511. He shocked and angered the congregation; in time, they succeeded in having him sent back to Spain. Just one year after Montesino's sermon, Spain promulgated the Laws of Burgos, the first legislation intended to regulate the colonists' supervision of the Indians.

QUESTIONS TO CONSIDER

1. If you were a colonist in Hispaniola and had been granted Indians to help search for gold and plant and harvest sugar cane on your land, would you have modified your treatment of the Indians on your lands? Explain.
2. What other factors besides excessive work might have led to such widespread death of the Indians?
3. By preaching a radical gospel in favor of the Indians, why did Montesinos, and the Dominicans generally, present a dilemma for the Spanish colonists in Hispaniola?

"In order to make you aware of your actions I have come here as a voice of Christ in this deserted island . . . listen with attention and with all your heart and senses, so that you may hear it; for this will be the strangest voice that you ever heard, the severest, hardest, and most awful and dangerous that you ever expected to hear . . . This voice says that you are in mortal sin, that you live and die in it, because of the cruelty and tyranny you practice in dealing with these innocent people. Tell me, by what right and with what justice do you keep these Indians in such cruel and horrible servitude? With what authority have you waged a detestable war against these people, who lived gently and peacefully on their own land . . . ? Why do you keep them so oppressed and fatigued, neither giving them enough to eat nor taking care of them in their illnesses, for with the excessive work you demand of them they become ill and die, or rather you kill them with your desire to extract and acquire gold every day? And what care do you take that they should be instructed in the doctrine of your religion and know your God and Creator, become baptized, hear mass, honor feast days and Sundays? Are these not men? Do they not have rational souls? Are you not obliged to love them as you love yourselves? Do you not understand this? How could you be in such a deep, lethargic sleep? Be certain that, in the state in which you are, you can no more be saved than the Moors or Turks who lack and do not believe in the Christian faith."

From Bartolomé de Las Casas, *Historia de las Indias* (Mexico: Fondo De Cultura Economica, 1951), Vol. II, 441–42, trans. Frank A. Gerome.

100

Bartolomé de Las Casas, *Destruction of the Indies* and The Only Method of Converting the Indians

Bartolomé de Las Casas was born in Seville in 1474, educated in law at Salamanca, and came to Hispaniola as a soldier of fortune in 1502. He acquired land and Indians and in 1510 was ordained to the priesthood but maintained his position as an *encomendero.*[1] He was present when Montesinos delivered his sermon to the colonists and strongly resented it, as did others who heard it. In 1514, however, Las Casas gave up his lands and Indians and for the rest of his life worked to abolish Indian slavery and the forced labor of the encomienda. To a considerable degree, his efforts led the Spanish Crown to issue the New Laws of 1542, which intended to abolish the encomienda system in the New World. Las Casas is best known for his strong indictment of Spanish cruelty to the Indians in his famous work, *The Brief Account of the Destruction of the Indies* (1552). In the following excerpt from this work, Las Casas describes the Spanish conquest of Cuba. The final selection is taken from another of his writings, *The Only Method of Attracting All People to the True Faith,* arguing that conversion should be accomplished by peaceful means.

QUESTIONS TO CONSIDER

1. What advice does the Indian ruler, Hatuey, suggest to his followers in an effort to survive the arrival of Spaniards?
2. Might Las Casas have exaggerated his account of the decimation of the native inhabitants?
3. Did the realities of colonial existence in the New World overrule the voice of morality and religion? What other examples could you cite where this occurred?
4. Why were many of Spain's competitors and enemies in Europe eager to seize on Las Casas's descriptions of the Spanish character? In what ways did this reflect national rivalries and stereotypes of the era?

In the year 1511 the Spaniards passed over to the island of Cuba, which as I said, is as long as from Valladolid to Rome, and where there were great and populous provinces. They began and ended in the above manner, only with incomparably greater cruelty. Here many notable things occurred.

A very high prince and lord, named Hatuey, who had fled with many of his people from Hispaniola to Cuba, to escape the calamity and inhuman operations of the Christians, having received news from some Indians that the Christians were crossing over, assembled many or all of his people, and addressed them thus.

[1]The person in charge of an *Encomienda,* an assignment of Indians who were to serve the Spanish grantee with tribute and labor.

"You already know that it is said the Christians are coming here; and you have experience of how they have treated the lords so and so and those people of Hayti (which is Hispaniola); they come to do the same here. Do you know perhaps why they do it?" The people answered no; except that they were by nature cruel and wicked. "They do it," said he, "not alone for this, but because they have a God whom they greatly adore and love; and to make us adore Him they strive to subjugate us and take our lives." He had near him a basket full of gold and jewels and he said: "Behold here is the God of the Christians, let us perform *Areytos* before Him, if you will (these are dances in concert and singly); and perhaps we shall please Him, and He will command that they do us no harm."

All exclaimed: it is well! it is well! They danced before it, till they were all tired, after which the lord Hatuey said: "Note well that in any event if we preserve the gold, they will finally have to kill us to take it from us: let us throw it into this river." They all agreed to this proposal, and they threw the gold into a great river in that place.

This prince and lord continued retreating before the Christians when they arrived at the island of Cuba, because he knew them, but when he encountered them he defended himself; and at last they took him. And merely because he fled from such iniquitous and cruel people, and defended himself against those who wished to kill and oppress him, with all his people and offspring until death, they burnt him alive.

When he was tied to the stake, a Franciscan monk, a holy man, who was there, spoke as much as he could to him, in the little time that the executioner granted them, about God and some of the teachings of our faith, of which he had never before heard; he told him that if he would believe what was told him, he would go to heaven where there was glory and eternal rest; and if not, that he would go to hell, to suffer perpetual torments and punishment. After thinking a little, Hatuey asked the monk whether the Christians went to heaven; the monk answered that those who were good went there. The prince at once said, without any more thought, that he did not wish to go there, but rather to hell so as not to be where Spaniards were, nor to see such cruel people. This is the renown and honour, that God and our faith have acquired by means of the Christians who have gone to the Indies.

On one occasion they came out ten leagues from a great settlement to meet us, bringing provisions and gifts, and when we met them, they gave us a great quantity of fish and bread and other victuals, with everything they could supply. All of a sudden the devil entered into the bodies of the Christians, and in my presence they put to the sword, without any motive or cause whatsoever, more than three thousand persons, men, women, and children, who were seated before us. Here I beheld such great cruelty as living man has never seen nor thought to see.

Once I sent messengers to all the lords of the province of Havana, assuring them that if they would not absent themselves but come to receive us, no harm should be done them; all the country was terrorized because of the past slaughter, and I did this by the captain's advice. When we arrived in the province, twenty-one princes and lords came to receive us; and at once the captain violated the safe conduct I had given them and took them prisoners. The following day he wished to burn them alive, saying it was better so because those lords would some time or other do us harm. I had the greatest difficulty to deliver them from the flames but finally I saved them.

After all the Indians of this island were reduced to servitude and misfortune like those of Hispaniola, and when they saw they were perishing inevitably, some began to flee to the mountains; others to hang themselves, together with their children, and through the cruelty of one very tyrannical Spaniard whom I knew, more than two hundred Indians hanged themselves. In this way numberless people perished.

There was an officer of the King in this island, to whose share three hundred Indians fell, and by the end of the three months he had, through labour in the mines, caused the death of two hundred and seventy; so that he had only thirty left, which was the tenth part. The authorities afterwards gave him as many again, and again he killed them: and they continued to give, and he to kill, until he came to die, and the devil carried away his soul.

In three or four months, I being present, more than seven thousand children died of hunger, their fathers and mothers having been taken to the mines. Other dreadful things did I see.

Afterwards the Spaniards resolved to go and hunt the Indians who were in the mountains, where they perpetrated marvellous massacres. Thus they ruined and depopulated all this island which we beheld not long ago; and it excites pity, and great anguish to see it deserted, and reduced to a solitude.

The Only Method of Converting the Indians

The one and only method of teaching men the true religion was established by Divine Providence for the whole world, and for all times: that is, by persuading the understanding through reasons, and by gently attracting or exhorting the will. This method should be common to all men throughout the world, without any distinction made for sects, errors, or corrupt customs.

This conclusion will be proved in many ways: by arguments drawn from reason; by examples of the ancient Fathers; by the rule and manner of preaching which Christ instituted for all times; by the practices of the Apostles; by quotations from holy teachers; by the most ancient tradition of the Church and by her numerous ecclesiastical decrees.

And first, this conclusion will be proved by arguments drawn from reason, among which let this be the first. There is only one method peculiar to Divine Wisdom by which it disposes and moves created beings gently to actions and to their natural ends. But among created beings, rational creatures are higher and more excellent than all others which were not made in the image of God. . . . Therefore, Divine Wisdom moves rational creatures, that is, men, to their actions or operations gently. . . . Therefore, the method of teaching men the true religion ought to be gentle, enticing, and pleasant. This method is by persuading the understanding and by attracting the will.